SLAYER

An Expanded and Updated Unofficial and Unauthorised Guide to *Buffy the Vampire Slayer*

Keith Topping

This edition published in 2002 by

Virgin Books Limited
Thames Wharf Studios
Rainville Road
London
W6 9HA

First published in 2000, updated in 2001

ISBN 0 7535 0631 9

A catalogue record for this book is available from
the British Library.

Typeset by Galleon Typesetting, Ipswich
Printed and bound in Great Britain by
Mackays of Chatham PLC

For Martin Day.
My Watcher. My guru, my brother and my friend.

And

Kathy Sullivan.
Without whom there would have been *no* book.

And

Wendy Comeau.
True support. And thanks for all the scones.

And

Lily Topping.
The only critic that matters.

By the same author:

*Hollywood Vampire: A Revised and Updated Unofficial and
    Unauthorised Guide to Angel*
*High Times: An Unofficial and Unauthorised Guide
    to Roswell*

By the same author with Paul Cornell and Martin Day:

The New Trek Programme Guide
X-Treme Possibilities
The Avengers Dossier

By the same author with Martin Day:

Shut It! A Fan's Guide to 70s Cops on the Box

Acknowledgements

'I think I need help,' I said. And they came like bats out of the Hellmouth . . .

The author wishes to thank the following friends and colleagues for their encouragement and contributions to *Slayer*: Ian and Janet Abrahams, Becki Ablett, Jessica Allen, Marie Antoon, Rebecca Barber, Jeremy Bement, Robyn Bennett, Daniel Ben-Zvi, Stephen Booth, Jo Brooks, Anthony Brown, Paul Comeau, Allison Costa, Rob Crowther, Davy Darlington, Peter Darvill-Evans, Keith RA DeCandido, Alexandre Deschampes, Clay Eichelberger, Jeff Farrell, Irene Finn, Simona Fischer, Paul Gibson and Colleen Laffey, Jeff Hart, Lea Ann Hays, Claire Hennessy, Ralph Holland, Alan Hufana, Alryssa Kelly, Tony and Jane Kenealy, Kevin Lamke, Helen Lane, Sarah Lavelle, Di Lawson, Fawn Leibowitz, Gary Lewis, Peter Linford, Shaun Lyon, Jackie Marshall, Dave and Lesley McIntee, Paul McIntyre, John and Lucy McLaughlin, Jon Miller, John Mosby, Ingrid Oliansky, Tara O'Shea, Mark Phippen (who doesn't even *like* the show), Alex Popple, Ian Reid, Shaun Reid, Leslie Remencus, Justin Richards, Gary Russell, John Seavey, Jill Sherwin, Trina Short, Jim Smith, Matt Springer, Paul Steib and Wendy Wiseman, Angela and Ian Stewart, Dave Stone, Jim Swallow and Mandy Mills, Ruth Thomas, Caroline Trevelyan, Iain Truskett, Jason Tucker, Martin Wiggins and the *Fat Dragon Ladies*. Plus, everyone at *Gallifrey One* in Los Angeles, *Neutral Zone* in Newcastle and *CONvergence* in Minneapolis (especially my fellow campaigners for a Tasteful-Lesbian-Shower-Scene, Anna Bliss, Jody Wurl, Stephanie Lindorff and Windy Merill). Not forgetting David Bailey, Paul Condon, Paul Cornell, Simon Guerrier, Jim Sangster and all my pals on the *BuffyWatchers* mailing list. Chris Cornwell and Steve Purcell provided several (desperately needed) business lunches during the writing of this book.

The Watcher's Web (www.watchers.web.com/) remains an invaluable source of information from a largely British perspective. Thanks are due to numerous website custodians who spared the time to answer my, no doubt annoying, emails. Details of many of these sites can be found in the chapter 'Buffy and the Internet'. Also my gratitude to Will Cameron, Tony Dryer, Beth Kiefner, Judy Pykala, Carol Stoneburner and Deb Walsh who helped fill a few *vital* gaps.

A special thank you to the awesome *Scooby Gang*: my editor Kirstie Addis, Suzie Campagna (*my* angel), Diana Dougherty, Rob Francis (who *again* went for the doughnuts), Robert Franks and Mike Lee (invaluable critique), Paul Simpson (who provided unedited transcripts of his interviews with many of the cast and crew and generally kept me sane), Susannah Tiller (the best proofreader in the business), Graeme Topping (who spotted the *South Park* link) and Mark Wyman, all of whom, once again, loaned the project their boundless enthusiasm and talent for the duration.

And to my family, as always, for their support – particularly Maureen and Gudi, who never seem to get mentioned.

Contents

Xander: 'He did a spell just to make us think he was cool?'
Giles: 'Yes.'
Xander: 'That is so cool!'

– 'Superstar'

Preface

When I first proposed *Slayer* to Virgin Publishing late in 1998, my main reason for wanting to write the book was that there was no episode guide to *Buffy the Vampire Slayer* available in Britain. By the time it was commissioned two months later, there were *three* in the shops. Such is the pace at which a cult can grow into a mainstream success. OK, so there *are* other *Buffy* books on the shelves and some of them are very good. *Slayer* is different to *all* of them, however. Certainly it covers the same episodes, but it covers them in very different ways. The aim of *Slayer* is to offer a British perspective to this most Californian of subjects, to recognise the sometimes very adult nature of the series and to provide a touch of critical analysis where other books may fear to tread.

Buffy is, on one level, a quasi-fairy tale in which a group of young people are the focus of a battle between the forces of good (as represented by themselves) and evil (represented, mostly, by an older generation). In other words, it's the Brothers Grimm with a rock-and-roll soundtrack and its own syntax. Yet there is more to this series than sharp one-liners and eye-candy set pieces. Without getting too pretentious, *Buffy* has more in common with *Hamlet* than a blond hero and death on a large scale. *Buffy* is about growing up and facing the totally mundane horrors of the adult world. About a time when the game of life is still being played by *our* rules but with the knowledge that this is changing. It concerns the point where childhood ends and the ordinary, everyday realities of career, relationships and responsibilities appear on the horizon. Thus as the viewer explores Sunnydale we see a world that we can, hopefully, recognise. Because it was *our* world too. A world of hormone-charged teenagers with their own secret language. A world where educational establishments play host to the epic battle between the forces of light and darkness. A world where the body count (physical *and* emotional) is astronomical. These themes are universal and timeless, not tied to a particular part of the United States in the dying days of the twentieth century.

The story is simple: Buffy Summers and her mother move from Los Angeles to the small Californian town of Sunnydale after her expulsion from a previous school (there was that nasty business of the gym burning down). On her first day at Sunnydale High, she befriends two local nerds, Xander Harris and Willow Rosenberg, which excludes her from the cool set led by the formidable Cordelia Chase. Buffy also meets her Watcher, Rupert Giles, because (as we discover) she is a Vampire Slayer: a one-per-generation clan of stake-wielding super-babes who rid the world of vampires, demons and the forces of darkness. As *SFX* said, when placing the series in their 'Top Fifty SF TV Shows of All Time', '*Buffy* should be awful . . . In the land where the one-line pitch is king, *Buffy* rules . . .'

But *Buffy* is also a peek into a toy shop of magnificent conceit – a series fixated in equal measure by the claustrophobic 'outsider' constraints of the adolescent years and by a battle fought by a heroine, not because she *wants* to (indeed, she's initially a reluctant Slayer), but because she's good at it and because, like most dirty jobs, *someone*'s got to do it. Into this mix come elements of high (and sometimes extremely *low*) comedy and much confident and self-aware dialogue. *SFX* believes that the main reason for *Buffy*'s success is that it has 'the three cornerstones of quality TV: good writing, good characters and good acting. More to the point, *Buffy* is the perfect combination of both cynicism and quality; a well-written, well-acted series that just happens to star gorgeous teenagers in soap-style situations.' The heavyweight US critic Matt Roush also wrote of the series' genre-crossing appeal: 'A show as terrific as *Buffy*, with its kicky commingling of humour and horror, may be aimed at the youth market. But it deserves a following as wide as its buzz is loud. If only it could overcome the perception of its silly sounding title . . . I'd argue that it has a bigger emotional resonance than any youth soap on the air.'

Anthony Stewart Head, who plays the erudite Giles, told *DreamWatch* about his first impressions of the script: 'I was sitting in the Border Grill in Santa Monica . . . I laughed out loud and suddenly found myself having to stop because people were looking at me! As I was reading it, I couldn't wait to turn the page and find out what happened next. I thought this is an extraordinary combination. I'm no judge of what is going to be a success on TV but this *has* to be a success.' And so it has proved. Along with series like *Xena: Warrior Princess*, *Buffy* has brought an audience to mainstream SF that covers a wide demographic and gender range (put simply, lots of women like these series for their powerful female characters and hunky male icons).

The episode category headings remain pretty much the same as in the previous editions: Joyce's regular denials, the pop-culture references and the bits when logic flies out of the window. However, there are some new ones this time around. Most should be fairly self-explanatory. **Critique** details what the press made of it all while **Comments** from the production staff and cast have been added where appropriate. **Soundtrac**k highlights the series' excellent use of music. Songs marked '*' appear on *Buffy the Vampire Slayer – The Album* (see 62, 'Wild at Heart').

We begin each season with a list of the regular cast to help those of you who don't know who all of the actors are. Remember them, they are quite important. Sarah Michelle Gellar is Buffy, Nicholas Brendon is Xander, Alyson Hannigan is Willow, Anthony Stewart Head is Giles, Charisma Carpenter is Cordelia, Kristine Sutherland is Joyce, Seth Green is Oz, James Marsters is Spike, Emma Caulfield is Anya, David Boreanaz is Angel (in several episodes he plays a character called Angelus, who occupies the same body as Angel but is very different), Robia LaMorte is Jenny, Mercedes McNab is Harmony, Marc Blucas is Riley, Amber Benson is Tara, Alexis Denisof is Wesley and Danny Strong is Jonathan.

Preface to the Third Edition

Another year, another edition; but it's different this time. Buffy Summers is dead for a start.

Now an established and acclaimed part of the TV landscape, *Buffy* found itself this year at the centre of controversy both off- and on-screen, and with a critically praised story-arc that has taken the series into new dramatic areas and to an ever-widening audience around the globe. Conventions (such as N3K in London) continue to remind us past-it cynics what genuine passion and fanaticism there is for this great show (and its spin-off, *Angel*) amongst its, predominantly young, fanbase. And how much *love* there is for the people who make it, and star in it (and even, occasionally, those of us who merely write about it). It's good to be reminded of these things sometimes. The negativity that one can pick up from some of the more vocal sections of Internet fandom do neither the series nor its many positive achievements any credit.

So, as the audience grows, the need for *Slayer* grows with it. This book remains – as, hopefully, all my books do – the work of, first-and-foremost, a fan of the series he writes about. Someone who *adores* watching such series and talking about them with friends and fellow fans. The opinions expressed in this book are exactly those that you'll hear me spouting when I'm having a beer and a pizza with three or four mates in Newcastle, Los Angeles, Minneapolis or London (the four cities in which *Slayer* was written). If you like this book, or if there's anything in it that you disagree with, then please let me know. Feedback is what TV journalism *and* TV fandom is all about.

Keith Topping
His Gaff
Merrie Albion
August 2001 (Common Era)

A Short History of the Vampire in Myth, Literature and Film

'The children of the night, what sweet music they make.'

'**Vampire** *n.* 1. (in European folklore) a corpse that rises nightly from its grave to drink the blood of the living. 2. a person who preys mercilessly upon others.' – *Collins Dictionary*.

They've been with us for so long that it would require a book considerably larger than this to untangle the myriad legends and myths that concern them. They are the fabric of our nightmares. They are central to much of our literature and movie culture. 'Even today,' wrote Montague Summers in 1928, 'in remoter districts of Europe, [like] Transylvania, Slovenia, the isles and mountains of Greece, the peasant will . . . utterly destroy the carrion who at night will issue from his unhallowed grave . . . Assyria knew the vampire long ago, and he lurked amid the primaeval [sic] forests of Mexico before Cortes came. He is feared by the Chinese, the Indian, and the Malay; while Arabian stories tell us . . . of the ghouls who haunt ill-omened lonely crossways.'

The origins of the word 'vampire' (or 'vampir', or 'vampyre') are hazy. Matthew Bunson notes that it 'may have come from the Lithuanian *wempti* ("to drink")'. It arrived in the English language in 1732 via a translation of the case of Serbian vampire Arnold Paole. As early as 1198, however, William of Newburgh's *Historia Rerum Anglicarum* recorded examples of vampiric activity in Northumberland. Other important historical works include Leo Allatius's *De Quorundum Graecorum Opinationibus* (on the Greek *vrykolakas* legends), Michael Ranftius's *De Masticatione Mortuorum in Tumulus Liber* and Dom Augustine Calmet's *Traité sur les Apparition des Esprits, et sur les Vampires*. Some scholars suggest ancient Egypt as the birthplace of vampirism (with so many death cults in Egyptian mythology, it's not an unreasonable starting point). Others look to India and the *bhuta* creatures of Hindu folklore, China and the Taoist *chiang-shi* or the Mesopotamian Empire. 'Bloodsuckers' (*sanguisugga*) are mentioned in the Old Testament (Proverbs 30:15), though the *utukku* of Assyria and Greek legends of the *callicantzaro* and the *vrykolakas* probably predate this. These myths of the Aegean are very different from the more familiar Slavic and Germanic tales of the walking dead that influenced Gothic literature, fascinated Paris in the 1820s and led (via a plethora of 'penny bloods') to Bram Stoker and *Dracula*.

The vampire in literature can be found in the work of German poets, such as Heinrich Ossenfelder's 'Der Vampir' and Gottfried August Bürger's 'Lenore', while Johann Wolfgang von Goethe's *Die Braut von Korinth* and Johann Ludwig Tieck's *Wake Not the Dead* are examples in the Gothic movement. But it was *The Vampyre* by John Polidori that caught the imagination of the public, particularly in England and France. Polidori was physician to Lord Byron and accompanied the poet on his notorious 1816 trip to Europe, before they parted company less than amicably. On the shores of Lake Geneva in June, they met Percy and Mary Shelley and a competition in writing ghost stories led to what Stephen King describes as 'one of the maddest British tea parties of all time'. The outcome is legendary: Mary Shelley wrote *Frankenstein*, while Byron's fragment (*The Burial*) was acquired by Polidori and fleshed out into *The Vampyre* (as an act of revenge against his former employer). First published in the *New Monthly Magazine* in April 1819 under Byron's name before the true author took credit, the charismatic 'Lord Ruthvan' was a thinly veiled caricature of Byron. Subsequent important vampire stories include Edgar Allen Poe's 'Ligeia', Tolstoy's 'Upry', the remarkable 'Varney the Vampire, or Feast of Blood' by James Malcolm Rymer and Guy de Maupassant's 'Le Horla'.

Sheridan Le Fanu's *Carmilla*, first published in 1872, was one of the first novels to pursue the link between vampirism and sensuality and in Carmilla Karnstein, Le Fanu created a lesbian icon of extraordinary power. The character was based on one of the Middle Ages' most notorious mass murderers, the Hungarian noblewoman Elizabeth Bathory (1560–1614), who was said to bathe in the blood of young women in an attempt to retain her youth. Bathory was one of two figures from the history of the Carpathians that became the basis for much of what we know today as the vampire genre. The other was Vlad Tepes (1431–76), a warlord prince of Transylvania. The son of Vlad Dracul of Wallachia, Tepes was a butcher who gained his sobriquet ('the impaler') from his delightful hobby of executing his enemies on wooden stakes. Now regarded in Romania as a symbol of nationalistic pride for his defeat of the Ottoman Turks, Vlad was also known by another name, in honour of his father: *Draculae* – Son of the Dragon.

Bram Stoker's 1897 novel is a stylistic summation of the genre. Influenced by Rymer, Poe and Le Fanu and with a majestic grasp of the Central European mythology, *Dracula* was an entirely new kind of vampire novel in which the combination of evil and human weakness continued to be exploited, but which also dealt with psychology and sex. In *Danse Macabre*, Stephen King discusses the most sexually explicit moment in the book (Harker's 'languorous ecstasy' as he encounters the voluptuous but lethal 'sisters'):

> In the England of 1897, a girl who 'went on her knees' was not the sort of girl you brought home to meet your mother; Harker is about to be orally raped, and he doesn't mind a bit. And it's all right because *he is not responsible*. In matters of sex, a highly moralistic society can find a psychological escape valve in the concept of outside evil.

These strong sexual overtones, notes King, are one reason why the movies based on Stoker's work have continued to be successful no matter how radical the treatment. AA Gill suggests that 'Dracula and his clan are all metaphors for sex, specifically virginal girls' yearnings and their consequent sense of guilt . . . Vampires have no reflections: being able to look yourself in the face is a sign of purity and innocence.'

Following Stoker's lead, the vampire novel has gone through a series of thematic changes but with, basically, the same ingredients that Stoker mixed in the 1890s. The early twentieth century saw such classics as Marion F Crawford's *For the Blood is the Life*, Algernon Blackwood's *The Transfer*, Reginald Hodder's *The Vampire* and MR James's *An Episode of Cathedral History*. One would have thought that the horrors of the Great War would have ended the public's fascination with such stories but EF Benson's *Mrs Amsworth* was the first of a series of genre-stretching novels that have taken the vampire into the fabric of modern literature: *Revelation in Black* (Carl Jacobi), *The Cloak* (Robert Bloch), *Dreadful Hollow* (Irina Karlova), *The Devil Is Not Mocked* (Manly Wade Wellman), *The Girl With the Hungry Eyes* (Fritz Leiber), *I Am Legend* (Richard Matheson), *Doctors Wear Scarlet* (Simon Raven), *Salem's Lot* (Stephen King), *The Hunger* (Whitley Strieber), and the works of Anne Rice, beginning with *Interview with the Vampire*, are among the most celebrated of modern vampire texts.

Cinema's love affair with the vampire began as early as 1922 when FW Murnau's expressionist masterpiece *Nosferatu* (starring Max Schreck as the Dracula-like Count Orlok) suggested the enormous possibilities for cinematic horror. In America, Universal Films acquired the rights to Hamilton Deane's 1898 stage-adaptation of *Dracula* (directed by Tod Browning and starring Bela Lugosi) and fashioned a movie that, as Matthew Bunson notes, 'influenced the way the Count was forever after depicted, shaping the general style of succeeding Universal projects and proving the financial potential of horror'. The company went on to produce many variants on the theme before a dispiriting spiral into low-budget parody in the 1940s (e.g. *Abbott and Costello Meet Frankenstein*).

A decade later the British company Hammer revived the genre and produced a series of beautifully made bloodthirsty shockers on minimalist budgets, in the process turning Peter Cushing and Christopher Lee into icons of equal status to Lugosi. Hammer's *Dracula* cycle, eight films between 1958's *Dracula* (US title: *Horror of Dracula*) and 1973's *The Satanic Rites of Dracula*, are highly recommended to lovers of the genre, as is the company's 'Karnstein trilogy' (*The Vampire Lovers*, *Lust for a Vampire* and *Twins of Evil*). At the same time the French director Jean Rollin's series of vampire movies (which explored the sex angle to a greater degree than Hammer) were becoming both influential and popular.

Comedy and vampirism may seem strange bedfellows but Roman Polanski's 1967 *Dance of the Vampires* (US title: *The Fearless Vampire Killers*) showed that such a merging of seemingly incompatible genres *was* possible. RW Johnson noted in 1982, 'we have actually got round to really funny films about vampires – not burlesques, which refuse to take the myth seriously, but comedies which accept the myth head on, and still laugh at it.' In the 1980s, at the very moment when the vampire novel was becoming a serious literary subgenre with the success of Anne Rice's novels, numerous teenage vampire films were made in America. Mostly low-budget, often sneered at by 'serious' critics who regarded the horror motif as not worthy of study and equally loathed by horror fans for not including capes, castles and bats, from *Fright Night*, *Once Bitten*, *Vamp*, *The Lost Boys*, *Near Dark* and *Beverly Hills Vamp* it's a very short step to *Buffy the Vampire Slayer*, a critical and artistic failure upon its release in 1992.

Did You Know?: Interviewed in 1996, Hammer's chairman Roy Skeggs noted that Miramax Films wanted to remake the camp classic *Dracula A.D. 1972* as '*Dracula 1999* reset in Los Angeles, [with] the modern whizz-kids fighting vampires.' Hang on, that sounds a bit like . . .

Awakenings

A shopaholic teenager discovers that she is the latest in a line of mythical warriors.

Whether **M1**, *Buffy the Vampire Slayer* should be regarded as an example of Joss Whedon's talent or a triumph for his persuasive skills is unclear, but the fact that the concept ever made it beyond that one-line description suggests the latter.

Asked how much like Xander Harris he was as a teenager, Joss admitted: 'Less and less as he gets laid more and more.' Whedon is a third-generation Hollywood scriptwriter (his grandfather wrote for *Leave it to Beaver*, his father worked on *The Golden Girls*). His education included a period at Winchester Public School in England ('My mother was a teacher,' he told Rob Francis. 'She was on sabbatical in England so I had to go somewhere'). After writing many speculative scripts in his teens, he landed a writing job on *Roseanne* (he also produced the TV version of *Parenthood*). 'My life was completely about film,' he told *teen movieline*. '[I] learned about filmmaking by analysing two particular movies, *Johnny Guitar* and *The Naked Kiss*.' However, with an encyclopaedic knowledge of horror movies and comics, Whedon had always wanted to write for that market (his favourite film remains Kubrick's *The Shining*), acknowledging two stylistically fascinating modernist vampire movies – *The Lost Boys* and *Near Dark* – as an influence on *Buffy*. 'Sometimes we have fruity European Anne Rice-type vampires,' notes Whedon. 'Sometimes we have the dusty, western *Near Dark*-type vampires. And sometimes we just have a bunch of stuntmen.'

'I watched a lot of horror movies,' Whedon told *The Big Breakfast*. 'I saw all these blonde women going down alleys and getting killed and I felt bad for them. I wanted one of them to kill a monster for a change so I came up with *Buffy*.' His movie script for **M1**, *Buffy the Vampire Slayer* suffered four years of rejection before finding a supporter in producer Howard Rosenman. Next to arrive was the Czech director Fran

Rubel Kuzui (whose previous work included *Tokyo Pop*), who fell in love with *Buffy* as soon as she heard the preposterously silly title. Kuzui rewrote Whedon's script, introducing many of the elements that are now part of the mythos (like the John Woo-influenced martial arts fight sequences) but losing something vital in the process.

What followed was an interesting failure: a false dawn that nevertheless contained moments that help to explain why nearly a decade later Buffy Summers is still around whupping vampire ass.

'Since the dawn of man, the Vampires have walked among us. Feeding. The only one with the strength or skill to stop their heinous evil is the Slayer. She who bears the birthmark, the mark of the coven. Trained by the Watcher, one Slayer dies and the next is chosen.'

**A Kuzui Enterprises/Sandollar Production/
20th Century Fox**

M1
Buffy the Vampire Slayer – The Movie

**Theatrical Release: September 1992; 86 minutes
(rated PG-13)**

Co-Producer: Dennis Stuart Murphy
Executive Producers: Sandy Gallin, Carol Baum,
Fran Rubel Kuzui
Producers: Kaz Kuzui, Howard Rosenman
Writer: Joss Whedon
Director: Fran Rubel Kuzui

Cast:
Kristy Swanson (Buffy), Donald Sutherland (Merrick),
Paul Reubens (Amilyn), Rutger Hauer (Lothos), Luke Perry (Pike),
Michele Abrams (Jennifer), Hilary Swank (Kimberly),
Paris Vaughan (Nicole), David Arquette (Benny),
Randall Bantinkoff (Jeffrey), Andrew Lowery (Andy),
Sasha Jenson (Gueller), Stephen Root (Gary Murray),
Natasha Gregson Wagner (Cassandra), Candy Clark (Buffy's Mom),
Mark DeCarlo (Coach), Tom Janes (Zeph), James Paradise (Buffy's Dad),
David Sherrill (Knight), Liz Smith (Reporter),
Paul M Lane (Robert Bowman), Toby Holguin (Vampire Fan),
Eurlyne Epper-Woldman (Graveyard Woman), Andre Warren (Newscaster),
Bob 'Swanie' Swanson (Referee), Erika Dittner (Cheerleader), JC Cole (Biker),
Michael S Kopelow (Student), Ricky Dean Logan (Bloody Student),
Bobby Aldridge, Amanda Anka, Chino Binamo, Al Goto, Terry Jackson,
Mike Johnson, Sarah Lee Jones, Kim Robert Kosci, Clint Lilley, Chi-Muoi Lo,
Jimmy N Roberts, David Rowden, Kenny Sacha, Ben R Scott,
Kurtis Epper Sanders, Sharon Schaffer, Lincoln Simonds (Vampires)
French title: *Buffy Contre Les Vampires*

Southern California – the 'Lite Ages': 'killing time' takes on a new meaning at Hemery High when Buffy (a blonde-brained cheerleader) is told by the mysterious Merrick that she is the Chosen One – the Vampire Slayer. But, when Lothos and his cackling sidekick Amilyn seek vengeance on the Slayer, Buffy finds herself up to her neck in trouble, battling against the undead and her rapidly dwindling popularity with her Valley girlfriends, with only the help of a seriously gorgeous drifter and a pointed stick. *Totally*.

Dudes and Babes: For the girls, Luke Perry. Say no more.

Authority Spanks!: In Administrator Murray's office, a green spanking paddle is visible, even though corporal punishment is banned in California (see **9**, 'The Puppet Show').

A Little Learning is a Dangerous Thing: Buffy: 'Excuse me not knowing about El Salvador. Like I'm ever going to Spain anyway?' Cassandra's question about the ozone layer is met with Buffy's reply, 'Gotta get rid of that.'

Mom's Apple Pie: Buffy's mom (unnamed and clearly a *very* different character from Joyce in the TV series) calls Jeffrey 'Bobby'. Buffy offers the sulky opinion that she probably thinks Buffy's name is Bobby too. One of the best scenes in the film occurs when Buffy comes home extremely late and her mother apprehends her at the door asking if she knows what time it is. Buffy replies, 'It's around ten', which her mom wanted to know as her watch had stopped. (See **33**, 'Becoming' Part 1, for an interesting variation.)

It's a Designer Label!: Buffy's electric-blue cheerleader leggings and red flower-patterned miniskirt in the opening scenes are tame compared to her gym-wear during her first meeting with Merrick. Yellow sports bra, multicoloured pants and shocking-pink leggings. Is she colourblind? (Possibly, if her desire for that lemon-yellow jacket is anything to go by.) The Grace Kelly-style prom dress and hairdo don't suit her and when Pike stands on the end of the dress, ripping it, she's wearing jogging pants underneath. Which is *very* convenient.

References: 'It's time to put away such childish things' alludes to I Corinthians 13:11. 'The rest is silence' are the eponymous hero's dying words in *Hamlet*. Buffy sings a few lines from Louis Gost and Morris Albert's 1975 easy-listening standard 'Feelings'. Also, Sting's battle to save the rain forests, the 'Elvis Lives' myth, actor Christian Slater (*Heathers*, *Kuffs*, *Very*

Bad Things), *Kung Fu*, a misquote from *The Wizard of Oz* and an oblique reference to the circumstances surrounding Jimi Hendrix's death.

The Drugs Don't Work: Administrator Murray claims to have 'done acid' at a Doobie Brothers concert and believed he was a giant toaster before freaking out when his friend Melissa's head turned into a party balloon.

'You May Remember Me From Such Films and TV Series As . . .': Kristy Swanson's movies include *Highway to Hell*, *Marshal Law*, *Flowers in the Attic*, *The Phantom*, *Bad to the Bone* (TV) and *The Chase*. She played Erica Paget on *Early Edition*. Luke Perry was Dylan in *Beverly Hills 90210*, and 'Sideshow' Luke Perry in *The Simpsons*. Paul Reubens is best known as Pee-Wee Herman in *Pee-Wee Herman's Big Adventure*. Donald Sutherland's CV includes many of this author's favourite movies (*Dr Terror's House of Horror*, *The Dirty Dozen*, *M*A*S*H*, *Klute*, *Don't Look Now*, *The Eagle Has Landed*, *The First Great Train Robbery*, *Murder by Decree*, *Backdraft* and *JFK*). During the 60s, Sutherland was a British TV regular; he's the voodoo god Dwumbala in an episode of *The Champions* for instance, and also appeared in *Man in a Suitcase*, *The Saint* and *The Avengers*. Dutch actor Rutger Hauer is a cult figure in Britain via his adverts for Guinness during the 80s and films like *Blade Runner*, *The Hitcher*, *The Osterman Weekend* and *Fatherland*. Hilary Swank played the lead in *The Next Karate Kid* and recently won an Oscar for her transsexual performance in *Boys Don't Cry*. David Arquette is a star of the *Scream* movies and also features in *Never Been Kissed* and *Muppets from Space*. Stephen Root's credits include *Crocodile Dundee II*, *Ghost* and *Robocop 3*, while he provides the voice of Bill Dauterive in *King of the Hill*. Candy Clark was Mary-Lou, Thomas Newton's girlfriend in *The Man Who Fell to Earth*. She's also in *American Graffiti*, *Amityville 3-D* and *Stephen King's Cat's Eye*. Natasha Gregson Wagner was in *High Fidelity* and *Stranger Than Fiction*.

Don't Give Up the Day Job: Liz Smith is now a famous gossip columnist in the US. JC Cole's brief appearance was in addition to his production role on the film, as dolly grip. Stuntwoman Kim Koscki would later work on *The Flintstones* and *Apollo 13*, while the TV announcer is played, uncredited, by Jeff Coopwood, a voice artist who worked on *The Rock* and *Star Trek: First Contact* and was the voice of Captain Panaka in *Star Wars Episode 1: The Phantom Menace*.

Stun-Your-Friends Trivia!: The basketball player wearing No. 10 is a young Ben Affleck (before starring roles in *Chasing Amy*, *Good Will Hunting*, *Shakespeare in Love*, *Armageddon* and *Dogma*). And the small plump girl playing Charlotte the waitress . . .? Can that *really* be future talkshow diva Ricki Lake?

Valley-Speak: The movie as a celebration and a critique of Valley-girl culture is full of such contrivances as: 'Mr Howard is *so heinous*', 'This is *so lush*' and 'Does the word "*Duh!*" mean anything to you?'

Buffy and Jennifer, on why they aren't going to a movie theatre: '*Bogus* corn.'

Kimberly's opinion of the jacket Buffy wants: 'Pur-leeze. It's *so* five minutes ago.'

Surfer-kid: 'This party sucks, man.'

Pike: 'Pity, you seem like such a *flink*.'

Cigarettes and Alcohol: 'You're *thrashed*,' Buffy tells Pike. 'That,' he says, 'would explain the slurred speech.'

Logic, Let Me Introduce You to This Window: When Pike fights the vampire wearing the varsity jacket, Buffy leaps on the vampire's shoulders and wraps her legs around his head. The next shot has her falling on Pike with the vampire nowhere to be seen. The implication is she's killed him – but how, exactly? (An answer is given in **2**, 'The Harvest', and it's not pretty.)

Quote/Unquote: Andrew, trying not to touch Buffy's bottom as she leans over him to kiss Jeffrey: 'I don't want to sound sexist or anything, but can I borrow her?'

Buffy's dad: 'Have fun. Be good. Stay away from the Jag.'

Buffy, on Merrick's claims: 'Does Elvis talk to you?'

Amilyn, after Pike has caused his arm to be severed: 'Kill him. A lot.'

Buffy on her ambitions: 'All I want to do is graduate from school, go to Europe, marry Christian Slater and die.'

Lothos, after Buffy stakes him: 'Now I'm *really* pissed off.'

Notes: 'I'm in a graveyard with a strange man, hunting for vampires, on a school night.' Imagine a cross between *Beverly*

Hills 90210, *Clueless* and *Interview with the Vampire* and you're about a third of the way to how weird **M1**, *Buffy the Vampire Slayer* is. It's a badly plotted film (Whedon's script was extensively rewritten). Donald Sutherland is great but the movie dies on its feet the moment his character is written out with half an hour to go. It's also a very shallow tale: we care little about these people. This is particularly true of Buffy herself, who in this incarnation is a selfish moron, hanging around with her sycophantic tittering girlfriends long after she realises that there are more important things in life. There *are* nice realistic moments, like her discussion with Merrick about suffering from the cramps ('my secret weapon is PMT'). In places the film is actually quite (conceptually) dark. The bottom line is see it if you get the chance, but don't be surprised if it's not to your taste.

Buffy owns a teddy bear (see **5**, 'Never Kill a Boy on the First Date'; **10**, 'Nightmares'; **21**, 'What's My Line?' Part 1). She used to do gymnastics and still knows the moves. She wants a career as a 'buyer', even though she doesn't know what one does. She had the 'hairy mole' birthmark that identified her as the Slayer removed (an element that was, along with the PMT references, not picked up on during the series).

Differences between the movie and the series: vampires can fly and don't turn to dust when staked. They can't enter a building unless invited, including public areas like the school gym (see **7**, 'Angel'; **30**, 'Killed By Death') and leave no image on film (see **21**, 'What's My Line?' Part 1; **46**, 'Helpless'). Merrick (in a confusing speech that suggests reincarnation, but also extreme longevity) says he has 'lived a hundred lifetimes' and that it's been the same life over and over with the knowledge to prepare the Slayer. But when he's killed by Lothos, there's no evidence of soul transference, so maybe he's simplifying things for Buffy by not telling her there are other Watchers. The implication of Buffy's dreams (the Slayer is reborn each generation) also suggests reincarnation. Among the previous Slayers mentioned are a Magyar peasant girl, an Indian princess, a slave in Virginia and a serving girl (possibly in medieval England, certainly somewhere where there were knights). The Hemery High basketball team are called The

Hogs. Much of the location filming took place in North Hollywood, Sherman Oaks and Pasadena. Marshall High School
(also used in *Pretty in Pink*) is the location of Hemery High.

Soundtrack: 'Keep it Comin' (Dance Till You Can't Dance No
More)' by C&C Music Factory, 'In the Wind' by War Babies,
'Man Smart, Woman Smarter' by Dream Warriors, 'I Fought
the Law (And the Law Won)' by Mary's Danish, 'I Ain't Gonna
Eat Out My Heart Anymore' by Divinyls, The Cult's 'Zap City',
'Silent City' by Matthew Sweet, 'Inner Mind' by Eon, Toad the
Wet Sprocket's 'Little Haven', 'Party with the Animals' by
Ozzy Osbourne, 'Light Comes Out Black' by Rob Holland and
'We Close Our Eyes' by Susannah Hoffs.

Did You Know?: One of the uncredited extras on the film was
Seth Green (playing a dorky teenage vampire). The scene in
which he appeared was cut before release. However, his photo
can be seen on the sleeve of the 1997 commercial video.

The Comic: In an attempt to marry the continuity of the movie
with the many variations of these events described in the TV
series, January 1999 saw the publication by Dark Horse of a
three-part comic, *Buffy the Vampire Slayer – The Origin*,
adapted from Whedon's original screenplay by Daniel Brereton
and Christopher Golden, pencilled by Joe Bennett and inked by
Rick Ketcham. This drew heavily on the movie, but included
elements subsequently changed by the series (such as Buffy's
first meeting with Merrick, seen in **33**, 'Becoming' Part 1) and
parts of the screenplay only alluded to in *Buffy* folklore (the
burning down of the Hemery High gym). Some of the story is
told in the form of a (possibly unreliable) narrative by Buffy's
former friends, while an intriguing coda has Buffy telling
Willow and Xander about a trip to Las Vegas with Pike before
she came to Sunnydale. (See 'The Buffy Novels': *Sins of the
Father.*)

Novelisation: Richie Tankersley Cusick's tie-in novel appeared
in August 1992 shortly before the movie premiered. Based on
Whedon's script rather than the actual film, it features several
sequences that are radically different from the movie, including
a much lengthier prologue set in Europe in the Dark Ages.

U1
The untransmitted TV pilot

The film wasn't what Joss had in mind (Robia LaMorte told *DreamWatch*, 'I know Joss was really upset about the movie, because he wasn't in the position to have the creative control over it.') In 1996 Whedon (having worked on the scripts of *Twister*, *Waterworld*, *Toy Story* – for which he was Oscar nominated – *Speed* and *Alien: Resurrection*) was asked by Sandollar to revive *Buffy* as a TV format. Whedon wrote and partly financed a 25-minute 'presentation' show-reel. The script (the first draft of which was dated 26 Jan. 1996) was a work-in-progress version of **1**, 'Welcome to the Hellmouth'. Tony Head has indicated that Whedon also directed the 'presentation', recalling, 'He's now an incredible director, but he had a fairly unhelpful crew.'

Head, Sarah Michelle Gellar, Nicholas Brendon, Charisma Carpenter, Mercedes McNab, Julie Benz and Danny Strong were all featured, although there was a different Willow, a different Principal Flutie and no trace of Angel. Having chosen his cast, Whedon invited them all to his home for a script readthrough. 'The chemistry was remarkably good,' Head told *Xposé*. 'I think one of the successes of the show is that Joss's casting is bang on.' The editing was, according to *The Watcher's Guide*, the work of future co-producer David Solomon. Head also remembers that, 'It wasn't as polished as the pilot became. The effects were great but . . . the end scene that I did was horrible.'

The Blonde Leading the Blonde: Here, Buffy is a brunette.

No Fat Chicks!: The script describes Willow as: 'Bookish and very possibly dressed by her mother. The intelligence in her eyes and the sweetness of her smile belie a genuine charm that is lost on the unsubtle highschool [sic] mind'. Casting her as a shy obese girl with a *very* unflattering skirt length and then (when a series was commissioned) dropping her in favour of someone thinner was unfortunate. Who knows what a self-esteem boost for millions of fat kids an overweight character could have achieved? (Given that the entire population of the USA will, according to recent statistics, be clinically obese by the year 2032, how likely is it that a group of high school misfits like the Scooby Gang would all be slim to the point of anorexia?) Having said that, Riff Regan is clearly nervous and fluffs some of her lines badly. 'She was lovely,' Tony Head remembered. 'I was very fond of her but there was no doubt about it, when I read the script that wasn't . . . Willow at all.'

Thankfully, Alyson Hannigan was just a phone call away.

It's a Designer Label!: Darla's flowery dress and black leggings clash with the faded 80s soul-boy look of her male counterpart. Buffy's blue-suede shoes, ginger miniskirt and Technicolour-yawn top show little sign of what we would come to expect, though in this incarnation, Willow *does* seem to have seen 'the softer side of Sears'. If the 'presentation' shows one thing that the series needed to get sorted, it's what they were trying to say about clothes. As Cordelia notes, 'I know flannel is *so* over, but I can never tell what's coming next.' Taste, seemingly.

References: Fashion guru Laura Ashley (see **11**, 'Out of Sight, Out of Mind'), Martha Stewart (see **37**, 'Faith, Hope and Trick'), The Beach Boys' 'Surf's Up', *The Muppets Take Manhattan*, *Crossroads* and Lionel Ritchie; allusions to *Terminator II: Judgment Day* ('She's back, and this time it's personal'), *Bambi*, The Smiths' 'Meat is Murder' and *The Flintstones*. Giles quotes *Hamlet* ('There are more things in heaven and earth . . . than are dreamt of in your philosophy.') A poster of FW Murnau's *Nosferatu* decorates the final scene.

Bitch!: Cordelia to Xander: 'Has any girl ever spoken to you of her own free will?'

Awesome!: Loads of cool images (like the close-up on a skull in the opening scene) and Buffy's fight with three vampires in the auditorium. Her gymnastic way of getting from the first floor of the library to the ground is a particular highlight. There's a terrific sequence (dropped from **1**, 'Welcome to the Hellmouth') in which Xander shows Buffy around school.

'You May Remember Me From Such Films As . . .': Stephen Tobolowsky, who played Principal Flutie, appeared in *Thelma and Louise*, *Spaceballs*, *Single White Female* and

Basic Instinct. Readers may know him best as 'Ned, the Insurance Man' in *Groundhog Day*.

'Is The Band Any Good?': Long before their debut on the series (see **16**, 'Inca Mummy Girl'), Dingoes Ate My Baby are mentioned. One of the Cordettes (see *Angel*: 'Rm w/a Vu') think 'They Rock!' but Xander tells Buffy 'They don't know any actual chords yet, but they have *really* big amps.' (See **50**, 'Doppelgängland'; **62**, 'Wild at Heart'.)

Dust to Dust: Only one vampire death is seen in close-up and it's interesting to compare the rather slow and ordinary 'crumbling skeleton' effect seen here to the beautifully realised explosion of dust featured in the series itself.

Valley-Speak: Girl #2: 'Chatter in the caf is that she [Buffy] got kicked out and that's why her mom had to get a new job.' Girl #1: '*Neg!*' Girl #2: '*Pos!*'

Buffy: 'I was *totally* phasing.' And: 'I'm *way* sure.' And: 'I'm *totally jammin'* on your dress.' And: 'It's *lush*.' And: 'I've both been there, and done that . . .'

Xander: '*Dudes*! Surf's always up somewhere in the world.'

Logic, Let Me Introduce You to This Window: Why does Buffy immediately assume, when Xander tells her that Willow has a date, that it's with a vampire?

You Can See Why They Dropped *That* Idea: Flutie's habit of calling Buffy 'Bunny', 'Bambi', 'Betty' and 'Wilma'. They would have run out of pun names by episode three.

What a Shame They Dropped . . .: This gem from the shooting script. Guy: 'My parents grounded me! It's *so* not fair.' Other Guy: 'You should sue.' Guy: '*No way*. My dad's lawyer is *way* better than mine.'

Quote/Unquote: Xander: 'Those guys are the Howzers. They'd be *total hardcore gangstas* except for the upper-class white-guy stigma. Total wannabes, but they're OK.'

Flutie's 'School Rules': 'No gang colours. No fur. No hanging from the rafters in the cafeteria screaming "Meat is Murder" during Sloppy Joe day.' And: 'We *almost never* have dead kids stuffed in the locker.'

Buffy: 'What is it with vampires and clothes? You always think the march of fashion stopped dead the day you did.'

Notes: As Buffy says: 'Relax. The world's in beauty hands.'

One has to agree with Tony Head's assessment of this oddity – that is, nice ideas (and clearly with potential) but *how* did they sell a series out of it? It's unfair to apply the same criteria to something that was never intended for public consumption as to the actual series, but there was obviously still much to be done. The characterisation is odd too, although Cordelia and Xander are excellently played (*love* Nick Brendon's demonstration of Buffy's 'crane technique').

The school is Berryman High, whose football (or basketball) team are called The Bulls. Buffy chews gum (a habit we don't see her repeat until **58**, 'Living Conditions'). She is taking 'Eurocentric history' (it's not her best subject). She was thrown out of her last (unnamed) school for 'causing trouble' (there's no reference to burning down the gym). She was on the student council. She mentions the football team and Xander jokingly asks if she was on that too. She seems to be referring to her time as a cheerleader (see **3**, 'The Witch'). She implies that her last Watcher died (is it Merrick she's talking about?). The history teacher is Mr Bron, and Mr Worth teaches maths.

Of course, the series *was* picked up. As Tony Head told *DreamWatch*: 'Several people have said it's one of the few instances where a TV spin-off improves on what people originally knew as the project. It's basically what Joss originally envisaged. He had no real say in the way the movie was made, in the way that writers *do* have very little say . . . I'm just glad to be part of what he eventually got made.'

Did You Know?: 'Mutant Enemy', Joss Whedon's production company, takes its name from a line in the song 'And You, And I' by prog-rock dinosaurs Yes.

*'We can do this the hard way, or . . . actually,
there's just the hard way.'*

– 'Welcome to the Hellmouth'

*'In every generation there is a Chosen One. She will
stand against the vampires, the demons and the forces
of darkness. She is the Slayer.'*

First Season (1997)

Mutant Enemy Inc./Kuzui Enterprises/
Sandollar Television/20th Century Fox
Created by Joss Whedon
Producer: Gareth Davies
Co-Producer: David Solomon
Executive Producers: Sandy Gallin, Gail Berman,
Fran Rubel Kuzui, Kaz Kuzui, Joss Whedon
Co-Executive Producer: David Greenwalt

Regular Cast:
Sarah Michelle Gellar (Buffy Summers), Nicholas Brendon (Xander Harris),
Alyson Hannigan (Willow Rosenberg),
Charisma Carpenter (Cordelia Chase, 1–5, 7, 9–12),
Anthony Stewart Head (Rupert Giles),
David Boreanaz (Angel, 1–2, 4–5, 7, 11–12),
Mark Metcalf (The Master, 1–2, 5, 7, 10, 12),
Ken Lerner (Principal Flutie, 1–2, 4, 6),
Kristine Sutherland (Joyce Summers, 1–3, 7, 9–10, 12),
Julie Benz (Darla, 1–2, 7), Mercedes McNab (Harmony Kendall, 2, 11),
Elizabeth Anne Allen (Amy Madison, 3),
Amanda Wilmshurst (Cheerleader, 3[1]),
William Monaghan (Dr Gregory, 3–4),
Andrew J Ferchland (the Anointed One, 5,[2] 7,[3] 10, 12),
Robia LaMorte (Jenny Calendar, 8, 12),
Dean Butler (Hank Summers, 10),
Armin Shimerman (Principal Snyder, 9, 11)

[1] Credited as 'Senior Cheerleader' in **3**, 'The Witch'.
[2] Credited as 'Boy' in **5**, 'Never Kill a Boy on the First Date'.
[3] Credited as 'Collin' in **7**, 'Angel'.

1

Welcome to the Hellmouth

US Transmission Date: 10 Mar. 1997
UK Transmission Date: 3 Jan. 1998 (Sky)
30 Dec. 1998 (BBC2)

Writer: Joss Whedon
Director: Charles Martin Smith
Cast: Brian Thompson (Luke), J Patrick Lawlor (Thomas),
Eric Balfour (Jesse), Natalie Strauss (Teacher), Amy Chance (Girl #1),
Tupelo Jereme (Girl #2), Persia White (Girl #3),
Carmine D Giovinazzo (Boy)
French title: *Bienvenue À Sunnydale, Première Partie*
German title: *Das Zentrum des Bösen*

On her first day at Sunnydale High, the Vampire Slayer Buffy
Summers befriends Xander and Willow, to the chagrin of resident snob Cordelia. In the library, Buffy meets Mr Giles, who
reveals he is her Watcher. A corpse is discovered and Buffy
finds the victim was killed by a vampire. She argues with Giles
about her responsibilities, both unaware that Xander has over-
heard. On her way to the Bronze club Buffy encounters a
stranger who warns her that she is living at 'the Mouth of
Hell'. He gives Buffy a crucifix and tells her that 'the Harvest'
is coming. At the cemetery Willow is attacked by a female
vampire, Darla, who has also brought another offering to The
Master, Xander's friend Jesse. Buffy and Xander overpower
Darla, just as The Master's henchman, Luke, appears.

Dudes and Babes: Angel's first appearance set many a female
heart aflutter (Buffy describes him as 'dark, gorgeous in an
annoying sort of way'). Darla is cute until she turns all
vampiry, at which point the attraction becomes somewhat
obscure (see **7**, 'Angel'). But Miss Summers in *that* skirt . . .
Hubba. Xander's fumbling attempts to chat her up are a highlight ('You forgot your . . . stake').

Authority Sucks!: Principal Flutie ('All the kids here are free
to call me Bob. But they don't') seems prepared to let Buffy's
past lie until he reads about the gym burning down.

A Little Learning is a Dangerous Thing: Xander tells
Willow he has a problem with 'the math'. When she asks

which part, he replies 'the math'. She advises that he borrows *Theories in Trig* from the library. We're informed that 25 million people died in the Black Death and that it was 'an early form of germ warfare'.

Mom's Apple Pie: Joyce's plea to Buffy before she starts her first day at Sunnydale High is, 'Try not to get kicked out.' Buffy says stakes are being used for self-defence in LA as pepper sprays are 'so passé'.

It's a Designer Label!: Cordelia would kill to live in LA to be so close to 'that many shoes' (see *Angel*: 'City Of'). Buffy recognises a vampire by his jacket, noting that only someone who has 'lived underground for ten years' would wear something so unfashionable. Willow's dress was one that her mom picked out (see **78**, 'Restless'). Buffy's red miniskirt and knee-length leather boots are smashing, but the two skirts she considers wearing to the Bronze make her look, she believes, either like a slut or a Jehovah's Witness.

References: Cordelia's 'coolness factor' test includes what Buffy thinks of James Spader (*Pretty in Pink*, *Less than Zero*, *Sex, Lies and Videotape*, *Stargate* and *Crash*) and former TV host and musician John Tesh, and the opinion that vamp nail polish is '*so* over'. Also department stores Neiman-Marcus and Sears, coffeehouse chain Starbucks, the Jehovah's Witness magazine *Watchtower* and 80s pop group De Barge.

Awesome!: The montage that forms Buffy's nightmare (many fans believe these to be scenes from the movie – they aren't). Buffy's fight with Luke in the mausoleum is impressive, though her first meeting with Angel tops it for emotional impact, *and* gymnastic stunts.

'You May Remember Me From Such Films and TV Series As . . .': Sarah Michelle Gellar was a child star, appearing in Burger King adverts as a four-year-old and having a starring role in *Swans Crossing*. She won a Daytime Emmy for her role as Kendall Hart in the soap *All My Children*. Her movies include *I Know What You Did Last Summer* (as Helen Shivers), *Cruel Intentions* (as Kathryn Merteuil) and *Scream 2*. Alyson Hannigan was also a child actor, making her debut in *My Stepmother is an Alien*. She has guested on series as diverse as *Roseanne*, *Picket Fences* and *Touched By An Angel* and her movies include several films that explore the dark underbelly of the US high school system, *Indecent Seduction*, *Dead Man on Campus*, *Boys & Girls* and *American Pie*. Tony Head will be known to British audiences for his Gold Blend commercials opposite Sharon Maughan in the 1980s (the adverts were also popular in the US where the coffee is called 'Taster's Choice'). He played Adam Klaus in the pilot of *Jonathan Creek* and appeared in two episodes of the *The Comic Strip Presents . . .* along with series like *Secret Army*, *Bergerac* and *Howard's Way*. Fans of *The X-Files* will recognise Brian Thompson as the enigmatic Alien Pilot. He was also in *The Terminator* and *Star Trek: Generations* (playing a Klingon). J Patrick Lawlor had a small role in *Pleasantville*.

Don't Give Up the Day Job: With his enormous success on *Buffy*, Joss Whedon remains much in demand in Hollywood, writing *Titan A.E.*, though sadly his script for *The X-Men* was one of several not used by the production. His next movie project will be an SF thriller called *Afterlife*. Director Charles Martin Smith is also an actor appearing in *Deep Impact*, *The Untouchables*, *Starman*, *American Graffiti* and *Pat Garrett and Billy the Kid* and TV series including *The X-Files*, *The Outer Limits* and *The Twilight Zone*.

Valley-Speak: Buffy: 'OK? What's the sitch?' And: 'Gee, everyone wants to know about me. How *keen*.' 'The wiggins' is Buffy's personal version of 'the willies'. Many subsequent episodes feature it, or a variation.

Cordelia: '*Totally* dead. *Way* dead.' And: 'My mom doesn't even *get* out of bed any more. And the doctor says it's Epstein-Barr. I'm like, *pleeease*! It's chronic hepatitis, or at least chronic fatigue syndrome. I mean, *nobody* cool has Epstein-Barr any more.'

Xander, on Buffy: 'Pretty much a *hottie*.' And: 'You're certainly a font of nothing.'

Logic, Let Me Introduce You to This Window: In the library, Giles piles several books into Buffy's arms, while telling her about all of the mythical creatures that exist. He stacks them so that the bindings are facing Buffy. Before she gives them back, Buffy raises the pile and the bindings are facing Giles. When she hands them over, they are again facing her. When Buffy looks for Willow in the Bronze, she breaks off a stool leg to use as a weapon. Next time we see her, it has become a stake.

I Just *Love* Your Accent: Asked by *The Watcher's Web* whether his time in England and exposure to British Tele-fantasy had scarred him for life, Joss Whedon noted: 'I saw *Blake's 7*, *Sapphire and Steel* and *Doctor Who* but not a great deal. I was at boarding school and didn't have much opportunity. What we watched were our heroes like *Starsky and Hutch* but I watched a huge amount of British TV while I lived in America. That's one of the reasons I was so anxious to come. I was an entire PBS kid. *Masterpiece Theatre*, *Monty Python*, BBC Shakespeares.' 'You want the contrast between Giles and Buffy,' he told Rob Francis when asked if his time in Britain had helped to get characters like Giles right. 'But at the same time I hope he's been a little more human than just stuffy. The great thing is there are dirty words that the American audience don't know.'

Giles was the curator at a British museum, or 'possibly *the* British Museum'. His ideal night is staying home with a cup of Bovril (can you *get* Bovril in the US?) and a good book (see **8**, 'I Robot . . . You Jane'). Producer Gareth Davies worked for the BBC in the 1960s on *The Wednesday Play* (including Dennis Potter's groundbreaking dramas *Vote, Vote, Vote For Nigel Barton*, *Alice*, *Where the Buffalo Roam*, *Message for Posterity*, *Angels Are so Few* and the notorious *Son of Man*). He subsequently produced *Tales of the Unexpected* and *Boon* before moving to America to work on *Remington Steele*.

Motors: Joyce Summers drives a Jeep Cherokee Sport (see **40**, 'Band Candy').

Quote/Unquote: Giles on zombies, werewolves, incubi and succubi: 'Everything you ever dreaded was under your bed but told yourself couldn't be in the light of day. *They're all real.*'

Buffy's reply to Giles's surprise that the vampire she's tracking isn't dead: 'No, but my social life is on the critical list.'

Notes: 'This is Sunnydale. How bad an evil can there be here?' A great debut, well paced, superbly characterised (we already feel as if we've known these people for *years*) and with a wicked sense of humour. 'Welcome to the Hellmouth' is an intricate doll's house of a plot, with many knowing winks to the audience. If you don't find something of interest in this, you're probably dead.

Buffy's previous school was Hemery High in Los Angeles (see **M1**). She burned down the gymnasium because 'it was full of vampires' (real reason), or 'asbestos' (official excuse). Xander's skateboarding skills leave much to be desired. Xander and Willow used to go out, but split up when he stole her Barbie doll (they were five). Willow says that when she's with a boy it's hard for her to say anything 'cool or witty. Or at all. I can usually make a few vowel sounds and then I have to go away.' The book Giles shows Buffy to establish his Watcher credentials is an ancient volume called *Vampyr*. When Giles tells Buffy about all of the mythical creatures that exist, she asks, 'Did you send away for the *Time Life* series?' Giles confirms he *did* and that he received the free calendar instead of the free phone. Giles says, of Sunnydale: 'Dig a bit in the history of this place. You'll find a steady stream of fairly odd occurrences. I believe this area is a centre of mystical energy, that things gravitate towards it', and 'The influx of the undead, the supernatural occurrences, it's been building for years. There's a reason why you're here and a reason why it's now' (see **51**, 'Enemies'; **56**, 'Graduation Day' Part 2).

The Bronze ('they let anybody in, but it's still the scene') is in 'the bad part of town', which is 'half a block from the good part of town'. It is said that the whole of Sunnydale can be seen from the top of the gym, which ties in with there not being 'a whole lot of town' (see **15**, 'School Hard'), even if it has got an airport (see **21**, 'What's My Line?' Part 1). If a vampire sucks someone's blood, this will kill the person being attacked. The victim will only turn into a vampire themselves if they suck the vampire's blood in return (see **33**, 'Becoming' Part 1, though the series occasionally contradicts this. See **46**, 'Helpless'). The vampires refer to themselves as 'the Old Ones' (as does Giles in **2**, 'The Harvest'). The history teacher is called Mr Chopski. The female gym coach, Foster, has 'chest hair' according to Cordelia. The two girls discussing Buffy in the locker room are called Aphrodisia and Aura (they appear to belong to 'the Cordettes', see *Angel*: 'Rm w/a Vu').

Another of their friends, the one who finds out about Buffy having been expelled from Hemery, is called Blue.

All US transmissions are accompanied by a pre-episode caption warning *tonight's presentation is rated TV-PG and contains action scenes which may be too intense for younger viewers* (or a variation). When the BBC purchased the series, they edited the episodes with a blunt hacksaw instead (notably any fight sequences). Overseas prints of this episode do not feature the voice-over concerning two previous Slayers – Lucy Hanover in Virginia in 1866 and a nameless woman in Chicago in 1927.

Nick Brendon told *Spectrum*: 'Being on a network like WB at the time was beneficial for both parties. I think that *Buffy* has helped to launch that network and make it the fastest-growing on TV.' The school used is Torrance High in Los Angeles. It's also used for *Beverly Hills 90210* and *She's All That*.

Novelisation: By Richie Tankersley Cusick as *The Harvest* (Pocket Books, September 1997).

Soundtrack: The theme music is by Nerf Herder [*] whose name is an insult Princess Leia hurls at Han Solo in *The Empire Strikes Back*. Sprung Monkey perform 'Believe', 'Swirl' and 'Things Are Changing' in the Bronze. Another song, 'Saturated', is heard when Buffy tries to decide which dress to wear.

Did You Know?: David Boreanaz's audition scene was the sequence in which Angel warns Buffy about the coming Harvest. It was shot at two in the morning 'in some god-awful street' according to Boreanaz.

2

The Harvest

US Transmission Date: 10 Mar. 1997
UK Transmission Date: 10 Jan. 1998 (Sky)
30 Dec. 1998 (BBC2)

Writer: Joss Whedon
Director: John T Kretchmer
Cast: Brian Thompson (Luke), Eric Balfour (Jesse), Deborah Brown (Girl),
Teddy Lane Jr (Bouncer), Jeffrey Steven Smith (Guy in Comp. Class)

French title: *Bienvenue À Sunnydale, Seconde Partie*
German title: *Die Zeit der Ernte*

Buffy escapes from Luke and saves Xander and Willow, but Jesse has been taken by the vampires. Luke and Darla tell The Master about Buffy. Suspecting she may be the Slayer, they use Jesse as bait. Buffy and Xander return to the cemetery and meet the stranger who warned Buffy about the Harvest. He introduces himself as Angel and tells her that it will take place that night. They find Jesse, but he's now a vampire. Buffy and Xander escape through a ventilation duct. At the Bronze, Luke begins to drain victims of their blood, becoming The Master's 'Vessel'. Buffy battles with Luke as the others lead the frightened teenagers out of the Bronze. Xander fights Jesse, and kills him. Buffy tricks Luke into believing it is sunrise and, with the Vessel dead, the Harvest is prevented.

Dudes and Babes: Xander's inadequacy when Buffy won't let him help is touching. Buffy complains about Angel's 'cryptic wise-man act'. For the boys, there's Cordelia dancing.

Mom's Apple Pie: Buffy's mom grounds her for skipping class. 'If you don't go out it'll be the end of the world? *Everything*'s life or death to a sixteen-year-old girl.'

A Little Learning is a Dangerous Thing: Cordy discovers how to save a computer file. Not.

It's a Designer Label!: Willow's dungarees are horrible. *Love* Angel's disco threads. Buffy's Raybans and her leather jacket give the final scenes a touch of class.

References: Luke burning himself on Buffy's cross mirrors a device used in many vampire films, notably Hammer's *Dracula, Prince of Darkness*. Buffy mentions Sam Peckinpah's notoriously violent *The Wild Bunch*.

Bitch!: Cordelia: 'Hello, Miss Motormouth, can I get a sentence finished?' And: 'Excuse me, who gave you permission to exist?' Cordelia and Harmony call Buffy a 'psycho loony'.

'You May Remember Me From Such Films and TV Series As . . .': Both Nick Brendon and David Boreanaz made guest appearances on the popular sitcom *Married: With Children*. Nick's also appeared in movies like *Children of the*

Corn III and *Psycho Beach Party*. A former cheerleader for the San Diego Chargers, Charisma Carpenter began her acting career with a small part in *Baywatch*, playing Hobie's girlfriend Wendie (probably the only time you'll see 'Baywatch' and 'small part' in the same sentence). Aaron Spelling personally auditioned her for the 'über-vixen-bitch' Ashley Green in NBC's *Malibu Shores*. She was also Beth Sullivan in the *Josh Kirby: Time Warrior* TV movies and appeared in a legendary advert for Spree sweets ('It's a kick in the mouth').

Mark Metcalf played Doug Neidermeyer in the classic *National Lampoon's Animal House*. Kristine Sutherland was Matt Frewer's wife in *Honey I Shrunk the Kids* and appeared in *Legal Eagles*. Ken Lerner is in dozens of films including *Robocop 2* and *The Running Man* and was Fonzie's love rival Rocko in *Happy Days*. Mercedes McNab played the young Sue Storm in *The Fantastic Four* and was in both *The Addams Family* and *Addams Family Values*. Former ice-skater Julie Benz (once ranked twelfth in the US) was one of many actresses who auditioned for the role of Buffy. She later played Kate Topolsky in *Roswell* and was in *As Good As It Gets, Jawbreaker, A Fate Totally Worse Than Death, Darkdrive, Shriek If You Know What I Did Last Friday the 13th* and *Satan's School for Girls*.

Don't Give Up the Day Job: John T Kretchmer was assistant director on the first two *Naked Gun* movies and *Jurassic Park*. The first female victim was played, uncredited, by Kerry Zook.

Valley-Speak: Buffy: 'We *so* don't have the time . . .' Her description of the Harvest is: 'A suck-fest.'

Logic, Let Me Introduce You to This Window: Why is that globe spinning in the library while Giles is talking about the Earth's ancient history? In the computer class, Harmony asks: 'Are we going to the Bronze tonight?' Cordelia: 'Of course we're going to the Bronze. Friday night, no cover.' If it's Friday night, why are they at school the next day? And, as we see, there clearly *is* a cover charge. When Xander and Buffy are climbing to the surface, watch Xander's left hand grabbing Buffy's breast after the vampire reaches out for her foot.

I Just *Love* Your Accent: Flutie refers to the British royal
family and to 'all kinds of problems' in the UK. Oh really?
Wish we had a crime rate as low as California, mate. Giles
hates computers, an attitude he describes as 'a bit British',
which is pretty insulting to perfectly respectable UK-based Net
nerds like this author. And most of his friends. (See **8**, 'I
Robot . . . You Jane'.)

Quote/Unquote: Buffy notes that the first time she saw a
vampire, she tried to rationalise their existence: 'Once I'd done
with the screaming part.' (See **33**, 'Becoming' Part 1.)

Luke on Jesse: 'I thought you were nothing more than a meal,
boy. Congratulations, you've just been upgraded. To "bait".'

Buffy asks Giles what he can say that will make the day any
worse. 'How about the End of the World?' '*Knew* I could rely
on you.'

Notes: 'Yesterday, "Uh-oh Pop Quiz". Today, it's "rain of
toads".' Even better. Here we see the various strands that make
Buffy work meshing perfectly. This concludes the first part
with an apocalyptic storyline and lots of cool jokes and gets
better every time you see it.

Giles indicates that the world is older than most people
realise and is dismissive of Christianity, noting that 'contrary
to popular mythology' it did not begin with a paradise. (This
doesn't fit with a crucifix and holy water being deadly to a
vampire, not to mention the very Christian presentation of Hell
in the series, the plethora of biblical lore either quoted or
alluded to and references to the crucifixion in **15**, 'School
Hard'. See also **44**, 'Amends'; **45**, 'Gingerbread'.) Giles notes
that for untold eons demons walked the Earth. They made it
their home, but in time they lost their purchase on this reality.
'The way was made for mortal animals, for man. All that
remains of the old ones are vestiges, certain magicks . . . The
books tell that the last demon to leave this reality fed off a
human, mixed their blood. He was a human form possessed,
infected by the demon's soul. He bit another, and another, and
so they walk the Earth, feeding . . .'

Willow has 'accidentally' decrypted the city council's computer security system allowing her access to all sorts of classified material. Luke recounts the last time someone attacked

him and survived: '1843, Madrid. He caught me sleeping.' Things that will kill a vampire (aside from a wooden stake) include garlic, fire, holy water, sunlight and beheading. Buffy has done a little of the latter, including the story she tells Xander about her hacking off a varsity football left-tackle's head with a small penknife. (So *that* explains that garbled scene in **M1**.) She beheads a vampire, using a cymbal (unless you were watching on BBC2). There was an earthquake in Sunnydale in 1937 during The Master's last bid for freedom (see **12**, 'Prophecy Girl'; **67**, 'Doomed'). Sunnydale was first settled by the Spanish, who called it *Boca del Infierno* (roughly translated, 'Hellmouth'). It's a portal between this reality and the next ('other dimension' references crop up regularly too). When the BBC broadcast this episode (as a double feature with **1**, 'Welcome to the Hellmouth'), several cuts were made including the almost complete ruination of the 'Just say you're sorry' eye-poking sequence. Thankfully, Sky left it in uncut. Interestingly, *Buffy*'s first broadcast was in New Zealand, its run there beginning on 2 February 1997, a full six weeks ahead of the US debut.

Novelisation: By Richie Tankersley Cusick as *The Harvest* (Pocket Books, September 1997), which includes scenes and dialogue cut from the transmitted episodes.

Soundtrack: Sprung Monkey's 'Right My Wrong' and the Dashboard Prophets' 'Ballad for a Dead Friend' and 'Wearing Me Down'.

3
The Witch

US Transmission Date: 17 Mar. 1997
UK Transmission Date: 17 Jan. 1998 (Sky)
6 Jan. 1999 (BBC2)

Writer: Dana Reston
Director: Stephen Cragg
Cast: Robin Riker (Catherine), Jim Doughan (Mr Pole),
Nicole Prescott (Lishanne)
French title: *Sortilèges*
German title: *Verhext*

It's the cheerleading tryouts, and Buffy hopes to make the squad. However, horrible things happen to leading contenders (including the blinding of Cordelia). Willow's friend Amy, whose mom was a great cheerleader, is an obvious suspect and when Buffy, Xander and Willow perform an experiment to confirm if Amy is a witch, the test is positive. Amy concocts a spell that will kill Buffy. Desperate to reverse it, Giles and Buffy meet Amy's mom, Catherine, and discover that she has switched bodies with her daughter so that she can relive her glorious past. While Giles prepares the reversal, 'Amy' realises what is happening. She attacks Buffy, but Giles completes the spell. Catherine, back in her own body, unleashes an energy bolt but Buffy uses a mirror to trap the witch in her own cheerleading trophy.

Dudes and Babes: 'You were pretending seeing scantily clad girls in revealing postures was a spiritual experience,' Willow tells Xander, who spends the episode trying to date Buffy, including giving her a chain with 'Yours Always' written on it. He says it 'came that way'. Poor lad, he obviously has a lot on his plate once Buffy tells him he's '*totally* one of the girls' (a reversal of his informing Willow she is 'like a guy'). Let's not forget that Buffy has needs too, as we're reminded by her reaction to an African fertility statue: 'Jeepers!'

Authority Sucks!: Giles forbids Buffy to join the cheerleading squad, to which she asks, 'And you'll be stopping me, how?'

Mom's Apple Pie: The issue of parental pressure is central (with the implication of child abuse in Buffy's description of Catherine as 'Nazi-like'). Joyce (who is seemingly more concerned with her gallery's first exhibition than Buffy) doesn't come out of the episode too well, but the closing scenes are well done as she admits she doesn't understand her daughter. She says she wouldn't want to be sixteen again (judging by the uncool 'wannabe' girl we see glimpses of in **40**, 'Band Candy', it's obvious why not).

It's a Designer Label!: Let's start with Buffy's cheerleading outfit (those red sports knickers they wear are *outstanding*). The discerning male viewer is also pointed in the direction of Cordelia's jogger shorts. Minus points for Amy's horrible sweatshirt, with a CND logo.

References: 'Count the ways' is a reference to Elizabeth Barrett Browning's epic love poem *Sonnets from the Portuguese*. Also, the LA Lakers, *Sabrina the Teenage Witch*, *Mommie Dearest* (the biography of actress Joan Crawford), Marvel's *Fantastic Four* character Johnny Storm, the Human Torch, and HG Wells's *The Invisible Man*. Buffy sings a couple of lines from the Village People's 'Macho Man'.

There's an oblique reference to Farrah Fawcett Majors (of *Charlie's Angels*) when Buffy looks at her mom's yearbook photo and says, 'I've accepted that you've had sex, I am not ready to know you had Farrah-hair.' Joyce says it was actually '*Gidget*-hair', referring to the Sally Fields sitcom based on the *Gidget* novel by Frederick Kohner. Giles gives a precise little essay on Spontaneous Human Combustion.

Bitch!: Buffy believes Giles should 'get a girlfriend . . . if he wasn't so old'.

Cordelia's response to Willow saying Amber is on fire. 'Enough of the hyperbole.'

Willow, after Giles wonders why anyone would wish Cordelia harm: 'Maybe they *met* her?'

Awesome!: Giles's reaction to Buffy enslaving herself 'to this cult', which turns out to be the cheerleading squad. Plus Amber's hands on fire and the girl with no mouth.

'You May Remember Me From Such Films and TV Series As . . .': Robin Riker was the female lead in the seminal 1980 horror movie *Alligator*. She's also made guest appearances on *M*A*S*H*, *The A-Team* and *Murder She Wrote*. Elizabeth Anne Allen, like Julie Benz, auditioned for the role of Buffy and was rewarded with a slot as fan favourite Amy. She was Shelly in *Silent Lies*, Carri in *Green Sails* and appeared in *Illegal Blue*.

Don't Give Up the Day Job: Writer Dana Reston was story editor and producer on the Fran Drescher sitcom *The Nanny*. Jennifer Badger, Charisma Carpenter's stunt double, was one of the stunt team on *Austin Powers: The Spy Who Shagged Me*. Sarah Michelle Gellar's stunt double on the first four seasons was London-born Sophia Crawford who played Chameleon in *WMAC Masters* and Carmella in *Night Hunters*.

Valley-Speak: Buffy: 'He totally lost his water.' And: 'I've seen some pretty cringeworthy things, but nobody's hands ever got toasted before.' And: 'I need to get the skinny on Amber.' And: 'Get *down* with your bad self.'

Cordelia: 'You're going to be so very *beyond* sorry.'

Cigarettes and Alcohol: Willow says Amber only ever got detention once, for smoking. ('Regular smoking . . . With a cigarette.')

Logic, Let Me Introduce You to This Window: Sunnydale must have the most dangerous parcel delivery service in America. One would have expected the van driver to, at least, slow down after crashing into a parked car and nearly running a blind girl down. Maybe he was on a time bonus? Amber Grove's hair is significantly shorter when seen from behind as Buffy is putting out the fire on her hands. When Giles and Buffy arrive at the Madison home, Giles's car is missing its front licence plate. (This 'error' was spotted by lots of American fans, which is odd because in many states such plates are not required by law. The same thing crops up in **26**, 'Innocence' and **27**, 'Phases'.) When did Amy steal Buffy's bracelet? On overseas prints, the credits list the band who play the theme tune as 'Nerfherder' (one word). The sign in the gym reads, 1996 CHEERLEADING TRYOUTS. It should be 1997.

Motors: A first look at Giles's 1963 Citröen DS Coupé. Unfortunately, it's fallen greatly into disrepair.

What a Shame They Dropped . . .: Giles repeats the mistakes of *Monty Python's Holy Grail*: 'The ducking stool. We throw her in the pond. If she floats, she's a witch. If she drowns, she's innocent . . . Some of my texts are a bit outdated.'

Quote/Unquote: Xander tells Buffy he laughs in the face of danger. 'Then, I hide until it goes away.'

Giles, at the cynical looks the others give him as he talks enthusiastically about the 'cornucopia of fiends, devils and ghouls' that inhabit the Hellmouth: 'Pardon me for finding the glass half full.'

Notes: 'This witch is casting horrible and disfiguring spells so that she can become a cheerleader?' *Major* revaluation time: initially dismissed as one of the lesser episodes of the season, 'The Witch' improves *hugely* with repeated viewing although half the episode *is* made up of non-sequiturs. Extreme eye-candy, certainly, but with a depth and intelligence.

Xander has checked the books *Witches: Historic Roots to Modern Practice* and *The Pagan Rites* out of the library. ('It's not what you think.') To look at the semi-nude engravings. ('OK, maybe it *is* what you think.') Willow describes herself and Xander as 'the Slayerettes'. Catherine led her team to be tri-county champions, still a unique achievement. She and Amy's father were Homecoming King and Queen. They got married immediately after graduation. Amy's father was 'a big loser . . . Ran off with Miss Trailer Trash when I was twelve', but since this is really Catherine speaking it's difficult to know how much is true. Sunnydale's basketball team are The Razorbacks.

Soundtrack: 'Twilight Zone' by Dutch techno duo 2 Unlimited.
What's In a Name?: Willow shares her unusual name with the character played by Britt Ekland in Robin Hardy's dreamlike horror masterpiece *The Wicker Man*. Cordelia first appeared in the Holinshed's *Chronicles* and was used by Shakespeare in *King Lear*. It's also the name given to the smallest of Uranus's moons, discovered by *Voyager 2* in 1986. Variations on the surname Giles appear in England as far back as *The Domesday Book* in 1086. St Giles lived as a hermit in France and the name derives from the Celtic word for 'servant'. A large number of English churches were dedicated to him, though the name itself was not popular, possibly because of St Giles's association with beggars and cripples of whom he is the patron saint.

4
Teacher's Pet

US Transmission Date: 25 Mar. 1997
UK Transmission Date: 24 Jan. 1998 (Sky)
13 Jan. 1999 (BBC2)

Writer: David Greenwalt
Director: Bruce Seth Green

Cast: Musetta Vander (She-Mantis), Jackson Price (Blayne),
Jean Speegle Howard (Natalie French),
Jack Knight (Homeless Guy),
Michael Robb Verona (Teacher), Karim Oliver (Bud #1)
French title: *Le Chouchou du Prof*
German title: *Die Gottesanbeterin*

When biology teacher Dr Gregory goes missing, the school
assigns a substitute, the alluring Ms French. Dr Gregory's body
is found in the cafeteria, minus his head. Believing a clawed
vampire who attacked Angel to be responsible, Buffy sees it
about to attack Ms French, then flee in terror. Buffy concludes
that Natalie French is a She-Mantis. Giles calls a friend who
went mad hunting such a creature for details on how to kill it. At
Natalie's home Xander is drugged and locked in a cage in the
basement, next to another boy from school, Blayne. When
Xander awakens, he sees Ms French in her true form. Blayne
says she has already eaten the head of her mate. Buffy uses the
clawed vampire to lead her to the She-Mantis. With the help of
Giles and Willow, she breaks in and hacks the creature to death.
Dudes and Babes: Xander is jealous of Angel. Mind you,
anybody who has dreams like young Mr Harris (finding time to
'finish my solo and kiss you like you've never been kissed
before') deserves what they get, frankly. He may have been
distracted by the cheerleaders modelling their 'new short
skirts' (see **3**, 'The Witch'). Giles's description of Natalie is
'lovely, in a common, extremely well-proportioned way'. Her
slinky black dress reveals *how* well-proportioned. As Xander
says: 'It's a beautiful chest . . . dress.'
A Little Learning is a Dangerous Thing: How ants communicate. With other ants. The sexually charged lesson on the
praying mantis and its wily ways reveals that there are 1,800-
plus species worldwide, in most of which the females are larger
and more aggressive.
School Dinners: The following items are on a notice board in
the cafeteria: 'salad bar, meat loaf, lasagna, sloppy joes, maca-
roni and cheese, fajitas, cheeseburger, blueberry pie, orange
jello, brownies'. Buffy and Willow are horrified to find out
they're getting 'hot dog surprise' for lunch. Cordelia has a medi-
cally prepared lunch, prescribed by her doctor (implication: it's

to keep her weight steady), but finding Dr Gregory's body in the kitchen seems to put her off her food. Anybody eating during this episode, beware of Natalie's insect sandwich.

It's a Designer Label!: Buffy's red dress in Xander's dream and her extremely short light-blue skirt are impressive, but the highlight is her yellow stretchpants. Angel gives Buffy his leather jacket. The She-Mantis's fashion sense is 'predatory'.

References: Xander's flashbacks bear similarity to techniques used in another seminal high school series, *Parker Lewis Can't Lose*. There are name checks for *The Exorcist*, the legends of 'virgin thieves' (the Greek sirens and the Celtic maidens) and an oblique reference to *Godzilla* and its sequels ('We're on Monster Island').

Awesome!: Buffy's fight with the claw-handed vampire. Twenty seconds of unrestrained violence. Or, in the case of the BBC edit, *five* seconds of unrestrained violence.

'You May Remember Me From Such Films As . . .': Jean Speegle Howard is the mother of Ron Howard and has a great role in his movie *Apollo 13* (as Jim Lovell's confused mom).

'You May Remember Me From Such Video Games, Films and TV Shows As . . .': Musetta Vander had a starring role in the *Voyeur* computer game (circa 1991). She also plays Munita in *Wild Wild West* and appeared in the excellent *Stargate SG-1* episode 'Crossroads'.

Don't Give Up the Day Job: One of writer David Greenwalt's first jobs was as Jeff Bridges' body double before becoming a director on *The Wonder Years* and writer/producer on *The X-Files* and *Doogie Howser MD*. His film scripts include *Class*, *American Dreamer* and *Secret Admirer* (which he also directed) and *one* acting role as 'Uniformed Cop' in the 1981 horror-spoof movie *Wacko*. Director Bruce Seth Green's TV work includes series like *Knight Rider, Airwolf, MacGyver, She-Wolf of London, V, SeaQuest DSV, Xena: Warrior Princess, TJ Hooker, Hercules: The Legendary Journeys, American Gothic* and *Jack & Jill*.

Cigarettes and Alcohol: Xander drinks the Martini that Ms French gives him.

Logic, Let Me Introduce You to This Window: Xander throws a chair leg into a vampire's chest during his dream. It goes into the right side of the chest, as opposed to where the heart is. Since it's a dream, we could excuse this as Xander's naïveté in the ways of killing (though he's already staked one vampire: Jesse in **2**, 'The Harvest'). The door shouldn't be left open during a private session with a counsellor. Dr Gregory's narration on the ant features a slide of a beetle. As Natalie eats her insect sandwich, for most of the scene her sweater sleeves are pulled up to her elbows. However, for the close-up of her hands pouring the insects on to the bread, the cuffs cover her wrists. When Xander is tied up in Natalie's basement, he has a flashback to her first class with him. If Blayne was heading straight to biology when Buffy and friends were sitting outside, we can assume that it was the first class of the day. Certainly the group are seen at lunch *afterwards*. However, as Natalie approaches Xander, the clock behind him says 1.45. After Buffy hacks the She-Mantis to death, she wipes the machete blade on the seat of her pants. Bet she caught it from her mom on the next washing day (see **34**, 'Becoming' Part 2). Angel's scar from his encounter with the clawed vampire: although vampires seem to heal quickly (Angel being shot in **7**, 'Angel', for instance), this doesn't always work (see **43**, 'The Wish'; **55**, 'Graduation Day' Part 1).

I Just *Love* Your Accent: Giles's former colleague, Carlisle, first discovered references to the She-Mantis in old German texts. He tried to hunt her after boys were murdered in the Cotswolds, but went insane. (Giles tells him in a telephone call that he *was* right about the She-Mantis, but probably wrong about his mother being reincarnated as a Pekinese.)

Quote/Unquote: Giles on bat sonar: 'Soothingly akin to having one's teeth drilled.'

Notes: 'A perfect end to a wonderful day.' Loads of fun with a dangerous, sexy villainess – a complete subversion of the 'pretty girl in peril' form of horror fantasy. The She-Mantis is so over-the-top that it moves into areas of grand kitsch. Isn't the monster costume gloriously pants? Proof that in the best traditions of *Doctor Who* a witty, entertaining series can still do crap monsters on a budget and get away with it.

Xander's middle name is LaVelle (he's embarrassed by it). He says he likes cucumber. He's also a virgin (which we *all* knew anyway). The real Natalie French's address is 837 Weatherley Drive.

Novelisation: By Keith RA DeCandido in *The Xander Years Vol. 1* (Pocket Books, February 1999).

Soundtrack: Superfine perform 'Already Met You' [*] in the Bronze (the singer is less than impressed with Xander's dancing). Their song, 'Stoner Love', is also featured.

Critique: *Buffy* received its first UK publicity with this episode, as 'Today's Choice', in the satellite section of *Radio Times* (though it had been previously mentioned in the magazine's John Peel column). It was described as 'a huge hit in the States', a 'supernatural drama' and 'a sort of *Beverly Hills 90210* meets *The X-Files*'. Extremely 'sort of . . .'

Did You Know?: One of David Boreanaz's previous movie roles had been playing 'Vampire Victim' in a movie called *Macabre Pair of Shorts* (1996).

5
Never Kill a Boy on the First Date

US Transmission Date: 31 Mar. 1997
UK Transmission Date: 31 Jan. 1998 (Sky)
20 Jan. 1999 (BBC2)

Writers: Rob Des Hotel, Dean Batali
Director: David Semel
Cast: Christopher Wiehl (Owen), Geoff Meed (Andrew Vorba),
Paul-Felix Montez (Mysterious Guy), Robert Mont (Van Driver)
French title: *Un Premier Rendez-Vous Manqué*
German title: *Ohne Buffy Lebt Sich's Länger*

Giles discovers a dead vampire's ring belongs to the Order of Aurelius, just as Buffy's crush Owen Thurman arranges a date. Unfortunately, Buffy learns that an ancient prophecy, the rising of the Anointed, will be fulfilled tonight and by the time she has finished her patrol she finds Owen dancing with Cordelia at the Bronze. A shuttle bus crashes and all of the passengers are killed by the vampires. Giles asks Buffy to check out the funeral home where the bodies were taken. She refuses, saying that she needs a break. Giles goes himself and encounters two vampires. Xander and Willow alert Buffy, though she is unable to get rid of Owen. Buffy finds Giles in the storage room, and she and Owen fight the vampire, whom Giles believes to be the Anointed One. Enraged when Owen is hurt, Buffy tosses the vampire into the incinerator. Owen wants to go out with Buffy again, but only to relive the adrenaline rush. Buffy refuses. Meanwhile, The Master meets the *real* Anointed One.

Dudes and Babes: Owen seems a little bookish for Buffy (and Cordy for that matter), despite Buffy's brattish outburst to Giles ('Cute guy; teenage post-pubescent fantasies').

Cordelia on Angel: '*Hello*, salty goodness!'

A Little Learning is a Dangerous Thing: Owen's 'Emily Dickinson for beginners' gives a nice introduction to the works of the poet (1830–1886). It's certainly a more impressive overview than Giles stuffily noting that she was 'quite a good poet . . . for an American'.

School Dinners: There's a big discussion on what the 'green stuff' served in the cafeteria is.

It's a Designer Label!: Buffy's green and white dress ('Does this outfit make me look fat?'). Let's heave a sigh of delight for her tigerskin anorak, too.

References: Nick Brendon impersonates Jerry Seinfeld: 'Everyone forgets, Willow, that knowledge is the ultimate weapon.' Vorba sings the hymn 'Gather at the River'. Also, *Soylent Green*, *The Untouchables* ('Here endeth the lesson') and *Superman* ('even Clark Kent had a job'). Xander has a Tweety Pie wristwatch. There's a possible reference to Patrick McGoohan's 1960s series *Danger Man* but, as that show was called *Secret Agent* in the US, it's more likely a coincidence.

Bitch!: Buffy: 'Boy, Cordelia's hips are wider than I thought.'

Valley-Speak: Buffy: 'I *totally* blew it.' And her legendary taunt to Vorba: 'Bite me!'

Logic, Let Me Introduce You to This Window: If a vampire's clothes turn to dust when they are killed, why does the ring remain intact? In the first shot of the shuttle bus, we can see the interior lights illuminated. When the scene cuts inside, all of its lights are off. As Buffy tells Giles 'if the Apocalypse comes, beep me', she reaches forward, grabs her pager and holds it up. The next shot is from the side and there is no table or platform on which the pager could have been resting.

Quote/Unquote: Buffy, when Giles shows an interest in the ring of the dead vampire: 'That's great. I kill 'em, you fence their stuff.'

Giles: 'I'll just jump into my time machine, go back to the twelfth century and ask the vampires to postpone their ancient prophecy for a few days while you take in dinner and a show?'

Notes: 'Prophecy. Anointed One. Yadda yadda yadda.' A solid, if rather uneventful episode, with not much to get excited about except the usual array of great one-liners. The climax, however, is clever as the identity of the Anointed One is revealed.

Giles was ten when his father told him he was destined to be a Watcher (as part of a 'tiresome speech about responsibility and sacrifice'). Giles had plans to be a fighter pilot (or a grocer). At least two previous members of the Giles family were Watchers: Giles's father, and his paternal grandmother. He has volumes of lore, prophecies and predictions, but he says he doesn't have an instruction book on how to be a Slayer (this is contradicted in **22**, 'What's My Line?' Part 2).

Soundtrack: Three Day Wheely's 'Rotten Apples', Rubber's 'Junkie Girl' and 'Let the Sun Fall Down' by Kim Richey. Velvet Chain perform the dramatic 'Strong' [*] and 'Treason' in the Bronze.

6

The Pack

US Transmission Date: 7 Apr. 1997
UK Transmission Date: 7 Feb. 1998 (Sky)
3 Feb. 1999 (BBC2)

Writers: Matt Kiene, Joe Reinkemeyer
Director: Bruce Seth Green
Cast: Eion Bailey (Kyle), Michael McRaine (Rhonda), Brian Gross (Tor), Jennifer Sky (Heidi), Jeff Maynard (Lance), James Stephens (Zookeeper), Gregory White (Coach Herrold), Jeffrey Steven Smith (Adam), David Brisbin (Mr Anderson), Barbara K Whinnery (Mrs Anderson), Justin Jon Ross (Joey), Patrese Borem (Young Woman)
French title: *Les Hyènes*
German title: *Das Lied der Hyänen*

On a zoo trip, Kyle and his gang of bullies are confronted by Xander in the quarantined hyena house. All of the teenagers leave with yellow eyes and changed personalities, Xander acting cruelly particularly to Willow. Buffy and Giles discover an African tribal legend concerning hyena spirits that possess men. The pack find Herbert, the school's pig mascot, and eat him. Buffy is attacked by Xander but she locks him in the book cage. The rest of the pack are sent to the principal's office, where they eat Flutie. Buffy and Giles talk to the zookeeper, who describes a way of reversing the curse. Buffy leads the pack, including Xander, to the zoo, where the keeper plans to create a transfer to gain the hyena spirits himself. He is successful but is tossed into the hyena pit by Buffy and a recovered Xander.

Dudes and Babes: Willow tells Buffy that Xander makes her head 'all tingly'. Xander seems similarly excited by the sight of zebras mating. He says he's been waiting for Buffy 'to jump on [his] bones'.

A Little Learning is a Dangerous Thing: Willow's attempts to teach Xander basic geometry are hindered by his possession.

School Dinners: Xander's hunger isn't satisfied by Buffy's croissant or various hotdogs so he goes for a giant, uncooked bacon sandwich. Without the bread. As Buffy asks: 'Didn't your mom teach you, don't play with your food?'

It's a Designer Label!: Ouch! The Rupert Bear pants on the girl walking behind Buffy in the opening scene and Xander and Willow's near-matching Nerds-On-Tour gear. Buffy wears the jacket Angel gave her (see **4**, 'Teacher's Pet') – it goes with her shoes. It may, but her pink miniskirt definitely doesn't go with the black ski-cap she's wearing in the final scene.

References: The signs in the zoo are in the same font as those in *Jurassic Park*. The line 'all shiny and new' *may* be a nod to Madonna's 'Like A Virgin'. Noah's Ark is referred to (see Giles's Christianity-baiting speech in **2**, 'The Harvest'). Also, *The X-Files* ('I can't believe you, of all people, are trying to Scully me'), *The Wizard of Oz* ('Oh great, it's the Winged Monkeys'), and *Silence of the Lambs* ('a bottle of Chianti'). Buffy makes a sarcastic comment about Yanni, the notorious US easy-listening synth-musak guy.

Bitch!: Rhonda and Heidi do their best to make Buffy's life a misery in the opening scene.

Awesome!: Buffy's practice session with Giles. His reaction to her aggression is priceless.

'You May Remember Me From Such Films As . . .': David Brisbin is in *Twin Peaks: Fire Walk With Me, Forrest Gump* (as 'Newscaster') and plays Nicolas Cage's landlord in *Leaving Las Vegas*. Jennifer Sky played Amarice in *Xena: Warrior Princess*.

Valley-Speak: Buffy: 'Xander has been acting *totally* wiggy since that day at the zoo.'

Logic, Let Me Introduce You to This Window: When Xander is locked in the cage, Willow watches a documentary about hyenas. However, while the first clip shows a pack of hyenas, all subsequent ones depict African wild dogs (you can tell by the white fur at the end of their tails). Why would Willow keep viewing this, especially with Xander caged behind her? Seems a touch masochistic.

Cruelty to Animals: Two words: bacon sandwich (see **School Dinners**).

Quote/Unquote: Giles, when told that Xander has been teasing the less fortunate, has noticeably changed in demeanour, and is spending his time lounging about: 'It's devastating. He's turned into a sixteen-year-old boy. Of course, you'll have to kill him.'

Willow: 'Why couldn't Xander be possessed by a puppy? Or some ducks?'

Notes: 'Once they separate them, the pack devours them.' The silliest episode of the season, though, in a lot of ways, the most disturbing. Xander makes an extremely credible bully (it's in the eyes). There's not enough plot to fill the screen-time requirements, however, and what there is, is often a bit inconsequential (an act closing with the implied death of a pig for instance). But it's an effective and occasionally scary piece.

Buffy seems to have an affinity with pigs. Willow knows Xander's blood pressure is 130 over 80. There are references to Buffy rescuing Willow and Xander in **2**, 'The Harvest', and Xander's knowledge of guitar music (given his daydream in **4**, 'Teacher's Pet', we presume he can play. But, see **47**, 'The Zeppo'). The Razorbacks is the name of the Sunnydale High basketball team (see **3**, 'The Witch'), and also of their football team (using the same name for all sports teams is not uncommon in US high schools). Wretched Refuse are a local rock band. The opening scenes were shot at San Diego Zoo.

Novelisation: By Jeff Mariotte in *The Xander Years Vol. 2* (Pocket Books, April 2000).

Soundtrack: Sprung Monkey's 'Reluctant Man', Dashboard Prophet's 'All You Want' and Far's 'Job's Eyes'. The incidental music is some of the best of the season.

Around The World in 45 Minutes: Just to prove that *Buffy* isn't purely an English-language phenomena the series is broadcast in a bewildering array of countries and dubbed languages. For instance, it can be seen in Argentina, Australia, Brazil, China, Denmark, Finland (as *Buffy Vampyyrintappaja*), France (*Buffy Contre Les Vampires*), Germany (*Buffy Im Bann der Dämonen*), Israel, Hungary (*Buffy, a Vámpírok Réme*), Italy, Japan, the Netherlands, Norway, Poland, Portugal (*Buffy A Caça Vampiros*), Spain and Sweden (*Buffy Vampyrdödaren*). The iron fist of American cultural imperialism inside the velvet glove of quality television.

7
Angel

US Transmission Date: 14 Apr. 1997
UK Transmission Date: 14 Feb. 1998 (Sky)
17 Feb. 1999 (BBC2)

Writer: David Greenwalt
Director: Scott Brazil
Cast: Charles Wesley ('Meanest Vamp')
French title: *Alias Angelus*
German title: *Angel – Blutige Küsse*

The Master sends the Three (a trio of vampire super warriors) after Buffy, who is saved by Angel. He tells Buffy that he is attracted to her, and they kiss. Angel suddenly reveals that he is a vampire, and Buffy screams as he escapes out of her window. Giles discovers that Angel's real name is Angelus, and he and Xander believe it's Buffy's duty to kill the vampire.

Angel meets Darla who suggests Angel tell Buffy about his 'curse'. Darla goes to Buffy's house and attacks Joyce, leaving her for Buffy to find in Angel's arms. Buffy hunts down Angel, and finds him in the Bronze. They fight, but Angel tells Buffy that this is a trap, just as Darla shoots Angel. During the struggle Angel kills Darla with a crossbow bolt.

Dudes and Babes: Drool factor eleven, on a scale of one to ten as far as *everybody* is concerned. Xander dancing is a bit special . . . in terms of comedy. Darla's 'Catholic schoolgirl' look is disturbingly effective.

Denial, Thy Name is Joyce: Joyce believes her neck wounds were caused by her passing out and falling on a barbecue fork, despite the fact that she doesn't own one.

It's a Designer Label!: Xander's greeny-yellow shirt and Willow's horrible stripy top clash for the worst clothes of the season. Cordy is horrified that somebody has a carbon copy of her Todd Oldman 'one-of-a-kind' dress: 'This is exactly what happens when we sign these free-trade agreements.' She tells Xander to, 'Please get your extreme oafishness off my two-hundred-dollar shoes.'

References: Friar Tuck of the Robin Hood legends. The Master's line, 'out of the mouths of babes', is from Psalms 8:2. The Darla/Angel reminiscences about their past may have been conceptually inspired by *Highlander* and *Forever Knight*. Watch out for a SMOKING SUCKS poster, and issues of the fanzine *Twisted* on the wall at the Bronze.

Bitch!: Xander tells Cordelia: 'I don't know what everybody's talking about. That outfit doesn't make you look like a hooker.'

Surprise!: End of act one: Angel turns towards Buffy with his face contorted and fangs bared. *Gasp*. One of the most shocking and brilliantly timed moments of 90s television that has every viewer shouting 'But . . .?' at their TV sets.

Logic, Let Me Introduce You to This Window: When Angel hears Joyce scream from inside the Summers's home, Sarah Michelle Gellar's scream from earlier in the episode is used on the soundtrack. Just before Buffy is attacked by the Three, she passes a green-lit window. After Angel saves her, the pair run off in the opposite direction to that from which Buffy arrived, but pass the same window. When Buffy takes Angel dinner in her bedroom, she is wearing a shiny-red lipstick. After the discussion about her diary, she isn't. As noted in **4**, 'Teacher's Pet', vampires' healing properties are sometimes spectacular. The cross mark on Angel's chest is missing from future bare-chested scenes. At what point did Buffy tell Giles about the Three so that he could research them 'from midnight until six'? How did Darla know when Angel would arrive at Buffy's home for her plan to work? Does Darla have an unlimited supply of ammunition during the climax?

Quote/Unquote: Willow on 'speaking up': 'That way lies madness, and sweaty palms.'

Darla: 'It's been a while.' Angel: 'A lifetime.' Darla: '. . . Or two, but who's counting?'

Willow: 'So he *is* a good vampire? I mean on a scale of one to ten. Ten being someone who's killing and maiming every night. One being someone who's . . . not.'

Notes: 'You're living overground. Like one of *them*.' *The* revelation of *Buffy*'s first season. *Everything* you know is wrong. Beautifully filmed and acted, easily the highlight of the first year and, as things would turn out, a pilot episode for a spin-off series three years later.

Buffy and Joyce live at 1630 Revello Drive. Giles is a master with the quarterstaff (except when fighting Buffy). Angel confirms the legend about a vampire being unable to enter a building unless invited (see **M1**), though this doesn't apply to public domain (see **15**, 'School Hard'; **30**, 'Killed By Death'). Angel says his family are dead, killed by vampires long ago. In fact, *he* killed them. And their friends. And their friends' children. Angelus is approximately 240 years old and was 'made' by Darla in Ireland (see **33**, 'Becoming' Part 1; *Angel*: 'The Prodigal'). He spent decades creating havoc in Europe (The Master regards him as 'the most vicious creature I ever met'). Eighty years ago (actually ninety-eight, see **33**, 'Becoming' Part 1; **44**, 'Amends'; *Angel*: 'City Of') he left Europe after killing a Romany gypsy girl whose clan cursed him and restored his soul, giving him a conscience. He came to America but shunned other vampires (see *Angel*: 'Are You Now Or Have You Ever Been?'). He drinks refrigerated blood, the implication being it's not human (see **11**, 'Out of Sight,

Out of Mind'; **21**, 'What's My Line?' Part 1; **54**, 'The Prom'). He has a tattoo on his back. Angel and Darla last met in Budapest, Hungary, at the turn of the century (see **85**, 'Fool for Love'; *Angel*: 'Darla'). Darla is approximately 400 years old (Buffy says she's been 'around since Columbus' but is clearly making a sarcastic 'ageist' comment). *Angel*: 'Darla' confirms the date of her sireing by The Master as 1609 in Virginia. Bullets can't kill vampires, but they can 'hurt like hell'.

Novelisation: By Nancy Holder in *The Angel Chronicles Vol. 1* (Pocket Books, July 1998).

Soundtrack: 'I'll Remember You' by Sophie Zelmani.

8
I Robot ... You Jane

US Transmission Date: 28 Apr. 1997
UK Transmission Date: 21 Feb. 1998 (Sky)
24 Feb. 1999 (BBC2)

Writers: Ashley Gable, Tom Swyden
Director: Stephen Posey
Cast: Chad Lindberg (Dave), Jamison Ryan (Fritz),
Pierrino Mascarino (Thelonius), Edith Fields (School Nurse),
Damon Sharp (Male Student),
Mark Deakins (Voice of Moloch)
French title: *Moloch*
German title: *Computerdämon*

Cartona, Italy, 1418: a horned demon, Moloch the Corrupter, is trapped in a book. Sunnydale 1997: the computer-science teacher Ms Calendar and her students are scanning books on to computer. Buffy finds the volume that Moloch was trapped in and Willow scans the pages. Some time later Willow tells Buffy she has met a guy online called Malcolm. Buffy asks computer nerd Dave to find out more about Malcolm, but he warns her to stay away from Willow. Buffy follows Dave to a computer facility. After Buffy survives near electrocution, and Dave apparently kills himself, Willow suspects that Malcolm is not all he seems, but she is kidnapped by his human acolyte, Fritz. Willow discovers that Moloch has created a robotic body for himself as Buffy and Xander break into the facility. Giles informs Ms Calendar that a demon is loose on the Internet. She tells him that she was already aware of this. Attempting to trap Moloch, they recant the spell, trapping him in his robot body. Enraged, he attacks Buffy, but she electrocutes him.

Dudes and Babes: 'That dreadful Calendar woman' – a technopagan babe ('there's more of us than you think'). How come we never had teachers like her at my school?

A Little Learning is a Dangerous Thing: Buffy: 'Woah! I *got* knowledge!' 'Nazi Germany was a model of a well-ordered society,' we are informed, which is *technically* correct. It was only when it came to the 'murdering half of Europe' thing that it all went pear-shaped.

It's a Designer Label!: Buffy's white vest-type T-shirt and *tiny* skirt in the opening scene. If Giles is ever on the *Jerry Springer Show* episode 'My Slayer Dresses Like A Hooker', this will be Exhibit A. The skirt puts in another appearance later, accompanied by a black T-shirt that leaves little to the imagination. Her dark glasses and trenchcoat for private investigations are much more restrained.

References: Buffy's pop-culture reference to her 'spider sense' concerns *Spider-Man*. The title is a homage to *Tarzan* and Isaac Asimov. It could be coincidental, but there are lots of references to *Macbeth* ('I'll see you anon'; 'We three'; 'Malcolm'). Xander refers to 'With a little help from my friends', which seems a bit retro for him. Maybe his parents have a copy of *Sgt. Pepper's Lonely Hearts Club Band* lying around. Or, given Xander's misquoting 'I Am The Walrus' in **22**, 'What's My Line?' Part 2, more likely *The Beatles 1967–70*. His self-aware 'for those in our studio audience who are me' is a homage to the many US sitcoms that were 'video-taped before a live studio audience' (*Happy Days*, *Cheers* etc.). The voice synthesiser that Moloch uses has more than a touch of *2001: A Space Odyssey* about it.

Fritz cutting a message into his arm: while self-mutilation is by no means rare (Elizabeth Wurtzel's *Prozac Nation* contains a harrowing autobiographical account of the disorder), one cannot help but think of Manic Street Preachers' guitarist Richie Edwards and his carving the slogan '4-Real' into his arm during

an interview with *NME* in the early 90s. The notorious case of
Internet couple Robert Glass and Sharon Lopatka who fanta-
sised about Glass killing Lopatka, to the point where she allegedly knowingly went to her death at his hands, gained much
publicity with Glass's arrest in October 1996 around the time
this episode was being written. It's possible that Buffy and
Xander's hysterical discussion about Willow's Net friend is a
reference to this.

'You May Remember Me From Such TV Series As . . .':
Chad Lindberg was excellent as the moody teenager Bobby
Rich in *The X-Files* episode 'Schizogyny'.

**'You May Remember Me From Such Pop Music Videos
As . . .':** Aside from a brief stint in *Beverly Hills 90210*, as Jill
Fleming, Robia LaMorte was 'Pearl' in Prince's videos 'Dia-
monds and Pearls' and 'Cream'.

Don't Give Up the Day Job: Stephen Posey was cinematographer on *Friday The 13th Part V: A New Beginning*, *The
Slumber Party Massacre* and *Bloody Birthday*.

Valley-Speak: Buffy: 'Let's focus here, OK?'

Not Exactly a Haven for the Bruthas: Jenny's angry rant
about knowledge being kept for 'a handful of white guys'.
Political correctness aside, there *is* an undercurrent of racial
tension in *Buffy*. Has anyone else noticed how few non-
caucasian people there are in Sunnydale? (See **37**, 'Faith,
Hope and Trick'.)

Logic, Let Me Introduce You to This Window: Buffy's
status changes from 'sophomore' to 'senior', between the
records that Moloch accesses and those Fritz is looking at. Her
date of birth also changes from 24 October 1980 to 6 May 1979
(see **10**, 'Nightmares'; **67**, 'Doomed'). It's also worth noting
that her full name is Buffy Summers, with no mention of her
middle name (see **35**, 'Anne'). Buffy attempts to delete Willow's file from the computer. However, when Buffy turns on
the monitor, the folder is already open. Watch the hand-held
scanner Willow is using – it doesn't cover more than
two-thirds of the page width, yet scans the entire text of
Moloch. How did Buffy keep track of Dave if he drove off in
his car? And why didn't she see Dave's hanging body as soon
as she entered the lab? Buffy is focused on through the PC

camera. If such cameras have a focusing element, it would be manual. More significantly, the camera centres on her. Not possible. The cameras have no motors and if this was some Moloch magic, you'd think Willow would notice the movement of a nonmovable object. Malcolm Black? OK, it's close to Moloch but what kind of a name is that for a demon to choose? 'Malcolm' is Gaelic: 'the followers of St Columbus'. Four kings of Scotland used it, and it's a character name in *Macbeth* (see **References**), but still . . .

Buffy telling Giles to call Willow at home seems dumb, when she's already talked to Willow about her being inaccessible when she's on the Net. If Willow *was* at home (in fact, where *was* she?) then they wouldn't be able to talk to her. When Giles leaves the library following his discovery of the blank book, why don't we see him through the window of the room he goes into? 'I know the secrets of your kings' – what is Moloch on about? He's become modern enough to hold convincing conversations with Willow, but he's unaware of a lack of kings in the modern world? As in many TV shows, there is a naïve correlation between the Internet and sources of all knowledge. Confidential information isn't stored on the Internet because it is not a safe medium (as the publishing of the Stephen Lawrence inquiry report in the UK proved).

I Just *Love* Your Accent: 'How am I going to convince her there's a demon on the Internet?' is an amusing (if probably unintentional) reference to the UK-based Internet provider Demon.

Quote/Unquote: Jenny: 'I know our ways are strange to you, but soon you will join us in the twentieth century, with three whole years to spare.'

Giles: 'I'll be back in the Middle Ages.' Jenny: 'Did you ever leave?'

Moloch: 'Right now a man in Beijing is transferring money to a Swiss bank account for a contract on his mother's life. Good for him.'

Notes: 'He's gone all binary on us.' The funniest episode of the first season. *Buffy* proves it can do sitcom, taking a technophobe's view of the Internet and having fun with it. Intelligent characterisation (Giles's horror of a world without books) adds a dose of realpolitik to the fantasy elements. Cyber-tastic.

Buffy's Grade Point Average is 2.8, according to her school record, which destroys the 'Buffy is doing lousy at school' idea. A 2.8 GPA, while not in Willow's league, still corresponds to C+ or B– level (see **42**, 'Lover's Walk'). Willow keeps a picture of her and Giles in her locker. Xander has an uncle who worked at CRD, 'in a floor-sweeping capacity'. There are references to Buffy and Xander's disastrous crushes on non-humans in **7**, 'Angel' and **4**, 'Teacher's Pet' respectively. Giles says he has a 'childlike terror' of computers and still prefers a good book (see **1**, 'Welcome to the Hellmouth').

Cool in-joke: Fritz uses a program called Watcher Pro Security. Elmwood, where Malcolm claims to live, is eighty miles from Sunnydale. The announcer's voice heard while Giles listens to the radio is, apparently, Joss Whedon. Among the news items reported are all FBI's serial-killer files being downloaded on to the Net and a fragment concerning financial irregularities involving an archbishop.

Novelisation: By Yvonne Navarro in *The Willow Files Vol. 1* (Pocket Books, December 1999).

9
The Puppet Show

US Transmission Date: 5 May 1997
UK Transmission Date: 28 Feb. 1998 (Sky)
3 Mar. 1999 (BBC2)

Writers: Rob Des Hotel, Dean Batali
Director: Ellen S Pressman
Cast: Richard Werner (Morgan), Burke Roberts (Marc),
Lenora May (Mrs Jackson), Chasen Hampton (Elliott), Natasha Pearce (Lisa),
Tom Wyner (Voice of Sid), Krissy Carlson (Emily (Dancer)),
Michelle Miracle (Locker Girl)
French title: *La Marionnette*
German title: *Buffy Lässt Die Puppen Tanzen*

Giles is assigned by Principal Snyder to produce the annual 'Talent(less) Show'. Snyder forces Buffy and friends to participate as punishment for their regular absences. They meet Morgan, who is doing a ventriloquist act with his puppet 'Sid'. One of the dancers is killed in the changing room, and Morgan seems a likely killer. Buffy breaks into his locker, but finds his puppet is missing. Buffy discovers Morgan's dead body with its brain removed. In her bedroom, Buffy is attacked by the puppet, and he later tries to stab her. They realise both believed they were fighting a demon. Sid explains that he is a demon hunter who is cursed to live inside a puppet's body. Marc, the real demon, straps Giles into a guillotine. Buffy saves Giles's life aided by Sid, who kills the demon and frees himself from his wooden existence.

Authority Sucks!: The appointment of the new school principal gives plenty of opportunity for power-crazed megalomania. His line, 'Sunnydale has touched and felt for the last time' serves notice that Buffy and her friends have more than vampires and demons to worry about. However, Snyder's dialogue suggests that he is less knowledgeable about the Hellmouth than he will subsequently become: his 'There's something going on here' seems genuine. At this point he may be on the outside of whatever conspiracy it is that he is most certainly on the inside of by **15**, 'School Hard'. (See also **31**, 'I Only Have Eyes for You'; **34**, 'Becoming' Part 2; **53**, 'Choices'.)

A Little Learning is a Dangerous Thing: Giles tells Willow: 'Concentrate on reanimation theory, I'll poke about in organ harvesting.' Mrs Jackson's history class gets a minimal overview of the 'Monroe Doctrine', as well as a (somewhat simplistic) definition of the word 'eponymous'. Willow knows the square root of 841 is 29 off the top of her head.

Mom's Apple Pie: Buffy appeals to her mother *not* to attend the talent show.

It's a Designer Label!: Buffy's slip-on tortoiseshell dress is great, compared to Willow's duck T-shirt. But, what *are* they all wearing at the end?

References: Cordelia sings 'The Greatest Love of All' (*very* badly). Originally a hit for George Benson, it's probably more familiar via Whitney Houston's cover version. Xander's cries of 'Redrum' are from Stephen King's novel *The Shining* and Stanley Kubrick's film adaptation. 'Does anyone else feel like we've been Keyser Soze'd' concerns the mysterious (and possibly fictitious) villain in *The Usual Suspects*. There's a reference to *The Sting*, while aspects of the plot may have been influenced by the 'Prey' segment of the 1975 TV movie *Trilogy of Terror* or any number of other 'devil-doll' stories (e.g. *Magic*). After Willow flees during the *Oedipus Rex* sequence, Xander and Buffy move together in imitation of artist Grant Wood's *American Gothic* painting (see **10**, 'Nightmares', for Willow suffering stage fright again).

Bitch!: Xander, replying to Cordelia's self-pitying whinge that the murdered Emily could have been her: 'We can *dream*.'

Awesome!: Xander's double-take when discovering Sid is missing. Pure *Tom and Jerry*.

'You May Remember Me From Such Films and TV Series As . . .': Armin Shimerman played Pascal on *Beauty and the Beast* and then became a TV comedy icon as the Ferengi bar owner Quark in *Star Trek: Deep Space Nine*. He also has a semiregular role as a judge in *Ally McBeal*. His films include *Blind Date*, *The Hitcher* and *Stardust Memories*. Krissy Carlson was in *Sunset Beach*.

Valley-Speak: Buffy: 'However did you finagle such a permo assignment?'

Willow: 'Creep factor is also heightened.'

Logic, Let Me Introduce You to This Window: While Buffy says, 'I'm never going to stop washing my hands', you can hear Willow typing and the computer beeping. However, the monitor is visible and there is no program running.

Buffy lives a fair distance from school (her mom drives her there each day) and Sid's only got little legs, so how did he manage to get all the way from school to Buffy's house and back in a night? After Sid stabs the demon, the knife is sticking out of Marc's body. When Buffy picks up Sid, the knife has disappeared. Why would the teacher let Morgan keep his puppet on his desk during class? Where were the rest of the talent-show participants when Buffy was fighting the demon just before the curtain opened?

Quote/Unquote: Snyder: 'There are things I will not tolerate. Students loitering on campus after school. Horrible murders with hearts being removed. And also smoking.'

And on where Flutie went wrong: 'That's the kind of woolly-headed liberal thinking that leads to getting eaten.'

Giles advises a nervous Cordelia on overcoming stage fright by imagining all of the audience in their underwear. Cordelia: 'Euw. Even Mrs Franklin?' Giles: 'Perhaps not.'

Notes: 'I don't get it, what is it, avant garde?' Outrageously over the top, the impression of 'The Puppet Show' is of some sort of 'Plan B' in operation (did another script fall through?). It's very different from the surrounding episodes and nearly everyone is out of character; but it's a memorable debut for Armin Shimerman, with good jokes and top-quality direction.

Willow plays the piano, though not in public. Snyder is obviously well read on the events of previous episodes, making specific reference to the death of his predecessor in **6**, 'The Pack', and the case of 'spontaneous cheerleader combustion' in **3**, 'The Witch'. Buffy has never liked ventriloquist's dummies (there is no story behind it, she just doesn't). The day before these events Buffy, Willow and Xander left school to fight a demon. Since this doesn't sound like the plot of **8**, 'I Robot . . . You Jane', we must presume there's at least one missing adventure in-between.

Sid says he knew a Slayer in the 1930s who was a Korean girl. There's a rivalry between the dancers and the school band.

Critique: Peter Fairly reviewed this episode in *The Journal*: 'Last night, they stretched the plot line, in a series in which the credibility factor is rapidly approaching warp nine, to breaking point. Take a school play, another corpse – Buffy's school has already seen its headmaster eaten alive and various staff and pupils dispatched in unsavory ways – and a moody scholar with headaches whose best friend is a wooden ventriloquist's dummy, and you have a ready-made scenario for Buffy to strut her ghoul-slaying stuff.'

10

Nightmares

US Transmission Date: 12 May 1997
UK Transmission Date: 7 Mar. 1998 (Sky)
10 Mar. 1999 (BBC2)

Writer: David Greenwalt
From a story by Joss Whedon
Director: Bruce Seth Green
Cast: Jeremy Foley (Billy Palmer), Justin Urich (Wendell),
J Robin Miller (Laura), Terry Cain (Ms Tishler),
Scott Harlan (Aldo Gianfranco), Brian Pietro (Coach),
Johnny Green (Way-Cool Guy),
Patty Ross (Cool Guy's Mom),
Dom Magwili (Doctor), Sean Moran (Stage Manager)
French title: *Billy*
German title: *Die Macht Der Träume*

Everyone is having nightmares, and some of them are starting
to affect reality, but only Buffy can see the strange little boy
hanging around school. A girl, smoking in the boiler room, is
attacked by an ugly man saying 'Lucky Nineteen'. Buffy and
Giles learn that the girl is the second victim of the same
attacker. The first was a Junior League baseball player, Billy
Palmer, currently in a coma. Giles theorises that Buffy saw an
astral projection of the comatose boy. Buffy finds Billy, who
explains that he is trying to hide from 'the Ugly Man'. Buffy
dreams that The Master is free and, when Giles, Willow and
Xander find Buffy, she has become a vampire. They rush to
the hospital to try to wake Billy. The Ugly Man appears again
and Buffy kills him, restoring reality.

Dreaming (As Blondie Once Said) is Free: Among the
nightmares-made-flesh is Buffy walking into The Master's lair
but being powerless against him. She also has fears concerning
a history test she hasn't studied for, her father telling her that
she was the reason for her parents' divorce, and being turned
into a vampire. Giles's two nightmares are probably the most
emotionally effective; losing his ability to read and Buffy's
death. Xander faces twin fears – nakedness (except for his
underwear) in class and a clown who terrorised him at his sixth
birthday party (that this is a dream sequence is evidenced by
the swastikas, echoing Xander's earlier comment about being
more frightened of Nazis than spiders). Willow suffers from
stage fright (see **9**, 'The Puppet Show'; **78**, 'Restless'), while
Cordelia is having a bad-hair day and turns into a chess-club
geek. Wendell's arachnophobia is understandable once he
explains the background and the Way-Cool Guy's fear of his

mom embarrassing him in front of his friends is one we've all shared. But, *come on*, who dreamed about giant flies destroying Sunnydale? Own up . . .

A Little Learning is a Dangerous Thing: Xander didn't pay much attention in Ms Tishler's 'active-listening' class, being more interested in her midnight-blue angora sweater. He is surprised to find that spiders are 'arachnids' ('They come from the Middle East?'). Buffy shouldn't find this too amusing ('What am I, knowledge girl now?'). She gets 'astral' and 'asteroid' mixed up. Giles can read five languages. On a normal day.

Mom's Apple Pie: Xander's birthday party sounds like the kind of nightmare many children suffer; but a darker side to the competitiveness of American life is highlighted in Billy being beaten by his baseball coach for dropping a catch that lost the game. Joyce's attempts to convince Buffy that her father loves her, without weakening her own position ('No more than I do'), are hilarious, if a bit scary.

It's a Designer Label!: Buffy's T-shirt manages to take our attention away from Xander's horrible shirt (does he get them in bulk?), Cordy's pink pants and Willow's yellow tights.

References: Visual references to Poe's 'The Premature Burial' and Hansel and Gretel (Xander following a trail of chocolate. See **45**, 'Gingerbread'), and dialogue samples from *The Wizard of Oz* ('You were there. And you'), *Star Trek* ('Red alert'), *Cinderella* ('a dream is a wish your heart makes') and *Rosemary's Baby* ('This *isn't* a dream'). *Evita* is mentioned concerning Cordelia's delusions of grandeur. The opera that Willow dreams herself into is Puccini's *Madame Butterfly* (as Cio-Cio-San).

Bitch!: Cordelia on Buffy's panic over how she'll be able to pass a test she hasn't studied for: 'Blind luck?'

'You May Remember Me From Such TV Series As . . .': Dean Butler is best known as Almanzo in *Little House on the Prairie*.

Don't Give Up the Day Job: Sean Moran was one of the dancers in *Grease*. Dom Magwili is also a writer; his credits include the movie *Bikini Hotel*.

Valley-Speak: Xander: 'Which is a fair wiggins, I admit . . .'

Logic, Let Me Introduce You to This Window: When Buffy

is talking about her parents' separation, Willow slips her back-pack off. In the next shot, it is on her shoulder again. How did Buffy get to the hospital in daylight if she was a vampire?

Quote/Unquote: Xander tells the clown: 'Your balloon animals were *pathetic*. Anyone can make a giraffe.'

Notes: 'Our nightmares are coming true.' A surreal and well-structured episode with some of the most memorable images of the season, 'Nightmares' highlights are in the area of characterisation, subtly playing with the secret fears of the regulars. The climax is overdrawn, but scenes such as Xander overcoming his terror of clowns more than make up for that.

Buffy has a red stuffed animal (see **M1**). Her parents divorced last year, although they were separated for some time before that (see **33**, 'Becoming' Part 1). Willow says *her* parents don't bicker, though they do occasionally 'glare'. Given that Buffy was born in both 1979 and 1980 in **8**, 'I Robot . . . You Jane', it's little surprise to see her gravestone read 'Buffy Summers 1981–1997' (see **100**, 'The Gift'). Though, as this takes place as part of Giles's nightmare, it's possible this is his mistake. Similarly, when Buffy sees The Master in the graveyard he says, 'You're prettier than the last one', indicating that he met the Slayer before Buffy, but we have to ask ourselves if this is a *real* conversation or just Buffy's overactive imagination. Willow has a Nerf Herder sticker on the inside of her locker door. She attended Xander's sixth-birthday party at which he ate a chocolate hurricane and was chased by the clown (we never find out exactly why, or what happened, but the experience has scarred Xander's life).

11

Out of Sight, Out of Mind
[a.k.a. Invisible Girl]

US Transmission Date: 19 May 1997
UK Transmission Date: 14 Mar. 1998 (Sky)
17 Mar. 1999 (BBC2)

Writers: Ashley Gable, Tom Swyden
Story: Joss Whedon
Director: Reza Badiyi
Cast: Clea DuVall (Marcie Ross), Ryan Bittle (Mitch),
Denise Dowse (Ms Miller), John Knight (Bud #1),
Mark Phelan (Agent Doyle),
Skip Stellrecht (Agent Manetti),
Julie Fulton (FBI Teacher)
French title: *Portée Disparue*
German title: *Aus den Augen, Aus Dem Sinn*

Cordelia's boyfriend Mitch and her friend Harmony fall victim
to attacks by an invisible force as Cordy is running for May
Queen. Willow and Buffy link the attacks to missing student
Marcie Ross, whom no one can remember. Buffy finds
Marcie's yearbook, but the entries suggest she had no friends.
Cordelia, having worked out that she may be the next target,
asks Buffy for help. Marcie sets a trap for Giles, Willow and
Xander in a gas-filled basement. While Angel saves their lives,
Buffy and Cordelia wake up in the Bronze, tied to chairs.
Marcie has gone mad during her isolation and wants to disfig-
ure Cordelia, but Buffy overcomes the difficulties of fighting
an opponent she cannot see. Two FBI agents take Marcie into
custody, and tell Buffy and Cordelia to forget what happened.
Cordelia thanks Buffy and her friends for their help, though
she is unable to publicly admit this.

Dudes and Babes: Naked guys alert. Plus Angel in leather-
jacket-and-vest mode. Xander says he would use the power of
invisibility to 'guard the girls' locker room'.

Authority Sucks!: Snyder's hysterical reaction to Harmony
breaking her ankle is to tell her not to sue the school.

A Little Learning is a Dangerous Thing: Ms Jackson's
English class is doing *The Merchant of Venice*, focusing on
'the anger of the outcast': this episode and, indeed, this series
all over. Xander's research leads him to note: 'Great myths
speak of cloaks of invisibility, but they're usually for the gods.'

It's a Designer Label!: Cordelia says she's having her May
Queen dress specially made as off-the-rack clothes give her
'the hives'. Check out Harmony's kitten T-shirt, Willow's

Tasmanian-devil T-shirt, Buffy's pink skirt and the peach skirt she wears in the final scene.

References: Writer and scholar Helen Keller (1880–1968), *Poltergeist*, *The Merchant of Venice*. 'Gee, it's fun we're speaking in tongues,' says Buffy, referring to the spiritual gift of glossolalia. 'Crush! Kill! Destroy!' was the catchphrase of the robot in *Lost in Space*. On the blackboard, there's a reference to Irish playwright Samuel Beckett (1906–89).

Bitch!: Even when she's trying to be nice, Cordy asks Buffy: 'You were popular? In what alternate universe?' And, in response to Giles saying he doesn't recall seeing her in the library before: 'Oh no. I have a life.' And, when seeing a picture of Marcie: 'Oh my God. Is she *really* wearing Laura Ashley?'

'You May Remember Me From Such Films As . . .': Clea DuVall's movies include a starring role in *The Faculty* and *Can't Hardly Wait* (with Seth Green).

Valley-Speak: Cordelia on Shylock: 'Colour me *totally* self-involved . . .'

Buffy: 'I think I speak for everyone here when I say, "*Huh*?"'

Willow, on Marcie: 'No wonder she's miffed.'

Logic, Let Me Introduce You to This Window: As Giles says, 'I've never actually heard of anyone attacked by a lone baseball bat before', Xander puts a potato chip in his mouth. In the next shot from a slightly different angle Xander is holding a sandwich as he says: 'Maybe it's a vampire bat.' There is clearly something strange going on in the cafeteria, as Buffy's french fries change into a drink during the same scene. After Snyder announces Cordelia as May Queen, he steps to the left as Cordelia comes to the microphone. For the distance shots, Snyder is standing behind Cordelia's left shoulder, but in close-up Cordy is the only person in shot. The board at the Bronze reads: CLOSED FOR FUMIGATION (stock footage from **7**, 'Angel'). How does Angel get to the school during daylight? After Marcie slashes Cordelia's face, Buffy kicks the instrument table, knocking Marcie out of the way. Buffy rushes to Cordelia's chair and tries to loosen the rope. As Buffy is attacked by Marcie, the rope around Cordy's left hand comes free. For the rest of the scene, however, the rope is still tightly tied. Why did Marcie's clothes become invisible as well as her body? If it's something to do with them being in contact with her body then why isn't the knife she holds also invisible? How did Marcie get Cordelia and Buffy to the Bronze without anyone noticing? When Marcie goes into the classroom full of other invisible students, how does she know the chair she sits on isn't occupied?

Quote/Unquote: Angel's moment of Byronic anguish: 'Looking in the mirror everyday and seeing nothing there. It's an over-rated pleasure.'

Giles: 'Once again, I teeter on the precipice of the generation gap.'

Notes: 'Being this popular is not just my right, it's a responsibility.' Conceptually the most extreme episode of *Buffy* yet, focusing on one of Joss Whedon's cornerstones, the anger of the outcast. An intriguing and mysterious opening gives way to a thoroughly slovenly middle ten minutes, however, before the episode comes to an excellent climax. Great direction, particularly during the flashbacks. The scene between Giles and Angel is particularly well written (Giles notes that Angel and Buffy's affection is 'rather poetic, in a maudlin sort of way').

There's also the rehabilitation of Cordelia Chase. This is very much Cordy's episode and a first hint that, far from being a simpering bad girl with mush for brains, she is actually a tough cookie. Her eyes are hazel. She once 'sort of' ran over a girl on a bicycle in her car (she must, therefore, have passed her driving test sometime after **3**, 'The Witch', and prior to this episode). Willow and Xander tell a (seemingly amusing) story about something that happened to Cordelia in sixth grade that involves antlers and a man in a hat. Sounds like quite a story behind *that* one. Cordelia refers to Buffy 'attacking' her in **1**, 'Welcome to the Hellmouth'. Buffy was the equivalent of May Queen at Hemery. When Giles suggests witchcraft may be involved Willow says, 'We can fight a witch' (see **3**, 'The Witch'). It is confirmed that Angel casts no reflection and that he hasn't fed from a human for 'a long while' (see **7**, 'Angel'; **33**, 'Becoming' Part 1). Xander invites Willow home for dinner. 'Mom's making her famous "phonecall to the Chinese place".' Willow doubts the Harrises even *have* a stove. *Entertainment Weekly* observed that Xander's family life 'beyond his parents fighting, his mother's [lack of] cooking, and his dad's unemployment remains a mystery'. 'He was abused as a child,' deadpans Brendon. 'I've got two people in mind for his dad – George Hamilton and Steven Seagal.' (See **78**, 'Restless'.)

Mitch's dad is Sunnydale's most powerful lawyer if Willow and Xander aren't lying to Snyder. Angel tells Giles that The Master is planning something big (see **12**, 'Prophecy Girl', for the climax to *that* story arc). Salient books of Slayer prophecy have mostly been lost, including *The Tiberius Manifesto* and *The Pergamum Codex* (which Angel manages to acquire. Did he get it from the demon bookseller in **53**, 'Choices'?). Giles is currently reading the Hindi text *Legends of Vishnu*. When Buffy shows Marcie's yearbook picture to Cordelia, Willow's photo is next to Marcie's, which makes the fact that Willow can't remember Marcie even sadder. Page 54 of the textbook at the end of the episode contains the heading: 'Chapter 11: Infiltration and Assassination'. The subheading states, 'Case D: Radical Cult Leader as Intended Victim'. The paragraph begins, 'August 2nd 19XX'. The rest of the page consists of lyrics from the Beatles' 'Happiness is a Warm Gun'.

12
Prophecy Girl

US Transmission Date: 2 Jun. 1997
UK Transmission Date: 21 Mar. 1998 (Sky)
31 Mar. 1999 (BBC2)

Writer: Joss Whedon
Director: Joss Whedon
Cast: Scott Gurney (Kevin)
French title: *La Manuscrit*
German title: *Das Ende der Welt*

Xander asks Buffy to the Spring Fling but is turned down. Giles translates an ancient codex, and discovers a prophecy predicting the death of the Slayer as Jenny tells him that portents suggest the apocalypse is coming. As Giles and Angel discuss the prophecy, Buffy overhears them. She says she doesn't want to be the Slayer any more. When Cordelia and

Willow discover several murdered students, Buffy decides she must follow her destiny, entering The Master's lair alone. Xander and Angel find Buffy's drowned body but Xander performs mouth-to-mouth resuscitation and revives her. An army of vampires attack Giles, Cordelia, Willow and Jenny in the library as the Hellmouth is about to open. Buffy faces The Master again and pushes him through the library skylight where he is impaled on a beam of wood. With the Hellmouth closed, at Xander's suggestion they all leave for the Bronze.

Dudes and Babes: Poor Xander, he hasn't got a *clue* has he? ('Just *kill* me.') Trying to get Willow on the bounce from Buffy is dumb. There's a fragile beauty to Buffy that can inspire exchanges such as Angel: 'You're in love with her.' Xander: 'Aren't you?'

Mom's Apple Pie: The dress Joyce buys her daughter is, indeed, beautiful. Joyce tells Buffy that she attended Homecoming during her freshman year without a date. (*With* 'Gidget-hair'? See **3**, 'The Witch'.) It was horrible for an hour until she met Buffy's father (who *did* have a date). This fits in with the uncool girl that Joyce describes herself as in **3**, 'The Witch', and whom we see in **40**, 'Band Candy'.

It's a Designer Label!: Buffy's grey T-shirt and blue skirt, plus Willow's green trainers and zigzag jumper.

References: Xander describes Country as 'the music of pain'. The Master's 'Where are your jibes now?' is a question Hamlet asks Ophelia in *Hamlet*. A few seconds of a *Porky the Pig* cartoon are seen on the TV in the room where the vampires killed the boys. There's a quotation from Isaiah 11:6 ('The wolf shall lie with the lamb'). Xander refers to the *Star Trek: The Next Generation* episode 'The Best of Both Worlds': 'Calm may work for Locutus of the Borg.' The rising of the dead and their descending on the library owes much to Romero's *Night of the Living Dead*, while The Master's death may have been suggested by the climax to Hammer's *Dracula Has Risen from the Grave*, in which Dracula is impaled on a cross.

Bitch!: Cordelia being 'nice' to Willow (to gain her help in setting up the sound system for the dance). At least she's honest about it. Indeed, the stunning scene between the pair as they discover the bodies of Kevin and his friends is so well played, it's almost voyeuristic. In no other series would we be made to care so much about Cordelia's loss.

Awesome!: The pre-title sequence of Buffy taking on a vampire mostly in slow motion. The scene of Xander asking Buffy out to the dance is both sweet and heart-rending because you *know* what the answer is going to be.

***That* Scene:** Highlight of the episode is the sequence where Cordelia and Willow find the bodies of the boys (see **Bitch!**). Alyson Hannigan told *DreamWatch*: 'We did two different versions of the scene where we walk into a room and find a bunch of dead kids. We did the tame version for America and . . . a bloodier version that we thought we could get away with in Europe. We poured blood everywhere . . . It's probably non-existent now.'

Valley-Speak: Xander, on the results of asking Buffy for a date: 'On a scale of one to ten? It sucked.'

Willow, when Xander reveals Buffy died: 'Wow. Harsh.'

Logic, Let Me Introduce You to This Window: While Buffy is walking in the tunnels the shadow of one of the production team can be seen on the wall. When Xander asks Buffy to the prom, keep an eye on his backpack. In distance shots it's resting on the bench beside his legs; in close-ups, the strap is on his right shoulder. When Buffy falls into the pool, her arms are under her body while her hair is tied up in a ponytail. But when Angel and Xander find her, her arms are spread out and her hair is undone and floating in the water. Everyone leaves for the Bronze at the end of the episode. However, it's clearly daylight outside the library (Angel should burn to death from the sun coming through the broken skylight). How does Angel pay his phone bills? Or his rent for that matter? (Direct debit, probably.) How could Angel and Giles not notice Buffy coming into the library? Did Buffy *really* tell Xander where Angel lives? (How else would he know?)

What a Shame They Dropped . . .: After Buffy has rejected Xander, the original script called for a scene in which it rains pebbles. 'Check it out,' says a student. 'It's raining stones!' 'Figures,' notes a heartbroken Xander.

Quote/Unquote: Buffy: 'I'm sixteen years old. I don't want to die.' And, after knocking Giles unconscious: 'When he wakes up, tell him . . . Think of something cool, tell him I said it.'

Willow on finding the bodies: 'It wasn't our world any more. They [the vampires] made it theirs. And they had fun.'
Notes: 'By the way, I like your dress.' A staggering season finale. Once again the direction is stunning and the story features a circular feeling, as elements from the initial episodes are again referred to. One of the finest aspects is the juxtaposition between Giles and Jenny talking about Armageddon, and Cordelia and Kevin discussing their trivial dance.

Willow checks with Xander that nerds are still 'in'. Xander doesn't handle rejection well which, he notes, is odd since he's had a lot of practice at it. Giles finally realises that the vampire Buffy killed in **5**, 'Never Kill a Boy on the First Date', *wasn't* the Anointed One. Among the portents of the 'end days' are a cat giving birth to a litter of snakes, a boy being born with his eyes facing inward and blood pouring from the sink in the girls' bathroom. This was the first episode to be rated TV-14.
Soundtrack: 'I Fall to Pieces' by Patsy Cline, and 'Inconsolable' by Jonathan Brooke.
***Buffy the Vampire Slayer* Will Return . . .:** At this point the production team and cast didn't know whether *Buffy* would be picked up for a second season (indeed, the lateness of the renewal is why Anthony Stewart Head had to vacate his potentially recurring role in *Jonathan Creek*). Therefore, the final scenes have an added poignancy since (at the time of shooting) this may have been our last look at the characters. Fortunately a second season *was* eventually commissioned.
Did You Know . . .?: Sarah Michelle Gellar originally screen tested for Cordelia (we get a vague idea of how she may have played the role from her performance in *Cruel Intentions*). According to an *FHM* interview, Katie Holmes (*Dawson's Creek*, *Disturbing Behaviour*, *The Gift*) turned down the part of Buffy so that she could finish school.

'I wish dating was like slaying.
Simple, direct, stake to the heart . . .'

– 'Bewitched, Bothered and Bewildered'

Second Season (1997–98)

Mutant Enemy Inc./Kuzui Enterprises/
Sandollar Television/20th Century Fox
Created by Joss Whedon
Producer: Gareth Davies
Co-Producers: David Solomon, Gary Law (19–34)
Consulting Producer: Howard Gordon (13–25)
Executive Producers: Sandy Gallin, Gail Berman,
Fran Rubel Kuzui, Kaz Kuzui, Joss Whedon
Co-Executive Producer: David Greenwalt

Regular Cast:
Sarah Michelle Gellar (Buffy Summers), Nicholas Brendon (Xander Harris),
Alyson Hannigan (Willow Rosenberg), Charisma Carpenter (Cordelia Chase),
Anthony Stewart Head (Rupert Giles),
David Boreanaz (Angel/Angelus,[4] 13–15, 17–34),
Kristine Sutherland (Joyce Summers, 13, 15–16, 23–6, 28–30, 33–4),
Julie Benz (Darla, 33), Mercedes McNab (Harmony Kendall, 25,[5] 28),
Elizabeth Anne Allen (Amy Madison, 28),
Amanda Wilmshurst (Cheerleader, 14),
Andrew J Ferchland (the Anointed One, 13, 15),
Robia LaMorte (Jenny Calendar, 13–15, 19, 23, 25–6, 28–9, 34),
Dean Butler (Hank Summers, 13),
Armin Shimerman (Principal Snyder, 13, 15, 18, 21, 31–4),
James Marsters (Spike, 15, 18–19, 21–2, 25–6, 28–9, 31, 33–4),
Juliet Landau (Drusilla, 15, 18–19, 21–2, 25–6, 28–9, 31, 33–4),
Brian Reddy (Bob, 15, 31),
Seth Green (Daniel 'Oz' Osborne, 16, 18, 21–2, 25–8, 33–4),
Jason Hall (Devon, 16, 28),
Danny Strong (Jonathan Levinson, 16–17, 22,[6] 24, 29,[7] 32),
Larry Bagby III (Larry, 18, 27), Robin Sachs (Ethan Rayne, 18, 20),
Julia Lee ('Chantarelle'/'Lily'/Anne Steele, 19)

[4] For episodes **26**, 'Innocence', to **34**, 'Becoming' Part 2, the character is
referred to as Angelus – Angel's demonic persona.
[5] Credited as appearing in **25**, 'Surprise', but the scene was cut before
transmission.
[6] Credited as 'Hostage Kid' in **22**, 'What's My Line?' Part 2.
[7] Credited as 'Student' in **29**, 'Passion'.

Bianca Lawson (Kendra, 21–2, 33), Eric Saiet (Dalton, 21, 25),
Saverio Guerra (Willy, 21–2), James G MacDonald (Detective Stein, 23, 34),
Jeremy Ratchford (Lyle Gorch, 24), James Lurie (Mr Miller, 26,[8] 31)

13
When She Was Bad

US Transmission Date: 15 Sep. 1997
UK Transmission Date: 28 Mar. 1998 (Sky)
8 Apr. 1999 (BBC2)

Writer: Joss Whedon
Director: Joss Whedon
Cast: Brent Jennings (Absalom), Tamara Braun (Tara)
French title: *La Métamorphose de Buffy*
German title: *Im Banne Des Bösen*

Buffy's back from summer vacation, but to Giles's surprise
she recommences her training immediately. Buffy suffers a
nightmare and awakens to find Angel in her room. He warns
her that the Anointed One has been gathering vampires, but
Buffy is dismissive. Willow, Xander and Cordy all realise that
Buffy is not acting like herself. Cordelia and Jenny are kidnapped by vampires and Buffy is told to go to the Bronze.
Assuming she is walking into a trap, Buffy realises too late that
it is actually a diversion to allow the abduction of Giles and
Willow, as the blood of the people closest to The Master when
he died is needed for his revivification. With Angel and
Xander's help, Buffy tracks the vampires to a warehouse and,
in a whirlwind of violence, deals with the 'issues' that Giles
believes she still has outstanding.
Dreaming (As Blondie Once Said) is Free: Buffy's nightmare features The Master (wearing Giles's face) trying to
strangle her.
Dudes and Babes: Buffy working out. Oh, sweet mother . . .
Lads, if you *have* access to a cold shower, now might be a good
time. Buffy and Xander dancing is erotic in all sorts of ways
but is clearly designed to make Angel jealous. It's actually a

---

[8] Credited as 'Teacher' in **26**, 'Innocence', but the scene was cut before
transmission.

nasty, cruel trick Buffy pulls since Willow doesn't look too pleased, while poor Xander is left completely baffled as to where he stands. As he says: 'I'm a man, I have certain needs.'

Authority Sucks!: Snyder: 'That Summers girl. I smell trouble. I smell expulsion and just the faintest aroma of jail.'

A Little Learning is a Dangerous Thing: Xander has genuine trouble working out what 'B-I-T-C-H' spells.

Mom's Apple Pie: Joyce tells Hank that she hasn't been able to get through to Buffy for a long time and that she'll be happy if Buffy gets through the year without getting expelled (see **34**, 'Becoming' Part 2).

It's a Designer Label!: Cordy's trousers in the final scene. *Hot damn.* Willow sports yet another pair of *horrible* tights (these are yellowy-green).

References: The title is an allusion to nursery rhyme 'Jemima'. ('There was a little girl, and she wore a little curl, right in the middle of her forehead. When she was good, she was very very good, but when she was bad, she was horrid.') Xander and Willow's 'dumb game' includes dialogue misquotes from *The Terminator, Planet of the Apes, Star Wars* and *Witness.* Xander refers to Giles as 'G-Man', a nickname given to the FBI, which was first used (allegedly) by bank robber Machine Gun Kelly in 1934. Cordy uses *The Three Musketeers* as an insult. After Willow points out that they were actually quite cool, Xander suggests Three Stooges would have been more appropriate. Again, it's possible to spot the influence of Hammer's *Dracula, Prince of Darkness* (both contain a victim suspended above a vampire's corpse so that their blood can be used to reanimate it).

Bitch!: Buffy telling Cordelia: 'Your mouth is open, sound is coming from it. This is never good.' And: 'You won't tell anyone that I'm the Slayer. I won't tell anyone you're a moron.'

Cordy considers that Buffy is 'really campaigning for Bitch of the Year', to which Buffy replies, 'As defending champion, are you nervous?'

Awesome!: The opening: Buffy kicking the crap out of a vampire and throwing him against a tree with a conveniently placed stake-shaped branch with a cheeky, extremely postmodern nod to the audience: 'Hi guys. Miss me?' You've *gotta* love this girl, haven't you?

Subtext: the audience assumes that Buffy is addressing *them*, but the theme of the story is the fear of rejection and of finding that your friends don't need you any more. Buffy is actually targeting Willow and Xander.

Don't Give Up the Day Job: This episode marked the debut of Sophia Crawford's husband, Jeff Pruitt, as *Buffy*'s stunt coordinator. In addition to a list of stunt credits as long as your arm, Jeff has acted in films like *The Bad Pack*, *Scanner Cops* and *Martial Law*.

Act Naturally?: A bit of bad acting can slip into even the classiest of productions. When Xander is telling Cordelia not to mention Buffy's slaying abilities in public, watch the guy in the blue shirt on the right of screen. Is that the most dreadful piece of ham you've seen this side of a bacon commercial? He does another little cameo of scene-stealing a moment later, walking behind Willow as she says, 'A little too good?'

Valley-Speak: Xander: 'Please, I'm *so* over her.'

Logic, Let Me Introduce You to This Window: Watch the tree with the 'conveniently stake-shaped branch' in the pre-titles. In the preceding scene the pointy branch is missing. The morning after Angel's visit, Buffy rides to school with her mom. In the car, Buffy is wearing a pink camisole. However, in her next scene at the school, Buffy sports a white tank top. The pink camisole shows up again the next day. Nobody seems to notice Cordelia or Jenny's absence for an entire day. As Buffy, Angel and Xander spy on the revivification ritual, the vampires gather around The Master's skeleton. The long-haired vampire moves into position, to his right stands the vampire wearing the tan jacket. Moments later as Buffy stakes the long-haired vampire, all the other vampires turn towards her. The tan-jacket vampire is now on the opposite side to where he was earlier. As Giles hangs above the skeleton, his left hand brushes it and the 'bones' bend. Buffy's sledgehammer skills leave a bit to be desired. Her first blow destroys the skull. The second smashes the left side of the rib cage. The next nine occur off screen. When we see the skeleton again during sledgehammer blow twelve, it still looks remarkably intact. Did she miss a lot? Buffy tells Giles, 'I put my best friends in mortal danger on the second day of school.' Willow later confirms it's Wednesday. However, Buffy actually put her friends in mortal danger on the *third* day of school, so it should be Thursday. The Anointed One sees the remains of The Master's skull at the climax, but Buffy smashed it earlier.

Quote/Unquote: Hank: 'At least when she was burning stuff down I knew what to say.'

Snyder: 'There are some things I can just smell. It's like a sixth sense.' Giles: 'Actually, that would be one of the five.'

Cordy's advice: 'Whatever's causing the Joan Collins 'tude, deal with it. Embrace the pain. Spank your inner moppet. Whatever.'

Xander telling Buffy: 'If they hurt Willow, I'll kill you.'

Notes: 'Come on. Kick my ass.' A slow, but alluring opener. Good fight sequences aside, the best bits are the Buffy/Cordelia scenes which add depth to both characters. It's certainly the finest of what was to become an annual reinvention by Joss Whedon, with the first episode of this and subsequent seasons becoming, in effect, pilots for a new series. It's just a pity that after some fine approach play, several goal-scoring opportunities are missed until the exciting climax. And, is it just me or does this episode look *cheap*?

Buffy spent the summer in LA with her dad, partying and shopping. She says she never thanked Xander for saving her life in **12**, 'Prophecy Girl'. Xander always does 'scissors' in 'rock-scissors-paper'. He bets Willow that Giles will need to 'consult his books' within ten minutes of the start of school. He wins, with over a minute to spare. Cordy spent the summer with her parents in Tuscany. Suffering, apparently. Jenny says she went to a couple of 'stirring' festivals (including naked mud dancers, which sounds like fun).

Two pieces of stock footage are used across a scene break. The first (the front of school with a bus passing in the foreground) crops up in many episodes. The second shows the water fountain in the plaza. The guy walking away in a purple shirt is Owen from **5**, 'Never Kill a Boy on the First Date', which gives us a clue where this came from.

Soundtrack: 'It Doesn't Matter' by Alison Krauss and Union Station [*]. 'Spoon' and 'Sugar Water' by Cibo Matto, featuring

Sean Lennon (who perform in the Bronze and get name-checked by both Xander and Willow).

Did You Know?: Sarah Michelle Gellar has a phobia about cemeteries. As she told *FHM* (in the issue in which readers voted her top of 1999's *100 Sexiest Women*), 'I used to cry if I went near one . . . The first series was a horrible nightmare, so for the second they had to build fake cemeteries.'

14

Some Assembly Required

US Transmission Date: 22 Sep. 1997
UK Transmission Date: 4 Apr. 1998 (Sky)
14 Apr. 1999 (BBC2)

Writer: Ty King
Director: Bruce Seth Green
Cast: Angelo Spizzirri (Chris), Michael Bacall (Eric),
Ingo Neuhaus (Daryl), Melanie MacQueen (Mrs Epps)
French title: *Le Puzzle*
German title: *Operation Cordelia*

After the discovery of the robbed graves of three cheerleaders, suspicion falls on two of Willow's acquaintances from science club, Chris and the ghoulish Eric. In their lab, the boys only require a head to perfect a mate for Chris's formerly dead brother, Daryl. Daryl kidnaps Cordelia during a football game, but Buffy defeats him and Xander rescues Cordelia from the burning lab. Cordelia tries to express her gratitude to Xander for saving her life, but he brushes her off.

Dudes and Babes: Eric's pornography collection is so huge it scares even Xander. Cordelia hangs on to Angel's arm when Buffy enters the library and gets him to take her home ('I always pegged him as a one-woman vampire').

A Little Learning is a Dangerous Thing: Buffy is worried that slaying is interfering with her trigonometry homework. As Cordelia notes, 'I don't think anyone should be made to do anything educational in school if they don't want to.'

It's a Designer Label!: Check out Eric's nasty shirt, Willow's multicoloured patterned blouse and Jenny's tight cream stretchpants. When Eric ties Cordelia up he lifts her skirt; we get a look at those red cheerleader knickers again (see **3**, 'The Witch').

References: Giles refers to Cyrano de Bergerac while Buffy provides an oblique reference to film critics Gene Siskel and Roger Ebert. There's a homage to *Batman* ('it's the Bat signal'). Eric sings a few lines from the Temptations' 'My Girl'.

Bitch!: Another episode full of glorious Cordy/Xander exchanges. Cordelia: 'Why are these terrible things always happening to me?' Xander: 'Karma?'

Awesome!: Buffy falling into the grave. Xander and Cordy's escape on the medical trolley through the burning lab is pure James Bond.

Surprise!: The first appearance of Daryl.

'You May Remember Me From Such Films As . . .': Michael Bacall played Perry in *Free Willy*.

Valley-Speak: Buffy's advice to Giles on dating: 'Just say, "Hey, I gotta *thing*, you maybe have a *thing*. Maybe we could have a *thing*."'

Jenny: 'Is this normal strategy for a first date? Dissing my country's national pastime.'

Logic, Let Me Introduce You to This Window: The cheerleaders were students at Fondren High so why do they have the letter 'J' on their uniforms? None of the pictures that Eric develops matches the shots he took. There was no boy in a striped shirt walking on the stairs behind Buffy, Willow was looking at her clipboard when she was photographed and Cordelia's eyes were aimed away from the camera for the first two shots, then her hand covered her face for the last photo. How did the keys roll that far under Cordelia's car? Look at the depressions in the earth caused by dragging the body from the grave. Either the ground was *immensely* soft, or the body was that of the world's first thirty-two-stone cheerleader.

I Just *Love* Your Accent: Buffy: 'Speak English, not whatever it is they speak in . . .' Giles: 'England?'

Quote/Unquote: Buffy refuses to dig graves: 'Sorry, but I'm an old-fashioned gal. I was raised to believe that men dig up the corpses and women have the babies.'

Cordelia: 'Hello, can we deal with my pain please?' Giles

(uninterestedly patting her on the back): 'There, there.'

Giles on American football: 'I just think it's rather odd that a nation that prides itself on its virility should feel compelled to strap on forty pounds of protective gear just in order to play rugby.'

Notes: 'Love makes you do the wacky.' An overt homage to *Bride of Frankenstein* which takes far longer to get to the point than it should (in a series as sharp as this, it's surprising somebody doesn't say, 'This is *just* like *Frankenstein*!'). Includes lots of cool bits (Xander's heroic rescue of Cordy, for instance) that transcend the obvious denouement. The episode has aged rather better than several around it and repeated viewing is recommended.

Buffy owns a yo-yo. There are references to Buffy's dance with Xander in **13**, 'When She Was Bad'. Jenny likes Mexican food (Buffy somehow guessed she would). Willow believes she's the only girl in school who has the coroner's office website bookmarked. Her science project is 'Effects of subviolet light spectrum deprivation on the development of fruit flies'. That sounds a more likely winner than Cordelia's 'The Tomato – fruit or vegetable?' When Cordy asks for help, Willow tells her, 'It's a fruit.' There's at least one issue of *Scientific American* that Willow hasn't read. Angel reveals that he is 241 years old (see **33**, 'Becoming' Part 1; *Angel*: 'City Of'). Giles assumed that Jenny spent her evenings downloading incantations and casting bones. In fact, she *does*, but she likes football too. She tells Giles that 'Ms Calendar' is her father's name. This may imply a sex-change operation but as Calendar isn't her real surname (see **25**, 'Surprise') she's almost certainly teasing.

Tony Head's voice replaces the original narrator in the opening monologue.

15

School Hard

US Transmission Date: 29 Sep. 1997
UK Transmission Date: 11 Apr. 1998 (Sky)
15 Apr. 1999 (BBC2)

Writer: David Greenwalt
Story: Joss Whedon, David Greenwalt
Director: John T Kretchmer
Cast: Alexandra Johnes (Sheila), Keith Mackechnie (Parent),
Alan Abelew (Brian Kirch), Joanie Pleasant (Helpless Girl)
French title: *Attaque À Sunnydale*
German title: *Elternabend Mit Hindernissen*

Snyder assigns the organisation of Parent–Teacher Night to his two worst students, Sheila and Buffy. Vampire couple Spike and Drusilla arrive in town but are coldly received by the Anointed One. The Night of St Vigeous will occur on Saturday, the time when a vampire's strength is at its peak. Spike watches Buffy at the Bronze and tells her that he will kill her on Saturday. He then lures Sheila to his warehouse and feeds her to Drusilla. At Parent–Teacher Night Buffy is unable to keep Snyder and Joyce apart and is in big trouble with her mom until Spike and an army of vampires attack the school. Buffy herds the parents into a room, while Willow and Cordelia hide in a nearby closet, and Giles, Xander and Jenny barricade the library. Buffy takes on the vampires, including Sheila. After an angry confrontation with his former guru, Angel, Spike almost kills Buffy but Joyce smashes an axe over Spike's head. Joyce tells Buffy how proud she is of her daughter's bravery and says that those qualities are more important than her problems at school. Spike and Dru, however, are here to stay and end 'the Annoying' One's term as leader.

Dudes and Babes: Buffy worries about whether she has a split end. Some people are just never satisfied. Xander, once again, dances like somebody trying to crush cockroaches.

Authority Sucks!: Snyder says he wants his students to think of him not as their pal but as their judge, jury and executioner.

A Little Learning is a Dangerous Thing: Xander learns a very important lesson in this episode: never rummage through a girl's handbag, because you don't know what you might find. It's a little mousie, right?

Mom's Apple Pie: 'In the car – now.' Buffy and Joyce have a mini-argument about Parent–Teacher Night, including the explicit threat that Buffy will be stopped from going out with her friends. However, despite Snyder's attempts to paint Buffy as a troublemaker, Joyce comes to realise that Buffy is a resourceful and brave girl who cares about other people (but, see **24**, 'Bad Eggs'). Snyder now has *two* problems called Summers, noting, 'I'm beginning to see a certain mother–daughter resemblance.'

It's a Designer Label!: What *is* Xander wearing? That shirt should carry a public-health warning. Willow's dungarees also deserve attention. Buffy has a cute purple top. Sheila has one of the same colour, but several degrees sluttier, and an extremely short skirt to match.

References: Spike's bravado in front of the other vampires (see **Valley-Speak**) may be an oblique reference to the famous 'Show us your yarbles' scene in *A Clockwork Orange*. The title and aspects of the plot are taken from the classic action movie *Die Hard*. The works of novelist Anne Rice (*Interview With the Vampire* et al.) are referred to in a derogatory way. Spike calls Angel 'my Yoda' (from *The Empire Strikes Back*) and 'an Uncle Tom', a cynical term normally applied to a black whose behaviour towards whites is regarded as servile after the character in HB Stowe's novel *Uncle Tom's Cabin* (1852). There are possible references to the Beatles' 'From Me to You' and 'Jack and the Beanstalk'.

Bitch!: Xander: 'Does anybody remember when Saturday night meant date night?' Cordelia: '*You* sure don't.'

Awesome!: Giles swearing for the first time ('*Bloody* right I will . . .'). Buffy's fight with the vampire behind the Bronze is so good it gets a round of applause from Spike. Cordy's prayer in the final scene is one of the funniest sequences they've ever done.

The Drugs Don't Work: Spike says he was at Woodstock (presumably he had a tent and slept through the day). He fed on a flower person and spent the next six hours 'watching my hand move'. Snyder and Bob's 'official' explanation for the outbreak of violence at the school is: 'Gang-related. PCP' – a reference to the hallucinogenic narcotic 'phencyclidine', the street name of which is 'Angel Dust'.

'You May Remember Me From Such Films and TV Series As . . .': Juliet Landau, despite appearances in films such as *The Grifters*, *Pump Up the Volume*, *Theodore Rex* and *Citizens* *of Perpetual Indulgence*, and series like *Parker Lewis Can't Lose* and *La Femme Nikita*, is best known for her performance as Loretta King opposite her father Martin in Tim Burton's *Ed Wood*. James Marsters isn't from London, though the accent is good enough to fool many UK fans. He's actually from California and he can also be seen (using his 'real' voice) in a guest slot on *Millennium* and, briefly, in the movie *House on Haunted Hill*.

Valley-Speak: Spike: 'Any of you wanna test who's got the biggest wrinklies around here, step on up.'

Cigarettes and Alcohol: Willow notes Sheila was already smoking in fifth grade (age ten).

Logic, Let Me Introduce You to This Window: Buffy and Willow leave their books on the table as they dance at the Bronze. These have vanished when Xander returns to the table to fetch a stake from Buffy's bag. Of course, someone may have stolen them, but why not take the bag too? Why does Buffy not confront Spike when he tells her he is going to kill her? Willow and Cordelia run into a room next to a trophy cabinet to hide from the vampires. When we see them inside the closet, the cabinet is nowhere near the door. It is located on the opposite side of the hall. The vampires cut the power in the school, so why is the cabinet still illuminated? Why was Snyder turning off all the lights in the lounge while some of the parents were still there?

Motors: Spike's 'deathmobile' is a 1963 DeSoto.

What a Shame They Dropped . . .: This brilliant exchange: Buffy: 'I don't suppose this is something about happy squirrels?' Giles: 'No, vampires.' Buffy: 'That was my next guess!'

Quote/Unquote: Spike: 'If every vampire who said he was at the crucifixion was actually there, it would have been like Woodstock.'

Jenny tells Giles: 'You have *got* to read something that was published *after* 1066.'

Joyce's triumphant: 'Nobody lays a hand on my little girl.'

Notes: 'So, who do you kill for fun around here?' A *gorgeous* episode. Funny in all the right places, but with a real tension and menace. The introduction of the drop-dead- sexy Spike and Drusilla is the point at which *Buffy* went from being merely a very good show into being a *great* one.

In reply to Snyder referring to Buffy burning down a school building, Buffy says this was never proved (the fire marshal said it could have been mice). Given that she freely admitted to burning down the Hemery gym in **1**, 'Welcome to the Hellmouth', and that she later tells Sheila she burned down more than one building, are we to assume that this refers to the destruction of the old science lab in **14**, 'Some Assembly Required'? Spike's reference to the crucifixion begs the question: were the vampires who attended afraid of crosses? This is the first time that Mrs Summers is referred to as Joyce. Sheila stabbed a horticulture teacher with some pruning shears, which seems to put Buffy's antisocial activities into context. Spike, also known as 'William the Bloody' (he gained his nickname by torturing his victims with railroad spikes) is younger than his mentor and hero Angelus, who 'sired' him (a term Angel is reticent to explain to Xander). Giles notes he is 'barely two hundred' (which is flatly contradicted in **63**, 'The Initiative'. See **85**, 'Fool for Love'). He has killed two Slayers in the last century. One was during 'The Boxer Rebellion' which *just* fits into that timescale (this was an anti-foreign uprising in China during the years 1898–1900). He says that the last Slayer he killed begged for her life (he's lying, of course, see **85**, 'Fool for Love'). His (childlike) lover, Drusilla, collects dolls. Before coming to Sunnydale they were in Prague. This episode includes the first hints that Snyder, in collaboration with others (in this case Bob), knows *something* odd is occurring in Sunnydale, but that they are actively engaged in a cover-up (see **31**, 'I Only Have Eyes for You'). According to the sign Spike's car knocks down, Sunnydale has a population of 38,500. And decreasing (see **42**, 'Lover's Walk'). The French teacher is called Mr Dujon.

Soundtrack: Nickel perform '1000 Nights' and 'Stupid Thing' in the Bronze.

16

Inca Mummy Girl

US Transmission Date: 6 Oct. 1997
UK Transmission Date: 18 Apr. 1998 (Sky)
5 May 1999 (BBC2)

Writers: Matt Kiene, Joe Reinkemeyer
Director: Ellen S Pressman
Cast: Ara Celi (Ampata), Henrik Rosvall (Sven), Joey Crawford (Rodney),
Kristen Winnicki (Gwen), Gil Birmingham (Peru Man),
Samuel Jacobs (Peruvian Boy)
French title: *La Momie Inca*
German title: *Das Geheimnis der Mumie*

Sunnydale's student exchange programme brings the beautiful Ampata to town. Unbeknown to her new friends, Ampata is a mummy girl who escaped from her tomb when the seal was stolen. While Xander and Ampata develop a mutual attachment, Giles asks Ampata to translate the pictograms on the seal, but she is frightened by the object and tells him to destroy it. Buffy and Giles discover that the mummy has the ability to drain the life-force of its victims. Buffy finds a shrivelled corpse in Ampata's trunk, proving that her new friend is the mummy. Giles begins to piece together the broken seal to send Ampata back to her mummified state. Ampata attacks him, also throwing Buffy into an open tomb. But Xander tells her that if she wants another life it must be his and Buffy pulls the disintegrating Ampata apart in her hands.

Dudes and Babes: A Xander love story that lets us see the sensitive and vulnerable side of X-boy. Ampata's gorgeous and Xander can't believe how lucky he is ('You're not a praying mantis?' he asked, referring to **4**, 'Teacher's Pet'). There's a severe lack of Angel, however.

A Little Learning is a Dangerous Thing: Willow helps the inordinately stupid Rodney with his chemistry. He says he's almost memorised the '14 natural elements'; Willow notes there are 103. However, since the discovery of the 103rd (lawrencium in 1961), a further eight had been identified by 1998.

Mom's Apple Pie: Is Joyce's pleasure at how quickly Ampata is fitting into Sunnydale society a sly dig at her daughter's inability to do likewise?

No Fat Chicks!: Buffy is seen drinking a can of (non-diet) Pepsi. She should have a look over her shoulder at the three girls with enormous bottoms who wobble through shot and reflect on America, the land of the pancake breakfast.

It's a Designer Label!: Good stuff: Buffy's very low-cut top in the scenes investigating Rodney's disappearance and her kick-boxing vest and stretchpants, Ampata's night shorts, Cordelia's blue miniskirt. *Very* bad stuff: Buffy's 'white-trash' look, Willow's bobble-hat. Willow's Eskimo costume could also be a contender but it seems to do something for Oz, so the jury is still out on that one. Xander says lederhosen make his calves look fat. There's also a delicious double entendre between Buffy and Giles over the word 'trunks'.

References: Willow makes specific reference to the mummy-film genre and the plot bears a similarity to Hammer's *Blood From the Mummy's Tomb*. Buffy makes a pun concerning *Mommie Dearest*. The name of Oz's band, Dingoes Ate My Baby, is a reference to the case of Australian mother Lindy Chamberlain, wrongly imprisoned for murdering her infant daughter. Readers may know the film dramatisation *A Cry in the Dark*. Xander's '*Ay carumba*' is a probable nod to *The Simpsons*, while 'I am from the country of Leone – it's in Italy pretending to be Montana' identifies someone as a fan of Sergio Leone's spaghetti Westerns.

Bitch!: Cordelia on Willow's Eskimo suit: 'Near *faux pas*. I nearly wore the same thing.'

Awesome!: A big girly cat-fight! Encore! Xander's fight with the bodyguard is rather good. He's beginning to be able to handle himself (in a Xander kind of way . . .).

'You May Remember Me From Such Films and TV Series As . . .': Seth Green's movies include *Stephen King's It*, *Radio Days*, *Can't Hardly Wait*, *Idle Hands*, *Enemy of the State*, *Knockabout Guys*, *Austin Powers: International Man of Mystery* and *Austin Powers: The Spy Who Shagged Me* (as Scott Evil) and *My Stepmother is an Alien* (as Alyson Hannigan's boyfriend). He played a very Oz-like character in *The X-Files* episode 'Deep Throat' and he provides the voice for Chris Griffin in *Family Guy*. Seth's a great actor and his (often understated) contribution to *Buffy* can't be praised highly enough. 'He can *own* a scene he has no lines in,' notes Joss Whedon. Danny Strong, who originally screen tested for the role of Xander, was Juke Box Boy in *Pleasantville* and appeared in *Saved By the Bell: The New Class*, the *Clueless* TV series and *Spoof! An Insider's Guide to Short Film Success*. Jason Hall can be seen in *No Child of Mine* and *Play Dead* and was one of the voice artists on *The 10th Kingdom*.

Valley-Speak: Buffy: 'It's the *über*-suck.'

Cordelia on her Swedish exchange student: 'Isn't he lunchable?'

Logic, Let Me Introduce You to This Window: When Buffy opens Ampata's trunk the head of the mummified corpse is on the right. Later, when she opens the trunk, it's moved to the left. With Rodney Munson attending how could Buffy and Sheila (see **15**, 'School Hard') be the two 'worst students in school'? (With Snyder you get the feeling it's all about appearances.) Xander and Ampata sit on the bleachers with Xander's bag lying on the seat in front of them. When the bodyguard attacks them the bag is knocked off and lands on a footrest. When Xander gets up and runs off with Ampata, the bag is in its original position. Ampata tells Buffy that she doesn't have any lipstick. However, she applied some in the school restroom. In the museum Giles is about to reassemble the final piece of the seal when Ampata grabs it from him. In the next shot, just before Ampata smashes it, the seal appears whole. Given that Cordelia has a book showing (presumably) all the exchange students, why does nobody question Ampata's credentials? How well could Xander drive so soon after almost having his life-force sucked out of him? But, given that Xander can drive, why does he need Cordelia to give him a lift in **21**, 'What's My Line?' Part 1?

Quote/Unquote: Buffy's sarcastic impression of Giles: 'I'm so stuffy, give me a scone.'

What impresses Oz in a girl involves: 'A feather boa and theme from *A Summer Place*.'

Xander on Sunnydale bus depot: 'What better way to welcome somebody to our country than the stench of urine?'

And: 'We're in the Crime Club, which is kind of like the Chess Club. Only with Crime. And no Chess.'

Notes: 'I can translate salivating boy talk.' Nobody ever sets out to make a deliberately bad hour of television, but sometimes nothing goes according to plan. This is one such instance. 'Inca Mummy Girl' is an uneven story which lacks explanations, a focus and a degree of rationality. The direction, on the other hand, is terrific, so at least this hollow tale of unrequited love and betrayal isn't a complete loss.

Xander claims his dad tried to give him to some Armenians. He can drive and knows approximately four words of Spanish ('*dorritos*', 'Chihuahua' and '*Ay carumba*'). Buffy refers to how upset she was at the prophecy of her death in 12, 'Prophecy Girl'. During the dance at the Bronze, a 'WP' sticker is seen representing the band Widespread Panic (these stickers crop up in many episodes, so it's fair to assume somebody on the production team is a fan).

Novelisation: By Keith RA DeCandido in *The Xander Years Vol. 1* (Pocket Books, February 1999).

Soundtrack: The Dingoes Ate My Baby songs, 'Shadows' and 'Fate', are by Four Star Mary.

17

Reptile Boy

US Transmission Date: 13 Oct. 1997
UK Transmission Date: 25 Apr. 1998 (Sky)
6 May 1999 (BBC2)

Writer: David Greenwalt
Director: David Greenwalt
Cast: Greg Vaughan (Richard), Todd Babcock (Tom),
Jordana Spiro (Callie),
Robin Atkin-Downes (Machida), Christopher Dahlberg (Tackle),
Jason Posey (Linebacker), Coby Bell (Young Man)
French title: *Dévotion*
German title: *Der Geheimbund*

Buffy discovers a bracelet in the graveyard. She accepts Cordelia's invitation to a fraternity house party, much to

Xander and Willow's surprise. While Buffy and Cordelia attend the party, Willow discovers that the bracelet belonged to a missing student called Callie. When confronted by Giles and Angel, Willow tells them where Buffy is. Xander gatecrashes the party but is humiliated and thrown out. Buffy is drugged, waking next to Cordelia and Callie in the basement. They discover that the fraternity is a cult who worship a snake-demon called Machida to whom the girls are to be offered as sacrifices. Giles, Angel and Xander invade the ceremony just as Buffy frees herself and kills Machida.

Dudes and Babes: Buffy says her dreams about Angel contain 'surround sound'. You and every other female on the planet, girl. Plus, frat party! Babes!

Authority Sucks!: Giles's chastising Buffy ('And don't think sitting there pouting is going to get to me because it won't') is worthy of Snyder.

A Little Learning is a Dangerous Thing: Willow explains the plot of the Hindi movie she, Xander and Buffy are watching on Channel 59: 'She's sad because her lover gave her twelve gold coins, but then the wizard cut open the bag of salt and now the dancing minions have nowhere to put their big maypole fish thing . . .'

It's a Designer Label!: A nice collection of miniskirts – Cordelia's blue one we've seen before, Buffy's green effort also looks familiar, but Willow's dark-purple skirt is a beaut. Cordelia states that Buffy shouldn't wear black, silk, chiffon or spandex to the frat party as these are Cordelia's trademarks. She also tells Buffy not to 'do that thing with your hair'.

References: Herman's Hermits' 'There's a Kind of Hush', Nancy Sinatra's 'These Boots Are Made for Walkin'', *The Incredible Hulk, Godzilla* and the *Superman* comics ('You could go on to live among rich and powerful men . . . In Bizarro World').

Bitch!: Cordelia: 'Buffy, it's like we're sisters. With *really different hair.*'

Awesome!: Buffy taking on the entire frat coven *and* the snake-demon while Xander, Angel and Giles muck about upstairs with the varsity footballers.

'You May Remember Me From Such TV Series As . . .':

Robin Atkin-Downes, hiding inside the snake costume, is best known as the poetry-spouting telepath Byron in *Babylon 5*.

Valley-Speak: Tom: 'And you are?' Buffy: '. . . *So* not interested.'

Cigarettes and Alcohol: Buffy and Cordelia both drink in this episode. The implication is that it's the first time Buffy has ever had alcohol (though after a summer of partying mentioned in **13**, 'When She Was Bad', you've got to wonder what sort of parties she gets invited to).

Logic, Let Me Introduce You to This Window: The student lounge seems to have the quickest Coke machine in the world. Willow buys a can of Coca-Cola Classic, which is delivered almost before the coins have left her hand. What kind of glass was that balcony door made out of? Callie just runs through it. Greg Vaughan's name is misspelled as 'Vaughn' in the opening credits. Willow asks a question that most of us have been *dying* for *someone* to articulate for years. If Angel casts no reflection then how does he (and other vampires) shave? Sadly, she doesn't get an answer. Why does Buffy wear black to the party when Cordelia specifically asked her not to (or perhaps we shouldn't need to ask!).

Motors: Cordelia's car is a red Chrysler Sebring convertible with the licence plate 'Queen C'.

Quote/Unquote: Angel: 'This isn't some fairy tale. When I kiss you, you don't wake up from a deep sleep and live happily ever after.' Buffy: 'When you kiss me, I want to die.'

Willow's rant at Giles and Angel: 'She's sixteen going on forty. And *you* . . . You're going to live forever, you don't have time for a cup of coffee?'

Xander's beating up the frat boy who made him dance in women's clothes: 'And *that's* for the last sixteen and a half years.'

Notes: 'Party's over, jerkwater.' Two substandard episodes in a row is almost unique in a series this good. A pity really, as a lot of the ideas in 'Reptile Boy' are very good and David Greenwalt's script is quite well structured. But . . . it's just so *obvious*. And the acting of a lot of the nonregulars is really poor. If you're going to do *Animal House*-with-demons, at least make it funny. The local paper is called the *Sunnydale Press*.

Novelisation: By Nancy Holder in *The Angel Chronicles Vol. 1* (Pocket Books, July 1998).
Soundtrack: 'Wolves' by Shawn Clement and Sean Murray, 'Bring Me On' by Act of Faith, and 'She' by Louie Says.

18

Halloween

US Transmission Date: 27 Oct. 1997
UK Transmission Date: 2 May 1998 (Sky)
28 Oct. 1999 (BBC2)

Writer: Carl Ellsworth
Director: Bruce Seth Green
Cast: Abigail Gershman (Girl)
German title: *Die Nacht der Verwandlung*

Halloween, a traditionally quiet time in the supernatural community, is interrupted by the opening of a new costume store owned by warlock Ethan Rayne. Forced by Snyder into accompanying groups of children on their trick-or-treating, Buffy, Xander and Willow find themselves in a clothes-created nightmare as Rayne's spell transforms people into the reality of their costumes. While the children turn into monsters and ghouls, Xander becomes a soldier, Willow emerges from her body as an intangible ghost and Buffy becomes a helpless noblewoman. Willow leaves Xander and Buffy with the unaffected Cordelia to get Giles's help. Angel arrives, but is confused by the transformations and frightens Buffy who runs from the house and hides in a warehouse, pursued by Spike who is about to kill Buffy when Giles forces his 'old mate' Ethan to reverse the spell. Later, Buffy and Angel finally spend some time together and share a kiss. Giles finds a note on the counter of Ethan's shop saying, 'Be seeing you.'
Dudes and Babes: Buffy and Angel kissing at the climax. Aaah. Buffy tells Giles that Ms Calendar thinks he is 'a babe' and 'a hunk of burning . . . something'. Giles wants to know 'of what?' Of course, it's a lie to allow Willow to steal the Watcher Diaries, but Giles doesn't seem too displeased by it.

Plus Cordelia in her pussycat costume.

Authority Sucks!: Snyder 'volunteers' Xander, Buffy and Willow for Halloween chaperone patrol duty. 'Bring them back in one piece and I won't expel you.'

A Quiet Night In?: The subversion of Halloween being a festival for the undead by having them all 'stay home' that night and let the children get on with it! (See **60**, 'Fear Itself'.)

It's a Designer Label!: Xander likes his women in spandex but 'completely renounces it' when he sees Buffy in the eighteenth-century dress. It's certainly preferable to the checky flares she wears. Willow's 'hooker' look is effective but she's right: it isn't her (though again, it gets Oz's attention).

References: Name checks for the Care Bears, *Xena: Warrior Princess* (a compliment *Xena* returned by referring to 'Buffus the Bachae Slayer'), Catwoman (from *Batman*), US sitcom clichés ('Hi honey, I'm home') and a misquote from *The Godfather*. 'Be seeing you' echoes the catchphrase of *The Prisoner* (Robin Sachs has confirmed that this *was* deliberate).

Bitch!: Cordelia on Buffy after a fight: '*Love* that hair. It screams "street urchin".'

Awesome!: The black-and-white 'camcorder' footage of Buffy's fight with the vampire in the pumpkin patch. The best bit of the episode is Giles's reaction to Willow walking through the wall (*what* was that he almost said?).

Surprise!: Giles's entire conversation with Ethan ('Hello, Ripper!') despite being nothing more than innuendo just screams 'back-story alert . . .'

'You May Remember Me From Such Films and TV Series As . . .': Robin Sachs was in one of this author's favourite films, Hammer's notoriously sexy *Vampire Circus*. *Babylon 5* fans will recognise him as Hedronn. He provided the voice for the Silver Surfer in *The Fantastic Four* and, unrecognisably, appeared as the villain Sarris in *Galaxy Quest*.

Logic, Let Me Introduce You to This Window: When Buffy slams Larry against the drinks machine, a Diet Dr Pepper falls out. However, this was not a choice according to the selection buttons (see **55**, 'Graduation Day' Part 1). While reviewing the video of Buffy's fight, Spike orders the vampire with the remote control to rewind. At this point both Buffy and the vampire are standing and fighting. However, after the tape is 'rewound', Buffy has the vampire on the ground and is raising the wooden sign for the death blow. Perhaps he hit 'fast forward' by mistake? Vampires cast no reflection in a mirror (see **11**, 'Out of Sight, Out of Mind'), so how do they appear on video tape which uses mirrors as part of the focusing/view-finding mechanism? (See **46**, 'Helpless'.) After Giles tells Willow to leave when he confronts Ethan, you can see Willow bump a curtain and hear her close the door despite supposedly being an intangible ghost. If the editing during the sequence in the warehouse is done in real-time, then why does Giles hold the sculpture over his head for so long? Buffy and Angel are attacked in the Summers's kitchen by what appears to be a vampire (Angel even asks for a stake), so who invited this vampire in?

I Just *Love* Your Accent: Aside from the episode featuring two fine British actors, the van that Oz drives has its steering wheel on the right, which suggests it's also British.

Quote/Unquote: Xander: 'A black eye heals, but cowardice has an unlimited shelf life.'

Spike on the mayhem Ethan causes: 'This is just . . . neat!'

Cordelia's reaction to Willow telling her that she isn't a cat, she's in high school and that they are her friends, well sort of: 'That's nice, Willow. And you went mental *when* . . .?'

Notes: 'This could be a situation.' One of the best of the season, showing that *Buffy* had come out of the lethargy of the previous episodes. A story about perception with a cool subplot in which the clothes, literally, maketh the man (or the Slayer). Plus an icy cold, yet very funny, performance from the excellent Robin Sachs. Willow gets to do all the groovy detection stuff, Xander becomes *macho* and Buffy faints a lot. What more could one ask for?

This episode answers the question of whether or not Cordelia knew about Angel's vampirism. Amusingly, it appears not. Giles says he has many relaxing hobbies including cross-referencing. The dark hints about his past would be explored further in **20**, 'The Dark Age'. Cordelia is still dating Dingoes Ate My Baby's singer, Devon (see **16**, 'Inca Mummy Girl'), although a break-up is on the cards given her conversation with Oz.

Novelisation: By Richie Tankersley in *The Angel Chronicles Vol. 2* (Pocket Books, January 1999).

Soundtrack: 'Shy' by Epperley and 'How She Died' by Treble Charger.

Head On . . . : One of the great things about interviews with Tony Head are his insights into Giles's view of Buffy and her friends, as he told Paul Simpson: 'I think Giles likes Buffy, but she annoys him. The mere fact that she doesn't want the job that he's offering her – she frustrates him. She represents everything he doesn't understand. Ultimately he becomes extremely fond of her. People have said, what is it? A father/daughter relationship? And it's not quite. There's nothing like it on TV. It's difficult to pigeonhole. He becomes extremely fond of her and gets into all sorts of terrible trouble because of it . . . Xander is complete anathema to him. A great annoyance because he never seems to take anything seriously. Cordelia is . . . Who knows where she's coming from? Willow he respects greatly, but it's all a confusion to him. He's never really sure of anybody or anything. The only thing he is sure about is what he's supposed to do.'

19

Lie to Me

US Transmission Date: 3 Nov. 1997
UK Transmission Date: 9 May 1998 (Sky)
4 Nov. 1999 (BBC2)

Writer: Joss Whedon
Director: Joss Whedon
Cast: Jason Behr (Billy Fordham), Jarrad Paul (Marvin), Will Rothhaar (James)
French title: *Mensonge*
German title: *Todessehnsucht*

Billy 'Ford' Fordham, Buffy's boyfriend at Hemery, arrives in Sunnydale. At the Bronze, she introduces Angel to Ford but the situation is awkward. Outside, Buffy hears a scuffle and sends Ford back while she confronts a vampire. She makes up a story explaining her actions, but Ford simply says that he knows she is the Slayer. After Buffy goes home, Ford returns to a club full of groupies who dream of joining the undead. Angel asks Willow to find out what she can about Ford. She discovers that he never registered at Sunnydale High, confirming Angel's suspicions. Buffy and Ford encounter two vampires. Ford tackles the female but, instead of staking her, he lets her go. At the library she attacks Buffy and Giles to steal a book. Ford meets Spike and offers him the Slayer in exchange for immortality. Buffy goes to the club and while they wait for Spike to arrive she tries to reason with Ford, who reveals he has incurable brain cancer. Spike and his cohorts arrive and begin to feed. Buffy grabs Drusilla and tells Spike to let the clubbers go. Later, Buffy returns and finds Ford's body. Buffy and Giles attend Ford's grave and discuss the complexities of life. Ford rises from the dead and Buffy kills him.

Dudes and Babes: The idea of a Goth club full of vampire worshippers would be *so* cool if only Ford's friends weren't such a bunch of dweebs. Especially Marvin in that cape.

Willow tells Xander why Angel was in her room: 'Ours is a forbidden love!'

A Little Learning is a Dangerous Thing: Cordelia says she can relate to Marie Antoinette (the executed wife of King Louis XVI of France). Unfortunately she gets 'oppressed' and 'depressed' mixed up.

It's a Designer Label!: Willow's high-collared blouse in the Bronze. Giles claims not to have any clothes other than those he wears to school (which, judging by the stripy tie he takes to his date with Jenny, seems to be true). And what about Xander's red Adidas top and Ford's orange shirt? Chantarelle's low-cut red dress is a definite highlight.

References: The film that Ford is so fascinated by is a 1973 TV movie adaptation of *Dracula* starring Jack Palance. Buffy notes that when Ford ignored her in fifth grade she sat around in her room for months 'listening to that Divinyls song "I Touch Myself"'. Before adding, 'Of course I had no idea what it was about.' For anybody who *doesn't* know, it was about masturbation and was a worldwide hit in 1991. Joss Whedon seems to be a fan of The Doors judging by references to 'The End' ('This is the end') and a misquote from 'Five to One' ('No one gets out of here alive').

Awesome!: Angel and Drusilla in the playground is about as sinister as *Buffy* has ever got. I'm sure we've *all* got people we'd like to shout 'lying scumbag' at, as Buffy does at Ford, so *that's* an extremely satisfying moment.

Don't Give Up the Day Job: The make-up supervisor Todd McIntosh has a cameo in the club as the man dressed as a vampire standing in a coffin who says 'Hi' to Xander.

'You May Remember Me From Such TV Series As . . .': Jason Behr would go on to deserved stardom as the alien schoolboy Max Evans in *Roswell*.

Valley-Speak: Buffy: 'Do we have to be in total share mode?'

Logic, Let Me Introduce You to This Window: Before they leave for the club, Spike gives specific orders to all the vampires to make the Slayer their first priority. When they enter, however, they attack everybody *but* the Slayer. When Buffy fights in the alley behind the Bronze as Ford watches, pay attention to the length of her hair. From behind it seems much longer than Buffy's normal shoulder-length (it's very obviously Sarah's stunt double Sophia Crawford). Again we don't see Willow's parents, though we do hear her mom's voice. It's also worth asking exactly *when* (and *how*) Ford worked out that Buffy is the Slayer? Remember, when he first tells her he knows, he hasn't met Spike at that point.

Quote/Unquote: Xander, upon learning that the vampires are known as 'the lonely ones': 'We usually call them "the nasty, pointy, bitey ones".'

Drusilla on Angel's infatuation with Buffy: 'Your heart *stinks* of her.'

Buffy on the stupidity of the club teenagers: 'Spike and all of his friends are going to be pigging out at the All You Can Eat Moron Bar.'

Buffy: 'Does it get easy?' Giles: 'What do you want me to say?' Buffy: 'Lie to me.' Giles: 'Yes, it's terribly simple. The good guys are always stalwart and true, the bad guys are easily distinguished by their pointy horns or black hats, and we always defeat them and save the day. No one ever dies, and everybody lives happily ever after.'

Notes: 'I know you're the Slayer.' A highly effective tear-jerker, 'Lie to Me' potters along for a while seemingly concerned with jealousy, before becoming a pointed essay on betrayal and obsession (the juxtaposition of what Angel did in the past to Drusilla, with Billy's attempted manipulation of Buffy, is nicely realised) and ends up with one of the finest climaxes of the season. Highlights include Angel entering Willow's house for the first time and a quite lovely and philosophical finale.

Ford was Buffy's fifth-grade crush (though he was a year older). Something embarrassing seems to have happened to Buffy during the swimsuit section of her ninth-grade beauty contest. Willow has upgraded from a desktop computer to a laptop sometime between **8**, 'I Robot . . . You Jane', and this episode. Angel was obsessed by Drusilla when she was still human. He sent her insane by killing everyone she loved and tortured her before following her to a convent, where she sought refuge and he sired her (see **33**, 'Becoming' Part 1 and *Angel*: 'Dear Boy'). Angel is said to have cold hands, which fits in with the idea first presented in **12** 'Prophecy Girl', that his body is, basically, dead (see **26**, 'Innocence'; **55**, 'Graduation Day' Part 1). Giles thought Drusilla had been killed by a mob in Prague (see **15**, 'School Hard'). Jenny takes Giles to a Monster Truck rally, at which he seems to have a *really* bad time. Drusilla's mother used to sing her to sleep. Coffee is said to make Willow 'jumpy' (something she shares with Angel, see **54**, 'The Prom').

Novelisation: By Nancy Holder in *The Angel Chronicles Vol. 1* (Pocket Books, Jul. 1998).

Soundtrack: On first US transmission, a voice-over stated 'tonight's presentation of *Buffy* included music from Sisters of Mercy' (the song 'Never Land') and a caption featured the cover of the band's *Floodland* LP. This credit (to become something of a regular feature in the third season) was shown between the final scene and the preview for the next episode. However, due to copyright problems, all subsequent broadcasts (including those in the UK) have removed 'Never Land' and replaced it with 'Blood of a Stranger' by Shawn Clement and Sean Murray. Also: 'Lois On the Brink' by Willoughby and 'Reptile' by Creaming Jesus.

20

The Dark Age

US Transmission Date: 10 Nov. 1997
UK Transmission Date: 16 May 1998 (Sky)
11 Nov. 1999 (BBC2)

Writers: Dean Batali, Rob Des Hotel
Director: Bruce Seth Green
Cast: Stuart McLean (Philip Henry), Wendy Way (Deirdre),
Michael Earl Reid (Custodian), Daniel Henry Murray (Creepy Cult Guy),
Carlease Burke (Detective Winslow), Tony Sears (Morgue Attendant),
John Bellucci (Man)
French title: *La Face Cachée*
German title: *Das Mal des Eyghon*

Giles identifies a body found at the school as Philip, an old
friend from London. He is asked about the tattoo on Philip's
arm, but denies any knowledge. Buffy prevents a vampire
attack on the hospital blood supplies with Angel's help, but is
surprised that Giles didn't turn up as planned. At his apartment, she finds him drinking. After she leaves, Giles rolls up
his sleeve, revealing an identical tattoo. Buffy finds Ethan
Rayne who tells her about the Mark of Eyghon that both he
and Giles wear. Buffy locks the resurrected Philip into the
book cage while Giles argues with Ethan, but they are dis-
rupted by Philip breaking open the doors. He dissolves into a
liquid puddle, which touches Jenny's unconscious body trans-
forming her into Eyghon. Buffy stops her from killing Giles,
who explains that in their youth he and his friends conjured up
the demon Eyghon, who is trying to kill everyone who wears
his mark. Ethan knocks Buffy out and tattoos her, burning off
his own tattoo with acid. Eyghon enters Angel's body but is
destroyed by the demon within.

Dudes and Babes: Giles and Jenny's kiss. ('I trust I gave good
squirm?') Is it any wonder Tony Head has such a following
among the ladies? Xander believes that he could live without
the thought of Giles and orgies in the same sentence.

A Little Learning is a Dangerous Thing: Willow informs
Xander that hot lava is used to kill a heretic, not a demon.

It's a Designer Label!: Buffy's green training vest, Giles's blue pyjamas and Willow's fluffy green jumper. Rather cruelly, Buffy speculates that Giles's diapers were tweed.

References: A bizarre array include *Hamlet* ('The rest is silence'), *ER*, *Lost Weekend*, *The Sound of Music*, Frank Sinatra's 'I've Got You Under My Skin' and Bill Withers's 'Lean on Me'. 'Be seeing you' crops up again (see **18**, 'Halloween').

'Anywhere But Here . . .': A game anyone can play: Buffy wants to be on a beach having her feet massaged by Gavin Rossdale (singer with British grunge band Bush). Willow's contribution is a dinner date in Florence with actor John Cusack *(True Colours, Grosse Pointe Blank, The Thin Red Line, Being John Malkovich, High Fidelity, Serendipity)*. Xander implies that both have recently changed their fantasies, though his remains large-chested actress Amy Yip 'at the Waterslide Park'.

Bitch!: Xander's moment of Premier League sarcasm: 'A bonus day at class, plus Cordelia? Mix in a little rectal surgery and it's *my best day ever.*'

   Cordelia: 'Do you know what you need Xander – besides a year's supply of acne cream? A brain.'

Awesome!: Willow's anger at Xander and Cordy bitching (and their reactions to it). Giles's nightmares (the first one, especially). Cordelia tripping Ethan.

Surprise!: The photograph of a much younger (and rockier) Rupert. '*That* is Giles?'

Never Mind the Warlocks!: Tony Head, interviewed on the BBC's *Fully Booked*, confirmed that the photo of Giles playing bass was his head superimposed on the body of Sid Vicious!

Valley-Speak: Cordelia: 'It's *totally* bogus.'

Cigarettes and Alcohol: A clearly drunk Giles answers the door to Buffy.

Logic, Let Me Introduce You to This Window: Cordelia says the police were asking Giles about a homicide. However, she entered the library after that was mentioned. After Giles learns of Deirdre's death and hangs up the phone, he removes his spectacles and puts them on the desk some inches away from his notebook. In the next shot, the glasses are on top of the notebook. After Philip bursts from his cage, Buffy lunges at him. When the camera angle switches, Buffy's kicking leg switches with it. It's midnight when Giles phones Britain where, he says, it's 5 a.m. The West Coast of the USA is *eight* hours behind UK time.

Quote/Unquote: Giles: 'I know music. Music has notes. This is noise.'

Buffy: 'Have I ever let you down?' Giles: 'Do you want me to answer that, or shall I just glare?'

Eyghon: 'You're like a woman, Ripper. You cry at every funeral.'

Notes: 'You're back?' A direct sequel to **18**, 'Halloween', the only disappointment of this cracking episode is that the viewer expects the revelations about Giles's past to be bigger than a university dropout experimenting with Bad Magik. Clever ending, though, and some great stunts (Jenny crashing through the window).

This was the first episode since **12**, 'Prophecy Girl', to earn the TV-14 rating (the subject matter is pretty dark, but the violence is no worse than normal). Buffy thinks Giles counts tardiness as a deadly sin. Notice the look Willow shoots at Xander when he asks, 'When are we gonna need computers for real life?' Xander tells Cordelia, 'Twelve years of you and I'm snappin'', which implies they've known each other since kindergarten (in the prologue to *The Xander Years Vol. 1*, Keith RA DeCandido provides a lovely cameo of the five-year-old Xander dumping a bowl of ice cream on Cordelia's head). Xander's uncle Rory was a 'stodgy taxidermist' by day, while by night it was 'booze, whores and fur flying' (see **47**, 'The Zeppo'). Giles studied history at Oxford. When he was twenty-one, he dropped out and lived in London. He played bass in a band (see **40**, 'Band Candy') and fell in with a 'bad crowd' of occultists who included Ethan, Philip Henry, Deirdre Page, Thomas Sutton and Randall (whom Eyghon killed). Giles's approximate age (mid-forties) and his reference to The Bay City Rollers, should place this in the mid-1970s. But weren't the Rollers a bit 'tame' for such badass mothers as Giles and his gang? Black Sabbath or Led Zeppelin would seem more their gig. Of course, this could be 'English humour'.

Soundtrack: The music Buffy uses for her callisthenics: the riff sounds like the KLF's 1991 hit '3 AM Eternal'; however, it's a common sample and it could be almost anything.

21
What's My Line? Part 1

US Transmission Date: 17 Nov. 1997
UK Transmission Date: 23 May 1998 (Sky)
18 Nov. 1999 (BBC2)

Writers: Howard Gordon, Marti Noxon
Director: David Solomon
Cast: Kelly Connell (Norman Pfister), Michael Rothhaar (Suitman),
PB Hutton (Mrs Kalish)
French title: *Kendra, Première Partie*
German title: *Die Rivalin*

Buffy interrupts two vampires robbing a mausoleum of artefacts. Frustrated by her thwarting his schemes, Spike summons the Order of Taraka, a society of deadly assassins, to deal with the Slayer. Several strangers arrive in Sunnydale, including a girl who stowed away in an aircraft cargo hold. That night, Buffy skates on the empty ice rink while waiting for Angel to meet her. A one-eyed man attacks her, but Angel helps Buffy kill the assassin. Giles tells Buffy that the Order will not stop until they complete their mission. Distraught, Buffy goes to Angel's apartment. Angel asks his usual informant, Willy, for information but is attacked by the mysterious girl. She traps Angel in a cage, soon to be flooded with sunlight, and tells him that she is going after his girlfriend. Buffy wakes as an axe swings towards her. She asks whom she is fighting, and is told, 'I am Kendra, the Vampire Slayer.'

Dudes and Babes: Kendra the, seemingly Caribbean, *second* Slayer. Initial impressions: *phwoar!*

Authority Sucks!: Although Snyder's hardly seen, his shadow hangs over the episode. His 'hoop of the week' for Buffy to jump through is the Career Fair. He tells Xander, 'Whatever comes out of your mouth is a meaningless waste of breath.'

A Little Learning is a Dangerous Thing: Willow checks with

Giles that both 'slayed' and 'slew' are acceptable past tenses for 'slay'.

It's a Designer Label!: Cordy and Buffy both have extremely cute black miniskirts. Check out Kendra's red satin pants.

References: The title is from a legendary 1950s TV show in which members of the public mimed their jobs for celebrities to guess their occupations. (That was the British version at least. The US game show of the same name was apparently quite different.) There are dialogue allusions to *The Simpsons* ('Have a cow!'), *Highlander* ('There can be only one'), *My Fair Lady* ('By George, I think he's got it') and *Scooby Doo Where Are You?* (this is the first time Buffy's friends, in this case Xander, refer to themselves as 'the Scooby Gang'). Plus another biblical reference, this time to King Solomon.

Bitch!: Cordelia: 'I aspire to help my fellow man. Check. As long as he's not smelly, dirty or something gross.' Cordelia asks if she's 'mass transportation'. Xander replies, 'That's what a lot of the guys say but it's just locker-room talk.'

Awesome!: The location filming of Buffy and Giles in the graveyard. Kendra's fight with Buffy and the triple cliffhanger.

Surprise!: The last six words of the episode. Give me a '*what?*'

'You May Remember Me From Such Films As . . .': Eric Saiet was in *Felicity, Roswell, Home Improvements, Ugly Naked People, Groundhog Day, Godzilla* and played Shermerite in *Ferris Bueller's Day Off.* Saverio Guerra was Benny in *Blue Streak*, Woodstock in *Summer of Sam* and Bob in *Becker*.

Don't Give Up the Day Job: Howard Gordon was previously co-producer on *The X-Files* (co-writing the episode 'Synchrony' with David Greenwalt). David Solomon was first editor, then producer on *Perry Mason*.

Logic, Let Me Introduce You to This Window: When the bus carrying the first bounty hunter arrives, the flooring of the steps is white and a WATCH YOUR STEP sign is stuck to the side of each. However, when the hunter steps down the flooring is now red and the signs have disappeared. In the sequence where Pfister's right arm is generated, the cuff of his shirt sleeve is three or four inches above his elbow. Later, the sleeve ends at elbow level. During the 'chick fight', Kendra slams Buffy on to Angel's table and it collapses. In the next shot, a dazed

Buffy lies on the broken table. However, for the remainder of the fight the debris is nowhere to be seen. How does Kendra know where Angel's apartment is? It's possible that she followed him from the ice rink, but why didn't she attack him then? (It could be reconnaissance, of course.) How does Dalton manage to carry the cross of du Lac? Surely (like all crosses) it should be *deadly* (or at least very unhealthy) to a vampire? Angel's reflection is briefly seen in the frame of a picture in Buffy's bedroom.

Quote/Unquote: Willow wakes up in a panic: 'Don't warn the tadpoles.'

Giles tells Buffy she'd be amazed at how 'numbingly pompous and long-winded' some of the Watcher diaries are. Buffy: 'Colour me stunned.'

Notes: 'She's a bloody thorn in my bloody side.' What a *great* episode this is, full of fine dialogue, terrific action sequences and a sense of impending horror. The Buffy/Angel scenes at the ice rink are a little undiscovered treasure, while the episode ends with the biggest 'Ohmigod!' moment on the series since we discovered Angel's true nature.

Buffy owns a stuffed pig called 'Mr Gordo' (see **57**, 'The Freshman'). Buffy wanted to be an ice skater (her heroine was Dorothy Hamill, the 1976 Olympic figure-skating champion). Willow suffers from fear of frogs (see **30**, 'Killed By Death'). Angel is supplied his blood (pigs, seemingly) by Willy the Snitch (see **54**, 'The Prom'). Sunnydale is on Route 17.

Kendra's Voice: When Fox Home Entertainment began their release of *Buffy* video box-sets in the UK in 1999 they hit some initial teething problems. One of these was a faulty batch of one of the tapes in the *Season 2, Box 1* set (**13**, 'When She Was Bad', to **22**, 'What's My Life?' Part 2) many of which featured a lack of synch between the soundtrack and the picture on a portion of **16**, 'Inca Mummy Girl'. One concerned online retail outlet, who had delivered hundreds of sets, wrote to their customers alerting them to the problem and asking if anyone who has purchased the box had noticed any other problems. 'Yes,' replied one joker, 'Kendra's voice is all funny.' It was left to this author to inform the company that, actually, it was *supposed* to sound like that.

Novelisation: By Richie Tankersley in *The Angel Chronicles Vol. 2* (Pocket Books, January 1999).
Soundtrack: 'Spring' from Vivaldi's *The Four Seasons*.

22

What's My Line? Part 2

US Transmission Date: 24 Nov. 1997
UK Transmission Date: 30 May 1998 (Sky)
2 Dec. 1999 (BBC2)

Writer: Marti Noxon
Director: David Semel
Cast: Kelly Connell (Norman Pfister), Spice Williams (Patrice)
French title: *Kendra, Seconde Partie*
German title: *Das Ritual*

Giles realises that Kendra must have been called when Buffy briefly died. Kendra informs the others about her encounter with Angel. They go to Willy's bar but Angel has been taken by Spike who needs him as part of a ceremony to restore Drusilla's strength. Xander and Cordelia discover the perfume salesman is not human and take refuge in the basement. They argue, then passionately kiss, before escaping. There is an attempt on Buffy's life by the third assassin dressed as a policewoman, during which Oz saves Willow and is shot in the arm. Buffy and Kendra force Willy to lead them to Spike. Kendra refuses to go with Buffy and reports back to Giles. At the church, Buffy discovers that she has walked into a trap. Kendra attacks the assassins who are holding Buffy. Giles and Willow take on a couple of vampires, while Xander tricks Pfister into becoming stuck in liquid adhesive and he and Cordelia stomp the worms to death. Spike takes Drusilla but Buffy knocks him out and everyone flees the burning church. However, Spike and Drusilla are far from dead.
It's a Designer Label!: Cordy's wet dress. Kendra's best shirt is her *only* shirt; she's a bit peeved when it gets torn in a fight.
References: Disneyland is mentioned, along with John Wayne, Kate Douglas Wiggin's novel *Rebecca of Sunnybrooke Farm*, *Mighty Morphin Power Rangers*, brat-pack actress Molly

Ringwald (*Pretty in Pink, The Breakfast Club*) and a sarcastic reference to Chevy Chase. Plus a misquote from the Beatles's 'I Am The Walrus' ('I am the bug man, coo coo ca choo').

Bitch!: Buffy's Sigourney Weaver moment: '*Nobody* messes with my boyfriend.'

Awesome!: Every scene featuring Xander and Cordelia (particularly when he turns the hose on her).

Surprise!: Xander and Cordy in the basement. 'Coward!' 'Moron!' 'I hate you!' Dramatic music. *The kiss.* Now *who* guessed *that* was going to happen?

Valley-Speak: Cordy: 'We *so* need to get out of here.'

Willow notes that Oz is experiencing 'computer nerd solidarity'.

Xander discovers that Angel sired Drusilla: 'Man, that guy got some *major* neck in his day.'

Cordelia: 'I know what it means, dork-head.'

Logic, Let Me Introduce You to This Window: As with the previous episode, how is Spike able to hold the cross without it burning him? Cordelia pulls a worm from her hair and drops it on to a book marked 'Biology', which Xander then slams shut. In later shots, it's a different book. Spike says that the full moon is required for the ritual; Giles that it must take place on the night of the new moon. You can't have both on the same night, so one of them must be wrong. If Kendra was sent to her Watcher at an early age, long before she was called to be the Slayer, then how many potential Slayers exist at any one time? In **M1,** Merrick suggests that Watchers are given only one Slayer and that it's up to them as to when they tell the girl of her destiny and begin training – although Merrick talking of getting a new Slayer if Buffy dies and Giles asking Gwendolyn in **41,** 'Revelations', if she's had a Slayer before seems to refute this. The suggestion from this episode, plus **37,** 'Faith, Hope and Trick', is that there are always dozens of would-be Slayers awaiting the call. Joss Whedon has noted: 'There is only one active Slayer at a time (except now cuz of the *wacky* circumstances). Inactive, I don't know. The Watchers pinpoint the potentials if they can. In some cultures (like Kendra's) they can announce their presence and whisk the girl off. In some, they can't. And sometimes they can't pinpoint the girl until she is called, which is what happened with Buffy.'

I Just *Love* Your Accent: The only episode to feature the word 'flummoxed'. Xander asks, 'Who sponsored Career Day today? The British soccer fan association?' – which shows that he knows as much about the complexities of a serious social phenomena as he does about everything else.

Quote/Unquote: Willy: 'I swear on my mother's grave . . . Should something fatal ever happen to her, God forbid.'

Notes: 'You've been a very bad daddy.' The series' first attempt at a two-part storyline is helped by the hilarious (yet strangely attractive) Xander/Cordelia subplot. The episode does become a bit of a runaround in the middle, sagging under the weight of such a stretched storyline, but that is, surely, the best 'burning church' climax you're likely to see *anywhere*.

Kendra's Watcher is Sam Zebuto. Giles has never met him but knows him by reputation (and seemingly speaks to him on the telephone during this episode). There are continuity references to Buffy's 'death' in **12**, 'Prophecy Girl', as well as the 'praying-mantis lady' from **4**, 'Teacher's Pet'. There *is* a Slayer handbook (which Giles has never thought it necessary that Buffy read, directly contradicting what he said in **5**, 'Never Kill a Boy on the First Date'; see also **80**, 'Real Me'). There are 43 churches in Sunnydale. Drusilla and Spike have previously lived in Paris. Drusilla's mother (whom Angel killed, along with most of the rest of her family) ate raw lemons. Oz eats animal crackers. Despite being something of a computer expert and brilliant at tests, he doesn't want a career, instead describing his ambition as to be able to play 'E flat diminished ninth' ('a *man's* chord'). That's a fancy name for a pretty bog-standard chord, telling us something about Oz's confidence in his own ability (see **47**, 'The Zeppo'; **52**, 'Earshot').

Novelisation: By Richie Tankersley in *The Angel Chronicles Vol. 2* (Pocket Books, January 1999).

23
Ted

US Transmission Date: 8 Dec. 1997
UK Transmission Date: 6 Jun. 1998 (Sky)
9 Dec. 1999 (BBC2)

Writers: David Greenwalt, Joss Whedon
Director: Bruce Seth Green
Cast: John Ritter (Ted Buchanan), Ken Thorley (Neal),
Jeff Pruitt (Vampire #1), Jeff Langton (Vampire #2)
French title: *La Fiancée*

Buffy finds her mother kissing a man. Joyce introduces Ted, who makes a good impression on Xander and Willow, but not Buffy. While playing mini-golf Ted takes exception to Buffy's sullenness and threatens her, but regains his pleasant personality when Xander, Willow and Joyce join them. Buffy tells her mother about Ted's threat but Joyce doesn't believe her. After patrol, Buffy finds Ted reading her diary. Buffy attempts to get it back but he throws her against the wall. Enraged, Buffy sends him tumbling down the stairs, killing him. Xander, Willow and Cordelia discover a drug in the cookies that Ted baked. At Ted's home, they find the bodies of his previous four wives in a closet. Ted appears again in Buffy's room. Buffy stabs Ted with a nail file, revealing wires and circuits. The android Ted knocks Buffy unconscious and confronts Joyce. She believes his lies at first, but then grows suspicious. Buffy regains consciousness and smashes a frying pan over Ted's robotic skull.

Dudes and Babes: Xander and Cordelia's utterly strange relationship continues to develop, if that's the right word. Xander asks Cordy if she'd like to accompany him to the utility closet to make out. Cordelia asks if *that's* all he ever thinks about (it is, see **52**, 'Earshot'). Before adding 'OK'. Jenny refers to Giles's 'puppy dog eyes' and Xander talks about Buffy playing games of 'the naughty stewardess'.

Authority Sucks!: Another walk along the tightrope of child abuse. (See **3**, 'The Witch'.)

A Little Learning is a Dangerous Thing: 'How was school

today, Buffy? Did you learn anything?' There's very little in the way of classroom scenes, though news of Ted's death seems to have made it to school before Buffy did.

Mom's Sticky Buns: 'Seeing my mother Frenching a guy is definitely a ticket to therapy-land.' The secret of Ted's great mini-pizzas is after baking, fry them in herbs and olive oil in a cast-iron skillet. Joyce asks Buffy if she wants any sticky buns, which is a bit of innuendo crying out for a suitable reply.

Denial, Thy Name is Joyce: Even by her own standards some sort of award is due to Mrs Summers for even *thinking* about believing Ted's story of *not* having died.

It's a Designer Label!: *What* is that on Willow's head? It looks like a tea cosy. 'Hey Cordy, nice outfit,' says Xander. That's a lie. The yellow miniskirt is particularly unfortunate.

References: Xander ('Somebody was raised in a culture-free environment'), Willow and Buffy have a pointless argument about 70s popstars The Captain and Tennille ('Love Will Keep Us Together'). There's a discussion on the psychology of Sigmund Freud (1856–1939). Both *Psycho* and *The Terminator* seem to be influences (the heroine cheating at golf may be a subtle *Goldfinger* reference) and *Thelma and Louise, Licence to Kill* and *Superman* all get name-checked along with John Stanley's legendary Saturday night horror movie slot *Creature Features*, which ran for several years on KTVU in Oakland, California. There's an allusion to *The Stepford Wives*. 'Good morning, sunshine' is a misquote from *Hair*.

Awesome!: A terrified Giles holding up a cross . . . to Jenny ('I get that reaction from men all the time'). Plus Buffy kicking the stuffing out of the vampire ('You don't normally beat them into quite such a bloody pulp').

Surprise!: 'You killed him.' Not as surprising as Ted's return from the dead minutes later.

The Drugs Don't Work: Or, in this case, *do*. Willow identifies the drug Ted uses in his cookies as demotoran, which shares properties with Ecstasy, the street name for MDMA (methylenedioxymethamphetamine), the powerful hallucinatory stimulant popularised by rave culture in the 90s.

'You May Remember Me From Such Films and TV Series As . . .': John Ritter was the star of the sitcom *Three's*

Company (the American version of *Man About the House*). He also had the leading role in the two *Problem Child* movies and *Stay Tuned*. Ken Thorley was the Bolian barber Mr Mott in *Star Trek: The Next Generation*.

Valley-Speak: Xander: 'You *rock!*'

Logic, Let Me Introduce You to This Window: When Buffy climbs into her room her nightstand is in darkness. However, in close shots it's well illuminated. After Buffy punches Ted, he drops her diary and it can be seen on the floor. However, when Ted picks Buffy up the diary has vanished. Xander opens Ted's closet door with his left hand while holding a torch in his right, down by his side. As the door opens, the shot cuts to a different angle and the torch is by his head. Where is the miniature golf course? At the end of **13**, 'When She Was Bad', Willow says that there's no such course in Sunnydale. Silly explanations about 'layers of tweed' aside, how did Giles not only survive a point-blank hit in the back with a crossbow bolt, but also have the strength to pull it out *and* stab the vampire with it? Without fainting? And what was Willow looking at under the microscope when examining Ted's cookies? Crumbs? Analysing a foodstuff for its chemical make-up requires lots of complicated tests, but magnifying wouldn't seem to be one of them.

Quote/Unquote: Giles: 'I believe the subtext here is rapidly becoming the text.'

Xander on his triumphant discovery that Buffy is having 'parental issues': 'Freud would have said the exact same thing. Except, he might not have done that little dance.'

Giles, after Cordelia mentions Eyghon in a conversation about facing responsibility for someone's death: '*Do* let's bring that up as often as possible.'

Stepford Dad: There are two schools of thought on this episode. One is that it's almost the definitive *Buffy*-as-teenage-horror tale in a series in which hyena-kids, vampires and witches are *de rigueur* as opposed to real life where we have bullies and stepfathers. The implication is that Joss Whedon uses the clichés of the horror genre to represent the terrors of being a teenager (Joyce's new boyfriend is a violent robot because, to a teenage girl, that's exactly how a prospective stepfather appears). Put simply, in *Buffy the Vampire Slayer* the obsessions and fears of teenagers are made flesh. All valid. But there is another, more logical, critical analysis on 'Ted' which is nowhere near as positive. What ruins the episode for many is that this is not a 'Buffy-Universe story': it's straight SF. This is the *only* episode in the series in which there is *no* supernatural element whatsoever. There's no magic or demons at work – instead we are asked to believe (in a series that, for instance, takes its technology pretty seriously) that in the 1950s (with the components of the era) a convincing android/replicant could be made. Even Moloch in **8**, 'I Robot . . . You Jane', utilising the peak of research technology, could only come up with something like *Robocop*. (See **93**, 'I Was Made to Love You'.)

Notes: 'I'm not wired that way.' A disturbingly uneven episode. 'Ted' contains one of *the* great performances in *Buffy*: John Ritter's chilling portrayal of a psychotic control freak on the verge of screwing up two people's lives. Unfortunately, *Buffy*'s *raison d'être* required some form of 'demonisation' of the central character and a huge opportunity to explore an important, relevant issue is lost. He's a robot – it's no longer scary, so you can come out from behind the sofa and laugh at the risible final scenes. Otherwise, 'Ted' contains all you'd expect from two of *Buffy*'s best writers: pithy dialogue, intelligent characterisation and superb timing. It's a pity that it couldn't have contained more *feeling*.

There are continuity references to the previous episode (Angel's absence for most of the episode is touched upon). According to Jenny it's been three weeks since the events of **20**, 'The Dark Age' (she says she is still having trouble sleeping). Buffy says she doesn't bruise easily, which suggests that Slayers have abnormally high recuperative powers (see **30**, 'Killed By Death'; **56**, 'Graduation Day' Part 2).

24
Bad Eggs

US Transmission Date: 12 Jan. 1998
UK Transmission Date: 13 Jun. 1998 (Sky)
16 Dec. 1999 (BBC2)

Writer: Marti Noxon
Director: David Greenwalt
Cast: James Parks (Tector Gorch), Rick Zieff (Mr Whitmore),
Brie McCaddin (Mall Girl), Eric Whitmore (Night Watchman)
French title: *Oeufs Surprises*
German title: *Faule Eier*

Buffy encounters cowboy vampires: Lyle Gorch, and his idiot
brother Tector. Mr Whitmore gives eggs to his students for a
parenting assignment. When Buffy goes to sleep a tentacle
slithers from her egg and attaches itself to her face. Xander
reveals he boiled his egg to prevent it from breaking. When
Buffy notices her egg shaking, a purple insect-like creature
bursts out and Buffy stabs it with a pair of scissors. At school,
Buffy and Xander are knocked unconscious by Cordelia and
Willow. A parade of students march robot-like to the basement. Joyce arrives looking for Buffy. Giles places one of the
creatures on her back, and they join the others in their effort
to dig up Mother Bezoar, a pre-prehistoric parasite. While
searching for a weapon, a recovered Buffy is faced with Lyle
and Tector. They fight and both Tector and Buffy are pulled
into the parasite creature, but seconds later Buffy emerges,
having killed it. Giles invents a story involving a gas leak to
prevent awkward questions.

Dudes and Babes: The opening shot of the legs of the Mall
Girl suggests more than we actually get. Tector says that
Sunnydale doesn't have a decent whore in the city limits,
which doesn't fit in with what we know about the place.

A Little Learning is a Dangerous Thing: Mr Whitmore's sex
education class descends into farce. 'That was a rhetorical
question, Mr Harris, not a poll.'

Mom's Apple Pie: 'I swear sometimes I don't know what goes
on in your head.' The nadir of Joyce and Buffy's relationship
with Buffy getting about four levels of punishment as the
episode progresses. (When Joyce told Buffy in **15**, 'School
Hard', that it would be 'at least a week and a half' before her
pride in her daughter wore off, it seems she wasn't exaggerating.
'Bad Eggs' takes place in a weird parallel universe where the
close relationship established in **15**, 'School Hard', never happened and where Joyce still thinks her daughter is an

irresponsible tearaway.) Buffy says, 'Did I ask for back-seat parenting?' and notes she doesn't want to be a single parent (even a surrogate one to an egg) like her mother.

It's a Designer Label!: The dress that Buffy wanted made her look 'like a streetwalker' according to Joyce. Cordy's little grey skirt and leather slit miniskirt, and a bear bag (she claims she started the nationwide craze for bags shaped like animals).

References: Lyle and Tector Gorch were the names of the brothers played by Ben Johnson and Warren Oates in *The Wild Bunch*, a film that also includes a character called 'Angel' (see **2**, 'The Harvest'). 'Bad Eggs' includes dialogue and textual references to *Die Hard* ('Yippie kai-aye'), the Beatles' 'Dig a Pony' ('All I want is you'), *Batman* ('Think about the future'), *Dial M For Murder* (the scissors scene), and William Castle's *The Tingler*.

Bitch!: Xander, kissing Cordelia: 'This would work a lot better for me if you didn't talk.'

Don't Give Up the Day Job: Both James Parks (a carpenter on *Reality Bites*) and Rick Zieff (the casting assistant on *Breakdown*) have film-industry jobs other than acting.

Valley-Speak: Buffy: 'I just feel all funky.' And: 'My egg. It went postal on me.'

Logic, Let Me Introduce You to This Window: The opening scenes are set during the day, therefore how is Lyle not a small pile of ash on the floor? In the arcade, the girl with Lyle plays the pinball machine. In the initial shot, her handbag is hanging from her right wrist. However, in the next shot the straps are further up her arm. During Buffy's fight with Lyle in the arcade, both of them collide with the same pinball machine that the girl was playing earlier and the machine is now turned off. How does the shell of Buffy's egg repair itself? Watch closely in the scene in the library where Buffy put her egg on the desk close to a chain. The respective positions of the chain and the egg change from shot to shot about four times. It's so obvious, one almost suspects it's been done deliberately to provide books like this with something to talk about! The 'walking around zombified' cliché enables Giles to converse with some intricacy with Joyce, allows Cordelia to knock Buffy out with a single blow, but also renders its slaves incapable of attacking a concrete floor in anything more than a 'slo-mo slave action'. Isn't it lucky that a pre-prehistoric creature lays eggs that look *exactly* like hens' eggs? After she loses consciousness, the parasite falls from Willow's back. However, when everyone else collapses no parasites can be seen dropping from their backs.

Quote/Unquote: Giles on Xander boiling his egg: 'I suppose there is a sort of Machiavellian ingenuity to your transgression.' Xander: 'I resent that . . . or, possibly, thank you.'

Joyce on children: 'They're such a . . . oh, I don't want to say burden, but . . . actually, I kind of *do* want to say burden.'

Notes: 'Long story.' *And* a tall one. And not a very good one either. This is such a lopsided episode that it's surprising it doesn't collapse under its own weight. The main focus is the subplot about the parasitic eggs, while the two hick vampires serve absolutely no purpose – they're far too stupid to be a threat to anyone. 'Bad Eggs' also seems to think it's really funny in places where it clearly isn't. That the episode has to resort to devices such as Xander's pratfall when he and Buffy enter the cave is an indication of just how desperate a production this is. My least favourite episode, because you *know* this series is capable of so much more.

Buffy had a giga-pet, but she sat on it and it broke. Xander implies Cordelia has bad breath. Cordelia says she has 'a friend' ('not me') who once had sex in a car at the top of a hill and accidentally kicked off the handbrake. Angel cannot have children. Before they became vampires, Lyle and Tector massacred a Mexican village in 1886. The mall used at the beginning is the Sherman Oaks Galleria north of Los Angeles. After Willow enters the science lab and stands next to the dead hatchling, on the blackboard behind her is written POSTING BOARD. This was an acknowledgement (by Jeff Pruitt) to all the regulars on the *BtVS* Posting Board. When Joyce enters the library, keep your eyes on the standing sign. Under SUNNYDALE HS LIBRARY, it says, WEBSITE COMING and BVS BRATS TALK – more in-jokes for the series' Internet fans.

25
Surprise

US Transmission Date: 19 Jan. 1998
UK Transmission Date: 20 Jun. 1998 (Sky)
6 Jan. 2000 (BBC2)

Writer: Marti Noxon
Director: Michael Lange
Cast: Brian Thompson (the Judge), Vincent Schiavelli (Uncle Enyos)
French title: *Innocence, Première Partie*
German title: *Der Fluch der Zigeuner*

Buffy has a nightmare in which Drusilla kills Angel. Jenny is visited by her Uncle Enyos who tells her that Angel's fear is weakening. Jenny reveals Angel's involvement with Buffy to Enyos who demands that she keep them apart. Due to his injuries, Spike is confined to a wheelchair while Drusilla (now stronger) takes delivery of mysterious boxes. A surprise birthday party is arranged for Buffy, but ruined by a fight with some vampires. Angel realises that the vampires are collecting body parts of the Judge, an ancient demon who (when assembled) can destroy humanity. Drusilla throws a party in celebration of the coming of the Judge. Buffy and Angel gatecrash, then escape. Angel finally professes his love for Buffy and they consummate their relationship. Angel gets out of bed in agony.

Dreaming (As Blondie Once Said) is Free: Buffy's nightmare: like all good dreams, it's got a rock'n'roll soundtrack; Willow speaks French accompanied by a small monkey; crockery smashes and, in a moment dripping with Freudian symbolism, Angel is staked by Drusilla. Sexy. Buffy also mentions a dream she had – she and Giles opened an office warehouse in Las Vegas – which sounds a good series in itself.

Dudes and Babes: Oz says he's 'groupie free' these days which, frankly, isn't nearly rock-and-roll enough (see **55**, 'Graduation Day' Part 1). Xander tells Buffy he feels 'a pre-birthday spanking coming on'. Drusilla dancing is certainly provocative.

It's a Designer Label!: Drusilla's red party dress, Buffy's short black skirt, green pants and cool white jacket, Giles's stripy tie, plus another tea cosy on the head for Willow. There's a lovely close up of Oz's Fender Stratocaster.

References: Xander mentions the diner chain Denny's. There are references to *Dead Poets Society* ('Seize the day') and 'Jack and the Beanstalk' ('grind his bones to make your bread'). 'Discretion is the better part of valour' is a misquote from *Henry IV, Part 1*.

Bitch!: Giles: 'A true creature of evil can survive the process. No one human ever has.' Xander: 'What's the problem? We send Cordy to fight this guy and go for pizza!'

Awesome!: The reassembly of the Judge, followed by Dalton's rather messy death ('do it again!'). Buffy crashing into her own surprise party and killing a vampire with a drumstick. Plus the charming scene where Willow and Oz ask each other out.

'You May Remember Me From Such Films and TV Series As . . .': For Brian Thompson, see **1**, 'Welcome to the Hellmouth'. Vincent Schiavelli will also be well known to *X-Files* fans for his sympathetic performance as Lanny in 'Humbug'. His movies include *Ghost, One Flew Over the Cuckoo's Nest* and *Tomorrow Never Dies*.

Valley-Speak: Buffy: 'You can't spend the rest of your life waiting for Xander to wake up and smell the hottie.'

Xander to Giles: 'Are you ready to get down, you funky party weasel?'

Logic, Let Me Introduce You to This Window: When Buffy approaches Willow's table in her dream, the monkey is facing Buffy. In the next shot it's facing Willow, then it turns around to face Buffy as Willow waves (maybe it's just following the action?). Why would Angel take the time to get dressed before running outside if he was in extreme pain? How do the boxes containing the body parts of the Judge fit together? When the panels open, inside is one big chamber instead of six small ones. The gypsy-curse subplot is indescribably dumb. The punishment for Angelus is to give him a soul. Fine. But to take it away again if he gets happy, turning him *back* into Angelus, the vicious creature that has killed thousands . . .? This whole thing shrieks plot device and never really makes sense.

I Just *Love* Your Accent: Xander asks Giles: 'Are all you Brits such drama queens?'

Quote/Unquote: Enyos: 'Vengeance demands that his pain be eternal.'

Spike, on Dalton: 'He's a wanker, but he's the only one we've got with half a brain.'

Notes: 'The time for watching is past.' *This* is teen-drama? An astonishingly sensual, erotic episode. 'Surprise' is about as far removed from traditional horror clichés as it's possible to get. Buffy takes her first, faltering steps into the adult world of passion. And the *real* horrors to come. Grown-up, intelligent, beautiful television. And with barely a joke in sight.

Buffy loses her virginity (would it be too indelicate to ask whether the thought that she's committed what amounts to necrophilia occurred to anybody in Broadcast Standards and Practices?). Willow speaks to the monkey in French, saying: '*L'hippo a piqué ton pantalon*', which means 'The hippo stole your trousers', a reference to Oz's joke at the end of **22**, 'What's My Line?' Part 2, that all of the monkeys (who are French) in boxes of Animal Crackers have pants and the hippos are jealous. Angel refers to the Irish as 'my people' when giving Buffy the Claddagh ring. Jenny's real name is Janna. She is a Kalderash Romany gypsy and has been sent to America by her clan specifically to watch Angel. In addition to Prague and Paris, Spike and Drusilla also spent time in Vienna and Spain.

Novelisation: By Nancy Holder in *The Angel Chronicles Vol. 3* (Pocket Books, August 1999).

Soundtrack: 'Transylvanian Concubine' by Rasputina [*] and 'Anything' by Shawn Clement and Sean Murray, featuring vocals by Care Howe.

26

Innocence

US Transmission Date: 20 Jan. 1998
UK Transmission Date: 27 Jun. 1998 (Sky)
13 Jan. 2000 (BBC2)

Writer: Joss Whedon
Director: Joss Whedon

Cast: Brian Thompson (the Judge), Ryan Francis (Soldier),
Vincent Schiavelli (Uncle Enyos),
Carla Madden (Woman),
Parry Shen (Student)
French title: *Innocence, Seconde Partie*
German title: *Der Gefallene Engel*

Angel reverts to his old self, Angelus, and visits Spike and
Drusilla. The Judge attempts to disintegrate him, but there is no
humanity left to kill. Drusilla tells Angelus they plan to bring
forth Armageddon, but he asks for one night to punish the
Slayer. Buffy goes to her lover's apartment but finds him cruel
and dismissive. Angelus turns up at school, intending to kill
those close to Buffy, starting with Willow. He is prevented by
Xander and Jenny. Xander forms a plan to steal an army rocket
launcher to defeat the Judge and with the help of Willow, Oz and
Cordelia he succeeds. Buffy and Giles discover Jenny's dark
secret and that the curse cannot be reinvoked. Putting Xander's
plan into action, they follow the Judge, Angelus and Drusilla to
a shopping mall, where Buffy uses the weapon to destroy the
Judge. Giles drives Buffy home and assures her that she has not
lost any of his respect.

Dudes and Babes: The semipornographic flashback to Buffy
and Angel, ahem, 'getting it on' is, of course, all done in the
best possible taste. Soft focus, unruffled sheets (without stains)
and no sweating. Just like sex *isn't*.

Mom's Birthday Muffin: Mrs Summers doesn't notice that
Buffy arrives home in different clothes to the ones she had on
when she left the previous day. Very observant. Her birthday
muffin for Buffy is both affectionate and stupidly pointless.

It's a Designer Label!: 'Wear something trashy . . . er.'
Xander's palm-tree shirt, Cordelia's extremely short tartan
skirt and Buffy's white socks all fit the bill.

References: The Judge zapping everyone in the mall may be a
homage to the climactic scene in *Raiders of the Lost Ark*. The
movie theatre where Buffy and Angelus fight is lined with
posters for Warner Bros' animated feature film *Quest for
Camelot*. At the end, Buffy and Joyce are watching *Stowaway*
(starring Shirley Temple). Also, software giants IBM ('Big
Blue') and the Smurfs.

Bitch!: Willow on Xander and Cordelia's attraction to each other: 'Weird? It's against all laws of God and man.'

Awesome!: The scene where Angelus threatens Willow in front of Jenny and Xander. The slow-motion killing of the Judge as Angelus and Dru are thrown away from the explosion (yes, *just* like that scene in *Die Hard*). Buffy fighting Angelus and kicking his goolies.

Surprise!: The moment we discover, along with Dru, Spike and the Judge that Angel is Angelus again. 'Yeah, baby, I'm back.'

'You May Remember Me From Such Films As . . .': Ryan Francis played the young Peter in Spielberg's *Hook*.

Valley-Speak: Xander: 'Now, I'm having a wiggins.'

Cigarettes and Alcohol: Angelus gives 'blowing off' a whole new meaning. (See **Logic, Let Me Introduce You to This Window.**)

Logic, Let Me Introduce You to This Window: When Angel ran outside in **25**, 'Surprise', it was raining heavily. At the beginning of this episode, however, the rain has stopped. When Buffy cries herself to sleep and dreams about her intimate night with Angel, she is wearing silver nail polish. But, in **25**, 'Surprise', she wasn't wearing any. The episode's time frame is completely up the spout. Buffy runs home distressed, as Xander tells Cordelia to meet him at Willow's house in half an hour. Willow, meanwhile, is supposed to bring Oz and his van. The scene then shifts to Buffy's bedroom, where she weeps and falls asleep. Buffy wakes up the next day and goes to school to force the truth out of Jenny. The following scene depicts Xander and Cordy stealing the rocket launcher, events that happened the night before. Presumably Giles managed to keep Buffy's attack on Jenny from Snyder, otherwise she'd be suspended on the spot. (One of the students even asks, 'Shall I get the principal?') How many vans does Oz have? In **18**, 'Halloween', he drove a zebra-striped van with a steering wheel on the right. Here he drives a dark-coloured left-hand drive van. In **12**, 'Prophecy Girl', Angel confirmed he had 'no breath' so how does Angelus exhale all that smoke after feeding on the cigarette-smoking prostitute? In **34**, 'Becoming' Part 2, we find out that vampires in general, and Spike in particular, are at pains *not* to see the end of the world, so what's the deal with the bringing on of Armageddon here?

Quote/Unquote: Drusilla: 'Psst . . . We're gonna destroy the world. Wanna come?'

Willow, angry at discovering Xander and Cordelia kissing: 'I *knew* it. Well, knew it in the sense of not having the slightest idea, but I *knew* there was something I didn't know.'

Spike to Angelus: 'I know you haven't been in the game for a while, mate, but we *do* still kill people. Sort of our *raison d'être*, you know?'

Cordelia sums up the plot: 'This is *great*. There's an unkillable demon in town, Angel's joined his team, the Slayer's a basket case, I'd say we've hit bottom.' Xander: 'I have a plan.' Cordelia: 'Oh no, here's a lower place.'

Cordelia asks Xander if looking at guns makes him want to have sex: 'I'm seventeen. Looking at linoleum makes me want to have sex.'

Notes: 'It's not justice we serve, it is vengeance.' Strangely, nowhere near as effective as **25**, 'Surprise', despite containing numerous impressive performances. Highlights include Alyson Hannigan's uncanny ability to be angry and funny at the same time (as in the sequence where she can't think of a nasty word to call Giles and the others). I think what holds the episode down is the unnecessary subplot about the rocket launcher that pushes the viewer away from the important relationship stuff. And there's that odd, downbeat ending with Joyce and Buffy and the birthday muffin, which deserved better direction.

Buffy says she beat up Willy the Snitch to get information about Angel (see **21/22**, 'What's My Line?'). There are references to Xander's military expertise in **18**, 'Halloween'. He says he can still put together an M16 rifle in 57 seconds. Xander is the treasurer of the 'We Hate Cordelia Club', of which Willow is also a founder member.

Novelisation: By Nancy Holder in *The Angel Chronicles Vol. 3* (Pocket Books, August 1999), in which the author used the opportunity to correct the timing mistakes on TV.

27
Phases

US Transmission Date: 27 Jan. 1998
UK Transmission Date: 4 Jul. 1998 (Sky)
20 Jan. 2000 (BBC2)

Writers: Rob Des Hotel, Dean Batali
Director: Bruce Seth Green
Cast: Camila Griggs (Gym Teacher), Jack Conley (Cain),
Megahn Perry (Theresa Klusmeyer), Keith Campbell (Werewolf)
French title: *Pleine Lune*
German title: *Der Werwolfjäger*

Xander and Cordelia make out in her car. Without warning, they are attacked by a werewolf. Giles is excited, having never encountered a lycanthrope before. One of Buffy's classmates, Theresa, walks home alone and meets Angelus. Buffy and Giles investigate the woods and discover a very unpleasant werewolf hunter named Cain. They drive to the Bronze, arriving as teens flee from the werewolf inside, but it escapes before Buffy can capture it. Buffy and Giles hear on the radio that Theresa has been found dead. As the sun rises, the werewolf slowly transforms back into its human form. Oz. Willow invites Oz to help her do some research, but he refuses and runs off. Before he can lock himself up, Willow calls at his home. He tries to warn her of the danger, but it is too late and he is transformed. A lengthy chase begins, climaxing in Willow shooting Oz with a tranquilliser. The next day, Oz tells Willow that he'll be fine as long as he locks himself up around the full moon every month. To his surprise, Willow is still interested in continuing their relationship.

Dudes and Babes: As relationships become clearer (Oz and Willow, Xander and Cordy), poor Buffy is left to trail around with Giles for most of the episode. Theresa's cute, but something about her screams 'Angelus bait'.

A Little Learning is a Dangerous Thing: Willow is helping Cordelia with her history homework (or possibly doing it for her).

It's a Designer Label!: Willow's got another of those tea-cosy bobble-hats, a smiley-face backpack and a pair of sickly yellow overalls. Oz's *New York City Yoga* T-shirt, Theresa's red 'burial' miniskirt (!), Buffy's miniskirt (also red).

References: Contains visual and dialogue references to classic werewolf films including *The Wolf Man*, *Curse of the Werewolf*, *Dr Terror's House of Horror*, *The Beast Must Die*, *The Howling* and *An American Werewolf in London*. Also, Kraven the Hunter from *Spider-Man*, Calvin Klein's Obsession aftershave, Robbie the Robot from *Forbidden Planet* and the exercise device the Thigh Master™. Larry's 'outing' may be a nod to *Heathers* ('I *lurv* ma dead-gay son!'). Xander's sexuality denial (as with Chandler in *Friends*) is completely in character – he's witty, knows way too much about films and is lousy with women (even though all his best friends are girls). For Larry, the clichéd bully, to be revealed as gay – and subsequently transformed into a decent, likeable human being by the experience (see **52**, 'Earshot') – is significant for both gay and straight audiences.

Bitch!: Willow says she has never got a 'mi-aow' before, but she's certainly awarded one for 'What's his [Xander's] number? Oh yeah, 1-800-I'm-dating-a-skanky-ho.'

Awesome!: Xander accidentally 'outing' Larry. Oz's telephone conversation with his aunt concerning his cousin ('and *how long* has that been going on?') and his reassuring Willow that bunnies can 'really take care of themselves'.

Surprise!: Who the werewolf changes into. Hands up who was surprised by *that*?

The Drugs Don't Work: 'Phenobarbitone' (which Giles mispronounces as 'phenabarbitol') is a powerful barbiturate used to treat insomnia, so it's a perfect tranquilliser.

'You May Remember Me From Such Films As . . .': Jack Conley often gets meaty detective-type roles in films like *Payback*, *Mercury Rising*, *L.A. Confidential* and *Get Shorty*.

Don't Give Up the Day Job: Keith Campbell was Tom Cruise's stunt double in both *Mission: Impossible* movies and doubled for Val Kilmer in *Batman Forever* and *The Saint*. He was on the stunt team for *Blaze*, *Supernova*, *Analyze This*, *Face/Off*, *Wolf*, *Patriot Games*, *Stargate* and *Deep Impact*. As an actor, readers may recognise him as Perp in *Men In Black*; he also appeared in *Fatal Instinct* and *Suburban Commando*.

Valley-Speak: Willow: 'I want smoochies.'

Cordelia: 'It could be a crock.'

Oz: 'That's fairly freaksome.'

Logic, Let Me Introduce You to This Window: Two men push Giles's car as it arrives in front of the Bronze. Keen-eyed viewers can spot the tops of their heads through the rear window. While Buffy is trapped in the net her flashlight is off, but it's on again when the net lowers to the ground. After everyone evacuates the Bronze, Buffy runs inside putting her backpack on. She bumps someone and one of the straps falls off her left shoulder. As she walks inside, the camera angle switches and the strap has returned to its former position. After Buffy senses the werewolf's movement, she slides off the left strap and walks upstairs and parts a curtain. The angle switches again, and now the backpack is in her right hand. During the chase through the woods, Willow trips. As she gets up notice the stains on her overalls. When she gets to the library, they're spotless. In the library scene, for several shots Giles is not wearing glasses but in others he is. After knocking the gun out of Buffy's hands, the werewolf shoves her backwards but she falls face first over Giles. What are Oz and Larry, two seniors, doing in a self-defence class full of juniors? If Oz didn't realise he was a werewolf until the morning after the full moon, then where did he wake up the morning after 'the night before the full moon'? Shouldn't the bullet Cain makes be too hot to handle seconds after having been molten silver? Buffy says a werewolf is human 'twenty-eight days each month'; it should be twenty-five days each lunar month.

I Just *Love* Your Accent: Giles, on Cain: 'Pillock!'

Cruelty to Animals: Cain: 'First they tell me I can't hunt an elephant for its ivory. Now I've got to deal with People for the Ethical Treatment of Werewolves.'

Quote/Unquote: Larry: 'I would love to get some of that Buffy and Willow action, if you know what I mean.' Oz: 'That's great, Larry, you've really mastered the single entendre.'

Cordelia: 'We came here to do the thing I can never tell my father about because he still thinks I'm a good girl.'

Buffy asks Xander if he's sure he was attacked by a werewolf: 'Six feet tall, claws, a big old snout in the middle of his face, like a wolf? Yeah, I'm sticking with my first guess.'

Giles: 'You hunt werewolves for sport?' Cain: 'No, I'm in it purely for the money.'

Notes: 'Good doggy, now play dead.' A *really* fun episode, taking all the best bits of recent (and ancient) werewolf texts and playing with them in an amusingly postmodern way. Lovely direction more than makes up for the terrible werewolf make-up (which actually *adds* to the kitschy, sub-*Howling* homage that the episode is). Stellar performances from Seth Green and Alyson Hannigan. A template for how *Buffy* was changing and growing into something very different from the series when it began.

Giles's delight on discovering a werewolf case ('It's one of the classics. I'm sure my books and I are in for a fascinating afternoon') makes Buffy remark, 'He needs to get a pet.' Oz notes that the cheerleading statue has eyes that follow him around the room, referring to **3**, 'The Witch'. He doesn't smoke. He took Willow to the movies last night and, although he's forgotten the movie itself, he did enjoy the popcorn. He was bitten by his cousin, Jordy, whose parents are called Maureen and Ken. There are references to Xander becoming doglike in **6**, 'The Pack', and to his allegedly being unable to remember those events, and a very funny PMT reference – Willow noting 'three days out of the month, *I'm* not much fun to be around either.' Cordelia has dated lots of guys in bands before (see **16**, 'Inca Mummy Girl'). On patrol, Buffy sees Brittany Podell making out with Owen Stadeel, who is supposed to be going with Barrett Williams. Buffy's locker has a Velvet Chain (see **5**, 'Never Kill a Boy on the First Date') sticker on it.

Novelisation: By Yvonne Navarro in *The Willow Files Vol. 1* (Pocket Books, December 1999).

Soundtrack: 'Blind for Now' by Lotion.

Did You Know?: Joss Whedon gave Seth Green a copy of the script for 'Phases' to persuade the actor to become a regular: 'It had all this metaphorical stuff and gave strong shades to the character,' says Seth. 'I said, "Yeah, I want to be part of this!"'

28

Bewitched, Bothered and Bewildered

US Transmission Date: 10 Feb. 1998
UK Transmission Date: 11 Jul. 1998 (Sky)
27 Jan. 2000 (BBC2)

Writer: Marti Noxon
Director: James A Contner
Cast: Lorna Scott (Miss Beakman), Jennie Chester (Kate),
Kristen Winnicki (Cordette), Tamara Braun (Frenzied Girl),
Scott Hamm (Jock)
French title: *Un Charme Déroutant*
German title: *Der Liebeszauber*

Harmony and her friends mock Cordelia for dating Xander.
Giles warns Buffy that Angelus has a long history of commit-
ting horrid acts on Valentine's Day. Buffy receives a box of
roses and a card with the word 'soon' on it. At the Bronze,
Xander gives Cordelia a gift. After admiring the necklace,
Cordelia breaks up with him. Xander is furious and it only gets
worse for him the next day as everyone in school seems to
know what happened. Xander tells Amy that he knows she's
practising her mother's art of witchcraft. Xander blackmails
Amy into casting a love spell on Cordelia, so that he can then
dump *her*. Much to Xander's dismay, the spell has no effect on
Cordy. However, every other female in Sunnydale seems
attracted to him. Xander spends his time running away from all
of the women in his life (including Buffy, Willow, Jenny,
Harmony and Drusilla) while Giles and Amy try to reverse the
spell. And also reverse a spell that's turned Buffy into a rat.
While a mob of girls battle each other, Xander and Cordelia
arrive at Buffy's house. Joyce starts seducing Xander, so he
and Cordelia barricade themselves in the basement. Giles
and Amy perform the reversal spells. Next day Harmony
mocks Xander, but Cordelia comes to his defence telling her
(former) friends that she will date whom she wants to.
However lame.
Dudes and Babes: In an episode all about the shallowness of
relationships based purely on physical attraction, let's nail this

one right away. Does anybody else wish there hadn't been a convenient object for Buffy to hide behind when she suffers from 'a slight case of nudity'? Glad to know I'm not alone. A pig-out and a vid-fest are said to be the time-honoured tradition of the loveless. Which sounds about right.

A Little Learning is a Dangerous Thing: Or, *no* learning in Amy's case, since she uses her 'mojo' to con Miss Beakman into believing she handed in a test paper.

Mom's Apple Pie: Joyce coming on to Xander is a bit strong, even given the implications concerning what a little raver she used to be (see **12**, 'Prophecy Girl'; **40**, 'Band Candy').

Denial, Thy Name is Joyce: How on *earth* could Joyce fall for Cordelia's utterly lame 'scavenger hunt' excuse in reply to the obvious question: 'What are you twenty girls and one boy doing in my basement and why am I holding a carving knife?' Since everybody seems to have retained their memories of these events (note Buffy's 'sudden-need-for-cheese' confession) it's reasonable to assume that Joyce has also, and that she's just (as Buffy suggests) 'repressing' after 'hitting on one of my friends'.

It's a Designer Label!: Buffy's big red coat and black gloves and Xander's overcoat (it can get pretty cold in California once the sun goes down in February). Harmony's gang have some *horrible* clothes, including the blonde girl with the big bottom wearing a very unflattering navy-blue miniskirt, a scarlet PVC coat and a lime-green blouse. Buffy's light-blue (sheep-motif) vest and leopardskin slit miniskirt and Cordelia's red Valentine dress are better. And Xander's 'nice shirt' is, actually, rather good. Cordelia admires his clothes and he admits he allowed Buffy to dress him. As John Travolta circa 1977, seemingly. Is Oz's hair going to remain the same colour two episodes running?

References: The title derives from Rodgers and Hart's 'Bewildered' (made famous by Frank Sinatra). Xander's reference to a 'parallel universe' takes us into a whole SF subgenre. Elvis gets name-checked. Oz's guitar is inscribed 'Sweet J', a possible reference to Lou Reed's Velvet Underground song 'Sweet Jane' (see **59**, 'The Harsh Light of Day'. This is also a really subtle *Austin Powers* in-joke, 'Sweet J' being the name of Scott Evil's best friend). The sequences of Joyce asking Xander to let her in and attacking the door with a carving knife may have been influenced by *The Shining*.

Bitch!: Xander, surprised that Cordelia hasn't been affected by the spell: 'Is this love? Coz maybe on you it doesn't look any different.'

Cordelia to Joyce: '. . . And keep your mom-age mitts off my boyfriend. *Former*.'

Awesome!: Cordelia's 'sheep' speech to Harmony.

The Drugs Don't Work: Midol is an over-the-counter medicine frequently used in the US as a treatment for PMT. 'Roofie' is the street name for the 'date rape' drug, Rohypnol.

Don't Give Up the Day Job: Director James A Contner's previous work includes *Midnight Caller, 21 Jump Street, Wiseguy, The Equalizer, Miami Vice, The Flash, Lois and Clark: The New Adventures of Superman, SeaQuest DSV, Hercules: The Legendary Journeys, American Gothic, Dark Skies, The X-Files* and *Charmed*. Before that he was a cinematographer on movies like *Heat, Monkey Shines, Jaws 3-D, The Wiz, Superman* and *Times Square*. It's his camera work on the concert footage in *Rock Show: Wings Over the World*.

Valley-Speak: Buffy: 'I'm glad you guys are getting along. Almost nearly.'

Harmony: 'A girl wants to look good for her geek.'

Guy in orange shirt: 'Dude, way to get dumped.'

Xander: 'I made her put the love whammy on Cordy.' And: 'Every woman in Sunnydale wants to make me her cuddle monkey.'

Logic, Let Me Introduce You to This Window: Xander nails three boards to the basement's doorframe. When Joyce's knife pokes through, sending Xander and Cordy running down the stairs, we see one of the boards runs all the way from the bottom left corner to the upper right. However, when Willow and the others open the door, the board is much higher. The timescale of the end of the episode is impossible. Xander saves Cordelia from the mob of girls early in the day, yet when they arrive at Buffy's house to hide, it's evening.

Cruelty to Animals: Angel's past is littered with depraved displays of ultraviolence on Valentine's Day (including, on one occasion, nailing a puppy to something).

Quote/Unquote: Xander, after Cordelia has dropped her bombshell: 'Were you running low on dramatic irony?'

Xander, when Buffy suggests they should comfort each other: 'Would lap-dancing enter into that scenario at all? Coz I find that *very* comforting.'

Drusilla asks Xander how he feels about eternal life: 'We couldn't just start with the coffee?'

Notes: 'It's funny how you see someone every day, but not really *see* them.' I once reviewed this episode for a magazine and tried to give it twelve out of ten, but they wouldn't let me. Taking an old sitcom idea (loser-guy-becomes-babe-magnet-through-nefarious-skulduggery) and peppering it with so many great one-liners you lose count, this is *really funny*. The best episode of the season.

Willow has been in Xander's bed before, but they were both (much) younger. We get our first decent look at Xander's room (it's got a HAZARDOUS WASTE sticker on the door). Among the Marvel and pop-art posters (including one for Widespread Panic, see **16**, 'Inca Mummy Girl'), it's nice to spot an acoustic guitar (so, maybe the daydream in **4**, 'Teacher's Pet', wasn't all fantasy. But see **47**, 'The Zeppo').

Two stickers for the band Lotion, who performed in **27**, 'Phases', are visible: the first on the locker behind Giles when we first see him; the second on the locker next to Cordelia's, best seen when Harmony slaps her. Chris Beck's incidental music is some of the best in the series, wonderfully fitting the tone. Sarah Michelle Gellar was missing for most of this episode as she was hosting *Saturday Night Live* that week.

Novelisation: By Keith RA DeCandido *The Xander Years Vol. 1* (Pocket Books, February 1999).

Soundtrack: Four Star Mary's anthem 'Pain' [*] is the song Dingoes Ate My Baby mime to in the Bronze. Also 'Drift Away' by Naked and 'Got the Message' by 70s funksters the Average White Band. *Niiice.*

Sky Nil: After this episode, Sky TV in the UK pulled *Buffy* from its 8 p.m. Saturday slot citing low viewing figures as a reason (it was replaced by *3rd Rock from the Sun* which promptly drew *lower* ratings). It would be over a year before the series was shown on Sky again, and then only after a long and often bitter campaign by fans.

Did You Know?: This is producer Gareth Davies's favourite episode, but for unusual reasons. As he told *Entertainment Weekly*, with Gellar off the set for five days, the writers turned Buffy into a rat. 'Nothing against Sarah, but that rat was *marvellous*. It was a real trouper!' In the same interview, London-born Davies confided that the character he most relates to is Giles, because 'I can understand every word he says'.

29

Passion

US Transmission Date: 24 Feb. 1998
UK Transmission Date: 16 Jul. 1999 (Sky)
3 Feb. 2000 (BBC2)

Writer: Ty King
Director: Michael E Gershman
Cast: Richard Assad (Shopkeeper), Richard Hoyt Miller (Policeman)
French title: *La Boule De Thésulah*
German title: *Das Jenseits Lässt Grüßen*

Buffy wakes up to discover a drawing from Angelus on her pillow. She pleads with Giles for a way of stopping Angelus entering her home. She tells her mother that Angelus has been stalking her and that Joyce should never invite him in. Jenny, hoping to restore Angel's soul, purchases an Orb of Thesulah. The shopkeeper warns her that the spell's translation has been lost, but Jenny tells him that she's working on the text. With Jenny's help, Giles devises a spell to exclude Angelus from places he had previously been invited into. Angelus asks Joyce to help him get Buffy back and mentions that they made love, but he is unable to enter the Summers's house as Willow and Buffy perform the spell. Jenny completes her programme, but Angelus knows what she is planning and kills her, leaving her body in Giles's bed. Giles attacks Angelus at the factory. Buffy arrives in time to prevent Angelus from killing her Watcher, but Angelus escapes. Giles is furious at Buffy for interfering, but she won't allow him to kill himself. Willow takes over as substitute teacher and accidentally misplaces the computer disk that is the key to Angel's soul.

A Little Learning is a Dangerous Thing: Jenny asks Willow to take her computer class for her and after Jenny's death Snyder makes the same request.

Mom's Apple Pie: Joyce claims to have read 'all the parenting books' as she shares dinner with Buffy (roast chicken and vegetables). After Angelus tells Joyce that he and Buffy had sex, she and Buffy have the 'were you careful?' talk. Joyce regains a lot of plus points with her sympathetic handling of the situation.

It's a Designer Label!: Features some really lousy clothes such as Willow's orange sweater, Buffy's grey pants and Xander's red shirt and checky strides.

References: The mass-murdering dictator Joseph Stalin (1879–1953), US book chain Barnes and Noble, *A Charlie Brown Christmas* (see **81**, 'The Replacement') and Russ Meyer's notorious biker-sex movie *Faster, Pussycat! Kill! Kill!* are mentioned.

Ménage à Trois: Interviewed by *TV Guide*, David Boreanaz, James Marsters ('resembling an undecayed version of Billy Idol') and Juliet Landau described the Angel, Spike and Dru relationship. Boreanaz: 'Angel has a very sarcastic side and he knows how to torment Spike. Every time Spike pushes my buttons, I push his . . . He's all talk. It's like tennis, and Drusilla is in the middle, watching.' Marsters: 'Angel was my mentor, [but] I'm grown up now and I don't need him any more.' When interviewer Tim Appelo described the relationship as 'the scariest romantic triangle since the *Archie* comics', Landau replied: 'In a funny way [Drusilla and Spike] have, like, a healthy relationship. I mean, we do go out and kill people, but we have a loving, giving relationship. But with Angel, it's almost like an incestuous, abusive relationship. That's why when I chained him to a bed and burned him with holy water, it was . . . a strange cross between sexuality and power.'

Bitch!: Cordelia: 'I'd do the same for you if you had a social life.'

Awesome!: Angelus killing Jenny against every dramatic convention that the viewer thinks they are party to, followed by the horribly voyeuristic sequence in which he watches Buffy and

Willow's reaction to the phone call informing them of Jenny's death. Giles's murderous attack on Angelus and the moment when Buffy tells Giles that she won't let him kill himself because she can't do this alone.

Don't Give Up the Day Job: Michael Gershman began his career as a camera operator on movies like *The Gauntlet*, *The Deer Hunter*, *Blow Out*, *The Golden Child* and *Die Hard 2* before a stint as second unit director on *Under Siege 2: Dark Territory*.

Logic, Let Me Introduce You to This Window: The object Willow is nailing to her wall is referred to as a crucifix. It isn't, it's a cross. How did Willow not notice that her aquarium was empty as she poured fish food into it? Who put Jenny in Giles's apartment? We must assume it's Angel though we've never seen him in Giles's apartment before.

Cruelty to Animals: Willow on her dead fish: 'We hadn't really had time to bond yet.'

A Death in the Family: According to Alyson Hannigan 'Angel . . . had to kill somebody we loved – we were all warned about that. Actually I think it was supposed to be Oz that was killed, then they decided they'd keep Oz around and they killed Ms Calendar.' According to Robia LaMorte, '[The filming of] the confrontation in the classroom was one day in itself, that took probably four or five hours because of all the fire and explosions . . . On a separate day we did the rest . . . to the point of my death. A lot of running in high heels! The good thing about TV is, as soon as the camera goes to those tighter shots, put those sneakers on.'

Quote/Unquote: Giles: 'Yes, Xander, once again you've managed to boil a complex thought down to its simplest possible form.'

Angel's final words of wisdom: 'If we could live without passion, maybe we'd know some kind of peace. But we would be hollow. Empty rooms, shuttered and dank. Without passion, we'd be truly dead.'

Notes: 'Passion. It lies in all of us. Sleeping, waiting and though unwanted, unbidden, it will stir. Open its jaws and howl.' Not the masterpiece it's often made out to be because it spends half the episode building towards a signposted climax, but contains a

dramatic intensity that is frequently overpowering and performances to match (Tony Head has never been better). 'Passion' is
another example of how adult a series *Buffy* can be. Once again,
a note on just how effective the direction is.

Willow's parents would never let her have a puppy. Her
father's name is Ira and the Rosenberg family are Jewish (as
hinted in previous episodes). Once invited into a house, a
vampire is always welcome (except if, as in this case, a reversal spell is performed). The sign on the front of the school
says (in Latin) ENTER ALL YE WHO SEEK KNOWLEDGE, which
Angelus claims is his invitation (but, see **30**, 'Killed By
Death', concerning vampires and public places). The places
that Angelus can no longer visit include Buffy's house,
Willow's house (which he entered in **19**, 'Lie to Me') and
Cordelia's car (**14**, 'Some Assembly Required'). Joyce
remembers Angel as 'the college boy' who tutored Buffy in
history (see **7**, 'Angel').

In the scene where Buffy and Joyce are eating dinner, look
over Joyce's shoulder at the picture. It's a publicity photo of
Sarah Michelle Gellar that appeared in the August 1997 issue
of *Entertainment Weekly*.

Novelisation: By Nancy Holder in *The Angel Chronicles
Vol. 3* (Pocket Books, August 1999).

Soundtrack: 'Never an Easy Way' by Morcheeba, Puccini's
'Acte 10 Soave Fanciulla' from *La Bohème*. During the graveyard scene, a choral voice can be heard. It belongs to Tony
Head who suggested to Christophe Beck that he provide the
accompaniment.

30
Killed By Death

US Transmission Date: 3 Mar. 1998
UK Transmission Date: 23 Jul. 1999 (Sky)
17 Feb. 2000 (BBC2)

Writers: Rob Des Hotel, Dean Batali
Director: Deran Sarafian
Cast: Richard Herd (Dr Stanley Backer), Willie Garson (Security Guard),

Andrew Ducote (Ryan), Juanita Jennings (Dr Wilkinson),
Robert Munic (Intern), Mimi Paley (Little Buffy),
Denise Johnson (Celia),
James Jude Courtney (Der Kindestod)
French title: *Réminiscence*
German title: *Der Unsichtbare Tod*

Buffy is in hospital with a nasty dose of flu. Overcome with fever, she sees a terrifying demonic figure stalking the halls, and children are dying. A boy, Ryan, tells her that Death is coming for them and that he is invisible to adults. Angelus tries to visit Buffy, but Xander stops him. Buffy tells her friends about Death and they investigate. The prime suspect is one of the doctors, Backer, but Buffy sees him killed by an invisible force. Willow helps Buffy investigate Backer's office for clues, while Giles and Cordelia discover the legend of Der Kindestod, a demon who sucks the life from children. Buffy ingests some of the flu virus so that she can see her enemy and (with Willow creating a diversion) she and Xander follow him to the basement where the children are hiding. Buffy kills the demon while Xander leads the children to safety.

Dudes and Babes: A sick Buffy in her fluffy bed socks is so cuddlesome, you want to hug her till she pops.

A Little Learning is a Dangerous Thing: Willow has done Buffy's homework for her. All she has to do is sign it and the ruse will be complete.

It's a Designer Label!: There's some horrible stuff on display here, including Buffy's white trainers, Willow's red tights and Cordy's green-lined parka. But Cordelia's short dark skirt and black booties are heavenly.

References: Gwyneth Paltrow, 'Mr Potatohead', Humphrey Bogart, Death-as-a-chess-player in Ingmar Bergman's *The Seventh Seal* and *Bill & Ted's Bogus Journey*, the DC superheroine Power Girl, Greek poet Homer. Angelus hums a snatch of Beethoven's famous ninth symphony 'Ode to Joy' (see *Angel*: 'Rm w/a Vu'). Obliquely, Sherlock Holmes and *The Invisible Man* ('If I see a floating pipe and a smoking jacket, he's dropped'). Dare I mention how reminiscent of *Nightmare on Elm Street* (notably the third movie, *Dream Warriors*, which is set in a hospital) the whole thing is?

Bitch!: Cordelia's inept sympathy for Buffy: 'We're all concerned about how *gross* you look.' As Giles notes, 'Cordelia, have you ever actually *heard* of tact?'

Angelus: 'It must just eat you up that I got there first.'
Xander: 'You're going to die and I'm going to be there.'

'You May Remember Me From Such Films and TV Series As . . .': Richard Herd played James McCord in *All The President's Men*, Henry Skerridge in *Midnight in the Garden of Good and Evil*, and Commander John in *V*, though readers may remember his performance as 'Captain Galaxy', Moe Stein, in the 'Future Boy' episode of *Quantum Leap*. His other TV credits include *Starsky and Hutch, The A-Team* and *Hart to Hart*. Willie Garson, in addition to small parts in *There's Something About Mary, Mars Attacks!, Groundhog Day* and *The Rock* and a recurring role (as Henry Coffield) in *NYPD Blue*, has made something of a career out of playing Lee Oswald, appearing in both the movie *Ruby* and the *Quantum Leap* episode 'Lee Harvey Oswald'. Denise Johnson is one of the voice artists on *A Bug's Life*.

Valley-Speak: Xander: 'I gotta get me a life.'

Xander: 'Increased ooginess. That's a danger signal.'

Cordelia's attempts to articulate what Der Kindestod does to children consist of several repetitions of 'Euw!'

Logic, Let Me Introduce You to This Window: When Buffy rants about killing vampires, Dr Wilkinson gives her a tranquilliser injection straight to her arm. The drug should have been administered intravenously. Before Buffy sees Der Kindestod, her bedside clock changes from 2.26 to 2.27. In the next shot, the clock reads 2.15. When Buffy looks into the children's ward for the first time, there is no blue BASEMENT ACCESS plaque on the exit door. Why is there an unlocked, clearly labelled door that leads from the children's ward straight to the hospital basement? Reports differ on the actual number, but there are very few Krispy Kreme doughnut takeaways in Southern California, so Cordelia must have driven *miles* to get Xander his doughnut breakfast. It *must* be love.

I Just *Love* Your Accent: Giles visits Buffy in hospital carrying a brown paper bag. It wouldn't contain *grapes*? It does.

A ubiquitous gift for the invalid and a cultural stereotype that should be executed with extreme prejudice.

Quote/Unquote: Cordelia: 'I was using "watch her back" as a euphemism for "looking at her butt".'

Buffy, on how she intends to stop Der Kindestod: 'Thought I might try violence.'

Notes: 'Fear is for the weak.' Again well directed (the weirdly angled corridors for instance) and, despite the obvious Freddie Kruger riffs, for the most part a clear and simple story about the bogeyman. It gets a bit confusing towards the end, but the characterisation (particularly of Cordelia and Xander) is impressive. The plot is a bit like a jigsaw that has a couple of pieces missing, but it does (eventually) make sense.

When Buffy was eight her cousin Celia (to whom she was close) died in hospital while Buffy was alone with her. It is subsequently revealed that the invisible Kindestod sucked the life from her. This presumably means either there is more than one Kindestod, or that Buffy is a victim of 'Jessica Fletcher's Syndrome', having *always* been a magnet for these kinds of deadly events. Or it's just a huge coincidence and an excuse for a contrived plot device. Your choice. There's an oblique reference to Buffy's amazing self-healing power as previously hinted (see **23**, 'Ted'). Joyce tells Giles how sorry she was to hear about Ms Calendar's death (see **29**, 'Passion'). Xander and Willow used to play 'doctor' (literally, since Willow had lots of medical text books and Xander never had the heart to tell her she was playing it wrong). Buffy claims never to have played the game. Cordelia's raised eyebrows at this suggest a) she doesn't believe Buffy and b) she herself has. Frequently. There's another reference to Willow's frog-phobia (see **21**, 'What's My Line?' Part 1). Buffy likes peanut butter and jelly sandwiches without the crust, and drinks juice that is two parts orange to one part grapefruit. This episode explains how vampires can enter factories and school buildings. After Willow asks if Angelus can attack Buffy while she's in the hospital, Xander says: 'He can come in. It's a public building.'

31

I Only Have Eyes for You

US Transmission Date: 28 Apr. 1998
UK Transmission Date: 30 Jul. 1999 (Sky)
24 Feb. 2000 (BBC2)

Writer: Marti Noxon
Director: James Whitmore
Cast: Meredith Salinger (Grace Newman),
Christopher Gorham (James Stanley), John Hawkes (George),
Miriam Flynn (Ms Frank), Brian Poth (Fighting Boy),
Sarah Bibb (Fighting Girl), Ryan Taszreak (Ben),
Anna Coman-Hidy (50s Girl #1),
Vanessa Bodnar (50s Girl #2)
French title: *La Soirée De Sadie Hawkins*
German title: *Ein Dämon Namens Liebe*

Buffy finds a boy and girl fighting in the school hallway. He holds a gun and shouts, 'Don't walk away from me, bitch.' Buffy stops the boy from shooting, but the couple are confused about why they are arguing and where the gun came from. Or went to, since it is nowhere to be seen. More weirdness occurs, including a teacher writing the same words on a blackboard as Buffy has a daydream about the school in the 50s. Xander is attacked by a rotting arm in his locker. Willow looks up shooting incidents at school and finds a case from 1955, where a student (James) shot his teacher (Grace), then himself. Buffy recognises their faces from her daydream. In the cafeteria all of the food turns into snakes. Willow plans to exorcise the spirit with Buffy, Xander and Cordelia chanting from different locations in the school at midnight. However, a swarm of wasps invades the hallways. Giles, after initially thinking that the troubled spirit is Jenny, believes James's soul is haunting the school, seeking forgiveness from Grace, but this can never happen, since each time the scenario is re-enacted, Grace dies. Buffy returns to school and meets Angelus and the pair are possessed by the ghosts. Buffy (acting out James's role) 'kills' Angelus. Buffy prepares to shoot herself, when Angelus stops her, forgives her and they share a kiss before the souls depart, leaving Buffy and Angelus in an embrace. Angelus escapes, feeling violated. He takes Drusilla to find blood. After they leave, Spike rises from his wheelchair.

Authority Sucks!: Snyder tells Buffy he intends to carefully look over the details of the gun incident until he can work out how it's all her fault. He's interrupted mid-rant by a vegan chaining himself to the snack machine.

The Conspiracy Starts at Home Time: In one short exchange between Snyder and Bob, an entire back-story is created and the suspicions that viewers had from the scene featuring the same pair in **15**, 'School Hard' (about a conspiracy), is confirmed. We learn that Snyder was given his job by the City Council. Snyder refers to 'you people' which suggests that whatever is taking place, it involves the Sunnydale PD (or perhaps he's talking in a wider context, see **33**, 'Becoming' Part 1) and the little flinch he gives when Bob suggests that he talk to the Mayor speaks volumes. But, when Snyder states 'we're on a Hellmouth', suddenly a lot of things become clear. They *know*.

A Little Learning is a Dangerous Thing: Buffy notes she 'pretty much repressed anything math-related' (nice to know repression runs in the family). Willow wants her students to read the chapters on 'information grouping' and 'binary coding'. Xander doesn't know the difference between a 'scapula' and a 'spatula'. There's an essay on the New Deal (before 1935 it concentrated on revitalising stricken businesses and agricultural communities). Also Giles's completely bonkers Fox Mulder-like leap to the wrong conclusion about the identity of the malevolent ghost.

School Dinners: Snakes in the spaghetti. If you have lunches, get ready to part with them.

It's a Designer Label!: A *big* round of applause for Cordelia's tight red sweater. Buffy's suede boots and impossibly short brown skirt (it's really a long vest, isn't it?) cop similar reactions. There's also the red and gold dress worn by the singer with Splendid. On the minus side, Willow's rainbow jumper and pale-green top.

References: Misquotes from *Julius Caesar* ('You came, you saw, you rejected') and *The Merchant of Venice* ('The quality of mercy is not Buffy'), plus references to OJ Simpson, the Nazi 'Final Solution', Ernest Hemingway, the Loch Ness Monster,

Alice Cooper's rebellion anthem 'School's Out' and *The Exorcist* ('I saw that movie. Even the priest dies'). *Poltergeist* is mentioned and parts of the plot seem influenced by it (notably Cordelia's mirror-sequence). 'You've got to roll with the punches' is from Van Halen's 'Jump'. Snyder's line 'I'm no stranger to conspiracy. I saw *JFK*' is the series in microcosm. The characters of James and Grace share their names with those of the leading actors in Hitchcock's *Rear Window* (Stewart and Kelly respectively). 'I'm dead-as-hell and I'm not gonna take it any more' is a paraphrase of Peter Finch's Oscar-winning dialogue in *Network*.

Awesome!: That incredibly touching scene between Giles and Willow at the start. And Buffy and Angelus playing out the James/Grace scenario.

'You May Remember Me From Such Films and TV Series As . . .': Christopher Gorham played Walt in *A Life Less Ordinary*. John Hawkes was Pete Bottoms in *From Dusk Till Dawn* and was terrific as the writer Phillip Padgett in *The X-Files* episode 'Milagro'. Miriam Flynn was the voice of Maa in *Babe*.

Don't Give Up the Day Job: Although director James Whitmore's credits include *Melrose Place*, *Quantum Leap*, *The X-Files*, *Nowhere Man* and *The Pretender*, he is also an actor playing Bernie Terwilliger in *Hunter*.

Valley-Speak: Cordelia's incantation: 'I shall *totally* confront and expel all evil.'

Xander: 'Oh yeah, baby, it's snakealicious in here.' And: 'I don't want to *poo-poo* your wiggins.'

Logic, Let Me Introduce You to This Window: After Buffy has re-entered the wasp-surrounded school, Giles and the others stand in front of the building. The shot of them staring at the wasps is the same one used earlier in the episode after they had escaped. Look closely and you'll be able to spot Buffy's legs. After Snyder leaves Buffy alone in his office, the 1955 yearbook falls from the bookshelf. When it hits the floor, you can see the cover flip open. As Buffy bends down the book is closed. 'I Only Have Eyes For You' by the Flamingos is used during the flashbacks to 1955. However, the song wasn't released until 1959. Why is Cordelia, who had her own diet in

4, 'Teacher's Pet', eating spaghetti in the school cafeteria?

Quote/Unquote: Giles: 'You should never be cowed by authority. Except, of course, in this instance where I am clearly right and you are clearly wrong.'

Xander: '"Something weird is going on"? Isn't that our school motto?'

Notes: 'Love is for ever.' Serious stuff. Marti Noxon's combination of ghost story and pop-culture angst combines to produce an episode that flirts with saying something really quite profound, but never quite delivers. The redemption theme is wonderfully handled and there's a (genuinely) *great* last scene, but when you're dealing with something as horrific as teen suicide, you need more than gestures. Like **13**, 'When She Was Bad', this focuses on what an intolerant character Buffy can be (there are narrative links between Buffy ranting at her friends' stupidity here and her rows with Angel in the season opener).

Buffy says she's not seeing anybody, ever again. Willow gives Giles a rose-quartz stone that belonged to Jenny. It's been suggested that Willow should be unable to retrieve any of Jenny's computer files, as her PC was destroyed in **29**, 'Passion'. In the former episode, when Angelus threw the computer from her desk, the monitor smashed and burst into flames. The hard drive, however, fell on the ground away from the monitor. It's perfectly possible that it suffered no significant damage. Of course, there may have been backup disks. (Indeed, if *anyone* is going to keep backups it would be a computer teacher.) The original US broadcast was followed by a public service announcement by Sarah Michelle Gellar on behalf of the American Association of Suicideology.

Soundtrack: Aside from the Flamingos' recording, 'Charge' by Splendid [*].

32
Go Fish

US Transmission Date: 5 May 1998
UK Transmission Date: 6 Aug. 1999 (Sky)
2 Mar. 2000 (BBC2)

Writers: David Fury, Elin Hampton
Director: David Semel
Cast: Charles Cyphers (Coach Marin), Jeremy Garrett (Cameron Walker),
Wentworth Miller (Gage Petronzi), Conchata Ferrell (Nurse Greenliegh),
Shane West (Sean), Jake Patellis (Dodd McAlvy)
French title: *Les Hommes-Poissons*
German title: *Das Geheimnis Der Fischmonster*

A victory party for the swim team sees everyone celebrating
except Buffy. But, when two team members disappear, she and
her friends become involved. Snyder encourages Willow to
raise the (failing) grade of Gage, another swimmer. Giles
believes that since the two victims were the best swimmers in
school, Gage is the next likely target. While keeping Gage
under surveillance, Buffy saves him from an attack by
Angelus. With a position open due to the deaths, Xander
makes it on to the swim team. Buffy sees Gage tear away his
own skin, emerging as a monster. Xander learns that steroids
are passed to the team in the steam room, meaning that he has
been exposed to the substance that transformed the others.
Coach Marin tells Buffy about Russian experiments with fish
DNA on their Olympic swimmers. He forces Buffy into the
sewer so his boys can satisfy their 'other needs'. Xander struggles with Marin, as Buffy fends off the creatures and the coach
ends up in the sewer, with his boys.

Dudes and Babes: Xander in red Speedo swim wear ('I'm
undercover', 'Not under much'). The double takes on the faces
of Cordy, Buffy and Willow are wonderful. It must be said,
Xander's far too well built to be a total geek – it *must* be his
personality.

Authority Sucks: Xander on Snyder's manipulation of Willow
to up Gage's grades: 'It's a slap in the face to every one of us
that studied hard and worked long hours to *earn* our 'D's.'

A Little Learning is a Dangerous Thing: Since Willow is
still in charge of the computer class, everybody's pie charts
look like they're supposed to. Except Gage's. Xander
seemingly doesn't know who wrote the constitution. His take
on history is little better ('the discus throwers got the best
seats at all the crucifixions'). Cordelia's opinion on the
'all-men-are-created-equal thing': 'Propaganda spouted out

by the ugly and less deserving.' And on Abraham Lincoln: 'Disgusting mole and stupid hat.'

It's a Designer Label!: Cordelia's miniskirts take much of the viewer's attention, but Buffy's stretchpants are practical *and* fun. She lets the side down, wearing leather trousers in the sewer scenes – just the sort of thing for chasing fish monsters. Willow's usual hippychick look is further emphasised by a pair of flared orange loon pants.

References: The title is from Rose Troche's 1994 lesbian movie. Xander's favourite teams include the New York Yankees, Abbot and Costello, and *The A-Team*. Also referenced are Gertrude Edderley (the first woman to swim the English Channel), Twisted Sister (the 80s glam-metal band), *The Creature from the Black Lagoon* and the Brooke Shields film *Blue Lagoon*. Willow's line about the 'chocolatey goodness' of Oreo cookies may be an in-joke (Alyson Hannigan has done commercials for Oreo). There are dialogue and visual nods to *Jaws*. Xander misquotes The Commodores' 'Three Times a Lady' and there's an oblique reference to Thomas Dolby's 'She Blinded Me With Science'. Magazines seen in the library include *Women's Sports and Fitness* (and let's face it, we've *all* got a subscription to that), *Sports Illustrated*, *Vegetarian Times*, *National Geographic*, *PC World*, *Slam! Smithsonian*, *Horseman*, *Skin Diver* and *Art News*.

Bitch!: Cordelia's suggestion after Xander asks what he can do to help the investigations: 'Go out into the parking lot and practice running like a man.'

Awesome!: Buffy taking on two monsters in the dressing room (nice use of a lacrosse stick) and Buffy and Angelus battling ('Why, Ms Summers. You're beautiful'). Cordelia's pride in Xander when he becomes the hero ('You were so courageous. And you looked really hot in those Speedos!') is perfectly in character. A highlight is Willow's interrogation of Jonathan and her reaction to his 'confession' that he peed in the pool ('Euw!').

'You May Remember Me From Such Films and TV Series As . . .': Charles Cyphers was one of John Carpenter's repertory company appearing in *Assault on Precinct 13*, *Escape from New York*, *The Fog* and the first two *Halloween* movies.

On TV he appeared in *The Dukes of Hazzard*, *Wonder Woman*, *Charlie's Angels* and *Starsky and Hutch*. Conchata Ferrell was Susan Bloom in *L.A. Law*, and was in *True Romance*, *Edward Scissorhands* and *Network*.

Valley-Speak: Xander: 'Last month he's the freak with jicama breath who waxes his back. He wins a few meets and suddenly inherits the cool gene?'

Gage: 'Aw, dude, what *is* that foulness?'

Logic, Let Me Introduce You to This Window: The first shot of the Bronze features a blank chalkboard. However, when Buffy observes Gage with Angelus, it has gained an advert DJ 2NITE NO COVER. Coach Marin is concerned that the swim team will find out about the recent deaths. In the Bronze, Gage seems unaware of Cameron's death. When Buffy tells him of the killer, she doesn't mention Cameron by name. But Gage's question after Angelus's attack is, 'Was that the thing that killed Cameron?' In the final shot, we see three fish creatures in the ocean. Where's the fourth? Watch out for Buffy's *Wonder Woman*-style leap from the sewers to the trap door. Didn't know she could do that.

Quote/Unquote: Xander: 'It's officially nippy. So say my nips.'

Cordelia gets most of the best lines, including 'Xander, I know you take pride in being the voice of the common wuss.' And, when believing that Xander had become an aquatic monster: 'We can still date . . . Or not. I'd understand if you want to see other fish. I'll do everything I can to make your quality of life better, whether that means little bath toys or whatever.'

Buffy: 'I think we'd better find the rest of the swim team and lock them up before they get in touch with their inner halibut.'

Notes: 'Is steroid abuse usually linked with "Hey, I'm a Fish"?' Another Xander-led episode and another comedy classic. Amid the hilarity of one of *Buffy*'s funniest episodes, however, is a very cynical essay on drug-enhanced performance and the ceaseless search for winners that the US school system seem hell-bent on. Few other series could have got away with the sexual overtones of this episode. Astonishingly 'Go Fish' has a low reputation with some of the series' Internet fans, regularly appearing alongside **16**, 'Inca Mummy Girl', and **24**, 'Bad Eggs', in *Least Favourite Episode* polls. Seldom has an episode less deserved such a fate.

The school board are having trouble finding a competent teacher late in the term, so Willow is asked to continue subbing through finals (see **29**, 'Passion'). Although we had previously seen Sunnydale docks (**25**, 'Surprise'), this episode confirms it as a coastal town with its own beach. Did the fish creatures eat Coach Marin, or did they have something else in mind? They leave at least half of Nurse Greenliegh intact and the coach specifically states that they've had their dinner and have 'other needs'. Xander's smirk when Buffy says, 'Those boys really loved their coach', suggests some horrible ideas.

Novelisation: By Jeff Mariotte in *The Xander Years Vol. 2* (Pocket Books, April 2000).

Soundtrack: 'Mann's Chinese' by Naked and 'If You'd Listen' by Nero's Rome.

33

Becoming Part 1

US Transmission Date: 12 May 1998
UK Transmission Date: 13 Aug. 1999 (Sky)
9 Mar. 2000 (BBC2)

Writer: Joss Whedon
Director: Joss Whedon
Cast: Max Perlich (Whistler), Jack McGee (Doug Perren),
Richard Riehle (Buffy's First Watcher[9]),
Shannon Weller (Gypsy Woman), Zitto Kazann (Gypsy Man),
Ginger Williams (Girl), Nina Gervitz (Teacher)
French title: *Acathla, Première Partie*
German title: *Wendepunkte*

Galway, 1753: Angel encounters Darla, who offers to show him her world. Sunnydale, 1998: Giles is asked by the museum

---

[9] There is considerable debate in the *Buffy* fan community as to whether this character is supposed to be Merrick or not. Certainly the scenes set in Hemery High are conceptually close enough to the movie to suggest that the film's events are canonical. Additionally, at least one 'official' book on the series lists the character as Merrick.

to look at a stone artefact. London, 1860: Drusilla enters a church, and is told by Angelus that she is the 'spawn of Satan'. Sunnydale, 1998: Buffy and Willow discover the disk on which Jenny stored the spell to restore Angel's soul. Romania, 1898: the body of a gypsy girl lies on the ground, while a curse of restoration is cast. Angelus is told that he will be haunted by the souls of those he has killed. Sunnydale, 1998: Angelus tells Spike about the demon Acathla, who possesses the power to swallow the Earth into Hell. Kendra arrives, having been sent by her Watcher because another dark force is threatening Sunnydale. Manhattan, 1996: Angel, living as a tramp, is approached by a demon, Whistler, who offers Angel the chance to regain his dignity. Los Angeles, 1996: Whistler shows Angel the Chosen One, observing Buffy's initial meeting with her first Watcher. Whistler says Buffy will need Angel's help. Sunnydale, 1998: Angelus fails to revive Acathla. A girl vampire walks into an exam room, tells Buffy that she must meet Angelus that night, then bursts into flames. Buffy finds Angelus at the cemetery and they fight, but it is a trap to get the Slayer away from her friends. At the library the vampires attack. Drusilla kills Kendra; Willow and Xander are left unconscious, and Giles is taken away. Buffy arrives as a police officer orders her to freeze.

Dudes and Babes: This is the episode that gets all the girls banging on about how tragic (and therefore sexy) a figure Angel is. Mind you, the Irish accent could use a bit of work, David. *Begorrah*. (See also *Angel*: 'Somnambulist'.)

Authority Sucks!: Snyder on his students having relationships: 'These public displays of affection are not acceptable in my school. This isn't an orgy, people, it's a classroom.' He then asks Buffy to give him a reason to kick her out (see **34**, 'Becoming' Part 2).

A Little Learning is a Dangerous Thing: Willow is enjoying teaching and helps Buffy with some chemistry homework. 'When, in the real world, am I going to need chemistry? Or history? Or math? Or . . . the English language?' asks Buffy.

Mom's Apple Pie: A clever reversal of the 'Do you know what time it is?' scene from **M1**: Joyce catches Buffy coming in late from slaying and has a blazing row with her.

School Dinners: Xander's re-enactment of Buffy's killing a vampire using two fish fingers is certainly worth seeing.

It's a Designer Label!: Watch out for Buffy's red dress and her brilliant trouser suit and ice-blue frock coat. Cordy's red sweater from **31**, 'I Only Have Eyes for You', puts in another appearance. On the minus side, Buffy's hooded top, her yellow coat and horrible pants in the 1996 sequences and Whistler's green shirt.

References: Allusions to *The Sword in the Stone*. Buffy calls Acathla 'Alfalfa' from *The Little Rascals*. The sequence in which Darla cuts her chest with her fingernail and makes Angel drink from it is yet another moment that seems to have been inspired by *Dracula, Prince of Darkness* (see **2**, 'The Harvest'; **12**, 'Prophecy Girl'). Angel's mentor shares his name with one of the vampire killers in *Blade*.

Bitch!: After Cordelia is really nice to Willow, Xander notes: 'And almost sixty-five per cent of that was actual compliment. Is that a personal best?'

Cordy on Snyder: 'A tiny impotent Nazi with a bug up his butt the size of an emu.'

Xander: 'So, this spell might restore Angel's soul? Well, here's an interesting angle: Who cares?'

I'd love to know what word it was that Willow calls Xander that causes Buffy to say, 'Do you kiss your mother with that mouth?'

'You May Remember Me From Such Films and TV Series As . . .': Max Perlich was Johnny Hardin in *Maverick* and was a regular on *Homicide: Life On the Streets* (as James Brodie). Jack McGee is one of those actors that seems to be in *everything*: he's in *Backdraft, Lethal Weapon 2* and *Showgirls,* plays a Sheriff in *Basic Instinct* and is the cop who sprays Val Kilmer with mace in *The Doors*. Richard Riehle had lots of film credits including *Fear and Loathing in Las Vegas, Casino, The Fugitive* and *Fried Green Tomatoes at the Whistle Stop Cafe*. Zitto Kazann is in *Waterworld*.

Valley-Speak: Buffy: 'Ready to rock.'

Plus her *total* Valley-girl act: 'Call me!'

Logic, Let Me Introduce You to This Window: In **14**, 'Some Assembly Required', Angel is 241 years old. Assuming that episode took place in 1997, he would have been born in 1755 or 1756. According to **18**, 'Halloween', Angel was 18 years old in 1775 and still human, which ties in with this. However, here Angel is bitten by Darla in 1753, three years before he was born. It seems Buffy isn't the only character with a variety of birthdays (see **Angel's Age**). According to the flashbacks, Angel saw Buffy at least twice before they met in **1**, 'Welcome to the Hellmouth', despite him saying in the opening episode, 'I thought you'd be taller.'

What a Shame They Dropped . . .: A marvellous Whistler line: 'There are three kinds of people that no one understands. Geniuses, madmen, and guys that mumble!'

Quote/Unquote: Drusilla: 'Met an old man. I didn't like him. He got stuck in my teeth.'

Willow has been researching the Black Arts – for fun.

Spike: 'It's a big rock. Can't wait to tell my friends. They don't have a rock this big.'

Notes: 'So, what are we? Helpless puppets? No, the big moments are gonna come, you can't help that. It's what you do afterwards that counts.' 'Becoming' Part 1 explores the nature of destiny and does it *beautifully*. Sharing similarities with the *Highlander* TV series isn't the worst of crimes as this poetic exercise in controlled storytelling delves into two centuries of Angelus's past with a series of conceptually ingenious flashbacks. However, Kendra's arbitrary death (well played as it is) is a real disappointment.

Giles has been using his Orb of Thesulah as a paperweight, which is a clever in-joke referring to what the Magik-Store guy told Jenny he had sold a couple of the Orbs for in **29**, 'Passion'. Xander says Buffy has killed five vampires over the previous three nights. Buffy's boyfriend when she first became the Slayer was called Tyler. Kendra calls the stake which she gives to Buffy 'Mr Pointy'. We see another copy of *The Sunnydale Press* (see **17**, 'Reptile Boy'; **55**, 'Graduation Day' Part 1). The episode includes flashbacks to events first mentioned in **7**, 'Angel'; Darla's 'siring' of Angel and his being cursed by the Romany people. The 1860 sequence shows that Drusilla was psychic before she became a vampire (she predicted a pit disaster). She refers to her mother in the present tense, which means this must have taken place at the beginning of Angelus's relationship with her, as **19**, 'Lie to Me', makes clear he killed all of those close to her before finally killing her. Indeed, this could be their first meeting (although Angelus is certainly taking lots of risks to be close to her – entering a church, for example). Whistler's reference to Buffy as little more than a child seems to imply that the Slayer is normally older (see **46**, 'Helpless'). The Hemery High set is a façade on the Universal backlot in Studio City. It was also the Hill Valley Clock Tower in the first two *Back to the Future* films. The Latin that Giles speaks during the restoration curse translates as 'That which was lost shall be found'.

Angel's Age: *Angel*: 'The Prodigal' nails the problem of exactly how old Angel is. Liam, it states, was born in 1727 and became a vampire in 1753. Although the date of Liam's death confirms the on-screen information in **33**, 'Becoming' Part 1, it contradicts several other bits of dating in *Buffy* (notably Willow's observation, taken from *The Watcher's Diaries*, in **18**, 'Halloween', that Angel was 18 years old in 1775 and still human). It seems that vampires take their 'age' from the time that they actually become a vampire (see, for instance, Spike's age as given in **63**, 'The Initiative') though in Angel's case this is *still* a couple of years away from the dates given in *Buffy* episodes during 1997–98 (that Angel was either 240 or 241). See also **85**, 'Fool for Love'; *Angel*: 'Dear Boy' and 'Darla' for further continuity.

34
Becoming Part 2

US Transmission Date: 19 May 1998
UK Transmission Date: 13 Aug. 1999 (Sky)
16 Mar. 2000 (BBC2)

Writer: Joss Whedon
Director: Joss Whedon
Cast: Max Perlich (Whistler), Susan Leslie (First Cop),
Thomas G Waites (Second Cop)
French title: *Acathla, Seconde Partie*
German title: *Spiel Mit Dem Feuer*

Buffy is arrested for murder, but escapes and visits the hospital in disguise. Xander tells her Willow is in a coma and Giles has disappeared. At Giles's apartment, Buffy meets Whistler, who tells her Angel was destined to stop Acathla, not revive him. A patrol cop recognises Buffy but Spike helps her escape, explaining that he wants to stop Angelus. Buffy takes him back to her house, where a vampire attacks her mother. Buffy kills it and explains to Joyce that she is a Vampire Slayer. Joyce is angry at having been kept in the dark and tells Buffy, if she leaves now, not to bother coming back. Giles refuses to divulge the information Angelus needs, despite being tortured. Willow recovers and tells the others that she will try the curse again. Buffy returns to the library to retrieve Kendra's sword. Snyder finds her and gleefully expels her, calling someone to tell the Mayor the good news. Drusilla tricks Giles by making herself look like Jenny. Giles says Angelus's blood is the key to the awakening. Xander frees Giles as Buffy sword-fights Angelus, leaving Spike to hustle Drusilla away. Willow restores the curse on Angelus's soul just as Buffy is about to deliver the final blow. However, Acathla is awakening and Buffy must send Angel to Hell. Homeless and expelled, Buffy boards a bus and leaves Sunnydale.

Dudes and Babes: Buffy's claim to be the drummer in a rock band with Spike as the singer is such a wonderful image we almost wish it were true.

Authority Sucks!: 'You stupid little troll, you have no *idea*.' But Snyder *does*, as Buffy discovers in the scene where he expels her.

Denial No More!: 'Mom, I'm a Vampire Slayer.' There's not much even Joyce can say to that, although 'Have you tried *not* being a Slayer' is an impressive comeback. Buffy rages at her mother's inability to see what's been staring her in the face for the last two years, asking how many times Joyce has washed blood out of Buffy's clothes (see **4**, 'Teacher's Pet').

It's a Designer Label!: Buffy's undercover hat is so funny, you'll fall on the floor and kick your legs in the air laughing. Xander's purple jumper crops up again. There's also Oz's yellow shirt and a pink one in the final scene. Cordelia's lemon dress is a highlight.

References: Snyder's 'Your point being?' echoes Homer Simpson's reply in *The Simpsons* episode 'Marge on the Lam', when asked if he is just holding on to the coke cans that have got both his arms stuck in two drinks machines. 'A gay old time' is a reference to *The Flintstones*. 'Goodbye Piccadilly, farewell bloody Leicester Square' is a misquote from the First World War song 'It's a Long Way to Tipperary'.

Bitch!: Buffy to Snyder: 'You never got a single date in high school, did you?'

Awesome!: Willow's 'resolve' face. The lengthy Buffy/ Angelus sword fight. Plus the delightful comedy scene with Joyce and Spike (see **42**, 'Lover's Walk').

'You May Remember Me From Such Films As . . .': Thomas G Waites played Windows in *The Thing* and Fox in *The Warriors*.

Valley-Speak: Buffy to Xander: 'That was equal parts protecting me and copping a feel?'

Logic, Let Me Introduce You to This Window: Why does Buffy invite Spike into her home? You'd think she would have learned something from the events of **29**, 'Passion'. When did Xander show Buffy the 'funky-looking mansion' on Crawford Street? Buffy couldn't have known Drusilla was responsible for Kendra's death (Xander was unconscious before Drusilla entered the library) yet that's what she tells Spike. Principals cannot expel students without a school board hearing. If Spike is so anti-the-End-of-the-World then what was all that business with the Judge in **26**, 'Innocence'? During the final battle scene, Buffy's hair changes from loose to ponytailed several times. Spike drives out of the garage and turns the steering wheel hard to the left, keeping it in that position for several seconds (the car should be going in circles). Angelus's sword-fighting double looks more like Xander than Angelus. Major logic flaw: the script implies that only Angel's blood could call Acathla, even though it is supposed to be his destiny to stop this happening. Without Angel turning into Angelus, this story would never have happened.

I Just *Love* Your Accent: Spike says he likes dog racing and Manchester United (in that, he's typical – most of their supporters live *anywhere* but Manchester). Whistler says, 'Raiding an Englishman's fridge is like dating a nun: you're never going to get to the good stuff.'

Quote/Unquote: Buffy to Whistler: 'If you're gonna crack jokes, I'm gonna pull out your rib cage and wear it as a hat.'

Spike: 'I don't fancy spending the next month trying to get librarian out of the carpet.'

Go Straight to Hell: Angelus: 'You're going to Hell.' Buffy: 'Save me a seat.'

Notes: 'I've had a *really* bad day.' Initially more concerned with power politics and characterisation than plot. For twenty minutes the episode stutters (despite the hospital scenes contrasted with the grotesque brutality of Angelus torturing Giles) before a magnificent recovery to its tragic conclusion. It is *impossible* to watch the final moments of this episode without a lump in the throat and a prickly sensation behind the eyes.

Xander tells an unconscious Willow that she is his best friend and that he loves her. Significantly, the first word Willow says on coming out of her coma is 'Oz'. The last time Angelus tortured someone the chainsaw hadn't been invented. Spike refers to Joyce hitting him with an axe in **15**, 'School Hard'. Snyder says the Sunnydale police are deeply stupid, which seems accurate on the evidence we've seen (see **48**, 'Bad Girls'). The road sign at the end of the episode reads NOW LEAVING SUNNYDALE. COME BACK SOON!

Soundtrack: 'Full of Grace' by Sarah McLachlan. (On the same CD is a song called 'Angel'. Coincidence?) Christophe Beck's magnificent score won a deserved Emmy. The love theme 'Close Your Eyes', [*] which accompanies the final Buffy–Angel scenes, is truly epic.

'I Need a Hug': The Mutant Enemy vampire on the closing credits replaced his usual 'Grrr Arrrgh' with this touching sentiment. Most viewers probably agreed with him.

> 'This girl has a history of mental problems dating back
> to early childhood. I'm a blood-sucking fiend! Look at
> my outfit!'
>
> – 'Doppelgängland'

Third Season (1998–99)

Mutant Enemy Inc/Kuzui Enterprises/
Sandollar Television/20th Century Fox
Created by Joss Whedon
Producer: Gareth Davies
Executive Producers: Sandy Gallin, Gail Berman,
Fran Rubel Kuzui, Kaz Kuzui, David Greenwalt, Joss Whedon
Co-Producers: Marti Noxon, David Solomon, Kelly Manners

Regular Cast:
Sarah Michelle Gellar (Buffy Summers), Nicholas Brendon (Xander Harris),
Alyson Hannigan (Willow Rosenberg), Charisma Carpenter (Cordelia Chase),
David Boreanaz (Angel), Anthony Stewart Head (Rupert Giles),
Mark Metcalf (The Master, 43),
Kristine Sutherland (Joyce Summers, 35–7, 40, 42, 44–6, 48–9, 51–5),
Mercedes McNab (Harmony Kendall, 43, 55–6),
Elizabeth Anne Allen (Amy Madison, 45), Robia LaMorte (Jenny Calendar, 44),
Armin Shimerman (Principal Snyder, 36–7, 40, 45, 50, 53, 55–6),
James Marsters (Spike, 42), Seth Green (Daniel 'Oz' Osborne, 35–48, 50–6),
Jason Hall (Devon, 36, 39–41, 50),
Danny Strong (Jonathan Levinson, 36, 39, 43, 52, 54, 56),
Larry Bagby III (Larry, 35, 43, 52, 56), Robin Sachs (Ethan Rayne, 40),
Julia Lee ('Chantarelle'/'Lily'/Anne Steele, 35),
Saverio Guerra (Willy, 44, 47), James G MacDonald (Detective Stein, 49),
Jeremy Ratchford (Lyle Gorch, 39), James Lurie (Mr Miller, 35,[10] 55),
Fab Filippo (Scott Hope, 37–9), Eliza Dushku (Faith, 37–9, 41, 44, 47–51, 53–6),
K Todd Freeman (Mr Trick, 37, 39–40, 48–9),
Harry Groener (Mayor Richard Wilkins III, 39–40, 42, 45, 48–51, 53–6),
Jack Plotnick (Deputy Mayor Allan Finch, 39, 42, 48–9),
Emma Caulfield (Anya Jenkins, 43, 50, 54–5),
Harris Yulin (Quentin Travers, 46),
Alexis Denisof (Wesley Wyndam-Pryce, 48–56),
Amy Powell (TV News Reporter, 49), Megan Gray (Sandy, 50),
Ethan Erickson (Percy West, 50, 52, 55–6),
Andy Umberger (D'Hoffryn, 50), Bonita Friedericy (Mrs Finkle, 53,[11] 54)

[10] Credited as 'Teacher' in **35**, 'Anne'.
[11] Credited as 'Manager' in **53**, 'Choices'.

35

Anne

US Transmission Date: 29 Sep. 1998
UK Transmission Date: 20 Aug. 1999 (Sky)
30 Mar. 2000 (BBC2)

Writer: Joss Whedon
Director: Joss Whedon
Cast: Carlos Jacott (Ken), Mary-Pat Green (Blood Bank Doctor),
Chad Todhunter (Rickie), Michael Leopard (Roughneck),
Harley Zumbrum (Demon Guard), Barbara Pilavin (Old Woman),
Harrison Young (Old Man), Alex Toma (Aaron),
Dell Yount (Truck Guy)
German title: *Anne – Gefangen In Der Unterwelt*

Willow, Xander and Oz try to carry on Buffy's work in her absence, but they aren't very good at it. Buffy, meanwhile, is working as a waitress in an LA diner. There she meets 'Lily', whom she knew as 'Chantarelle' in Sunnydale. Lily tells Buffy that her boyfriend, Ricky, is missing. Buffy reluctantly agrees to help and finds an old man dead in the street, whom she identifies as Ricky from his unique tattoo. 'Lily' is ensnared by Ken, who runs the Family Home, a refuge for homeless teenagers. Clues lead Buffy to the home, where she finds Lily about to be initiated. Lily, Buffy and Ken pass through a black pool into an other-dimensional factory where hundreds of missing teenagers are working as slave labour with demonic guards. Ken says a day on Earth equates to a hundred years in this dimension. Buffy organises a rebellion among the slaves and helps them to freedom. Buffy gives her apartment and job (along with her 'name') to Lily and returns home.

Dreaming (As Blondie Once Said) is Free: Buffy and Angel on a beach at sunset with the classic line: 'I'll never leave you, not even if you kill me.'

Dudes and Babes: Willow: 'Come and get it, big boy.' 'Lily' (see **19**, 'Lie to Me') is *still* as wet as a slap in the face with a haddock and now has 'dead-boyfriend issues' to deal with.

Buffy's Peach Pie: Buffy tells 'Lily' that she can't guarantee the peach pie at the diner actually contains peaches.

Denial, Thy Name is Joyce: Joyce says she doesn't blame

herself for Buffy leaving; she blames Giles (which is pretty hypocritical since it was she who threw Buffy out).

It's a Designer Label!: The pink flowery dress Buffy wears in her dream is the same one she has in **36**, 'Dead Man's Party'. Cordelia wears a tasteful green skirt but Willow's at it again, with a short purple skirt and tea-cosy hat (this is, incidentally, the only episode in which 'tea cosy' is mentioned; it's something Buffy says she's always wanted, even though she doesn't know what one is. She ought to have a look on her best friend's head). There are some nice pants on display, including Cordelia's blue flares, the tight red pair worn by the lead singer of Belly Love and the cream hipsters worn by Lily.

References: 'Duck and cover' was a 50s information campaign aimed largely at children on how to protect themselves in the event of a nuclear attack. Buffy beats up Ken, telling him it's her impression of Mahatma Gandhi (1869–1948) when he was 'really pissed-off'. Buffy's assumed name, Anne Summers, raised a lot of smiles in Britain where this is the name of a leading erotica store.

Bitch!: Cordy notes that Xander has always been attracted to monsters (see **4**, 'Teacher's Pet') and refers, caustically, to the Inca Mummy Girl. Xander gets his own back with 'The vampire kills you, we watch, we rejoice.' Then there's a repeat of the **22**, 'What's My Line?' Part 2, kiss-sequence (with *that* music again).

'You May Remember Me From Such Films As . . .': Harrison Young played the old Private Ryan in *Saving Private Ryan*. Carlos Jacott was tremendous as the agent in *Being John Malkovich* and also appears in *She's All That*, *The Last Days of Disco*, *Grosse Pointe Blank* and as Ramon the Pool Guy in *Seinfeld*.

Don't Give Up the Day Job: Stunt co-ordinator Jeff Pruitt has a cameo role as the Family Home doorman. He previously played a vampire in **23**, 'Ted'.

Logic, Let Me Introduce You to This Window: Willow's scream interrupts Xander and Cordelia's fight and we see Cordy run towards Willow with Xander behind her. In the following shot, Oz is running in the same direction while Xander and Cordy are standing still. For most of the episode Buffy wears a purple T-shirt under a black hooded sweatshirt. After she tells the other prisoners, 'Anyone who's not having fun here, follow me', she's wearing a different top beneath her sweatshirt. Buffy wears a pair of white Nike shoes but after Lily pushes Ken off the balcony, watch Buffy's shoes as she climbs up. They're light-grey deck shoes. How could Willow have not known that Oz didn't finish school? Larry was a senior last year, wasn't he? What were those slaves working on? A *huge* MacGuffin that's as yet unexplained.

Quote/Unquote: Ken: 'You've got guts. I'd like to slice you open and play with them.'

Notes: 'I didn't ask for you to come to me with your problems. I just wanted to be left alone.' Clever opening (particularly Oz's incompetent attempt at throwing a stake) but this is a *real* disappointment. A downbeat story about the sick underbelly of LA, and an exercise in reformatting, 'Anne' tries hard to say something about society, but it's uninvolving stuff and after a while the viewer simply wants the episode finished and Buffy back in Sunnydale. It's a *long* forty minutes to sit through just to get to 'I'm Buffy the Vampire Slayer . . . And you are?'

Buffy's middle name is Anne. She has a fluffy toy duck in her rented apartment. Cordelia spent the summer in Mexico where, she says, they have cockroaches big enough to own property (see **13**, 'When She Was Bad'). Giles has a friend in Oakland who gives him a (false) lead on vampire activity.

Soundtrack: Belly Love perform 'Back to Freedom' in the Bronze.

Critique: The third season began with a glowing write-up in *TV Guide*: 'Can we tell you how great it is not to have to choose between *Buffy* and *Ally McBeal* any more? Kicking off a hot Tuesday line-up (followed by the much anticipated *Felicity*), this smart-sexy-funny-scary original is at the top of its game.' The piece also included a few gems from Joss Whedon, including a comment that Angel has 'been in Hell, so he's going to be a little cranky'!

36
Dead Man's Party

US Transmission Date: 6 Oct. 1998
UK Transmission Date: 27 Aug. 1999 (Sky)
6 Apr. 2000 (BBC2)

Writer: Marti Noxon
Director: James Whitmore Jnr
Cast: Nancy Lenehan (Pat), Paul Morgan Stetler (Young Doctor),
Chris Garnant (Stoner #1)
French title: *Le Masque De Cordolfo*
German title: *Die Nacht Der Lebenden Toten*

A Nigerian mask Joyce bought for her gallery proves to be an
even bigger headache for Mrs Summers than organising a
homecoming that will please her (still confused) daughter.
First a cat is raised from the dead, then an elaborate party with
all of Buffy's friends and Oz's band is ruined by the arrival of
gatecrashing zombies. Buffy, whose sulky demeanour proves
trying even to Xander and Willow, manages to fight the demon
of the mask Ovu Mobani, the Evil Eye, which is inhabiting the
body of Joyce's neighbour Pat. Killing the demon makes the
zombies vanish and leaves Buffy alone with those closest to
her, to come to her senses and start acting like herself again.

Dreaming (As Blondie Once Said) is Free: For the second
episode running, Angel appears only in a dream sequence. And
a very surreal one at that, set in a deserted school with weird
music and Buffy in a very revealing top.

Authority Sucks!: Snyder's reply to Joyce saying that Buffy
was cleared of all charges surrounding Kendra's death: 'While
she may live up to the "not a murderer" requirement for enrol-
ment, she *is* a troublemaker.' And he advises Buffy that 'Hot
Dog on a Stick' are hiring. Joyce later describes Snyder as a
'nasty little horrid bigoted rodent-man'.

The Conspiracy Starts at Home Time: The Mayor is mentioned twice. When Joyce says she will take Buffy's expulsion
up with him, Snyder says *that* will be an interesting meeting.

Mom's Apple Pie: Joyce believes that Buffy has 'no appreciation of primitive art' (this is a *bad* thing?). Buffy says she was

starving until the four-course snack Joyce made her after dinner. The 'mom's-not-perfect' scene is a tremendously effective one – and, for once, we're actually on Joyce's side.

It's a Designer Label!: Joyce's orange mom-pants. Giles wears a very tasteful three-piece suit in grey. Buffy's jogging pants are also good. On the minus side, Devon's brown shirt.

References: Fashion designer Tommy Hilfiger, popular 70s children's toy the Weebles, *Rambo*, *The Bad Seed*, UK techno group Shut Up and Dance, newspaper *USA Today*, sitcom *Mr Belvedere* (1985–90) and Jacquelyn Mitchard's novel *The Deep End of the Ocean*. The title comes from a song by Oingo Boingo. Aspects of the story may have been influenced by *Night of the Living Dead* and *Mask*.

Awesome!: Buffy's fight on (and off) the roof with the demon, especially the garden-spade ending.

'You May Remember Me From Such Films As . . .': Both Nancy Lenehan and Paul Morgan Stetler are in *Pleasantville*.

Valley-Speak: Oz's hilarious bit on the differences between a 'gathering', a 'shindig' and a 'hootenanny'.

Xander: 'It's great to have the Buffster back.'

Stoner on whose party it is: 'Heard it was for some chick that just got out of rehab.'

Logic, Let Me Introduce You to This Window: Buffy sets the table for six. However, Joyce invited seven (eight counting Pat). When Xander asks the group to vote on how Buffy's homecoming should be celebrated, Willow raises her right hand with a pencil in it. When the camera returns to Willow, her hand is still raised, but where's the pencil? When Buffy goes to her room and starts to pack her bag, she leaves the door slightly open. After the commercial break, when Willow finds Buffy, the door is fully open. (Despite a *major* party taking place downstairs, these scenes have virtually no background noise.) When Buffy stakes the zombie to see if it is a vampire, it raises its left arm in reaction. Next shot, the arm is still on the floor. The wallpaper pattern changes between shots after Buffy and Pat fall out of the window. Will Dingoes Ate My Baby ever do their guitarist another personal favour after *this*? And grabbing the principal like that could easily cost a librarian his job. (There *has* to be more to this scene than we see. Why does Giles believe he can get away with it? And why does Snyder give in?)

Quote/Unquote: Buffy: 'What about home schooling? It's not just for scary religious people any more.'

Giles: ' "Do you like my mask? Isn't it pretty? It raises the dead!" *Americans*!'

Xander: 'Generally speaking, when scary things get scared, not good.'

Notes: 'So, is this a typical day at the office?' A long-winded way to get Buffy and her friends back together again, though it's much funnier than 35, 'Anne', and, consequently, more interesting. At least the effects are very good, but the party scenes of Buffy bitching the Scooby Gang are painful to watch.

Giles hot-wires his car (he says it's 'like riding a bloody bicycle', which suggests he's done some of this during his 'dark' past. See 45, 'Gingerbread'). Willow isn't a fully fledged witch yet, that takes years (see 45, 'Gingerbread'; 50, 'Doppelgängland'). Xander's call sign during the patrol is 'Night Hawk'. The Summerses have skis in their closet.

Critique: '*Buffy* works against atmospherics, going for the contrasts implicit in a horror story setting that looks like the subject of a Beach Boys song,' wrote Lloyd Rose in the *Washington Post*. 'Impossibly fit, gorgeous teens stroll the halls. Buffy, in the person of Sarah Michelle Gellar, is a major babe, way too good-looking to ever be the nerd she's portrayed as . . . The movies' response to feminism has been to create heroines who might be called "Boys With Breasts". But though Buffy batters bad guys with the best of them, she's all girl. She's emotional. She has bad hair days (which Cordelia is always quick to comment on). She worries about her boyfriend. And with Gellar in the role, she's the sexiest nerd in history. And Whedon isn't above the more traditional S&M images: Who can forget how Buffy looked after killing a snake-demon, her little black dress clinging to her lithe figure, broken manacles dangling from her wrists like saucy bracelets?'

Novelisation: By Yvonne Navarro in *The Willow Files Vol. 1* (Pocket Books, December 1999).

Soundtrack: Dingoes Ate My Baby mime to 'Never Mind', 'Sway' and 'Pain' (see 28, 'Bewitched, Bothered and Bewildered') by Four Star Mary.

37

Faith, Hope and Trick

US Transmission Date: 13 Oct. 1998
UK Transmission Date: 3 Sep. 1999 (Sky)
13 Apr. 2000 (BBC2)

Writer: David Greenwalt
Director: James A Contner
Cast: Jeremy Roberts (Kakistos), John Ennis (Manager)
French title: *La Nouvelle Petite Sœur*
German title: *Neue Freunde, Neue Feinde*

At Sunnydale's Happy Burger, two vampires search for the Slayer. Principal Snyder readmits Buffy to school, under orders from the board. Giles tells Buffy he needs to perform a binding spell on Acathla to keep the demon dormant and asks for details of Angel being sent to Hell. At the Bronze, Cordelia points out a couple on the dance floor. Buffy follows and discovers the boy is a vampire. What takes her by surprise is the girl's ability to deal with him, stopping only to greet Buffy and introduce herself as Faith, the new Slayer, called forth in response to Kendra's death. Faith tells Buffy that her Watcher is at an annual retreat, but Giles discovers that the Watcher is dead. Buffy and Faith are attacked by Kakistos, Mr Trick and their acolytes. The Slayers defeat Kakistos. Unable to keep her secret any longer, Buffy tells Giles and Willow that Angel was cured before she killed him. Buffy revives plans for her weekend date with Scott Hope just as, unknown to her, Angel is returned from Hell.

Dudes and Babes: Faith, the new Slayer is 'personable' according to a green-eyed Buffy. She says slaying makes her 'hungry and horny' (Buffy agrees about the hungry part). Willow notes that Buffy does 'that thing with your mouth that boys like. No not *that* thing . . .' What on earth is she talking about? Also debuting is Scott Hope, Buffy's 'nice normal non-boyfriend'. Angel appears naked in the final scene. Quite popular with the girls, this one . . .

Authority Sucks!: Joyce tells an outmanoeuvred Snyder, 'What I believe my daughter is trying to say is "Nyah-nyah-nyah".'

A Little Learning is a Dangerous Thing: The preconditions of Buffy becoming a schoolgirl again are that she takes make-up tests on all of the classes she skipped last year, along with providing a letter of recommendation from a member of the faculty who 'isn't an English librarian' and that she sees the school psychologist (see **38**, 'Beauty and the Beasts'). She eventually passes all of these, although her initial reaction to the English test ('they give you a credit for speaking it, right?') makes us wonder how, exactly. (See **42**, 'Lover's Walk'.)

Mom's Apple Pie: Faith seems to enjoy the fries Joyce serves for dinner.

It's a Designer Label!: Willow's fluffy light-blue sweater sums up her personality. Ditto, Cordelia's vampy Raybans. And Faith's impressive trouser wardrobe (tight multicoloured hipsters in her first scene, crimson leathers later on). She says she sometimes sleeps naked, unlike Buffy who's seen in a lime-green nightshirt. Oz's horrible dyed shirt puts in another appearance.

References: The episode title is derived from I Corinthians 13:11 (see **M1**). Martha Stewart (American 'home-and-garden' guru) is mentioned (see **U1**). Mr Trick says that Sunnydale's death rate makes 'DC look like Mayberry' (a reference to *The Andy Griffiths Show*). The 70s disco kings KC & The Sunshine Band are name-checked and there are allusions to George Gershwin's 'Summertime' and *Single White Female*. Scott wants to take Buffy to a festival of films by silent comedy genius Buster Keaton (what a fabulous chat-up line *that* is). Angel's climactic return is a tribute to *The Terminator* with him falling from the sky, naked, in a blaze of light.

Bitch!: Buffy and Faith get their claws out (chiefly over what little the latter knows about Angel). As usual, though, neither can hold a candle to Cordy, particularly her assessment of Faith: 'Does anyone believe that's her *actual* hair colour?'

Awesome!: The pre-title sequence at the Happy Burger ('*now* I'm hungry') is a classic.

'You May Remember Me From Such Films As . . .': Eliza Dushku made her film debut aged eleven in *That Night*. She played Emma in *Bye Bye Love*, Missy in *Bring It On*, Dana Tasker in *True Lies* and was in *This Boy's Story*, *Jay and Silent*

Bob Strike Back and *Soul Survivor*. K Todd Freeman was McCullers in *Grosse Pointe Blank* and Muddy in *The Cider House Rules*.

Valley-Speak: Faith: 'The Vamps, they better get their asses to *Def Con 1*.'

Not Exactly a Haven for the Bruthas: Let's have this one in full. Mr Trick: 'Admittedly, it's not a haven for the bruthas . . . Strictly the Caucasian Persuasion here in the 'Dale. But you just gotta stand up and salute that death rate.'

Logic, Let Me Introduce You to This Window: During the tour of Sunnydale High, Willow identifies one of the class-rooms as the cafeteria. After Buffy tries to stake Kakistos the second time, she leaves the stake sticking out of his chest. When Faith drives the huge beam through Kakistos's chest, the smaller stake is gone.

Quote/Unquote: Buffy's idea of 'girly stuff' is: 'Date and shop and hang out and go to school and save the world from unspeakable demons.'

Xander's reaction to Faith's semierotic slaying tale: 'Wow, they should film that and show it every Christmas.'

Buffy mispronounces Kakistos as 'Khaki Trousers'.

Mr Trick: 'There's a reason these vengeance crusades are out of style. The modern vampire, we see the big picture.'

Buffy's first rule of slaying: 'Don't die.'

Notes: 'If doing violence to vampires upsets you, you're in the wrong line of work.' A great David Greenwalt script, with many fine moments (the 'uncoupling' scene, Buffy's silent exasperation at her friends' sudden desire to be with Faith while she has to study). A subtle game played by Giles to get Buffy to confront her own demons leads to a shocking conclu-sion. A little gem.

Buffy doesn't believe in two things: coincidence and lepre-chauns. Giles tells her the former *does* exist but, as far as he knows, the latter do not. In the final scenes Buffy is wearing a heart-shaped pendant instead of her usual crucifix. Willow says that when Giles is mad he makes a 'cluck, cluck' sound with his tongue. Giles likes kayaking. A Watcher retreat is held in the Cotswolds each year (Giles had never been invited). Buffy tells Faith that Oz is a werewolf. 'It's a long story.' 'I got bit,' says Oz. 'Obviously not *that* long,' notes Buffy (see **27**, 'Phases'). Faith grew up in South Boston. She had a female Watcher (the second time a female Watcher has been alluded to. See **5**, 'Never Kill a Boy on the First Date'; **41**, 'Revelations'). Faith tells a vampire, 'My dead mother hits harder than that' (see **51**, 'Enemies'). Whatever Kakistos did to Faith's Watcher before killing her, it wasn't pleasant. Interesting fan theory: was Kakistos Faith's *Cruciamentum* (see **46**, 'Helpless')? A Watcher test that 'went wrong', causing the death of Faith's Watcher, may help to explain (almost) all of Faith's subsequent actions.

Soundtrack: 'Going to Hell' by The Brian Jonestone Massacre, 'The Background' by Third Eye Blind, and 'Cure' and 'Blue Sun' by Darling Violetta.

Novelisation: By James Laurence in *The Faith Trials* (Pocket Books, April 2001).

38

Beauty and the Beasts
[a.k.a. All Men Are Beasts]

US Transmission Date: 20 Oct. 1998
UK Transmission Date: 10 Sep. 1999 (Sky)
4 May 2000 (BBC2)

Writer: Marti Noxon
Director: James Whitmore Jnr
Cast: John Patrick White (Pete), Danielle Weeks (Debbie),
Phill Lewis (Mr Platt)
French title: *Les Belles Et Les Bêtes*. Très Cocteau
German title: *Dr Jeckyll and Mr Hyde*

It's Oz's 'time of the month', but Xander sleeps during his watch and a brutal murder may mean that Oz escaped. Buffy meets her counsellor Mr Platt and discusses her relationship with Angel. At the morgue, Willow collects evidence which proves the victim was mauled by a savage animal. Buffy encounters someone running through the woods. To her horror, it's Angel. Chaining him up, Buffy is unable to tell her friends about her discovery. Buffy visits Mr Platt's office, ready to confess that she needs help, but finds him dead. Scott's friend Pete and his girlfriend Debbie are in a storage room. Pete transforms into a monstrous creature and strikes Debbie. Oz notices Debbie's bruised eye, but she says she walked into a door. While Buffy and Willow confront Debbie, Pete goes to the library and finds Oz ready for transformation. Insane with jealousy, Pete attacks Oz as it begins. A chase follows in which Oz is tranquillised and Pete kills Debbie. He attacks Buffy but she is saved by Angel, who has escaped his chains. He recognises Buffy before collapsing.

Dudes and Babes: Faith appears not to have been joking when telling Buffy that Slaying makes her 'horny'. Their discussion about boys and Faith's observation about 'a good, down-low tickle' is only half-a-notch above *filthy* (compare Buffy's handling of the phallic crystal in **46**, 'Helpless'). In an episode all about repressed male sexual aggression, it's interesting that the two most direct references to sex are both from girls. (Willow tells Xander she and Oz have done a 'half monty', though, tactfully, she refuses to reveal which half.) Angel appearing almost naked and Faith dancing to her Walkman in the library are highlights.

It's a Designer Label!: Willow's nasty crimson and green jumper and Scott's yellow shirt vie for attention. Buffy's green top is great, but the last word goes to Willow's grey tights.

References: Willow seems to have an affinity for *Scooby Doo, Where Are You?* We've seen her wearing a *Scooby* T-shirt in an earlier episode and now we learn that she owns a *Scooby* lunchbox. Also, Jack London's *The Call of the Wild*, *The Full Monty*, 'Monopoly', Barbie and Ken dolls, *The Strange Case of Dr Jekyll and Mr Hyde*, *The Sound of Music*, *The English Patient* and the series *Manimal*.

Awesome!: Willow, Xander and Cordelia in the morgue examining the first victim's body. Giles is shot in the back by one of his friends aiming for someone else *again* (see **23**, 'Ted').

'You May Remember Me From Such Films As . . .': Phill Lewis was Steve Jessup in *City Slickers* and Dennis in *Heathers*.

Valley-Speak: Pete: 'Check out Scotty liking the manic-depressive chick.'

Xander: 'This guy is pretty barf-worthy. Can't we be else-where?'

Logic, Let Me Introduce You to This Window: When Oz transforms, he doesn't remove his clothes. During the trans-formation, there's no indication that Oz's clothes are ripping apart, but when we see Wolf-Oz, his clothes are gone. When Cordelia says 'Now I'm gonna be stuck with serious thoughts all day', a close shot of Xander reveals the strap of his bag is covering the right side of his collar. In the next shot, it's under his collar. Why is everybody sitting around in the library, waiting for Buffy to come in, at 5.25 p.m.?

Quote/Unquote: Mr Platt: 'Lots of people lose themselves in love, it's no shame. They write songs about it.'

Oz: 'You know that thing where you bail in the middle of an upsetting conversation? I have to do that.'

Notes: 'Pete's not like other guys, is he Debbie?' The issue of domestic violence is dealt with in much the same way as paren-tal abuse is in **23**, 'Ted' – by avoiding and demonising it. The episode is disturbingly misanthropic (for example, Faith's 'all men are beasts' speech, which I'm *very* uncomfortable with for all sorts of reasons, not least that the – female – writer has the same character talking about 'down-low tickles' in the same scene). Not only that, but the way to stop male violence towards women seems, from the resolution, to be female vio-lence back at them. Well, that's *one* solution, but it becomes even more suspect when Buffy (who, let's be honest, has taken out far more dangerous opponents than Pete) suddenly requires Angel to rescue her. There's an unpleasant, aggressive and thuggishly PC side to some of the points the episode makes. Too well written to be easily dismissed, but far too wrapped up in a handbag full of hate to be likable.

Giles says he has dreams that he saved Jenny (see **29**, 'Pas-sion'). He notes there is no record of anyone returning from the demon dimension, adding that time runs a very different course there. Buffy says, 'I know' (see **35**, 'Anne'). Sunnydale High has a marching jazz band in which Debbie and Jeff, the first victim, played.

Soundtrack: 'Teenage Hate Machine' by Marc Ferrari.

Joss Whedon's (Ironic) Comments: 'Someone mentioned

that the show has developed a feminist subtext. Well, I never! I just wanted to show a quiet, obedient girl learning to attract men through cosmetics and physical weakness. (Probably a mistake to cast the off-puttingly plain Miss Gellar, in that case.) But sometimes we can't control our creations. Forgive me.'

39

Homecoming

US Transmission Date: 3 Nov. 1998
UK Transmission Date: 17 Sep. 1999 (Sky)
11 May 2000 (BBC2)

Writer: David Greenwalt
Director: David Greenwalt
Cast: Ian Abercrombie (Old Man), Billy Maddox (Frawley),
Joseph Daube (Hans Gruenshtahler),
Jermyn Daube (Frederick Gruenshtahler),
Lee Everett (Candy Gorch), Tori McPetrie (Michelle Blake),
Jennifer Hetrick (Ms Mason), Chad Stahelski (Kulak)
French title: *Le Bal De Fin D'Année*
German title: *Die Qual Der Wahl*

While Cordelia plans her campaign for Homecoming Queen and Buffy breaks up with Scott, Mr Trick assembles a team of specialists to take part in Slayerfest '98 and rid him of Buffy and Faith. Buffy is furious she missed the yearbook photo session because of Cordelia's thoughtlessness and runs against her friend for Queen, putting Xander, Willow and Oz in an awkward position. They get Buffy and Cordelia together in a limo and tell them to work out their problems. Unfortunately the car is hijacked by Trick's men and Buffy and Cordelia take refuge in a cabin. Disposing of some of their enemies, they return to school and defeat the rest just in time to attend the Homecoming Queen announcement. They have both lost. Mr Trick arrives at City Hall, where Mayor Wilkins introduces himself.

Babes and Babes (Bring Your Own Subtext): Buffy tells Angel about Scott ('a nice solid guy – he makes me happy'), at which point Scott breaks up with Buffy and attends the

Homecoming with another girl. Trick refers to Buffy's 'nubile flesh', which proves what we already suspected, he's a vampire with *taste*. Xander notes that Buffy and Faith 'are in the library getting all sweaty', which *presumably* means they're training. Throw in Oz's reference to Buffy and Cordelia mud-wrestling and you have a slash-fiction fan's delight. In response to an Internet question about a lesbian relationship between Slayers, Joss Whedon commented, 'I just read the piece on Buffy and Faith . . . and by God, I think she's right! I can't believe I never saw it! (Actually, despite my facetious tone, it's a pretty damn convincing argument. But then, I think that's part of the attraction of the Buffyverse. It lends itself to polymorphously perverse subtext. It encourages it. I personally find romance in every relationship (with exceptions), I love all the characters, so I say Bring Your Own Subtext!)'

The Conspiracy Starts at Home Time: We finally meet the dirt-obsessed Mayor Wilkins. He reveals that he's aware Mr Trick is a vampire and he wants his help in eliminating the 'rebellious element' from Sunnydale. Wilkins says he's been Mayor for 'quite some time' and that this is 'an important year' (see **48**, 'Bad Girls'; **49**, 'Consequences'; **51**, 'Enemies'; **53**, 'Choices' and **55/56**, 'Graduation Day').

It's a Designer Label!: Buffy's gym shorts. Willow asks Xander if he remembers 'that eighth-grade cotillion and you had that clip-on?' It's worth noting that *everyone* looks great in their Homecoming clothes (Xander in a tux, Willow's long black dress, Buffy and Cordy's dresses). Watch out for Trick's crimson crushed-velvet jacket and orange tie. Candy Gorch's pink feather boa and purple satin pants are equally desperate.

References: Oz's line 'as Willow goes, so goes my nation' refers to a famous quote about General Motors. Cordelia says she's been doing 'the Vulcan Death-Grip' since she was four. Of course, as all Trekkies know, the Vulcan Death-Grip doesn't exist. Mr Trick makes an ironic comment about American frontiersman Daniel Boone (1735–1820). Flying ace Amelia Earhart (1898–1937) and author Maya Angelou (born 1928) are name-checked alongside an allusion to English evangelist John Wesley (1703–1791).

Bitch!: Faith's revenge on Scott over his break-up with Buffy, telling him, in front of his date, that the doctor says the itching, swelling and burning should clear up 'but we have to keep using the ointment.' 'And speaking of big heads, if I had a watermelon as big as Cordelia's, I'd be rich.' Buffy's strategy board lists the strengths and weaknesses of her opponents: Cordelia's strengths are: 'Popular with boys', 'Makes friends easily', 'Expensive clothes' and 'Perfect teeth'; while her weaknesses include 'Manipulative', 'Two-faced', 'Fake smile', 'Bad in sports', 'Superficial', 'No sense of humour' and 'Xander!' (Anyone else think the exclamation mark makes this *incredibly* mean?) Michelle's entries include (strengths): 'Nice', 'Popular', 'Friendly', 'Good cook' and 'Athletic'; (weaknesses): 'Bad skin', 'Wears polyester', 'PB Crazy', 'Dandruff' and 'Too much make-up.' Holly's list includes (strengths): 'Debating skills', 'Straight A', 'Nice' and 'Sweet'; (weaknesses): 'Few friends', 'Introvert' and 'Always studying'. Cordelia's opinion of 'I laughingly use the phrase "competition"' is: 'Holly Charlston: nice girl, brain-dead, doesn't have a prayer. Michelle Blake: open to all mankind, especially those with a letterman's jacket and a car. She could give me a run.' Once Buffy joins the race, it gets nasty: 'Crazy freak!', 'Vapid whore!', 'Do you have parents?', 'Yes, two of them, unlike some people!' Et cetera.

Awesome!: One of the *great* sequences as Buffy battles the yellow-skinned demon while Cordelia hits it with a cooking spatula. 'Cor, the gun!' shouts Buffy. Cordelia picks up the gun and fires wildly. 'Cordelia,' says Buffy, in resignation, 'the spatula!' 'Homecoming' also contains fine characterisation as Willow and Xander remember old times, speculate on the future, dance and kiss. Wonderful stuff. But it's Buffy and Cordelia's episode, with highlights being the scenes in the cabin, Cordy facing down Lyle Gorch and the disgusted looks on their faces at the end.

'You May Remember Me From Such Films and TV Series As . . .': Three-time Tony-nominated, German-born Harry Groener played Tam Elburn in the *Star Trek: The Next Generation* episode 'Tin Man'. He also appeared in *Amistad* and *Dance With Me*, the US version of *Dear John* (as Ralph Drang) and *Mad About You* (as Brockwell). Jack Plotnick was Edmond Kay in *Gods and Monsters* and had a recurring role as Barrett in *Ellen*. Ian Abercrombie was Justin Pitt in *Seinfeld*. Jennifer Hetrick played Jean Luc Picard's girlfriend Vash in *Star Trek: The Next Generation* and *Deep Space Nine* and Walter Skinner's wife in *The X-Files*. She was also Corrine Hammond in *L.A. Law*.

Don't Give Up the Day Job: Chad Stahelski, in addition to being David Boreanaz's stunt double, also worked on such films as *The Matrix, 8mm* and *Alien: Resurrection*.

Logic, Let Me Introduce You to This Window: After Buffy and Faith finish their training session Faith lays the punching pads on the table. Next shot, she's still holding them. The position of the rifle in Frawley's hands as Mr Trick introduces the Slayerfest participants changes between shots.

Quote/Unquote: Mr Trick: 'We all have the desire to win. Whether we're human, vampire . . . Whatever the hell you are, my brother. You got a spiny-looking head thing, I never seen that before.'

Willow: 'I'm not a friend, I'm a rabid dog who should be shot. But there are forces at work here. Dark, incomprehensible forces.'

Xander: 'How do you get from "chick fight" to "our fault"?' Willow: 'Because we felt so guilty about "The Fluke", we overcompensated helping Cordelia and we spun the whole group dynamic out of orbit and we're just a big meteor shower heading for Earth . . .'

Giles: 'We have to find Buffy. Something terrible's happened. Just kidding. Thought I'd give you a scare.'

Cordelia: 'Listen up, needle-brain. Buffy and I have taken out four of your cronies, not to mention your girlfriend.' Lyle: 'Wife!' Cordelia: 'Whatever!'

Notes: 'You've awakened the Prom Queen within.' What an astonishing piece of work. *Buffy*-as-sitcom taking such an *obvious* idea (two friends fight over who will be Homecoming Queen) and throwing in a bunch of misfit monsters for them to kill. This is what we probably all imagine American teenage life is like. If we've taken enough acid. The Buffy–Cordelia scenes in the cabin are some kind of series highlight to date. One of two back-to-back jewels that illustrate everything that is *great* about this series. Another twelve out of ten.

Buffy refers to **36**, 'Dead Man's Party', saying that lots of people came to her 'Welcome Home' party. Willow helpfully adds, 'They were killed by zombies.' Ms Moran was Buffy's favourite teacher in her class called 'Contemporary American Heroes'. Unfortunately, she doesn't remember Buffy at all. At Hemery, Buffy was 'Prom Princess', 'Fiesta Queen' and on the Cheerleading Squad (see **M1**; **3**, 'The Witch').
Soundtrack: 'Fell into the Loneliness' by Lori Carson, 'Jodie Foster' by The Pinehurst Kids, 'How' by Lisa Loeb, 'Fire Escape' by Fastball and 'She Knows' by Four Star Mary (the song that Oz supposedly wrote for Willow).

40
Band Candy

US Transmission Date: 10 Nov. 1998
UK Transmission Date: 24 Sep. 1999 (Sky)
18 May 2000 (BBC2)

Writer: Jane Espenson
Director: Michael Lange
Cast: Peg Stewart (Ms Barton)
French title: *Effet Chocolat*
German title: *Außer Rand und Band*
Spanish title: *Los Chocolates Embrujados*

The Mayor asks Mr Trick to help him collect a tribute to a demon and Trick subcontracts the sale of cursed chocolate to Ethan Rayne. Snyder makes the students sell the chocolate to raise money for the school band. Buffy sells her bars to Joyce and Giles and is surprised when Giles doesn't show up for school. She finds him at his home with Joyce, apparently working out a schedule to make it easier for Buffy to spend time with both of them. At the Bronze, Buffy and Willow notice lots of adults acting like rowdy teenagers. Buffy realises that there is something wrong with the candy. At the factory, she discovers her mother and Giles making out. Inside, Buffy finds Ethan, whose job was to divert the adults from the main objective, paying tribute to the demon Lurconis, who eats babies. In the sewers Buffy finds the babies, the demon and Mr Trick. While Buffy fights the vampires, Giles and Joyce move the babies out of harm's way. Lurconis, a huge serpentine creature, emerges. Buffy detaches a gas pipe and creates a blowtorch to defeat the demon.

Dreaming (As Blondie Once Said) is Free: One that we don't get to see. Buffy being chased by 'an improperly filled-in answer bubble screaming, "None of the above".'

Dudes and Babes: Joyce: 'So, why do they call you Ripper?' Giles: 'Wouldn't you like to know?' Oz imagines Giles was a 'pretty together' teen. Buffy corrects him: 'Giles at sixteen? Less "Together-Guy" more "Bad-Magik-Hates-the-World-Ticking-Time-Bomb-Guy".' When Joyce gives Buffy her pair of handcuffs, Buffy orders her to '*Never* tell me.' In **52**, 'Earshot', we find out what interaction occurred between Giles and Joyce. There are more gratuitous bare-torso shots of David Boreanaz and two plump miniskirted cheerleaders who walk behind Giles and Buffy in the final scene.

Authority Sucks!: 'Everybody expects me to do everything around here because I'm the principal. It's not fair.' Snyder says he got a commendation for being principal from the Mayor, who shook his hand twice. (Knowing what we subsequently do about Wilkins, it's to be hoped that Snyder wore gloves.) But he still ends up getting the kids to clean up the graffiti off the lockers. Some things never change.

The Conspiracy Starts at Home Time: The Mayor tells Mr Trick, 'I made certain deals to get where I am today. This demon requires its tribute', adding, 'That's what separates me from other politicians. I keep my campaign promises.' We see that his cupboard is full of skulls.

A Little Learning is a Dangerous Thing: Willow says Oz is the highest-scoring person (on SATs) never to graduate. It's unclear whether she's talking about just Sunnydale High or the whole country. Xander is against a system which 'discriminates against the uninformed'. But Cordelia is looking forward to the SATs, noting that she usually does well on standardised tests (see **42**, 'Lover's Walk'). Buffy says, 'We can study at the Bronze. A little dancing, a little cross-multiplying.'

Mom's Apple Pie: Buffy tells Joyce she's a good mom, but not the best, as she won't let her daughter drive. While they eat Chinese food (with chopsticks) there is a lengthy discussion on responsibility ('I don't need this much Active Parenting'). Once the cursed chocolate kicks in, we have something of a paradox.

Denial, Thy Names are Joyce and Rupert: Buffy: 'At least I got to the two of you before you actually did something.' Joyce: 'Right.' Giles: 'Indeed.' (Liars! See **52**, 'Earshot'.)

It's a Designer Label!: 'Mom started borrowing my clothes. There should be an age limit on Lycra pants,' notes Cordelia. One could say the same about Joyce and that miniskirt. On the plus side there's Buffy's red top and grey jogging pants, her green skirt, Willow's light-blue miniskirt and Cordy's tartan skirt. Minus points for Oz's yellow T-shirt, Willow's fluffy red jumper and orange trainers and Trick's purple shirt.

References: Cordy's dad takes copies of *Esquire* magazine and locks himself in the bathroom. Also, MTV's *The Real World*, Charles Dickens's *A Christmas Carol* ('The Ghost of Christmas Past'), Willy Loman from Arthur Miller's play *Death of a Salesman*, TV show *Nightline,* 70s soft-rockers Seals & Crofts, *The Rocky Horror Picture Show* ('Let's do the time warp again'), singer Billy Joel, the US sitcom *Welcome Back Kotter* (and the character Vinnie Barbarino played by John Travolta), country-and-western singer Juice Newton, actor Burt Reynolds, a misquote from *The Wild Ones* ('I just gotta see what you got') and Bow Wow Wow's 'I Want Candy'. 'Kiss Rocks!' refers to the American glam metal band. 'Louie Louie', a hit for the Kingsmen in 1963 and a classic song of teenage rebellion, is performed a cappella by lots of old guys. 'Now for the bonus question – and believe me when I say that a wrong answer *will* cost you all your points' is a general parody of game shows.

Bitch!: Giles and Joyce are at it this week: 'For God's sake, let your mum have a sodding candy bar' and 'You wanna slay stuff and I'm not allowed to do anything about it. Well, this is what I wanna do, so get off my back.' Respectively.

Awesome!: Buffy hitting Giles with the ball, blindfolded, and her double take when spotting her mother and Giles kissing ('Go away, we're busy'). Top marks for the characterisation of Giles,

Joyce and Snyder as teenagers with Tony Head's incredible cockney wide-boy ('Ooo, copper's got a *gun*!') *just* outdoing Armin Shimerman's equally valid interpretation of Snyder as a cowardly nerd who desperately wants to be part of the cool kids' scene ('I am *so* stoked'). Joyce, meanwhile, becomes what we suspected she was: a totally uncool, over-talkative, rather sly wannabe hanging around with the coolest guy in town (note the disgusted look on Giles's face when she asks if he likes Seals & Crofts). Kristine Sutherland's view of this is interesting: 'I found particularly painful the scene where we're listening to the music in Tony's apartment, and I thought Joss captured it perfectly. He's really ignoring me, he's completely into the music and I'm trying to figure out, as the girl, how to connect with him. It brought up a lot of those horribly painful adolescent feelings . . .'

Best moment of this remarkable episode: the *'Yes!'* from Giles, punching the air as Buffy hits Ethan.

Don't Give Up the Day Job: Writer/Producer Jane Espenson is a sitcom veteran who has written for *Dinosaurs*, *Ellen* and *Star Trek: Deep Space Nine*.

Valley-Speak: Buffy: '*Voilà*! Driveyness!' And: 'You guys are just wigging me out.'

Sex and Drugs and Rock'n'Roll and Cigarettes and Alcohol: Giles smokes and drinks red wine with Joyce while listening to Cream's 'Tales of Brave Ulysses'. ('I gotta get a band together,' he says as Eric Clapton's guitar solo starts and he adds, 'Listen to this bit.') 'You've got good albums,' notes Joyce (see **59**, 'The Harsh Light of Day').

'Whoa, Summers. You Drive Like a Spaz!': Snyder's comments are echoed by Buffy: 'Look at that dent the size of New Brunswick. I did that.' Joyce: 'Oh my God. What was I thinking when I bought that geek machine?' Later Joyce notes, 'Buffy assures me that it happened battling evil, so I'm letting her pay for it on the instalment plan.'

Logic, Let Me Introduce You to This Window: When Buffy drives her mom's jeep, a pair of headlights can be seen behind. The car appears to be no more than a few feet away, but when Buffy makes the right turn, it's much further. When Buffy bends down to switch on the radio, you can still see the headlights through the jeep's rear window, but seconds later there's no sign of it. Although the boxes of candy say 'Milkbar', Giles says that Buffy convinced him to buy twenty 'Cocoariffic' bars. Why do all of the spell-affected adults, regardless of their age, speak and act as though their teenage years were during the 70s? Giles's white T-shirt has a hole in the chest in some scenes, but this disappears in others. When he emerges after falling into the sewer, he seems remarkably dry and clean.

I Just *Love* Your Accent: Joyce says it must be very cool being from England. Giles's reply is: 'Not particularly!'

Quote/Unquote: Giles on the SATs: 'It's a rite of passage.' Buffy: 'Is it too late to join a tribe where they just pierce something or cut something off?'

Ms Barton: 'Willow. That's a tree . . . Are there any nachos in here, little tree?'

Mr Trick: 'That's the reason I love this country. You make a good product and the people will come to you. Of course, a lot of them are gonna die, but that's the other reason I love this country.'

Giles on Buffy's interrogation technique: 'You're *my* Slayer. Go knock his teeth down his throat.' And, to Snyder: 'You filthy little *ponce*. Are you afraid of a little demon?'

Buffy on Trick's parting shot: 'They never just leave. Always gotta say something.'

Notes: 'And *don't* do that.' It was going to take a work of *genius* to better **39**, 'Homecoming'. Here then, ladies and gentlemen, is 'Band Candy'; a work of *genius*! Again, the central idea is not new (adults acting like children, to the chagrin of the *real* children), but there's a cleverness to the presentation here that charms the viewer while they are rolling on the floor laughing. *Still* one of my favourite episodes. Thirteen out of ten.

Buffy says Giles is allergic to being late. Cordelia refers to her life before Xander as 'BX'. Snyder claims to have taken tae kwon do 'at the Y'. Scott Hope is mentioned by Angel (Buffy hasn't told him that she and Scott have broken up. See **39**, 'Homecoming').

Soundtrack: Aside from the Cream classic, 'Blasé' by Mad Cow, 'Violent' by Four Star Mary and 'Slip Jimmy' by Every Bit of Nothing.

Did You Know?: In Mike Hodges' 1987 film *A Prayer For The Dying*, Tony Head plays a cockney thug named Rupert. For his legion of female fans, it's a movie worth checking out as he removes most of his kit in the course of it.

Jane Espenson's Comments: Asked on the *Posting Board* how scripts are assigned, Jane noted, 'Usually it kind of rotates. Whoever has had the longest break writes the next one. But if one person pitched a specific idea, they usually get to write it (like 'Band Candy'). Or if a specific story calls for a specific kind of writing strength – Marti [Noxon] tends to get the big love-relationship stories. And then sometimes a writer's personal schedule will dictate which episodes they're available for . . .' Jane continues to cite 'Band Candy' as her favourite episode ('It was the first, and my original idea').

41

Revelations

US Transmission Date: 17 Nov. 1998
UK Transmission Date: 1 Oct. 1999 (Sky)
25 May 2000 (BBC2)

Writer: Douglas Petrie
Director: James A Contner
Cast: Serena Scott Thomas (Gwendolyn Post), Kate Rodger (Paramedic)
German title: *Der Handschuh Von Myhnegon*

Faith's new Watcher, Gwendolyn Post (Mrs), sets the group a task, the recovery of the Glove of Myhnegon. Gwendolyn has little respect for Giles and his frustration grows as he is unable to find any information on the demon Lagos, also searching for the glove. Xander sees Angel, and follows him back to the mansion, where he observes Buffy and Angel kissing. Buffy is quizzed by her friends, Giles feeling she has let him down. Faith finds an angry Xander at the Bronze and decides to kill Angel. Giles tells Gwendolyn he has recovered the Glove and she smashes a statue over his head. Xander alerts Buffy to Faith's intentions. Arriving at the mansion, Faith sees her new Watcher wrestling with Angel for the Glove and she attacks him but is stopped by Buffy. Gwendolyn finds the Glove and gains the ability to fire bolts of lightning. Buffy picks up a shard of glass and severs the glove from Gwendolyn, leaving Faith feeling betrayed.

Dudes and Babes: Gwendolyn is a typically Hitchcock-style villainess. Faith refers to Buffy's liaison with Angel, asking what it was like 'boinking the undead?' (See **25**, 'Surprise'.) Faith lists some of her ex-boyfriends as 'Ronnie (deadbeat); Steve (klepto); Kenny (drunk)'. She says her motto now is 'get some, get gone' (see **47**, 'The Zeppo'; **48**, 'Bad Girls').

A Little Learning is a Dangerous Thing: Books that the library *doesn't* possess include Hulme's *Paranormal Encyclopaedia* and *The Labyrinth Maps of Malta* (which *is* on order). Giles *does* have a copy of Sir Robert Kane's *Twilight Compendium*.

It's a Designer Label!: Oz's gold-lamé waistcoat is extremely rock-and-roll. So is Buffy's pink Bronze dress, though her 'bomb' ski-cap isn't. Faith's crimson leathers appear again.

References: *Mary Poppins*, *Marathon Man*.

Bitch!: Gwendolyn: 'Faith, a word of advice. You're an idiot.'

Awesome!: An exercise in 'synchronised Slaying': about ten minutes is taken up with one fight or another including Faith and Angel battling and the Buffy–Faith fight. Plus the effects as Gwendolyn is killed. Angel and Buffy's t'ai chi-style exercises are impressive. Best bit: the series of facial expressions Willow gives as Buffy fights the demon.

The Drugs Don't Work: 'Cold turkey', mentioned in this episode, is a euphemism for heroin withdrawal without the aid of a secondary drug, and is now used as a general term for quitting any form of addiction.

'You May Remember Me From Such Films As . . .': Serena Scott Thomas was in *The World is Not Enough*, *Let Him Have It* and played the Princess of Wales in *Diana: Her True Story*.

Don't Give Up the Day Job: Doug Petrie wrote the 1996 movie *Harriet The Spy* and episodes of *Clarissa Explains It All*.

Logic, Let Me Introduce You to This Window: While a frustrated Giles instructs Xander to find whatever information he can on Lagos, Willow stands on the upper level of the library. As Xander ascends the stairs, Willow is standing some distance from where she was in the previous shot. In the scene at Willow's locker, she hoists her backpack on to her right shoulder, then starts to close the locker door with her right hand. In the reverse-angle shot, Willow's right hand is on her shoulder strap while she closes the locker with her left. Why is Faith's door unlocked in the last scene when Buffy enters?

I Just *Love* Your Accent: Giles gets flustered when Gwendolyn arrives. (Buffy says, 'Interesting lady. Can I kill her?') Gwendolyn says there is talk within the Council that Giles has become a bit 'too American'. 'Him?' asks Buffy. (This is later revealed to be a lie, along with much else Gwendolyn says.) She notes at one point that she is 'completely knackered' training with Faith, who refers to her as 'Mary Poppins'. Gwen also uses lots of supposedly British expressions, such as 'everything's gone to Hell in a hand basket', and shares Giles's obsession with tea. *Must* be British, then. Xander believes Giles needs a qualified surgeon to remove the British flag from his butt.

Notes: 'Keeping secrets is a lot of work.' A case of 'after the Lord Mayor's Show'. There's little *wrong* with 'Revelations', indeed it's a Tasmanian devil of an episode, a whirlwind of manic violence. Perhaps it's only subtlety that's missing, although the final scenes and Faith's growing cynicism at the world signal the way her character will develop.

Giles indicates that a Watcher may have more than one Slayer, which contradicts what we thought we knew about the Watcher–Slayer relationship (see **21/22**, 'What's My Line?'). There are twelve cemeteries in Sunnydale. Xander notes Buffy has been 'killing zombies and torching sewer monsters' – references to **36**, 'Dead Man's Party', and **40**, 'Band Candy', respectively. Gwendolyn was sacked by the Watchers' Council for 'misuse of Dark Power'.

Soundtrack: 'Run' is the Four Star Mary song that Dingoes Ate My Baby mime to. Also 'West Of Here' by Lotion and 'Silver Dollar' by Lolly.

Novelisation: By James Laurence in *The Faith Trials* (Pocket Books, April 2001).

True Faith: 'The [script] said "Faith dancing wildly; a mix between Biker Chick and Trailer Trash",' Eliza Dushku told *Science Fiction World*. 'It's fun to play the animal instinct and get away with it, and get paid and have it called work. Totally kinky, but totally fun.'

42

Lover's Walk

US Transmission Date: 24 Nov. 1998
UK Transmission Date: 7 Oct. 1999 (Sky)
1 Jun. 2000 (BBC2)

Writer: David Vebber
Director: David Semel
Cast: Marc Burnham (Lenny), Suzanne Krull (Clerk)
French title: *Amours Contrariées*
German title: *Liebe Und Andere Schwierigkeiten*

Spike is back, having split with Drusilla. Desperate to win her back, he kidnaps Willow and Xander and threatens to kill them unless Willow performs a love spell. Buffy arrives home to find Spike telling his sob story to her mom, while a horrified Angel is unable to enter the house. Spike tells them what he's done with Willow and Xander, and they reluctantly agree to help him get what he needs and then get out of Sunnydale. Realising that their situation seems hopeless, Xander and Willow kiss, unaware that Oz and Cordelia have just arrived to rescue them. As Cordelia runs away upstairs, she falls and is impaled on a steel rod. Spike, Buffy and Angel fight a group of vampires. Spike is reawakened by the battle and decides to forget about the love spell and win Drusilla back by good old-fashioned torture. Cordelia survives but will not forgive Xander's betrayal.

Dudes and Babes: Spike's arrival mirrors the opening scene of **15**, 'School Hard' (his car crashing into the WELCOME TO SUNNYDALE sign). Everyone has a bad time, relationship-wise, in this episode but it's hard not to feel for poor Xander. That final scene with Cordy is heartbreaking.

The Conspiracy Starts at Home Time: The Mayor practising his putting says he would sell his soul for 'a decent short game' before adding, 'It's a bit late for that now.' He was aware of Spike's activities last year (and approved) but says this year is different and agrees with the deputy's suggestion to ask Mr Trick to send a 'welcome committee'.

A Little Learning is a Dangerous Thing: Willow's SAT score for English verbal of 740 (which she is disappointed with) is more than all of Xander's scores added up (since the maximum score in one subject is 800, this suggests that Xander's likely occupation once he finishes school will include the words 'Do you want fries with that?'). Buffy's combined score, 1,430, surprises not only everybody else, but also herself. Cordelia also seems to have done very well (as she predicted she would in **40**, 'Band Candy').

Mom's Apple Pie: Spike's talk with Joyce over a cup of hot chocolate is hilarious (he asks if she has any of those 'little marshmallow things'). She tells Buffy, 'You belong at a good old-fashioned college with keg parties and boys, not here with Hellmouths and vampires.' So, replace slaying with alcohol and sex? Interesting . . .

It's a Designer Label!: Horrible stuff first: Willow's red pants and stripy miniskirt, Xander's purple shirt. Buffy's green vest-type T-shirt and tight training pants make up for these. Willow's fluffy pink sweater appears (see **50**, 'Doppelgängland').

References: The title is an Elvis Costello song. Also, 'Cletus the Slack-Jawed Yokel' (from *The Simpsons*), *The Exorcist* and *Scanners* ('Her head span around and exploded') and *Weird Science*. The book Angel reads is *La Nausée* by French existentialist philosopher Jean-Paul Sartre (1905–80).

Bitch!: Spike on Drusilla after she gave him the 'we can be friends' nonsense: 'She just left, she didn't even care enough to cut off my head, or set me on fire. Is that too much to ask? Some little sign that she cared.'

Buffy to Spike: 'I violently dislike you.'

Awesome!: Spike at the Magic Box, asking for a leprosy curse to make Angel's 'parts fall off'! The brilliant action sequence of Buffy, Angel and Spike taking on dozens of vampires. The excellently timed funeral sight-gag.

Cigarettes and Alcohol: Spike spends half the episode wasted on Jack Daniel's.

Logic, Let Me Introduce You to This Window: While Spike holds the broken bottle to Willow's face, the position of her

hair changes from shot to shot. Something similar happens to
Spike's red shirt when he's pinned to the kitchen table by
Buffy and Angel. Why did Joyce leave the back door
unlocked? With all her concerns over her daughter's occupation (and after the events of **29**, 'Passion', and **36**, 'Dead Man's
Party'), you'd think she'd be more protective of the sanctity of
her own home.

I Just *Love* Your Accent: With Spike around the insults get
rather 'football-terrace', telling Buffy to 'shut your gob' and
referring to Angel as 'your great *pouf'* (see **85**, 'Fool for Love').

Quote/Unquote: Cordelia: 'What if they were kidnapped by
Colombian drug barons? They could be cutting off Xander's
ear right now? Or other parts.'

Spike on Buffy and Angel: 'You'll be in love till it kills you
both. You'll fight and you'll shag and you'll hate each other
till it makes you quake, but you'll never be friends. Love isn't
brains, children, it's blood. Blood screaming inside you to
work its will. I may be love's bitch, but at least I'm man
enough to admit it.'

Notes: 'Love's a funny thing.' Yet another confident, articulate, amusing vehicle for a production at the peak of its creativity. Very little happens, but it's a pivotal reaffirming link to the
past while pointing a way forward. It's *great* to see Spike back
(his scenes with Joyce are a joy) and he's, by far, the most
level-headed character in the episode. Simply gorgeous.

Xander wanted to be a fireman in sixth grade (see **81**, 'The
Replacement'). Cordelia has pictures of Xander and herself (and
some group shots) inside her locker. She says they were taken on
the pier. Oz can smell Willow when she's nearby (Cordy speculates it's 'some residual werewolf thing', see **75**, 'New Moon
Rising'). Spike says he used to bring Dru rats in bed along with
the morning paper. After leaving Sunnydale, they went to Brazil
but she never forgave him for his pact with Buffy. She flirted
frequently, including a tryst with a 'Chaos Demon' (who Spike
describes as 'all slime and antlers, they're disgusting', see **85**,
'Fool for Love'). The US broadcast was followed by an advert
for the phone service '1-800-Collect' featuring Sarah Michelle
Gellar and David Boreanaz in character with a prize of a walk-
on part in an upcoming *Buffy* episode (see **54**, 'The Prom').

Soundtrack: Contrary to fan-myth the version of 'My Way' at the end is *not* by Sid Vicious, but rather is a sound-alike cover by Gary Oldman from the soundtrack of *Sid and Nancy*.

Critique: *Shivers* reviewer Ian Atkins was fulsome in his praise: 'You would have to be undead if you did not think "Lover's Walk" was a classic episode of *Buffy*, and a beautiful piece of television too. After "Homecoming" and "Band Candy", it's good to see that the show does not need to rely on laughs for an episode to work . . . The main reason is because the episode presents a situation most viewers have been in: of love going wrong when reality breaks through the violins and roses. Pretence, and denial, can only go so far. It's almost painful to watch . . . The sad final montage of broken-hearted, lost souls is remarkably powerful and needs no words.'

The Comic: In another continuity-knitting exercise, April 1999 saw Dark Horse's one-shot comic *Spike and Dru: Paint the Town Red*, co-written by James Marsters and Christopher Golden, which takes place between **34**, 'Becoming' Part 2, and **42**, 'Lover's Walk', with the couple living (and killing) in Turkey.

43
The Wish

US Transmission Date: 8 Dec. 1998
UK Transmission Date: 8 Oct. 1999 (Sky)
7 Jun. 2000 (BBC2)

Writer: Marti Noxon
Director: David Greenwalt
Cast: Nicole Bilderback (Cordette #1), Nathan Anderson (John Lee),
Mariah O'Brien (Nancy), Gary Imhoff (Teacher),
Robert Covarrubias (Caretaker)
French title: *Meilleurs Vœux De Cordelia*
German title: *Was Wäre Wenn . . .*

When new girl Anya asks Cordelia if she wishes things were different, Cordy wishes Buffy had never come to Sunnydale, since that was when all of her problems started. In the blinking of an eye, Cordy finds herself in the world she wished for: a terrifying grey place of tiny classes, horrible clothes and rampant vampire activity; a world where Xander and Willow are still together, even in death; where The Master lives and is about to unleash the ultimate terror on mankind. Giles and his 'white hats' try to fight forces against which their weapons are useless, in a world made by Anyanka the 'Patron Saint of Scorned Women' and Cordelia's wish. Buffy arrives but she dies at the hands of The Master just as Giles smashes Anyanka's amulet and puts the world to rights.

It's a Wonderful What?!: Lots of shows have done 'what if?' treatments, *Moonlighting*'s 'It's a Wonderful Job' being a good example. The 'dark' versions of the regulars may have been suggested by the 'Mirror Universe' in *Star Trek*. (The characterisation of Evil-Willow owes much to the mirror Major Kira in *Deep Space Nine*.)

Dudes and Babes: Willow in leather, licking Angel. *Oh yes*!

It's a Designer Label!: Cordelia has a Prada bag, which Anya recognises (Cordy says most people in Sunnydale can't tell the difference between Prada and Payless – a discount shoe chain). She asks if Anya's amulet is a Gucci. There's a reference to *W* ('the fashion magazine for the discerning woman').

References: Buffy calls Giles 'Jeeves', referring to PG Wodehouse's Jeeves and Wooster novels. 'What's done is done' is from *Macbeth*, while there are allusions to Smokey Robinson and the Miracles' 'Tears of a Clown', Sam and Dave's 'Soul Man', Aldous Huxley's *Brave New World*, *Superman* comics ('Bizarroland') and *Star Trek* ('Your logic doesn't resemble our Earth logic').

Bitch!: Harmony suggests Cordy date Jonathan: 'He won't cheat on you. At least for a week.'

Awesome!: The sequence in which Willow and Xander kill Cordelia (while Giles can only watch) is one of the most disturbing in the series, while the slow-motion deaths of Xander, Willow and Buffy are extraordinary.

Surprise!: The end of act one, Anya revealed as a demon. 'Done!'

'You May Remember Me From Such TV Series As . . .': Emma Caulfield played Lorraine Miller in *General Hospital* and Susan Keats in *Beverly Hills 90210*.

Valley-Speak: Buffy: 'You're acting a little schizo.' And: 'Slaying's a rough gig.'

Xander: 'Slap my hand, soul man.'

Logic, Let Me Introduce You to This Window: The last cut that Cordelia makes to Xander's photograph is around chin level. However, when we see it burning the photo includes Xander's chest.

Quote/Unquote: Cordelia: 'Buffy changes it. It was better, I mean the clothes alone. The people were happy. Mostly.'

Buffy: 'We fight, we die. Wishing doesn't change that.'

Buffy: 'This is a "get in my pants thing"? You guys in Sunnydale talk like I'm the Second Coming.'

Anya: 'You trusting fool. How do you know the other world is any better than this?' Giles: 'Because it *has* to be.'

Those Prosthetics?: Alyson Hannigan confirmed: 'They're quite comfortable . . . They're squishy. It was fun to be evil for a week, but if you had to do it week in and week out your face would fall off with all that glue.'

Notes: 'Don't you kind of wish . . .?' Fan-fiction-in-the-area. Such an *obvious* idea, so well done. The characterisation of the alternative-universe regulars is magnificent with Tony Head's anguished, out-of-his-league Giles just topping Sarah Michelle's portrayal of a scarred Buffy who has never experienced Giles's influence and, as a result, is hardened and cynical (like Faith) living only for slaying. Plus the little things like the cloves of garlic on the school lockers to remind us that we've wandered into another world. And Willow in leather, mustn't forget *that*.

There's a reference to Cordelia being bitten by a snake in **31**, 'I Only Have Eyes for You', to Angel having previously seen Buffy in 1996 in **33**, 'Becoming' Part 1, and Amy (see **3**, 'The Witch'; **28**, 'Bewitched, Bothered and Bewildered'; **45**, 'Gingerbread'). In the world in which Buffy never came to Sunnydale, Willow and Xander were turned into vampires and the Harvest happened. Giles runs a motley band of vampire hunters called 'the white hats' (who include Oz and Larry). He speaks to Buffy's Watcher (is it Merrick?), who tells him that she is currently in Cleveland. Giles refers to Sunnydale as '*a* Hellmouth', which indicates there is more than one. Nancy notes that vampires are attracted by bright colours.

Soundtrack: 'Tired of Being Alone' by The Spies, 'Dedicated to Pain' by Plastic and 'Never Noticed' by Gingersol.

Critique: According to *SFX*, 'The Wish' was: 'Another chance for the main cast to play against type . . . It's a sign of a series that is supremely confident in its writers and actors, that they feel they can do fun like this. The final scene is comic genius, with Cordelia making increasingly nasty wishes and Anya desperately but impotently trying to grant them.'

44

Amends
[a.k.a. A Buffy Christmas]

US Transmission Date: 15 Dec. 1998
UK Transmission Date: 14 Oct. 1999 (Sky)
14 Jun. 2000 (BBC2)

Writer: Joss Whedon
Director: Joss Whedon
Cast: Shane Barach (Daniel), Edward Edwards (Male Ghost),
Cornelia Hayes O'Herlihy (Margaret), Mark Kriski (Weatherman),
Tom Michael Bailey (Tree Seller Guy)
French title: *Le Soleil De Noël*
German title: *Heimsuchungen*

Christmas is coming, but for Angel (reliving, in his dreams, the numerous murders he has committed) it isn't a time of festive cheer. Angel visits Giles for help but is distracted by the 'ghost' of Jenny Calendar. Buffy confides in Giles that she shared Angel's dream. Jenny tells Angel that he is losing his soul again and killing Buffy is the only act that will bring him peace. Giles links these manifestations to the Harbingers, a group of priests who can summon the First, a name given to Absolute Evil. Angel contemplates suicide but is saved by a combination of Buffy's persuasion and a freak snow storm.

Dreaming (As Blondie Once Said) is Free: Buffy's line about making 'guest spots' in Angel's dreams may be a reference to the *Angel* spin-off. His dreams (shared with Buffy) contain an interesting balance of historical fact (the murders of Daniel and

Margaret), surrealist nightmares (the scary monks, Buffy appearing at the Victorian dinner party) and erotic stimulation of the moist variety (*that* night with Buffy – see **25**, 'Surprise').

Dudes and Babes: Nice hair and moustache combination in the 1838 sequences but Boreanaz's Irish accent is still woefully naff (see **33**, 'Becoming' Part 1). Margaret's description of Angel before Darla got to him is of a 'drunken, whoring layabout' who was a disappointment to his parents and whose only success in life was to die before he got syphilis.

Mom's Apple Pie: Christmas in the Summers household seems nice and relaxed, despite Buffy suggesting, 'You're still number one with the guilt trip, Mom.'

Denial, Thy Name is Joyce: Watch Joyce's reaction to Buffy's suggestion that they invite Giles around to Christmas dinner.

It's a Designer Label!: Xander's trampy red sweatshirt is a definite black mark, but on the plus side we have Buffy's blue shirt and white overcoat, Willow's slinky red dress and Faith's extremely short miniskirt.

References: A cheesy version of 'Joy to the World' is heard when Buffy and Joyce visit the tree farm. Also, David Bowie's 'Scary Monsters (And Super Creeps)'. Giles quotes from the Crystals' 'He's a Rebel'.

Bitch!: Cordy will spend Christmas skiing in Aspen, she gleefully tells her former friends.

Awesome!: Two great sequences – Giles inviting Angel into his home at the point of a crossbow and Oz and Willow deciding *not* to have sex.

'You May Remember Me From Such Films and TV Series As . . .': Cornelia Hayes O'Herlihy played the teenage Princess Margaret in *Gods and Monsters*. Before moving to America, she appeared in a couple of episodes of *Newman and Baddiel in Pieces*.

Don't Give Up the Day Job: Although Mark Kriski often plays news reporters (he's in both of the *Speed* movies) he's a *real* weatherman for KTLA Morning News in Los Angeles.

Valley-Speak: Buffy: 'These are the guys working the mojo on Angel?'

Logic, Let Me Introduce You to This Window: The snowdrift seems to be the quickest in meteorological history. (Is it supposed to be magical and/or at the intervention of some higher power? If so, then we're getting frighteningly close to *Quantum Leap* territory. See **Joss Whedon's Comments**.)

I Just *Love* Your Accent: Buffy reads an ancient text about a child being born of a man and a goat, who had two heads the first of which 'shall speak only in riddles'. 'No wonder you like this stuff,' she tells Giles. 'It's like reading the *Sun*' – a reference to the British tabloid newspaper. I always had Giles figured for a *Times* man.

Quote/Unquote: Angel asks 'Jenny' what she wants: 'I wanna die in bed surrounded by fat grandchildren, but I guess *that's* off the menu.'

Xander: 'That's the Christmas spirit.' Willow: 'Hello? Still Jewish. Hanukkah spirit, I believe that was.'

'Jenny': 'I'm not a demon, little girl, I'm something you can't even conceive . . . I am the thing the darkness fears.'

Notes: 'I think we're losing him.' Redemption is the theme of this variant on *A Christmas Carol*. In places the ideas are far better than the execution. As with **35**, 'Anne', this deals with potentially massive subjects that then get pushed into the background. This is, theoretically, the most dangerous enemy that Buffy has ever encountered, but there's no real ending. The good stuff on offer is mostly in the way of characterisation.

Angel says vampires aren't 'big on Christmas'. Is it the commercialisation they object to, or just the Christianity? Xander always sleeps outdoors on Christmas Eve (he says it's so that he can look at the stars and feel the 'nature vibe' though, in reality, Cordelia reveals it's so he can avoid his family's drunken fights). What drink is chilling in the ice bucket on Willow's coffee table? It looks like a two-litre bottle of either Sprite or 7-Up. Two (seemingly fictitious) films are playing at the Sunnydale cinema. *Abilene* (rated PG), and one that begins *Pray For* . . . The two books Giles gives Xander and Buffy for research purposes are *The Black Chronicles* and *The Diary of Lucius Temple*.

Joss Whedon's Comments: 'The snow was not evil! The snow was good. It was "hope",' Joss told the *Posting Board*. 'Was the snow a cheap *Deus Ex Machina*? Well, obviously I don't think so or I would avoid the question . . . I know some people here thought it was corny, but I didn't just pull it out of a hat. The whole episode was leading to that, it was the point, not just a way to end it . . . Was it God? Well, I'm an atheist, but it's hard to ignore the idea of a "Christmas miracle" here (though "Pray" on the marquee was an unintentional coincidence). The Christian mythos has a powerful fascination to me and it bleeds into my storytelling. Redemption, hope, purpose, Santa, these all are important to me, whether I believe in an afterlife or some universal structure or not. I certainly don't mind a strictly Christian interpretation being placed on this episode by those who believe that – I just hope it's not limited to that.'

Soundtrack: Willow's attempt to seduce Oz is accompanied by 'Can't Get Enough of Your Love, Babe' by the Walrus of Lurv himself, Barry White.

45

Gingerbread

US Transmission Date: 12 Jan. 1999
UK Transmission Date: 15 Oct. 1999 (Sky)
21 Jun. 2000 (BBC2)

Teleplay: Jane Espenson
Story: Thania St John, Jane Espenson
Director: James Whitmore Jnr
Cast: Jordan Baker (Sheila Rosenberg), Lindsay Taylor (Little Girl),
Shawn Pyfrom (Little Boy), Blake Swendson (Michael),
Grant Garrison (Roy), Roger Morrissey (Demon), Daniel Tamm (MOOster)
French title: *Intolérance*
German title: Appropriately, *Hänsel Und Gretel*

The discovery of two children's bodies by Joyce Summers has a profound effect on life in Sunnydale. Apparently the work of occultists, it leads to a witch hunt within the town from which no one is immune. Willow, Amy and eventually Buffy are targeted while Giles's books are confiscated, leaving him to rely on the Internet. Oz sends a message to Willow, who discovers that these same children have been repeatedly murdered every fifty years back to their origins in the 'Hansel and Gretel' fairy tale. Buffy, Willow and Amy are tied to stakes in City Hall to be burned alive. Giles and Cordelia stop the ceremony and reveal the children to be a hideous demon which Buffy impales with the stake she is tied to.

Authority Sucks!: Snyder's glee at being given the power to search the lockers: 'This is a glorious day for principals everywhere. No pathetic whining about students' rights. Just a long row of lockers and a man with a key.'

Mom's Milk of Human Bigotry: Joyce's 'bonding visit' to see what Buffy does (complete with thermos flask and sandwiches) goes disastrously wrong and she finds herself in her worst nightmare. She says that for too long she's been too afraid to speak out and that silence is 'the town's disease'. Her setting up of Mothers Opposed to the Occult ('nice acronym, Mom') turns Sunnydale into Salem. Oh well, we all make mistakes.

Denial, Thy Names are Joyce and Rupert: The awkward scene between them is really funny. ('It's been a while', 'Not since . . . a while'.)

Denial, Thy Name is Sheila Rosenberg: Willow's mom is an academic, the co-author of a recent paper on 'The Rise of Mysticism Among Adolescents'. The implication (of not noticing her daughter's five-month-old haircut and the last long chat they had being about a children's TV show) is that she and Willow don't talk much. She believes Willow's claim to be a witch is delusional and 'a cry for discipline', though she later says, 'It seems I've been rather closed-minded.' Willow later tells Buffy that her mother is doing 'that selective-memory thing your mom used to be so good at'. Sheila *does* remember that Willow is dating a musician and Oz must attend the Rosenbergs for dinner next week.

It's a Designer Label!: Buffy's blue frock coat and pink jumper. Cordelia says her hairspray is imported and costs $45.

References: *My Friend Flicka,* the pre-school TV show *Mr Roger's Neighbourhood* and the puppet King Friday (1968 to date) and *Apocalypse Now* ('I love the smell of desperate librarian in the morning') are referenced, along with the Salem witch trials. Xander says, 'Oh man, it's Nazi Germany and I've got *Playboy*s in my locker', and refers to 'Jack and the Beanstalk'. The writer of the article Willow finds is 'Howard Fine', the name of two of the Three Stooges.

Bitch!: Cordelia: 'Everyone knows that witches killed those kids and Amy is a witch. And Michael is whatever a boy witch is, plus being the poster child for "yuck". If you're going to hang with them, expect badness 'coz that's what you get when you hang with freaks and losers. Believe me, I know. That was a pointed comment about me hanging with you guys.'

Giles refers to Snyder as 'that twisted little homunculus'.

Awesome!: The shocking pre-title sequence (Joyce's horrified cry of 'It's Mr Sanderson from the bank' would be comical in other circumstances). The Giles, Xander, Oz and Buffy scenes in the library; an example of a minimalist setting helping with the development of a storyline. And Oz and Xander's incompetent attempts to save Buffy and Willow.

It's *That* Idea Again: Willow's mother calls Buffy 'Bunny' (see U1).

Don't Give Up the Day Job: Co-writer Thania St John would subsequently write for and produce the WB's other *great* fantasy show of the era, *Roswell*. Grant Garrison also has a flourishing career as a carpenter and art labourer on films like *Dreammaster: The Erotic Invader* and *Cyberella: Forbidden Passions*. Roger Morrisey started his career as a dolly grip on films like *Access Denied* and *Silent Lies* before acting in *Dizzyland* and *Tale of the Mummy*.

Valley-Speak: Buffy on Joyce: 'She's completely wigging.'

Logic, Let Me Introduce You to This Window: During the locker search, a cop is looking through a coin purse behind Snyder. Some time later the same cop is looking through the same purse (maybe Snyder was right about how stupid the Sunnydale police are). For the final scene with Buffy and Willow in the bedroom, we first see an establishing shot which reveals it's night and the lighting is appropriate for this. However, the rest of the scene looks like it takes place in the middle of the day. Where did those pictures of Hans and Greta Strauss come from? It's pretty strange that the residents of Sunnydale are holding a witch burning indoors. A more politically correct name for Joyce's group would have been '*Parents* Opposed to the Occult', but that would have made the acronym even more unfortunate.

I Just *Love* Your Accent: Giles: 'There is a fringe theory, held by a few folklorists, that some regional stories have actual, very literal antecedents.' Buffy: 'And in some language that's English?' Giles believes the murders may be the work of European Wiccan covens.

Quote/Unquote: Joyce: 'Good, honey! Kill him!'

Buffy: 'We need those books.' Giles: 'Believe me, I tried to tell that to the nice man with the big gun.'

Snyder: 'Just how is *Blood Rites and Sacrifices* appropriate material for a public school library? Chess Club branching out?' (As with a lot of questions asked in this episode, you've got to wonder why somebody hasn't asked it before.)

Buffy, on MOO: 'Who came up with that lame name?' Snyder: 'That would be the founder. I believe you call her "Mom".'

Willow: 'I'm a witch. I can make pencils float. And I can summon the four elements. OK, two, but four soon. And I'm dating a musician . . . I worship Beelzebub. I do his biddings. Do you see any goats around? No, because I sacrificed them . . . Prince of Night, I summon you. Come fill me with your black, naughty evil.'

Buffy: 'I'm like that kid in the story, the boy that stuck his finger in the duck.' Angel: 'Dyke. It's another word for dam.' Buffy: 'OK, that story makes a lot more sense now.'

Willow: 'Another step and you will all feel my power.' Buffy: 'What're you gonna do, float a pencil at them?'

Notes: 'How many of us have lost someone who just disappeared? Or got skinned?' There's a *lot* of anger in this episode. Its *probable* target are those people who use sudden violent incidents to pursue an agenda of censorship. How ironic it was that just months afterwards they'd be out in force again, with *Buffy* on their hitlist (it was really disturbing watching this episode mere days after the Littleton High School massacre with news programmes full of similarly hysterical reactions from people in search of *anyone* to blame). The anger in 'witch hunt' stories is often blind, but I'll give any episode that rages against being judgemental in such a refreshingly honest manner ten out of ten for effort. And, astonishingly considering the subject matter, 'Gingerbread' is also, in places, *really* funny.

Slayers are not supposed to kill people (see **23**, 'Ted'; **48**,

'Bad Girls'), though Buffy's horrified 'someone with a *soul* did this?' suggests breaking that rule is on her mind. It's Buffy's birthday next week (see **46**, 'Helpless'). Cordelia asks Giles how many times he's been knocked out and (as with Buffy constantly allowing herself to get distracted by diversionary tactics) he does, indeed, seem to fall for that one rather a lot (see **39**, 'Homecoming'). He has the ability to pick locks with a hairpin (Cordelia notes, 'You really *were* the little youthful offender, weren't you?' see **36**, 'Dead Man's Party'; **40**, 'Band Candy'). Amy performs the same spell as she did on Buffy in **28**, 'Bewitched, Bothered and Bewildered', with similar results, turning *herself* into a rat. Buffy and Willow are still trying to reverse the spell at the end of the episode (see **46**, 'Helpless'). Giles has somehow found his way into the 'Frisky Watchers' Chat Room'.
Novelisation: By Yvonne Navarro in *The Willow Files Vol. 2* (Pocket Books, February 2001).
Should the Bible Be Banned?: Buffy: 'Maybe next time that the world is getting sucked into Hell, I won't be able to stop it because the anti-Hell-sucking book isn't on the Approved Reading List.' It was inevitable that this episode would happen sooner or later. The Christian Right in America have never quite known what to make of *Buffy* – the plethora of Wiccan elements was an immediate cause for concern, but essentially it was about teenage good fighting evil so they couldn't complain on that score without dragging *The Hardy Boys* and *Nancy Drew* into the equation and, despite never quite knowing if it took place in a Christian universe or not, *Buffy* seemed to achieve 'moral acceptability'. That was until the magic 's' word ('sex') started cropping up. When Buffy slept with Angel in **25**, 'Surprise', it was open target practice on the series for anybody with access to the Old Testament and a computer and the Net was swamped with warning articles emanating from the Bible Belt (real 'Watch *Buffy the Vampire Slayer* and be damned for eternity' stuff). Whether 'Gingerbread' was a reaction to this (albeit brief) wave of hysteria is unknown (certainly the episode has been used by fans to rub in the face of any religious objector ever since). Interestingly, however, there is little criticism of religion in either the series in general or 'Gingerbread' itself (that would be commercial suicide in a TV industry still dominated by

advertising and network nervousness of offending *anyone*). Instead, what 'Gingerbread' *does* question, vocally and angrily, is a more disturbing saga. In America, many school and public libraries ban certain books. The website http://www.cs.cmu.edu/People/spok/most-banned.html lists the fifty most commonly suppressed, including works by William Shakespeare, John Steinbeck, JD Salinger, Mark Twain, Roald Dahl, Maya Angelou, William Golding, Kurt Vonnegut, Alice Walker and Margaret Atwood. It's sad that a nation that promotes freedom of speech has within it elements that seek to limit this on their own people. (Joyce's line 'MOO just wants to weed out the offensive material' seems chillingly realistic.) Readers can find more information at http://www.ala.org/bbooks/ the American Library Association's webpage.

Pagan Man Wasn't *Just* an Aftershave: Recognised by both the Home Office and the Church of England as a bona fide religion, paganism involves a wide body of beliefs, including Wicca, druidry and shamanism, which have their roots in the world's pre-Christian nature religions. The Pagan Federation was set up in 1971 to help counter misconceptions about Satanism and the like. It is estimated that today there are over 50,000 pagans in the UK alone. Federation spokesperson Andy Norfolk was quoted in *Alternative Metro* as saying that TV programmes such as *Buffy* and *Charmed* have greatly helped to increase the profile of paganism: 'Stories of young women who use magic to battle bad guys could be seen as positive role models.'

Jane Espenson's Comments: Jane explained 'Gingerbread's creation on the *Posting Board*: 'Thania St John and I never met. She pitched the "parent's group, witch-burning" idea a long time ago. I pitched a "book burning" idea. Joss meshed 'em, I added "Hansel and Gretel" and someone arranged the shared "story by" credit. I did talk with Thania on the phone after the episode had aired and she seemed great – I'm glad she's doing well on *Roswell*.' In another interview with the *Raven's Realm* website, Jane explained in detail her interaction with the cast: 'I have the opportunity to see the actors every day if I want to. This morning I had a long talk with Tony [Head]. So far I really haven't had actors pitching story ideas at me. I think they know that has to go through Joss.'

46

Helpless

US Transmission Date: 19 Jan. 1999
UK Transmission Date: 21 Oct. 1999 (Sky)
12 Jul. 2000 (BBC2)

Writer: David Fury
Director: James A Contner
Cast: Jeff Kober (Zackary Kralik), Dominic Keating (Blair),
David Hayon-Jones (Hobson), Nick Cornish (Guy),
Don Dowe (Construction Worker)
French title: *Sans Défense*
German title: *Die Reifeprüfung*

As her eighteenth birthday approaches Buffy suffers dizzy spells and weakness that suggests she is losing her powers. In reality she is being drugged by Giles as part of the *Cruciamentum*, a ritual that the Slayer undergoes to prove their resourcefulness. The weakened Slayer must survive an encounter with a vampire, in Buffy's case the insane Zackary Kralik. All does not go according to the plans of Chief Watcher Quentin Travers, Kralik escaping and abducting Joyce. Giles tells Buffy the truth, to her disgust. Buffy goes in search of Kralik, despite her lack of strength. She cleverly manipulates Kralik into drinking holy water. Travers commends Buffy on her successful passing of the test. However, since Giles demonstrates a relationship with Buffy that the Council deems too close, he is relieved of his Watcher duties.

Dudes and Babes: Giles is at his most toe-curlingly sexy in this episode, while there's an extremely gratuitous shot of Boreanaz's rippling biceps. If that had been one of the girls, everybody would be crying 'exploitation'.

Authority Sucks!: Quentin's treatment of Giles. This is the first hint that the Watchers' Council is a subdivision of a small fascist dictatorship. (See **90**, 'Checkpoint'.)

A Little Learning is a Dangerous Thing: Cordelia has a paper to research on Bosnia.

Mom's For Dinner: Kralik killed and ate his own mother, something he takes great delight in telling Joyce.

It's a Designer Label!: Buffy's All Saints-style combat pants. Another triumph for Willow: a pair of suitably horrible hats (a red tea-cosy-bobble one and a yellow abomination), a nasty yellow jumper and pink miniskirt.

References: The 1988 Olympic figure-skating champion and *South Park*-icon Brian Boitano, Bizet's opera *Carmen*, and *Superman*. Angel's present for Buffy is *Sonnets from the Portuguese* by Elizabeth Barrett Browning (see **3**, 'The Witch') inscribed 'Always'. *Cruciamentum* is Latin for torment.

Bitch!: Cordelia tells one potential suitor that he shouldn't take her flirting seriously as she is on the rebound (from Xander).

Awesome!: Buffy and Angel working out, Kralik's death sequence and Xander and Oz's discussion on what sort of kryptonite is deadly to Superman (Oz is right: green is deadly, red mutates and gold drains power).

The Drugs Don't Work: The pills that Kralik so desperately needs get both Blair and Kralik himself killed.

'You May Remember Me From Such Films, TV Series and Adverts As . . .': Jeff Kober played Bear in the memorable *X-Files* episode 'Ice', was Dodger in *China Beach* and Booga in *Tank Girl*. Readers may recognise him as 'Ray, the voice of Reef Radio' in those annoying Bacardi adverts. Harris Yulin is a character actor *par excellence*, appearing in *Bean*, *Clear and Present Danger*, *Scarface* and *Ghostbusters II*. In one of those coincidences that only seems to crop up in the crazy world of TV books, on the day that I viewed this episode, I stopped the video tape and playing on TV at that moment was an episode of *Ironside* featuring a younger Mr Yulin.

Valley-Speak: Buffy: 'Did I zone out on you?' And she gives Quentin that old standby: 'Bite me!'

Cordelia: 'First of all, *posse*? *Passé*! Second of all, anyone with a teaspoon of brains knows not to take my flirting seriously. Especially with my extenuating circumstances.'

Logic, Let Me Introduce You to This Window: The last knife that Buffy throws in the library breaks a glass object. However, whenever the camera focuses on the target, there's nothing made of glass nearby. Were Hobson and Blair's deaths part of Quentin's plan from the beginning? Kralik can be photographed (see **M1**, the movie) despite a camera using mirrors as part of its focusing mechanism (see **11**, 'Out of Sight, Out of Mind'; **21**, 'What's My Line?' Part 1 and *Angel*: 'Are You Now or Have You Ever Been?'). Buffy says she and her dad go to the Ice Show every year for her birthday, but there was no mention of this last year during **25**, 'Surprise'. Buffy seems to push the bookcase on to Blair rather easily considering how weak she is. She must have switched Kralik's water with the holy water amazingly quickly.

I Just *Love* Your Accent: Where is Quentin from? He certainly doesn't sound English. Giles says he doesn't give 'a rat's arse' about the Council's orders, and refers to the *Cruciamentum* as a dozen-century-old 'archaic exercise in cruelty'.

Quote/Unquote: Angel on Buffy's heart: 'I could see that you held it before you for everyone to see and I worried that it would be bruised or torn. More than anything in my life, I wanted to keep it safe, to warm it with my own.' Buffy: 'That's beautiful. Or, taken literally, incredibly gross.'

Buffy: 'Hummers. Big turnoff. I like guys who can remember the lyrics.'

Notes: 'I don't *know* you.' A story that manages to rise above voyeurism just long enough to become a hymn to the power of intelligence over superstition. Betrayal is the key theme in a modern 'Little Red Riding Hood' variant that relies on an old fan-fiction standby, setting up a character to be hurt, so they can be comforted. An important piece of the developing story-arc, but 'Helpless' is hard work at times, and difficult to enjoy.

Willow went to see *Snoopy on Ice* when she was small (her father took her backstage and she got so scared she threw up on Woodstock). Faith is on one of her 'unannounced walk-abouts'. There are numerous continuity references, including Giles saying Buffy may have a 'bad flu bug' (see **30**, 'Killed By Death'), Angel telling Buffy he saw her before she became the Slayer (see **33**, 'Becoming' Part 1), references to the parties in **25**, 'Surprise', and **36**, 'Dead Man's Party', Buffy's love of skating in **25**, 'Surprise', 'Mr Pointy' the stake from **33**, 'Becoming' Part 1, and Buffy's birthday present last year being 'a severed arm in a box' (see **25**, 'Surprise'). Amy is still a rat (see **45**, 'Gingerbread'). There is no evidence that Blair fed on Kralik to become a vampire (Kralik's dialogue with both Blair and Buffy suggests that the process has more to do with the quantity of blood the vampire takes rather than on cross-feeding as stated in **1**, 'Welcome to the Hellmouth'. See **33**, 'Becoming' Part 1; **56**, 'Graduation Day' Part 2). Blair also rises remarkably quickly and seems very focused for someone who has undergone such a radical change (see Angel's observation in **15**, 'School Hard', about how confusing it all is for a vampire at first). Quentin says the Slayer must undergo the *Cruciamentum* '*if* she reaches her eighteenth birthday', which suggests that most Slayers are called before that age (Buffy was fifteen, see **68**, 'A New Man'). However, as both Kendra and Faith seem to prove, older girls *have* been called. This also suggests that the calling is not, necessarily, in any fixed order and that had Buffy not 'died' in **12**, 'Prophecy Girl', and lived for several years thereafter, Kendra may not have automatically been the next choice.

Electra on Azalea Path: What's going on in the Buffy–Giles relationship? Quentin says Giles has 'a father's love' for Buffy and the implication from Buffy's (unsubtle) attempt to get Giles to take her to the Ice Show in her dad's place indicates her (possibly subconscious) need for a father substitute. She spends a lot of time trying to get Giles and Joyce together, only to be *horrified* when they *do* (see **40**, 'Band Candy'; **52**, 'Earshot'). Poet Sylvia Plath (1932–63) was a great exponent of Electra (the female equivalent of Oedipus Complex proposed by Freud based on the Greek myth of Agamemnon's daughter). In such poems as 'Full Fathom Five', 'Electra on Azalea Path' and 'Daddy' she explored her own relationship with her father, and (particularly in the third poem) her search for a replacement figure in her life.

Who Watches the Watchers?: 'Joss and I had similar but differing back-stories,' Tony Head has recalled. 'Joss had an idea of who the Watchers were and what their place in the world is. I had a slightly different picture which informed me better . . . Joss's vibe was that like some villages in England are famous for their cheese, there's a village in Cheshire or something that is famous for its Watchers!'

47

The Zeppo

US Transmission Date: 26 Jan. 1999
UK Transmission Date: 22 Oct. 1999 (Sky)
19 Jul. 2000 (BBC2)

Writer: Dan Vebber
Director: James Whitmore Jnr
Cast: Channon Roe (Jack O'Toole), Michael Cudlitz (Bob),
Darin Heames (Parker), Scott Torrence (Dickie),
Whitney Dylan (Lysette), Vaughn Armstrong (Cop)
French title: *Un Zéro Pointé*
German title: *Die Nacht Der Lebenden Leichen*

Combining their talents, Giles, Willow, Faith and Buffy defeat
a group of female demons, the Sisterhood of Jhe. Xander,
however, can only watch. Stung by Cordelia's jibes that he is a
passenger in a group of superheroes, Xander attempts to find
his own speciality and borrows his uncle's car, but succeeds
only in coming to the attention of a local psychopath, Jack
O'Toole. O'Toole, however, needs a 'wheels man' for his
quest to raise his three friends from the dead and leads Xander
into one of the strangest nights of his life – the night on which
he will lose his virginity and prove to himself that he is the
equal of his friends. Unfortunately, they're too busy with the
End of the World to notice.

Dreaming (As Blondie Once Said) is Free: Every nightmare
that Willow has that doesn't involve academic failure or public
nudity concerns the Hellmouth creature seen in **12**, 'Prophecy
Girl'. In fact, she once dreamed it attacked her while she was
late for a test *and* naked.

Dudes and Babes: Lysette, the girl Xander takes out to the
Bronze, seems to prove the old theory about it being a guy's
car that's the biggest turn-on for the girls. The ridiculousness
of his liaison with Faith is emphasised when he's pushed out of
her room semi-clothed, with his pants in his hands and an idiot
grin on his face. Yeah, we've *all* had those sorts of nights . . .

It's a Designer Label!: What on earth is up with Buffy's hair?

It looks like a perm's gone wrong somewhere. Xander's pink jumper takes few prisoners.

References: Superman's pal Jimmy Olsen is mentioned twice. Also, fast-food chain Taco Bell, the Beastie Boys' 'Hello Nasty' and Michael Jackson's 'Wanna Be Startin' Something'. Bob's overriding concern after eight months in his grave is 'Whoa! *Walker, Texas Ranger*. You been taping 'em?' Nice to see even the undead have their priorities right. The title, as alluded to by Cordelia, refers to Herbert 'Zeppo' Marx (1901–79), the fourth Marx Brother and the one that everyone forgets alongside his illustrious siblings Groucho, Chico and Harpo. (Does that make Cordy herself Gummo, the fifth – and even more obscure – member?)

Bitch!: Cordelia to Xander: 'Boy, of all the humiliations you've had that I've witnessed, that was the latest.' And: ' "Cool". Look it up. It's something that a subliterate that's repeated twelfth grade three times has and you don't. There was no part of that that wasn't fun.'

Xander tells Cordy: 'Feel free to die of a wasting disease in the next twenty seconds.'

Awesome!: The Xander–Oz 'essence of cool' scene. Plus the sequence in the boiler room with some of Xander's dialogue seemingly inspired by *Dirty Harry*.

'You May Remember Me From Such Films As ...': Channon Roe played Surfer in *Boogie Nights*.

Don't Give Up the Day Job: Michael Cudlitz worked as a construction co-ordinator on *American History X* and *Beverly Hills 90210*, a series he also starred in as Tony Miller.

Valley-Speak: Faith: 'These babes were wicked rowdy.' ('Wicked' is an all-purpose New England slang adjective cementing Faith's Boston background. See **55**, 'Graduation Day' Part 1.)

Logic, Let Me Introduce You to This Window: The cafeteria scene begins with a shot of the lunch counter. The camera rises and we see Xander in the background with Buffy and Willow; Oz is nowhere to be seen and Xander is wearing different clothes from the rest of this scene. (This is footage from **31**, 'I Only Have Eyes for You'. The episode also features that stock shot from **5**, 'Never Kill a Boy on the First Date', with

Owen again.) Jack says he couldn't raise his dead friends earlier because he 'had to wait eight months for the stars to align', but he died three weeks ago himself and yet his grand-pappy (presumably) raised him the same night. Throughout the scene in the boiler room, the bomb is heard beeping as the seconds tick by. But the digital countdown is all over the place, jumping from 10 to 13, down to 7, and taking many more than six beeps to reach 2, when Jack finally disarms the bomb.

Motors: Xander's green 1957 Chevrolet Bel Air.

Quote/Unquote: Willow: 'Occasionally, I'm callous and strange.'

Xander, on his car: 'It's my thing.' Buffy: 'Is this a penis metaphor?'

Cordelia: 'It must be really hard when all your friends have, like, superpowers. Slayer, werewolf, witches, vampires . . . You must feel like Jimmy Olsen.'

Jack brandishes a knife: 'Are you scared?' Xander: 'Would that make you happy?'

Notes: 'Did I mention I'm having a very strange night?' I'm a sucker for Xander-led episodes and, as with **28**, 'Bewitched, Bothered and Bewildered', and **32**, 'Go Fish', the decision to use Nick Brendon's comic talents to the fore is an inspired one. 'The Zeppo' was *hated* by many online *Buffy* fans who completely missed the point and demanded to know why we kept cutting back to Xander and his trivial chase through the school when the fate of the world was at stake. I love the way everything keeps happening just out of Xander's reach and we see things for once through his eyes (for instance, in the scene where Buffy and Angel kiss, the dialogue seems trite and melodramatic; are we seeing real events or Xander's over-the-top version of it?). True heroism isn't always about saving the world from unspeakable demons; sometimes it's about facing up to your fears and being yourself, as this episode demonstrates – showing that Alexander Harris is every bit as much of a hero as his friends. Great music too.

Giles says most of his sources have dried up since he was relieved of his duties by the Watcher Council. He tries to contact the Spirit Guides who 'live outside of time' and 'have knowledge of the future', but he gets no luck there either. Giles is always the one who asks for jellied doughnuts in the mix during research sessions and is horrified when Buffy eats the last one (*top* bit of snitching by Willow on Buffy: 'She ate *three*!'). Xander asks Oz if learning the guitar is hard (Oz: 'Not the way I play', see **22**, 'What's My Line?' Part 2), which proves that Xander's dream in **4**, 'Teacher's Pet', *was* just a dream and the guitar we see in his bedroom *is* just for show. He reveals some musical talent, having played the flugelhorn in eighth grade. Xander tells Jack he is *not* retarded. 'I had to take that test when I was seven. A little slow in some stuff, mostly math and spatial relations, but certainly not challenged.' He mentions his Uncle Rory again (see **20**, 'The Dark Age'). He loses his virginity to Faith.

Novelisation: By Jeff Mariotte in *The Xander Years Vol. 2* (Pocket Books, April 2000).

Soundtrack: 'G-Song' by Supergrass and 'Easy' by Tricky Woo. The acoustic-guitar riff played as Xander walks away from Cordelia at the end sounds like the opening chords of Oasis's 'Talk Tonight'. But it isn't.

Critique: In *Shivers*, Ian Atkins observed: 'That "The Zeppo" is an immensely clever episode can be seen by just how few fans originally got the joke: the story polarised opinion into hate it and love it and yet it's hard to understand the former: the story of Buffy and her friends' experience is little more than a retread of **12**, "Prophecy Girl", with a bigger budget. What the viewer gets instead is a brave and playful experiment in the mechanics of point of view, and it's just as exciting, witty and dramatic as any of the surrounding stories . . . "The Zeppo" isn't just a comedy episode. But you've got to get the joke to see that.'

48
Bad Girls

US Transmission Date: 9 Feb. 1999
UK Transmission Date: 28 Oct. 1999 (Sky)
26 Jul. 2000 (BBC2)

Writer: Douglas Petrie
Director: Michael Lange

Cast: Christian Clemenson (Balthazar),
Alex Skuby (Vincent), Wendy Clifford (Mrs Taggert)
French title: *El Eliminati*
German title: *Der Neue Wächter*

The arrival of a replacement Watcher sees Buffy and Faith
question to whom their loyalties belong. Hunting a vampire
sect called El Eliminati, the girls become reckless despite
Angel's warning that the Demon Balthazar is not as dead as
the new Watcher, Wesley, believes. In need of weaponry, the
Slayers break into a hunting equipment shop, but their shoplift-
ing spree is cut short by two cops. Though they escape, Buffy
recognises the dangerous game she is playing and that the time
she is spending with Faith has upset Willow and Xander. But
when Giles and Wesley are captured by Balthazar's vampires,
Buffy helps them before she can deal with the consequences of
Faith's most irresponsible act of all – the staking of the Deputy
Mayor. Mayor Wilkins performs a ritual in his office and
becomes invincible. Buffy visits Faith to discuss their crime
but is disturbed by Faith's lack of guilt.

Dudes and Babes: In the opening scene, Faith is astonished
that Buffy and Xander have never . . . you know. ('Not even
once?') Buffy says they are just friends, to which Faith replies,
'What else are friends for?' Faith is very descriptive about her
need for sex ('A little after-hours [grunt]') and about how
'sweaty' Slaying makes her (see **37**, 'Faith, Hope and Trick';
38, 'Beauty and the Beasts'). Xander's eye twitches whenever
Buffy mentions Faith.

The Conspiracy Starts at Home Time: The strands of innuendo that have been building all season start to come together.
The Mayor, who again hints at a non-human longevity, says
that it will be one hundred days to his 'ascension', during
which time nothing can harm him (not even getting his head
sliced in half). After this process Earthly affairs will not
concern him as he will be on 'a higher plane'. Balthazar seems
to know what is coming, telling Buffy and her friends, 'When
he rises, you'll wish I'd killed you all.'

A Little Learning is a Dangerous Thing: Having been
accepted for 'early admission' to university, Willow is being
'wooed' by both Harvard and Yale (see **50**, 'Doppelgängland').

She says chemistry is a lot like witchcraft, 'only less newt'. Xander, meanwhile, is hoping to get into 'appliance repair or motel management' post-school, though he had yet to hear back from The Hot-Dog Emporium. Buffy cuts class in the middle of a chemistry test (a silly thing to do considering that Snyder is looking for any excuse to expel her again).

Mom's Waffles: Joyce is on a diet, though she seems to be seeking an excuse to have some waffles. When Buffy says she doesn't want any, Joyce notes that they only don't have calories if she's making them for Buffy. ('Mom logic'.)

It's a Designer Label!: Is that underwear Faith is washing in her sink at the end? Why does Willow's jumper look like the Swiss national flag?

References: Wesley's middle name is a reference to the king of British science fiction, John Wyndham (1903–1969) author of *The Day of the Triffids*, *The Midwich Cuckoos*, *The Kraken Wakes* and *Random Quest* among others. There's a lengthy discussion on comic strips: *Family Circus* (by Bill Keane, a rather twee story of family life, and the most widely syndicated strip in the world), *Marmaduke* (by Brad Anderson about a troublemaking Great Dane) and *Cathy* (by Cathy Guisewite concerning the trials of a single woman). Also *Sesame Street*, *Magnum Force*, Kipling's *Captains Courageous* and Hot Chocolate's 'Every One's a Winner'. Balthazar looks a lot like the vampire archivist Pearl in *Blade*.

Bitch!: Judging by a horrible comment Cordy makes to Xander, his father seems to have recently become unemployed. Oh, *that's* nasty (see **54**, 'The Prom'). Mind you, his suggestion that she start modelling her own line of 'hooker-wear' is almost as bad.

Awesome!: Buffy and Faith shaking their funky stuff in the Bronze. Balthazar is the most disgusting villain we've had in a while, with the scariest face this side of Keith Richards. His scenes with Giles and Wesley ('Stay calm, Mr Giles', 'Thank God you're here, I was planning to panic') are funny, though the action sequence that follows seems to go on for *ever*.

'You May Remember Me From Such Pop Videos As . . .': Alexis Denisof can be seen in George Harrison's 'Got My Mind Set On You'.

'You May Remember Me From Such Films and TV Series As . . .' Alexis Denisof later shot to prominence as Richard Sharpe's love rival, Johnny Rossendale, in *Sharpe* and appeared in *Rogue Trader*, *First Knight* (as Sir Gaheris) and *True Blue*. Recently, he portrayed an American hitman in the Vic Reeves–Bob Mortimer remake of *Randall and Hopkirk (Deceased)*. Christian Clemenson has a blink-and-you'll-miss-him part in *Armageddon* and more substantial roles in *Apollo 13* (as Dr Chuck), *The Big Lebowski*, *The Fisher King*, *Broadcast News* and *Hannah and Her Sisters*.

Valley-Speak: Faith, on dead vampires: 'They're toast.'
  Willow: 'I can *totally* handle myself.'

Not Exactly a Haven for the Bruthas: Mr Trick thinks El Eliminati should use Uzis instead of swords: 'Would've saved your ass right about now.'

Cigarettes and Soft Drinks: The Mayor and Mr Trick are about to share a root beer at the end.

Logic, Let Me Introduce You to This Window: When Buffy breaks into the display case containing the dagger, the weapon falls and she catches it between her index and middle fingers. In the next shot it's between her thumb and index finger. Why didn't Buffy bandage her wound before going to the Bronze with Faith? When telling Wesley about the three vampires she and Faith killed, Buffy says, 'One of them had swords. I don't think he was with the other two.' All three of the vampires were dressed in the same Eliminati uniform, so why would she think they weren't together?

I Just *Love* Your Accent: *Two* British Watchers. (Love the bit where Giles and Wesley simultaneously clean their spectacles.) Giles uses the *very* British insult 'twerp' to Wesley. The new Watcher's three most important words ('Preparation, preparation, preparation') could be a reference to Tony Blair's famed speech during the 1997 election campaign when he said that the three most important things in Britain were 'education, education, education'. The song that Faith and Buffy dance to is 'Chinese Burn' by British indie band Curve.

Quote/Unquote: Buffy on Wesley: 'Is he evil?' Giles: 'Not in the strictest sense.'

Buffy: 'Whenever Giles sends me on a mission, he always says "please". And afterwards I get a cookie.'

Wesley says that El Eliminati were a fifteenth-century duellist cult whose numbers dwindled after, among other things, 'a lot of pointless duelling'.

Notes: 'Want. Take. Have.' An up-and-down trip. 'Bad Girls' has lots of good ideas that aren't followed up in the next episode so, sadly, it's a case of guilt by association. The introduction of Wesley allows Giles to get into the action more, which has both positive and negative aspects (attempting to turn him into 'Bruce Willis in Tweed' is a definite negative, as his OTT stunts in the warehouse prove). However, Alexis Denisof's performance is genuinely funny. It was amusing to see Internet fans getting annoyed at how 'irritating' Wesley is. That's the whole *point*, kids, he's *supposed* to be. Sadly, another inclusion in the growing family of characters means that Oz, Cordelia and Xander hardly appear.

There are continuity references to **41**, 'Revelations', and Gwendolyn Post, and an oblique reference to Xander and Faith's liaison in **47**, 'The Zeppo'. Giles's first entry in the Watcher Diary noted that Buffy was wilful and insolent and that her abuse of the English language was such that he understood only 'every other sentence'. Wesley says he has faced two vampires himself, under controlled conditions (no word on whether he killed them. Was this, perhaps, a Watcher equivalent of *Cruciamentum*?). There seem to be girl gangs in Sunnydale. Just how stupid *are* the police in Sunnydale? (See **33**, 'Becoming' Part 1.) The complete Mayoral 'Things to Do' checklist is: 'meet scouts', 'Lumber Union reschedule', 'call temp agency', 'become invincible', 'meeting with PTA', 'haircut'. Mrs Haggard is the chemistry teacher.

Novelisation: By James Laurence in *The Faith Trials* (Pocket Books, April 2001).

Alexis Sold: Although born in the US, Alexis Denisof had done most of his work in Britain and, seemingly, has an old friend to thank for the part of Wesley. 'They were looking for somebody "who thinks he's Pierce Brosnan but is actually George Lazenby",' Tony Head told Paul Simpson and Ruth Thomas. Head suggested Alexis with whom he had worked in a 1993 theatre production of *Rope* in Chichester. 'He played one of the two guys who did the murder and he was fantastic, as indeed they've found on *Angel*. I'm hoping to get a little guest spot in *Angel* because I'd love to do some more work with Alexis. I had one scene with David [in **64**, 'Pangs'], which was really nice. I miss the tension between the characters. It's nice to keep it alive. We've talked about it, but it's probably going to be next season . . .'

49
Consequences

US Transmission Date: 16 Feb. 1999
UK Transmission Date: 4 Nov. 1999 (Sky)
2 Aug. 2000 (BBC2)

Writer: Marti Noxon
Director: Michael Gershman
Cast: Patricia Place (Woman)
French title: *Au-Dessus Des Lois*
German title: *Konsequenzen*

The Deputy Mayor's murder is discovered. Buffy tries to convince Faith to confess without success, but they break into his office and spot the Mayor and Mr Trick together. Buffy is concerned by Faith's lack of conscience, though Faith says slaying puts them above the law. Buffy confesses to Willow, who advises that she see Giles. When she gets to the library, she finds Faith has told Giles that Buffy was responsible. Giles assures Buffy that he's aware of Faith's lies and they ask Angel to help Faith face up to the horror of what she has done. Unfortunately, Wesley overhears the conversation and he and his men subdue Angel and capture Faith. She escapes and seems to have gone rogue, but Buffy finds her at the docks and Faith saves Buffy from an attack by Mr Trick, whom she kills. However, the Mayor gets a visit from Faith at his office. With Mr Trick out of the picture, Faith wants the available job. **Dreaming (As Blondie Once Said) is Free:** Buffy's nightmare has her drowning, with Finch holding on to her foot. When she struggles to the surface, Faith pushes her back under.

Dudes and Babes: Faith and Xander are (but for Angel's intervention) at it again, only with more strangulation involved. Presumably, the sequence that got the TV-14 rating. Faith and Angel's use of the term 'safety words' suggests a knowledge of the BDSM community!

A Little Learning is a Dangerous Thing: Cordelia checks out books from the library by Sigmund Freud (see **23**, 'Ted') and Carl Gustav Jung (1875–1961) for her psychology class.

Mom's Apple Pie: The pained expression on Joyce's face when Buffy arrives home to find a policeman waiting for her speaks volumes. Joyce cuts a lonely figure watching TV alone in the early hours of the morning.

Denial, Thy Name is Faith: Faith attempts to shift the blame for the murder on to Buffy (Giles notes that Faith may be good at a lot of things, but lying isn't one of them).

It's a Designer Label!: Faith's leather strides previously seen, plus a pair of incredibly tight jeans, and her 'Motor City Baby' T-shirt. Buffy's pink overcoat is also worth a mention.

References: Obliquely, *Star Trek: The Next Generation*. Also, MasterCard, the Troggs' 'Wild Thing', England's most underrated band the Kinks, Carolyn Crawford's Motown classic 'My Smile Is Just A Frown Turned Upside Down' and 'Zip a Dee Doo Dah' from *Song of the South*. 'We *are* the Law' may be a nod in the direction of *Judge Dredd*.

Bitch!: When Buffy says Cordelia is 'a friend', Cordy replies, 'Let's not exaggerate.'

Awesome!: Xander confessing that he slept with Faith to Giles, Buffy and Willow and their different reactions to it.

Surprise!: Faith turning up at the Mayor's office at the end. Didn't see *that* coming at all.

Don't Give Up the Day Job: A genuine TV news reporter, Amy Powell has also appeared in similar roles in *White Man's Burden* and *The Bird Cage*.

Valley-Speak: Faith: 'You'd *dig* that, wouldn't you? To get up in front of all your geek pals and go on record about how I made you my boy-toy for the night.'

Logic, Let Me Introduce You to This Window: The day after Finch's murder (see **48**, 'Bad Girls'), Buffy went to Faith's motel (in daylight and a clean outfit). 'Consequences' begins with Buffy waking up from a nightmare; then she goes to school. This means it is at least the second day since the murder. But the detective questioning the witness at the scene of the crime says, 'You heard the man scream at about what time last night?' (Finch didn't scream.) Later, Buffy tells Faith, 'Less than twenty-four hours ago, you killed a man', when it's closer to forty-eight. When Angel watches the police at the crime scene, blood is smeared down the dumpster where Finch was killed. However, in **48**, 'Bad Girls', Faith didn't stab Finch until he had already slumped to the ground. Is Detective Stein the only officer in the police department making house calls on a regular basis? (Or, more to the point, is he part of the ongoing police conspiracy?) How does Wesley know where Angel is living? The calendar in Giles's office is for April 1997.

I Just *Love* Your Accent: The Watchers' Council is referred to by Wesley as 'The Watchers' Council of Britain'. Is it just me or did anyone else feel really sorry for Wesley when he's left alone in the library after Buffy's caustic put-down?

Quote/Unquote: Mr Trick's death-line: 'Oh no, this is no good at all.'

Notes: 'We're warriors, we're built to kill.' A really awful episode that attempts to look at what creates human weakness, but fudges it completely. Even the best bits of 'Consequences' feature heavy-handed moralising and bad characterisation that would be unacceptable from a series novice let alone one of its most accomplished writers. Top-heavy with a claustrophobic atmosphere that stifles creativity, 'Consequences' squats in a hole, afraid to actually *say* anything worthwhile.

Giles says this isn't the first time a Slayer has killed a human ('It's tragic, but accidents happen'). The Council, however, take a dim view of such events, suggesting that Faith will be locked up for a long time (that would have been self-defeating if this was their approach to previous cases. Locking up your only Slayer!). Wesley speaks to Quentin on the telephone (the password is 'monkey'). Angel's entrance into Faith's room isn't the first time we've seen this phenomenon (in **26**, 'Innocence', Angel was able to enter Uncle Enyos's hotel room without an invitation). Presumably hotels

and motels are public domain (see **30**, 'Killed By Death'). There's a reference to the Scooby Gang's confrontation with Buffy over her keeping Angel's return a secret in **41**, 'Revelations'. Michael is mentioned; he and Willow are *still* trying to 'de-rat' Amy (see **45**, 'Gingerbread').
Soundtrack: 'Wish We Never Met' by Kathleen Wilhoite.
Novelisation: By James Laurence in *The Faith Trials* (Pocket Books, April 2001).

50

Doppelgängland

US Transmission Date: 23 Feb. 1999
UK Transmission Date: 5 Nov. 1999 (Sky)
9 Aug. 2000 (BBC2)

Writer: Joss Whedon
Director: Joss Whedon
Cast: Michael Nagy (Alfonse), Norma Michaels (Older Woman),
Corey Michael Blake (Waiter), Jennifer Nicole (Body-Double Willow)
French title: *Les Deux Visages*

Desperate to end her time as a mortal, Anyanka begs a demon to create a temporal fold allowing her to retrieve her amulet, but it refuses. So she seeks Willow's help. The spell is broken before the necklace is returned, but it does have one unexpected side effect: the calling into this dimension of the vampire Willow from the world created by Cordelia's wish. After various confusing meetings in which her friends believe that Willow has become a vampire, the truth is discovered and the two Willows meet. Evil-Willow convinces some vampires to work for her and restore chaos to Sunnydale and Anya promises to help in the hope of getting her necklace back. But their plans are defeated by Willow, who pretends to be her evil self in a game of double bluff. However, she cannot bear to see her evil twin killed and arranges to send her back to her own dimension.
Dreaming (As Blondie Once Said) is Free: Evil-Willow wakes up in a pink cardigan: 'Oh no, this is like a *nightmare*.'
Dudes and Babes: There are numerous references to sex

(even more than **43**, 'The Wish', 'Doppelgängland' is *full* of lesbian overtones). The Mayor tells Faith: 'No Slayer of mine is gonna live in a fleabag hotel. That place has a very unsavoury reputation. There are immoral liaisons going on there.' Faith notes: 'Yeah, plus all the screwin'.' When Evil-Willow finds Xander in the Bronze, they embrace, much to Xander's discomfort: 'This is verging on *naughty touching* here. Don't want to fall back on bad habits. Hands! Hands in new places!' When Evil-Willow is discovered, a conversation ensues on how she is *exactly* like Willow, except, as Buffy says: 'Your not being a dominatrix. As far as we know.' Willow replies: 'Oh, right. Me and Oz play Mistress of Pain every night.' Which leads Xander to ask, 'Did anyone else just go to a scary visual place?' Willow finds her other self 'So evil and skanky. And I think I'm kind of gay.' Buffy tells her to remember that a vampire's personality 'has nothing to do with the person it was'. Angel says, 'Well, actually . . .' Then, thankfully, he shuts up (see **75**, 'New Moon Rising').

Authority Sucks!: Snyder, as in **32**, 'Go Fish', manipulates Willow, in this case to help Percy with his history paper on Roosevelt: 'I just hate the way he bullies people. He just assumes everyone's time is his,' notes Willow as Giles emerges from another room and says, 'Willow, get on the computer. I want you to take another pass at accessing the Mayor's files.' And, meekly, she does.

A Little Learning is a Dangerous Thing: Xander gets Willow's new nickname 'Old Reliable' mixed up with the film *Old Yeller* and the geyser 'Old Faithful'.

It's a Designer Label!: Oz's yellow 'El Speedo' shirt is a sight for sore eyes. Or a cause of them. Willow's pink fluffy jumper puts in another appearance, as do Evil-Willow's leathers.

References: *Vanity Fair* magazine, *Bill and Ted's Excellent Adventure* ('No way', 'Yes way'), *Old Yeller*, *The Creature from the Black Lagoon*, PlayStation, *Arts & Entertainment Channel*'s *Biography*, the psychiatry of Rorschach patterns and John Wayne.

Bitch!: Cordelia finds Evil-Willow in the book cage: 'It occurs to me that we've never really had the opportunity to talk. You know, woman to woman, with you locked up . . . What could we talk about? How about the ethics of boyfriend stealing?'

Awesome!: Willow finding Giles, Xander and Buffy in the library mourning her death ('Oh God, who died?') and their reactions to, first, seeing her and then to discovering that she's not a vampire (Xander seems to think there's something wrong with the cross he's holding). And her reaction to their reaction. This is closely followed by a subsequent scene as Angel tries to give them the bad news about Willow and the facial expressions of Buffy, Giles and Xander at his double take. Xander's 'We're right there with you, buddy' sums up the whole thing. In an episode full of such tiny gems, there's also Willow pretending to be Evil-Willow asking Anya and Alfonse, 'Could a human do this?' and then screaming loudly. Xander's joy that in Evil-Willow's world he's a 'bad-ass vampire', the special effects as Willow and Anya attempt to bring forth the amulet ('Have you tried looking behind the sofa? In Hell?'); Willow's discovery of her breasts ('Gosh, look at *those*!'); her control of a pencil (see **45**, 'Gingerbread'); and Percy's 'apple-for-teacher' bit.

'You May Remember Me From Such TV Series As . . .': Andy Umberger was in *The West Wing*, *NYPD Blue* and *Angel*. Ethan Erickson played Dane Sanders in *Jawbreaker* (alongside Julie Benz) and appears, uncredited, in *Scream 3*.

The Drugs Don't Work: Willow on Xander, Buffy and Giles acting strangely: 'Say, you all didn't happen to do a bunch of drugs, did you?'

Valley-Speak: Willow: 'Aren't you sort of naturally buff, Buff?'

Cigarettes and Alcohol: Anya, despite being 1,120 years old, still can't get a beer in the Bronze without ID and has to settle for a Coke instead.

Logic, Let Me Introduce You to This Window: When Evil-Willow throws Willow over the library counter, Willow lands on her right side when she rolls off the edge. In the following shot, Willow is on her left side. The entire episode is based on a *HUGE* flaw of logic. **43**, 'The Wish', created 'Dark Sunnydale' not as an alternative dimension but to *replace* normal Sunnydale. With the destruction of the amulet, things snap back into place and version two of reality never existed. Either one Sunnydale can exist, or the other, but not both. So, at the end of 'The Wish', Evil-Willow and all of the other 'Dark Sunnydale' characters never existed. Pure 'paradox theory'. Explain *that*, Einstein. How did Wesley get into the bathroom before Cordelia and Evil-Willow? He was running towards them in the hallway, but somehow got in there first and came from behind Cordelia.

I Just *Love* Your Accent: Faith sarcastically refers to Wesley as 'Princess Margaret'.

Quote/Unquote: Anya: 'For a thousand years I wielded the power of the Wish. I brought ruin to the hearts of unfaithful men. I brought forth destruction and chaos for the pleasure of the lower beings. I was feared and worshipped across the mortal globe. And now I'm stuck at Sunnydale High. Mortal. A child. And I'm flunking math.'

A bewildered Willow as Buffy and Xander, realising she's not a vampire, hug her: 'Oxygen becoming an issue.'

Oz: 'Professional bands can play up to six, sometimes seven, completely different chords.' Devon: 'That's just, like, fruity jazz bands.'

Evil-Willow: 'This is a dumb world. In my world, there are people in chains and we can ride them like ponies.'

Notes: 'Aren't you gonna introduce me to your . . . *Holy God*, you're Willow.' Odd, isn't it, that it's the 'funny' episodes that contain the best characterisation? 'Doppelgängland' is a superb example. It's a story about loss on several levels (Anya's lost her power, Cordelia's lost her boyfriend, Evil-Willow's lost her world) and also about how reality is sometimes less 'real' than fantasy ('This world's no fun,' says Evil-Willow. 'You noticed that, too?' replies Willow). This is a genuinely groundbreaking piece of work in any context – all the way to the suddenly explained 'oh f–' reprise from **43**, 'The Wish'. It's a favourite of many of the *Buffy* cast and crew.

Buffy has been undertaking sessions with the Watchers' Council psychiatrist after the events of **49**, 'Consequences'. Willow wanted to be a florist. Evil-Willow remembers Oz was a 'white hat' in her world. Dingoes Ate My Baby had a gig in Monterey on Sunday night. They don't have a roadie. Snyder refers to the 'swim team debacle of last year' (see **32**, 'Go Fish') and says that Willow has a letter of acceptance from 'every university with a stamp'. The Mayor tells Faith he is a family man. The movies playing at the Sunnydale cinema are an 'R' rated film the last word of which is *Hotel*, and one which begins *The Goose Ran* . . .

Soundtrack: 'Virgin State of Mind' by K's Choice [*], Spectator Pump's 'Priced 2 Move'.

Novelisation: By Yvonne Navarro in *The Willow Files Vol. 2* (Pocket Books, February 2001).

51
Enemies

US Transmission Date: 16 Mar. 1999
UK Transmission Date: 11 Nov. 1999 (Sky)
16 Aug. 2000 (BBC2)

Writer: Douglas Petrie
Director: David Grossman
Cast: Michael Manasseri (Demon), Gary Bullock (Shrouded Man)
French title: *Trahison*
German title: *Gefährliche Spiele*

Buffy and Faith encounter a demon who offers to sell them the Books of Ascension. Faith reports to the Mayor, who orders her to retrieve the books and kill the demon. Faith and the Mayor plan to banish Angel's soul and, with the aid of a mysterious Shrouded Man, succeed. Angelus and Faith plan to torture Buffy. At the Hall of Records, Oz locates a photograph of Mayor Wilkins. Xander reveals the return of Angelus. Buffy taunts Faith, but when an angry Faith blurts out more information about the coming events Angel tells her that his 'Angelus' role is an act. Faith escapes and is comforted by the Mayor, who reminds her that once the Ascension takes place, her broken friendship with Buffy will be irrelevant.

Dudes and Babes: The movie that Buffy and Angel see is *Le Banquet D'Amelia*, a sexy arthouse affair ('I thought it'd be about food,' notes Buffy). Angel remarks that there was some food involved). 'Check out the lust-bunny,' says Faith when she sees Angel and the episode sees the pair almost becoming entangled (it gets explicit when Faith is astride Angel and he says, 'I should have known you'd like it on top,' before asking her to 'wriggle'). There are also lots of allusions to bondage.

The Conspiracy Starts at Home Time: The Ascension will happen on Graduation Day (see **56**, 'Graduation Day' Part 2). Faith notes that the Mayor 'built this town for demons to feed on'. Oz discovers Mayor Wilkins is over one hundred years old and Wesley guesses that he isn't human. The implication is that far from being a recent phenomena, demonic activity has been rife in Sunnydale for decades, hence it *is* possible to rationalise people turning a blind eye to the town's mortality rate (see **37**, 'Faith, Hope and Trick'; **45**, 'Gingerbread'). They've never known any different. (See, for instance, Oz's 'It all makes sense' comments on vampires in **25**, 'Surprise'.)

A Little Learning is a Dangerous Thing: Cordelia is doing an English paper and wants Wesley's help . . . because he's English.

Mom's Apple Pie: Joyce seems to have reduced every aspect of Buffy's life into two categories: 'vampire problem', and 'nonvampire problem'. When Angel flirts with her, we find that she's recently had highlights added to her hair.

It's a Designer Label!: Some disastrous stuff like the demon's orange shirt and Willow's sheepskin coat (see **53**, 'Choices'). Buffy's blue dress and Faith's tarty leather jacket are better.

References: *Reader's Digest*, the Hanna-Barbera cartoon *Super Friends*, the final words of murderer Gary Gilmore before his execution ('Let's do it'), another allusion to *Scooby Doo Where Are You?* and to Samuel Beckett's *Waiting for Godot*. The music is reminiscent of *The Omen*.

Awesome!: Angel punching Xander ('that guy just *bugs* me'). Most of the best bits involve Giles, particularly the scene with the Shrouded Man where he informs everyone that the 'debt' settled was over the introduction of the Shrouded Man to his wife.

Surprise!: Faith: 'What can I say? I'm the world's best actor.' Angel: 'Second best!'

Valley-Speak: Buffy: 'So, "Ascension", possibly *not* a "love-in"?'

    Faith: 'Sure. Fine. Whatever.'

'You May Remember Me From Such Films As . . .': Gary Bullock was in *Robocop 2* and *3* and also appeared in *Species* and *The Handmaid's Tale*.

Logic, Let Me Introduce You to This Window: When Cordelia enters the library to ask Wesley to dinner, the sound effect of her shoes on the floor doesn't match the action on screen. When Angel slides the Mayor's letter opener across the desk, you can see the reflection of his hand on the nameplate. After Faith runs from the mansion, we cut to a night-time exterior shot of the high school. However, the following scene – in which Giles thanks the Shrouded Man – takes place during the day (sunlight is pouring through the windows). Exactly how much of Buffy, Angel and Giles's scheme was preplanned and how much was improvised? For instance, did Angel know about the Mayor's invincibility, or was he aiming to kill him?

I Just *Love* Your Accent: Buffy wears a Union Jack shirt. Xander refers to Wesley as a 'limey bastard'. Giles uses the expression 'sod all'.

Cruelty to Animals: The Mayor knows the saying 'there's more than one way to skin a cat' is a factually accurate statement.

Quote/Unquote: Giles: 'Demons after money? Whatever happened to "the still-beating heart of a virgin"? No one has any standards any more.'

    Mayor Wilkins's two words that will make all of Faith's pain go away: 'Miniature golf!' (What is it with *Buffy* villains and miniature golf? See **23**, 'Ted'.)

Notes: 'You had to tie me up to beat me. There's a word for people like you, Faith. Loser.' The story of a Slayer going rogue should have been the crowning jewel in this often brilliant season. Sadly, 'Enemies' never begins to hit the mark – the ideas are good, but the script is slow moving. There are some serious problems with the narrative viewpoint of the episode too, a lot of which makes no sense once Angel's deception is revealed (even *with* hindsight and some artistic licence). This is a long-winded 'one-joke' story that runs out of steam well before the climax.

It's been a while since Angel went to the movies. Buffy doesn't own a kimono. Xander says he 'applied some pressure' to Willy the Snitch (so he *did* survive **47**, 'The Zeppo') for information on the demon; he subsequently reveals he bribed Willy with $28. The Watchers' Council won't reimburse without a receipt. Faith's mother was a drunk who never loved her and wouldn't let her have a puppy (see **37**, 'Faith, Hope and Trick').

52

Earshot

Original Scheduled Transmission Date: 27 Apr. 1999[12]
US Transmission Date: 21 Sep. 1999
Australian Transmission Date: 14 Sep. 1999
UK Transmission Date: 12 Nov. 1999 (Sky)
24 Aug. 2000 (BBC2)

Writer: Jane Espenson
Director: Regis B Kimble
Cast: Keram Malicki-Sanchez (Freddy),
Justin Doran (Hogan), Lauren Roman (Nancy),
Wendy Worthington (Lunch Lady), Robert Arce (Mr Beach),
Molly Bryant (Ms Murray), Rick Miller (Student),
Jay Michael Ferguson (Another Student)
French title: *Voix Intérieures*
German title: *Fremde Gedanken*

While battling a demon, Buffy is infected by its blood, making her telepathic. At first it seems the only drawback for the Slayer is that she knows exactly what her friends are thinking. However, as the horror of being able to read *everyone*'s thoughts threatens to overwhelm her, Buffy overhears someone in the cafeteria planning a killing spree. Angel, Giles and Wesley battle to find a cure, while the rest of the gang try to

---

[12] Some sources list 52, 'Earshot', as initially advertised for transmission on 13 Apr. 1999 in the trade press. Confirmation of this has proved impossible.

discover who would be alienated enough to commit such an atrocity. Buffy recovers in time to save Jonathan from a foolish act and stop the real would-be assassin.

The Caption: 'Mindful of the tragic events last week at Columbine High School, the originally scheduled episode of *Buffy the Vampire Slayer* will air at a later date.'

Dudes and Babes: Buffy says the boys of Sunnydale are seriously disturbed. The thoughts of the lad who wants to 'shove her against that locker' suggest she's right.

A Little Learning is a Dangerous Thing: 'Maybe I'll take French. How hard can it be? French babies learn it!' *Othello* is used as a metaphor in the same way *The Merchant of Venice* was in **11**, 'Out of Sight, Out of Mind'. Buffy uses her power to read both Nancy Doyle and Ms Murray's minds in English class (Ms Murray: 'Jealousy's merely the tool that Iago uses to undo Othello. But what is his motivation? What reason does Iago give for destroying his superior officer?' Buffy: 'He was passed over for promotion. Cassio was picked instead, and people were saying that Othello slept with his wife.') Xander thinks four times five is thirty and six times five is thirty-two (see **1**, 'Welcome to the Hellmouth'; **47**, 'The Zeppo').

Mom's Apple Pie: As Joyce asks, 'How about some soup? Chicken and stars?' Buffy notices that her mother seems nervous about spending any time with a telepath.

Then . . . 'You had *sex* with *Giles*?' (See **40**, 'Band Candy'.)

Denial, Thy Names are Joyce and Rupert: Which leads to . . . 'It was the candy! We were teenagers!' Buffy: 'On the hood of a police car? . . . *twice*!' As she later informs Giles: 'We can work out after school. If you're not too busy having *sex with my mother*!' (See **72**, 'Who Are You?'; **94**, 'The Body'.)

It's a Designer Label!: Buffy tells Giles: 'When I walked in a few minutes ago, you thought "Look at her shoes. If a fashion magazine told her to, she'd wear cats strapped to her feet".' Willow's pussycat T-shirt and sun hat, Oz's 'Eater' shirt, Xander's tasteful yellow sweater and Buffy's white miniskirt. Buffy tells Giles she has a hard time finding jeans that fit her.

References: Principal Snyder has the Bangles's hit 'Walk

Like an Egyptian' stuck in his head. Oz misquotes René Descartes, while there are references to *Othello* and Pierce Brosnan. The clock-tower finale shares conceptual and visual links with Hitchcock's *Vertigo*, *The X-Files* episode 'Blood' and the 1966 Charles Whitman murders. Mr Beach's history class are doing Henry VIII, judging from the blackboard.

Bitch!: Giles: 'I was just filling Buffy in on my progress regarding the research of the Ascension.' Wesley: 'What took up the rest of the minute?'

Oz, on the Sunnydale cheerleaders: 'Their spelling's improved.'

Awesome!: *All* of the Scooby Gang's 'thought' sequences are wonderful and Oz's are extremely Zen. (Xander's are the funniest, naturally, though Cordelia's are a bit disturbing – can she *really* be that shallow?) Best bit of a clever climax (full of red herrings) is Nancy's unimpressed reaction to Buffy's astounding gymnastic feat ('*I* could have done that'). *Love* the box of rat poison with RAT POISON! written on it. And Giles walking into the tree (Tony Head confessed this was his idea and never thought that Joss would let him get away with it).

'You May Remember Me From Such Films and TV series As . . .': Lauren Roman was Laura English in *All My Children*. Keram Malicki-Sanchez appeared in *American History X*.

Don't Give Up the Day Job: Director Regis Kimble began as *Buffy*'s film editor (a role he also filled on *Matlock*). Over on *Angel*, he designed the stunning title sequence.

Valley-Speak: Buffy: 'Scabby demon number two got away. Scabby demon number one, *big check* in the slay column.'

Student: 'Wait till I'm a software *jillionaire* and you're all flipping burgers. Who's the loser then?'

Buffy: 'Prison, you know, it's a lot like high school. But instead of *noogies* . . .'

Not Exactly a Haven for the Bruthas: Nancy says race is an issue. In *Othello*.

Logic, Let Me Introduce You to This Window: If the demons are telepathic, how come they don't anticipate Buffy's attack? What's all that rubbish Angel spouts about vampires' thoughts being unreadable for the same reason that their reflections can't be seen? Abject nonsense! Isn't a high-velocity rifle a bit of an ostentatious suicide weapon? Couldn't Jonathan find a handgun?

I Just *Love* Your Accent: A jealous Xander refers to Wesley's 'Pierce Brosney-eyes' being all over Cordelia. When we hear what Wesley actually *thinks* about Cordelia, we're forced to agree. ('I'm a *bad, bad* man!') Giles calls Wesley a 'berk'.

Quote/Unquote: Willow: 'According to Freddy's latest editorial, "The pep rally is a place for pseudo prostitutes to provoke men into a sexual frenzy which, when thwarted, results in pointless athletic competition." ' Xander: 'And the downside being?'

Buffy: 'I'm suddenly gonna grow this demon part . . . It could be claws, or scales . . .' Willow: 'Was it a *boy* demon?'

Angel: 'No matter what, I'll always be with you. I'll love you even if you're covered in slime.' Buffy: 'I liked everything until that part.'

Buffy: 'God, Xander! Is that *all* you think about?'

Cordelia tries to discover if Mr Beach is the would-be murderer: 'I was just wondering, were you planning on killing a bunch of people tomorrow?'

Jonathan: 'Stop saying my name like we're friends . . . You all think I'm an idiot. A *short* idiot!'

Notes: 'You read my mind.' In 'Earshot', Jane Espenson taps into something dark and nasty at the core of the American psyche. Fear. The whole episode is marbled with the hidden terrors that are at the heart of the teenage years. Each character must face their own fears in an isolated environment because no one has any time to help them; they're too busy dealing with fears of their own. That's the point of Buffy's little speech at the end – like the song says, 'Everybody Hurts'. But where Espenson's study of these social misfits *really* scores is characterised by the points in the episode where she allows us to actually *see* how confused and alone everyone feels. 'Earshot' is a glorious meditation on isolation, regret, the belief that knowledge is power, paranoia and self-loathing. And, magnificently, redemption. The episode takes events like those that it (with horrible irony) predicted, and gives them contextualisation – a face, rather than merely a number. That such an epic, lyrical episode fell victim to its own prophecy merely adds to its greatness. In twenty years' time there'll be *legends* about 'Earshot'.

Willow is still tutoring Percy (see **50**, 'Doppelgängland'). Giles says that Angel's charade in **51**, 'Enemies', was important in bringing Faith's treachery into the open. When Oz reads the school newspaper he goes straight to the obituaries (in any other school I'd think he was joking). Angel says he's been with dozens of bad girls like Faith but that in 243 years he's loved one person. Larry is much happier since Xander helped 'out' him in **27** ,'Phases'. These days even his grandma is fixing him dates with guys. The demon Azareth was ritually flayed. The headlines of various issues of *Sunnydale High Sentinel* are: TEACHERS FAIL COMPETENCY EXAM; DROPOUTS FIND HAPPINESS; APATHY ON THE RISE, NO ONE CARES and BIG GAME DRAWS MINDLESS BRAIN DEAD MOB. Freddy also writes that: 'Dingoes Ate My Baby play their instruments as if they have plump Polish sausages taped to their fingers.' Oz agrees this is fair. The Sunnydale basketball team is in the divisional championships.

Despite the best intentions of all concerned, WB still managed to put their foot in it when replacing the postponed episode with, of all things, **48**, 'Bad Girls'. As the *St Paul Pioneer Press* noted: 'Tonight's regularly scheduled new episode . . . has been pulled by the WB Network in the wake of the Littleton High-School shootings. The episode centred on Buffy's clairvoyant ability in which she read the thoughts of someone who was contemplating killing other students . . . Instead, WB airs a repeat, "Bad Girls", in which Buffy craves a taste of the wild side and follows the character Faith into her reckless world. *The repeat seems about as bad as the scrapped one*' (my italics). The first *legal* broadcast of 'Earshot' actually occurred in some regions of Australia a week before the US eventually got to see it in September 1999.

Jane Espenson's Comments: Jane fascinatingly spelled out on the *Posting Board* what happens to an average *Buffy* script: 'Joss and the whole staff work out the story for each episode together and in detail. In theory. In actuality, we all sit and pretend we're being helpful while Joss works out the whole story. Then the writer for that episode writes a "beat sheet", then a "full outline", based on that work. An outline is usually fourteen pages of single-spaced text in which each scene is described [as per] what Joss worked out. What the writer has added at this point is an indication of the shape of the scene – the order the information comes out in, some more specifics about what each character thinks and expresses during the scene, how it transitions into the next scenes, a few sample jokes. Joss gives the writer notes on the outline. He nixes bad things, adds good things, makes sure it's on track. Then the writer writes the first draft. From 14 pages you go to approximately 50–55 pages of fun-filled description and dialogue. It may sound like this doesn't leave much room for individual creativity, after all the writer knows exactly what will happen in each scene but, in fact, there are many ways to write each scene and the writer has to pick the best way. Then Joss gives notes on the first draft. These can be minor or enormously detailed, or "This scene? Make it better." It takes several days, usually, for the writer to implement the changes he asks for, because it [can] require rethinking in a big way. There may be further drafts after that, time permitting. Eventually, Joss takes the script away from the writer, into his lair of genius and does his own rewrite. Again, [it can be] minor or enormous. Then it gets filmed. So I laugh when people say that one of us has better "plotting" than another or that Joss wouldn't have let a character say that if he'd written the episode. It *all* goes through the big guy and it's all the better for it . . . When Joss writes an episode, Joss writes an episode *himself*. It's a beautiful process of aloneness. Actually, quite inspiring.'

Reality Bites: The reaction of some online *Buffy* fans to the postponement of 'Earshot', in light of the terrible events that took place in Colorado, says much about TV fans' occasional lack of priorities. WB's decision to delay broadcast was supported by Joss Whedon who told the *Posting Board*: 'We're taking it out of the order. It's about how lonely everybody is . . . and how somebody just snaps.' (Whedon also noted: 'Oddly enough, when we were shooting it I thought it felt like the final High School episode. The last three are very personal, but 'Earshot' sort of contains the show's *thesis statement* in a way, though I wish it could have aired in order.') Seth Green added: '[It was] the right decision to postpone . . . It would have seemed really callous and inappropriate. But the actual episode has nothing to do with school violence. It's a red herring in the story.' WB's main concern was one exchange: Xander: 'I'm still having problems with the fact that one of us is just gonna gun everyone down for no reason.' Cordelia: 'Yeah, because that *never* happens at American high schools?' Oz: 'It's bordering on trendy'; plus Xander's: 'Who hasn't just idly thought about taking out the whole place with a semi-automatic?' 'I don't think I have ever been suicidal at the point that Jonathan was at in "Earshot", so I can't really say that I could relate to that emotional state,' Danny Strong told *The Watcher's Web*. 'As far as the decision to pull it, I agreed with it. I thought it would have been totally insensitive to air the episode in the same week as Columbine. I still can't believe that Columbine happened.' A study of the *Buffy* newsgroups following the decision showed some posters allowing their disappointment to cloud both judgement and taste. The sad fact is that fifteen people in Colorado were unable to watch 'Earshot' when it was eventually transmitted, whether they were fans or not. At the end of the day, it's still *just* a TV series.

53
Choices

US Transmission Date: 4 May 1999
UK Transmission Date: 18 Nov. 1999 (Sky)
31 Aug. 2000 (BBC2)

Writer: David Fury
Director: James A Contner
Cast: Keith Brunsmann (Vamp Lackey), Jimmie F Skaggs (Courier),
Michael Schoenfield (Security Guard #1), Seth Coltan (Security Guard #2),
Jason Reed (Vamp Guard), Brett Moses (Student)
French title: *La Boîte De Gavrok*
German title: *Die Box Von Gavrock*

The final preparations for the Mayor's Ascension are under-way but the last piece of the jigsaw, the Box of Gavrok, comes to the attention of Buffy and her friends. An attempt to capture the Box from the Mayor's office succeeds, but Willow is taken hostage by Faith and a swap is arranged in the school cafeteria at night. Snyder unwittingly interferes and the Box is briefly opened, revealing its deadly contents. Meanwhile, Buffy and Willow have some hard choices to make about where they will go to college, and Cordelia faces an uncertain future.

Authority Sucks!: Wesley gives a little Masonic-type crossed-fingers sign when he starts his 'by the power invested in me by the Council' bit.

The Conspiracy Starts at Home Time: The Mayor receives the Box of Gavrok from Central America. It contains 'fifty billion' of the spider-crab creatures. He finally meets Buffy (although they were in the same room in **45**, 'Gingerbread', and almost met in the sewers in **40**, 'Band Candy').

A Little Learning is a Dangerous Thing: Buffy has received acceptances from Northwestern University in Illinois and UC Sunnydale. Willow, inevitably, has the pick of 'every school in the country' (Harvard, Yale and MIT are mentioned) and 'four or five in Europe' (including Oxford). Cordelia's include USC, Colorado State and Columbia.

Mom's Apple Pie: Joyce's pride in Buffy's university acceptances is touching.

Denial, Thy Name is Joyce: Willow: 'Sounds like your mom's in a state of denial.' Buffy: 'More like a continent.'

Denial, Thy Name is Willow: When Buffy says her mother has to realise she can't leave Sunnydale, Willow says, 'Maybe not now, but soon . . . Or maybe I too hail from Denial Land.'

It's a Designer Label!: *What* is Willow wearing? (The pink dress thing with nonmatching sheepskin coat and Doctor Martens.) Also, Xander's 'Bean Sprout' T-shirt and Giles's kipper tie, Buffy's green dress and Faith's *incredibly* revealing top.

References: Faith turning to 'the dark side of the Force' refers to Darth Vader in the *Star Wars* movies. Also, the 'Duck and Cover' campaign (see **35**, 'Anne'), *Batman* ('Think about the future', see **24**, 'Bad Eggs') and Nancy Drew. Xander is reading Jack Kerouac's *On the Road*, preparing for his sojourn as a bohemian. Willow refers to Friedrich W Moller's song

'The Happy Wanderer'. 'Raise 'em up my inner flagpole, see which one I salute,' misquotes *Twelve Angry Men*.

Bitch!: Xander: 'I think it'll be good for me, help me to find myself.' Cordelia: 'And help us to lose you. Everyone's a winner.' Xander: 'Look who just popped open a fresh can of venom!' Plus Cordy's memorable put-down of all the schools Willow has been accepted for: 'Oxford? Whoopee. Four years in teabag central, sounds thrilling. MIT is a Clearasil ad with housing and Yale is a dumping ground for those who didn't get into Harvard.' When Buffy tries to intervene with: 'You guys, don't forget to breathe between insults,' Cordy's comeback is, 'I'm sorry Buffy, this conversation is reserved for those who actually *have* a future.' 'She was just being Cordelia, only more so,' notes a conciliatory Willow. Later, Cordelia and Xander have another go. Xander: 'Ten minutes with you and the admissions department decided that they'd already reached their mean-spirited, superficial-princess quota.' Cordelia: 'And once again, the gold medal in the Being Wrong event goes to Xander "I'm as stupid as I look" Harris.'

Awesome!: Willow leaving Oz and Xander a diagram on how to mix the ingredients for her spell (Oz: 'There's you, there's me.' Xander: 'How can you tell which is which? They both kind of look stick-figurey.' Oz: 'This one's me. See the little guitar?'). Oz's violent outburst, Angel and Buffy taking on two vampires in the Mayor's office and Snyder with the chair clamped to his chest. The Mayor telling Angel and Buffy their relationship is doomed is a defining moment in the series. Given that so much of the show is about denial (from Buffy's continual denial of who she is, to the populace's denial of their surroundings), it's interesting that it needs the series' most heinous villain to make the point . . .

Denial, Thy Names are Buffy and Angel: But, of course, they don't take any notice. It'll all end in tears. (See **54**, 'The Prom'.)

Surprise!: The revelation that Cordelia is *working* in that dress shop. (See **54**, 'The Prom'.)

The Drugs Don't Work: Snyder: 'OK, what's in the bag?' Student: 'My lunch.' Snyder: 'Is that the new drug lingo?' Snyder's quest seems to be a single-handed campaign to stamp out drugs even where they don't exist. As he asks the Scooby

Gang, 'Why couldn't you be dealing drugs like *normal* people?'

Valley-Speak: Buffy: 'I gotta have a plan? Really? I can't just be proactive with pep?'

Logic, Let Me Introduce You to This Window: Did David Boreanaz dye his hair? It looks a lot darker than normal. When Cordelia shows Xander her acceptance letters, she hands him three envelopes saying, 'USC, Colorado State, Duke'. She then produces two more, one with a USC logo, 'and Columbia'. After the Gavrok spider-crab thing is killed by Buffy, Angel helps her up, but where has the dead creature gone?

I Just *Love* Your Accent: Buffy: 'I can't believe you got into Oxford.' Oz: 'There's some deep academia there.' Buffy: 'That's where they make Gileses!' Willow: 'I could learn and have scones.' If *Inspector Morse* is to be believed, Oxford's got a mortality rate higher than Sunnydale.

Quote/Unquote: Mayor Wilkins on his present to Faith: 'You be careful not to put somebody's eye out with that thing. Till I tell you to.'

Buffy, when Wesley reminds her that she is the Slayer: 'I'm also a person. You can't just define me by my Slayerness. That's . . . "something-ism".'

Faith on the courier: 'I made him an offer he couldn't survive.'

Willow to Vampire: 'Did you get permission to eat the hostage?'

Mayor Wilkins: 'This is exciting, isn't it? Clandestine meetings by dark of night, exchange of prisoners . . . I feel like we should all be wearing trenchcoats.'

Notes: 'Now we're supposed to decide what to do with our lives.' A pleasant way to snuggle into the Ascension story-arc. 'Choices' isn't the greatest of episodes (there's not much plot but there *is* a lot of capture-escape-capture), but it has much energy and humour. And, in Willow's confrontation with Faith, a key moment in the series.

Buffy's Aunt Arlene lives in Illinois. She and Angel recently found a fire demon's nest in a cave by the beach (which Angel considered 'a nice change of pace'). There's a reference to 'Mr Pointy' (see **33**, 'Becoming' Part 1). It's established that Buffy will 'live in' at college next season. The Mayor had an Irish setter called Rusty. He married his wife, Edna Mae, in 1903 and was with her until she died, wrinkled and senile and cursing him for his youth, which indicates she, at least, was human.

Novelisation: By Yvonne Navarro in *The Willow Files Vol. 2* (Pocket Books, February 2001).

54

The Prom

US Transmission Date: 11 May 1999
UK Transmission Date: 19 Nov. 1999 (Sky)
7 Sep. 2000 (BBC2)

Writer: Marti Noxon
Director: David Solomon
Cast: Brad Kane (Tucker Wells),
Andrea E Taylor (Sales Girl), Mike Kimmel (Butcher),
Tove Kingsbury (Tux Boy), Michael Zlabinger (AS Student at Mic),
Monica Serene Garnich (Pretty Girl), Joe Howard (Priest),
Damien Eckhardt (Jack Mayhew), Stephanie Denise Griffin (Tux Girl)
French title: *Les Chiens De L'Enfer*
German title: *Der Höllenhund*

The Senior Prom is coming and Xander has an interesting date. Anya. By chance he discovers Cordelia's part-time job and is shocked to learn that her family have lost all of their money. But they are interrupted by an attack from a creature Giles describes as a 'hell hound'. A bitter classman, Tucker has captured and trained the creatures to attack anyone wearing a tuxedo, after his failure to get a date to the prom. Buffy, angry after a break-up with Angel, averts the attack by the creatures and arrives in time to receive a surprise award from her classmates. And to enjoy a dance with her former lover.

Dreaming (As Blondie Once Said) is Free: The king of *all* dream sequences: Angel dreams that he and Buffy marry in church, walk down the aisle and out on to a beautiful sunny day at which point she, rather than Angel, bursts into flames. A photo of the pair in their wedding attire appeared in *TV Guide*, leading to all sorts of weird fan rumours.

Dudes and Babes: Anya says she has witnessed a millennium of treachery and oppression by the male species and she has nothing but contempt for the gender. But she'd like Xander to go to the prom with her. (Anya: 'I have all these feelings . . . I know you find me attractive; I've seen you looking at my breasts.' Xander: 'Nothing personal, but when a guy does that, it just means his eyes are open.') Buffy writes, 'Buffy and Angel 4ever' on one of her school books.

Mom's Apple Pie: Joyce finally has a heart-to-heart with Angel (probably half a season too late) which, along with much of the rest of this episode, sets up the parameters for *Angel*. As with Mayor Wilkins in the previous episode and Spike in **42**, 'Lover's Walk', Joyce tells Angel that there *can* be no future for him and Buffy as a couple. The crucial difference is that she's putting the onus on Angel, saying that if he *really* loves Buffy he must make the hardest choice of all.

It's a Designer Label!: Check out Willow's pussycat T-shirt. All the cast look gorgeous in their prom outfits (especially Buffy's Pamela Dennis dress). When everyone gets obsessed with what they'll be going to the prom in, Giles says: 'I shall be wearing pink taffeta, as chenille will not go with my complexion. Now can we *please* talk about the Ascension!'

References: 'Miles to go before we sleep' refers to Robert Frost's 'Stopping By Woods On A Snowy Evening'. Also, *Carrie*, *Psycho*, Prince's '1999' and Sister Sledge's 'We Are Family'. The videos that Tucker has forced the hell hounds to watch are *Prom Night* (1 and 4!), *Pump Up the Volume*, *Pretty in Pink*, *The Club* and *Carrie* (most of which concern disastrous events on prom nights). Many mythologies have 'hell hounds', the most famous being the three-headed dog Cerberus in Greek mythology, which stood guard over the entrance to the Underworld. The creatures in this episode, however, seem more like werewolves, doglike demon foot-soldiers left over from 'the Makhesh War'.

Awesome!: Xander's disgust when someone else wins the 'Class Clown' award. Oz's reaction to Xander's prom partner ('Interesting choice').

Don't Give Up the Day Job: In addition to playing Larry in *Starship Troopers*, Brad Kane was the singing voice for Aladdin in Disney's *Aladdin*. See **73**, 'Superstar'.

Cigarettes and Alcohol: Buffy describes the prom to Angel as a 'cotillion with spiked punch and Electric Slide'. (A cotillion is a formal ball, usually given for debutantes to be introduced to society. The Electric Slide is a line dance, often performed at weddings.)

Logic, Let Me Introduce You to This Window: The positioning of Angel's bed – facing a panoramic window – is stupid. True, the window is covered by a thick drape, but all it needs is for Buffy or Angel himself to get a bit careless with opening the curtain at the wrong time (as here), or to come in a bit drunk the night before and forget to close it (we've all done that) and it's a question of how they'll get the ash stains from the bedsheets. Similarly, when Joyce calls at Angel's during the day, why does he answer the door in clear sunlight? It could have been anybody asking him to step outside. In **52**, 'Earshot', the entrance to Angel's place was covered by a black drape (as the windows are), so when did he have the doors installed? When the hell hound bursts through the store window, the boy it attacks remains calmly adjusting his tuxedo. When Buffy takes her prom dress out of her bag she leaves the bag (full of lethal weapons) outside the school. We never saw Buffy put a knife in her jacket, yet she stabs one of the hell hounds with one. Does she carry it around all the time? (It looks like the knife she got at the library, but she put that one in her bag, not her jacket.) 'Blueberry scones', though very common in California, are rare (and virtually unknown) in England. Derby or fruit scones are a more likely object of a conversation between Giles and Wesley. Where did Angel get his tuxedo from? (Is there an all night tux-hiring shop in Sunnydale?)

I Just *Love* Your Accent: Aside from half the songs being by British artists (Fatboy Slim, the Sundays), there's Giles's rant at Wesley (see **'Quote/Unquote'**). Cordy thinks that Wesley will look 'way-007 in a tux'.

Cruelty to Animals: Buffy says she killed her goldfish (presumably accidentally) when Angel talks about her possibly wanting to have children one day.

Quote/Unquote: Anya (asking Xander to the prom): 'You're not quite as obnoxious as most of the alpha males around here.'

Giles (on Buffy's break-up with Angel): 'I understand this sort of thing requires ice cream of some kind.'

Wesley asks Giles's opinion on whether he should ask Cordelia to dance: 'For God's sake, man, she's eighteen. And you have the emotional maturity of a blueberry scone. Just have at it, would you? And stop fluttering about!'

Notes: 'Once again, the Hellmouth puts the special into special occasion.' Simply beautiful, a story about hidden feelings in which Buffy loses Angel but learns how appreciated she is, even if it's usually unspoken. Cordelia discovers how much Xander cares for her and where love ultimately triumphs. Interestingly, two weeks before this episode, **52**, 'Earshot' (which concerned a student apparently planning a spree-killing), was withdrawn and yet this episode (which *does* concern a student planning a spree-killing) escaped completely unchallenged. Maybe it was the *modus operandi*? (Hell hounds are acceptable, guns aren't.)

There are references to the 'weird stuff' that goes on around Sunnydale including 'zombies' (see **36**, 'Dead Man's Party'), 'hyena people' (see **6**, 'The Pack') and 'Snyder' (student humour, seemingly). Jonathan says that the Class of '99 has the lowest mortality rate of any class in Sunnydale High's history, which fits in with supernatural nastiness having gone on for decades rather than starting when Buffy arrived (see **51**, 'Enemies'). Given the events of **52**, 'Earshot', Jonathan's personal endorsement of Buffy's award is sweet and touching. Buffy is given the title of 'Class Protector'. The clothing store where Cordelia works is called April Fools (see **53**, 'Choices'). Her family has lost all of their money after her father made 'a little mistake on his taxes – for the last twelve years'. (One fan theory is that Cordelia's medical bills from her injury in **42**, 'Lover's Walk', didn't help and this may explain her continued blaming of all of her problems on Buffy – see **43**, 'The Wish'.) Xander pays for Cordy's prom dress with money from his 'road trip fund' (see **53**, 'Choices'), a selfless act that makes me want to grow up to be Xander Harris. Giles states that there are thousands of species of demons (see **55**, 'Graduation Day' Part 1; **84**, 'Family'). Angel has no mirrors at home (which stands to reason, despite Buffy's surprise). He gets his blood from a local meat factory (see **21**, 'What's My Line?' Part 1). He doesn't drink coffee as it makes him jittery. Anya still hasn't got her powers back (see **43**, 'The Wish'; **50**, 'Doppelgängland'). Wesley went to an all-male preparatory.

An unconfirmed rumour is that the winner of the '1-800-Collect' competition (see **42**, 'Lover's Walk'), Jessica Johnson of Maryland, appears in this episode. The prize was a three-day trip for two 'to participate in the taping of an upcoming episode' and $2,000 cash.

Soundtrack: One of the best: 'Praise You' by Fatboy Slim, 'The Good Life' by Cracker, 'El Rey' by The Lassie Foundation and The Sundays' beautiful version of 'Wild Horses' [*]. A ten-second snatch of Kool & The Gang's 'Celebration' brings a less-than-enthusiastic response from Buffy ('that song *sucks*!').

Did You Know?: A highlight of the *1999 MTV Movie Awards* was the appearance of Alyson Hannigan in a series of spoofs used to introduce the various categories. Among the films parodied were *I Know What You Did Last Summer*, *The Breakfast Club*, *Varsity Blues*, *She's All That*, *Say Anything* and (brilliantly) *Cruel Intentions*. The show, hosted by Lisa Kudrow, also saw Seth Green reprise his role as Scott Evil in an *Austin Powers* sketch. Around this time Seth also appeared on the *Conan O'Brien* chatshow and revealed that, although he is seldom pestered by fans, he *is* continually asked by shady characters if he would like some of their drugs! A couple of weeks later Sarah Michelle Gellar hosted the season finale of *Saturday Night Live*, going (almost) topless for a 'Holding Your Own Boobs' sketch.

55
Graduation Day Part 1

US Transmission Date: 18 May 1999
UK Transmission Date: 26 Nov. 1999 (Sky)
14 Sep. 2000 (BBC2)

Writer: Joss Whedon
Director: Joss Whedon

Cast: Hal Robinson (Professor Lester Worth),
John Rosenfeld (Vamp Lackey #2), Adrian Neil (Vamp Lackey #1)
French title: *La Cérémonie, Première Partie*
German title: *Das Blut Der Jägerin*

With the Mayor's transformation at hand, the Scooby Gang prepare for what they believe may be their last day on Earth. Angel walks into a trap and is shot with a poisoned arrow by Faith. Buffy is told that only the blood of a Slayer will be enough to save his life. She goes to Faith's apartment and the Slayers fight to the death on the rooftop. Buffy stabs Faith with Faith's own knife, but, as a final desperate act, Faith topples on to a passing truck.

The Conspiracy Starts at Home Time: The Mayor tells Snyder that his help in maintaining order at Sunnydale High will be rewarded. He's dead meat, right?

A Little Learning is a Dangerous Thing: Mr Miller's class are playing 'Hangman' instead of studying (a 'last-day-of-school' tradition the world over).

Mom's Apple Pie: 'Looking back,' notes Joyce, 'maybe I should have sent you to a different school.' There's a great scene as Buffy tells Joyce she wants her to leave town until after the graduation as she won't be able to concentrate on fighting the demon if she's also worrying about Joyce.

It's a Designer Label!: Cordelia: 'I can't believe this loser look. I lobbied so hard for the teal. No one ever listens to me. Lone fashionable wolf.' Xander: 'I like the maroon. It has more dignity.' There are a whole bunch of cool clothes: Faith's pink dress, Buffy's red leather pants, Wesley's mauve shirt and the reappearance of Buffy's blue frock coat.

References: 'Big Sister's Clothes' is an Elvis Costello song (see **42**, 'Lover's Walk'). Willow asks if the commencement speaker will be 'Siegfried? Roy? One of the tigers?' referring to 'The Masters of the Impossible'. 'This is mutiny' is from *Mutiny on the Bounty*. Xander quotes from *Jaws* ('We're gonna need a bigger boat'). The motto on the school yearbook is 'The Future is Ours', a possible reference to the Stone Roses song 'She Bangs A Drum'.

Bitch!: Cordelia to Xander: 'Dignity? You? In relation to clothes? I'm awash in a sea of confusion.' Willow says she'll miss Harmony. Buffy: 'Don't you hate her?' Willow: 'Yes, with a fiery vengeance. She picked on me for ten years. Vacuous tramp.' (See **59**, 'The Harsh Light of Day'.)

Awesome!: Giles and Wesley's fencing is hilarious, while Oz and Willow's final surrendering to intimacy is worth waiting for. Buffy and Faith's five-minute fight in Faith's apartment is a Hong Kong action movie in miniature.

Valley-Speak: Faith: 'I feel *wicked* stupid in this.'

Xander to Anya: 'That humanity thing's still a "work in progress", isn't it?'

Logic, Let Me Introduce You to This Window: Anya mentions her car. Where did she get the money? Indeed, where does she live? As Angel and Buffy argue in the street, he's holding a cardboard box with two hands. The camera moves to Buffy, but Angel is still at the edge of the shot and he doesn't move. When it cuts back to him, he has the box in one hand. When Buffy tends to Angel in the library, the shots from the front show sweat on his face, but from the side it looks dry. Buffy says that the Mayor will have a hundred helpless kids to feed on at graduation. That's a pretty small graduating class for a city with a population of 38,500 (see **15**, 'School Hard'; **42**, 'Lover's Walk') and a university. (There are other high schools in Sunnydale – see **14**, 'Some Assembly Required', and **17**, 'Reptile Boy' – and this *is* a place where teenage mortality is on the high side.) When Angel is shot with Faith's arrow Giles notes that he is bleeding. If Angel is a walking corpse (in **54**, 'The Prom', Buffy confirms that his heart doesn't beat; see also **12**, 'Prophecy Girl'; **26**, 'Innocence') this is impossible.

I Just *Love* Your Accent: Xander refers to Wesley as 'Monarchy Boy'. Wow, *top* insult. When Wesley says Buffy can't turn her back on the Council, she replies: 'They're in England. I don't think they can tell which way my back is facing.'

Cruelty to Animals: The Mayor eats some of the Gavrok spider-crab things.

Quote/Unquote: Xander on Anya's perception of men: 'Yes, men like sports. Men watch the action movie. They eat of the beef and enjoy to look at the bosoms. A thousand years of avenging our wrongs and that's all you've learned?'

Buffy: 'The whole senior class has turned into the 60s. Or

what I would've imagined the 60s would've been like, you know, without the war and the hairy armpits.'

Anya: 'I've seen some horrible things in my time. I've been the cause of most of them actually.'

Mayor Wilkins after Giles stabs him: '*That* was a little thoughtless. Violent outbursts like that in front of the children. You know, Mr Giles, they look to you to see how to behave.'

Anya: 'When I think that something could happen to you, it feels bad inside, like I might vomit.' Xander: 'Welcome to the world of romance.'

Mayor Wilkins to Vampire: 'We don't knock during dark rituals?'

Notes: 'That's one spunky little girl you've raised. I'm gonna eat her.' A fine example of how to move pieces into position without losing narrative cohesion. There *are* contrived elements (why turn Buffy into a murderer so pointlessly?) but as a series of mini-climaxes, the episode works. The characterisation of the Mayor is interesting. Trouble is he's so *sympathetic* – it's a bold thing for a series to have its most dangerous character *not* going around eye-gouging subordinates or doing over-the-top baddy things that undermine credibility. Wilkins is someone who one feels *would* kill without a second thought if he felt it necessary, rather than spend time boasting like a hackneyed Bond villain. He gets two glorious scenes with the Scooby Gang in **53**, 'Choices', and this episode, which give the impression of a slightly eccentric, but basically decent, family man who just has a hobby of wanting to rule the world. Well, it's more sane than stamp collecting, isn't it?

Willow says she'll miss PE, though this seems to be a touch of temporary insanity. Her scene with the 'trusty soda machine', which gives her coke instead of root beer could be a reference to the mistake with the Dr Pepper can in **18**, 'Halloween'. Percy thanks Willow for helping him with his history and for not kicking his ass like she did in the Bronze (see **50**, 'Doppelgängland'). The implication of the Willow/Oz bed scene could be that both were previously virgins (though Oz's postcoital 'Everything feels different' may simply mean that Willow is the best he's ever had. He's certainly mentioned having groupies before and claimed in **44**, 'Amends', to have previously 'done it'). When Oz and Willow get intimate they do so without covering Amy's cage (*this* could be considered 'cruelty to animals'?), which is an incentive to keep Amy rat-like if *ever* there was one. Faith's childhood in Boston is mentioned (see **37**, 'Faith, Hope and Trick'; **47**, 'The Zeppo'). About 800 years ago in the Urals, a sorcerer achieved Ascension, becoming the embodiment of the demon Lohesh (a four-winged soul killer). Anya witnessed this while cursing a local shepherd. All of the demons that walk the Earth are tainted, human hybrids like vampires. Those demons not of this realm are different. They're certainly *bigger*.

Soundtrack: Spectator Pump's 'Sunday Mail'.

Did You Know . . .?: The first – four-second – trailer for *Angel* appeared during the initial US broadcast of this episode. Against a red background, David Boreanaz turns towards camera with the words '*Angel*. This Fall' superimposed.

56
Graduation Day Part 2

Original Scheduled US Transmission Date: 25 May 1999
Canadian Transmission Date: 23 May 1999
US Transmission Date: 13 Jul. 1999
UK Transmission Date: 26 Nov. 1999 (Sky)
21 Sep. 2000 (BBC2)

Writer: Joss Whedon
Director: Joss Whedon
Cast: Paolo Andres (Dr Powell), Susan Chuang (Nurse),
Tom Bellin (Dr Gold), Samuel Bliss Cooper (Vamp Lackey)
French title: *La Cérémonie, Seconde Partie*
German title: *Der Tag Der Vergeltung*

Buffy saves Angel's life by offering herself for him to feed on, although he is still determined to leave her. Surviving (with the subconscious help of the comatose Faith), Buffy, the Scooby Gang and the students of Sunnydale High surreptitiously arm themselves against the Mayor's coming Ascension. The Mayor begins to transform during his speech and kills Principal Snyder. The students attack using what weapons they have and, ultimately, Buffy destroys the demon, though at the cost of many lives. As she and her friends prepare for college, Angel leaves Sunnydale and Buffy behind.

The Caption (Slight Return): 'Mindful of recent tragic events affecting America's schools, the conclusion to *Buffy the Vampire Slayer*: Graduation Day, originally scheduled for tonight's broadcast will air at a later date.'

Dreaming (As Blondie Once Said) is Free: Buffy: 'Is this your mind or mine?' Faith: 'Beats me.' The shared coma/dream/whatever-it-is takes on the dream in **54**, 'The Prom', for weirdness and beats it hollow. (Sample dialogue: Buffy: 'A higher power guiding us?' Faith: 'I'm pretty sure that's not what I meant.') The sequence's climax is among Whedon's most beautifully realised scenes: Faith places her hand on Buffy's cheek; in a flash of light Buffy wakes up in her hospital bed. She slowly gets up and walks across the room to Faith, still in a coma, and kisses her. Stunning.

Question: was this a psychic transference of Slayer powers from one Slayer to the next (or, in this case, previous)? Some of the dialogue (Buffy: 'How are you going to fit all this stuff?' Faith: 'Not gonna, it's yours') suggests as much. Interviewed by *DreamWatch*, however, Joss denied this: 'It's not really a transfer of Slayer powers, more just, emotionally, I wanted to take Buffy and Faith to a place . . . where their relationship *could have been* rather than just play them as arch enemies. There was a great deal of love between them and that would manifest itself when Faith was no longer in a position to be attacking.'

As for what 'Little Miss Muffet, counting down from 7-3-0' means . . . (See **71**, 'This Year's Girl'; **78**, 'Restless'; **79**, 'Buffy vs Dracula'; **100**, 'The Gift'.)

Dudes and Babes: One final moment of greatness for Cordelia. In many ways she was at the core of why *Buffy* is so special. In *any* other series Cordy would have been a cardboard cipher. A hollow archetypal bad girl, laughed at and given her comeuppance once per episode. That's probably how the character was devised, but in the hands of a gifted actress and sympathetic writers, she blossomed. Angel drinking Buffy's blood is the clearest link in *Buffy* between vampirism and sexual awakening. Joss Whedon has suggested that he was unsure if he'd get away with this scene but that, in the furore over the students attacking the Mayor, WB missed it completely.

Authority Spanks!: Mayor Wilkins to his minions: 'No snacking. I see blood on your lips, it's a visit to the woodshed for you boys.'

Authority Sucks!: Snyder, begrudgingly: 'Congratulations to the class of 1999. You all proved more or less adequate. This is a time of celebration so sit still and be quiet. Spit out that gum!' When the Mayor ascends: 'This is simply unacceptable . . . This is not disciplined. You're on my campus, buddy, and when I say I want quiet . . .' Followed, inevitably, by death.

A Little Learning is a Dangerous Thing: Giles saves Buffy's diploma from the flames. Oz notes they survived not just the battle but also high school, leading Buffy to ask if someone will 'wake me up when it's time to go to college'.

It's a Designer Label: Difficult to work out which is worse, Buffy's leather pants or Jonathan's red anorak.

References: The Mayor on Angel eating spinach refers to Popeye the Sailor and another reference to 'Stopping By Woods On A Snowy Evening' (see **54**, 'The Prom').

Bitch!: Xander: 'I need to talk to you . . .' Harmony: 'You mean in front of other people?'

Awesome!: Angel feeding on Buffy. Wilkins changing into a sixty-foot snake. The following battle sequences are breathtaking. Xander's sarcastic line about how much he'll miss Angel.

'You May Remember Me From Such TV Series As . . .': Tom Bellin's impressive CV includes appearances on *The Monkees*, *Alias Smith and Jones*, *The Streets of San Francisco*, *The Rockford Files*, *The Bionic Woman*, *Charlie's Angels*, *Matlock* and *Beverly Hills 90210*.

The Drugs Don't Work: When Angel takes Buffy to hospital, Doctor Powell asks, 'You two been doing drugs?'

Valley-Speak: Cordelia: 'My point, however, is, crazy or not it's pretty much the only plan. Besides, it's Buffy's. Slay gal, you know, little Miss Likes-to-fight?' Xander: 'I think there was a "yea" vote buried in there somewhere.'

Xander: 'Angel, in his "Non-Key Guy" capacity, can work

with me.' Angel: 'What fun.' Xander: 'Hey, "Key Guy" still talking!'

Willow: 'Man, just *ascend* already.'

Surrealism Rules – Fish: Cordelia: 'I personally don't think it's possible to come up with a crazier plan.' Oz: 'We could attack the Mayor with hummus.' Cordelia: 'I stand corrected.'

Logic, Let Me Introduce You to This Window: Sunnydale is said to have been founded a hundred years ago by Wilkins (the WELCOME TO SUNNYDALE sign in **15**, 'School Hard', and **42**, 'Lover's Walk', says 'Founded in 1900'). This doesn't square with **2**, 'The Harvest', which suggests that the town is much older, originally settled by the Spanish in the 1700s. If the Mayor set up Sunnydale as demon-feeding ground then is *he* behind Buffy being there too? Consider the numerous occasions when world-threatening stuff has only been averted because Buffy is on hand. The Master, the Judge, Acathla, the Hellmouth creature in **47**, 'The Zeppo', the thing 'the darkness fears' in **44**, 'Amends', all Armageddon scenarios. **39**, 'Homecoming', and **42**, 'Lover's Walk', both indicate that the Mayor had full knowledge of what was going on in Sunnydale during the two years prior to his introduction, so one has to wonder if there is something in how he's set the city up that means they will always fail, or if he's been depending on Buffy all along.

I Just *Love* Your Accent: Xander, after his discussion with Giles on tea ('you're destroying a perfectly good cultural stereotype'), makes reference to cricket batting averages. Cordelia demands an 'explanation for Wesley'. 'In-breeding?' suggests Xander.

Quote/Unquote: Willow on Angel: 'He's delirious. He thought I was Buffy.' Oz: 'You too?'

Cordelia, to Giles concerning Wesley: 'Does he have to leave the country? I mean you got fired and you still hang around like a big loser, why can't he?'

Wilkins: 'I'd get ready for some weeping if I were you. I'd get set for a world of pain. Misery loves company, young man, and I'm looking to share that with you and your whore.'

Xander: 'It's just good to know when the chips are down and things look grim you'll feed on the girl that loves you to save your own ass.'

Cordelia: 'We'll attack him with germs.' Buffy: 'Great, we'll get him cornered, then you can sneeze on him.' Cordelia: 'We'll get a container of Ebola virus . . . It doesn't have to be real, we can just get a box that says Ebola on it and chase him. With the box.' Xander: 'I'm starting to lean towards the hummus offensive!'

Wesley: 'It's rather a lot of pain actually. Aspirin anyone . . . Perhaps I could just be knocked unconscious.'

Giles: 'There's a certain dramatic irony attached to all of this. A synchronicity that borders on predestination one might say.' Buffy: 'Fire bad, tree pretty.'

Notes: 'The show's not over but there will be a short intermission. Don't want to miss the second act, all kinds of excitement.' A suitably intense finish to a remarkable six months of television. The build-up is well handled though the effects-overload finale lacks some finesse. Of the series' three major semi-regular school-age characters – Harmony, Larry and Jonathan – Larry sadly appears to die in the Graduation mêlée. The others survive for memorable returns in Season Four, though, in Harmony's case, it's as a vampire.

Angel says that Buffy has no allergies (how does he know?). Buffy's amazing healing properties are again demonstrated (see **30**, 'Killed By Death'); indeed she refers to them. The doctor's astonishment that Faith is still alive suggests that this is something all Slayers share. Buffy also notes that Angel heals fast (see **4**, 'Teacher's Pet'). Angel confirms that Buffy will not become a vampire as she did not feed off him (see **46**, 'Helpless'). Xander believes that Giles's coffee is 'brewed from the finest Colombian lighter fluid'. Giles prefers tea, but 'tea is soothing. I wish to be tense'. There's another reference to Xander's military knowledge (see **18**, 'Halloween'; **26**, 'Innocence'). Wesley says a solar eclipse is 'standard procedure for an Ascension'. Cuts were made to the episode before its first scheduled transmission, including Xander loudly celebrating the blowing up of school, and some effects footage.

Soundtrack: Elgar's *Pomp & Circumstance March No 1*.

What the Papers Said: Many newspapers sprang to the defence of *Buffy* when WB's decision to postpone was announced. Robert Bianco, TV critic for *USA Today*, named

Buffy as one of the ten best shows of 1998–9: 'This consistently surprising and enormously entertaining comic morality play from the incredibly talented Joss Whedon is one of the wittiest, smartest series on TV. Too smart for WB, maybe, which insulted the audience's intelligence and the show's integrity by shelving the season finale because of sensitivity concerns, even though no series has been more adept at teaching teens about responsibility and consequences. Never fear: Buffy will triumph, as she always does.' *Entertainment Weekly* also attacked WB: 'This post-Columbine squeamishness is not just idiotic (not airing one of the few programs that portray teens in powerful, responsible positions is being "respectful" of the tragedy?); it also gives strength to the notion that TV shows should be censored to fit whatever is politically prominent at the moment.' *Chicago Sun Times*' Richard Roeper added: 'Cloaking itself in a veil of disingenuous good intentions while combining cowardice with stupidity, WB squelched Tuesday's *Buffy the Vampire Slayer* because of fears that impressionable young minds might be influenced by watching teenagers doing battle in the hallways of their High School with the town mayor, transformed into a 60-foot, serpentlike creature . . . Here's a thought. If you lose a child or a friend or a loved one in a school shooting, I would imagine your grief would be so overwhelmingly complete that you really wouldn't give a rat's behind about what they're doing on *Buffy* . . . Most American TV shows and movies, including stuff like *Buffy* and *The Matrix*, also play in dozens of foreign countries, including places where they have strict gun-control laws. And guess what? It turns out that the lack of access to handguns actually translates to fewer killings, regardless of what's playing on TV or at the local multiplex.' *The Newark Star-Ledger*'s Alan Sepinwall said: 'Virtually every episode of *Buffy* features some plot or another to kill students, their parents, their dogs, etc. If you start pulling every episode in which a massacre either happens or is planned, you won't have a show left. But if anything in television is an unwitting culprit, it's not the likes of *Buffy*, but TV news. Kids aren't stupid; they see the way CNN, MSNBC, *Dateline, 20/20*, etc., descend on these tragedies and cover them wall-to-wall for weeks at a time. If some troubled teenager decides he wants to go out in a blaze of glory, the cable news channels and news magazines have clearly established that they will make him famous.'

Mark Wyman's superbly balanced piece in *Shivers*, concentrated on the leaking of the episode on to the Internet: 'Something unprecedented happened this spring, after a major real-life horror incident prompted the postponement of two crucial episodes of *Buffy the Vampire Slayer*. The novelty wasn't the cancellation, but how that temporary censorship was evaded, which puts in doubt the ability of censors at any level to prevent material from reaching public circulation.' And, when the episode aired, Matt Roush wrote an impassioned *TV Guide* article, concluding with his assessment that: 'If Emmy voters weren't such snobs about fantasy and youth genres, *Buffy* and its gifted creator Joss Whedon . . . would merit recognition. The writing is *that* sharp, the performances *that* good, the tone *that* consistent – a unique blend of ironic whimsy and tumultuous passion amid the carnage.'

Finally, Sarah Michelle Gellar, in a dignified statement noted: 'I share WB's concern and compassion for the recent tragic events . . . I am, however, disappointed that the year-long culmination of our efforts will not be seen by our audience. *Buffy the Vampire Slayer* has always been extremely responsible in its depiction of action sequences, fantasy and mythological situations. Our diverse and positive role models battle the horror of adolescence through intelligence and integrity and we endeavor to offer a moral lesson with each new episode. There is probably no greater societal question we face than how to stop violence among our youth. By cancelling intelligent programming like *Buffy the Vampire Slayer*, corporate entertainment is not addressing the problem.'

Joss Whedon's Comments: On 27 May, Joss Whedon told the *Posting Board*: 'How about that season finale, eh? Although, looking at it objectively, it WAS a little like "Band Candy".' ('Graduation Day' Part 2 was replaced by a repeat of **40**, 'Band Candy'.) Whedon continued, 'For the record, I don't think the WB had to pre-empt the episode, but I understand why they did. When those of you who haven't seen it do, you'll wonder what all the fuss was about. But one violent graduation incident and the WB and I would feel like collective @$~%. So, July. At least we won't be up against the final *Home Improvement*. Crazy people with guns bother me.' Whedon also noted: 'It's nice to see how much people care about seeing the episode – although there were threats made against WB execs, which is most creepy. Look to poor Britain who get it [the series] in clumps, out of order, on different networks or not at all.' Nice to see somebody's aware of what we have to put up with over here.

This was a hectic period for Joss, as he explained: 'Today's schedule, an example of a typical day: Watch filming. Edit. Production meeting re the next episode. Prep next director, explain tone and meaning in script. Pick song for the Bronze. Casting. Drink huge amount of tea. Talk to Sarah about the script. Discuss directors for next season. Panic. More tea. Work on *Angel*.' And then he goes online for an hour to talk about it. On the future of *Buffy*, in the wake of the furore over **56**, 'Graduation Day' Part 2, Joss told concerned fans: 'The show will not change. I made a couple of trims in the final episodes, but I was on board for that – they just seemed tasteless (by pure coincidence). But nothing will change in the creative process. If someone tries to start interfering with the show, I'll not make it any more. Very simple.' But then Joss Whedon is a remarkable man. When told by *USA Today* that there was a flourishing black market in videotapes and computer downloads of the withheld episodes, his advice to fans was simple: 'I'm having a Grateful Dead moment here . . . Bootleg the puppy!'

The Comic: Issue 20 of Dark Horse's, by now hugely popular, *Buffy* comic series (April 2000) was a Doug Petrie story entitled 'Double Cross' (pencilled by Jason Minor and inked by Curtis Arnold) set in the aftermath of **56**, 'Graduation Day' Part 2, and featuring Angel and Buffy fighting one last foe together in dreams.

City of Angel: Crawling from the apocalyptic emotional wreckage of *Buffy*'s third season, *Angel* was a chance for Joss Whedon and David Greenwalt to escape the world they had fashioned in Sunnydale and step into the adult morass of Los

Angeles. If one element defines the fundamental differences between the two series, then it's *Angel*'s ability to get down into the gutter of The Big City while *Buffy* is stuck in the confines of small-town America. Creators of cult shows often fail to strike lucky with their second projects (*Crusade* and *Millennium* are recent examples). In a revealing interview with Rob Francis, Joss was asked the secret of getting a spin-off up-and-running while simultaneously maintaining the standards on the parent-show: 'We were very careful to learn while we were doing *Angel* not to set a formula until we had seen the results – what they meant, how people responded to them. I was determined not to have a second show that brought down the quality of the first.' It was during the *Buffy* episode **31**, 'I Only Have Eyes for You', that Whedon began thinking about a spin-off: 'Seeing David open himself up to playing this really emotional female role and doing it excellently – without overdoing it or being silly, without shying away from it as a lot of male action stars might have – was extraordinary. That was the moment when I thought, "This guy could carry his own show".'

> Xander: 'College not so scary after all?'
> Buffy: 'It's turning out to be a lot like high school,
> which I can handle.'

> – 'The Freshman'

Fourth Season (1999–2000)

**Mutant Enemy Inc/Kuzui Enterprises/
Sandollar Television/20th Century Fox**
Created by Joss Whedon
Producers: Gareth Davies, David Fury
Co-Producers: Jane Espenson, David Solomon,
James A Contner (59, 63, 69, 75, 77)
Consulting Producer: David Greenwalt
Supervising Producer: Marti Noxon
Executive Producers: Sandy Gallin, Gail Berman, Fran Rubel Kuzui,
Kaz Kuzui, Joss Whedon

Regular Cast:
Sarah Michelle Gellar (Buffy Summers), Nicholas Brendon (Xander Harris),
Alyson Hannigan (Willow Rosenberg), David Boreanaz (Angel, 64, 76),
Anthony Stewart Head (Rupert Giles),
Kristine Sutherland (Joyce Summers, 57, 60, 71–2, 78),
Mercedes McNab (Harmony Kendall, 59, 63–4, 78),
Elizabeth Anne Allen (Amy Madison, 65),
Armin Shimerman (Principal Snyder, 78),
James Marsters (Spike, 59, 62–78),
Seth Green (Daniel 'Oz' Osborne, 57–62, 75, 78),
Jason Hall (Devon, 59), Danny Strong (Jonathan Levinson, 73),
Robin Sachs (Ethan Rayne, 68), Saverio Guerra (Willy, 70),
Eliza Dushku (Faith, 71–2[13]), Harry Groener (Mayor Richard Wilkins III, 71),
Emma Caulfield (Anya Jenkins, 59–60, 64–6, 68–70, 72–8),
Amy Powell (TV News Reporter, 70[14], 72), Andy Umberger (D'Hoffryn, 65),
Ethan Erickson (Percy West, 67), Marc Blucas (Riley Finn, 57, 60–78),
Mace Lombard (Tom, 57, 63), Dagney Kerr (Kathy Newman, 57–8),
Lindsay Crouse (Professor Maggie Walsh, 57, 60–3, 66, 68–9, 72–8),
Phina Oruche (Olivia, 57, 66, 78), Paige Moss (Veruca, 58[15], 61–2),
Adam Kaufman (Parker Abrams, 58–61, 63),
Bailey Chase (Graham Miller, 63–4, 67, 69–71, 73–5, 77),

[13] Credited (onscreen) as 'Buffy' in **72**, 'Who Are You?'
[14] Credited as 'Reporter' in **70**, 'Goodbye Iowa', and **72**, 'Who Are You?'.
[15] Uncredited in **58**, 'Living Conditions'.

Leonard Roberts (Forrest Gates, 63–4, 66–7, 69–72, 76–7),
Amber Benson (Tara Maclay, 66, 68–78),
George Hertzberg (Adam, 69–70, 72–3, 75–8),
Jack Stehlin (Doctor Angleman, 69–70, 77),
Robert Patrick Benedict (Jape, 73, 75[16]),
James Michael Connor (Scientist #1, 74[17], 75),
Conor O'Farrell (Colonel McNamara, 75–7),
Bob Fimiani (Mr Ward, 76–7), Sharon Ferguson (Primitive[18], 78)

57

The Freshman

US Transmission Date: 5 Oct. 1999
UK Transmission Date: 7 Jan. 2000 (Sky)
28 Sep. 2000 (BBC2)[19]

Writer: Joss Whedon
Director: Joss Whedon
Cast: Pedro Balmaceda (Eddie), Katharine Towne (Sunday),
Mike Rad (Rookie), Shannon Hillary (Dav),
Robert Catrini (Professor Riegert), Scott Rinker (R.A.),
Denice J Sealy (Student Volunteer), Evie Peck (Angry Girl),
Jason Christopher (Non-Serious Guy), Jane Silvia (Conservative Woman),
Mark Silverberg (Passing Student), Walt Borchert (New Vampire)
French title: *Disparition Sur Le Campus*
German title: *Frischlinge*

On the first day of term Buffy wanders disorientated around
university, unlike Willow and Oz, who seem completely at
home. Buffy accidentally drops books on the head of teacher's
assistant Riley Finn. She meets her roommate, Kathy, and has
a horrible first day; kicked out of one class by an overzealous

---

[16] Credited as 'Adam's Lackey' in **73**, 'Superstar'. Although he appears in the
credits for **75**, 'New Moon Rising' (as 'Jape'), his scenes were cut.
[17] Credited as 'Scientist' in **74**, 'Where the Wild Things Are'.
[18] Character referred to in dialogue as 'the first Slayer' (see **96**, 'Intervention').
[19] The BBC's transmission of Season Four is the first-ever broadcast of *Buffy*
in widescreen/stereo. Although not filmed as such, Mutant Enemy were able to
offer widescreen prints for overseas sales as a by-product of using bigger and
better film-stock from Season Three onwards. Joss Whedon noted that, as the
episodes weren't framed with 16:9 transmission in mind, lights and
microphones occasionally intrude into the picture.

tutor, while another professor, Maggie Walsh, refers to herself as 'the evil bitch-monster of death'. Buffy meets a kindred lost soul, Eddie, but he goes missing soon afterwards and she's further shocked by Giles's refusal to help her since he feels that she no longer requires a Watcher. Eddie subsequently turns up as a vampire and Buffy is forced to kill him, watched by a vampire gang led by the sarcastic Sunday, who realises that Buffy is the Slayer. The girls exchange insults and fight and Buffy has her ass kicked, eventually having to flee. At the Bronze, Buffy meets Xander who raises her spirits. While Xander goes for help, Buffy attacks Sunday's gang alone. Sunday breaks Buffy's Class Protector award, which finally gets the Slayer angry enough to kill them. Buffy determines that college isn't so bad after all. Elsewhere on campus, a vampire is captured by men in military gear.

The Trailer: For the start of the season, a highly charged trailer of clips from the first four new episodes was broadcast accompanied by flash-captions: 'From the darkness . . . of a new beginning . . . shines the light . . . of a new challenge . . .'

Dudes and Babes: Eddie: '*Of Human Bondage.* Have you ever read it?' Buffy: 'I'm not really into porn . . .' So, Riley Finn . . . lots of fans *hate* him with a passion. I rather like him, though it's obvious that at this stage the writers weren't sure of what to do with the character. What a shame, on the other hand, that they couldn't have found some way of keeping Sunday alive – her pissed-off hands-on-hips pose as she's killed is particularly impressive.

Xander and Oz don't hug as they are 'too manly'.

A Little Learning is a Dangerous Thing: Willow says Buffy waited until the last minute before making her course selection, unlike Willow who, Buffy notes, chose her major in 'playgroup'. Classes Buffy considers include 'Introduction to the Modern Novel' ('I'm guessing I'd probably have to read the modern novel . . . do they have an introduction to the modern blurb?') and 'Images of Pop Culture' (Willow: 'They watch movies, TV shows, even commercials.' Buffy: 'For credit?') Maggie Walsh notes: 'If you're looking to coast I recommend "Geology 101". That's where the football players are.' Buffy manages to confuse 'reconnaissance' with 'the

Renaissance'. 'I've had a *really* long week,' she tells Xander.
Mom's Cardiac Arrest: 'Can't wait till Mom gets the bill for these books, I hope it's a funny aneurysm.'
Denial, Thy Name is Buffy: The episode concerns Buffy's inability to adapt to the changes taking place in her life. Until pushed.
Work is a Four-Letter Word: Xander spent the summer working in the kitchen (and, it is implied, the stage) of Oxnard's *The Fabulous Ladies Night Club*.
It's a Designer Label!: Sunday, on Buffy's clothes: 'I think you had a lot of misconceptions about college. Like that anyone would be caught dead wearing *that*.' Rookie adds: 'The best part was when you ragged on her clothes. She was like, *No! Not the ensemble!*' Sunday hates 'those jeans with the little patches', and refutes the idea that they're coming back into fashion by saying she intends to 'kill every single person who wears them'. Willow's orange pants and yellow hooded top are garish, though they're matched by Kathy's blue-mottled miniskirt and Buffy's pink dress and jacket. Was the idea of sticking Buffy in pink for most of the episode to emphasise her femininity?
References: 'Remember before you became Hugh Hefner, when you used to be a Watcher?' refers to the *Playboy* billionaire. Also, *Planet of the Apes* ('pretty much a madhouse. A madhouse'), Randy Newman's 'Short People', the Nuremberg rallies, Dietrich von Freiberg's *Treatise of the Intellect and the Intelligible*, W Somerset Maugham's *Of Human Bondage*, Lay's potato crisps slogan 'You can never eat just one', *Grand Canyon*, French impressionist Claude Monet (1840–1926) and the founder of the Vienna Sezession, Gustav Klimt (1862–1918). Kathy hangs a Celine Dion poster on her wall. *Must* be evil, then (see **58**, 'Living Conditions'). Xander misquotes 'America, the Beautiful' ('There's some purple mountains majesty'), Joan Armatrading's 'Love and Affection' ('once more, with even less feeling') and *Scarface*, name- checks the Marvel superhero team *The Avengers* and produces a hilariously mangled version of Yoda's advice to Anakin Skywalker in *Star Wars Episode 1: The Phantom Menace* (' "Fear leads to anger. Anger leads to hate. Hate leads to anger." No wait, hold

on. "Fear leads to hate. Hate leads to the dark side . . . First you get the women, then you get the money" ').

Bitch!: Rookie: 'Are we gonna fight? Or is there just gonna be a monster sarcasm rally?'

Sunday to Buffy: 'Don't take this the wrong way, but . . . you fight like a girl.'

Buffy: 'That's my skirt. You're never going to fit in it with those hips.'

Awesome!: Willow and Buffy too engrossed choosing courses to notice the vampire emerging behind them. Willow's enthusiastic reaction to university ('this penetrating force. I can just feel my mind opening up and letting this place thrust into and spurt knowledge . . . That sentence ended up in a different place than it started . . .'). Sunday and her hapless gang of vampire misfits are hilarious – particularly their stealing prints from the freshmen rooms they raid. But the best bit is Xander and Buffy at the Bronze. Funny *and* touching.

'You May Remember Me From Such Films and TV Series As . . .': A former professional basketball player with the Manchester Giants, Marc Blucas played the basketball hero in *Pleasantville*. He was also Buddy Wells in *The 60s* and Billy in *Undressed*, a series that also featured Pedro Balmaceda. Katharine Towne, the daughter of Hollywood screenwriter Robert Towne, can be seen in *Mulholland Drive*, *The In-Crowd*, *But I'm a Cheerleader* and *She's All That*. Lindsay Crouse has a huge CV that includes *Out of Darkness*, *Chantilly Lace*, *House of Games*, *The Verdict*, *Slap Shot*, *All The President's Men*, *L.A. Law* and *The Outer Limits*. Readers may remember her as Kate McBride in *Hill Street Blues*. Robert Catrini's movies include *The Lottery* and *A Kiss So Deadly*, while Phina Oruche was in *If Looks Could Kill*, *How Stella Got Her Groove Back*, *Punks* and *The Sky is Falling*. Denice J Sealy played Betty in *The Ditchdigger's Daughters*.

Valley-Speak: Buffy: 'I'm all for spurty knowledge.' And: 'I didn't mean to . . . suck.'

Xander: 'OK Buff, what's the "what" here?'

Sunday: 'This is *totally* mine.'

Xander: 'The point is, you're Buffy.' Buffy: 'Maybe in high school.' Xander: 'Now, in college, you're Betty Louise?'

Buffy: 'Yeah, I'm Betty Louise Plotnick of East Cupcake, Illinois. Or I might as well be.'

It's Snore Joke for the Afflicted: Kathy's snoring may be caused by sleep apnoea, a disorder in which breathing is restricted.

Cigarettes and Alcohol: During Buffy's visit Giles drinks Scotch on the rocks. However, he later hands it to Olivia, so presumably it's *her* drink rather than his.

This Season's Obligatory Religious Joke: Girl: 'Have you accepted Jesus Christ as your personal Saviour?' Buffy: 'You know, I meant to and then I just got really busy.'

The Drugs Don't Work: 'Slayer's blood's gotta be, *whoa*, like Thai-stick', refers to particularly potent marijuana usually laced with another drug like speed.

Logic, Let Me Introduce You to This Window: When lost on campus, Buffy is carrying a bag. Its stripes are slightly different on either side in different shots. In the scene in which Buffy tries to sleep while Kathy snores, Buffy's bedclothes are at chin level during close-ups, but several inches lower in the long-shots. When the vampires clean out Eddie's room, they can be seen in the mirror above the sink. It appears that Rookie is involved in packing Eddie's stuff, but after a cut to the stereo that Dev is stealing, Rookie is now sitting at a desk, finishing the forged 'goodbye note'. Several fans noted that the vampires live in a building with a skylight, which doesn't seem very sensible.

I Just *Love* Your Accent: Buffy: 'Gentleman of leisure? Isn't that British for *unemployed*?'

Cruelty to Animals: Xander: 'You're sitting here alone . . . looking like you just got diagnosed with cancer of the puppy.'

Quote/Unquote: Oz: 'My band's played here a lot. It's still all new. I don't know what the hell's going on. (Sees someone) Hey, Doug!'

Willow on Xander's road trip: 'He said he wasn't coming back until he had driven to all fifty states.' Buffy: 'Did you explain about Hawaii?' Willow: 'He seemed so determined.'

Professor Riegert: 'There are two people talking at once and I know that one of them is me. The other is . . . a blonde girl.'

Dav: 'Does this sweater make me look fat?' Sunday: 'No.

The fact that you're fat makes you look fat. That sweater just makes you look purple.'

Giles after Buffy has met Olivia: 'I'm not supposed to have a private life?' Buffy: 'No. Because you're very, very old. And it's *gross*.'

Buffy: 'Thanks for the Dadaist pep talk, I feel much more abstract now.'

Xander saves the episode: 'When it's dark and I'm all alone and I'm scared or freaked out . . . I always think, "What would Buffy do?" *You're my hero*.'

Notes: 'Freshmen. They're so predictable.' For the third season running *Buffy* gets off to a slow start, 'The Freshman' beginning like an episode of *Felicity the Vampire Slayer*. You get the feeling that Joss Whedon, great writer that he is, just hasn't got the hang of these season openers *at all*. The episode takes a long time to make its points and wastes Giles completely. Two major points in its favour, however – a marvellous performance by Katharine Towne and one of the series' finest scenes, as Buffy is reunited with Xander.

Buffy notes it has been a 'slay-heavy summer'. UC Sunnydale is five miles from the centre of town. Buffy, Willow and Oz are taking Introduction to Psychology 105 with Professor Walsh. Willow is also taking Ethnomusicology (instead of 'Modern Poetry'). Dingoes Ate My Baby have played at UCS on numerous occasions (and are playing again on Thursday night). Campus buildings include: Richmond Hall, Weisman Hall and Fischer Hall (site of Buffy's dorm here but, see **58**, 'Living Conditions'). In 1982, the Psi Theta fraternity house was abandoned and it has been dormant while zoning issues have dragged on. When Buffy answers the phone and no one speaks, it's Angel on the other end (we see him make the call during *Angel*: 'City Of'). Oxnard, where Xander spent most of his summer, is about forty miles southeast of Sunnydale. He tells Buffy: 'The engine fell out of my car, and that was literally. So, I ended up washing dishes at *The Fabulous Ladies Night Club* for about a month and a half while I tried to pay for the repairs. No one really bothered me, or even spoke to me, until one night when one of the male strippers called in sick, and no power on this earth will make me tell you the rest of that story. Suffice to say I traded my car in for one that wasn't entirely made of rust, came trundling back home to the arms of my loving parents, where everything was exactly as it was except I sleep in the basement and I have to pay rent.' Oz and his bandmates are living in a house off-campus.

Xander mentioned his proposed road trip in **53**, 'Choices'. Buffy tells Eddie that she doesn't have a security blanket, unless one counts Mr Pointy (see **33**, 'Becoming' Part 1). Interestingly, Buffy told Owen in **5**, 'Never Kill a Boy on the First Date', that she had a security blanket. Buffy sees that Sunday and friends have Mr Gordo, her stuffed pig (see **21**, 'What's My Line?' Part 1). Willow mentions 'the one time [Buffy] disappeared for several months and changed her name' (see **34**, 'Becoming' Part 2; **35**, 'Anne'). Sunday breaks the staff of the gold parasol presented to Buffy as Class Protector in **54**, 'The Prom'. Buffy's diary has been seen on two previous occasions – when she thought Angel had read it in **7**, 'Angel', and when Ted actually *did* in **23**, 'Ted'.

Soundtrack: 'Universe' by Stretch Princess, 'Freaky Soul' by Paul Riordan and 'I Wish I Could Be You' by the Muffs, along with another example of Giles's impressive record collection, David Bowie's 'Memory of a Free Festival' (see **20**, 'The Dark Age'; **40**, 'Band Candy'; **59**, 'The Harsh Light of Day'). Splendid perform 'You and Me' at the Bronze, having previously appeared in **31**, 'I Only Have Eyes for you.'

Ad Break, Part 1 – 'Maybe She's Born with It': The initial US broadcast coincided with the debut of Sarah Michelle Gellar as 'The Maybelline Girl' advertising '3-in-1 express make-up'.

Ad Break, Part 2 – 'Barq's *Does* Have Bite': Also during early October 1999, Barq's ran a TV advertising campaign featuring Nick Brendon in a graveyard accidentally staking a vampire and saying that a lucky viewer who bought a can or bottle with a gamepiece matching the name of a cast member announced during 12 October episode (see **58**, 'Living Conditions') would have the chance to 'party with members of the *Buffy* cast'.

Critique: By the beginning of season four, *Buffy*'s critical standing among genre sections of the media was at its zenith.

A relative latecomer to *Buffy*, *SFX* columnist and TV writer Paul Cornell used an issue of his *Sound and Vision* diary to praise *Buffy* along with *Ally McBeal*, contrasting these series with the kind of fantasy programmes that many genre fans seem to want: '*Buffy*'s metaphors are character-based rather than visual. "My boyfriend turned into an animal", "Be careful what you wish for", "Nobody seems to notice me". When you're a kid, the world seems a place of melodrama, of heroes and monsters. In *Buffy*, these concepts are made flesh. Sunnydale is the hypocrisy capital of adulthood: nice on the surface, run by demonic authorities, infested by creatures who are literally too old to care about the needs of those new to this world they never made. The characters are complex enough to grapple with the gap between being archetypes and individuals, like we all do at that age. Willow, for instance, is turning into an insecure, nervy, Jewish witchy wise-woman. (And it's good, incidentally, to see the first positive portrayal of a Wiccan in series television.) Do you embrace being what your peers want you to be, like Cordelia does, or do you settle for not quite knowing who you are, like Buffy? More complex than that, even, Cordelia's a person, not a foil, someone who has awkward relationships with our heroes. Creator Joss Whedon is so good at real world interaction that he's even letting his characters grow up, because he can deal with them at every age.'

Joss Whedon's Comments: Joss described to the *Posting Board* the inspiration for Buffy's media professor: 'I freely confess that he's based on an old professor of mine, Joe Reed, who kicked my friend David out of the class one day in front of two hundred kids. Joe is cool, by the way.'

58

Living Conditions

US Transmission Date: 12 Oct. 1999
UK Transmission Date: 14 Jan. 2000 (Sky)
5 Oct. 2000 (BBC2)

Writer: Marti Noxon
Director: David Grossman

Cast: Clayton Barber (Demon 1), Walt Borchert (Demon 2),
Roger Morrissey (Tapparich), David Tuckman (Freshman)
French title: *Cohabitation Difficile*
German title: *Keine Menschenseele*

Buffy encounters cohabitation problems with Kathy, a girl who irons her jeans, listens to Cher and labels her food. But these are nothing compared to the horrifying demon-riddled dreams they share. Buffy is encouraged to tolerate Kathy's idiosyncrasies but decides that Kathy is evil and intends to kill her. Giles, Xander, and Oz tie Buffy up to stop her from making a terrible mistake. Giles believes demons have possessed Buffy, but research proves that she was right all along, just as an escaped Buffy finds Kathy, a demon's runaway daughter, attempting to procure Buffy's soul so that when her family come for her, they will take the wrong girl. While Giles and Willow perform a spell to right the damage, Kathy's father arrives. The demon opens a portal in the floor and takes Kathy home. Willow becomes Buffy's new roommate.

Dreaming (As Blondie Once Said) is Free: Buffy's dreams are terrifying. A demon pours blood into her mouth, puts a scorpion on her and sucks out a representation of her soul.

Dudes and Babes: Kathy (introduced in **57**, 'The Freshman') reappears. We also get a first look at Parker Abrams who will become significant over the next few episodes. Initial impression? Smooth git.

A Little Learning is a Dangerous Thing: Buffy confuses two proverbs, 'A stitch in time saves nine', and 'The early bird catches the worm.'

Denial, Thy Names are Giles, Oz, Willow and Xander: After all of the weird stuff they've seen, one would have thought the Scooby Gang willing to trust Buffy's instincts.

It's a Designer Label!: Lots of interesting clothes, starting with a yellow miniskirt worn by an extra in the opening scene. Kathy's various brightly coloured T-shirts and red shorts, Buffy's grey hooded top and red boob-tube, Willow's strange woollen shawl and rich-blue top and Oz's peach 'Libertyville' and green 'The Wheel' T-shirts and sheepskin coat (a literal wolf in sheep's clothing).

References: Kathy's musical taste provokes references to chronically unhip TV station VH-1 and the 90s trends of 'trip-hop' and 'riot grrl'. In a similar, diva, vein Parker notes: 'There's lots of popular artists who don't get their dues: Madonna, Whitney . . .' Also, German printer Johann Gutenberg, oblique references to *The Terminator* ('He'll be back'), *Really Bad Things*, *Austin Powers: The Spy Who Shagged Me* ('Mini-Mom of Momdonia'), Detroit ice-hockey team the Red Wings, *Titanic* and *The Exorcist* ('been doing a Linda Blair on us'). Buffy's dreams may have been influenced by *Rosemary's Baby*, while the bit where Kathy plays with her hard-boiled egg is similar to a scene in *Angel Heart*.

Bitch!: A girly cat-fight fest. Kathy: 'I just wanted to make sure that we didn't have a thief or something.' Buffy: 'Like who? Sid the Wily Dairy Gnome?' Buffy tells Giles: 'It's probably just me having a bitch attack.' Kathy feels that: 'Your problem is you're spoiled. Maybe the world revolved around you where you used to live, but it's share-time now.'

Awesome!: Oz's reaction after Buffy has reduced a park bench to matchwood: 'On the plus side you've killed the bench, which was looking shifty.' The Buffy–Kathy fight is hugely impressive (Sophia Crawford really earning her money, being thrown around the room like a rag doll). But it's the scenes of Buffy trying to convince her friends that Kathy is evil that impress most. (Xander, to the captured Buffy: 'This hurts me more than it hurts you.' Buffy: 'Not yet, but it will.')

Surprise!: Kathy's human face coming off in Buffy's hands, revealing her green eyes and orange skin.

'You May Remember Me From Such Films and TV Series As . . .': Adam Kaufman plays Ethan in *Dawson's Creek*, while Paige Moss was Tara Marks in *Beverly Hills 90210*. Her movies include *Can't Hardly Wait*, *Murder Live!* and *Killer Instinct*.

Don't Give Up the Day Job: Clayton Barber, one-time Angel stunt double, also worked on *Blade*, doubled for Chris O'Donnell in *Batman and Robin* and was in *Summer of Sam*.

Valley-Speak: Buffy: 'I'm looking for something *lurky* here.' And: 'I'm still going *ick* from the last time you tried to recapture your youth.' (See **40**, 'Band Candy'.) And: 'It's no big. I just figured I'd hang.'

Willow: 'So, spill. What was that all about, with the *cutie patootie*?' And: 'I have a *sucky* roomie too. You just have to deal.'

Buffy: 'Listening to *The Best of VH-1* all day sort of put me on edge.' Willow: 'Kathy's still spinnin' the divas?' Buffy: '"Coz it's *the fun-est*!" No big.'

Xander: 'Hit the girl with your best shot, then *hasta*.' Oz: 'Gotta respect the drive-by.' Xander: 'Low rejection, fond memories.'

Kathy: 'Quit it!'

Cigarettes and Alcohol: Oz refers to a Bloody Mary (vodka and tomato juice), 'without the Mary'.

Logic, Let Me Introduce You to This Window: Kathy shows Buffy her phone-call logging system and points at a pad of paper. In one shot, the uncapped end of the pen is pointing at the paper, but in the next the pen is the other way round. As Buffy and Willow are walking away from Buffy's dorm, Willow is carrying a bag, the straps of which are solid colour on one side and camouflage print on the other. The straps flip back and forth between shots. When Kathy joins Buffy on patrol, watch Buffy's ponytail, which is in a different position each shot. Giles tosses a towel over his shoulder when he sits down. When he stands up later, the towel is in his hand, but it returns to his shoulder seconds later. When Oz and Xander walk towards the tied-up Buffy, Oz is on Xander's right. Buffy knocks their heads together and they fall down, but in the shot of them on the floor, they've switched sides. During the Buffy–Kathy fight, the phone ends up between their night-stands. When the portal is opened, the phone is nowhere to be seen. Contrary to the implication of **57**, 'The Freshman', Buffy's dorm is Stevenson, not Fischer Hall.

Quote/Unquote: Buffy: 'Kathy's like, "It's share-time." And I'm like, "Oh yeah? Share this".' Oz: 'So either you hit her or you did your wacky mime routine for her?' Buffy: 'I didn't do either, actually. But she deserved it, don't ya think?' Oz: '*Nobody* deserves mime.'

Willow, on the telephone: 'Giles, I just talked to Buffy and I think she's feeling a little insane. Not *bitchy crazy*, more like *homicidal maniac crazy*. So I told her to come to you.'

Buffy: 'She has parts that can grow after they're detached. She irons her jeans. *She's evil*. She has to be destroyed.'

Taparrich: 'Do you have any idea how much trouble you're in young lady?' Kathy: 'I'm 3,000 years old. When are you going to stop treating me like I'm 900?'

Notes: 'Kathy's evil . . . I'm gonna have to kill her.' Better. An interesting premise (the, literal, 'roommate from Hell') and some lovely directional touches, but the pacing is hopeless with a crammed last five minutes and a convenient denouement spoiling earlier good dialogue and characterisation.

Buffy and Kathy's (and, later, Willow's) room is number 214. Both Buffy and Willow chew gum (see **U1**, the untransmitted pilot). Willow suggests that Buffy has become 'almost Cordelia-esque', the first reference to Cordy since **56**, 'Graduation Day' Part 2. Another of the courses Willow is taking is English. Her roommate seems to be a party animal. Willow hangs a Dingoes Ate My Baby poster at the end of the episode. Buffy refers to 'The Grotto', presumably a coffee shop on campus. The dining hall at UCS is called 'Rocket Cafe'. Kathy tells the Scoobies that she is originally from Nebraska. The ritual of Mok'tagar, a race of trans-dimensional demons, involves the forced ingestion of animal blood while the victim sleeps. But while the Mok'tagar can assume many forms, including human, they can always recognise their kind due to the lack of a soul.

Further to the 'Barq's Buffy Halloween Bash' (see **57**, 'The Freshman'), the winning character gamepiece was revealed to be *Riley Finn*.

Soundtrack: Cher's 'Believe'. Over and over . . . Willow listens to Four Star Mary's 'Pain' [*] on the stereo. Four Star Mary (see **78**, 'Restless') are the band that provide Dingoes Ate My Baby with their songs and this highlight of their 1999 CD *Thrown to the Wolves* previously featured in both **28**, 'Bewitched, Bothered and Bewildered' and **36**, 'Dead Man's Party'. Dingoes seem to have been in a studio and recorded at some stage (see **63**, 'The Initiative').

Joss Whedon Comments: 'Reaction seems mixed but OK. I can live with that,' Joss told the *Posting Board*. 'Some dug [it] some didn't but at least it's a *totally* accurate portrayal of roomies – I almost hired a man to kill mine when he straightened his rug one time. And he hated me even more. Marti wrote a script that I hardly had to touch, it was so tight. Taking/giving credit is a strange thing in TV. Sometimes you rewrite an episode completely, top to bottom, and no one ever knows. Sometimes five of us end up working on one script. Marti has done uncredited work on tons of *Buffy* and *Angel* scripts. Everyone compliments me on the "crane-game" scene in *Toy Story*, which I didn't write. Fact is, I've built an extraordinary staff. Wait till you see Jane Espenson's work next week.'

59

The Harsh Light of Day

US Transmission Date: 19 Oct. 1999
UK Transmission Date: 21 Jan. 2000 (Sky)
12 Oct. 2000 (BBC2)

Writer: Jane Espenson
Director: James A Contner
Cast: Melix (Bryan)
French title: *Désillusion*
German title: *Der Stein von Amara*

Harmony returns to Sunnydale as a vampire. She attacks Willow but Oz saves her. Harmony, meanwhile, heads underground to her new boyfriend . . . Spike, who is trying to dig into a crypt. Buffy and Parker Abrams go to a frat party and run into Spike and Harmony, who mentions 'the Gem of Amara', much to Spike's annoyance. Giles always believed the Gem (which renders the wearer invincible) was a myth. Xander, meanwhile, has to deal with the return of Anya and her suggestion that they have sex so that she can get Xander out of her mind. Afterwards Anya tells Xander that she is over him now, but gets upset when he agrees.

Buffy spends the night with Parker, but is hurt by his casualness afterwards. Spike finds the crypt and, eventually, the Gem and heads into the daylight. He attacks Buffy but she manages to wrestle the ring from his finger. He starts to burn, but makes it into a sewer. Buffy tells her friends that she wants Angel to have the ring. Oz has a gig in LA and will deliver it.

Dudes and Babes: Buffy: 'Does this always happen? Sleep with a guy and he goes all evil?' There's *loads* of sexual tension in Harmony and Spike's relationship, which veers perilously close to sadomasochistic ('I've got an extra set of chains'). Harmony suggests that Drusilla (or 'Dorkus') also shared an abusive relationship with Spike.

A Little Learning is a Dangerous Thing: Harmony is surprised that they have museums in France.

Denial, Thy Name is Anya: 'We went to the prom.' Xander: 'Our one and only date. Second date called on account of snake, remember? And the whole, you used to be a man-killing demon thing. Which, to be fair, is as much my issue as it is yours.'

Denial, Thy Name is Xander: Xander: 'So, the crux of this plan is . . .?' Anya: 'Sexual intercourse. I've said it like a dozen times.' Xander: 'Just working through a little hysterical deafness here.'

It's a Designer Label!: Oz (see **58**, 'Living Conditions') and Willow (see **51**, 'Enemies') wear matching sheepskins. There's *some* cool clothes – Buffy's girly dress and leather skirt, Oz's 'Dragon Inn' T-shirt, Anya's red dress. Also Willow's totally impractical ankle-length dress (a forerunner of several she'll wear this season), Anya's chunky sandals and Harmony's shiny blue pants and lace-up mauve top.

References: Giles refers to the Gem as 'the vampire equivalent of the Holy Grail'. Discount store Wal-Mart, Antonio Banderas (*Interview with the Vampire*, *The Mask of Zorro*, *Evita*, *Desperado*), his wife Melanie Griffith (*The Drowning Pool*, *Body Double*, *Something Wild*, *Stormy Monday*, *Working Girl* and *Tart*) and Cher's 'Love Hurts' are mentioned. Aspects of *Indiana Jones and the Last Crusade* seem to have been an influence.

Bitch!: Buffy: 'Harmony. A vampire? She must be dying without a reflection.' Willow: 'She just made me so mad. "My boyfriend's gonna beat you up" . . . *If* you believe her. She always lied about stuff like that. "Oh, he goes to another school. You wouldn't know him".'

Harmony: 'Hi. What a cute outfit. *Last year*.'

Buffy to Spike: 'And *you* with Harmony? What'd you do? Lose a bet?'

Awesome!: Xander squirting his cran-apple skyward as Anya strips naked. Who said the single entendre was dead? Buffy's casual lying about how she got the scar on her neck ('angry puppy') and Willow's delightfully wimpy 'band-aid, now?'

Valley-Speak: Willow: 'Buffy's looking at Parker. Who, it turns out, has a reflection, so *big plus* there. Buffy's having *lusty wrong* feelings.'

Buffy: 'Sleepy. Yawn. Bye.'

Cigarettes and Alcohol: A guy juggles beer bottles at the party. Most other guests drink it.

Act Naturally: The girl walking down the corridor of Buffy's dorm as she and Parker stand outside her door on whom the camera lingers . . . Whose relative is *she*?

Logic, Let Me Introduce You to This Window: In *Angel*: 'In the Dark' Oz says he only knows sixth-grade first aid, but here he seems remarkably proficient in bandaging a wound. When Harmony tells Buffy that Drusilla left Spike for a fungus demon, her hair changes between shots. Spike rips off the necklace that *isn't* the Gem, but a moment later it's back around his neck. Giles notes that 'there was a great deal of vampiric interest in locating it [the Gem] during the tenth century. Questing vampires combed the Earth, but no one ever found anything. It was concluded that it never existed.' Hardly surprising since it was buried in Sunnydale, part of a continent not discovered by Westerners until the fifteenth century.

I Just *Love* Your Accent: 'I *love* writing both Spike and Giles,' Jane Espenson told the *Posting Board*, although she confessed: 'I find that I've exhausted my supply of British slang. I better read more *Professionals* fanfic, that's where I find the words.' Presumably that's where she picked up 'stupid bint' as used by Spike – an extremely derogatory (and borderline racist) term. Spike also notes: 'I would be insanely happy if I heard *bugger all* about sodding France.' Spoken like a true Englishman.

Quote/Unquote: Xander, replying to Anya regarding sex: 'We hardly know each other . . . You have a certain directness that I admire. But sexual inter . . . What you're talking about, and I'm actually turning into a woman as I say this, but it's about expressing something. Accepting consequences.' Anya: 'I have condoms. Some are black.' Xander: 'That's . . . very considerate.' Anya: 'I like you. You're funny and you're nicely shaped and frankly it's ludicrous to have these interlocking bodies and not interlock. Please remove your clothing now.'

Harmony: 'Is Antonio Banderas a vampire?' Spike: 'No.' Harmony: 'Can I make him a vampire?' Spike: 'No. On second thought, yes. Go do that. Take your time. Do Melanie and the kids as well.'

Harmony: 'You love that tunnel more than me.' Spike: 'I love *syphilis* more than you.'

Notes: 'Sun beaming down in a nice, non-fatal way. It's very exciting.' Four returning characters signal the most *Buffy*-like episode of the season thus far. Xander's decidedly odd relationship with Anya is an obvious source of laughs, but inevitably most attention focuses on the return of Spike. A schizophrenic romp follows. The Spike subplot is great, the Buffy-gets-shoddily-treated-by-guy one isn't. Fortunately the former (eventually) gets more screen time.

A continuity fest. Buffy tells Parker that she once drowned (**12**, 'Prophecy Girl'). Xander says the last time he saw Anya, she was fleeing in terror (**55**, 'Graduation Day' Part 1) and refers to his and Anya's only date (**54**, 'The Prom'). He reminds her that she used to be 'a man-killing demon' (**43**, 'The Wish') and notes that Anya's brutally matter-of-fact invitation to sex is 'still more romantic than Faith' (**47**, 'The Zeppo'; **49**, 'Consequences'). Harmony reminds Spike that he almost killed Willow last year (**42**, 'Lover's Walk') and, from the same episode, there are references to Spike's inability to win back Drusilla (who left him for a fungus demon). Buffy has a scar from Angel feeding off her (**56**, 'Graduation Day' Part 2). The Willow–Harmony exchange 'I haven't seen you since . . .', 'Graduation. Big snake huh?' also refers to this episode. When Xander turns on Giles's TV, it is tuned to the news on Channel 14, the same channel that Joyce and Buffy watched in **49**, 'Consequences'. Spike says Sunnydale has witnessed some 'truly spectacular kickings of my ass', which include **15**, 'School Hard'; **18**, 'Halloween'; **22**, 'What's My Line?' Part 2, and **34**, 'Becoming' Part 2. Buffy has a copy of the Sunnydale High 1999 yearbook seen in **56**, 'Graduation Day' Part 2. Giles cleans his foil, which we last saw in **55**, 'Graduation Day' Part 1. There are two references to Angel.

Buffy and Willow's answering machine message has Buffy saying: 'Hey, this is Buffy and Willow. We're not in right now, so please leave a message.' Willow seems to have a new computer; the last one was a laptop, but she has a desktop in the dorm. Xander's basement flat has a fridge and a washing machine, as well as less practical adornments like a framed map of the US and a glitter ball. The frat house seems to belong to Gamma Alpha Pi, judging from the Greek letters on the wall. The house across the street is Tau Omega Alpha. Parker says he switched from Pre-Med to History as his major and that all of his scars are 'psychological'. His father died last year which made Parker develop a 'live for now' philosophy. All rubbish to get inside Buffy's knickers, of course.

Sunnydale is sometimes referred to by demons as the 'Valley of the Sun'. At some point, the gang (except, perhaps unsurprisingly, Xander) found out that Angel was in Los Angeles. They seem to know where he's living since Oz goes to Angel Investigations in *Angel*: 'In the Dark'. Devon used to date Harmony (presumably *after* he split-up with Cordelia in **18**, 'Halloween'. It's difficult to imagine Cordy accepting one of *Harmony*'s cast-offs). Giles owns a TV set ('he's shallow like the rest of us,' says a relieved Xander). He claims he only watches public access television.

Soundtrack: The album Oz finds at Giles's home is 'Loaded', by the Velvet Underground. Oz is a fan, but we already knew this (see **28**, 'Bewitched, Bothered and Bewildered'). Songs include Four Star Mary's 'Dilate' (which Dingoes Ate My Baby mime to), Psychic Rain's 'Take Me Down', Dollshead's 'It's Over, It's Under', 'Faith in Love' by Devil Doll and three at the party by the splendid Bif Naked, 'Moment of Weakness', 'Anything' and the epic 'Lucky' [*] (the song to which Buffy and Parker dance and then make love in one of the series' best uses of music and visuals).

Head On . . . Rupert's Record Collection: 'In one episode I had a wind-up gramophone,' Tony Head told Paul Simpson and Ruth Thomas. 'Now I've got a proper system. Still vinyl, though, and quite right too! A man of taste! Digital is all right but you miss a lot of ambient sound. I'd love Giles to open a record shop. If he ever has a shop it'll probably be a bookshop, but I'd love him to have a corner with all those old James Brown albums.'

Younger fans may be interested to know there was a UK psych/prog band in the late 60s called Rupert's Children. Never had a hit.

Jane Espenson's Comments: 'Harmony and Spike? Clearly not a love relationship like he had with Dru, but I think you can see that he considers her worth a dalliance,' Jane told the *Posting Board*. 'She's a pretty girl and seems to be up for a good time. I'm sorry that people found Buffy too naïve in her reaction to Parker, but I will remind you that she was taken very much by surprise by his rejection and that even though she was to a certain extent using him to try to get over Angel, she still *genuinely* liked the guy. We all know [how] hard it is when you like someone who doesn't like you back. Even once you learn that they're scum, you still wonder why . . .'

Subsequently On *Angel*: 'In the Dark': In LA, Oz gives Angel the Gem, but Spike, together with a vampire torturer, Marcus, kidnaps Angel demanding the ring as ransom. Angel is eventually rescued by his partner Doyle, Cordelia and Oz but not before Marcus has double-crossed Spike to obtain the ring. Angel kills Marcus, enjoys his first daylight in two hundred years, then destroys the ring so that it cannot fall into the wrong hands again.

60
Fear Itself

US Transmission Date: 26 Oct. 1999
UK Transmission Date: 28 Jan. 2000 (Sky)
26 Oct. 2000 (BBC2)

Writer: David Fury
Director: Tucker Gates

Cast: Marc Rose (Josh), Sulo Williams (Chaz),
Walter Emanuel Jones (Edward),
Adam Bitterman (Gachnar),
Aldis Hodge (Masked Teen), Darris Love (Hallmate),
Michele Nordin (Rachel),
Adam Grimes (Lobster Boy),
Larissa Reynolds (Present Girl)
French title: *Le Démon d'Halloween*
German title: *Der Dämon der Angst*

Buffy, still suffering from Parker-withdrawal, reluctantly joins Oz, Xander and Willow at a Halloween frat party. But, after an accident involving a demonic symbol, the gang find themselves in a house of horrors, in which a demon feeds on their hidden terrors. Anya realises that something is wrong and goes to Giles for help. In the house, each of the gang faces their greatest fear but, with the arrival of Giles, they are able to defeat the demon and discover that there is, literally, nothing to fear but fear itself.

Dudes and Babes: Frat Guy: 'Halloween isn't about thrills, chills and funny costumes, it's about getting laid.' Well, we know *that* . . .

A Little Learning is a Dangerous Thing: Xander: 'I tend to hear the actual words people say and accept them at face value.' Anya: 'That's stupid.' Xander: 'I accept that.'

Riley says: 'Halloween isn't a night for responsibility. It's when the ghosts and goblins come out.' Buffy replies: 'That's actually a misnomer.' It isn't. A misnomer is when something is incorrectly named; what she means is it's a fallacy (a misleading notion based on inaccurate facts).

Mom's Apple Pie: Joyce alters the length of Buffy's Red Riding Hood cape.

Denial, Thy Name is The Scooby Gang: The Scoobies greatest fears are: Buffy, of being alone and abandoned by her friends; Willow, that Buffy doesn't need her help or take her magic seriously ('I'm not your sidekick'); Oz, of being unable to control the wolf within and, Xander, of being superfluous and invisible to his friends (which had already been dealt with in **47**, 'The Zeppo'). Anya tells Xander that he doesn't fit in with the gang. From Xander's reaction, it's obvious that *this* is a real terror for him.

Work is a Four-Letter Word: Xander helps Giles catalogue his books.

It's a Designer Label!: Riley's white shoes with black trousers. Oz's 'La Farge' T-shirt and his 'Louisville 1988' basketball shirt. Buffy's flowery top and Xander's yellow and black sportshirt.

References: The title is from the phrase 'The only thing to fear is fear itself', famously used by Franklin D Roosevelt. The 'stupid video store' gave Xander the Disney classic *Fantasia* instead of the 1979 SF/horror movie *Phantasm*. Oz notes: 'Maybe it's because of all the horrific things we've seen, but hippos wearing tutus just don't unnerve me the way they used to.' Willow describes *Julius Caesar* in seven words: 'Brutus. Caesar. Betrayal. Trusted friend. Back stabby.' There's a mention of Arbor Day, a little celebrated US public holiday on the last Friday in April. Oz's reference to his Casio amplifier, 'Mi casio es su casio', is a clever pun on the Spanish phrase *Mi casa es su casa* ('My home is your home'). Giles owns a Frankenstein's monster doll and quotes from James Whale's *Frankenstein* ('It's alive!'). Buffy refers to ·*Abbott and Costello Meet Frankenstein*. Gachnar is reminiscent of the wizard in *The Wizard of Oz*, who pretends to be powerful, but proves to be harmless. Xander quotes *Star Wars Episode 1: The Phantom Menace* ('Sensing a disturbance in the Force, Master?'). Possible influences: *Kiss of the Vampire* (the bat attack), Polanski's *Repulsion*, *Night of the Living Dead*. The Halloween costumes are: Red Riding Hood (Buffy), Joan of Arc (Willow), James Bond (Xander) and God (Oz). 'Oh . . . my . . . God' is a catchphrase from *Friends*.

Bitch!: Oz: 'Xander's a civilian.' Frat Guy: 'Townie, huh? He looked so normal.'

Awesome!: Oz's God costume (his normal clothes with a sticker saying GOD), Giles's hilarious comedy sombrero (and chainsaw!), Anya's rabbit outfit. Buffy and Joyce share a touching scene concerning regret. Scariest moment: the girl that Anya sees hammering on the window before the building swallows her. Funniest bit: the last line.

'You May Remember Me From Such Films and TV Series As . . .': Marc Rose played Perryman in *Clockwork Mice*. Sulo

Williams was Manny in *Playing Mona Lisa*. Walter Emanuel Jones was the Black Ranger in *Mighty Morphin Power Rangers*, starred in *Malibu Shores* with Charisma Carpenter and appears in *Talisman* and *Malcolm X*. Adam Bitterman's movies include *Denial* and *Homicide*. Aldis Hodge was Raymond in *Die Hard: With a Vengeance* and features in *Big Momma's House*. Darris Love appears in *Passing Glory* and *Shrunken Heads*.

Don't Give Up the Day Job: Tucker Gates has directed episodes of *Angel*, *The X-Files*, *Roswell*, *Space: Above and Beyond*, *Nash Bridges* and the US version of *Cracker*.

Valley-Speak: Xander: 'I'd offer *my* opinion but you jerks aren't gonna hear it anyway. Not that *didn't-go-to-college* boy has anything important to say. I might as well hang out my new best friend, bleeding dummy head, for all you dorks care.'

Joyce: 'Your father *loved* to take you out.' Buffy: 'He was such a pain. Twelve years old and I can't go trick or treating by myself?' Joyce: 'He just wanted to keep you safe.' Buffy: 'No, he wanted the candy. I was just *the beard*.'

Buffy: 'That just paved right over memory lane, huh?'

Cigarettes and Alcohol: Bottles of beer at the party.

Logic, Let Me Introduce You to This Window: The Frankenstein's monster doll is swinging throughout Giles and Buffy's conversation, but in one shot it's stationary. The area on which the mark of Gachnar is painted is obviously different from the rest of the floor. In the scene in which Oz and Xander bring over the sound system, the hair dangling on Xander's forehead moves around in different shots. When Willow is checking Buffy's wound, her left braid is behind her. The camera then switches angles, and it's resting on her shoulder. The whole chainsaw thing is questionable. Giles's bag seems far too small for it to fit into, let alone pull out so easily.

I Just *Love* Your Accent: Giles: 'Oh, *bloody hell*.'

Quote/Unquote: Buffy: 'I was just thinking about the life of a pumpkin. Grow up in the sun, happily entwined with others. And then someone comes along, cuts you open and rips your guts out.'

Willow on the camouflaged guys: 'What are they supposed to be?' Oz: 'NATO?'

Xander on Oz's costume: 'I wish I'd thought of that before I put down my deposit. I could have been God.' Oz: 'Blasphemer.'

Giles: 'Don't taunt the fear demon.' Xander: 'Why? Can he hurt me?' Giles: 'No, it's just *tacky.*'

Xander: '*That's* your scary costume?' Anya: 'Bunnies frighten me.' (See **100**, 'The Gift'.)

Notes: 'If we close our eyes and say it's a dream it'll stab us to death. These things are real.' Straight-comedy-horror of the kind that *Buffy* excels in. There's much to laugh at but also lots of subtle characterisation and a clever ending.

Only one person dies and that's an accident. Buffy remembers 'when Ethan turned everyone into their costumes' (see **18**, 'Halloween'). That's why Xander wears the James Bond outfit (so if it happens again, he'll turn into someone cool). Giles repeats what he said in **18**, 'Halloween': 'Creatures of the night hate Halloween. They find it much too crass.' Xander refers to Uncle Rory (see **20**, 'The Dark Age'; **47**, 'The Zeppo'), who 'likes his schnapps'. Willow says she has much in common with Joan of Arc, 'being almost burned at the stake' (see **45**, 'Gingerbread') and 'having a close relationship with God'. She claims to be proficient in Wicca-basics like 'levitations, charms and glamours'. She calls on 'Aradia, goddess of the lost', for her guiding spell. She is arachnophobic. Anya and Xander 'copulated' in **59**, 'The Harsh Light of Day', which was a week ago. Joyce mentions that her 'last boyfriend' was a 'homicidal robot' (see **23**, 'Ted'). She didn't make any new friends the year she came to Sunnydale, largely through fear. 'I didn't believe I could trust anyone again. It's taken time and a lot of effort, but I've got a nice circle of friends now.'

Soundtrack: 'Kool' by 28 Days, 'Ow Ow Ow' by Third Grade Teacher and Verbena's 'Pretty Please'.

61
Beer Bad

US Transmission Date: 2 Nov. 1999
UK Transmission Date: 4 Feb. 2000 (Sky)
2 Nov. 2000 (BBC2)

Writer: Tracey Forbes
Director: David Solomon
Cast: Eric Matheny (Main Cave Guy),
Steven M Porter (Jack, the Pub Manager), Kal Penn (Hunt),
Jake Phillips (Kip), Bryan Cuprill (Roy), Lisa Johnson (Paula),
Joshua Wheeler (Driver), Patrick Belton (College Kid #1),
Kaycee Shank (College Kid #2), Steven Jang (College Kid #3),
Cameron Bender (Stoner), Kate Luhr (Young Woman)
French title: *Breuvage Du Diable*
German title: *Das Bier der Bösen Denkungsart*

Xander gets a job bartending while Buffy drowns her sorrows over Parker Abrams by drinking with a bunch of snooty upperclassmen. This, at the very moment that the bar manager has spiked the beer causing the drinkers to revert to a caveman mentality. Buffy is affected too, but when the cavemen start a fire, Cave-Slayer Buffy's instincts reactivate and she saves Willow's life. And batters Parker over the head with a stick.

Dreaming (As Blondie Once Said) is Free: Xander asks how Buffy's *fugue state* is coming along, referring to a state of altered consciousness that may last days. Buffy's daydream, saving Parker from the vampires, is hilariously over the top, including ice cream and flowers.

Dudes and Babes: Willow tells Parker: 'I got your number, *id-boy*. Only thing you're thinking about is how long before you can jump on my bones.'

Giles's description of Buffy is: 'Blonde. About this tall. Walks with a sort of a sideways limp.'

Authority Sucks!: Oz missed two classes of psychology (and perhaps more when he went to LA). This is interesting, since Professor Walsh told Buffy in **60**, 'Fear Itself', that if she missed a second class, she'd be kicked out. Perhaps Walsh simply didn't notice Oz's absences.

Denial, Thy Name is Buffy: Concerning Parker: 'Maybe he's just having trouble dealing. Don't guys sometimes put the girl they really like inside these deep little brain fantasy bubbles where everything's perfect? They do that, right? Maybe I'm in his bubble and then pretty soon he's going to realise that he wants more than just bubble Buffy and he'll pop me out and we'll go to dinner.'

Work is a Four-Letter Word: Xander is the new barman at the college pub ('got my lighter, my rag, my empathy face') which, needless to say, he's hopeless at. His fake ID features a photo with an obviously stuck-on moustache.

It's a Designer Label!: Emmy-nominated for 'Outstanding Hairstyling for a Series'. That's a joke category, right? Buffy's leather 'dream-pants' are fantastic but there are some crappy clothes, like Buffy's orange top, yellow skirt and butterfly pyjamas and Xander's Hawaiian shirt. Keep your eye open for the very tight red dress worn by a girl Oz passes in the Bronze.

References: Xander refers to *Cocktail* and Chan Romero's 'The Hippy Hippy Shake'. Also, St Thomas Aquinas (1225–74; Italian philosopher and theologian) and, obliquely, Tom Wolfe's *The Electric Kool-Aid Acid Test*.

Bitch!: Guy: 'I rudely interrupted and it sounds like the two of you were having quite the meeting of minds. Possibly debating the geopolitical ramifications of bioengineering. You got a take on that?' Xander: 'You want some beer?' Guy: 'A pitcher of Black Frost. I think we have a perfect venue here for conducting a little sociometry. A bipolar continuum of attraction and rejection. Now, given your sociological statuses I foresee a B-rejects-A dyad. I'm sorry, lemme clarify. You see, *we* are the future of this country and *you* keep our bowl of peanuts full.'

Willow: 'You heard of this Veruca chick? Dresses like Faith, voice like an albatross?'

Awesome!: Xander's incompetent barkeeping. And that's about it . . . Giles is completely wasted and hardly anybody other than Xander gets any decent lines. Very poor.

'You May Remember Me From Such Films and TV Series As . . .': Eric Matheny was Chuck Britz in *The Beach Boys: An American Family* and Adam Beam in *Time of Your Life*. Steven M Porter has been in *Mad About You* and *Friends*, and the movie *Favourite Deadly Sins*. Lisa Johnson featured in *The*

Next Step, while Patrick Belton appears in *Under the Bus*. Steven Jang is Sushi in *Mystery Men* and Vincent Wang in *One Fine Day*.

The Drugs Don't Work: Xander refers to Giles as '*Mister I spent the 60s in an electric-kool-aid-funky-satan-groove*.' Apart from correcting the era ('It was the early 70s'), Giles doesn't disagree (see **20**, 'The Dark Age'; **40**, 'Band Candy'). What, exactly, Jack puts in the beer is never revealed except that he learned its secrets from his warlock brother-in-law.

Valley-Speak: Buffy: 'Even if I had a pretend cigarette I couldn't tell you my pretend problems. The real ones have clogged up my headspace.' And: 'I'm suffering the afterness of a bad night of *badness*.'

Willow: 'That was me being tanked and friendless.' Xander: 'Gets my Oscar nod.'

Cigarettes and Alcohol: Willow refers to Wild Turkey, a brand of whisky. In California, you have to be 21 to work behind a bar, which is why Xander needs a fake ID. The two types of beer seen are Poker's Light and Black Frost. Buffy notes, 'My mother always said that beer was evil.'

Logic, Let Me Introduce You to This Window: As Xander tries to practise his bartending skills on Willow and Buffy, the coffee cups on the table move twice. When Xander holds up his fake ID, the shots from behind show that he's holding the licence with his thumb and middle finger, but in shots facing him, it's between his thumb and index finger. When Willow drinks from the cup that Oz brought her, she holds it at the top, but as the camera changes angle, her hand is lower. The second time Buffy is drinking with the guys, the pitcher of beer gets fuller between shots. There's a real logic problem with the end of the episode. It's established that the cave-people fear fire (Buffy even says, when smelling the smoke, 'fire bad'). Yet she still goes inside the burning building. Now *that*'s sloppy.

I Just *Love* Your Accent: There's a Welsh flag on the wall of the pub.

Quote/Unquote: Xander: '*Nothing* can defeat *The Penis*.' And: 'You're a bad, *bad* man.'

Buffy: 'I went to see Xander. Then I saw Parker. Then came beer.' Willow: '. . . And then group sex?'

Giles: 'I can't believe you served Buffy that beer.' Xander: 'I didn't know it was evil.' Giles: 'But you knew it was *beer*.' **Notes:** 'It's all about the sex . . . Men haven't changed since the dawn of time.' A thoroughly *rotten* episode. The comedy is lame and the lack of rationality in the plot is embarrassing. The ending suggests that the solution to betrayal and rejection is to clunk somebody over the head with a large piece of wood. Well, *thanks* Tracey, that *really* helps. One would have expected a debut writer could have produced something more adventurous or involving than this.

Buffy speaks a little French (more than Xander, anyway). Buffy likes open-shirted guys, pink roses and ice cream. One of the sororities at UC Sunnydale is Beta Delta Gamma. Oz knows the drummer of Shy ('He's cool').

Soundtrack: Lauren Christy's 'Perfect Again', 'I'm Gonna Fall' by Ash, Smile's 'The Best Years', 'Nothing But You' by Kim Ferron [*], 'Wonderland' by Collapsis and instrumental pieces 'It Feels Like I'm Dying', 'I Can't Wait' and 'People Will Talk' by Paul Trudeau. The music of Veruca's band, Shy, is by THC ('Overfire' features here). George Sarah, the group's composer/programmer appears as Shy's keyboard player in **61**, 'Beer Bad', and **62**, 'Wild at Heart'. The video Buffy watches is Luscious Jackson's 'Ladyfingers'. Jill Cunniff, the band's vocalist, was a childhood friend of Joss Whedon.

Critique: Tom Mayo in *SFX* didn't like the episode either: 'The Parker plot-thread feels artificially stretched out and the fact that his apology to Buffy is triggered by her hitting him with a stick is a strange message to send out . . . It doesn't help that the usual clever dialogue is largely replaced by wanky sociological technobabble and grunts.'

62
Wild at Heart

US Transmission Date: 9 Nov. 1999
UK Transmission Date: 11 Feb. 2000 (Sky)
9 Nov. 2000 (BBC2)

Writer: Marti Noxon
Director: David Grossman
French title: *Coeur De Loup-Garou*
German title: *Wilde Herzen*

Spike returns to Sunnydale but is immediately captured by the mysterious Commandos. It's full moon and Oz escapes from his cage and wakes naked next to another werewolf, Veruca. She scoffs at his cage-living habits and tells him that the wolf is part of him. Oz attempts to help Veruca by locking her up with him, but Willow finds them together next morning. Veruca tries to kill Willow but Oz kills Veruca and Buffy stops him from attacking Willow. Oz realises that he doesn't have control of the wolf and decides he must leave Willow, with whom he shares a heartbreaking farewell.

Dreaming (As Blondie Once Said) is Free: Wish we could have actually *seen* Willow's dream instead of just hearing the edited highlights ('It's in the sandblaster . . . All Geminis to the raspberry hats').

No Fat Chicks!: Veruca says she likes eating: 'I hate chicks who are like, *"does it have dressing on it?"*'

Dudes and Babes: Willow: 'I need a translator from the *Y* side of things.' Xander's views of sex fall into the categories: '*Wild-Monkey-Lurv*' and '*Tender-Sarah-McLachlan-Lurv*'.

Veruca appears in bra and pants in one scene.

A Little Learning is a Dangerous Thing: Buffy seems to be doing really well in Psych, Maggie Walsh giving her a discussion group to lead. It's got to the point where she has Willow academically jealous.

Denial, Thy Names are Oz and Willow: You name it, they're denying it: the wolf inside him, the fear of losing Oz in her . . .

Rent is a Four-Letter Word: Willow notes Xander's mom is 'cranky'. Xander: 'We're having a little landlord–tenant dispute, so I'm withholding rent. An effective, and might I add, thrifty tactic. She won't let me put a lock on my door. She's afraid I'll start having *the sex*.'

It's a Designer Label!: Willow's shirt makes her look like 'a crazy birthday cake'. Yep. Oz wears some ace T-shirts including a red Lou Reed one, and a mustard Clash design. Willow's sexy Veruca look doesn't work at all. Check out Shy's bass-player's boots.

References: The title is from a David Lynch movie. Buffy suggests Giles owns an Eight-Track (a chunky-cartridge audio format of the 70s), but she's probably being sarcastic. Also, the Rolling Stones, wild-child singer Fiona Apple, the late Jerry Garcia of the Grateful Dead, Elvis's 'Hound Dog', Sarah McLachlan and Habitrail (makers of pet 'environments', see **55**, 'Graduation Day' Part 1). Oz has a Cibo Matto poster in his room (who performed at the Bronze in **13**, 'When She Was Bad'), a Widespread Panic poster (whose stickers and posters have appeared in numerous episodes) and posters for Greg Gunn and Red Meat. Giles appears to be watching *Jeopardy* (knowing that the Thirty Years War ended with 'the Peace of Westphalia', and not 'Yalta' and bemoaning 'You moron. That dinette set should be mine'). Oz and Veruca enjoy an intense discussion on amplifiers, name-checking several brands.

Bitch!: Willow's spell: 'I conjure thee, by Borabis, by Satanis, and the Devil. As thou art burning, let Oz and Veruca's deceitful hearts be broken. I conjure thee, by the Saracen Queen, in the name of Hell. Let them find no love or solace, Let them find no peace as well. Let this image seal this fate, Not to love, only hate . . .'

Awesome!: Spike's twenty-second appearance, ranting about 'the Big Bad' being back just as he's captured by the Commandos.

Surprise!: The identity of the second werewolf.

Valley-Speak: Buffy: 'Yeah, she's *quelle-Fiona*. Colour me bored.'

Willow: 'The Bronze is more fun this year, isn't it?' Buffy: 'Coz of the gloating factor alone, you know? We're all about college now. We've got heady discourse.' Oz: 'Curfew-free nights of mom and popless *hootenanny*.'

Willow: 'It's like a big comfy blanky.' And: 'I don't speak musicianese.' And: 'I felt all *spazzy*.'

Giles: 'It's ages since I've been to a gig. Don't look that way. I'm *down* with the new music. And I have the albums to prove it.'

Oz: 'You're a . . .' Veruca: 'Werewolf groupie. Nobody else gets it done for me.'

Logic, Let Me Introduce You to This Window: When Professor Walsh hands Buffy her paper, Buffy accepts it in her left hand, but the next shot shows it in both hands. When Oz approaches Veruca in the café, she's holding her cup and about to take a drink, but as the camera switches away, she's just picking it up. During the Willow–Xander scene, Xander's hands change position on several occasions.

Cruelty to Animals: Call *People for Ethical Treatment of Werewolves*. Veruca suggests that werewolves eventually retain the memories of their time in wolf form, though Oz hasn't reached that stage yet.

Quote/Unquote: Buffy: 'I'm sure Oz is flogging and punishing himself . . . This is sounding wrong before I even finish.'

Veruca: 'God, somebody's domesticated the hell out of you.'

Willow: 'What if the girl wants to and the guy doesn't? That's a bad sign?' Xander: 'Could be. Or the girl caught the guy in one of the seven annual minutes he's legitimately too preoccupied.'

Willow: 'Don't you love me?' Oz: 'My whole life. I've never loved anything else.'

Notes: 'The wolf is inside me all the time, and I don't know where that line is any more between me and it.' From the ridiculous to the sublime. A brutal love story shot through with as much emotional impact as most series can manage in an entire season. Top marks to Seth and Alyson and to Paige Moss for an exercise in disturbing sexuality. If you don't cry at the end of this, you're a lost cause.

Buffy mentions running into the commando guys at Halloween (see **60**, 'Fear Itself'). She reminds Giles that she 'ran away and went to Hell', before she got over killing Angel (see **34**, 'Becoming' Part 2; **35**, 'Anne'; seemingly the demon dimension seen in 'Anne' *was* Hell, unless she's speaking metaphorically). Giles says he made 'a very interesting moussaka' last night. Though it's rare, this isn't the first time Giles has been to the Bronze (see **1**, 'Welcome to the Hellmouth'; **25**, 'Surprise'). Oz again refers to how cool Giles's record collection is (see **59**, 'The Harsh Light of Day'). Items seen in Xander's flat: a globe, a food blender, a CD rack (without many CD's) and a psychedelic 'Paris' poster.

Willow mentions that there's a Wicca group on campus, which she is joining (see **66**, 'Hush'). Oz's cage is in an underground crypt in one of the local cemeteries. He seems a dab-hand at welding. When Oz says he knows how Willow feels seeing him with Veruca, he's referring to finding her with Xander in **42**, 'Lover's Walk'. Willow says Oz gets a 'blushy thing behind his ears' when he's attracted to someone. Shy have a Wednesday night residency at the Bronze. The Dingoes were supposed to be playing there the following Friday but, presumably, that was cancelled unless they got a replacement guitarist quickly. Spike appears to believe in fate (which seems an odd attitude for a vampire).

Unconfirmed fan reports suggest that the building used for exterior shots of Giles's apartment is one used in *Melrose Place*. It certainly has the same number, 4616.

Soundtrack: 'Good Enough' by Eight Stops Seven, 'Dip' and 'Need To Destroy' by THC.

The Album: Released in November 1999, *Buffy the Vampire Slayer – The Album* (Columbia 496633 2) was a superbly put-together CD of music from the show (Nerf Herder's theme, Velvet Chain's 'Strong', Bif Naked's 'Lucky', a censored 'Slayer Mix' of Four Star Mary's 'Pain' and 'Transylvanian Concubine' by Rasputina) along with songs 'inspired' by the series, including heavyweight acts like Garbage. It was an odd, but very effective, mixture containing tiny nuggets of Britpop (Hepburn's 'I Quit', The Sundays' 'Wild Horses') and the shimmering beauty of Splendid's 'Charge' amid the more expected grunge bands like Guided By Voices (whose 'Teenage FBI' is the best thing on the CD) and Superfine's 'Already Met You'. The CD also included Chris Beck's Emmy-winning 'Close Your Eyes' (from **34**, 'Becoming' Part 2). Produced by Patricia Joseph, with Joss Whedon credited as 'Executive Soundtrack Producer', the CD, helped by some judicious advertising, sold by the bucketload.

63

The Initiative

US Transmission Date: 16 Nov. 1999
UK Transmission Date: 18 Feb. 2000 (Sky)
16 Nov. 2000 (BBC2)

Writer: Douglas Petrie
Director: James A Contner
Cast: Scott Becker (Lost Freshman)
French title: *Intrigues en Sous-Sol*
German title: *Die Initiative*

Spike is being held in a hi-tech facility underneath the university. Riley, who has a crush on Buffy, is a member of this military demon-hunting group (called the Initiative), run by Professor Walsh, which performs experiments on captured demons. Spike manages to escape and finds Willow, but is unable to bite her – the Initiative having put a chip in his head that renders him powerless. Buffy rescues Willow, while the Initiative and Buffy narrowly avoid discovering each other's secret identities.

Dudes and Babes: Three sex babes walk through shot in the opening seconds as a salivating Forrest notes: 'Women. Young, nubile, exciting. Each one a mystery, waiting to be unlocked.' When Riley tells Forrest that the next hot girl he is looking is 'Buffy', Forrest thinks it's a bit of Valley-Speak ('Girl's so hot, she's *Buffy*'). Riley thinks Buffy is 'peculiar' and prefers girls he can 'get a grip on'. The fact that she went out with Parker Abrams ('for about thirty seconds') seems common knowledge on campus. Parker says Buffy is: 'Definitely a bunny in the sack but, later on, well, you know the difference between a freshman girl and a toilet seat? A toilet seat doesn't follow you around after you use it.'

Authority Sucks!: 'Since I'm neither a freshman nor a narcissist,' Walsh tells Willow, 'I have to consider the whole class. If your friend can't respect my schedule, I think it's best he not come back.'

A Little Learning is a Dangerous Thing: Harmony doesn't know the difference between French and Italian.

The Conspiracy Starts at Home Time: Special Agent Finn, Riley, identity number 75329 and his colleagues Forrest Gates and Graham Miller form part of a government project known as the Initiative, run by Professor Walsh. Spike (Hostile 17) has been implanted with a chip that means he 'can't harm any living creature without intense neurological pain'.

It's a Designer Label!: Buffy: 'I need to go find something slutty to wear.' Yet at the party, as Willow notes, she's sporting a 'halter top with sensible shoes'. Riley, Forrest and Graham wear tastefully relaxed gear throughout. Minus points for Parker's horrible red sweatshirt, Harmony's tight scarlet pants and Buffy's gold dress.

References: Ouija-boards, the US Marine Corp's motto *semper fidelis*, the Denver Broncos, the Sex Pistols, *Star Trek: First Contact* and John Wayne. On the blackboard in Walsh's class are references to psychologists Ivan Pavlov (1849–1936) and BF Skinner (1904–1990).

Bitch!: Willow: 'You spend time together, feelings grow deeper and, one day, without even realising it, you find you're in love. Time stops and it feels like the whole world's made for you two alone, until the day one of you leaves and rips the still-beating heart from the other, who's now a broken, hollow, mockery of the human condition.' Riley: 'Yep, that's the plan.' Willow: 'I figured it was.'

Riley after Buffy has left the party with Xander: 'It's not like she blew me off. She just left with another guy, that's all . . .' Forrest: 'I hate to say it, but they're probably on their way to make crazy naked sex.'

Awesome!: Xander and Harmony's side-splittingly girly fight (made all the funnier by the dramatic music and slow motion). Riley punching Parker after he makes lewd comments about Buffy. Plus the entire sequence where Spike is unable to bite Willow, filled with impotence metaphors ('Maybe you're trying too hard. Doesn't this happen to every vampire?' 'I felt all right when I started. Let's try again'). 'The Initiative' set must have cost a fortune.

'You May Remember Me From Such Films and TV Series As . . .': Bailey Chase was Flicker in *Cosmo's Tale*. Leonard

Roberts played Emmet Taylor in *The 60s* and Tyrone in *Hoodlum* and also appeared in *Due South*.

The Drugs Don't Work: According to Tom, the Initiative drug the blood they give to captured vampires.

Valley-Speak: Forrest: 'She's a major-league *hottie*.'

   Spike: 'Your blondie bear is here to stay.'

   Buffy: 'Riley's a doof. He's not Teutonic.'

   Willow: 'I'll scream.' Spike: '*Bonus*!'

Cigarettes and Alcohol: Spike calls Harmony 'my little mentholated pack of smokes'.

Logic, Let Me Introduce You to This Window: Spike wakes up on the cell floor with his red shirt completely open. When the camera switches, the shirt is buttoned to his midriff. When Harmony strikes the match it seems to burn out, but next shot it's a large flame again. Walsh says Spike escaped at 2.47 p.m. This is odd since it would be daylight at that time and would also mean that she waited several hours before notifying Riley. Graham refers to Spike's 62.3-degree body heat as 'room temperature'. Standard room temperature is between 68 and 77 degrees Fahrenheit. Spike says that he's 'only 126', but in **15**, 'School Hard', Giles says he is 'barely 200'. Given that *Angel*: 'The Prodigal' finally answered the question of Angel's age and suggested that vampires take their age from the day they became a vampire, this, presumably, means that Spike was sired in or around 1873 (see **85**, 'Fool for Love'). Do vampires need to be invited into rooms in the dorm? Here it's a bit ambiguous, but in **76**, 'The Yoko Factor', Angel definitely does. Yet in **57**, 'The Freshman', Sunday's crew appear to be able to walk into any room.

I Just *Love* Your Accent: Spike uses the exclamation 'piffle'.

Quote/Unquote: Spike assumes the Initiative is Buffy's work: 'I always worried what would happen when that bitch got some funding.'

   Buffy: 'You know for someone who teaches human behaviour, you might try showing some.' Walsh: 'It's not my job to coddle my students.' Buffy: 'You're right. A human being in pain has nothing to do with your job.' Walsh to Riley: 'I like her.'

Notes: 'Remember, if you hurt her, I'll beat you to death with a shovel.' Six episodes of subplots begin to come together in this epic example of continuous narrative. There are key scenes involving Spike and Willow, and Xander and Harmony take part in one of the most deliberately ridiculous fight sequences in TV history.

Willow says Buffy likes cheese (see **28**, 'Bewitched, Bothered and Bewildered'; **78**, 'Restless') and 'Ice capades without the irony' (see **21**, 'What's My Line?' Part 1; **46**, 'Helpless'). Oz's full name is Daniel Osborne. Willow has been in 'a black hole of despair' since Oz left. Mr Gordo is mentioned again (see **21**, 'What's My Line?' Part 1). Giles likes raspberry fruit punch. Harmony berates Spike for trying to stake her (see **59**, 'The Harsh Light of Day') and has a unicorn poster in her lair. Spike notes he wanted to bite Willow last year when she was wearing 'the fuzzy pink number with the lilac underneath' (see **42**, 'Lover's Walk'). He speaks French. Buffy and Willow kept Kathy's stereo (see **58**, 'Living Conditions'). The Initiative HQ is under Lowell House where Riley lives. Riley says Dingoes Ate My Baby played at a Lowell House party last year.

63, 'The Initiative', was deliberately short on Buffy scenes to allow Sarah Michelle Gellar to film her part in *Angel*: 'I Will Remember You'. Production on *Angel* is generally one week ahead of *Buffy*. James Marsters' name is added to the opening credits of this episode in place of Seth Green. The voice of Xander's mother is heard for the first time.

Soundtrack: Jake Lee Rau's 'Welcome', Nikki Gregaroff's 'Like We Never Said Goodbye', Moby's 'Bodyrock', 'Never Say Never' by That Dog, Deadstar's 'Lights Go Down' and Four Star Mary's 'Fate' (also heard in **16**, 'Inca Mummy Girl').

Did You Know?: The list of Stevenson Hall residents, which Spike looks at, includes Jeff Pruitt (Stunt Coordinator), David Solomon (Co-Producer), and Lisa Rosenberg (Hair Stylist). Other names seen include: Cindy Rosenthal, Tim Speed and Brooks Tomb.

64

Pangs

US Transmission Date: 23 Nov. 1999
UK Transmission Date: 25 Feb. 2000 (Sky)
23 Nov. 2000 (BBC2)

Writer: Jane Espenson
Director: Michael Lange
Cast: Tod Thawley (Hus),
Margaret Easley (Curator/Anthropology Professor),
William Vogt (Jamie), Mark Ankeny (Dean Guerrero)
French title: *L'Esprit Vengeur*
German title: *Der Geist der Chumash*

At the groundbreaking ceremony for a new cultural centre Xander accidentally releases Hus, an Indian spirit, looking for vengeance on the white settlers who took his people's land. Meanwhile, Buffy wants to have a Thanksgiving with the people she loves, but must try to work out whom Hus will attack next. She and the Scooby Gang also have to deal with Spike, who arrives at Giles's home seeking help. When Angel – secretly in town to watch Buffy's back – tells Willow, Xander and Anya that Hus will target Buffy, they rush back into a war between Buffy and a band of Native American spirits. With the battle over, everyone sits down to enjoy the meal and Xander reveals Angel's presence.

Dudes and Babes: Anya loves watching Xander perform sweaty manual labour and imagines having sex with him while doing so.

Pompous, Thy Name is Willow: 'Thanksgiving isn't about blending of two cultures,' says Willow: 'It's about one culture wiping out another. And then they make animated specials about the part with the maize and the big belt buckles. They don't show you the next scene, where all the bison die and Squanto takes a musket ball in the stomach', which is historically accurate if, as with much Willow says in this episode, alarmingly politically correct.

Work is a Four-Letter Word: Xander's current job is as a construction worker digging the foundation for the new cultural centre. Anya thinks that his workclothes are 'so much sexier than the outfit from his last job'. Willow, however, misses 'the free hot dogs on sticks'.

It's a Designer Label!: Buffy's Stetson. Willow wears a garish pink 'Sal's Surf Shop' T-shirt and a 'peace symbol' sweater. Both her fluffy orange jumper and Angel's blood-red shirt again. Anya's multi-coloured pants and red top. Harmony wears a horrible blue and red sleeveless pullover.

References: The Village People are mentioned, along with Dutch post-impressionist Vincent Van Gogh (1853–90), the Californian supermarket chain Ralphs, *Superman* ('black-hat-tied-to-the-train-tracks, *soon-my-electro-ray-will-destroy-Metropolis* bad'), misquotes of Robert Frost's *The Death of the Hired Man* (Riley's line is wrong, Buffy's reply is correct) and Mighty Mighty's 'Is There Anyone Out There?' Iowa landscape artist Grant Wood (1891–1942), *Gentle Ben*, *Julius Caesar* and General George Custer (1839–76). Buffy points out that many Indian reservations now have casinos.

Bitch!: Anya: 'Have you ever seen anything so masculine?' Buffy: 'Guerrero or his wife?'

Buffy to Spike: 'So, you haven't murdered anybody lately? Let's be best pals.'

Spike: 'You know what happens to vampires who don't get to feed?' Giles: 'I always wondered that.' Spike: 'Living skeletons, mate. Like famine pictures from those dusty countries, only not half as funny.'

Awesome!: The scene between Giles and Angel (one of Tony Head's favourites). And the Giles–Willow confrontations (Willow: 'Angel? I saw him too.' Giles: 'That's not terribly stealthy of him.' Willow: 'I think he's lost his edge'). Sparkling dialogue in just about every scene (*love* the five-way argument about how to deal with Hus). The running joke about Angel being evil ('I'm *not* "evil again". Why does everyone think that?'). Plus the Scooby Gang bicycle challenge and Giles's hilarious phone call while under attack.

'You May Remember Me From Such Films and TV Series As . . .': Tod Thawley was Eddie in *Roswell* and the voice of Nightwolf in *Mortal Kombat: The Animated Series*. Margaret Easley appeared in *Slackers* and *Introducing Dorothy Dandridge*.

William Vogt was in *Murdercycle*.

Valley-Speak: Anya: 'It bites.'

    Buffy: 'It's *so* not fair.'

Cigarettes and Alcohol: Giles has brandy in the bookcase.

Logic, Let Me Introduce You to This Window: During the anthropology professor's speech, a car alarm goes and then abruptly stops. Anya acts as if she's never seen Angel before ('So this is Angel? He's large and glowery, isn't he?'), but they previously met in **50**, 'Doppelgängland'. As the Chumash spirits disappear, Spike is lying on the floor with the arrows still in him. One is missing from a previous shot. At dinner, Spike's shirt has no arrow holes in it. Spike complains that throughout 'an entire siege you'd think one of [the gang] would bleed'. Buffy bled twice (she was shot with an arrow and cut with a knife).

I Just *Love* Your Accent: Buffy: 'Native American. We don't say "Indian".' Giles: 'Always behind on the terms. Still trying not to refer to you lot as "bloody colonials".' Giles says he likes mushy peas.

Cruelty to Vampires: Spike on his implant: 'I'm saying that Spike had a little trip to the vet, and now he doesn't chase the other puppies any more.'

Cruelty to Animals: Anya: 'To commemorate a past event, you kill and eat an animal. It's a ritual sacrifice. With pie.' Xander throws bread rolls at the bear that Hus turns into, while Buffy stabs it.

Quote/Unquote: Willow: 'There's some great spells that work much better with an ear in the mix.' Buffy: 'That's one fun little hobby you've got there.'

    Giles: 'We should all keep a level head at this . . .' Willow: 'I happen to think that mine *is* the level head and yours is the one things would roll off.'

    Spike: 'I just can't take all this namby-pamby boo-hooing about the bloody Indians.' Willow: 'The preferred term . . .' Spike: '*You won*. All right? You came in and you killed them and you took their land. That's what conquering nations do. It's what Caesar did and he's not going around saying, "I came, I conquered, I felt really bad about it." The history of the world isn't people making friends. You had better weapons, and you massacred them. End of story.' Xander: 'Maybe it's the syphilis talking, but some of that made sense.' Giles: 'I made these points earlier, but fine, no one listens to me.'

Willow: 'At least we all worked together. It was like old times.' Xander: 'Especially with Angel being here and everything . . . Ooops.'

Notes: 'You exterminated his race. What could you possibly say that would make him feel better?' One of Espenson's best scripts, a comedy that takes time to examine political correctness (and literally *slays* it), the nature of custom and with wonderful lines for the regulars, including fan favourites Marsters and Caulfield. Every inch a gem, every scene a classic.

Buffy seems able to sense when Angel is nearby. Willow's mother does not celebrate Thanksgiving or Columbus Day ('the destruction of the indigenous peoples. I know it sounds a little overwrought, but she's right'). Buffy says that Joyce is spending Thanksgiving with Aunt Arlene in Illinois (see **53**, 'Choices'; this was the first explicit acknowledgement that Kristine Sutherland would be missing for most of the rest of the season. She was spending several months house sitting in Italy). Willow mentions 'the church The Master was in' (see **1**, 'Welcome to the Hellmouth'). Buffy lost Willow's hairbrush. Reference is made to Xander trying to avoid his family gatherings (see **44**, 'Amends'). Angel notes that his 'friend had a vision' in which Buffy was in trouble, referring to Doyle in *Angel*: 'The Bachelor Party'. Willow asks Angel: 'Is Cordelia really working for you? That's gotta be a special experience . . .' Anya inflicted a lot of putrefying diseases when she was an avenging demon and tells Xander: 'Looks like you're getting *all* of them.' There was an earthquake in 1812 which buried the Sunnydale mission. Riley is from Iowa and his grandparents live in Huxley. Harmony has 'been doing a lot of reading', says she's 'in control of [her] own power now', and doesn't need Spike to complete her. The dean of UC Sunnydale is Matthew Guerrero; his house is near the gym.

Head On: 29, 'Passion' remains Anthony Stewart Head's favourite *Buffy* episode, telling Paul Simpson and Ruth Thomas, 'I think it had fantastic performances.' However, he also rates **64**, 'Pangs' highly: 'I thought Alyson in "Pangs" was just extraordinary – you don't see such an emotional performance on television. **66**, "Hush" was fantastic too. It's the one episode we can't show the kids 'cos it's just so scary . . . Joss has some wonderful ideas. "Let's do two-thirds of the show in silence . . .! Just to see if we can . . ." Then [he] gives himself the task of writing it. I love that Joss plays with the medium. He's not content to say, "We've got something good, let's milk it dry." He wants to see where we can go with it . . . You've got **50**, "Doppelgängland" in which Alyson is brilliant as her alter ego. I respect Joss hugely for taking risks, not sitting back turning out the same old stuff.'

Subsequently On *Angel*: 'I Will Remember You': After Angel's visit, Buffy follows him to LA for a confrontation but, as they prepare to go their separate ways, a demon attacks Angel. They pursue the demon and Angel kills it, but a mingling of blood restores Angel's humanity. The Oracles, Doyle's link to The Powers That Be, confirm Angel's new status and he and Buffy share a perfect day. But Angel is unable to fight in his human form. After hearing that Buffy would perish if he were to remain human, he begs the Oracles to fold back time. They do, and despite Buffy's certainty that she will remember what they shared together, when time is reversed, only Angel has the knowledge of what might have been.

65

Something Blue

US Transmission Date: 30 Nov. 1999
UK Transmission Date: 3 Mar. 2000 (Sky)
7 Dec. 2000 (BBC2)

Writer: Tracey Forbes
Director: Nick Marck
French title: *Le Mariage de Buffy*
German title: *Mein Wille Geschehe*

One of Willow's spells goes awry, causing Giles to go blind, Xander to become attractive to demons and Buffy and Spike to fall in love and get engaged. As they plan their wedding, the demon D'Hoffryn notices Willow's abilities and offers to make her a vengeance demon as he once did with Anya. Riley meets a starry-eyed Buffy, who tells him that she is betrothed to a much older man (although not as old as her last boyfriend). Willow sticks with humanity and reverses the spell. Buffy tells a baffled Riley she made the whole thing up to tease him.

Dudes and Babes: The banner that Riley helps to hang says UC SUNNYDALE LESBIAN ALLIANCE.

Demonity Sucks!: Something that fans had suspected is established: some demons have the power to turn humans into demons. D'Hoffryn (who 'created' Anyanka) seems disposed to getting the human's permission first, though it's unknown whether this is always required.

It's a Designer Label!: An interesting mixture: Buffy's leopardskin skirt and the 'fluffy' orange slip-on that Spike holds up. Willow's multicoloured poncho, tartan pyjamas and 'Speak No Evil' shirt. Xander's orange and white 'flower' sweatshirt. Best of all, Anya's tight red top (goes beautifully with her short haircut).

References: The title is a reference to the wedding rhyme: 'Something old, something new, something borrowed, something blue.' 'I'm chained in a bathtub drinking pig's blood from a novelty mug. Doesn't rate huge in *The Zagat's Guide*', refers to a popular US guidebook. *The English Patient*, the daily soap *Passions* ('Timmy's down the bloody well'), KC and the Sunshine Band's 'Boogie Shoes', 'girl power', *One Million Years B.C.*, *The Brave Little Toaster*, Bette Midler's 'Wind Beneath My Wings', *Steel Magnolias* and Fruit Roll-Ups. Buffy hums *The Wedding March*. Willow misquotes Stevie Smith's 'Not Waving but Drowning'.

Bitch!: Buffy: 'How long are you going to pull this crap?'

Buffy: 'My mother gave me that name.' Spike: 'Your mother? Yeah, *she's* a genius.'

Anya on how she became a demon: 'I'd been dumped, I was miserable, doing a few vengeance spells – boils on the penis, nothing fancy . . .' (See **89**, 'Triangle'.)

Awesome!: Giles's novelty 'Kiss the Librarian' mug. A continuation of the excellent multi-handed dialogue scenes that impressed so much in **64**, 'Pangs'. (Buffy: 'Spike and I are getting married.' Xander: 'How? What? How?' Giles: 'Three excellent questions.')

Don't Give Up the Day Job: Nick Marck began as an assistant director on *10*, *Battlestar Galactica*, *The Postman Always Rings Twice* and *Rehearsal for Murder* before becoming a director on *The Wonder Years*, *The X-Files*, *Dawson's Creek* and *Malcolm in the Middle*.

Valley-Speak: Buffy: 'Cars and Buffy are, like, un-mixy things' (see **40**, 'Band Candy').

Anya: 'Off-topic Xander.'

Cigarettes and Alcohol: Willow gets extremely drunk in the Bronze on Miller Lite. Giles is drinking the hard stuff again (see **20**, 'The Dark Age'). In Giles's home we can see a decanter of whisky and a bottle of champagne.

Logic, Let Me Introduce You to This Window: Buffy's hair changes from crimped to straight throughout the episode. Willow tosses her bag on to her desk, hitting a hanging star. The star swings, but after a cut from Giles to Willow, it has stopped. Spike's reflection can be seen several times in Giles's glass bookcase. When the demon breaks through the door into Xander's basement, some wood falls to the floor. A moment later, it's leaning up against the door. As the demon throws Xander on to the tool bench, a piece of paper falls to the floor. When Xander gets up, the paper is back on the bench. According to some eagle-eyed fans, the rat used to portray Amy is male (this also occurs in **67**, 'Doomed').

I Just *Love* Your Accent: The first use of the word 'ninny'.

Quote/Unquote: Spike: 'I won't have you doing mojo on me if you can't read properly. You might turn me into a stink beetle.' Giles: 'It would be a generous ending for you.'

Spike: 'I don't like him. He's insipid. Clearly human.' Buffy: 'Red paint. We could smear a little on his mouth; blood of the innocent.' Spike: 'That's my girl . . .'

Spike on the Scooby Gang: '*This* is the crack team that foils my every plan? I am deeply shamed.'

Notes: 'Just say yes and make me the happiest man on earth.' Another cracker proving that Forbes's talent lies with satire rather than slapstick. Willow's disastrous attempts to rid herself of grief send the Scooby Gang into their worst night-mares (*nothing* could be more horrible for Buffy and Spike than what happens to them). It's a smart script with clever characterisation and a willingness to try something different.

Buffy mentions having seen Angel in LA 'for five minutes' (see *Angel*: 'I Will Remember You'). Giles refers to Oz's departure in **62**, 'Wild at Heart'. Willow remembers the spell that she almost cursed on Veruca. Buffy reminds Willow of her own 'beer fest', when she 'became *Cave-Buffy*' (see **61**, 'Beer Bad'). Willow mentions Amy turning herself into a rat (see **45**, 'Gingerbread') and all the demons who've been attracted to Xander: 'Insect Lady' (see **4**, 'Teacher's Pet'), Mummy Girl (**16**, 'Inca Mummy Girl') and Anya. D'Hoffryn was first seen in **50**, 'Doppelgängland', when Anya asked him to give her back her powers (he refused). Anya was originally human; D'Hoffryn made her a demon 1,120 years ago.

Devon is mentioned. Oz has been in touch with him and asked for his stuff to be sent on. UC Sunnydale has a park called Rugg's Field. Drowning is the only way to kill a Pargo demon. Spotted in Xander's flat: a dartboard, a portable TV, a basketball hoop and a poster for the band Red Meat (see **62**, 'Wild at Heart').

Soundtrack: Blink 182's 'All The Small Things' and 'Night Time Company' by Sue Willett. Excellent 'wacky' Chris Beck score.

Tracey Forbes's Comments: 'We spend a lot of time in the writers' room discussing real emotions [and] things that have gone on in our own lives,' Forbes told *Cinescape Online*. 'What we can remember from college and exactly how we felt. You become very close to the people who you work with. You really *do* end up talking about all the pain that you've ever been through in very open and honest ways so that we can best portray that on the show.'

66

Hush

US Transmission Date: 14 Dec. 1999
UK Transmission Date: 10 Mar. 2000 (Sky)
21 Dec. 2000 (BBC2)

Writer: Joss Whedon
Director: Joss Whedon
Cast: Brooke Bloom (Wanna Blessed-Be),
Jessica Townsend (Wanna Blessed-Be), Camden Toy (Gentleman),
Charlie Brumbly (Gentleman), Doug Jones (Gentleman),
Don W Lewis (Gentleman), Carlos Amezcua (Newscaster),
Elizabeth Truax (Little Girl), Wayne Sable (Freshman)
French title: *Un Silence de Mort*
German title: *Das Große Schweigen*

A group of skeletal demons called the Gentlemen come to
Sunnydale and steal everyone's voices. This is to enable them
to take the hearts of seven chosen victims without them being
able to scream. The Scooby Gang (as well as the Initiative) try
to devise a means of defeating the sinister villains while
deprived of the power of speech. Willow befriends a fellow
Wiccan, Tara, while Buffy and Riley fight the Gentlemen
together, thereby revealing their secret identities to each other.
The Trailer: The WB promoted this 'special' episode with a
series of unique trailers: 'Some fairy tales should not be told.
This one will come true', and 'Not a single word will be
spoken for 29 minutes.'
Dreaming (As Blondie Once Said) is Free: Riley: 'Tell me
about your dream. As a Psych major, I'm qualified to go
"hmm".' The opening – Buffy and Riley making out in front of
the class, before the little girl appears chanting her sinister
rhyme – almost seems to belong in a different episode. Is the
girl supposed to represent Buffy as a child?
Dudes and Babes: Anya: 'All you care about is lots of
orgasms.' Xander: 'Remember how we talked about private
conversations? How they're less private when they're in front
of my friends?' Spike: 'We're not your friends. Go on.'

Anya, after Xander has bravely fought Spike, makes a circle

with her thumb and forefinger and sticks another finger through it repeatedly. Yes, we get the message . . . Tara makes her first appearance. There are hints that she and Willow may become more than just friends as they hold hands to create a spell. An interesting fan theory at the time of Tara's arrival was subsequently proved to be accurate: the way Tara dresses and speaks bears the hallmarks of someone from a repressive, possibly abusive, home environment. See **84**, 'Family'.

The Conspiracy Starts at Home Time: Manipulation of the media: 'Big news item from Sunnydale, California. Apparently the entire town has been quarantined due to an epidemic of, as strange at this may sound, laryngitis.' An Initiative tactic?

It's a Designer Label!: Some horrible skirts: Buffy's cream model, Tara's very unflattering brown number and Willow's disgusting pink one. Xander wears a couple of remarkably tasteless shirts. He also sleeps in his vest.

References: Seemingly influenced by the dreamlike horror films of Tim Burton (*Batman*, *Edward Scissorhands*, *Sleepy Hollow*) and Stephen King's 'Insomnia'. References to the Earth Goddess Gaia, the festival of Bacchanal, Superman's alter ego Clark Kent, Revelation 15:1 and Pink Floyd. Buffy quotes Greek philosopher Terence: 'Fortune favours the brave.'

Bitch!: Willow on the Wicca group: 'Bunch of wanna-blessed-be's. Nowadays every girl with a henna tattoo and a spice rack thinks she's a sister to The Dark Ones.'

Spike: 'Like I'd bite you anyway . . . Not bloody likely.' Xander: 'I happen to be very biteable, pal. I'm moist and delicious.'

Awesome!: Has *any* series shown a tenth of the wit and imagination of, for instance, the scene in which Giles silently tells Buffy, Willow, Xander and Anya the plot (*everything* in the sequence is perfect, from Anya casually eating popcorn while graphic murder drawings are shown, to the horrified look on Buffy's face at Giles having sketched an unflattering cartoon of her with big hips and a miniskirt). Xander and Spike continue to bicker brilliantly (love Spike's impression of Anya). How ironic that, in a series about total female empowerment, it's a scream by the heroine that saves the day.

'You May Remember Me From Such Films and TV Series As . . .': Amber Benson played Meg in *Bye Bye Love*, 'Stoned Girl' in *Can't Hardly Wait* and also appears in *The Prime Gig* and *Imaginary Cries*. Don W Lewis was Major Keena in *Warrior of Virtue*.

Don't Give Up the Day Job: Doug Jones had behind-the-scenes roles on *Smooth Talk* (as set constructor) and *Untamed Heart* and *Equinox* (as a member of the 'swing gang'). Carlos Amezcua is a newscaster on KTLA's *Morning News*. KTLA is the WB affiliate in Los Angeles. The weatherman from the same show, Mark Kriski, appeared in **44**, 'Amends'.

Valley-Speak: Wanna-blessed-be: 'We need to get the message of blessing out to the sisters. Also, who left their scented candles dripping all over my women-power shrine?' And: 'One person's energy can suck the power from an entire circle. No offence.'

Willow: 'All talk. *Blah blah Gaia. Blah blah moon.* Menstrual-lifeforce-power thingy . . .'

Buffy: 'I start babbling. And he starts babbling and it's a babble fest.'

Cigarettes and Alcohol: Olivia seems to be on the whisky again (see **57**, 'The Freshman'). Later she and Giles share a bottle of red wine.

Logic, Let Me Introduce You to This Window: When we first see the clock tower, it's one o'clock. The camera cuts to the interior, looking out at the clock and the minute hand is pointing to the forty-minute mark. As the scene in the lecture hall starts, Anya is empty-handed. A moment later, she's eating microwave popcorn. In the same scene, Buffy holds her message board up to ask how she gets her voice back. The marker pen is in her right hand. After a quick cut away, it's in a slot on the board. As Spike opens the fridge, the cup of blood is full to the brim. He takes it out but, despite tipping it, doesn't spill any blood. When Riley smashes the bottle, a chunk of glass lands on top of the box. When he starts to swing at the box, the glass is gone. When the Gentlemen heads begin exploding, the shot of one of them is used twice. The list of Stevenson Hall residents that Tara prints out is not the same list that Spike looked at in **63**, 'The Initiative'. Some names are missing, they are in a different order, some students have moved to different rooms and this list includes phone numbers. The YES WE ARE OPEN sign seems to move location. Firstly it's seen on a building beside the coffee shop, then later it's on a premises close to the cinema. Spike is shown eating biscuits even though it's been long established that vampires don't eat.

I Just *Love* Your Accent: Spike mentions the British breakfast cereal Weetabix. The two-fingered reply he gives Xander is also *very* British. Amusingly, this gesture has turned up on a list of 'Obscure Cultural References' on a *Buffy* Internet newsgroup. What an odd idea of 'culture'.

Quote/Unquote: Spike: 'Sometimes I like to crumble up the Weetabix in the blood. Give it a little texture.'

Giles: 'I have a friend who's coming to town, and I'd like us to be alone.' Anya: 'You mean an *orgasm friend*?' Giles: 'Yes, that's *exactly* the most appalling thing you could've said.'

Anya: 'What about us? Our romantic evening?' Spike: 'I'm not having these two shag while I'm tied to a chair three feet away.' Xander: 'That's not exactly one of my fantasies either.'

Olivia: 'All the time you used to talk about witchcraft and darkness. I just thought you were being pretentious.' Giles: 'I was. I was also right.' Olivia: 'So everything you told me was true.' Giles: 'Well, no. I wasn't actually one of the original members of Pink Floyd. But the monster stuff, yes.'

Notes: 'Talking about communication, talking about language. Not the same thing.' One of the bravest, most experimental pieces of modern TV pulled-off in spectacular and confident fashion. A story about how people talk without actually communicating, 'Hush' is as good as anything *anywhere* in the last decade and maybe beyond. The scariest *Buffy* ever. And the funniest (Giles's projector-screen lecture for the Scooby Gang).

Willow says that she wants to float something 'bigger than a pencil' (see **45**, 'Gingerbread'; **50**, 'Doppelgängland'; **53**, 'Choices'). Giles takes delivery of *The Sunnydale Press*, the same newspaper seen in **48**, 'Bad Girls' (see **73**, 'Superstar'). Willow asks Tara how long she has been a practising witch. 'Since I was little,' says Tara, revealing that her mom 'had a lot of power. Like you.' (See **84**, 'Family'.) At the front of Giles's pile of LPs is the unmistakable cover of 'ChangesOneBowie'.

There's another Red Meat poster (see **65**, 'Something Blue'). Xander has a novelty clear-plastic phone in his flat.

The call letters of the TV station the Scooby Gang are watching are KOUS. Sunnydale has a liquor store called *Hank's Jr. Mart*. The full nursery rhyme is: 'Can't even shout, can't even cry, the Gentlemen are coming by. Looking in windows, knocking on doors, they need to take seven and they might take yours. Can't call to mom, can't say a word, you're gonna die screaming but you won't be heard . . .'

Soundtrack: The music that Giles plays during the lecture is Camille Saint-Saëns's *Danse Macabre*, also the theme music for *Jonathan Creek*. Both Tony Head and Joss Whedon have confirmed that this was a coincidence.

Did You Know?: Joss told *Ultimate TV* that he had planned for Buffy and Riley to have sex in this episode, but 'it became clear that it was too early for that'.

Critique: *TV Guide* were fulsome in their praise, calling 'Hush', 'A masterpiece of suffering in silence and one of the season's best episodes of *any* series . . . "Hush" was a largely wordless nightmare, thanks to some voice-stealing demons. Whedon devised any number of ingenious ways to propel the plot without dialogue, proving that the unsaid can be scarier than all the screams in Hollywood.'

The cover of *The Hollywood Reporter* from 19 June featured an ad encouraging Emmy voters to nominate 'Hush'. '*Buffy the Vampire Slayer*. For Your Emmy Consideration' accompanied by quotes from TV reviewers including: 'If *Buffy the Vampire Slayer*'s Joss Whedon doesn't get at least an Emmy nomination for "Hush", a horror masterpiece that played out its last half-hour in silence, there shouldn't be any Emmys at all'– Robert Bianco, *USA Today*, and '*Buffy*'s the best show on the air; brainy, good-hearted, gloriously expressive TV poetry'– Tom Carson, *Esquire*.

Joss Whedon's Comments: 'The idea came from a few different places,' Joss told Kate O'Hare. 'One of them being, I just wish everyone would shut up. I'm tired of writing dialogue. There was a nugget of that. It really came from just wanting to make something truly horrific and cinematic and pushing my own boundaries. It's easy in TV to devolve into what I call "radio with faces".' To achieve the Gentlemen's particular mode of above-the-ground transport required suspending the actors from overhead cranes or strapping them on to a dolly kept out of camera range. 'They were expensive and time-consuming,' continued Joss. 'I spent a long time working on the concept for them, because I had a very specific idea about what these creepy guys would look like, and the make-up guys just nailed it.' On the *Posting Board* Joss confirmed that 'inspiration for the Gentlemen came from: *Nosferatu* (both the Max Shreck and Klaus Kinski versions), *Dark City*, *Hellraiser*, Grimm's Fairy Tales, *The Seventh Seal* and much Victorian influence. They came from many storybooks and silent movies, horror movies and nightmares. And Mr Burns (from *The Simpsons*)!' When asked what actually scares *him*, Joss confessed: 'It's hard to describe. But I know the bad guys in "Hush" are as close to it as anything I've ever filmed. It was a monster to film and pulled the best (and most exhausted) work out of everyone. And it is, by-the-by, a Chris Beckathon. Give him an Emmy to go with his Emmy!'

When Emmy-time rolled around and Joss was, himself, nominated, he told *Variety*: 'It doesn't suck . . . I've had a steady diet of nothing, so I didn't expect a change. I wanted to make things harder on myself. It's easy to fall back on funny jokes and witty lines.' Sadly, 'Hush' didn't win.

67

Doomed

US Transmission Date: 18 Jan. 2000
UK Transmission Date: 17 Mar. 2000 (Sky)
4 Jan. 2001 (BBC2)

Writers: Marti Noxon, David Fury, Jane Espenson
Director: James A Contner
Cast: Anastasia Horne (Laurie), Anthony Anselmi (Partier)
French title: *La Fin de Monde*
German title: *Das Opfer der Drei*

Buffy and Riley argue about having kept secrets from each other, but an earthquake interrupts their conversation. Buffy worries that it may signify the end of the world and she turns out to be correct – yet another ancient prophecy is about to manifest itself. The Scooby Gang have to return to high school to stop the Hellmouth from opening yet again, while Riley tries to convince a wary Buffy that a relationship can work between them.

Babes and Babes (Bring Your Own Subtext): As it became clear that the relationship between Willow and Tara was something far more intimate than fans had initially believed, Joss Whedon told the *Posting Board*: 'We meant it to be *subtext*, but you guys have obviously worked it out. Yes, Willow is becoming a *Monkey-owner*. I just hope we don't get a lot of protest from Christian Right Groups over this. Marginally more seriously, Willow and Tara's relationship is definitely romantic. Thorny subject: the writers and I have had long topics about how to deal with the subject responsibly, without writing a story that sounds like people spent a long time discussing how to deal with it responsibly. To me it feels just right. *All* the relationships on the show are sort of romantic (hence the *Bring Your Own Subtext* principle) and this feels like the natural next step for her. I can only promise you two things: we're not going to do *Ally* or *Party of Five* in which we promote the hell out of a same sex relationship for exploitation value that we take back by the end of the episode, and we will never have a *Buffy* where someone gets on a soapbox. I just know there's a sweet story that would become very complicated if Oz were to show up again. Which he will.'

A Little Learning is a Dangerous Thing: Buffy: 'You're part of some military monster squad that captures demons, vampires . . . Probably have some official sounding euphemisms for them, like "unfriendlies" or "nonsapiens".' Riley: 'Hostile Sub-Terrestrials.' Buffy: 'So you deliver these HSTs to a bunch of lab coats, who perform experiments on them, which among other things turn some into harmless little bunnies. How am I doing so far?' Riley: 'A little too well.'

The Conspiracy Starts at Home Time: Riley says that the Vahrall demon is 'not a capture, it's a kill,' suggesting that the Initiative don't take all their specimens alive. Forrest believes that: 'the Slayer's some kind of bogeyman for the

Sub-Terrestrials. Something they tell their little spawn to make them eat their vegetables and clean up their slime pits.'

Work is a Four-Letter Word: Xander's new job is as a pizza delivery boy.

It's a Designer Label!: Spike wearing one of Xander's knee-length shorts and a Hawaiian shirt is a comedy zenith. Also, Buffy's orange top and red trousers, Laurie's slutty red blouse (*very* Faith) and Willow's 'Bunny's Dog Walking Service' T-shirt.

References: 'I was in the library during the quake, almost got buried under some nineteenth-century literature.' The title is a song by Julian Cope. When asked if he's heard of the Slayer, Forrest replies: 'Thrash band. Anvil-heavy guitar rock with delusions of Black Sabbath', a joke that's four years overdue, frankly. References to *Superman* (Smallville), the Easter Bunny, *Bad Omens*, Morley Safer of CBS's *60 Minutes*, US Navy recruitment commercials ('It's not just a job, it's an adventure'), the video game Donkey Kong, paintball, WB Yeats's 'The Second Coming' ('Things fall apart'), *End of Days*, *Survivors* ('What if the end of the world is coming in the form of a plague?'), GI Joe dolls and an oblique reference to Kentucky Fried Chicken ('Mayor meat. Extra crispy'). Porter, the hall where the party is taking place, is a college at UC Santa Cruz, which Marti Noxon attended. Both Kresge and Stevenson are also Santa Cruz colleges. Forrest tells Riley that he 'don't got game', a reference to the movie *He Got Game* in which Leonard Roberts appeared. Xander misquotes Smokey Robinson's 'I Second That Emotion'. Riley's room has a poster showing various sorts of 'balls'.

Bitch!: Xander: 'You look like a big mooch that doesn't lift a finger around here. But I have to get to work.' Spike: 'Delivering melted cheese on bread, doing your part to keep America constipated.'

Spike on Xander and Willow: 'I should think you would be glad to greet the end of days. Neither one of you is making much of a go at it. You, kids your age, are going off to university; you've made it as far as the basement. And Red here, you couldn't even keep dog boy happy. You can take the loser out of high school, but . . .'

Awesome!: Spike's fake American accent (think about this. James Marsters, an American, playing a British vampire doing a *bad* American accent – that takes some doing). Plus his closing rant: 'Sitting around watching the telly while there's evil still afoot. I say we go out there and kick a little demon ass . . . Come on. Vampires. *Grrr, nasty*. Let's annihilate them. For justice, and for the safety of puppies and Christmas, right? Let's *fight* that evil. Let's *kill* something. Oh, come *on*.'

'You May Remember Me From Such TV Series As . . .': Anastasia Horne was Lori in *Undressed* and Ana in *Kids Incorporated*.

Valley-Speak: Buffy: 'No offence, but you do look wicked conspicuous.'

Percy: 'Rosenberg? She's just some egghead who tutored me a little in high school. I mean, she's nice, but come on, captain of the nerd squad.'

Xander: 'Let's rock and roll.'

Cigarettes and Alcohol: Willow: 'Porter dorm is completely blacked out. So naturally they're dealing with the crisis the only way they know how: *Aftershock Party*.' Buffy: 'This from the dorm that brought us the *Somebody Sneezed* party and the *Day That Ends in Y* party.'

The murdered guy is mixing cocktails for a 'naked limbo' contest before he gets killed.

Logic, Let Me Introduce You to This Window: In the continuation from **66**, 'Hush', Buffy's hair changes between episodes. After Riley knocks out the demon, it looks as though its right horn is missing. When Willow finds the dead boy, his eyes are open. Close-up shows them closed. As the gang research the Vahrall demons and Willow reads about the ritual, Xander's pizza shirt is open over a white T-shirt. For one shot, though, it's buttoned up. Willow wears the same clothes to the Aftershock Party as she does in the rest of the episode (covering at least two days). Was everything else in the wash? When Spike attempts to stake himself, the stake flies off and cannot be seen when Spike is lying on the floor. Xander steps in front of him and picks the stake up.

I Just *Love* Your Accent: Spike: 'You want me to tear this place apart, you bloody *pouf*?' Plus 'almost-English' expressions (i.e. not very English at all) like: 'Bloody rot', 'fag off' and 'Stuck in this basement washing *skivvies* for a *blighter* I wouldn't have bothered to bite a few months ago.'

Cruelty to Demons: Forrest tells Riley demons are just animals.

Quote/Unquote: Buffy: 'I really thought that you were a nice, normal guy.' Riley: 'I *am* . . .' Buffy: 'Maybe by this town's standards, but I'm not grading on a curve.'

Giles: 'It's the end of the world.' Willow/Xander: '*Again*?' Buffy: 'I *told you*. I said "end of the world" and you're like *poo-poo. Southern California. Poo-poo.*' Giles: 'I'm so very sorry. My contrition completely dwarfs the impending apocalypse.' (See **2**, 'The Harvest'; **12**, 'Prophecy Girl'; **34**, 'Becoming' Part 2; **47**, 'The Zeppo'.)

Buffy: 'Do you know what a Hellmouth is? Do you have a fancy term for it? Because I went to high school on it for three years.'

Willow: 'We're not useless. We help people. We fight the forces of evil.' Spike: '*Buffy* fights the forces of evil. You're her groupies.'

Notes: 'I'm the Slayer. Chosen One. She who hangs out a lot in cemeteries . . . Look it up.' 'Doomed' can't quite overcome the 'written by committee' feel that inevitably comes from having three writers involved. Nevertheless, it's frequently amusing, a continuity fest (including a look at what Sunnydale High is like post-graduation) and the double act of Xander and Spike continues to work incredibly well.

Buffy says that she's 'Capricorn, on the cusp of Aquarius', which confirms that her birthdate is somewhere between 17 and 20 January, 1981. This corresponds with episodes featuring Buffy's birthday (**25**, 'Surprise'; **46**, 'Helpless') airing during the third week of January. She mentions that the last time there was an earthquake in Sunnydale she died, referring to **12**, 'Prophecy Girl'. She tells Riley that the last person who had 'fun' slaying is in a coma. This is the first time we've seen Basketball Percy since **56**, 'Graduation Day' Part 2. Willow and he haven't kept in touch though she was aware that he got a football scholarship to USC. Spike bids goodbye to Drusilla when he tries to kill himself. Buffy says that Riley is a psychology graduate student, which would mean that he already has a Bachelor's degree.

Marc Blucas becomes a series regular and part of the title sequence in this episode.

Soundtrack: 'Hey' by Hellacopters and Echobelly's 'Mouth Almighty'.

68

A New Man

US Transmission Date: 25 Jan. 2000[20]
UK Transmission Date: 24 Mar. 2000 (Sky)
11 Jan. 2001 (BBC2)

Writer: Jane Espenson
Director: Michael Gershman
Cast: Elizabeth Penn Payne (Waitress), Michelle Ferrara (Mother)
French title: *314*
German title: *Metamorphose*

Giles feels out of the loop when Buffy introduces Riley, and Maggie Walsh tells him that Buffy lacks a father figure. Giles subsequently discovers about the Initiative (and Riley's involvement in it) and that everyone knew but him. Ethan Rayne turns up and convinces Giles to go for a beer so that Ethan can warn him of some impending doom involving '314'. Giles gets drunk and wakes to find that Ethan has turned him into a Fyarl demon. Unable to speak English, he can't communicate with the gang, so he turns to Spike for help (which he gets, for $300 in cash) while Buffy hunts him down, thinking that the demon harmed Giles. Buffy almost kills him, but recognises his eyes. Back at the Initiative, Professor Walsh steps into a high-security room . . . 314.

Dudes and Babes: Anya hopes that Giles's story about a public-school prank will involve 'treacle and a headmaster'.

---

[20] 'A New Man' was originally announced to air on 18 January, but was rescheduled to 25 January.

Meanwhile Willow and Tara practise more magic, floating a rose with interesting results.

Denial, Thy Name is Giles: Poor Giles, his feelings of rejection that have been simmering all year finally burst: 'Twenty years I've been fighting demons. Maggie Walsh and her nancy ninja boys come in, six months later demons are pissing themselves with fear. They never even noticed me.'

The Conspiracy Starts at Home Time: The Initiative is a US military operation. They are able to tap into the 911 emergency call system. Riley says that Ethan will be taken to a detention facility in the Nevada desert. Riley has killed seventeen 'hostiles' (eleven vampires and six demons).

It's a Designer Label!: Giles's cool black shirt, sadly, gets ripped when he's a demon. Love the suede jacket, though. Willow's as-seen-on-TV T-shirt, Buffy's gold dress, Xander's orange trousers, Giles wearing Ethan's hideous silver satin shirt, and Spike, back in black.

References: Giles alludes to the legend of Theseus and the Minotaur. Also, *I Spy*, Spider-Man, Paul Weller's 'Broken Stones' and the Beatles' 'Run For Your Life'. A *Widespread Panic* sticker can be seen on the rec room notice board.

Bitch!: Walsh: 'It's only our methods that differ. We use the latest in scientific technology and state-of-the-art weaponry. You, if I understand correctly, poke them with a sharp stick.'

Spike on Xander's home: 'I've known corpses with a fresher smell. In fact, I've been one.'

Giles to Ethan: 'We've changed. Well, not you. You're still sadistic and self-centered.'

Awesome!: The scenes of Ethan and Giles in the bar are a great mixture of comedy and pathos ('We're just a couple of sorcerers. The night is still our time. Time of magic'). Demon-Giles waking up Xander is hilarious, but it's Giles and Spike in the car that gives the episode its greatness ('Do I have special powers? Like setting things on fire with my sizzling eye beams?' Spike: 'You got . . . paralysing mucous. Shoots out through the nose').

Surprise!: Yet *another* surprise birthday party for Buffy.

Don't Give Up the Day Job: Elizabeth Penn Payne was on the craft team of *Mid Summer*.

Valley-Speak: Riley: 'When I saw you stop the world from, you know, ending, I just assumed that was a big week for you. Turns out I suddenly find myself needing to know the plural of "apocalypse".'

Cigarettes and Alcohol: Ethan and Giles get drunk on beer and whisky. Spike spends most of the episode smoking.

Logic, Let Me Introduce You to This Window: As Ethan tells Giles that he has poisoned Giles's drink, the head on the beer increases and then decreases. There's a variety of strange things going on with the glasses in this scene, including an empty one that appears and disappears a few times. When Buffy and Willow are having breakfast, Willow picks up her orange juice while the camera is facing her. When the camera switches to Buffy, the glass is still on the table. When Demon-Giles wakes Xander, there are clothes hanging on a line. On the left is a pair of briefs dangling by one peg. A moment later, they're on two pegs. Then one. Then two . . . etc. Xander doesn't even go halfway up the stairs before coming back down and stating Giles isn't upstairs. When Spike and Giles talk in the cemetery, Spike puts a cigarette in his mouth. Next shot, he's holding it by his waist. Ethan is supposedly staying at the Sunnydale Motor Inn, but the shot outside his motel is of a place called the Downtowner Apartments. This is the same shot used in **37**, 'Faith, Hope and Trick'.

I Just *Love* Your Accent: Ethan: 'Religious intolerance. Sad. I mean, just look at "The Irish Troubles".' Bet *that* one doesn't make it on to the BBC. Spike refers to 'a few bob' which was, no doubt, understood by all of four people in the US, and all of zero in Britain under the age of 35. Giles calls Maggie Walsh a 'harridan' and a 'fishwife'.

Spike asking the waitress about Ethan and Giles: 'Two of them. English like me. But older. Less attractive.'

Motors: We finally get a car chase in *Buffy*. Granted it's between two Humvees and a Citroën . . .

What a Shame They Dropped . . .: Jane Espenson was asked during an online interview what happened to Spike after he crashed the car: 'That was cut . . . He got out of the car and said, "I can kill demons. I can crash cars. Things are looking up".' Both Robin Sachs and Tony Head have confirmed that the confrontation between Buffy and Ethan went on far longer than broadcast, that it was a scene both enjoyed and that they were sad that it got cut so much.

Quote/Unquote: Spike steals Xander's radio: 'And you're what? Shocked and disappointed? I'm *evil*.'

Walsh: 'We thought you were a myth.' Buffy: 'You were myth-taken.'

Ethan: 'I really got to learn to just do the damage and get out of town. It's the "stay and gloat" that gets me every time.'

Notes: 'The world has passed us by. Someone snuck in and left us a couple of has-beens in our place. This Initiative, their methods may be causing problems, but they're getting the job done. Where am I? An unemployed librarian with a tendency to get knocked on the head.' Yet another comedy diamond from Ms Espenson; a trio of outstanding performances from Head, Sachs and Marsters and the funniest moment of the season (Giles scaring Walsh for no other reason than he doesn't like her).

Buffy jokes that having her toes smashed would be better than her previous birthday surprises (see **25**, 'Surprise'; **46**, 'Helpless'). She tells Riley about the Mayor (see **56**, 'Graduation Day' Part 2). It's confirmed that Buffy was fifteen when she became the Slayer in 1996 (see **33**, 'Becoming' Part 1). She likes pancakes and waffles. She has been getting B– grades in psych. Giles's 'tendency to get knocked on the head' has included cranial trauma in **29**, 'Passion'; **12**, 'Prophecy Girl'; **41**, 'Revelations'; **33**, 'Becoming' Part 1; **45**, 'Gingerbread'; **64**, 'Pangs' and **52**, 'Earshot', among others. Giles went to a public school. He gets a new cordless phone. Riley owns a master key that opens every shop on Main Street.

Soundtrack: 12 Volt Sex's 'Over Drive', Other Star People's 'Then There's More', Scott Ellison's 'Down, Down Baby'.

Joss Whedon's Comments: '[Giles's] breakdown's been really funny,' Joss told *Ultimate TV*. 'And it's going to get worse. He's feeling really obsolete, and he gets turned into a demon for an episode and Buffy's hunting him. It's the perfect "I've been replaced, and now they want to get rid of me" metaphor. He's cute as a demon. He's scary-looking, but he's Tony.'

Jane Espenson's Comments: During an Internet convention

interview in July 2000, Jane noted: 'Some days you come in at nine, and you're immediately in the room with Joss all day breaking stories. Some days Joss is busy with *Angel*, or busy doing any of a million other things that he has to. And some days you don't even go to work because you're out on script. Some people come in and write their scripts in the office; I write mine at home or in the Beverly Hills Library. I pack up my computer and spend a day there.' Interestingly, Jane added that, 'Usually, nothing of great value is done without Joss in the room. Although, more and more, Marti is running it.' Both Jane and David Fury used time on the *Posting Board* to address comments from fans regarding the lower profiles of Xander and Giles during season four: 'Xander hasn't had a lot to do this year, I agree, but that will change. This year we had our first Giles-centric episode since **20**, 'The Dark Age'. The character is more peripheral in Buffy's life at the moment, but the actor is doing quite a lot.' Fury added, 'Perhaps it's not clear that Giles does not need to be near Buffy. Giles is the father figure going through an empty-nest syndrome. It's a phase he's slowly making his way out of. Be patient with him. And with us. Xander's current character arc will play out next season. The dynamics of a post-high school experience is that there is bound to be some splintering. It's natural. Any contrivance like making Giles the campus librarian and Xander his assistant [a widespread fan rumour] is forced and redundant.'

69

The I in Team

US Transmission Date: 8 Feb. 2000
UK Transmission Date: 31 Mar. 2000 (Sky)
18 Jan. 2001 (BBC2)

Writer: David Fury
Director: James A Contner
Cast: Neil Daly (Mason)
French title: *Piégée*
German title: *Schein und Sein*

Walsh and Riley familiarise Buffy with the Initiative, but

Willow worries that Buffy is getting involved with something she knows nothing about and that she's also not making enough time for her friends. On patrol with Riley, Buffy helps capture a Polgara demon. Afterwards, Buffy and Riley spend their first night together and, unbeknown to them, are watched by Professor Walsh. Concerned that Buffy is becoming a threat to her plans, Walsh sets a trap to have the Slayer killed. Assuming that Buffy is dead she tries to explain this to Riley, just as Buffy appears on video behind them, telling Walsh that her plan failed. Walsh goes to room 314 to check on her pet project, Adam, who wakes and stabs his creator to death.

Everybody Spanks!: Willow says Buffy is 'out with Riley. You know what it's like with a spanking new boyfriend.' 'Yes,' notes Anya, much to Xander's obvious discomfort, 'we've enjoyed spanking.' Later, Buffy finds that Riley's lunch is a Twinkie bar. 'He is *so* gonna be punished,' she notes. 'Everyone's getting spanked but me,' says a sad Willow.

The Conspiracy Starts at Home Time: The research area of the Initiative HQ is called the Pit. Walsh has surveillance cameras in the bedrooms of her boys.

Work is a Four-Letter Word: Xander's new job is selling Boost Bars – 'the natural food bar that provides a nutritional energy boost for active, health-conscious people.'

It's a Designer Label!: Buffy's very silly ankle-length skirt, Tara's electric-blue hooded top and Willow's star jumper.

References: The obvious inspiration for Adam is *Frankenstein*. The title is a reference to the adage 'There is *no* "i" in "team"', often used by sports coaches. Also, Twinkies, *Sabrina, the Teenage Witch*, the Discovery Channel, Lightning Seeds' 'The Life of Riley', David and Leigh Eddings's novel, *Polgara the Sorceress*, the Wal-Mart chain, *The Avengers* and the character of Mother, *Private Benjamin* and The Clash's 'Rock the Casbah'. Also an oblique reference to *A Hard Day's Night* ('it's very . . . clean'). The dialogue as Riley, Forrest and Graham track the tracer is similar to a famous sequence in *Aliens*.

Bitch!: Giles: 'Remind me. Why should I help you?' Spike: 'Because you *do that*. You're the goody-good guys. You're the bloody freaking cavalry.'

Awesome!: Best bit of the episode, the intercutting of Riley and Buffy fighting the demon with them, ahem, *performing the act* in bed later, all done like a combination of a slow-motion Jackie Chan movie and a sultry music video (with Delerium as the soundtrack). *Outstanding*. Xander spilling the cards when Anya talks about spanking is another highlight, though the slapstick ionisation scene is a letdown.

'You May Remember Me From Such TV Series As . . .': Jack Stehlin played David Reese in *General Hospital*.

Don't Give Up the Day Job: George Hertzberg wrote and starred in the movie *Too Much Magic*. He also played Tom in *The Pornographer*.

The Drugs Don't Work: Willow: 'Wha'cha got in the boxes, drugs?'

Valley-Speak: Buffy: 'This is unreal.' And: 'Sorry about the late-itude.' And: 'My *total* bad.'

Cigarettes and Alcohol: Giles has a bottle of cognac in the cabinet next to the sink.

Logic, Let Me Introduce You to This Window: When Walsh hands Buffy a stack of papers in the IHQ, Buffy holds them at chest height. But in some shots she holds them much lower. Walsh goes into room 314 and the door shuts behind her. Then we cut to a frontal shot of her coming in and the door shutting again. When Buffy and Riley have sex, the pillowcases are green and white, but afterwards, they're dark red, like the sheets. There's a hole in Spike's T-shirt from where he was shot with the tracer, but his jacket is intact. Buffy's clothes change between scenes. While Buffy is crouched over the map of the sewer system, her arms are crossed. In the next shot, her hands are clasped together. When the demon in the sewer knocks Buffy down, she falls in front of the gun, with her head towards it. Next shot, she and the gun are in different positions. The con-cam picks up audio, so when Buffy threw it down, Walsh should still have heard the fighting going on. The con-cam lands showing a sideways shot of the sewers. A few minutes later, the camera is shown flat on the ground, in a way that would result in a picture of the roof.

I Just *Love* Your Accent: Spike: 'You *right bastard*. That's all that's left. I spent the rest on blood and smokes.'

Giles: 'It's not for me, *you prat*.'

Cruelty to Animals: Walsh: 'They barely show up on the scanner and occasionally turn out to be raccoons.' She hands Buffy a weapon. Buffy: 'You're not crazy about raccoons, huh?'

Quote/Unquote: Anya: 'You haven't been paying any attention to me, tonight. Just peddling those process food breaks. I don't know why.' Xander: 'Let me put it in a way you'll understand. Sell bars. Make money. Take Anya nice places. Buy pretty things.' Anya: 'That *does* make sense. All right, I support you. Go sell more.'

Giles on the tracer: 'It's blinking.' Spike: 'I don't care if it's playing "Rockin' the Casbah" on the bloody Jew's harp, just get it out of me.'

Notes: 'She's becoming a liability.' A game of two halves. Some *great* stuff and the final scene is a real surprise, but there seems to be a sense of treading water for at least half the episode.

Giles pays Spike for his help during his 'recent metamorphosis', but he gets most of it back later. Riley tells Buffy that Walsh liked her before he did and told him so (see **63**, 'The Initiative'). Xander refers to his 'pseudo-soldier memory bank' (see **18**, 'Halloween'). Riley takes 'vitamins' at regular intervals (see **70**, 'Goodbye Iowa'). The government pulled him out of special operations training for this assignment.

Soundtrack: Lavish's 'Trashed', Black Lab's 'Keep Myself Awake' [*]. The song that plays throughout the Buffy–Riley fight–sex sequence is 'Window To Your Soul' by one of this author's favourite artists, Delerium.

70
Goodbye Iowa

US Transmission Date: 15 Feb. 2000
UK Transmission Date: 7 Apr. 2000 (Sky)
25 Jan. 2001 (BBC2)

Writer: Marti Noxon
Director: David Solomon

Cast: JB Gaynor (Little Boy), Andy Marshall (Scientist #1),
Paul Leighton (Rough-Looking Demon), Karen Charnell (Shady Lady)
French title: *Stress*
German title: *Die Kampfmaschine*

Riley is shocked that Walsh tried to have Buffy killed, but now that the Professor herself is dead, the Initiative is falling into disarray. Riley goes into withdrawal from missing the drugs he was unknowingly fed and begins to doubt everything he once thought he believed in, including Buffy. Meanwhile, Adam reveals information about himself, while trying to learn about people by investigating their insides.

Cyber-Dudes and Babes: Adam describes himself as a 'kinematically redundant, biomechanical demonoid, designed by Maggie Walsh. She called me Adam and I called her Mother . . . In addition to organic material, I am equipped with GP2D-11 infrared detectors, a harmonic decelerator, plus DC servo.'

The Conspiracy Starts at Home Time: 'The project', Adam, has been designed by Walsh and Angleman to be the 'ultimate warrior', pieced together from parts of demons, men and machines. Unfortunately, he has a design flaw.

Why does Tara sabotage Willow's spell to conjure the Goddess Thespia? 'It *will* get paid off,' Joss Whedon told *DreamWatch*. 'But not this season.' (See **84**, 'Family'.)

It's a Designer Label!: Buffy's crimson turtleneck and strawberry sweater and Giles's fleece jacket . . .

References: Adam's murder of the little boy is reminiscent of the monster killing a child in *Frankenstein*. Willow, Buffy and Anya watch the *Road Runner* cartoon 'Wild About Hurry'. The Weather Girls's 'It's Raining Men' (Buffy: 'Next thing I know, it's raining monsters.' Xander: 'Hallelujah'), *Goldilocks*, *Shazam* ('Holy moley'), Richard Wagner, GI Joe (again), *The Prisoner* ('I cannot be programmed. I'm a man') and Xerox.

Bitch!: Spike: 'Gotta hand it to ya, Goldilocks. You do have *bleeding tragic* taste in men.'

Awesome!: Spike's two-thumbs-up encouragement to the Initiative to kill Buffy. Riley cracking up in Willy's bar is dramatically intense, though the scene is a little too long.

'You May Remember Me From Such Films and TV Series

As . . .': JB Gaynor was Jeremy Gelbwaks in _Come On, Get Happy: The Partridge Family Story_. Andy Marshall played Alphonse in _Hoods_.

The Drugs Don't Work: Riley, and others in the Initiative, have been fed drugs in their food to increase their strength. When they stop, he suffers serious withdrawal symptoms.

Cigarettes and Alcohol: Several scenes in Willy's Place, where the distinctive bottles for Malibu, Blue Sapphire gin and Absolut Vodka can all be seen behind the bar.

Logic, Let Me Introduce You to This Window: When Buffy describes what happened in the sewers, she says the gate slammed down and then she tried to use the gun. However, she actually used the gun first. Buffy tells Giles Walsh sent her on a one-way recon, followed by a shot of Giles looking concerned. A few moments later, after Spike implies that Riley was in on it, the same shot of Giles is used. Spike no longer has a hole in his shirt where he was shot with the tracer in the last episode. Angleman slips in Walsh's blood and lands some way from her body. However, in the shot from above, the blood appears to stop much closer to the body. It's odd that Spike would have a TV in his mausoleum where one wouldn't normally expect electricity. There are a couple of continuity errors. The Polgara demon was captured the night before this episode starts. However, the second day into the episode, Riley says that 'the Polgara demon [we] captured last week' must have killed Walsh. Later, Willy says that he heard a Polgara demon was in town and taken off the streets 'a week or two ago'. Buffy takes the bandana from her hair and wraps it around Riley's hand. Moments later, she's wearing it again. Adam puts a second disk in his drive without having taken out the first. Riley doesn't have a tear in his shirt from being skewered by Adam. Angleman also doesn't have one in his lab coat, nor is he even bleeding (though there was blood on Adam's skewer). When the Commandos burst in, Forrest doesn't believe that there was a demon in the room, even though Adam should have been visible through the window.

I Just _Love_ Your Accent: Spike: 'Been a _real pisser_ of a day, isn't it (sic)? Those army blokes are on a tear.'

Quote/Unquote: Xander: 'Storm the Initiative? Yeah, let's take on those suckers.' Buffy: 'I was thinking more that we'd hide.' Xander: '*Oh, thank God.*'

Riley: 'That's Hostile 17.' Spike: 'No. I'm just a friend of Xander's . . . Bugger it. I'm your guy.' Buffy: 'This is Spike. He's . . . It's a really long story. But he's not bad any more.' Spike: 'What am I, a bleeding broken record? I'm bad. It's just . . . I can't bite any more, thanks to you wankers.'

Anya: 'You really should get yourself a boring boyfriend. Like Xander . . . You *can't have* Xander.'

Buffy: 'I'm the only one that can pass the retinal scan.' Xander: 'Euw. I don't wanna see *that*.' Buffy: '*Retinal. Scan. Xander.*'

Notes: 'I don't generally like to kill humans. But I've learned it pays to be flexible in life.' Noxon's dialogue is sharp, as usual, but there doesn't seem a lot of sparkle here. The episode drifts along for far too long without much happening.

Giles's tattoo, the Mark of Eyghon, is shown when he turns off the TV (see **20**, 'The Dark Age'). Willy the Snitch mentions the Apocalypse demons (i.e. the Jhe) who 'beat the crap' out of him in **47**, 'The Zeppo'. The Scooby Gang watch the news on Channel 14 again (see **49**, 'Consequences'; **59**, 'The Harsh Light of Day'). Spike has a cousin who is married to a regurgitating Phrivlops demon.

Soundtrack: Lou Reed's 'Romeo Had Juliet', 'My Last Romance' by Paul Singerman, Mark Cherrie's 'Big Ed'.

71
This Year's Girl

US Transmission Date: 22 Feb. 2000
UK Transmission Date: 14 Apr. 2000 (Sky)
1 Feb. 2001 (BBC2)

Writer: Douglas Petrie
Director: Michael Gershman
Cast: Chet Grissom (Detective), Alastair Duncan (Collins),
Jeff Ricketts (Weatherby), Kevin Owers (Smith), Mark Gantt (Demon),
Kimberly McRae (Visitor), Sara Van Horn (Older Nurse),
Brian Hawley (Orderly), Jack Esformes (Doctor)

French title: *Une Revenante*
German title: *Böses Erwachen*

Faith awakens from her eight-month, Buffy-induced coma and seeks revenge. After finding Buffy and the gang, she confronts her ex-friend on campus. The two Slayers fight but Faith escapes. Meanwhile, three mysterious men arrive in Sunnydale by helicopter. Faith, having received a final gift from the Mayor, goes to Buffy's house and attacks Joyce, telling her that Buffy doesn't care about either of them. Buffy arrives and the pair again do battle, but Faith uses her gift to switch bodies with Buffy. As an unconscious 'Faith' lies on the floor, Joyce asks 'Buffy' if she is OK. 'Five by five,' she replies.[21]

Dreaming (As Blondie Once Said) is Free: 'So that's my dream,' Faith tells Buffy. 'That and some stuff about cigars and a tunnel.' Initially, this takes place in the same setting as **56**, 'Graduation Day' Part 2, with Buffy and Faith *still* making the bed. Faith says: 'Little sis is coming' (a reference, seemingly, to the character of Dawn: see **'Grrr! Arrrgh!'**). The knife is still in Faith's stomach from **55**, 'Graduation Day' Part 1. 'Are you ever gonna take this thing out?' she pleads. Subsequently, Buffy is a ruthless monster, who murders the Mayor and then pursues Faith, literally, to the grave. The grass snake that the Mayor picks up is a reference to what he became in **56**, 'Graduation Day' Part 2.

Authority Sucks!: Buffy: 'We still have a decision to make. Do we hand [Faith] over to the cops? They wouldn't know what to do with a Slayer even if they knew we existed.' Willow: 'What about the Council?' Xander: 'Been there. Tried that. Not unlike smothering a forest fire with napalm as I recall.'

Denial, Thy Name is Joyce: Faith: 'Don't tell me you don't see it, Joyce. You've served your purpose. Squirted out the kid, raised her up and now you might as well be dead. Nobody cares, nobody remembers, especially not *Buffy, fabulous*

---

[21] The Buffy–Faith body-swop in 'This Year's Girl'/'Who Are You?': 'Buffy' refers to Faith inhabiting Buffy's body and 'Faith' refers to Buffy inhabiting Faith's body. Confused? You will be . . .

superhero. Sooner or later you're gonna have to face it. She was over us a long time ago.'

It's a Designer Label!: Faith's multicoloured top, Xander's stripy tank top and anorak. It's been a while since we've seen Willow in a stupid hat though not in a horrible skirt like the one seen here. Giles sorts the washing including a pair of spotty boxer shorts.

References: The title is a song by Elvis Costello (see **42**, 'Lover's Walk'). Faith, climbing from the grave and standing in the rain, may have been inspired by the prison escape in *The Shawshank Redemption*. Also, *Star Trek*, Talking Heads' 'Psycho Killer', Trey Parker's *Orgazmo* and Woody Allen's *Sleeper*, *The Terminator*, *Top Gun*, *The Patty Duke Show* and *Gunsmoke* ('If I were her, I'd get out of Dodge post-hasty'). Yet another Widespread Panic sticker can be seen. Faith calls Riley 'the clean Marine', the nickname given to John Glenn by the other Mercury astronauts in *The Right Stuff*.

Bitch!: Xander on Adam and Faith: 'I'd hate to see the pursuit of a homicidal lunatic get in the way of pursuing a homicidal lunatic.'

Willow on what they should do with Faith: 'Beat the crap out of her?'

Faith: 'You took my life, B. Payback's a bitch.' Willow: 'Look who's talking.'

Awesome!: Faith, generally.

'You May Remember Me From Such Films and TV Series As . . .': Alastair Duncan has appeared in TV shows as diverse as *Blossom*, *Sabrina the Teenage Witch*, *Babylon 5* and *Highlander*. Kevin Owers played a steward in *Titanic*. Sara Van Horn was in *Great Balls of Fire!* and *Devil in the Flesh*.

Don't Give Up the Day Job: Mark Gantt was assistant property manager on *The Siege* and *Barb Wire*.

Valley-Speak: Willow on Faith: 'She's like this *cleavagey slutbomb* walking around going "Ooh. Check me out, I'm *wicked cool*. I'm five by five".' Tara: 'Five what by five what?' Willow: 'See, that's the thing, no one knows.'

Forrest: 'The shish kebab that walks like a man.'

Willow: 'Flee. Maybe *skedaddle*. We're not here to engage. This is strictly recon.'

Cigarettes and Alcohol: Spike smokes when he meets Xander and Giles. It's interesting that The Watchers' Council have their own cigarette-smoking man, Collins.

Logic, Let Me Introduce You to This Window: Before Buffy finds the demon hanging from the trees, someone is in the bushes to her right. Willow and Xander should have noticed Riley coming down the stairs behind Buffy. Faith rips off her monitor and nothing happens. It should flatline at least. In Faith's dream, she climbs out of the grave and takes two steps forward. We then have a bird's-eye view of Faith where she's several feet from the grave. When Faith is watching the gang through Giles's window, Buffy has her arm around Riley. Between cuts, her arm goes back and forth from being draped around him to playing with his hair. As Buffy and Willow are talking, an extra in a striped sweater walks by on Buffy's left. Twice. When Faith is rummaging through Joyce's make-up, it's clear she doesn't have a tattoo. The nurse only dials four numbers when she calls to tell The Watchers' Council Faith has escaped, which suggests an internal call – yet they arrive in a helicopter. When Buffy unknowingly approaches Faith, she stops about a foot away. After the commercial break, she's much further back. As Faith climbs the wall, it moves a fraction. When Buffy looks over the wall, there are students sitting on the grass, which appears to be dry, even though on Buffy's side, it has clearly just rained. As Tara and Willow come down the stairs, the pendant on Tara's necklace continually moves from side to side between shots. Buffy throws Faith across the dining table, knocking everything off. A moment later, the tablecloth and pieces of fruit are back where they were.

Who rings Buffy at Giles's to tell her that Faith has woken up? Not Joyce, since Buffy doesn't react like it's her mother on the phone. The very brisk nature of her replies ('What sort of emergency?' 'Thank you, I'll let you know') suggest that she's talking to someone that she doesn't know. The police seems the obvious answer but why would they ring Buffy? Buffy, after a very brief call, knows lots of details about Faith's escape (that she knocked out someone at the hospital and stole their clothes). Do the words 'ludicrous plot device' seem applicable?

I Just *Love* Your Accent: Willow asks Buffy what she told

Riley about Faith. 'The truth. That she's my wacky identical cousin from England, and whenever she visits, hijinks ensue.'

Quote/Unquote: Xander: 'I'd say this qualifies for a *Worst Timing Ever* award.'

Buffy: 'I've been looking for you.' Faith: 'Been standing still for eight months, B. How hard did you look?'

Spike: 'I'll head out, find this girl, tell her exactly where you are and then watch as she kills you. Can't any one of your damn little Scooby Club at least try to remember that I hate you all? Just because I can't do the damage myself doesn't stop me from aiming a loose cannon your way.'

Faith: 'How do I look?' Joyce: 'Psychotic.'

Notes: 'I know what it's like. You think you matter, you think you're a part of something and you get dumped. It's like the whole world is moving and you're stuck . . . like those animals in the tar pits. It's like you just keep sinking a little deeper everyday and no one even sees.' Some people may try and convince you that season four of *Buffy* failed to capture the heights of previous years. 'This Year's Girl' gives the complete lie to this. Isn't it wonderful to see Harry Groener back, even if it's for only two scenes?

Xander refers to his 'history' with Faith (see **47**, 'The Zeppo'). Faith is told about the events of **56**, 'Graduation Day' Part 2: 'Sunnydale High School isn't even there any more . . . It was a tragedy. Lots of students died. The principal, the Mayor.' Buffy tells Riley: 'Giles used to be part of this Council. For years all they ever did was give me orders.' Riley: 'Ever obey them?' Buffy: 'Sure. The ones I was going to do anyway.'

The detective says that Faith is wanted for questioning for 'a series of murders', which suggests that the Sunnydale police have worked out a connection between the killings of Alan Finch and Professor Worth. Presumably stabbings aren't *that* common, even in Sunnydale.

72

Who Are You?

US Transmission Date: 29 Feb. 2000
UK Transmission Date: 21 Apr. 2000 (Sky)
14 Feb. 2001 (BBC2)

Writer: Joss Whedon
Director: Joss Whedon
Cast: Alastair Duncan (Collins), Chet Grissom (Detective),
Rick Stear (Booke), Jeff Ricketts (Weatherby), Kevin Owers (Smith),
Rick Scarry (Sergeant), Jennifer S Albright (Date)
French title: *Une Revenante 2*
German title: *Im Körper des Feindes*

'Buffy' eases herself into her new life, flirting with Spike,
sleeping with Riley and insulting Tara behind Willow's back.
Meanwhile, 'Faith' is kidnapped by the Watchers' Council to
be taken to England. Living as 'Buffy', however, opens Faith's
eyes to the realities of being a Slayer and she heroically saves
the day when a group of Adam's vampire protégés take hos-
tages in a local church. 'Faith' uses Willow and Tara's magic
to reverse the switch and an anguished Faith leaves town.

Dreaming (As Blondie Once Said) is Free: 'Buffy' daydreams
about stabbing Willow. That girl really has got some nasty
stuff floating around in her head.

Dudes and Babes: 'Buffy' on 'Faith': 'A little stint in the
pokey, show her the error of her ways. I'm sure there's some
big old Bertha just waiting to shower her ripe little self with
affection.' The lipstick shade Faith picks is called 'Harlot'.
'Buffy' asks Riley, 'What do you wanna do with this body?
What nasty little desire have you been itching to try out? Am I
a bad girl? Do you wanna hurt me?' When Riley says that he
loves her and doesn't want to play games, 'Buffy' is angry:
'Who are you? What do you want from her?'

'Faith': 'I don't have time for bondage fun.'

Babes and Babes (No Subtext Required): Tara: 'I am, you
know.' Willow: 'What?' Tara: '*Yours.*' 'Buffy' is the first to
spot the developing relationship: 'So Willow's not driving
stick any more? Who would have thought? I guess you never

really know someone until you've been inside their skin. And Oz is out of the picture? Never seen two people so much in love.'

A Little Learning is a Dangerous Thing: Willow: 'What's wetworks?' Xander: 'Scuba-type stuff.' Anya: 'I thought it was murder.' Xander: 'There could be underwater murder, with snorkels.'

Mom's Apple Pie: Joyce suggests that she and Buffy spend some time together, 'Some night when I'm not being held hostage by a raving psychotic.'

Denial, Thy Name is Faith: The first cracks begin to appear in Faith's façade. She hates what she is and this self-loathing explains why *becoming* Buffy had such an attraction for her. The final sequence features Faith, in Buffy's body, beating *herself* and screaming how 'disgusting' she is. This element would be taken further in the *Angel* sequels, 'Five By Five' and 'Sanctuary'.

It's a Designer Label!: Buffy's leather pants. Hot. Also, Willow's pink 'peace' T-shirt and Tara's chunky white sweater.

References: The title is a song by The Who. Spike misquotes Johnny Burke's jazz standard 'Misty' ('I'm just as helpless as a kitten up a tree'). In the Bronze, a sticker is visible for the band Split.

Bitch!: 'Buffy': 'I forgot how much you don't like Faith.' Willow: 'After what she's done to you? I wish those Council guys would let me have an hour alone in the room with her. If I was larger and had grenades.'

Anya says she and Xander were, 'Gonna light a bunch of candles and have sex near them.' 'Buffy': 'We certainly don't want to cut into *that* seven minutes.'

Awesome!: 'Buffy' in front of the bathroom mirror, practising her moves ('You can't do that. It's *wrong*'). Giles creating a diversion: 'Our families are in there. Our mothers and tiny, tiny babies.' 'Buffy's' confrontation with Forrest.

'You May Remember Me From Such Films As . . .': Rick Stear played Stan in *Went to Coney Island on a Mission for God . . . Be Back by Five*. Rick Scarry's movie CV includes *Wag the Dog*, *Naked Gun 33 1/3: The Final Insult*, *Us*, *Big Man on Campus* and *Fear* (which he also co-wrote).

The Drugs Don't Work: Riley mentions that the drugs that Professor Walsh gave him seem to have made him stronger and increased his healing abilities (see **70**, 'Goodbye Iowa', **82**, 'Out of My Mind'). 'Faith' is injected with a sedative.

Valley-Speak: 'Buffy': '*Wicked* obvious.'

Cigarettes and Alcohol: Spike drinks beer in the Bronze.

Logic, Let Me Introduce You to This Window: 'Buffy's' hair changes between the reprise from the previous episode and the next scene. When Joyce and 'Buffy' go into the house, the door Buffy smashed in **71**, 'This Year's Girl', appears to be intact. When the Watchers' Council squad jump out of the truck, they initially open the door on their left. When they close the doors, this one also *shuts* first. Not possible: for doors to latch-close correctly, whichever one opens first should close last. After 'Buffy' imagines stabbing Willow, there's a knife next to her on the desk that wasn't in the previous shot.

I Just *Love* Your Accent: Spike: 'Why don't you sod off?'
Weatherby: 'We're taking you back to the mother country . . . You've been a naughty girl.' And: 'Stop her, you *ponce*.'

Motors: The Council's big red armoured truck is stolen by Buffy and driven by Giles.

Quote/Unquote: Spike: 'You know why I really hate you, Summers?' 'Buffy': 'Coz I'm a stuck-up tight-ass with no sense of fun?' Spike: 'Yeah, that covers a lot of it.' 'Buffy': 'Coz I can do anything I want and instead I choose to pout and whine and feel the burden of Slayerness? I could be rich. I could be famous. I could have anyone. Even you, Spike. I could ride you at a gallop until your legs buckled and your eyes rolled up. I've got muscles you've never even dreamed of. I could squeeze you until you popped like warm champagne and you'd beg me to hurt you just a little bit more. And you know why I don't? Because it's *wrong*.'

Giles: 'Look, I know what you're going to say . . .' Faith: 'I'm Buffy.' Giles: 'All right, I *didn't* know what you were going to say . . .'

'Faith': 'What's a stevedore?'

Notes: 'Do you think I'm afraid of you? You're nothing. Disgusting, murderous *bitch*.' An extraordinary performance of a lifetime from Sarah as Faith-in-Buffy's-body (she even slips into the Bostonian accent occasionally: listen to her pronunciation of 'about') and Eliza is only half a heartbeat behind. A story about fear, self-loathing, trust and redemption, handled sympathetically. This is the best *Buffy* two-parter, taking on a *massive* challenge and doing it coherently, without resorting to melodramatic exposition.

'Buffy' makes a sarcastic comment about Wesley's attempt to capture Faith in **49**, 'Consequences'. The credit card 'Buffy' uses (it's probably Joyce's) has a number ending 6447 and an expiry date of May 2001. Willow worries that Buffy has been possessed by a hyena and tells Tara that such possessions are unpleasant (see **6**, 'The Pack'). 'Faith' wants Giles to question her to prove she is Buffy. Giles: 'Who's president?' 'Faith': 'We're checking for Buffy, not a concussion . . . You turned into a demon and I knew it was you. Can't you just look in my eyes and be all intuitive?' Giles asks how this happened. 'Faith': 'Oh, Ethan Rayne. And you have a girlfriend named Olivia. And you haven't had a job since we blew up the school, which is valid lifestyle-wise . . . When I had psychic power, I heard my mom think that you were like a stevedore during sex. Do you want me to continue?' Giles: 'Actually, I beg you to stop.' (See **68**, 'A New Man'; **57**, 'The Freshman'; **56**, 'Graduation Day' Part 2; **52**, 'Earshot' and **40**, 'Band Candy'.) Willow says, 'The Bronze is the coolest place in Sunnydale. Of course, there's not a lot of competition. I think the vending machine at Bergen's came in second' (see **1**, 'Welcome to the Hellmouth').

Willow notes that Buffy and Faith switched bodies, probably through 'a Draconian Katra spell'. Riley says he doesn't want 'a bunch of Marines' staring in at him during sex, which implies some of the Initiative are Marines rather than regular Army like Riley. He is a suit-wearing churchgoer and is able, in 'military situations', to get the local police to defer command to him. Giles's TV is again tuned to Channel 14. The Watchers' Council squad are described as a 'retrieval team' and a 'special operations unit' ('They handle the Council's trickier jobs. Smuggling, interrogation, wetworks') and are known to both Giles and, subsequently, Wesley (see *Angel*: 'Sanctuary'). Collins says that when they go on a job, they always put their

affairs in order, 'in case of accidents'. The Council can order a
kill if necessary including, seemingly, a Slayer.
Soundtrack: Nerf Herder's 'Vivian', The Cure's 'Watching
Me Fall', Headland's 'Sweet Charlotte Rose'.

73
Superstar

US Transmission Date: 4 Apr. 2000
UK Transmission Date: 28 Apr. 2000 (Sky)
22 Feb. 2001 (BBC2)

Writer: Jane Espenson
Director: David Grossman
Cast: John Saint Ryan (Colonel George Haviland), Erica Luttrell (Karen),
Adam Clark (Cop), Chanie Costello (Inga), Julie Costello (Ilsa)
German title: *Jonathan*

Suave, cool, successful – Jonathan Levinson is everyone's hero.
Among other things, he's a movie star, a singer/musician, a
basketball player and a better fighter than Buffy the Vampire
Slayer, who takes orders from and looks up to him. However,
Buffy begins to think that he's a little too perfect. How, for
instance, did he star in *The Matrix* without ever leaving
Sunnydale? His behaviour regarding a new monster is suspicious. Buffy concludes that he's altered the world to change
how people perceive him, and the Scooby Gang's research,
much to their disappointment, proves it. Jonathan admits to
performing an augmentation spell which created a balancing
force, the evil monster currently terrorising Sunnydale. With
Buffy's help, Jonathan destroys the monster to break the spell
and return everything to reality.
Dudes and Babes: Buffy has been pushing Riley away,
resentful about his having slept with Faith (in **72**, 'Who Are
You?'). Jonathan advises Buffy to forgive him, and Riley to let
Buffy know that she's the only one for him. And it works.
Mind you, this is a guy who shares his mansion with a pair of
Swedish blondes.

Marc Blucas removes his shirt to reveal his torso in *exactly* the way that they used to get Boreanaz to every three or four episodes. Run now, mate . . .

Denial, Thy Name is Anya: Anya on alternate realities: 'You could even make like a freaky world where Jonathan's some kind of not perfect mouth-breather if that's what's blowing up your skirt these days. Just don't ask me to live there.'

The Conspiracy Starts at Home Time: Haviland says that recovery of Adam is the Initiative's most important job. To this end he has asked 'our tactical consultant to address us today.' Graham to Riley: 'It's about time we brought out the big guns.' Jonathan notes that: 'Before we can locate Adam we need to understand him better. There's something that's bothered me almost from the start. We've known him to kill but never to eat the kill. So I've pulled some of Professor Walsh's original design schematics . . . His power source is not biological at all. It's here; the design attempts to hide it, but I believe that there's a small reservoir of uranium 235.'

It's a Designer Label!: Jonathan wears a dapper mohair suit with a lime-green shirt, together with his black poloneck, and a white tux. Anya's the one with the leather trousers this week, plus a yucky blue and yellow blouse. Also, Willow's fur coat and Buffy's fringy suede jacket.

References: Jonathan spots Giles's chess opening is 'the Nimzowitsch defence', named after Aron Nimzowitsch (1886–1935). Also, *Batman* (Jonathan crashing through the skylight of the vampire nest), *Wonder Woman*, *He-Man: Masters of the Universe*, vice-president Al Gore's assertion that he 'invented the Internet,' President McKinley (1843–1901), *The Matrix*, the US woman's soccer team and their victory in the 1999 World Cup and *Superman* ('He's like your Kryptonite'). The music is very James Bond-like. The movie playing at the Sun Cinema is *Being Jonathan Levinson* (a variation on *Being John Malkovich*, presumably?). The opening credits were redone to include shots of Jonathan interspersed with those of the regulars. The final shot of Jonathan walking away, coat billowing behind him, is an *obvious* nod to *Angel*.

Awesome!: Jonathan: 'So what do you think, Buffy? I mean, if I'm wrong, smack me. "Karen with a K" will lend you a book and it's pretty heavy.' What a star that Danny Strong is. Buffy and Anya's conversation is not only pivotal, it's funny too.

'You May Remember Me From Such Films and TV Series As . . .': Robert Patrick Benedict was Richard Coad in *Felicity*. Erica Luttrell played Jody in *Honey, We Shrunk Ourselves*.

Don't Give Up the Day Job: Brad Kane (see **54**, 'The Prom') is the voice behind Jonathan's performance at the Bronze.

Valley-Speak: Buffy: 'No talk, more dance.'

Buffy: 'What did this?' Tara: 'Big. Lumpy. Had something on its head. Like a Greek letter. Only not.'

Logic, Let Me Introduce You to This Window: A parallel universe was previously seen in **43**, 'The Wish', and **50**, 'Doppelgängland', but that universe was completely alternate, wished into existence in the manner Anya describes with her 'shrimp' example. In this case, only Jonathan is altered. Everyone else's *perceptions* have been affected, but the rest of the world is still exactly the same. The only person, apart from Jonathan, who realises is Adam . . . How? The explanation given is a load of waffle. As they dance at the Bronze, Buffy puts her hand on Riley's shoulder. A moment later, the same shot is used again.

I Just *Love* Your Accent: One for *Coronation Street* fans. John Saint Ryan spent a year in Weatherfield as Charlie Whelan.

Quote/Unquote: Buffy: 'He starred in *The Matrix* but he never left town. And how'd he graduate from med school? He's only eighteen years old.' Xander: 'Effective time management?'

Buffy: 'Tell them about the alternate universes.' Anya: 'OK. Say you really like shrimp a lot. Or we could say you don't like shrimp at all. "Blah, I wish there weren't any shrimp," you'd say to yourself . . .' Buffy: 'Stop. You're saying it wrong. I think that Jonathan may be doing something so that he's manipulating the world, and we're all like his pawns.' Anya: 'Or prawns.' Buffy: 'Stop with the shrimp . . .'

Xander: 'I'll always remember the way he made me feel about me. Valued, respected, sort of tingly. Now I'm just empty.' Buffy: 'Poor Xander. I guess Jonathan hurt you most of all.' Tara [raises her hand]: 'Umm.' Buffy: 'Except, of course, after Tara.'

Anya: 'Who really did star in *The Matrix*?' Riley: 'That wasn't real *either*?'

Notes: 'Sounds like you could use my help.' How many other series take the mickey out of themselves as successfully as this? What **47**, 'The Zeppo', did for Xander, this does for an even more unlikely hero. One of the best *Buffy* episodes because it scores on just about every level – comedy, 'what if?' scenario *and* drama. A criminally-underrated episode.

Buffy takes sugar in her coffee. In this reality, anyway. Jonathan mentions going to therapy after 'the thing with the bell tower and the gun' (see **52**, 'Earshot'). Xander has problems opening milk cartons.

Sunnydale Times's website is at www.sunnydaletimes.com.

Alternate Continuity: In the Jonathan universe, he seems to have taken over Buffy's role. Xander says that Jonathan crushed the bones of The Master and blew up the Mayor. Willow mentions that Buffy gave Jonathan the 'Class Protector' award at their prom. He calls Giles Rupert, and regularly beats him at chess. Jonathan has his own website, Jonathan. com. The *Jonathan* comic books (*Target: Jonathan*) are published by Dark Horse. Other 'officially endorsed' items include: Jonathan-O's cereal, a basketball poster, an I ♥ Jonathan T-shirt, an autobiography called *Oh, Jonathan*, shoe advertisements, trading cards, a swimsuit calendar (Giles has one. A gift, allegedly) and at least one CD (Tara says, 'Oh my God. He's going to do something off the new album').

Soundtrack: Four songs by Royal Crown Revue (the band on stage at the Bronze who back Jonathan): 'Trapped (in a Web of Love)', 'Jonathan's Fanfare', 'Serenade in Blue' (the song Danny Strong mimes to) and 'Hey Sonny'.

Danny Strong's Comments: When asked by Rob Francis whether the cast and crew played along with his 'superstar' status during filming, Danny confirmed: 'Unfortunately no. That would have been great. However, everyone has always treated me fantastically on the show. I was hoping that being the 'superstar' meant that I could get a date with Emma; unfortunately, anytime I got near her, the nerd, Jonathan, would come out and screw everything up. It's probably for the best; I don't think my girlfriend would've appreciated it.'

74

Where the Wild Things Are

US Transmission Date: 25 Apr. 2000
UK Transmission Date: 5 May 2000 (Sky)
1 Mar. 2001 (BBC2)

Writer: Tracey Forbes
Director: David Solomon
Cast: Kathryn Joosten (Mrs Holt),
Casey McCarthy (Julie), Neil Daly (Mason), Jeff Wilson (Evan),
Bryan Cuprill (Roy), Jeffrey Sharmay (Drowning Boy),
Jeri Austin (Running Girl), Danielle Pessis (Christie),
David Engler (Initiative Guy)
French title: *La Maison Hantée*
German title: *Die Unersättlichen*

While Buffy and Riley have reached a passionate stage of their
relationship, Anya believes that she and Xander are on the
verge of breaking up, and bonds with Spike (both of them
missing their ability to do evil things) while Xander flirts with
a girl named Julie at a Lowell House party. The party loses its
fun when the sexually repressed spirits of abused children who
lived there begin to assert themselves, prompted by Buffy and
Riley's love-making. The gang go to Giles for help and they
battle against the poltergeists, finally reaching a blissfully
unaware Buffy and Riley, with Xander and Anya rediscover-
ing their love for each other in the process.

Dudes and Babes *and* Authority Sucks!: '. . . You want sex?
Let's have sex. Hot, sweaty, big sex.' The pent-up sexual
tension from the children who where repressed at Lowell by
religious maniac Genevieve Holt manifests itself in what
would usually be classified as a poltergeist activity. It is
thought that more often than not, the owner of the poltergeist is
a woman going through puberty, beginning to grapple the
stress of womanhood – a metaphor that this episode takes
astonishingly literally.

Anya tells Xander: 'We have nothing in common besides
both of us liking your penis, and now I don't even have that.'
Xander's chat-up technique seems to be improving (compare,

for instance, some of his inept attempts during season one with his confident swagger here).

A Little Learning is a Dangerous Thing: Graham got a D in Covert Operations.

Work is a Four-Letter Word: Xander's new job is driving an ice-cream van.

It's a Designer Label!: Lots of short skirts seen at the party. Watch out for Buffy's silvery shiny pants and thick sweater, Forrest's orange jumper and Julie's pink top. A student at the party is wearing a UC✪D sweatshirt.

References: This episode shares its title (and some of its themes) with a book by Maurice Sendak. Buffy's 'Who says we can't all get along?' may be an oblique reference to Rodney King's much quoted plea for tolerance in 1992. Also, Martin Luther King (1929–68), Grace Jones's 'Slave to the Rhythm', the US series *Felicity* and the public furore over its star Keri Russell cutting her hair, 1 Kings 16:31 (first biblical reference of Jezebel) and *The Evil Dead*. Some of the condoms in the drawer appear to be the brand Durex. This is the first time condoms have been shown on *Buffy*, though Anya did mention them in **59**, 'The Harsh Light of Day'. Xander's ice-cream van has a 'giant insects' poster.

Bitch!: Willow on Riley and Buffy: 'They're probably going to . . .' Giles: 'Thank you, Willow, I *did* attend university in the Mesozoic era, I do remember what it's like.'

Awesome!: Xander and Anya in the ice-cream truck ('There's nothing wrong with my body.' Anya: 'There must be. I saw that wrinkled man on TV talking about erectile dysfunction . . .'). Giles produces a memorable *double entendre*: 'In the midst of all that, do you really think they were keeping it up? Oh, for a different phrasing.'

'You May Remember Me From Such TV Series As . . .': Kathryn Joosten plays Mrs Landingham in *The West Wing*.

There's a Ghost in My House: Xander: 'There's ghosts and shaking and people are going all *Felicity* with their hair.'

Valley-Speak: Buffy: 'You get Fang, I'll get Horny.'

Cigarettes and Alcohol and Rock'n'Roll: Giles: 'Much as I long for a good-kegger, I have other plans. The Espresso Pump . . . It's a meeting of grown-ups. It couldn't possibly be of any interest to you lot.' When the gang *see* Rupert Giles, *God of acoustic rock*, it actually turns out to be of *great* interest to Willow ('Now I remember why I used to have such a crush on him'), Tara ('He *is* pretty good') and Anya. Everybody, in fact, except Xander ('Could we go back to the haunted house? Coz this is creeping me out'). Spike and Anya drink whisky and beer (respectively) at the Bronze. Everybody's drinking at the party (mostly beer). Spike has taken to robbing people to keep himself in 'blood and beer'.

Logic, Let Me Introduce You to This Window: Considering a vine shoots through Anya's hand, there is a remarkable lack of blood. Spike's reflection can be seen first in the Lowell House window, then, even more clearly, on the glass door.

Quote/Unquote: Spike: 'I'm robbing you.' Anya: 'That's just ludicrous. You can't hurt me because you've got that chip in your brain. Also, I like my money the way it is . . . When it's *mine*.'

Xander: 'What do you feel?' Anya: 'Sad, afraid of being without you and a little hungry.' Xander: 'I meant about the house.' Anya: 'Oh. Still haunted.'

Notes: 'Seen a thousand relationships. First there's the love and sex and then there's nothing left but the vengeance. That's how it works.' Serious subject matter: child abuse. The episode tries hard not to get on its soap box, but occasionally can't help itself. To be fair, there are some good lines, and the erotic symbolism works quite well.

Xander wonders if every UC✪D frat house is haunted (see **60**, 'Fear Itself') and, if so, why people keep coming to these parties (it's not for the snacks). Anya mentions that she and Xander have only *not* had sex on two nights since they started going out. (Possibly when Spike stayed at Xander's in **66**, 'Hush', and when all the gang hid there in **70**, 'Goodbye Iowa'.) Willow had 'a bad-birthday-party-pony-thing' when she was four years old, leaving her fearful of both ponies and horses. Tara learned to ride when she was young.

Lowell House used to be the Lowell Home for Children, from 1949 to 1960, and housed upwards of forty adolescents: runaways, juvenile delinquents, and emotionally disturbed teenagers from the Sunnydale area.

Soundtrack: 'Parker Posey' by Crooner, Opus 1's 'Brit Pop Junkie', Caviar's 'I Thought I Was Found', 'The Devil You Know (God is a Man)' by Face to Face [*], Lumirova's 'Philo' and 'One of a Kind' by Fonda. Anthony Stewart Head sings a beautiful version of The Who's 'Behind Blue Eyes' at the Espresso Pump (the singing really *is* Tony, although the guitar is played by John King).

75

New Moon Rising

US Transmission Date: 2 May 2000
UK Transmission Date: 12 May 2000 (Sky)
22 Mar. 2001 (BBC2)

Writer: Marti Noxon
Director: James A Contner
Cast: Mark Daneri (Scientist #2)
French title: *Un Amour de Pleine Lune*
German title: *Abschiede*

Oz's sudden return to Sunnydale poses all sorts of complications in Willow's life, particularly as he has learned to control his wolf-side. At least until he discovers Willow's scent on Tara and draws the logical conclusion. As the wolf emerges, he's captured by the Initiative. The Scooby Gang work out an infiltration plan with Spike's help. But Spike is in cahoots with Adam, who has promised to get Spike's chip out in return for help with his plan. Inside the Initiative, Riley tries to free Oz but is locked up. Buffy holds Colonel McNamara hostage rescuing both Oz and Riley – now considered a traitor and a fugitive. Willow and Oz realise that they can't be together, as Willow is the one thing that can activate the wolf in Oz. Willow reveals that she is happy with Tara, and Oz leaves again. When Tara tells Willow that she should be with the one she loves, Willow replies, 'I am.'

No Thin Chicks: On 4 May 2000, in response to several very unkind postings about her, Amber Benson went online with an emotional message: 'I've been thinking a lot about what people said about Tara after the last episode. At first, I was very hurt. I tried to disassociate myself from feeling bad by saying: "This is Tara that they are talking about, not me." But I couldn't. I guess it hurts when someone calls you ugly or makes nasty comments about your weight whether or not it is really *you* they are referring to. I am just a human being and I feel like I deserve to be treated as such. I also feel that Tara deserves a little more kindness and compassion . . . A body is a beautiful thing to waste. Believe me, I have seen enough of my friends and peers waste away to *nothing* so that they could work in this industry. So that they could perpetuate the lie that anorexia is beautiful. Love yourself for who you are, not what others think you should look like. It's more important in this life to love each other despite our imperfections.'

Dudes and Babes: Willow tells Buffy about herself and Tara, much to Buffy's obvious discomfort.

Authority Sucks!: McNamara says that he will institute a court martial to investigate the extent of Riley's involvement with the Slayer. 'They're anarchists, Finn, too backwards for the real world. Help us take them down and you just might save your military career. Otherwise, you'll go to your grave labelled a traitor. No woman is worth that.'

A Little Learning is a Dangerous Thing: Buffy: 'Stay back, or I'll pull a William Burroughs on your leader.' Xander: 'You'll bore him to death with free prose?' Buffy: 'Was I the only one awake in English that day?'

Denial, Thy Name is Riley: Buffy on Riley's concern about Willow dating a werewolf: 'God, I never knew you were such a bigot.' Riley: 'I'm just saying it's a little weird to date someone who tries to eat you once a month.'

It's a Designer Label!: Return of the sheepskins (see **62**, 'Wild at Heart'). Anya is a vision in pink, while Buffy's light-blue roll-neck and bobble hat and Spike in combat green take some getting used to.

References: Radiohead, William Burroughs, The Jam's 'All Around the World', *The Fugitive* and Wheaties. The title is a reference to Credence Clearwater Revival's 'Bad Moon Rising', used to spectacular effect in *An American Werewolf in London* and now forever associated with werewolves. Riley quotes from The Sex Pistols' 'Anarchy in the UK' ('I am an anarchist'). Posters for the bands The String Cheese Incident and Devil Doll can be seen.

'You May Remember Me From Such Films and TV Series As . . .': Conor O'Farrell played James McDivitt in *From the Earth to the Moon*, was Detective Morrisey in *NYPD Blue* and appeared in *Eye of the Stalker*. Mark Daneri has a role in *When the Bough Breaks*.

The Drugs Don't Work: The Initiative scientists give Oz the drug Haldol to keep him quiet.

Logic, Let Me Introduce You to This Window: Oz's pendant keeps jumping in and out of visibility, even when he's not moving. When Oz is chasing Tara, he begins to run down a row of seats before the camera cuts to Tara. Next shot, Oz is at the beginning of the row again. When Tara throws the chair at Oz, Riley nails him with a tranquilliser dart at the same time. Oz falls to the floor, with no dart in his back. Riley steps over him and the dart is now in his back.

I Just *Love* Your Accent: Spike: 'None of that, or I won't help you get Red's mongrel back. Bad news travels fast with us demons. We all like a good laugh.'

Cruelty to Animals: The imminent arrival of Miss Kitty Fantastico (or whatever they end up calling her; Trixie is another of Tara's suggested names), provokes a discussion on witches' familiars. Those cruel lesbians are planning to make their new kitty 'go bonkers with string and catnip and stuff?'

Quote/Unquote: Spike: '*You* were a Boy Scout?' Adam: 'Parts of me.'

Giles: 'How did you get in?' Spike: 'The door was unlocked. You might want to watch that, Rupert. Someone dangerous could get in.' Buffy: 'Or someone formerly dangerous and currently annoying.'

Oz: 'It was stupid to think that you'd just be waiting.' Willow: 'I *was* waiting. I feel like some part of me will always be waiting for you. Like if I'm old and blue-haired and I turn the corner in Istanbul and there you are, I won't be surprised.'

Notes: 'I always suspected that stuff about werewolf transformations being based on a lunar cycle was campfire talk.' A rambling exercise in one step forward and eight sideways.

Oz's return gets mixed up in the ongoing plotline and the whole thing is ultimately unsatisfying.

Buffy still hasn't told Riley about her relationship with Angel. Willow says she is more a dog person than a cat person. Devon is mentioned. Oz has been to Mexico (where his van broke down and he traded his bass to have it fixed and garaged), Romania (where a warlock sent him to monks to learn some meditation techniques) and spent a long time in Tibet (where he 'got a lot of mileage out of the barter system' and traded Willow's present for a Radiohead record). Riley ends the episode hiding out at the ruins of Sunnydale High.

Critique: The 2 May edition of the *New York Daily News* ('"Buffy" Character Follows Her Bliss') declared that: 'Something really significant happens at the end of tonight's *Buffy the Vampire Slayer*. We don't see it, because the scene plunges into darkness and ends at that precise moment – but the dialogue leading up to that moment makes the episode a landmark in TV history. What happens is the shift from subtext to text of a very long-running, compelling and credible character development involving Alyson Hannigan's Willow ... A declaration of love between two women may not sound like a big deal, especially on a series so grounded in fantasy ... Beneath the literally monstrous surface of *Buffy the Vampire Slayer*, though, is a churning turmoil of metaphors about love, death, commitment and fear. Sex, on *Buffy*, is anything but casual; it can unleash demonic forces and change characters temporarily or permanently. Despite the silly-sounding fantasy elements, *Buffy* serves up more real angst, and more mature explorations of what it means to be a young person with emotions and responsibilities and insecurities and torn loyalties, than any of the more "realistic" youth dramas, such as *Beverly Hills 90210* or the WB's own *Dawson's Creek*, and *Felicity* ... This is, in fact, unlike anything else I can recall on regular prime-time television: a character evolving naturally over four seasons of stories and arriving at a place of sexual rediscovery. Once again, *Buffy* quietly, but assuredly, impresses and amazes.'

Jane Espenson's Comments: Jane fanned the flames on the *Posting Board*: 'Willow and Tara? Are you asking what they do in private? We don't write those scenes, so I guess you could say we don't know either. What you see is what there is.'

Joss Whedon's Comments: Finally, on 4 May, Joss told the *Posting Board*: 'OK. Let's be frank. Tuesday's episode was pretty controversial and a real eye-opener for me. Despite my fervent hatred of criticism, I do understand when I've made a mistake. I thought the Willow-arc made sense for her character, but the fact is, most people *aren't* like that, and it's hard for most normal people to understand a lifestyle that less than ten per cent of the population embrace. I don't want to be about issues – I just want to tell a story I think will engage and challenge, and this time I think I missed the mark. So I'm just hoping people understand we're feeling our way along here. We *are* listening. So we're going to shift away from this whole lifestyle choice Willow has made. Just wipe the slate. From now on, Willow will no longer be a Jew. And I think we can all breathe easier.' Nice to see that satire lives.

A couple of days later, Joss added: 'I may push the envelope a tad, I may make fun of the Standards and Practices guys, but I'm not actually out to stick it to them. We've had a pretty good relationship over the years. They have a family viewing audience to think about, I have a commitment to porn and between the two . . . I just want to say officially that I do know the difference between bigotry and someone just not liking the episode. And I have never spanked my creations. And by never I mean seldom . . .' Crazy guy.

Subsequently On *Angel*: 'Five By Five'; 'Sanctuary': Faith arrives in Los Angeles and is immediately recruited by the law firm Wolfram & Hart to assassinate Angel. To get Angel interested, she attacks Cordelia, and kidnaps and tortures her former Watcher, Wesley. Angel refuses to kill Faith despite having the opportunity to do so, and attempts to help her instead. This is hindered by the arrival not only of the Watchers' Council squad, led by Collins, but also of Buffy, outraged to find her enemy in the arms of her former lover. Eventually, Faith gives herself up to the police, in the hope of finding redemption, but Buffy and Angel part on bad terms.

76
The Yoko Factor

US Transmission Date: 9 May 2000
UK Transmission Date: 19 May 2000 (Sky)
29 Mar. 2001 (BBC2)

Writer: Douglas Petrie
Director: David Grossman
Cast: Jade Carter (Lieutenant)
French title: *Facteur Yoko*
German title: *Der Yoko-Faktor*

Colonel McNamara is ordered to get Riley back while Spike plays each of the gang against each other, resulting in a drunk Giles and a big argument between Willow, Xander and Buffy. Angel follows Buffy from Los Angeles to apologise, but gets into a fight with Riley before they can settle their differences. Buffy sees Adam kill Forrest and has to tell Riley. Buffy walks out on the gang after their Spike-induced falling out to fight on her own. A distraught Riley pays a visit to Adam.

Dudes and Babes: Willow on Buffy: 'I used to assume that we'd be roomies through grad school, well into little old ladyhood, you know, cheating at bingo together and forgetting to take our pills.' Anya says Xander is a 'Viking in the sack'.

The Conspiracy Starts at Home Time: McNamara tells his government contact, Ward, that morale's a problem and that controlling the HSTs is getting harder. He suggests that Riley fell in with a bad crowd and that he doesn't think that Riley was ever the soldier that the government hoped he was. 'Boy thinks too much.' Nevertheless, Ward says they want him back. Their databanks, however, don't have much on Buffy. 'She's just a girl,' says McNamara.

Work is a Four-Letter Word: Xander has worked for, and been fired from, Starbucks coffeehouse and a telephone sex line.

It's a Designer Label!: 'It's the pants, isn't it? It's OK, I couldn't take me seriously in these things either,' says Riley concerning the trousers he borrowed from Xander. Buffy's chunky sweater reappears.

References: Spike says that Adam is 'like Tony Robbins if he was a big, scary, *Frankenstein*-looking . . .' Also, The Doors' 'L.A. Woman', GI Joe (yet again), US Army adverts ('Be all you can be'), the New Jersey army base Fort Dix, *The Godfather* trilogy ('What kind of family are you, the Corleones?') and *The Wizard of Oz* (Spike: 'You're not exactly the whiz these days.' Willow: 'I *am* a whiz . . . If ever a whiz there was'). The Beatles (Spike: 'It's called "The Yoko Factor". Don't tell me you've never heard of the Beatles?' Adam: 'I have. I like "Helter Skelter".' Spike: 'What a surprise. The point is, they were once a real powerful group. It's not a stretch to say they ruled the world. When they broke up, everyone blamed Yoko, but the fact is, the group split itself up, she just happened to be there'). *Batman* (Xander: 'I'll stay behind and putt around the Batcave with crusty old Alfred.' Giles: 'You forget, Alfred had a job'). The cup Anya holds appears to be from the burger-chain In-N-Out. Another WP sticker can be seen in Buffy's room.

Bitch!: Spike: 'For someone who's got *Watcher* on his résumé, you might want to cast an eye to the front door every now and again.'

Anya: 'They look down on you.' Xander: 'And they hate *you*.' Anya: 'But they don't look down on me.'

Buffy: 'You've got to be kidding me. This is why you came?' Angel: 'No. This was an accident.' Buffy: 'Running a car into a tree is an accident. Running your fist into somebody's face is a plan.'

Angel on Riley: 'You actually *sleep* with this guy?' And: '. . . I don't like him!'

Awesome!: The Buffy–Xander–Willow–Giles argument. A defining moment as the Scooby Gang discover just how far they have drifted apart. Also, Giles's girly squeal when Spike interrupts 'Freebird' (see **Soundtrack**). Angel kicking Riley's ass and the beautiful scene between Angel and Buffy.

Valley-Speak: Xander: 'Give it up for an American chipmanship.'

Cigarettes and Alcohol: Buffy: 'Are you drunk?' Giles: 'Yes, quite a bit actually.' Spike owns a zippo lighter and drinks a can of lager.

Logic, Let Me Introduce You to This Window: When Spike rushes into Giles's home his reflection can be seen in a mirror behind Tara and Willow. Angel says that he needs an invitation to enter Buffy's dorm, but Sunday and her buddies didn't need one in **57**, 'The Freshman' (see also **63**, 'The Initiative'). When Tara and Anya are in the bathroom, some of the muffled arguments heard from the front room seem to be from the soundtrack of **64**, 'Pangs'.

I Just *Love* Your Accent: Spike: 'Little Miss Tiny's got a habit of *bollocksing-up* the plans of every would-be, unstoppable bad-ass who sets foot in this town.'

Cruelty to Demons: McNamara: 'They're animals, lieutenant. We pack them in until we're out of room and then we pack them in some more.' Lieutenant: 'They're going to start tearing each other apart, sir.' McNamara: 'I have no problem with that scenario.'

Pussy Galore: The author shares Willow's appreciation of Miss Kitty Fantastico's cuteness.

Quote/Unquote: Riley on Angel: 'Sometimes things happen between exes and when I saw that he was bad . . .' Buffy: 'He's not bad.' Riley: 'Seriously? That's a good day? Well, there you go. Even when he's good, he's all *Mr Billowy Coat King of Pain . . .*'

Giles: 'You never train with me any more. He's gonna kick your ass.' And: 'Whatever happened to Latin? At least when that made no sense, the church approved.'

Willow: 'You can't handle Tara being my girlfriend.' Xander: 'No. It was bad before that. Since you two went off to college and forgot about me. Just left me in the basement to . . . Tara's your *girlfriend*?' Giles (from upstairs): '*Bloody hell.*'

Buffy: 'We'll walk into that cave with you two attacking me and the funny drunk drooling on my shoe. Hey, maybe that's the secret way of killing Adam. Is that how you can help? You're not answering me . . . I guess I'm starting to understand why there's no ancient prophecy about "a Chosen One and her friends".'

Notes: 'At this point a cynical person might think that you're offering just what we need when we need it most.' Everything comes to a head in this marvellous drawing together of all of the various subplots that have been battling for prominence. Some of it works beautifully (the Buffy and the Scooby Gang stuff, especially), some of it seems contrived (Forrest's needless death, for instance), but at least we're heading *somewhere*.

Buffy *has* now told Riley about her relationship with Angel. She just edited out what actually *sends* Angel bad. So, Xander tells him instead. Xander says he doesn't hate Angel ('just the guts part'). Willow is thinking about taking drama next year (see **80**, 'Real Me'). She notes that there are 'off-campus places that are *way-cool* for groups' to live in. Spike tells Adam that he's previously killed two Slayers (see **15**, 'School Hard', **85**, 'Fool for Love'). Spike has a VCR, a Nintendo and a TV to replace the one Forrest destroyed in **70**, 'Goodbye Iowa', in his crypt.

Soundtrack: Tony Head sings a solo-acoustic version of Lynard Skynard's hippy anthem 'Freebird' until Spike, blissfully, interrupts him.

Critique: In their 11 May 2000 issue, *Rolling Stone* ran a gushing five-page cover-story on *Buffy*, going 'Behind the scenes at *the coolest show on TV*', with soundbites from many of the actors and production staff.

77

Primeval[22]

US Transmission Date: 16 May 2000
UK Transmission Date: 26 May 2000 (Sky)
5 Apr. 2001 (BBC2)

Writer: David Fury
Director: James A Contner
Cast: Jordi Vilasuso (Dixon)
French title: *Phase Finale*
German title: *Das letzte Gefecht*

---

[22] Confusion surrounded the title of this episode, with one 'official' book calling it 'Primevil', a mistake the last edition of this guide repeated. The matter was settled with the release of the Season Four video box, which confirmed the spelling as 'Primeval'.

Adam has activated a chip in Riley's chest and he is now under Adam's control. Riley finds that Forrest has been reanimated, along with Walsh and Angleman. Buffy guesses that Spike was behind the gang's strained relations and she manages to convince her friends of this. They realise that Spike is working for Adam, who is preparing to start a war inside the Initiative. To stop him, Giles, Willow and Xander perform a spell, combining themselves within Buffy's body. This creates SuperSlayer who fights and destroys Adam by ripping out his uranium core. With the demons loose in the Initiative, Riley overcomes his programming to fight Forrest. In the aftermath, the shadowy men in Washington realise that the Initiative has failed and decide to cancel the project.

The Conspiracy Starts at Home Time: Ward says that the Initiative represented the government's interests in not only controlling the otherworldly menace, but in harnessing its power for their own military purposes. An experiment that has failed. 'Once the prototype took control of the complex, our soldiers suffered a 40 per cent casualty rate' and it was only through the actions of the deserter and a group of civilian insurrectionists that their losses were not total. 'Maggie Walsh's vision was brilliant, but ultimately unsupportable. The demons cannot be harnessed' – or controlled. It is, therefore, 'our recommendation that this project be terminated and all records concerning it expunged. Our soldiers will be debriefed. Standard confidentiality clause. We will monitor the civilians and usual measures prepared should they try to go public. I don't think they will. The Initiative itself will be filled in with concrete. Burn it down, gentlemen . . . and salt the Earth.'

Unemployment is a Twelve-Letter Word: Anya: 'You said you wanted to check the board at the unemployment office this morning. You can't go like that. They won't even interview you if you're naked.'

It's a Designer Label!: Giles's dressing gown and Buffy's see-through top and huge boots.

References: Influenced by *The Matrix* (especially Buffy's fight with Adam), *The Terminator* (Adam's gun-arm) and *Jaws* (the death of Forrest). *Alice in Wonderland* is referenced, along with Nancy Drew, the Trojan Horse and *Must-See TV*.

Spike misquotes Apollo 11's first words on the moon ('The Slayer has landed'). *Manus, the Hands of Fate* was a B-movie made famous by *Mystery Science Theater 3000*.

Awesome!: Anya telling Xander that she loves him. Xander's reaction to Buffy and Willow hugging him ('Oh God, we're gonna die, aren't we?'). The battle at the end – 'I do appreciate violence,' notes Adam.

Valley-Speak: Willow: 'Why do you think Spike made with the head games?' Xander: 'He's all dressed up with no one to bite. He's gotta get his ya-ya's somehow.'

Cigarettes and Alcohol: Spike uses his cigarette as a weapon, stubbing it out in Forrest's eye.

Logic, Let Me Introduce You to This Window: Xander's blanket repositions itself several times. When Buffy pulls Adam's uranium core out, she holds it horizontally. In the next shot, she's holding it vertically. Giles's line: 'The enjoining spell is extremely touchy. It's volatile. We can't risk being interrupted', seems to have been overdubbed on to the soundtrack in post-production.

I Just *Love* Your Accent: Spike says it warms the cockles of his non-beating heart seeing 'you lads' (Riley and Adam) together. He also uses 'cripes' and 'blighters'; Giles adds 'piffle'.

Quote/Unquote: Giles: 'Xander, just because this is never going to work, there's no need to be negative.'

Xander being hugged by the girls: 'Giles, hurry up. You *definitely* wanna get down here for this.'

Adam: 'You can't last much longer.' Buffy: '*We* can. *We* are forever.'

Notes: 'I've got to shut him down. His final phase is about to start.' Cometh the hour, cometh the men. A huge engine of destruction that manages the impossible and ties virtually everything up. Top quality direction helps.

The photo of Buffy, Willow and Xander that Buffy looks at is the same one she found in the basement in **36**, 'Dead Man's Party'. It also featured in **18**, 'Halloween'. Xander wonders if anyone misses the Mayor. Giles speaks Sumerian. During the enjoining spell Xander takes the role of *Animus*, the heart, Giles is *Sophus*, the mind and Willow becomes *Spiritus*, the spirit. Buffy is *Manus*, the hand.

At some point immediately after this episode, Willow spends an hour on the phone to Cordelia in Los Angeles helping her old friend to decrypt the Wolfram & Hart files stolen by Angel in *Angel*: 'Blind Date'. Willow says 'hey' to Wesley, a cute wink by Alyson to her real-life boyfriend, Alexis Denisof.

78
Restless

US Transmission Date: 23 May 2000
UK Transmission Date: 28 May 2000 (Sky)
12 Apr. 2001 (BBC2)

Writer: Joss Whedon
Director: Joss Whedon
Cast: David Wells (The Cheese Guy), Michael Harney (Xander's Dad),
Sharon Ferguson (Primitive), Rob Boltin (Soldier)
French title: *Cauchemar*
German title: *Jedem sein Albtraum*

While Riley attends an Initiative debriefing, the Scooby Gang gather at Buffy's for a video night. Soon they're asleep and dreaming, their dreams exploring fears, fantasies and speculation about the past, the present and the future. But they all have something in common (besides a non-sequitur Cheese Man). The first Slayer, a wild primeval girl from the dawn of time, awoken by having her power invoked by the enjoining spell, is after them. Buffy, a hero even in dreams, puts a stop to the first Slayer's terrors, but is left with Tara's enigmatic statement: 'You think you know what's to come. What you are. You haven't even begun.'

Dreaming (As Blondie Never Said) is Forty-Five Minutes of Cheese: Dealing entirely with dreamscapes, 'Restless' is about secrets. Hidden laughter behind closed doors and shuttered windows. Abuse monsters, public nudity, what the future holds . . . These are the dreams that make us. And the cheese will not protect us.

Willow dreams that she is attending drama class, a surreal

adaptation of *Death of a Salesman*, starring her friends ('Your whole family's in the front row. And they look really angry'), in which she doesn't know her lines. Afterwards she finds herself back in class, wearing the clothes she did the day she first met Buffy while everyone laughs at her ('It's exactly like a Greek tragedy') and Tara and Oz whisper behind her back.

Xander's labyrinthine dream contains images of Joyce Summers's sexuality and Giles, Spike and Buffy playing like children while Xander ponders his future. Driving his ice-cream truck with Anya, who is thinking about getting back into vengeance, Xander finds himself attracted to Willow and Tara and unable to understand Giles and Anya, but all of his escape attempts lead him back to his basement where he meets Snyder, and his brutish father asks, 'Are you ashamed of us? Your mother's crying her guts out. The line ends here with us and you're not gonna change that.'

Giles dreams of himself, Olivia (pushing a pram) and a childlike Buffy at a funfair ('This is my business. Blood of the lamb and all that'), where Spike has hired himself out as a crass attraction. At the Bronze Giles meets Willow and Xander and, while Anya performs a terrible standup routine, he works out what is going on, telling his friends in song. All of the dreams end with a savage black girl attacking Willow, pulling out Xander's heart and scalping Giles. (The spirit, the heart, the mind . . . Remember that, it might be important.)

Buffy tells Tara she needs to find the others. 'Be back in time for Dawn' she is told (see **80**, 'Real Me', **100**, 'The Gift'). Buffy abandons her mother to a life of living in the walls, finds Riley (who's been made surgeon general) and a humanised Adam drawing up a plan for world domination. Finally, she finds herself in the desert with Tara and the first Slayer.

Buffy: 'At least you all didn't dream about that guy with the cheese. I don't know *where* the hell that came from.'

Dudes and Babes and Cheese: Xander's dream-image of Willow and Tara features Willow in a very short black leather dress and Tara in a short black skirt and revealing blouse. Both have heavy make-up. And they, ahem, 'get it on'. Off screen, obviously.

Authority Sucks!: Giles notes, 'Somehow our joining with

Buffy and invoking the essence of the Slayer's power was an affront to the source of that power.' Meaning that the first Slayer was able to hunt them in their dreams.

Tara tells the dreaming Willow: 'Everyone's starting to wonder about you. The *real* you. If they find out, they'll punish you; I can't help you with that.'

Riley on his world domination plan: 'Baby, we're the government. It's what we do.' (Concerning Riley and Adam sitting opposite each other at that table during Buffy's dream, Joss Whedon intriguingly notes, 'She was seeing that they were *two sides of the same coin*').

A Little Cheese is a Dangerous Thing: In Xander's dream both Giles and Anya speak French, which Xander doesn't understand. As Joss Whedon told the *Posting Board*: 'At the last minute I dragged my assistant Diego in to read it. He's Mexican, speaks a little French (yeah, he's *trilingual*, which for someone as barely unilingual as myself is both annoying and annoying) and he was reading off a script so it may not have sounded perfect to some but the effect was just great for the dream.'

Anya: 'I've figured out how to steer by gesturing emphatically.'

Denial, Thy Name is Cheese: Cheese Man: 'I wear the cheese. It does not wear me.'

Denial, Thy Name is Joyce: Buffy dreams of Joyce living in the college walls. 'I made some lemonade and I'm learning how to play mahjong. You go find your friends.' Buffy doesn't think that she should live there and Joyce notes, 'You could probably break through the wall.' But Buffy is already following Xander up the stairs.

The Conspiracy Starts at Cheese Time: Riley says that he has Graham, among others, testifying in his favour at the Initiative debriefing and that he may get out with an honourable discharge. 'Having the inside scoop on the administration's own Bay of Mutated Pigs is definitely an advantage,' he notes. 'You're blackmailing the government. In a patriotic way,' adds Willow.

It's a Designer Cheese!: The outfit Willow wears in her dream, after Buffy rips off her alleged costume, is the 'softer side of

Sears' clothes she wore in **1**, 'Welcome to the Hellmouth'. Also, Giles's black sweater, Willow's sun T-shirt, Joyce's red negligee, Spike in tweed, Xander's 'Sal's Surf Shop' T-shirt (see **64**, 'Pangs') and Riley wearing the loudest chaps since James Stewart in *Destry Rides Again*.

References: *Apocalypse Now* (Xander says it's 'a gay romp'). Willow asks for something 'less *Heart of Darkness*-y'. Giles feels the film is overrated, then realises that its theme is Willard's journey to Kurtz rather than the Vietnam war. Riley alludes to the Bay of Pigs. The Greek writing on Tara's back is the beginning of a poem by Sappho. 'This isn't *Madame Butterfly*, is it? Because I have a whole problem with opera' (see **10**, 'Nightmares'). Also, *Death of a Salesman* (though I've never seen a version with a cowboy either), *The Lion, The Witch and the Wardrobe* and the Chinese board game mahjong. Visually influenced by *Lawrence of Arabia* and conceptually by *An American Werewolf in London* (a dream within a dream within . . .).

Bitch!: Buffy: 'I'm going to ignore you, and you're going to go away. You're really gonna have to get over the whole primal power thing. You're *not* the source of me. Also, in terms of hair care, you really wanna say, what kind of impression am I making in the workplace?'

Awesome!: Giles *sings* the plot. ('The spell we cast with Buffy must have released some primal evil that's come back . . . Willow, look through the chronicles for some reference to a warrior beast . . . Xander, help Willow. And try not to bleed on my couch; I've just had it steam-cleaned.') Buffy with dark hair. The stunning recreation of *Apocalypse Now* (even the music sounds like The Doors). Oz's 'I've been here forever.' The monochrome sequence of Spike as a sideshow freak ('at least it's showbiz'). The lighters.

'You May Remember Me From Such Films As . . .': David Wells's movie CV includes *Beverly Hills Cops*, *Basic Instinct*, *Doorways*, *Crackin Up* and *The Progeny*. Michael Harney is in *Erin Brockovich* and *Turbulence*. Sharon Ferguson features in *Malcolm X*.

Valley-Speak: Xander: 'Got the sucking chest wound swingin'. I promised Anya I'd be there for her big night. Now I'll probably be pushing up daisies, in the sense of being in the ground underneath them and fertilising the soil with decomposition.' And: 'Don't get linear on me now, man.'

Logic, Let Me Introduce You to This Cheese: *Logic*?!

I Just *Love* Your Accent: Spike: 'Giles is gonna teach me to be a Watcher. Says I got the stuff.' Giles: 'Spike's like a son to me.'

It's Not Easy Being Cheesey: Joss Whedon: 'The Cheese Man is the only thing in the show that means nothing. I needed something like that, that *couldn't* be explained, because dreams always have that one element that is just *ridiculous*.' Having said that, many fans have come up with various extraordinary (and some quite convincing) theories on what he *might* represent.

Pussy Galore: The kitten stalks towards the camera in slow motion during Willow's dream.

Quote/Unquote: Xander: 'She does *spells* with Tara . . . Sometimes I think about two women doing *a spell*. And then I do a spell *by myself*.'

Snyder: 'I walked by your guidance counsellor's office one time. A bunch of you were sitting there waiting to be shepherded. I remember it smelled like dead flowers. Like decay. Then it hit me. The hope of our nation's future is a bunch of mulch.' Xander: 'I never got the chance to tell you how glad I was you were eaten by a snake.'

Anya: 'And then the duck tells the doctor, that there's a man that's attached to my ass. You see, it was the duck and not the man that spoke.'

Buffy: 'What else could I expect from a bunch of low-rent, no-account hoodlums like you? Your whole sex, throw 'em in the sea for all I care . . . and wait for the bubbles. Men, with your groping-and-spitting, all-groin-no-brain, three billion of you passing around the same worn-out urge.'

Notes: 'The Slayer does not walk in this world.' 'I walk. I talk. I shop. I sneeze. I'm gonna be a fireman when the floods roll back. There's trees in the desert since you moved out, and I don't sleep on a bed of bones.' *Major weird*. Completely inexplicable and yet, at the same time, utterly compelling to watch. In hindsight, 'Restless' alludes to the themes of the following season – Dawn's arrival, Xander's maturing, Willow and Tara's relationship – and to its fateful climax.

The clock in Buffy's dream reads 7.30, a likely reference to **56**, 'Graduation Day' Part 2, in which Faith mentioned 'counting down from 7-3-0.' ('It's so late,' says Buffy. 'That clock's completely wrong,' replies Tara. See **100**, 'The Gift'.) Buffy calls Xander 'big brother'.

Unlike every other episode the 'previously on *Buffy the Vampire Slayer*' montage is immediately followed by the title credits.

Soundtrack: Anthony Stewart Head (vocals), Christophe Beck (piano) and Four Star Mary (all other instruments) perform Joss Whedon's 'The Exposition Song'.

Did You Spot?: Xander dead at a weeping Harmony's feet during the *Death of a Salesman* sequence. The 'sheep' graffiti as Xander crawls from the back of the truck into his basement.

Joss Whedon's Comments: Asked by *DreamWatch* about the more experimental episodes and how they compare to those done by other series, Joss confessed: 'I don't want to do things that are just a wink to the audience. I thought the *X-Files/Cops* thing ['X-COPS'] made sense, it actually worked in a weird way. But *Felicity* did *The Twilight Zone*, *Chicago Hope* did a musical show and I don't want to be one of those shows that is self-indulgent. The episode that I did at the end of this season is all dreams and it is unbelievably bizarre, but it's in a world where it makes sense. As long as we don't start getting cutesy [or] stupid, we have opportunities to go to new places.'

'Death is your gift'

– 'Intervention'

Fifth Season (2000–2001)

**Mutant Enemy Inc/Kuzui Enterprises/
Sandollar Television/20th Century Fox**
Created by Joss Whedon
Co-Producers: Douglas Petrie, John F Perry, Marc David Alpert,
James A Contner (81, 93, 98)
Producers: Jane Espenson, David Solomon, Gareth Davies
Consulting Producer: David Greenwalt
Supervising Producer: David Fury
Co-Executive Producer: Marti Noxon
Executive Producers: Sandy Gallin, Gail Berman, Fran Rubel Kuzui,
Kaz Kuzui, Joss Whedon

Regular Cast:
Sarah Michelle Gellar (Buffy Summers),
Nicholas Brendon (Xander Harris), Alyson Hannigan (Willow Rosenberg),
David Boreanaz (Angel/Angelus, 85, 95),
Anthony Stewart Head (Rupert Giles),
Kristine Sutherland (Joyce Summers, 79–83, 85–94, 99),
Julie Benz (Darla, 85),
Mercedes McNab (Harmony Kendall, 80, 82, 84–85, 92),
Dean Butler (Hank Summers, 99), James Marsters (Spike, 79–94, 96–100),
Juliet Landau (Drusilla, 85, 92), Emma Caulfield (Anya Jenkins),
Harris Yulin (Quentin Travers, 90), Megan Gray (Sandy, 84, 86),
Marc Blucas (Riley Finn, 79–88), Bailey Chase (Graham Miller, 82, 87–88),
Amber Benson (Tara Maclay, 79–80, 82–84, 86–87, 89–100),
Sharon Ferguson (Primitive, 96, 99[23]),
Michelle Trachtenberg (Dawn Summers),
Bob Morrisey (Crazy #1, 80[24], 98–99),
Kelly Donovan (Xander Double, 81, 96),
Charlie Weber (Ben, 82–84, 86–87, 90, 92, 95, 97–100),
Clare Kramer (Glory, 83–84, 86, 90–91, 93, 95–100),
Paul Hayes (Older Night Watchman, 83, 87),
Kevin Weisman (Dreg, 86–87, 90), Nick Chinlund (Major Ellis, 87–88),
Randy Thompson (Doctor Kriegel, 87–88, 94),
Troy T Blendell (Jinx, 90–91, 93, 95–97), Justin Gorence (Orlando, 90–91, 98),

---

[23] Uncredited in **99**, 'The Weight of the World'.
[24] Credited as 'Crazy Guy' in **80**, 'Real Me'.

Paul Bates (Crazy #2, 91[25], 98–99), Carl J Johnson (Crazy #3, 91[26], 98–99),
Adam Busch (Warren Mears, 93, 96), Joel Grey (Doc, 95, 99–100),
Todd Duffey (Murk, 95–100), Lily Knight (Gronx, 98–99)

79
Buffy vs Dracula

US Transmission Date: 26 Sep. 2000
UK Transmission Date: 5 Jan. 2001 (Sky)

Writer: Marti Noxon
Director: David Solomon
Cast: Rudolf Martin (Dracula), EJ Gage (Mover #1),
Scott Berman (Mover #2), Marita Schaub (Vampire Girl #1),
Leslee Jean Matta (Vampire Girl #2), Jennifer Slimko (Vampire Girl #3)
French title: *Buffy contre Dracula*

Buffy and her friends come face-to-face with the greatest
vampire of all, Dracula. Whilst Buffy is under the Count's
influence, much to the chagrin of Riley, Xander becomes the
Dark One's emissary and leads his friends into peril. Giles
contemplates returning to England, feeling he is no longer
needed.

Denial, Thy Name is Riley: Jealous of Buffy's fascination with
Dracula, to the extent that he seeks out Spike for information,
Riley begins to realise that Buffy and he are walking different
roads (see **81**, 'The Replacement'; **88**, 'Into the Woods').

Desperate, Thy Name is Joyce: She seemingly invites Dracula
into the house for coffee because she's lonely. Joyce tells
Willow and Tara that she sometimes feels like giving up on
men altogether. 'A good Sunnydale rule of thumb?' notes
Willow. 'Avoid white-skinned men in capes.'

It's a Designer Label!: Willow's Wild Cherry Soda Pop
T-shirt. Buffy's two pairs of leather pants (scarlet and bright
pink). Xander's Hawaiian shirt.

References: Although based on a real-life Transylvanian
warlord, Vlad Tepes, Count Dracula as a character first

[25] Credited as 'Crazie #1' [sic] in **91**, 'Blood Ties'.
[26] Credited as 'Crazie #2' [sic] in **91**, 'Blood Ties'.

appeared in Bram Stoker's 1897 classic. Several aspects of the episode are drawn from this (the three sisters who menace Giles haunt Jonathan Harker in the book) and from Tod Browning's 1931 film adaptation (Xander's possession mirrors the character of Renfield. Nick Brendon's performance owes much to that of Dwight Frye in the movie). Also, *Sesame Street*, *The Horse Whisperer*, Lestat from Anne Rice's vampire novels, *Creature Feature* (see **23**, 'Ted'), The Clash's 'Complete Control', Chicago serial-killer John Wayne Gacy (a reference to painting clowns), *Frankenstein* and *Eurotrash*. Willow misquotes *Bull Durham* ('long, slow neckbites that last for days').

Bitch!: Riley thinks Buffy throws like a girl.

Awesome!: Giles and Dracula's sisters. Dracula possessing Xander ('You are strange and off-putting'). Spike, on the Count: 'That gloryhound's done more harm to vampires than any Slayer. His story gets out and suddenly everybody knows how to kill us.'

'You May Remember Me From Such Films and TV Series As . . .': German-born Rudolf Martin also played Vlad the Impaler in *Dark Prince: The True Story of Dracula*. He was Raoul in *Bedazzled*, Gilbert in *Punks* and Anton Lang in *All My Children* opposite Sarah Michelle Gellar and a preteen Michelle Trachtenberg, who played Lilly Montgomery. She was also Penny in *Inspector Gadget* and the eponymous *Harriet the Spy*. EJ Gage was in *My Uncle the Alien*. Marita Schaub appeared in *Southside*.

Don't Give Up The Day Job: Following the departure of Jeff Pruitt and Sophia Crawford at the end of Season Four, another key member of the *Buffy* team, Chris Beck, left to pursue a career in film scoring – his replacement was *Thirteenth Floor* orchestrator Thomas Wanker. Jeff Pruitt reassured fans that *his* replacement was a top choice: 'They've hired one of my good friends to be stunt co-ordinator,' Jeff told the *Posting Board*. 'His name is John Medlen and he's great.' Sophia Crawford's replacement as Buffy's stunt double was Melissa Barker who also doubled for Sarah on *Scooby-Doo*. Post Production Supervisor Brian Wankum played Roger in *True Crime*.

Valley-Speak: Xander: 'He *totally* looked shorter in person.' And: 'No big *whoop*!' Plus: 'I will serve you, your excellent spookiness.' And, to Buffy: 'There's this whole deal where I get to be immortal. You cool with that?'

Buffy: 'Am I *Repeato-Girl*?' And: 'It's a *total* drag.'

Sex and Drugs and Rock'n'Roll: Although Xander tells Willow that everyone knows about her relationship with Tara, Joyce doesn't seem to have realised yet (the appearance of Dawn appears to change this, see **80**, 'Real Me').

Logic, Let Me Introduce You to This Window: After Buffy and Joyce have eaten dinner, Joyce has a plate in front of her which disappears and is replaced by a bowl. And how come *everybody* (not just Riley) failed to notice the 'big honking castle' in the middle of Sunnydale?

I Just *Love* Your Accent: 'I patterned Spike's accent after a guy I was in a play with three years ago. Now I'm listening to Tony Head who sounds kind of like Spike in real life,' James Marsters told an online interview. 'His accent is just as fake as mine.'

Cruelty to Animals: Xander eats a spider and a fly.

Quote/Unquote: Buffy: 'Do you *know* what a Slayer is?' Dracula: 'Do *you*?'

Xander: 'Like any of that's enough to fight the dark master ... bator.' And: 'Where's the creep that turned me into a spider-eating man-bitch? I'm sick of this crap. I'm sick of being the guy who eats insects and gets the funny-syphilis.'

Notes: 'You're sure this isn't just some fanboy thing? 'Cos I've fought more than a couple of pimply, overweight vamps that called themselves Lestat!' Another sedate season opener in which the actors ease themselves back into their characters. But, with hindsight, there's a lot of setting up of the season's themes and some pointers towards its *denouement*.

Dracula, seeing the scar on Buffy's neck, concludes that she had been tasted (see **56**, 'Graduation Day' Part 2). Dracula tells Buffy, 'You think you know what you are, what's to come. You haven't even begun,' similar to Tara's line in **78**, 'Restless'. Giles owns an Apple Mac laptop and a scanner that he is using to create a database of his library. He has spent the summer labelling amulets and indexing his diaries. Anya met Dracula during her demon days – since she was a 'silly young thing' of 700, this would have been around the mid-sixteenth century. Spike sees Dracula as a rival (he still owes Spike £11, apparently). Dracula is different from other vampires – he can metamorphose into a bat or a wolf, control minds, appear in dreams and dissolve into mist – 'Swell party tricks' according to Riley; 'Showy gypsy stuff' adds an unimpressed Spike. He can, however, be killed just like other vampires. Or not. Jury's still out on that ('Think I don't watch your movies?' says Buffy. 'You *always* come back'). And this episode sees the debut of Buffy's feisty younger sister, Dawn.

Hang on . . . Buffy hasn't *got* a sister. Has she?

Soundtrack: Vertical Horizon's 'Finding Me'.

Did You Know?: The role of Dracula was originally intended for Sarah Michelle Gellar's boyfriend, Freddie Prinze Jr, until his movie schedule clashed with production.

Criminal Connections: Eliza Dushku fears her role as Faith may be a little too convincing as the nineteen-year-old has become an icon for some of America's worst criminals. 'I get mail from maximum security penitentiaries and Death Row,' she told *Entertainment Weekly*. 'What are the authorities thinking, playing a show with teenage girls to Death Row inmates? They send me photos: "Here's a picture of me before I was incarcerated!" It's way more creepy than *Buffy*.' When *Mean* magazine asked if it was true that Eliza was a spoiled child-star, she replied: 'I still am. The only time I [pull a star-fit] is with my brothers or my friends, and they know it's all bullshit. But I was the biggest brat on the planet. When you're ten and have people waiting on you hand and foot and then all of a sudden you go back to the real world, it's a little smack in the face.' She also discussed her Mormon upbringing and her feminist mother whom Eliza considers, 'a tough-ass. She's really liberal. She raised four kids by herself and kept a job as a professor and she's really into, like, sisterhood and bonding. She's amazing.'

Tributes: Other TV series seem keen to name check *Buffy* these days. *Xena*, for instance, mentioned their own Slayer, Buffus. *Friends* had Phoebe's porn-actress sister appearing in *Bouffet the Vampire Layer*, whilst both *Malcolm in the Middle* and *Popular* have featured characters watching *Buffy* on TV. In the WB comedy series *Grosse Point*, Sarah Michelle Gellar

appears to indulge in an on-screen lesbian kiss and win herself
an Emmy nomination – something she says she'd never
achieve on *Buffy*! How true.

David Fury Comments: David Fury, speaking at the Writer's
Guild of America West party and quoted in *The Richmond
Times Dispatch*, revealed: 'For all intents and purposes there is
a Dawn Summers [who has] always shared a house and parents
with Buffy. This creates a bizarre mystery that is not always
the focus of the episodes but will leave the audience wondering, who *is* she? We don't really learn anything until episode
five but Dawn will be a major part of what happens on
Buffy . . . She is pivotal to what the ultimate Big-Bad of the
season will be.'

80
Real Me

US Transmission Date: 3 Oct. 2000
UK Transmission Date: 12 Jan. 2001 (Sky)

Writer: David Fury
Director: David Grossman
Cast: Brian Turk (Mort), Chaney Kley Minnis (Brad),
Faith S Abrahams (Peaches), Tom Lenk (Cyrus)
French title: *Jalousie*

Buffy is forced to take Dawn with her when she and Giles visit
the Magic Box. They find the owner dead and the evidence
points to a vampire gang. When they learn its leader is
Harmony, though, nobody takes them very seriously. Until
Dawn is kidnapped.

Dudes and Babes: Harmony's bonehead gang of incompetent
vampires is hilarious, particularly when they vote to kill her
(except Brad, who abstains).

A Little Learning is a Dangerous Thing: Buffy has to drop
drama, which she was planning to take with Willow, due to
training pressures.

Work is a Four-Letter Word: Xander, Dawn believes, is
much cuter than anyone. And smarter too. 'He totally skipped

college and got a job working construction. And he's brave. Just last week he went undercover to stop that Dracula guy.'

It's a Designer Label!: Buffy's tie-around grey top. Harmony's shiny gold pants. Dawn's minxy blue dress.

References: The title is a song by the Who. Also, JK Rowling's Harry Potter novels ('I'm not going to Hogwarts'), *The Longest Day* ('It's not the Invasion of Normandy'), 'Little Miss Muffet' ('I know what you are. Curds and whey', see **56**, 'Graduation Day' Part 2; **71**, 'This Year's Girl'), the board games *Monopoly*™, *Clue*™ and *Game of Life*™, Ruffles potato chips, George Clooney, the *For Dummies* computer books, *This is Spinal Tap* (and the band's numerous drummers who die in bizarre gardening accidents and from spontaneous human combustion), *Superman* ('the Fortress of Solitude'), 'Time's Up' by the Buzzcocks, *The Banana Splits* and *Rowan and Martin's Laugh-In* ('Here come the judge'). Giles admits that when Spike lived with him, they watched *Passions* together (see **65**, 'Something Blue'; **90**, 'Checkpoint'). The technique of having a character speak the punctuation of their dialogue ('Underline. Exclamation point') was used to devastating effect in Dennis Potter's *The Singing Detective*. Among the items seen in Dawn's bedroom are a lava lamp, a Betty Boop doll, various fluffy toys and an R.E.M. poster. Outside the Magic Box, posters for a tour by the band Leftover and a performance at the Bronze by Todd Snider can be seen. A print by Dutch surrealist Maurits Cornelis Escher (1898–1972) is visible on Buffy's bedroom wall.

Bitch!: Harmony, to Xander: 'You're the hair-puller, you big girl.'

Buffy says she wouldn't even have had Harmony over to her house when she was alive.

Awesome!: Breakfast at the Summers' house. Xander and Harmony's bitching session. Harmony: 'So, Slayer, at last we meet.' Buffy: 'We've met, Harmony, you halfwit!'

'You May Remember Me From Such Films As . . .': Bob Morrisey was in *The Book of Stars* and *Total Reality*. Tom Lenk appeared in *Boogie Nights*. Brian Turk's movies include *Going Greek*, *A Civil Action* and *The Lost World: Jurassic Park*.

Valley-Speak: Dawn: '*I* could so save the world if somebody handed me superpowers.' And: 'Did not!'

Buffy, to Harmony: 'When you try to be bad, you *suck*.'

Xander: 'The whole enchilada.'

Sex and Drugs and Rock'n'Roll: As Dawn notes: 'Riley, my sister's boyfriend, is *so* into her. They're always kissing and groping. I bet they have sex.' Riley, himself, is more delicate, flattering Joyce before telling Buffy that 'I'm here to violate your firstborn' never goes over well with parents.

Logic, Let Me Introduce You to This Window: At the Magic Box, Dawn's hair length changes between shots. There's a book called *A Treatise on the Mythology and Methodology of the Vampire Slayer*, which directly contradicts Giles's statement in **5**, 'Never Kill a Boy on the First Date' (see also **22**, 'What's My Line' Part 2). When did Harmony try to be head cheerleader? Or chair the homecoming committee? (See **3**, 'The Witch'; **39**, 'Homecoming'.)

I Just *Love* Your Accent: Dawn has heard Giles use the word 'newfangled'. Willow tells Tara that Giles is British so he 'doesn't understand about stuff'. Spike says 'bollocks' (see **85**, 'Fool for Love').

Motors: Giles has a new 'red and sporty' BMW 328 iC. He doesn't like that it has automatic transmission.

Quote/Unquote: Dawn, on Willow and Tara: 'They do spells and stuff, which is so much cooler than slaying. I told Mom one time I wished they'd teach me some of the things they do together. Then she got really quiet and made me go upstairs.'

Spike, on killing his own kind: 'Bloke's gotta have a hobby, don't he?'

Notes: 'Most magic shop owners in Sunnydale have the life expectancy of a Spinal Tap drummer.' An excellent episode, instantly allaying fears that young Michelle Trachtenburg wouldn't be up to the task of making Dawn work. She's on *brilliant* form here, as are all of the cast (particularly James Marsters who does so much with his few scenes).

Dawn, like her sister, has a diary. She is fourteen and has a crush on Xander (see **92**, 'Crush'). Willow is Dawn's chess partner. Dawn eats Sunshine Chips for breakfast and likes chocolate ice cream. Mr Bogerty is the most recent former-owner of the Magic Box. One previous owner also died on-screen (see **42**, 'Lover's Walk'). Giles says that he had no idea that the profit margins on the shop were so high – 'It's no wonder there's never any trouble attracting new owners.' The latest of which is himself. Brad Konig once stood Harmony up in tenth grade. She repaid this by sireing him. Brad also beat up kids (possibly including Xander) in gym class. Spike has a new TV in his crypt (still no word on where his electricity supply comes from, see **70**, 'Goodbye Iowa'). He intends to steal a satellite dish to go with it.

Soundtrack: Grieg's 'Prelude from Holberg Suite' plays on the radio in Giles's car.

Did You Know?: Asked by *E! Online* about her relationship with former *Buffy* co-star Alexis Denisof, Alyson Hannigan noted: 'I had a crush on him the moment he showed up onset. He was the good one who said "Not while we're working together." We became friends, and I was dating somebody else [Marilyn Manson drummer Ginger Fish]. When that didn't work out, he was on *Angel* and we started dating.'

Alyson Hannigan's Comments: The Willow/Tara relationship was discussed during the same interview: 'At first it was a little awkward,' noted Alyson. 'Suddenly there would be more crew members watching [than normal]. But I never had a problem with it, because it was handled with such grace. I would trust Joss with my life. I'd never doubt his ability to tell a story and make it romantic.'

Fame, Fame, Fatal Fame: 'I love being in a cult hit,' Sarah Michelle Gellar told Australian magazine *Dolly*. 'You feel less pressure and you don't get typecast, because you've not become "Rachel from *Friends*".' Bet Jennifer Aniston *loved* that.

81
The Replacement

US Transmission Date: 10 Oct. 2000
UK Transmission Date: 19 Jan. 2001 (Sky)

Writer: Jane Espenson
Director: James A Contner

Cast: Michael Bailey Smith (Toth), Cathy Cohen (Building Manager),
David Reivers (Foreman), Fritz Greve (Construction Worker)
French title: *Le Double*

A demon attacks Buffy but accidentally zaps Xander instead,
splitting him into two (one with his strongest qualities, the
other with his weakest). Meanwhile, Anya is confronted with
her own mortality and Riley realises that Buffy doesn't return
his love for her.

Dudes and Babes: A major episode for Xander with his
sudden realisation (in both Cool and Uncool bodies) that he
must grow up, get out of the basement and assure Anya that he
is serious about their relationship. Which he does despite, as
Giles says, clearly being a bad influence on himself.

A Little Learning is a Dangerous Thing: Buffy is reading a
book on the Crusades; the eight Christian military expeditions
(1099–1291) to recapture the Holy Land from the Muslims.
Xander knows what the word 'olfactory' means.

Work is a Four-Letter Word: Xander has been working for a
construction firm for three months and, despite Uncool-
Xander's reservations, he seems quite good at it. The foreman
asks him to head the Carpentry crew on a new job in Carlton.

It's a Designer Label!: Willow's red jumper. Riley's bur-
gundy leather jacket. Buffy's spangly multicoloured top.

References: Allusions to *Star Trek*, Xander noting: 'There
comes a point when you either have to move on or buy yourself a Klingon costume,' plus the episode, 'The Enemy Within'
in which Captain Kirk is split in two ('kill us both Spock').
Also Spaghetti Os, *A Charlie Brown Christmas* (see **29**,
'Passion'. Here Xander *does* the Snoopy dance), BMW's
slogan 'The Ultimate Driving Machine', Samuel Coleridge's
The Ancient Mariner ('shiny things'), US Presidents George
Washington (1732–97) and Thomas Jefferson (1743–1809).
Xander owns a collection of *Babylon 5* commemorative plates
and mentions his kick-ass comic collection. Yet another
Widespread Panic sticker can be seen on the phone booth.
Giles hits Toth with a fertility statue of Oofdar, the Goddess of
childbirth.

Bitch!: Buffy, on Dawn: 'She's watching us like a big freak.'

Awesome!: Anya on why Xander's hot-plate is on the blink:

'We think the cat peed on it.' Toth's fight with Buffy. Every scene featuring the two Xanders.

'You May Remember Me From Such Films and TV Series As . . .': Michael Bailey Smith played Belthazor in *Charmed* and was in *Purpo$e*. Fritz Greve appeared in *To Protect and Serve*. David Reivers can be seen in *Malcolm X*.

Don't Give Up The Day Job: Kelly Donovan is Nick Brendon's identical twin. He's a set decorator on *Buffy* and played Jacob in *Undressed*. Special effects co-ordinator Bruce Minkus previously worked on *The Terminator 2: Judgment Day; Schindler's List* and *Jurassic Park*.

Valley-Speak: Anya: 'Things are looking pretty untogether.'

Cigarettes and Alcohol: Cool-Xander and Anya share champagne at his new apartment.

Sex and Drugs and Rock'n'Roll: Dawn's friend Sharon's older brother knew a girl who choked on her boyfriend's tongue. Allegedly. Anya asks the others to delay reintegrating the Xanders so that she can take them home and 'we can all have sex together.' One Xander is *appalled* at the prospect: '[It's] *wrong*. And it would be *very* confusing.'

'We should continue to pretend we heard none of the disturbing sex talk,' says Giles, wisely.

Logic, Let Me Introduce You to This Window: In the scene with the mannequin, Spike has a noticeable tan-line on his arms. Where can one get an answer machine like Anya's? – when you hit play it knows exactly which bit of the message you want. *Babylon 5* plates were planned but never released. In **80**, 'Real Me', Riley implied Anya had sustained a serious head-wound when attacked by Mort: however her only injury is a dislocated shoulder.

I Just *Love* Your Accent: Giles: 'Toth.' Buffy, to Riley: 'He called you a toth. It's a British expression. It means, like, "moron".' Xander can do a reasonable upper-class British accent when pretending to be Albert, his reference for the apartment (see **90**, 'Checkpoint').

Quote/Unquote: Spike, when asked what he's doing at the garbage dump: 'There's a nice lady vampire who set up a charming tea-room over the next pile of crap.'

Riley, on the Xanders: 'Psychologically, this is fascinating.

Doesn't it make everyone wanna lock them in separate rooms and do experiments on them? Just me then?'

Notes: 'A demon has taken my life from me, and he's living it better than I do.' A very good episode with a different take on the evil duplicate cliché to **50**, 'Doppelgängland', though a no less valid one ('Wait till *you* have an evil twin,' Xander tells Willow. 'See how you handle it.' 'I handled it *fine*,' Willow pouts). Plus, in one throwaway-line about Joyce Summers having a headache, an entire season-long story arc is set up.

On Xander's seventh birthday he wanted a toy firetruck but didn't get one. Then the house next door burned down and real firetrucks came. For years afterwards Xander thought Willow had committed arson especially for him ('And if you did, you can tell me'). Last year Xander believed he was lactose-intolerant, but it was just some bad Brie. When Xander is leaving his parents' basement he points out to Riley where Spike slept (a reference to **66**, 'Hush'), where 'Anya and I drowned the Sepavro demon' (**65**, 'Something Blue') and where he had his heart ripped out (**78**, 'Restless', though technically that was only a dream). Buffy has what Riley terms a 'bad ice-skating movie obsession' (see **21**, 'What's My Line?' Part 1). Anya has a list of what she wants from life. It includes a car, a puppy, a child and (possibly) a boat. She owns a hand gun. Xander's parents are heard arguing upstairs. He notes that Buffy has been to Hell (probably a reference to **35**, 'Anne'). Spike uses a mannequin in a blonde wig to simulate Buffy when he needs to release some pent-up aggression. As the season progresses, this will take on more sinister overtones (see **92**, 'Crush'; **96**, 'Intervention').

Did You Know?: Nick Brendon plays both Xanders. Kelly was used as a double, but did have some dialogue when the two were in the same shot (he mostly played Cool-Xander).

Joss Whedon's Comments: Interviewed by *TV Guide*, Joss explained the thought behind the creation of returning characters: 'It's not something that we take lightly. It's a question of how they fit into the group dynamic.' Whedon revealed that he felt the character of Anya could fill the smart-alecky void left by Charisma Carpenter. Regarding Anya, Joss noted: 'She speaks her mind rather bluntly and feels a bit on the outs with

people, so [it] makes perfect sense. Emma's extremely funny.
You don't usually get that much funny in a girl that pretty.'

82

Out of My Mind

US Transmission Date: 17 Oct. 2001
UK Transmission Date: 26 Jan. 2001 (Sky)

Writer: Rebecca Rand Kirshner
Director: David Grossman
Cast: Time Winters (Initiative Doctor), Dierdre Holder (Hospital Doctor)
French title: *Quand Spike s'en Mêle*

Joyce has a fainting spell. At the hospital Dawn discovers
Riley's heartbeat is irregular. When Buffy enlists the Initiative's help, Riley fights Graham rather than allow the government near his body again. Buffy manages to get Riley to an
Initiative doctor, but finds Spike is forcing the doctor to
remove his chip.

Dreaming (As Blondie Once Said) is Free: We don't see
Buffy's Hollywood-style *montage* of her college life (in which
she wears glasses) but, thankfully, Spike's obsession provides
one of the episode's few moments of class: Buffy bursts into
his crypt, he asks her to end his 'torment' and then they kiss;
'Oh God, no!' cries Spike, waking up.

Dudes and Babes: The debut of hunky young intern, Ben. At
this stage, no hint that he's anything more than that.

A Little Learning is a Dangerous Thing: Buffy and Willow
discuss aspects of the French Revolution including Jean-Paul
Marat (1743–93, author of *The Chains of Slavery*), Charlotte
Corday (a Girondin supporter who murdered Marat in his bath)
and Maximilien-François Robespierre (1758–94, the Jacobin
leader and instigator of The Reign of Terror). Buffy, however,
fails to spot Willow's witty allusion to the occipital lobe.

The Conspiracy Starts at Home Time: The Initiative are
monitoring Riley's phonecalls.

Work is a Four-Letter Word: Xander's carpentry skills are
being put to good use in the Magic Box.

It's a Designer Label!: Buffy's blue top and red leather pants appear again. Anya's fawn skirt.

References: Buffy says Xander, Giles and Riley are all her fairy godmother, Santa Claus and Q wrapped into one ('Q from Bond, not *Star Trek*'). Spike seems to be watching *Dawson's Creek* on TV ('Pacey, you blind idiot. Can't you see she doesn't love you?'). Also, *1984* (an allusion to Big Brother), the CIA's abortive attempts to assassinate Cuban dictator Fidel Castro, the Confucius proverb 'Better to light a candle than to curse the damn darkness' and Tinkerbell from *Peter Pan*. There's a Widespread Panic post on the college wall. Spike plays 'Twenty Questions' with Harmony. In the *South Park* movie, Cartman, like Spike, had a chip inserted in his brain. Only, in Eric's case, it stopped him swearing.

Awesome!: Spike's sinister threat to Buffy just before he falls into an open grave. The brilliant dream-sequence at the end.

'You May Remember Me From Such Films and TV Series As . . .': Time Winters appeared in *Gremlins 2: The New Batch*, *L.A. Story*, *Sneakers* and *True Vinyl*. Charlie Weber was Dillon Johnson in *Director's Cut*. Dierdre Holder was in *Jesus 2000* and *Code Blue*.

Don't Give Up The Day Job: Rebecca Rand Kirshner was a writer on *Freaks and Geeks*. One of the hospital paramedics is played by Dan Smiczek, an extra on many TV series. Dan's humorous and fascinating website, *The Adventures of Dan: Extra Extraordinaire*, at www.adventuresofdan.com/ details his experiences working on shows like *Roswell*, *The West Wing* and *The X-Files*. 'I'm about three feet from the [hospital] door when Sarah and Marc bust [in],' notes Dan. 'I open the door and immediately press myself up against it to let them through. Marc was hilarious. He did this thing where he puts his hand on my shoulder like "Thanks man for getting out of the way". The take was okay but they wanted to change some things around. In the meantime this guy came around with cookies for the crew and Sarah stocked up. The crew were asking him "Did you find Sarah to give her some?" I'm guessing she's a little bit of a cookie-monster.'

The Drugs Don't Work: Whatever the Initiative stopped

giving Riley last season, the results have been disastrous (his pulse is 150 per minute).

Valley-Speak: Harmony: 'I'm *totally* her arch-nemesis.'

Cigarettes and Alcohol: Harmony has taken up smoking (justifying this because she is evil).

Logic, Let Me Introduce You to This Window: After Riley's basketball game, the front of his shirt is drenched in sweat, but his back is completely dry. When he hits Graham, however, the back is wet too. Alyson Hannigan mispronounces the Latin word 'lux'. One of the shots of Buffy in the opening fight scene is clearly her stunt double.

I Just *Love* Your Accent: Spike calls Harmony a silly bint (see **59**, 'The Harsh Light of Day').

Cruelty to Animals: Giles won't sell newt-eyes in the Magic Box. Instead he stocks salamander eyes, the cataracts on which give them a newt-like appearance.

Quote/Unquote: Harmony: 'I'll do anything.' Spike: 'Anything, will you?' Harmony: 'I *said* I'll do anything. Oh, you mean will I have sex with you? Well, yeah.'

Notes: 'You're going to die over some macho-pissing contest?' After such a great start to the season, this episode is a real disappointment, and something of a rehash of **70**, 'Goodbye Iowa'. It's difficult to work up much sympathy for Riley who acts like a jerk throughout, nor for Buffy whose sadistic treatment of Spike threatens to come back and haunt her. Best bit: the doctor telling Harmony not to smoke whilst he's operating. And her reaction.

Buffy says she has the endurance of ten men. Dawn likes her omelettes with ketchup (urgh) and chicken fingers with mustard when she's ill. She prefers the free gifts you get in Sugar Bombs cereal to the actual cereal itself.

Soundtrack: Nickelback's 'Breathe'.

Did You Know?: 'I've pitched a couple of story ideas,' Tony Head told *DreamWatch*, 'and Joss, ever-so-sweetly, smiled and said "No". But he did tell me why on both occasions.'

Marti Noxon's Comments: Nervous WB execs gave the *Buffy* production team 'strong directions' on the Willow/Tara relationship. As Marti Noxon told *TV Guide Online*: 'They draw the line at any physical intimacy, so we have to be crafty in the way that we show it. One of the points that we try to make is that while the relationship is sexual, we don't want to play it for titillation. A lot of shows have done, "Come and watch the kiss" and then it never amounts to anything,' Noxon points out (referring specifically to *Ally McBeal*). 'In some ways the concerns that the network has about them being intimate doesn't feel like it's hindering us.'

83
No Place Like Home

US Transmission Date: 24 Oct. 2000
UK Transmission Date: 2 Feb. 2001 (Sky)

Writer: Douglas Petrie
Director: David Solomon
Cast: Ravil Isyanov (Monk), James Wellington (Night Watchman),
Staci Lawrence (Customer), John Sarkisian (Old Monk)
French title: *Soeurs Ennemies*

Buffy investigates a possible supernatural cause behind her mother's illness. Her search leads her to a woman called Glory who battles, and easily beats, the Slayer. Buffy discovers that she doesn't really have a sister – Dawn is The Key, sent to Buffy for protection. The gang help Giles open the Magic Box.
Dudes and Babes: An introduction to Glory, a disturbingly alluring young woman. She is incredibly strong, apparently needs (for reasons that will become apparent later) to suck the sanity from humans in order to maintain her own, and desperately wants The Key.
A Little Learning is a Dangerous Thing: Dawn is writing a report on rain forests.
The Conspiracy (Monastic Chant Mix): The Monk tells Buffy that many will die if she doesn't protect The Key. 'The Key is energy,' he says. 'It's a portal. It opens the door . . .' For centuries it had no form, and was kept by the Monk's brethren. Then Glory ('the abomination') found them. They performed a spell that made The Key flesh and sent it to Buffy,

as a sister, knowing that only the Slayer has the power to protect it. Buffy is horrified: 'You put *that* in my house?' Her memories and everyone else's were rebuilt, confesses the Monk. 'I don't even know, what is she?' says Buffy. 'Human,' notes the Monk. 'Helpless. She is an innocent.' Buffy still insists that Dawn is not her sister. '*She doesn't know that,*' replies the Monk, dying.

Work is a Four-Letter Word: Anya reveals a natural talent for shopwork and becomes Giles's assistant at the Magic Box.

It's a Designer Label!: Giles in a silly costume *always* gets a laugh (see **60**, 'Fear Itself'). Here, he wears a purple robe and pointed warlock's cap. And looks *ridiculous*. Also, Buffy's fur coat and tight mustard pants. Anya's leopardskin top. Willow's flowery blue jumper and Glory's awesome red dress.

References: The title is Dorothy's wish in *The Wizard of Oz*. Also, *The Oprah Winfrey Show*, *Iron Chef* (a Japanese cookery show), *The Uncanny X-Men* ('the danger room') and *The Amazing Spider-Man* ('Radioactive spider bite?'). Glory makes another oblique reference to 'Little Miss Muffet' with 'Someone's gonna sit down on their tuffet and make this birthing stop' (see **56**, 'Graduation Day' Part 2; **71**, 'This Year's Girl'; **80**, 'Real Me'). The concept of Dawn has similarities to a series of stories in *Doctor Who* known as 'The Key to Time' in which the Black and White Guardians split The Key into six pieces which the Doctor must reassemble to restore the balance of the universe (the final segment is a person). A sign in the Magic Box says: SHOPLIFTERS WILL BE TRANSFIGURED.

Bitch!: Anya: 'I've never had to afford things before and it's making me bitter.' Giles (sarcastically): 'The change is palpable.'

Glory: 'I don't even want to be here. And I'm not talking about this room or this city or this state or this planet. I'm talking about the whole mortal coil. It's disgusting. The food, the clothes, the people. I could crap a better existence than this.'

When Buffy asks Spike for an explanation of what he's doing outside her house in five words or fewer, he replies: 'Out. For. A. Walk. Bitch.'

Awesome!: Xander teaching Anya the joys of raging insincerity in retail. The stunningly directed trance scene, with its sinister music and lighting as Buffy wanders around the house and, in one of the series' great moments, sees a photo of herself, Joyce and Dawn, with Dawn fading in-and-out. Buffy's epic battle with Glory.

'You May Remember Me From Such Films and TV Series As . . .': Clare Kramer was Courtney Egbert in *Bring It On* and Heather in *Vig*. Ravil Isyanov was in *Octopus*, *The Saint* and *Hackers*. James Wellington appeared in *Roundabout*. John Sarkisian's movies include *Six-String Samurai*. Paul Hayes can be seen in *The Progeny*, *Chaplin* and *The X-Files*.

The Drugs Don't Work: The doctor's advice to Joyce concerning her fainting is to 'take four of some pills a day'. Ben gives the nightwatchman 9 cc's of Phenobarbitone to calm him. 'Have a nice trip,' Riley tells Buffy as she prepares for her trance.

Valley-Speak: Joyce: 'I can't be retro?'

Buffy: 'Whoever planted this doohickey's got answers.'

Willow, on Dawn: 'She's, you know, a big spaz.'

Dawn: 'Butthole.'

Cigarettes and Alcohol: A multitude of Spike's cigarette butts indicate that his obsession with Buffy has become stalking.

Logic, Let me Introduce You to This Window: General one: If The Key has only recently become human, how come blood is the key to the ritual? Glory specifically says, in **91**, 'Blood Ties', that The Key could be anything from a bicycle pump to a log, yet when the details of the ritual are revealed later in the season, it's obvious that The Key must be human since blood is the key to The Key. Bicycle pumps don't, generally, bleed.

I Just *Love* Your Accent: When Giles starts to panic about the number of shoppers, Xander's advice is: 'Stay British.'

Quote/Unquote: Joyce, after Buffy and Dawn have made her breakfast: 'So neither of you is pregnant, failing or under indictment? Just checking.'

Giles, on the Dagon-sphere: 'It appears to be paranormal in origin.' Buffy: 'How can you tell?' Giles: 'It's so shiny.'

Willow, after Giles's first sale: 'Congratulations. You're an official capitalist running dog.'

Spike, to Buffy: 'I'm just passing through. Satisfied? I really hope so, because God knows you need some satisfaction in life besides shagging Captain Cardboard. And I never really liked you anyway. And you have stupid hair.'

Glory, beating Buffy: 'You know that thing with worms where if you have one, you rip it in half, you get two worms? Do you think that'll work with you?'

Notes: 'You're not my sister . . . What *are* you?' The Dawn revelation episode, and it's a *beaut* on all levels. The Giles Opens A Shop subplot is really funny (especially Anya) but the real meat here is the introduction of Glory and the discovery that Dawn isn't a demon, which everyone had expected. Terrific.

This episode takes place two months after the final scene of **79**, 'Buffy vs Dracula', and Dawn's arrival. Buffy always wanted piano lessons. Joyce's nickname for Dawn was 'little punkin' belly'. Anya believes that the conjuring powder Giles sells is grossly overpriced and offers to hook him up with the Troll that sheds it (see **89**, 'Triangle'). Anya knew a legendary sixteenth-century French sorcerer, Cloutier, who perfected a spell to reveal demons, *tirer la couture* ('Pull the curtain back'). The magi enters a trance and is able to see a signature manifestation of the affliction. The Dagon-sphere has a history going back many centuries. It's a protective device, used to ward off primordial evil (specifically something referred to in the ancient texts as 'That Which Cannot be Named').

Did You Know?: In late 2000, an American pressure group, 'The Parents Television Council', posted an Internet guide to *Buffy*, noting that the series 'has earned red-lights for its sexual content, use of foul language and violence. Last season, sex was either shown or implied between Buffy and Parker, Buffy and Riley, Xander and Anya, Spike and Harmony and Oz and Veruca. In addition, homosexual undercurrents manifested between Willow and a fellow Wicca practitioner. Sexual content was at times graphic. In one episode a boy at a fraternity party became sexually aroused simply by touching a wall and grabbed his crotch. Other episodes have contained implied nudity, homosexual fantasies, masturbation, anatomical references, and references to orgasms and kinky sexual practices.' Don't know about other readers, but if I hadn't seen the series before hearing this I'd be tuning straight in afterwards.

Did You Spot: When Buffy is in her trance and enters Dawn's room, reality is fractured and she sees flashes of the room as it should be – dark and full of boxes. The room is the same one that Buffy walked into at the end of **78**, 'Restless', to be told by Tara, 'You think you know what's to come.' A piece of foreshadowing that impressed the hell out of this author.

Head On: In an interview with *E! Online*, long before the suggestion of a Giles spin-off was raised, Tony Head was asked about the possibility of *Buffy* taking a trip to London. 'In Season Three Joss wanted to shoot in Ireland,' noted the actor. 'The studio wouldn't let him. He was going to do three or four shows there, going back to find Angel's roots, which would have been nice.' On the subject of Tony's forthcoming CD, he says: 'A record company said they were interested in doing an album. My first reaction was "Actor in his 40s releases album. Put it on the shelf between William Shatner and David Hasselhoff." But I figured it was safe enough if I made it working with people I respect and love. So, Joss has contributed a song, James is on the album and so are Amber and Alyson.'

84
Family

US Transmission Date: 7 Nov. 2000
UK Transmission Date: 9 Feb. 2001 (Sky)

Writer: Joss Whedon
Director: Joss Whedon
Cast: Amy Adams (Cousin Beth), Steve Rankin (Mr Maclay),
Kevin O Rankin (Donny), Ezra Buzzington (Bartender),
Torry Pendergrass (Demon), Brian Tee (Intern), Peggy Goss (Crazy Person)
French title: *Les Liens du Sang*

Members of Tara's family arrive on her twentieth birthday. They announce that they want to take her home before she turns into a demon like her mother at the same age. When Glory sends demons to kill the Slayer, Tara inadvertently helps them whilst attempting to prevent her friends from seeing what she believes lies within her.

Dudes and Babes: Cousin Beth is outraged that Tara has

chosen education over her family: 'There's a house that needs taking care of. Donny and your dad having to do for themselves while you're down here living God-knows-what kind of lifestyle.' During the conflict at the Magic Box, Donny adds: 'Tara, if you don't get in that car, I swear by God I will beat you down.' Xander replies: 'And *I* swear by your full-and-manly-beard, you're gonna break something trying.'

Denial, Thy Name is the Maclay Family: 'I hoped maybe you'd gotten over the whole witchcraft thing,' Mr Maclay tells Tara. 'Your birthday's getting closer. You know what that means . . . It's the same age your mother was.' 'You've been lying to these people for a year,' adds Cousin Beth. 'You've put a spell on them. Is that a human thing to do?' Maclay says that the women of their family have demon in them. It's implied that Tara's mother stopped practising witchcraft at the age of twenty (see **Logic, Let Me Introduce You To This Window**). Interested in specifics, Anya asks 'What kind of demon is she? There's a lot of different kinds,' noting that whilst some are *very* evil, others have been considered useful members of society. Spike makes things simple by punching Tara in the nose and then collapsing in pain, proving that there is no demon in her. 'Just a family legend?' he asks Maclay. 'A bit of spin to keep the ladies in line?'

A Vastly Important Moment, Which No One Realised At The Time: Ben enters the hospital locker room, opens his locker and begins taking his clothes off. The camera pans back. A Lei-Ach demon comes into view, followed from behind, a few seconds later, by Glory. Ben and Glory are never in the same shot. Remember this for future reference.

It's a Designer Label!: Concerning Tara's present, Buffy has seen a cute sweater 'at Bloomy's. But, I think I want me to have it.' Willow's purple dress. Glory's leather skirt and everyone's excellent party clothes in the Bronze.

References: *Miss Congeniality*, French farce, an allusion to Sir Walter Scott's *Marmion* ('that was a tangled web of lies, sweetie') and Bob Marley and the Wailers' 'Rat Race'. There's a WP sticker on the University notice board.

Bitch!: Buffy describes Glory as 'like Cordelia', and is pretty sure Glory dyes her hair. Beth calls Tara a selfish bitch.

Willow: 'I don't need to be snuggled.' Tara: 'Vixen.'

Xander and Riley wrestle over whether Riley called Xander a bad name or 'something Latin'. When Tara cracks an obscure joke and then says 'That was funny if you studied Taglarin mythic rites. And are a complete dork,' Riley replies: 'How come Xander didn't laugh?'

Awesome!: Dawn saying that she is going to her friend Melinda's house across the street. Buffy, fearing that Glory might attack her, uses the excuse that Melinda is a bad influence. 'I don't like you hanging out with someone that ... short.' Afterwards, Riley notes: 'A lot of young people nowadays are experimenting with shortness. Gotta nip that in the bud.' Spike's way of proving that Tara isn't a demon. The beautiful ending with Willow and Tara literally dancing on air.

'You May Remember Me From Such Films and TV Series As . . .': Amy Adams took over Sarah Michelle Gellar's role, as Kathryn Merteuil, in *Cruel Intentions 2*. She's also in *Psycho Beach Party*, *Drop Dead Gorgeous* and *Pumpkin*. Steve Rankin was in *Mercury Rising*, *Men in Black*, *L.A. Confidential*, *Apollo 13* and *The West Wing*. Ezra Buzzington's movies include *Fight Club*, *Magnolia* and *Me, Myself & Irene*. Kevin O Rankin was in *After Diff'rent Strokes: When the Laughter Stopped*.

Valley-Speak: Buffy: 'Nothing like getting your ass kicked to make your ass hurt.' Dawn: 'You'll *totally* take her next time.'

Willow: 'There's Scoobyage afoot. Giles called a meeting about our spankin' new menace.'

Cigarettes and Alcohol: Riley has become a regular at Willy's Bar where he drinks whisky and buys Sandy (see **50**, 'Doppelgängland') vodka tonic, but tells her: 'My heart belongs to another. Besides, I don't go out with vampires. Never interested in my intellect.' Dawn is allowed to attend Tara's party at the Bronze and is provided with a stamp on her hand to prevent her from purchasing any booze. 'Only losers drink alcohol,' she says, as Riley, Xander, Giles and Buffy give each other worried looks.

Sex and Drugs and Rock'n'Roll: This is the first time we see Willow and Tara in bed together. Spike's daydream of him fighting the Slayer in the most erotic way imaginable occurs whilst he's in bed with Harmony and about to climax (just as Buffy says 'I'm coming right now'). Harmony: 'What are you thinking?' Spike: 'All about you, baby.'

Logic, Let Me Introduce You to This Window: In the last scene, Tara rests her head on Willow's shoulder. The camera cuts to a different angle and Tara has a large chunk of hair over her face. The angle switches back and it's gone. Much of this episode's revelations about Tara's mother don't really fit in with what Tara implies in **66**, 'Hush'.

Motors: The Maclays have a camper van.

Pussy Galore: The return of Miss Kitty-Fantastico. Tara and Willow devise a rather 'upsetting story' about a lost cat.

Quote/Unquote: Giles: 'You're in a magic shop and you can't think what Tara would like. I believe you're both profoundly stupid.' Xander: 'What, are we gonna get her some cheesy crystal ball?' Giles: 'Bloody well better not. I've got mine already wrapped.'

Glory: 'Pay attention. I am great and I am beautiful. And when I walk into a room all eyes turn to me, because my name is a *holy* name.'

Xander, to the Maclays: 'You're dealing with all of us.' Spike: ''Cept me.' Xander: ''Cept Spike.' Spike: 'I don't care what happens.'

Notes: 'We are her blood kin. Who the hell are you?' 'We're *family*.' So, the great revelation concerning Tara is that she's . . . a perfectly normal non-demon girl. Fine. Bit of an anti-climax there, but the episode's outrage at small-minded bigotry and blind tradition is worth the effort of wading through several *very* long-winded exposition sequences.

Buffy and Giles decide not to tell the others about Dawn's real status (see **83**, 'No Place Like Home'). Buffy's father (see **10**, 'Nightmares') is currently 'living the cliché' in Spain with his secretary and not returning Buffy's calls. Buffy says that, when Hank left, Dawn cried for a week: 'Except she didn't. She wasn't there, but I can still feel what it was like.' At some point (before the events of **83**, 'No Place Like Home', presumably), Buffy moved into a single corner suite at the University dorms. She's now decided to move back home to protect Dawn, telling the others it's to save money. Willow refers to the spell she and Tara attempted to reveal demons (which Tara secretly sabotaged, see **70**, 'Goodbye Iowa'). Xander, Anya, Willow and Tara play pool in the Bronze. Harmony shops at April Fools, the store where Cordelia worked (see **53**, 'Choices'). Anya exclaims during the demon attack that she's already been injured this month (see **80**, 'Real Me'). Riley mentions Graham and the government boys (see **82**, 'Out of My Mind'). Harmony says she met Carol Beets (who sired Brandon from the sewer gang) who told her that the Lei-Ach demon is recruiting his brethren to kill the Slayer for 'some big Nether-Wig'.

Soundtrack: Yo La Tengo's 'Tears Are In Your Eyes', Motorace's 'American Shoes', My Vitriol's 'Cemented Shoes' and Melanie Doane's 'I Can't Take My Eyes Off You'.

Critique: 'Wisely perhaps, "Family" doesn't attempt to go the whole distance by turning Tara into a fully sympathetic and likeable character,' John Binns noted in *Xposé*. 'The unspoken subtext of all this is arguably homophobia, personified by the irrational but clearly persuasive contention of Tara's father that his daughters become demons when they come of age.'

Did You Know?: Interviewed by Rob Francis, Amber Benson admitted she had no idea how much of a phenomenon *Buffy* was: 'I was actually in England. I truly believe that you guys are even more into *Buffy* than we are in the States. As an actor, the big hope is that you are able to eke out a living doing what you love and maybe if you're unbelievably, supremely lucky you get to actually become somewhat well-known. *Buffy* puts you on the map faster than you can say.'

Joss Whedon's Comments: 'I've always believed that a family is the people who love and respect you. That you create your own family,' Joss told *scifi_ign.com*. 'When we created the show, they said "Do you want [Buffy's] family?" I said, "Basically, she *has* a family. Her father is Giles, her sister is Willow. It's already in place." I really wanted to get this message out, that it's not about blood. Tara was the perfect vehicle for that. And I actually love my family.' Joss also mentioned in several interviews how real world disasters can create plotlines, revealing that Spike and Drusilla were supposed to return to Sunnydale together in **42**, 'Lover's Walk'. The

Spike/Dru break-up that persists to this day was initially simply to cover for Juliet Landau doing a movie and thus being unavailable for one episode.

85

Fool for Love

US Transmission Date: 14 Nov. 2000
UK Transmission Date: 16 Feb. 2001 (Sky)

Writer: Douglas Petrie
Director: Nick Marck[27]
Cast: Kali Rocha (Cecily Addams), Edward Fletcher (Male Partygoer),
Katharine Leonard (Female Partygoer), Matthew Lang (2nd Male Partygoer),
Chris Daniels (Stabbing Vampire), Kenneth Feinberg (Chaos Demon),
Steve Heinze (Vampire #1), Ming Liu (Chinese Slayer),
April Wheedon-Washington (Subway Slayer)
French title: *La Faille*

When a vampire stabs Buffy, she seeks information on the final battles of past Slayers from the only person she knows who has witnessed a Slayer's death: Spike. He not only details why his victims lost their lives, but his own history as a vampire. Meanwhile, Joyce's condition worsens.

Dudes and Babes: William was a very different character when he was alive, although there are lots of interesting little psychological reasons why he may have turned into the animal he did. Awkward and bookish, with none of the confident swagger we're used to from Spike, he was seemingly shaped by the pain of unrequited love. 'I know I'm a bad poet,' he tells Cecily, his muse. 'But I'm a good man.' She is horrified, telling William 'you're beneath me'. When Buffy uses the same phrase on Spike 120 years later, he is on the verge of tears, and it's impossible not to feel pity for this poor creature.

Once Angel told Spike about the legend of the Slayer, Spike was, he confesses, obsessed. To most vampires the Slayer was

---

[27] The Boxer Rebellion scenes were directed by Tim Minear during the *Angel* episode 'Darla'.

the subject of cold sweat and frightened whispers, 'but I sought her out. If you're looking for fun, there's death, there's glory and sod all else, right?' He gives Buffy some valuable lessons, such as the Slayer must always reach for her weapon whilst a vampire's are all in-built. The first Slayer he killed was 'business' but the second, a black girl in New York in 1977, Spike says had a touch of Buffy's style ('She was cunning, resourceful . . . hot. I could have danced all night with that one').

A Little Learning is a Dangerous Thing: The second lesson Spike teaches is to ask the right questions. Buffy wants to know how Spike beat the Slayers. The real question, Spike says, should be why did *they* lose?

Denial, Thy Name is the Slayer: 'You got off on it?' Buffy asks. She's talking about Spike killing the Slayers but his reply can be seen in a wider context: 'Suppose you're telling me *you don't*?' he asks. 'You can kill a hundred, a thousand, a thousand-thousand [of our kind] and all the enemies of Hell besides. And all we need is for one of us – *just one* – to have the thing we're all hoping for. One good day.' Every day, Spike continues, the Slayer wakes up with a question haunting her: 'Is today the day I die? Death is on your heels, baby, and sooner or later it's gonna catch you. Part of you wants it', he says, to stop the fear and uncertainty. He concludes that the secret is: 'Every Slayer has a death wish.' Spike also believes the only reason Buffy has lasted so long is that she has ties to the world. 'Your mum, your brat sister, the Scoobies. But you're just putting off the inevitable' (see **100**, 'The Gift').

It's a Designer Label!: Spike's leather coat originally belonged to the 1977 Slayer. The stabbing vampire's Anarchy-symbol leather jacket and Clash T-shirt are excellent, but several minus points for his *extremely* 1974 Afro haircut. Also, the horrible clothes worn by Willow (woolly hat and baggy sweater), Xander (orange sweatshirt) and Anya (impractical shoes and *Doctor Who*-style scarf) when patrolling.

References: The Boxer Rebellion (1898–1900) was an officially supported peasant uprising to drive foreigners (particularly Christian missionaries) from China. Boxers was the name given to a Chinese society known as the *I Ho Ch'üan*

('Righteous and Harmonious Fists'). They practiced callisthenics in the belief that this gave them supernatural powers and made them impervious to bullets. Also, Cheetos (the cheesy snack produced by Frito-Lay), the Discovery Channel, misquotes from the Bee Gees' 'Words', the Clash's 'Death or Glory' (see **It's a Designer Label!**) and *The Untouchables* ('Here endeth the lesson'). Xander eats Tito's potato chips. There's a possible oblique reference to 'Frankly, Mr Shankly' by the Smiths.

Bitch!: Even in the 1880s, Spike knew just how to put Angelus's back up, replying to his mentor's poetic rhetoric about the artistry of a kill with a succinct: '*Poofter!*'

Awesome!: From the moment that Buffy and Spike begin talking it's full-steam-ahead for one of the finest fifteen minutes in *Buffy*'s history. Particularly impressive is the inter-cutting between Buffy and Spike trading blows in the alley and Spike's memories of his battle with the Slayer on a New York subway train. At times the two become one, with a 1977-Spike talking directly to Buffy. It's a quite astonishing sequence, worthy of multiple viewing to catch little glances and lines that you miss in the heart-stopping suspense of the fight itself. Also, Giles telling Buffy that Watchers find the death of a Slayer too painful to talk about, the tiny Kung Fu movie that is Spike's battle with the 1900 Slayer, the girl's dying request that Spike tell her mother that she is sorry and Spike's (seemingly genuine) regret that he doesn't speak Chinese. Plus the touching scene in South America of Drusilla and Spike breaking up after her tryst with a Chaos Demon (who is *exactly* as described in **42**, 'Lover's Walk'), the Scoobies' incompetent idea of patrolling stealthily and the shot (reused in *Angel*: 'Darla') of the gang of four striding arrogantly amidst the chaos of the Boxer Rebellion as if they owned the world. *Magnificent*.

'You May Remember Me From Such Films and TV Series As ...': Kenneth Feinberg was in *Hard Hunted*. Edward Fletcher appeared in *Titanic*. Steve Heinze can be seen in *The Limey* and *Double Deception*. Kali Rocha was in *Meet the Parents* and *When Billie Beat Bobbie*. Matthew Lang appeared in *We Were Soldiers*.

Don't Give Up The Day Job: April Wheedon-Washington was Halle Berry's stunt double in *Swordfish*. She also played Faith in *General Hospital*.

Valley-Speak: Buffy: 'Do you think I'm a total wuss now?'

Dawn: 'Come on, who's *The Man*?'

Cigarettes and Alcohol: Spike notes that there are a few American beers that are underrated. Unfortunately, the one he's drinking isn't one of them. He also wants Buffy to order him spicy buffalo wings as part of his payment.

Logic, Let Me Introduce You to This Window: A retrospective one. In **15**, 'School Hard', Giles reads the details of Spike killing two previous Slayers from an ancient volume. But here we find that the second of them was as recently as 1977. It's confirmed that Spike was sired by Drusilla, despite him having said on two previous occasions (**15**, 'School Hard'; *Angel*: 'In the Dark') that it was Angel who made him. To be fair, Joss Whedon has said several times that Dru was always intended to be Spike's sire (on 2 January 1998 he told the *Posting Board*: 'Angel was Dru's sire. *She* made Spike. But sire doesn't just mean [the] guy who made you, it means you come from their line. Angel is like a grandfather to Spike'). In **15**, 'School Hard', Giles said Spike was 'barely 200 years old'. In **63**, 'The Initiative', Spike says he is 126. Here, the year he became a vampire is confirmed as 1880, making him approximately 120. Spike's reflection can be seen periodically in the subway during the fight. The word 'poofter' is possibly anachronistic for 1880 (in the *Oxford Dictionary of Slang* its first recorded usage is 1903). The New York Slayer moves her hand fractionally after Spike has killed her.

I Just *Love* Your Accent: Buffy says Watchers are prigs, a term referring to someone who displays an exaggerated sense of propriety. With his new name and Cock-er-nee accent, Spike was using 'bollocks' as an insult to Angel back in 1880. The English accents (Marsters and Landau's usual faultless delivery aside) are pretty woeful.

Quote/Unquote: William's poetry: 'My heart expands, 'tis grown a bulge in it. Inspired by your beauty, effulgent.'

Spike, on killing his first Slayer: 'The best night of my life. And I've had some sweet ones.'

Drusilla, to William: 'You walk in worlds the others can't begin to imagine.'

Buffy: 'You think we're dancing?' Spike: 'That's all we've ever done.'

Notes: 'Say I do want to. It wouldn't be you, Spike. It would *never* be you. You're beneath me.' Together with its *Angel* sequel, 'Darla' (shown immediately after this episode), this epic, extraordinary, lyrical and painful exercise in storytelling, crossing two hundred years and as many emotions, should be studied (long and hard) by anyone who still thinks *Buffy* is just kids stuff. That this series can get into the kind of philosophical and psychological areas that it does here, that it can make the audience genuinely *care* about a monster like Spike, speaks volumes for the intelligence and depth of the writing and the performance. Cherish this and episodes like it, because one day *Buffy* will be gone and things like 'Fool for Love' will only be memories.

Buffy mentions the Slayers' accelerated healing powers. Spike and Buffy play pool in the Bronze (see **84**, 'Family'). Spike had the nickname 'William the Bloody' when he was still human, as a result of his 'bloody awful' poetry. Spike was sired by Drusilla on the night he met her in 1880. Angel and Darla were unhappy with Spike's addition to their group, as he drew attention to them and forced them into hiding. Spike says that if he doesn't intend to hurt someone (if, for instance, he throws a punch intended to miss), his chip won't activate. He also indicates that there are varying levels of pain; that it sometimes lasts longer depending on what he does. Harmony refers to Spike staking her (see **59**, 'The Harsh Light of Day'). Giles refers to an eighteenth-century Slayer who forged her own weapons. Joyce announces that she is going into hospital overnight for a CAT scan.

Timeline Revisited: So much new information is revealed in this episode (and in *Angel*: 'Darla') that it's worth giving some praise to the writers as, the identity of Spike's sire aside (see **Logic, Let Me Introduce You to This Window**), the continuity is spot-on.

Born, as Liam, in 1725 (*Angel*: 'The Prodigal'), Angelus was sired by Darla, one of the Order of Aurelius (see **12**,

'Prophecy Girl') in 1753 (**33**, 'Becoming' Part 1). According to Darla, '[Angelus's] name would already be legend in his home village, if he had left anyone alive.' In 1760, the pair eventually travelled to London ('We cut a bloody swath through South Wales and Northern England') and Darla's sire, The Master (Darla had been sired in 1609, *Angel*: 'Darla'). Although Angelus insulted The Master and the pair left as enemies, at some stage there may have been a reconciliation as The Master remembers Angelus fondly in **7**, 'Angel'. Darla and Angelus travelled across Europe (they planned to go to Naples, though ended up in France in 1765, *Angel*: 'The Trial') creating mayhem and death wherever they went. They sometimes operated alone, as when Angelus sired Penn (*Angel*: 'Somnambulist') in the late 1700s, or when he was in Dublin in 1838 (**44**, 'Amends'), but they were together in 1860 in London. There Darla found Drusilla, a girl with frightening psychic ability; Angelus stalked her, killed her family, sent her mad and finally sired her (**19**, 'Lie to Me'; **33**, 'Becoming' Part 1; *Angel*: 'Dear Boy'), and also in London in 1880 when a sensitive young poet named William was sired by Dru. The gang then hid in Yorkshire, fleeing London barely ahead of an angry mob, due to William (now renamed Spike because of his habit of torturing his victims with railway spikes, **15**, 'School Hard') and his outrageous exploits.

In Borsa, Romania, in 1898, after killing a Kalderash Romany gypsy, Angelus was cursed to regain his soul (**33**, 'Becoming' Part 1) and, although Darla's initial reaction was to attempt to destroy him (*Angel*: 'Five By Five') Angel, with his soul intact, rejoined the gang in China in 1900 (**15**, 'School Hard') where Spike killed the then-current Slayer. However, when Angel saved a missionary family from Darla, she once again rejected him. It's possible they met on at least one further occasion (in **7**, 'Angel', he says that he last saw Darla in Budapest at the turn of the century). Around that time he was supposed to meet Penn in Italy, but missed the appointment, instead travelling to America and remaining there during the Depression (*Angel*: 'City Of'). He lived in L.A. in 1952 (*Angel*: 'Are You Now Or Have You Ever Been?') and New York in 1996 (**33**, 'Becoming' Part 1) before travelling to

Sunnydale in the same year.

Soundtrack: Crushing Velvet's 'XXX', 'Heal Yourself' by Elephant Ride, Avenue A's 'Run Cold', the Killington's 'Balladovie', Johann Sebastian Bach's 'Patita #3 in E Major' and Felix Mendelssohn's 'A Midsummer Night's Dream'.

Critique: 'An amazing episode,' wrote *SFX*'s Ed Gross, 'made even more astounding by the fact that this is the show's fifth season and the producers continually manage to pull the veritable rabbit out of the hat. It's fascinating to see Spike as a human, being rebuffed by the woman he has fallen in love with and heading outside to the darkness to seek solace. Instead, he literally bumps into Drusilla, Darla and Angelus.'

Did You Know?: 'It's just me and a guitar, I'm not going to be doing a lot of Smashing Pumpkins,' James Marsters told the press concerning his debut performance as acoustic rock-god at 14 Below in Santa Monica, opening for Barry Williams (from *The Brady Bunch*). 'I do Tom Waits, Neil Young, Bob Dylan. All the good stuff, when they had songs written for voice and guitar. I wish I could do Johnny Lee Hooker, but I'm not that good.' James was also a huge hit at the N2K convention in London when he entertained a sizeable audience with a set of covers and original material.

Joss Whedon's Comments: 'If I could write for any show, it would be *The Simpsons* or *Twin Peaks*,' Joss told the *Buffy* magazine. 'As much as you could say that *Buffy* is a cross between *90210* and *The X-Files*, you could also say it's a cross between *The Simpsons* and *Twin Peaks*. I want to kill Aaron Sorkin, eat his brain and gain his knowledge because I love *The West Wing* so much. His stuff is just amazing.'

Subsequently On *Angel*: 'Darla': A now-human Darla begins to feel guilt and confusion about her past. Wesley worries that Wolfram & Hart have planned this to distract Angel. Darla tries to contact Angel for help and then, with Lindsey's aid, attempts to escape. Lindsey gives Angel information as to where Darla is being kept and Angel saves her. Darla begs her former lover to sire her so she won't be plagued by her soul; Angel refuses.

86
Shadow

US Transmission Date: 21 Nov. 2000
UK Transmission Date: 23 Feb. 2001 (Sky)

Writer: David Fury
Director: Daniel Attias
Cast: William Forward (Dr Isaacs)
French title: *Incantation*

Joyce's scan reveals a shadow. A biopsy confirms that it's a brain tumour. Glory conjures up a supernatural snake to find The Key. The snake *does* find Dawn, but Buffy destroys it before it can report back. Riley, meanwhile, feels abandoned and begins to experiment with dark sexual games.

Dudes and Babes: The debut of Glory's spacious luxury apartment, her Imelda Marcos-style shoe fetish and her non-human minions (in this case, Dreg with his outrageous grovelling: 'Most tingly and wonderful Glorificus . . .').

Denial, Thy Name is Riley: Tired of waiting for Buffy to confide in him, wounded by constantly being reminded of Angel's presence and unsure of his position within the group, Riley goes to Willy's Bar again, gets drunk, and accepts Sandy's offer (see **84**, 'Family'). As she lovingly bites his neck, he stakes her.

It's a Designer Label!: Buffy's leather jacket and silver boots. Anya's sensible red dress. The long-haired shopper's spiderweb shirt. Glory's crimson leather dress. Spike steals a pair of Buffy's pink knickers as Riley throws him out of her room.

References: Allusions to *Destroy All Monsters*, Marvel's *Captain America*, Starkist Tuna's slogan 'Sorry Charlie', *The Usual Suspects*, *The Simpsons* (Giles uses Apu's catchphrase 'Thank you, call again') and the Beach Boys' 'Fun, Fun, Fun'. Xander mentions 'Bipperty, Bopperty, Boo' (from *Bedknobs and Broomsticks*). The Canadian comedy series *SCTV* featured a regular skit called 'Farm Film Celebrity Blowup' where two hicks (John Flaherty and John Candy) reviewed movies and then exploded them (and often their creators) with the catch-phrase 'They blew up *real* good' (see **Valley-Speak**).

Bitch!: Spike, to Riley: 'Face it, white bread. Buffy's got a type, and you're not it.'

  Dreg: 'Your creamy coolness has honoured me by speaking my name. Your voice is like a thousand sweet songbirds.' Glory, sarcastically: 'Yeah, I never tire of hearing *that*.'

Awesome!: Dawn telling Riley that Buffy 'cries a lot less with you than she did with Angel'. Buffy's fight with Glory in the zoo's reptile house. The lengthy chase and battle between Buffy and the snake.

'You May Remember Me From Such Films and TV Series As . . .': Kevin Weisman was in *Robbers*, *Gone in Sixty Seconds*, *Kat & Allison*, *Man of the Century*, *Felicity*, *Just Shoot Me* and played Larry in *Roswell*. William Forward appeared in *Thirst*, *D.O.A.*, *Chiller* and was Lord Refa in *Babylon 5*.

Don't Give Up The Day Job: Daniel Attias was producer on *Party of Five*, assistant director on *E.T. the Extra-Terrestrial* and helmed episodes of *The Sopranos*, *Ally McBeal* and *Sledge Hammer!* Just weeks after his second *Buffy* episode aired, Attias's son, David, was charged with murdering four pedestrians with his car in Santa Barbara.

The Spell *Will* Work: Giles, unknowingly, sells Glory a Khul's amulet and a Sobekian bloodstone. The Sobekites were an ancient Egyptian reptile cult and the amulet is a transmogrification conduit, though Giles says that the spells were lost thousands of years ago. When Buffy finds out that Glory has been to the shop, she asks: 'How did she get away with this bad-mojo stuff?' 'Giles sold it to her,' snitches Anya, brilliantly. 'If it's any consolation,' says a crestfallen Giles, 'I may have overcharged her.'

Valley-Speak: Xander: 'Captain America blowed it up real good. All by his lone-wolf lonesome.' And: 'This chick creamed you last time.'

  Glory: 'No problemo.'

Devil Worship and Rock'n'Roll: A customer asks if Giles stocks the LP 'Aleister Crowley Sings'. Giles, sadly, notes that they don't but says he *does* have some very nice whale sounds.

The advert for the Magic Box includes mention of CRYSTALS! POTIONS! and DEATH CHARMS!

Logic, Let Me Introduce You to This Window: Joyce's hair is different when she goes into the CAT scan from when she comes out. Glory hurts Buffy's right shoulder, but when Buffy is at the hospital she puts ice on the left. Watch out for the very obvious rubber snake when Glory pulls the cobra from the glass case. The first Sunnydale area telephone code, 803, is a real code for South Carolina. Seems it's a lot further from L.A. than we realised.

I Just *Love* Your Accent: Giles' slogan for the Magic Box is 'Your one-stop spot to shop for all your occult needs.'

Cruelty to Animals: Dawn asks what a CAT scan is. It's actually an acronym for 'Computed Axial Tomography', so she can rest assured that they don't 'test it on cats'.

Quote/Unquote: Xander: 'Am I right?' Giles: 'I'm almost certain you're not, but to be fair, I wasn't listening.'

Riley finds Spike in Buffy's room: 'Were you just smelling her sweater?' Spike: 'No. Yeah, all right, I did. It's a predator thing, nothing wrong with it. Just know your enemy's scent, whet the appetite for a hunt.'

Notes: 'Your mother has . . . low-grade glycoma. It's a brain tumour.' Welcome to the beginning of a very grim couple of weeks. Blowing about the next half-a-season's SFX budget on, let's face it, a pretty poor CGI snake was a questionable decision, but 'Shadow' is basically sound (if hardly laugh-a-minute stuff), with excellent performances from Sutherland, Trachtenberg and Gellar in particular.

This episode begins the day after the events of **85**, 'Fool for Love'. Buffy learns that Glory's name is Glorificus (see **84**, 'Family'). The Magic Box is located at 5124 Maple Court in downtown Sunnydale. The phone number is 803-555-8966 (the reason that 555 is used as a phone prefix in many US shows is that it's one of the few three-figure numbers that isn't a real area code. See, for instance, *Angel*, *The X-Files*, *Roswell*). Spike says Willow has recently performed two uninvitation spells on Buffy's home, locking out Dracula (**79**, 'Buffy vs Dracula') and Harmony (**80**, 'Real Me'). The Sunnydale Zoo was last seen in **6**, 'The Pack'. Buffy says that the snake demon isn't 'Mayor size' (see **56**, 'Graduation Day' Part 2). Dawn mentions celebrating her tenth birthday at the amusement park (just her, Buffy and Joyce as she hadn't made any friends by then) and notes that this was shortly after the family moved to Sunnydale. Anya refers to her fear of bunnies (see **60**, 'Fear Itself'). Joyce uses a cellphone with an ear piece.

Soundtrack: Thomas Wanker's beautiful piano score that accompanies the sad montage of characters at the end.

Did You Know?: 'The woman who owned the snake was like, "It's okay, we fed him a few days ago, he shouldn't be hungry,"' Clare Kramer told *FHM*. 'To be honest, I'd much prefer to hold a snake than a hamster. I don't dig little rodents.'

87

Listening to Fear

US Transmission Date: 28 Nov. 2000
UK Transmission Date: 2 Mar. 2001 (Sky)

Writer: Rebecca Rand Kirshner
Director: David Solomon
Cast: Keith Allan (Skinny Mental Patient),
Erin Leigh Price (Vampire Chick),
April Adams (Nurse Lampkin), Barbara C Adside (Creature),
Debbie Lee Carrington (Creature)
French title: *Météorite*

The gang investigates a suspicious death in the woods near a meteor crash site and discovers that the killer is an alien Queller demon, summoned to silence madmen. Riley secretly calls the military for help. Joyce – whose condition causes her flashes of incoherence – goes home rather than wait in the hospital for her surgery. The Queller follows.

Dudes and Babes: It was Ben who called forth the Queller Demon to clean up Glory's mess, 'just like I've done my whole damn life'. He is known to Dreg (who calls him 'sir'). Riley, meanwhile, is getting more vampire lurv (see **86**, 'Shadow'; **88**, 'Into the Woods').

Denial, Thy Name is Joyce ... : Joyce remembers the events of **82**, 'Out of My Mind', where, before fainting, she momentarily didn't know who Dawn was. It came to me like truth.' In her less lucid moments, she describes Dawn as 'nothing. You're a shadow.' 'She's not mine, is she?' Joyce asks Buffy. 'She *does* belong to us, though?' When Buffy confirms that Dawn does, Joyce continues, 'She's important. To the world.'

A Little Learning is a Dangerous Thing: The belief that the moon causes insanity is the origin of the term 'lunacy'. Friends of the afflicted would pray to the moon to send a shooting star to quell the madmen (which it would, due to the Queller demon inside them). Such meteoric anomalies go back to an incident in twelfth-century Reykjavik. In the Middle Ages there were sweeping plagues of madness, but the insanity would always subside after another meteor event.

Willow is studying the First World War in history ('underlying causes and trench foot'). She buys Dawn a book called *Spells*, and Buffy, a large book called *World History*. At the university library, Xander is reading a volume called *Meteors and You!* Tara notes that she and Anya have been scouring all the international periodicals for meteorite landings.

It's a Designer Label!: The leather-pants vampire-gang in the opening scenes. Buffy's hooded top. Tara's tasteful polo neck.

References: Tara says that Japanese commercials are weird. Spike mentions the fast-food chain Burger Barn. There's a sign in Dawn's bedroom saying PARENTAL ADVISORY LYRICS. Amongst Willow's presents are a yo-yo for Buffy and a beer-hat for Joyce.

Naming All the Stars: Willow identifies Canis Minor, a small constellation with two stars, Procyon and Gomeisa (in astronomy, it represents one of Orion's dogs). Cassiopeia is the 'W'-shaped figure beneath Polaris. In Greek mythology, Cassiopeia was Andromeda's mother, chained to her throne for eternity as a punishment for her boastfulness. Both are visible in North America between November and March. Willow says that some of the stars we look at don't exist any more. In the time that it takes for their light to reach Earth, they've exploded. She continues that she loved to look at the stars when she was little. They're supposed to make one feel insignificant, but they made Willow feel like she was in space. Tara describes various constellations that she has made up because she doesn't understand the real ones: The Big Pineapple, Short-Man-Looking-Uncomfortable, Moose Getting a Sponge Bath and Little Pile o'Crackers.

Bitch!: Joyce, to Buffy: 'You shouldn't eat any more, you're disgustingly fat.'

Awesome!: The finding of the meteor. When Anya says 'If there's radiation you could, like, go all sterile,' watch Riley looking alarmed and Xander jump hurriedly backwards. Willow: 'Something evil crashed to earth in this and then broke out and slithered away to do badness.' Giles: 'In all fairness, we don't really know about the slithered part.' Anya: 'No. I'm sure it frisked about like a fluffy lamb.' Plus the demon itself – nasty little bugger.

'You May Remember Me From Such Films and TV Series As . . .': Nick Chinlund may be familiar as Billy Bedlam in *Con Air*, Donnie Pfaster in *The X-Files* and Detective Tancredi in *Third Watch*. He was also in *Amy's Orgasm*, *Reform School Girl* and *Joshua Tree*. April Adams appeared in *Mission: Africa*. Debbie Lee Carrington played Felicity in *She's All That* and was in *Total Recall*, *Howard the Duck*, *Spaced Invaders* and *Return of the Jedi* (playing an Ewok).

Don't Give Up The Day Job: Keith Allan's usual industry job is title designer on *Hard* and *Zero Tolerance*. Barbara C Adside did stunts on *Bordello of Blood* whilst appearing in *Feds* and *Nemesis*. Randy Thompson was in *Singles*, *Chicago Hope* and directed the movie *Stages*.

The Drugs Don't Work: The doctor gives Buffy three bottles of pills for Joyce including sedatives and painkillers.

Valley-Speak: Willow, after killing two vampires: '*Yay* on me.'
    Anya: 'Big zippo.'

Logic, Let Me Introduce You to This Window: It's unusual for a doctor to respond to a call button; it would normally be a nurse's job. The nurse can hear a crazy guy screaming but, seemingly, not the demon. Buffy doesn't drive (she does, but really badly, see **40**, 'Band Candy'), and Joyce almost certainly can't in her condition, but one of them had to have driven home, as no other explanation is given for how they got there. Dawn says the crazy guy told her she wasn't real (see **80**, 'Real Me'); he didn't, merely telling her that she 'didn't belong here'. Willow mentions the Tunguska explosion in Russia and gives the date as 1917. It was actually 1908.

Motors: Xander, looking at a representation of the planets, observes how small Mercury is compared to Saturn. 'Whereas, in contrast, the cars of the same name . . .' Saturn is famous for the L-Series (sedans and station wagons), the SC-Series (sporty coupes) and the popular S-Series (compact sedans). Mercury is a subsidiary of Ford, and makes mid-size sedans and sports utility vehicles.

Cruelty to Animals: Dawn says a girl at school told her that gelatine is made from ground-up cows' feet and that if you eat Jell-O, there's a cow somewhere, limping.

Quote/Unquote: Willow: 'We're experienced.' Anya: 'Yes, it seems like we're always dealing with creatures from outer space. Except that we don't ever do that!'

Xander: 'I still don't know why we had to come here to look up information on a killer snot monster.' Giles: 'Because it's a killer snot monster from outer space.'

Willow says she feels like Santa Claus: 'Except thinner and younger. And female. And Jewish.'

Giles: 'It would appear that the world is not being invaded.' Tara: 'I'm pretty pleased about that.'

Notes: 'No matter what she is, she still *feels* like my daughter. I have to know that you'll take care of her.' One of the most unremittingly grim hours of television you'll ever see. Yet it's as darkly compelling as even the series' lightest moments.

The patient released from the hospital is the nightwatchman whom Glory attacked in **83**, 'No Place Like Home'. Previously, he mentioned his wife and two daughters, who we see with him in this episode. Willow says she doesn't want to be the one who finds the bodies anymore (see **12**, 'Prophecy Girl'; **67**, 'Doomed'; **80**, 'Real Me').

Did You Know?: Although he was surrounded by men like Giles during his time at Winchester, Joss actually got the name from his housematron, Barbara Giles. 'Mostly I knew people like the Watchers Council. There were some harsh old men teaching there.' Asked which of his characters he can most identify with, Joss notes: 'In school it was Xander. Obviously that's changed, because he's getting laid. Sometimes it's Giles, because I'm so appalled by everything around me.'

88

Into the Woods

US Transmission Date: 19 Dec. 2000
UK Transmission Date: 9 Mar. 2001 (Sky)

Writer: Marti Noxon
Director: Marti Noxon
Cast: Rainy Jo Stout (Junkie Vampire Girl),
Emmanuel Xuereb (Whip), Adam G (Tough Vamp)
French title: *Par Amour*

Joyce's surgery is successful. Buffy and Riley go home for celebratory sex. Riley sneaks out in the middle of the night, and Spike follows him to a vampire brothel, where Riley pays to have his blood sucked. Spike takes Buffy to the building to see for herself. Riley is approached by the military to return to the fold. He tells Buffy that he will leave if she doesn't give him a reason to stay, and a lecture from Xander makes Buffy realise how wrong she has been.

Dudes and Babes: Dawn says that when she was younger, she used to put chopsticks in her mouth and pretend to be a vampire. Buffy would chase her yelling 'I'm the Slayer, I'm going to get you.' 'That's disturbing,' notes Anya. 'You're emotionally scarred and will end up badly.'

A Little Learning is a Dangerous Thing: Buffy has been missing lots of school recently and says that she may have to take a few incompletes, but that she'll make it through the semester (see **97**, 'Tough Love').

Denial, Thy Name is Buffy: Xander perceptively notes that Buffy got burned with Angel and has been treating Riley like 'rebound guy' ever since, when he's actually the kind that comes along once in a lifetime. He has never held back from her, he's risked everything, Xander continues. Buffy is letting him leave because she doesn't like ultimatums. If he's not *the* guy, Xander says, let him go. 'But if you really think you can love this guy . . . then think about what you're about to lose.' Buffy begins to cry. 'Run,' Xander tells her. But it's too late. Just as in **57**, 'The Freshman', Xander is the only person who seems able to say honest things to Buffy when she most needs it.

The Conspiracy Starts at Home Time: Though the Initiative is dead (see **77**, 'Primeval'), there is still a branch of the army that hunts demons, led by Major Ellis (see **87**, 'Listening to Fear') of which Graham is a member. They apparently make their services available around the world (this job is in Belize, where a demon tribe is 'taking apart missionaries').

It's a Designer Label!: Buffy's 'With the Beatles'-style black polo neck. Xander's tan jacket.

References: Xander mentions Moo Goo Gai Pan, a Cantonese dish of chicken, mushrooms, vegetables and sautéed spices. 'The chimp playing hockey? Is that based on the Chekhov?' is a probable reference to the movie *MVP* and Anton Chekhov (1860–1904), Russian dramatist and author of *Uncle Vanya*, *The Seagull* and *The Cherry Orchard*. Also, *Game of Life* (see **80**, 'Real Me'), *The Graduate* ('are you planning to seduce me, Mr Finn?'), the *Rambo* movies, the State Farm insurance agency and *Penthouse*. The title is shared with an episode of *Buffy*'s WB-stablemate *Roswell* (presumably, a compliment for the other series using 'Surprise' as one of *its* titles). Posters for the bands String Cheese Incident and Mentor can be seen outside the vampire brothel.

Bitch!: Buffy, on Spike's sudden arrival: 'Every time you show up like this, you risk *all* of your parts.'

Awesome!: Xander and Giles *not* hugging at the hospital. Riley stabbing Spike with a plastic stake and then the pair getting drunk and maudlin afterwards. Buffy taking out seven vampires, including the junkie she saw biting Riley, with a javelin throw that would probably get her on the medal rostrum at the Olympics.

'You May Remember Me From Such Films and TV Series As . . .': Rainy Jo Stout was Nancy in *One*. Emmanuel Xuereb was in *Jerks*, *Natural Born Killers* and *Stonewall*. Adam G appeared in *The President's Man* and *Walker, Texas Ranger*.

Fun with Wigs: Joyce doesn't like the idea of wearing a wig and believes it will make her look like she has a cat on her head.

Valley-Speak: Dawn: 'I'm only sleeping here so Buffy and Riley can *boink*.'

Anya: 'They get off on the rush.'

Cigarettes and Alcohol: Anya thinks strawberry schnapps tastes like ice cream. Riley and Spike share a bottle of wine whilst discussing how much love *sucks*.

Vampire Sex and Drugs and Rock'n'Roll: Giles says he hasn't seen a vampire brothel since his Ripper days (see **20**, 'The Dark Age'). He explains such places – in which humans pay vampires to suck some of their blood because they find it arousing or like the thrill-factor – have been in existence for centuries. The vampires get cash and blood but it can be dangerous for the humans involved. People can die accidentally, or meet a vampire who only pretends to play by the rules.

Anya is desperate to tell Riley about some of her and Xander's 'sexcades' involving the vaulting horse in Buffy's training area.

Logic, Let Me Introduce You to This Window: After Spike is staked by Riley, whenever he removes his hand from his chest there's no hole in his shirt. Also, Spike reaches for the wine bottle and starts to open it. After a change of angle, he's got his hand on his chest, then starts to open the bottle again. Anya's hairstyle twice changes between scenes. When Buffy is hitting the punch-bag, both of her hands are taped. When Riley gets there, her left hand is taped but the right is not. Riley didn't tell Buffy what time he would be leaving (he just said 'tonight'), yet she somehow knew it would be at midnight. She also knows that he'd be leaving by helicopter when he didn't tell her that either. Several of the Scoobies have different clothes on to those that they wore in the final scene of **87**, 'Listening to Fear', despite the fact that these scenes take place just a couple of hours later.

I Just *Love* Your Accent: Giles notes that he is no longer a victim of crass holiday commercialisation but rather a purveyor of it as he hangs up a sign: DON'T FORGET! WINTER SOLSTICE, HANUKKAH, CHRISTMAS, KWANZAA & GURNENTHAR'S ASCENDANCE ARE COMING!

Cruelty to Animals: Anya's excitement at a film with a chimp playing hockey. 'That's hilarious. The ice is so slippery and monkeys are all irrational. We *have* to see this.'

Anya: 'Who ordered more chickens' feet? The ones we have aren't moving at all.' Xander: 'That's generally what happens when you cut them off the chicken.'

Quote/Unquote: Anya, to Willow: 'That's very humorous. Make fun of the ex-demon. I can just hear you in private. "I dislike that Anya. She's newly human and strangely literal."'

Spike, to Riley: 'Sometimes I envy you so much it chokes me. And sometimes I think I got the better deal. To be that close to her and not have her. To be all alone even when you're holding her. Feeling her beneath you. Surrounding you . . . No, *you* got the better deal.'

Xander, to Anya: 'I've gotta say something, 'cos I don't think I've made it clear. I'm in love with you. Powerfully, painfully in love. The things you do, the way you think, the way you move. I get excited every time I'm about to see you. You make me feel like I've never felt before in my life. Like a man. I just thought you might wanna know.'

Notes: 'What else do you want from me, Riley? I've given you everything that I have. My heart, my body and soul.' The end of a trilogy of *desperately* depressing episodes. 'Into the Woods', like the two immediately before it, abandons one of the series' great strengths, its humour, in favour of deep, dark and bitter truths. That these episodes work at all is a tribute to the writing; that they work as outstanding well as they do is all down to the cast, who play it like they mean it. I defy even the world's greatest Riley-hater not to be moved by the final shots of this episode. Fantastic stuff.

Anya says she sleeps with Xander. And feeds and bathes him. During her demon days Anya once made a man spontaneously combust, setting his village on fire in the process.

Soundtrack: Emilana Torrini's 'Summer Breeze'.

Did You Know?: According to *Soap Opera Weekly*, the 'In Memory of DC Gustafson' caption refers to Gustav Gustafson, a member of the *Buffy* crew and a close friend of Sarah who died in November 2000.

Joss Whedon's Comments: 'I love Marc and I loved Riley as a character,' Joss told the *Posting Board*. 'Some people responded to him and some didn't. Basically, it came down to nobody getting over Buffy and Angel. Because I'd done the tortured *Romeo and Juliet* "This is the wrong guy, he's gonna make me miserable" romance, I wanted to see Buffy have a nice relationship with a nice guy. America doesn't want to see that. So it became instead a scenario where people thought, "She has a nice guy. She's going to walk all over him." I think Marc really came into his own, particularly this season. He has a Gary Cooper quality. But Gary Cooper can't live in the Buffyverse.' Joss also acknowledged, bravely, some of the less than successful aspects of Season Four: 'We didn't have the money to make [The Initiative] look good, so they kept patrolling past the same bush. Spike was hiding behind that shrub and I was like, "Why don't you look in the shrub? It's the only shrub there is!" We wanted to bring a James Bondian world to the show but, quite frankly, it was too expensive.'

89

Triangle

US Transmission Date: 9 Jan. 2001
UK Transmission Date: 16 Mar. 2001 (Sky)

Writer: Jane Espenson
Director: Christopher Hibler
Cast: Abraham Benrubi (Olaf), Ranjani Brow (Young Nun)

With Giles in England meeting the Watcher's Council, a squabble over who was left in charge of the Magic Box, Anya or Willow, leads to a spell going wrong and the arrival of Olaf, a troll who hates both Anya and witches. Spike, meanwhile, tries to show Buffy his softer side.

Dudes and Babes: Anya has observed that humans make the same mistakes. Some guy dumps a girl, who calls on Anyanka to exact vengeance. The next year, same girl, different guy. 'After you smite a few you start going "My goodness, young lady. Maybe you're doing something wrong here too."' Buffy, meanwhile saves a nun from a vampire and asks: 'The whole abjuring the company of men? How's that working for you?' She has taken down the Riley pictures in her bedroom.

A Little Learning is a Dangerous Thing: Willow says that she uses the time between classes to copy over her notes with a system of different coloured pens. It has been pointed out to her that this is insane. 'I said *quirky*,' notes Tara defensively. Tara likes Greek Art which touches on mythology, history and philosophy. Buffy, however, says the professor spits too much when talking. Buffy has considered taking Central American Geopolitics but every time she hears the word 'jungle' she thinks of Riley.

There's more on alternative universes (see **43**, 'The Wish'; **50**, 'Doppelgängland') with Willow noting that trying to send someone to a specific place is like trying to hit a puppy by throwing a bee at it. She and Anya mention several such universes like the land of trolls, the land of perpetual Wednesday, the crazy-melty-land and the now legendary 'world without shrimp' (see **73**, 'Superstar').

Denial, Thy Name is Buffy: A definite case of guilt-transference here as she gets really upset over the possibility of Xander and Anya's 'miraculous love' being broken.

It's a Designer Label!: Buffy tells the others that the nun she saved let her try on her wimple. Buffy's fabulous pink silk blouse, Giles's grey tie, Willow's Rolling Stones T-shirt.

References: Willow describes Anya as the fish in the bowl, from Dr Seuss's *The Cat in the Hat*. Willow says 'I wish Buffy was here' and Buffy immediately walks in; she then adds 'I wish I had a million dollars' and looks around hopefully, a joke of Chandler's from the first episode of *Friends*. Also, Sea World, Julian Cope's 'Beautiful Love', *Lord of the Rings*. Magazines seen in the Magic Box racks include *Massage*, *UFO Tesla*, *Green Egg*, *Sharman's & Drums* and *Nexus*. A sign in the Magic Box says: MAGIC HAPPENS.

Bitch!: Dawn: 'Whatcha doin'?' Buffy, sarcastically: 'Playing soccer.'

Spike, to the mannequin: 'Ungrateful bitch.'

Willow, impersonating Anya: 'I like money better than people. People can so rarely be exchanged for goods and/or services.' And, when Anya says there are humans stranger than her: 'Unless I'm really wrong about Crazy Larry down at the bus stop, he's probably not gonna turn Xander into a troll.'

Awesome!: Spike practising giving Buffy chocolates with his mannequin and ending up having a violent argument with it. Buffy dealing nicely with her own break-up but becoming distraught and sobbing on Tara's shoulder at the suggestion that Xander and Anya are having difficulties. Olaf breaking Xander's arm, and calling him 'a tiny man'. Plus one of the best bits of comedy on the show: Buffy finds Spike tending an injured woman. Spike says, defensively, that he isn't sampling. 'You want credit for *not* feeding on bleeding disaster victims?' asks Buffy, walking away in disgust. Spike: 'What's it *take*?!'

'You May Remember Me From Such Films and TV Series As . . .': The great Abraham Benrubi was Larry Kubiac in the 90s cult classic *Parker Lewis Can't Lose*, Jerry Markovic in *ER* and appeared in *Twister* and *War Story*. Ranjani Brow was in *East of Hope Street*.

Don't Give Up the Day Job: Chris Hibler previously worked on *Matlock*, *Quantum Leap* and *Moonlighting*. He was assistant director on Disney's *Bedknobs and Broomsticks*.

Valley-Speak: Willow, on why she wouldn't try to have sex with Xander: 'Hello! *Gay now*?'

Cigarettes and Alcohol: Anya realises that Willow is exerting peer pressure. 'Any second now you're gonna make me smoke tobacco and have drugs.' Olaf drinks beer straight from the keg. Xander and Spike share a beer whilst they play pool in the Bronze (what's with all this pool? – that's three times in five episodes it's been used as a dramatic tool).

Logic, Let Me Introduce You to This Window: The Magic Box, in an exterior shot, is next to a book shop. This looks nothing like the location seen in **80**, 'Real Me'. Anya's hairstyle changes dramatically between shots whilst she and Xander are in bed, along with the level on his chest at which Nick Brendon has the bedclothes positioned. Xander gets hit in the face with a huge hammer. Twice. And *doesn't* have his skull crushed? (Look at the effect it had on Glory in **100**, 'The Gift'.) Buffy was nowhere near the falling gantry in the Bronze but still ends up beneath it when it lands. Xander and Anya's position in relation to Buffy, Willow and Tara changes several times between shots in the Bronze when confronted by Olaf. How does Buffy know so much about Riley's mission? He certainly didn't tell her where he was going. When Buffy and Dawn are talking in Buffy's room, Buffy is reading a magazine. Later, it disappears and she is holding a teddy bear. Anya says that she has never driven. In **55**, 'Graduation Day' Part 1, she told Xander she had a car outside, and suggested that they leave Sunnydale (and take turns driving).

I Just *Love* Your Accent: Tara is envious of Giles – a trip to England sounds exciting and exotic. 'Unless you're English.'

Cruelty to Animals: Willow used hellebore to 'de-rat' Amy (see **45**, 'Gingerbread'). It didn't work but Willow believes it might have made Amy really smart – 'She keeps giving me these looks like she's planning something.' Willow tried to emulate *The Cat in the Hat*'s balancing feats when she was six and, as a consequence, wasn't allowed to have pet fish for five years (see **29**, 'Passion').

Quote/Unquote: Anya: 'I have finesse coming out of my bottom!'

Buffy: 'I killed something in a convent last night.' Xander: 'In any other room, a frightening declaration. Here, a welcome distraction.'

Willow: 'I'm not stealing. I'm just taking things without paying for them. In what twisted dictionary is *that* stealing?'

Olaf: 'Do you know where there are babies?' Spike, to Xander: 'What do you think, the hospital?'

Notes: 'You told the witch to do that, Anyanka. You seem determined to put an end to all my fun. Just like you did when we were dating.' Maybe I'm just a sucker for Jane Espenson's deliciously less-than-serious take on *Buffy*, but this episode (which was absolutely *loathed* by many Internet fans and journalists: 'Shockingly bad' according to the review in *DreamWatch*) is one of my favourites of the season. The jokes are good, Abraham Benrubi is terrific and the music is a particular delight.

Anya dated Olaf when he was a big dumb guy. He cheated on her so she made him into a troll, which is how she got the job as a vengeance demon (see **65**, 'Something Blue'). Then some witches trapped him in a crystal for centuries before

Willow's spell released him. Giles returns to England to ask for the Council of Watchers' help in finding out more about Glory. They have no record of her, but will look into the matter (see **90**, 'Checkpoint'). Buffy says she trusts the Watchers as far as Giles could throw them. Spike likes the food in the Bronze, not just the chicken wings (see **85**, 'Fool for Love') but also Texas Tumbleweed ('a flower-shaped thing they make from an onion. It's brilliant'). Anya mentions the circumstances which saw Xander and Cordelia split (see **42**, 'Lover's Walk'). She notes that Willow has known Xander since they were squalling infants, and that Willow will always know him better than Anya does. Tara is allergic to shrimp. Buffy gets a souvenir from the fight with Olaf – his hammer (see **100**, 'The Gift').

Soundtrack: Blur's classic 'There's No Other Way' and 'Bohemian Like You' by the Dandy Warhols.

Critique: 'There are a lot of pluses to the episode,' noted *SFX*'s Ed Gross. 'Notably, Spike's growing obsession over Buffy which at times seems fairly psychotic.'

Did You Know?: 'In Santa Monica I'm completely anonymous,' James Marsters told Paul Simpson and Ruth Thomas. 'People notice me, but I'm not *that* famous. I'm not Leonardo DiCaprio. But when I come [to England] as a celebrity, there's hype. It's like *A Hard Day's Night* or something. In Britain they're better at expressing it. You guys know how to break the ice like nobody else. It's really nice, because it takes some of the pressure off meeting people.'

Joss Whedon's Comments: 'Every season has a unifying theme,' Joss told *E! Online*. 'Last year it was the liberation of college and how it fractures you as a group and as a person. This year was about family and identity and Buffy being a Slayer. And next year I refer to as "Oh, Grow Up". It's about realising that we're young adults, and now we're making choices like our parents did, and we're just as bad at it as they were.'

90
Checkpoint

US Transmission Date: 23 Jan. 2001
UK Transmission Date: 23 Mar. 2001 (Sky)

Writer: Jane Espenson, Douglas Petrie
Director: Nick Marck
Cast: Peter Husmann (Mailman), Kris Iyer (Nigel),
Cynthia Lamontagne (Female Council Member),
Wesley Mask (Professor Roberts), Oliver Muirhead (Phili),
Jack Thomas (Council Member #4), John O'Leary (Council Member #5)
French title: *L'inspection*

Buffy is visited by the Council of Watchers who say they know what Glory is, but refuse to give Buffy any information until she passes their tests. Glory stalks Buffy and threatens her family. And the Knights of Byzantium attack the Slayer, declare themselves her enemy and promise that legions will follow. Finally, Buffy realises why everyone is targeting her. She tells the Watchers that she is in charge and orders Quentin to reveal what he knows about Glory.

Dudes and Babes: Members of an ancient order, the Knights of Byzantium have a tattoo on their foreheads. They appear medieval in their speech and armaments, using swords and chain mail. They believe that The Key and its protector should be destroyed to prevent it from falling into The Beast's hands.

Authority Sucks!: Buffy's argument with Professor Roberts tackles such weighty topics as whether Rasputin was a vampire, did Columbus or the Vikings first discover America and the sleeping patterns of Prussian generals. 'You'd prefer I step aside?' asks the Professor, wearily. 'You can teach your own course. Speculation 101? Intro to Flights of Fancy?'

A Little Learning is a Dangerous Thing: The girl Watcher notes that the removal from Burma of one of Giles's statues is a criminal offence; when triggered, the statue has the power to melt human eyeballs. Nigel adds that most of the material in the Magic Box couldn't harm anyone, being mere dime store trinkets. But there *are* some potent elements including focusing crystals, runic artefacts and an amulet of Caldis.

Deportation is an Eleven-Letter Word: If Buffy fights the Council, Quentin threatens, they will have Giles deported and make sure he never sets foot in the US again. 'Perhaps you're used to idle threats and sloppy discipline, but you're dealing with grown-ups now.' Buffy asks Giles if they could really kick him out the country. 'In a heartbeat,' he replies. 'The rough stuff, they're all right [at]. A bit ham-handed but they get it done. But the bureaucracy, the pulling of political strings, they're the best in the world. They can kill you with the stroke of a pen ... Holding what they know hostage with a gun pointed at my green card. It's humiliating.'

Denial, Thy Name is Everyone: In a breathtaking speech, Buffy says that she's had people lining up to tell her how unimportant she is, but she now understands why. Power. She has it. They don't and this bothers *them*. She tells Giles and the Council about Glory's visit. 'She told me I'm a bug, a flea. She could squash me in a second. Only she didn't. We had what in her warped brain probably passes for a civilised conversation. Why? Because she needs something from me. Because I have power over her.' The Council, Buffy continues, haven't come all the way from England to determine whether or not she is good enough to be let back in. They came to beg her to give their lives some semblance of meaning. It is suggested that the Scooby Gang are mere children. Buffy replies: 'We're talking about two very powerful witches and a thousand-year-old ex-demon.' And Xander? 'The boy has clocked more field time than all of you combined. He's part of the unit.'

The Conspiracy Starts at Home Time: Jinx notes that the signs of the alignment are moving faster than expected and that if Glory is to use The Key, she must act quickly.

It's a Designer Label!: Glory's red towel. Dawn's pyjamas and *Pink Panther* T-shirt. Giles's leather jacket and Willow's lilac shirt. Buffy wears the first woolly hat seen in a year.

References: Grigori Yefimovich Rasputin (?1871–1916), a Siberian peasant monk, notorious for his debauchery, who wielded influence over the Romanov court. Also, *Born on the Fourth of July*, *Masterpiece Theatre*, *The Young Ones* ('Fascists!'), Christopher Columbus, the Japanese martial arts Aikido and Jujitsu, obliquely *The Ladies Home Journal* and

Snap's 'The Power'. Spike is still watching *Passions* (see **65**, 'Something Blue'), a one-hour daily soap targeted at teens, which began in July 1999, and is known for its supernatural storylines. The Knights of Byzantium take their name from the ancient free-city of Thrace – later Constantinople, and now Istanbul – at the mouth of the Bosphorus. It was founded c. 660 BC by the Greeks, then Roman occupied from AD 73, and became the centre of the Eastern Holy Roman Empire (also known as the Byzantine Empire), which lasted until 1453 when the Ottoman Turks conquered it. Byzantium of the Middle Ages was staunchly conservative and Christian, and launched several crusades against the Muslims.

Bitch!: Glory: 'I bet Mousy the Vampire Slayer has an idea where it is.'

Awesome!: Anya's terror that the Council may view her as a potential target leads to all sorts of hilarious panic: ' "Who's our little patriot?" they'd say, when I was younger, and therefore smaller and shorter than I am now.' When Buffy says her group contains an ex-demon, Anya is horrified: 'Willow's a *demon*?!' Nigel asking Willow and Tara a simple question about their relationship with the Slayer turns into a fab rant of lesbian pride, whilst the girl Watcher's giggly interrogation/ flirtation with Spike is a season highlight (especially her revelation that she did her thesis on him. Spike seems delighted!). Buffy's fight with the Knights. Plus yet another glorious Spike/Joyce scene (see **34**, 'Becoming' Part 2; **42**, 'Lover's Walk').

'You May Remember Me From Such Films and TV Series As . . .': Troy Blendell's movies include *Larceny* and *Love & Sex*. Kris Iyer was in *Some Girl* and *High Freakquency*. Wesley Mask can be seen in *Not of this Earth* and *Victim of Desire*. Oliver Muirhead appeared in *Friends* and *Austin Powers: The Spy Who Shagged Me*. John O'Leary was in *The Haunted*, *Airplane!*, *Demon Seed* and *Gene Pool*.

Don't Give Up The Day Job: Cynthia Lamontagne appeared in *American Virgin* and *The Cable Guy*, and was Brian DePalma's assistant on *Carlito's Way*.

Valley-Speak: Glory: 'I've been cooling my heels in this crappy little town long enough.'

Cigarettes and Alcohol: Travers notes that when the Council inventoried the Magic Box they found a bottle of single malt scotch behind the incense holders. He says he could use a glass after Buffy's triumphant demolition of their scheme.

Logic, Let Me Introduce You to This Window: Buffy mentions that the Vikings discovered an America-shaped continent in the 1400s. In fact it is believed that they discovered North America as early as 1000. In the first scene, the sleeves on Buffy's shirt continually change position.

I Just *Love* Your Accent: A further example of Xander's mastery of a British accent. Dick Van Dyke's British accent, that is. Tara thought English people were gentle. Xander says if the Council deport Giles, they're not just destroying his career, but also condemning him to a lifetime diet of blood sausage and bangers and mash. *Hardly*. Giles calls the Council 'Poncey sods'. Lots of tea is drunk. Love the way when the Council throw everyone out of the Magic Box, they're terribly English about it ('Very sorry for the inconvenience').

Quote/Unquote: Nigel: 'Magical proficiency level?' Willow: 'High. Very high. One of those top levels.' Tara, panicking: 'Five!'

Buffy: 'You're Watchers. Without a Slayer you're pretty much watching *Masterpiece Theatre*. You can't stop Glory. You can't do anything with the information you have, except maybe publish it in the *Everyone Thinks We're Insanos Home Journal*. So here's how it's gonna work. You're gonna tell me everything you know. Then you're gonna go away. You'll contact me if and when you have any further information about Glory. The magic shop will remain open. Mr Giles will stay here as my official Watcher, reinstated at full salary.' Giles (pretending to cough): 'Retroactive!'

Travers: 'Glory isn't a demon.' Buffy: 'What is she?' Travers: 'She's a god.'

Notes: 'That was excellent!' Another cracking episode, rounding off all the questions about the Council of Watchers posed in **46**, 'Helpless', and bringing Buffy and Giles back into the fold. But completely on *her* terms. Lots of great little moments, and a stunning climax.

Buffy refers to the life-endangering test that the Watchers

Council put her through on her 18th birthday (see **46**, 'Helpless') and to the time she and Faith switched bodies, resulting in her being kidnapped (see **72**, 'Who Are You?'). Buffy mentions the two instances when she was within slaying distance of Glory (**83**, 'No Place Like Home'; **86**, 'Shadow'). Xander tells the Council about the Scoobies' spell to create Super-Buffy (see **77**, 'Primeval'). His arm is still in a cast after Olaf's vicious pummelling in **89**, 'Triangle'. Reference is made to Riley (and his sweater). Willow and Tara are still working on the 'ball of sunshine' spell (see **89**, 'Triangle'). Dawn is in Junior High; since she's 14, she's likely to be in 8th grade. Anya's full name is Anya Christina Emmanuella Jenkins and she was born 4 July 1980 in Indiana. Technically, of course, none of that is *true*, since this is merely a persona that Anyanka created for herself when she tried to grant Cordelia's wish (see **43**, 'The Wish'). Nigel says there is an accredited institution for witches, with which he presumes Willow and Tara should be registered (they're not). Joyce shares Spike's passion for *Passions*. Dawn seemingly does not.

Did You Know?: As reported in several UK newspapers, 14-year-old schoolgirl Heidi Rogan, from Middlesbrough, bravely fought off an attack by five teenage male thugs using martial arts moves she learned from watching *Buffy*. Finding herself surrounded, Heidi pole-axed one assailant with a punch to the stomach. She followed this with a jump-kick to the groin of another. The other three cowards promptly fled. 'Buffy's my hero and I think she would have been proud,' Heidi was quoted as saying.

91

Blood Ties

US Transmission Date: 6 Feb. 2001
UK Transmission Date: 30 Mar. 2001 (Sky)

Writer: Steven S DeKnight
Director: Michael Gersham
Cast: Michael Emanuel (Burly Guard), Candice Nicole (Young Buffy),
Joe Ochman (Janitor), Elyssa D Vito (Young Dawn)

It's Buffy's twentieth birthday but, having told the Scooby Gang at last about Dawn's true purpose, she finds little time to celebrate. Particularly after Dawn, with Spike's help, breaks into the Magic Box, and discovers the truth about The Key.

Dreaming (As Blondie Once Said) is Free: Dawn has a flashback to playing on the swings with Buffy when she was younger.

Dudes and Babes: A first direct hint about Ben's relationship with Glory. Jinx telling Ben 'your fate is directly linked to her magnificently-scented Glorificus. She's been extremely forgiving of your considerable foibles up until now but if you persist in your defiance, she'll be forced to . . .' 'What?' asks Ben. 'Send a six-pack of minions to bore me to death? Glory can't lay a finger on me. You know it.' Ben tells Dawn that he has a sister too, and that he often wishes that she didn't exist. And just when everybody in the audience is lulled into thinking, Ah, so Ben is Glory's brother . . . see **Surprise!**

A Little Learning is a Dangerous Thing: Dawn's homework is to imagine what she will be like ten years from now and write a letter to her future self. When she finds out that she's The Key, Dawn announces that she isn't going to school as, 'blobs of energy don't need an education'. When she finally does go, she's suspended for yelling obscenities at a teacher.

Denial, Thy Name is Buffy: Spike suggests that, if Buffy had been more honest with Dawn, she wouldn't be trying to make herself feel better with a round of 'Kick The Spike'.

The Conspiracy Starts at Home Time: Using *The Book of Tarnis* (written by a twelfth-century monk, one of the founders of the Order of Dagon, who built the Dagon-sphere), the Council has discovered that Glory and two fellow gods ruled over one of the more unpleasant demon dimensions. Anya and Giles confirm there are thousands of such dimensions, all different and all pushing on the edges of our reality, trying to find a way in. Glory now has, though being in human form has limited her godlike powers. All the gang have to worry about is that she's immortal, invulnerable, and insane, as living in this world is affecting her mental state – she's only able to keep her mind intact by extracting energy from the human brain. Giles adds that she absorbs the energies that bind the human mind into a cohesive whole. Once drained, all that's left behind is crazy people, which explains the increase in the ranks of the mentally unstable in Sunnydale. The Key isn't described in any known literature, but research indicates an energy matrix vibrating at a dimensional frequency beyond normal human perception. Only those outside reality can see The Key's true nature (see **80**, 'Real Me'). The Key is also susceptible to necromanced animal detection, particularly those of canine or serpent construct (see **86**, 'Shadow').

Surprise!: Ben is Glory. Didn't see *that* one coming at all.

It's a Designer Label!: Glory's gold dress. Buffy's red blouse and fur coat. Willow's Cowboy City sweater. There's a fantastic bit of continuity to **84**, 'Family', as we see that Ben keeps Glory's red dress in his locker should he/she require a quick change. Willow and Tara's present for Buffy is a frilly dress that Anya takes a shine to.

References: The series' first reference to *Teletubbies*. Also, *Little Red Riding Hood*, Michael Jackson's 'Bad', allusions to Sly and the Family Stone's 'It's a Family Affair', The Beatles' 'Get Back' and Bob Dylan's 'Don't Think Twice (It's Alright)' ('this doesn't have to be a complete waste of my precious time'), *Movie of the Week*, *The Simpsons* ('Your point being?'), *Wheel of Fortune*, R.E.M.'s 'What's the Frequency, Kenneth', the get-out-of-jail-free card from *Monopoly*™, Uncle Ben (the rice producer) and *Gentle Ben*.

Bitch!: Glory: 'Is that the best you little crap-gnats can muster?'

Buffy: 'Conversation's over, hell-bitch.'

Awesome!: Dawn's confrontation with Orlando in the hospital.

'You May Remember Me From Such Films and TV Series As . . .': Joe Ochman was in *Never Been Kissed* and *That's My Bush!* Justin Gorence appeared in *Puzzled*, *Melrose Place* and *The Sexperiment*.

Don't Give Up The Day Job: Paul Bates was an electrician on *The Princess Stallion*, a generator operator on *The Winter Guest* and appeared in *Coming to America*. Carl Johnson was a puppeteer on *Men in Black*. Two of the stuntmen in this episode are W Glenn Malmskog, stunt co-ordinator on *Rumble in the Streets* and *The Protector*, and Scott Rhodes, a second

unit director on *Citizen Toxie: The Toxic Avenger Part 4*,
stunts on *Vampire Vixens from Venus* and *Legion of the Dead*
and technical advisor on *Dogma*.

The Spell *Will* Work: Willow and Tara perform an early
warning incantation at the Magic Box and Buffy's house. 'If
anything hellgodishly powerful comes within a hundred feet,
then screechy siren things will, you know, screech.'

Valley-Speak: Buffy: 'What's the homework *sitch*?'

Dawn, to Spike: 'Geez! Lurk much?'

Spike, on Glory: 'I thought you said this skank was tough?'

Cigarettes and Alcohol: When he breaks into the Magic Box,
Spike uses the Urn of Ishtar as an ashtray.

Sex and Drugs and Rock'n'Roll: Anya tells Dawn that she
and Xander were 'talking about sex. You know us, sometimes
we like to pretend stuff . . .' Which seemingly involves Xander
dressing as a fireman, or a shepherd.

Logic, Let Me Introduce You to This Window: When
Willow mentions that Dawn has been keeping her diaries for
years and Buffy replies 'since she was seven. I remember too,
Will', Willow shouldn't *remember* this since, even in the new
timeline, Dawn was approximately ten when they met (when
Buffy and Joyce arrived in Sunnydale). Glory doesn't remember anything Dawn said to her when she was Ben (presumably
this also means that Ben knows nothing from the times when
Glory inhabits his body, though later episodes fail to entirely
clear this question up, and it doesn't explain how he knows
who the Knights of Byzantium are. See, **98**, 'Spiral'; **99**, 'The
Weight of the World'). When Dawn goes to her room and
slams the door, part of the PARENTAL ADVISORY LYRICS
poster on the opposite wall can be seen shaking in the mirror
indicating that the wall isn't real. When Dawn is ripping up her
diaries there's a magazine on the chest at the end of her bed
that subsequently disappears. When Buffy enters Spike's
crypt, whenever the camera shows Buffy from Spike's point of
view, it's bright enough that she creates a shadow on the stone
coffin. However, whenever the camera is behind Buffy, it's
much darker.

Quote/Unquote: Willow: 'You know what they say. The bigger
they are . . .' Anya: '. . . the faster they stomp you into nothing?'

Spike: 'Brown-robe types are always protecting something. It's the only way they can justify giving up girls.'

Orlando, to Dawn: 'Cracked bones. The sun bleeding into the sky. The Key is the link. The link must be severed. Such is the will of God. Such is the will of God. SUCH IS THE WILL OF GOD!'

Notes: 'She probably feels like she can say or do anything right now. She's not real. We're not her family, we don't even know what she is.' Given that the Dawn/Glory arc has been so smoothly mixed in with other storylines, this episode is the first time this season where it's felt like the show is running on the spot. That said, there's a great central performance by Michelle Trachtenberg.

Both Willow and Tara used to be scared by candles that don't blow out. Dawn and Buffy visited Hank in San Diego one summer (probably in 1999, between Season Three and Four) where they picked shells on the beach. Dawn doesn't like marshmallows (when she was five, Buffy told her they were made from monkey brains), though she does like hot chocolate. Willow performs a teleportation spell on Glory, giving herself a nosebleed and materialising Glory high above Sunnydale. After the fight in the hospital, Dawn is unable to remember that Glory and Ben are one and the same (see **98**, 'Spiral'). The playground was last seen in **45**, 'Gingerbread'. Xander refers to Dawn's crush on him (see **92**, 'Crush') and calls himself 'the Xan-Man', much to Giles's disgust.

Soundtrack: Star Ghost Dog's 'Holiday'.

Joss Whedon's Comments: The reaction to Willow's lesbian storyline has been, Joss told *E! Online*, 'Overwhelmingly positive, except for some extremely vocal people who are like, "I will no longer watch the show. You've made Willow a fag." It's not like I want to drive people away; I want to be inclusive. But it felt like the right step for Willow, and Seth wanted to go make movies, so it all fell into place. We thought why not have two people fall in love?'

92

Crush

US Transmission Date: 13 Feb. 2001
UK Transmission Date: 6 Apr. 2001 (Sky)

Writer: David Fury
Director: Daniel Attias
Cast: Walter Borchert (Jeff), Frederick Dawson (Porter),
Joseph Diciandomenico (Matt), Asher Glaser (Boy in Bronze),
Jennifer Bergman (Girl in Bronze),
Nell Shanahan (Waitress), Greg Wayne (Student)

To Buffy's horror, she discovers that Spike has a crush on her. She's dealing with it pretty well until Drusilla returns to Sunnydale from her deranged rampage with Darla in Los Angeles, kills a trainload of passengers and tries to return Spike to his former glory.

Dudes and Babes: Drusilla leaves Sunnydale at the climax, as does Harmony, who is next seen seeking out her old friend Cordelia in LA in *Angel*: 'Disharmony'.

A Little Learning is a Dangerous Thing: Willow and Tara discuss Quasimodo's unrequited love for Esmeralda in Victor Hugo's *The Hunchback of Notre Dame* ('You can tell it's not gonna have a happy ending when the main guy's all bumpy').

Denial, Thy Name is Spike: 'The only chance you had with me was when I was unconscious,' Buffy tells him and, of course, she's right. Poor Spike, he loses every smidgen of dignity that he ever almost had in his relentless obsession with the Slayer. He even seems to know, telling Buffy: '*This*, with you, is wrong. I know it. I'm not a complete idiot.' Buffy slamming the door in his face at the end is the final cold insult.

It's a Designer Label!: Spike has stolen Buffy's tasteful blue cashmere sweater. Harmony's sexy negligee, the Bronze waitresses' silver pants, Buffy's leather trousers. Dawn thinks Spike's hair and leather coat are 'cool and stuff'.

References: Xander calls Spike 'Un-*Evil Dead*'. The porter at Sunnydale station has a copy of *The Amazing Spider-Man*. Instead of reading *The Hunchback of Notre Dame*, Buffy rented the movie. Not the Charles Laughton classic either, but rather the Disney version with singing gargoyles. Plus, obliquely the Beatles' 'Help!', *Quantum Leap* ('Oh boy'), *Family Fortunes* ('Survey says vampires'), The Small Faces' 'Tin Soldier', Anne Rice's *Queen of the Damned*, actress Charlize Theron (*2 Days in the Valley*, *The Devil's Advocate*, *The Astronaut's Wife*) and Morticia from *The Addams Family*. Drusilla alludes to the game 'musical chairs'.

In one of the documentaries on the *Buffy* Season 2 DVDs, Marti Noxon describes the inspiration for Spike and Drusilla, and their loving-yet-self-destructive relationship, as being Sex Pistols bassist, Sid Vicious, and his girlfriend Nancy Spungen (as played in Alex Cox's controversial *Sid & Nancy* by Gary Oldman and Chloe Webb). When Vicious was arrested for Spungen's murder in 1978, his reported confession to the police was: 'I done it. I'm a dirty dog.' Dru compares Spike to a 'bad dog' on several occasions.

Bitch!: Xander, to Spike: 'Listen, bleach boy, I don't have a chip in my head. I can do far more damage to you than you can ever do to me.'

Spike, on women troubles: 'Why do you bitches torture me?'

Awesome!: Anya dancing. Sexy. Buffy sitting down in the train carriage in the exact (tape-marked) position of one of Dru's victims. Dru's amused expression when Harmony calls Spike 'boo-boo'. Spike telling Dawn a horror story of him murdering a family and, just as he gets to the most gruesome part (finding the little girl), Buffy enters the crypt and demands that he finish: 'So I rip it open, very violent, haul her out of there . . . And then I give her to a good family in a nice home, where they're never ever mean to her, and didn't lock her in the coal bin!' As Dawn says: 'That's *so* lame!' Buffy and Dawn's subsequent soul-versus-chip debate continues when Buffy tells Spike he cannot love without a soul. Drusilla replies: 'We *can* love quite well. If not wisely.' Spike says if Buffy doesn't admit that there's something between them, he'll untie Dru and let her kill Buffy instead. Drusilla adds: 'Yes please. I like that game much more!' Plus Spike and Dru in the Bronze.

Don't Give Up The Day Job: Jennifer Bergman was a visual effects producer on *Blade* and *Firestorm*.

Valley-Speak: Tara: 'I'm down with that.'

Buffy: 'Hanging out with Spike is not cool, Dawn, OK? It's dangerous, and icky.'

Cigarettes and Alcohol: Spike drinks bourbon from a hip flask and Budweiser in the Bronze.

Sex and Drugs and Rock'n'Roll: The Bronze is having a Grand Reopening, having been extensively remodelled following its demolition by Olaf in **89**, 'Triangle'. Xander is horrified when he is told that Dawn may have a crush on Spike. Because 'It's always been me. Big funny Xander. What, she just suddenly decides I'm not cool any more?' (see **91**, 'Blood Ties').

When Harmony suggests that she and Spike 'play a game', to spice up their love life, the next shot is of Harmony wearing Buffy's blue sweater and a pair of stretchpants and holding a stake. She stalks round the crypt, saying: 'I'm gonna stake you . . . bad, evil vampire!' Spike, shirtless, then lunges from the darkness, aroused. Harmony says she isn't interested in threesomes unless it's boy-boy-girl, or Charlize Theron is involved. When Buffy is asked if she may innocently have encouraged Spike, she notes: 'I *do* beat him up a lot. For Spike that's like third base.'

The Base System: For readers unfamiliar with baseball or contact with the opposite sex (or both) it goes like this. First base is kissing, second base is groping, third base is oral sex ('Ah, *third base,*' remembers Chandler fondly in *Friends*; see also *American Pie*) and home run is intercourse itself.

'West Hollywood?': When Buffy notes that the two vampires have 'nested', Spike asks: 'You're saying they're a couple of *poofters*?'

Logic, Let Me Introduce You to This Window: When Spike and Buffy attack the two vampires, one is making popcorn over a lantern. They run away and Spike moves to follow, by which time the popcorn has disappeared, only to reappear a moment later. Why doesn't Spike's victim in the Bronze struggle or scream? Is she already dead? That seems to be the suggestion since Spike can drink from her, but *how*? Dru didn't appear to snap her neck or do anything other than push her gently in Spike's direction. There's no date on the issue of *The Sunnydale Press* that Buffy reads.

I Just *Love* Your Accent: Spike: 'Bleedin' crime, is what it is.

Jackin' up the bar-price to pay for fixin' up this sinkhole. Not my fault insurance doesn't cover Act of Troll.' And, to Buffy: 'You are completely off your bird?' He tells Buffy not to get her knickers twisted and uses both 'bint' and 'cock up' in casual conversation. One of Drusilla's victims on the train is wearing a cricket sweater.

Motors: Spike has a car in which he and Buffy stake out the vampires. Spike hums the Ramones' 'I Wanna Be Sedated', although as Buffy notes in **46**, 'Helpless', she can't stand guys who hum. So poor Spike never had a chance.

Quote/Unquote: Joyce, when Buffy returns from the Bronze: 'I wasn't feeling all that safe with you gone. At first. Then I remembered that Rupert was here and I felt much, much safer.'

Buffy: 'You're like a serial killer in prison.' Spike: 'Women marry 'em all the time!'

Drusilla: 'Electricity lies, Spike. It tells you you're not a bad dog. But you are.'

Spike, telling Buffy he will kill Drusilla to prove his love: 'You have the slightest idea what she means to me? It's the face of my salvation. She delivered me from mediocrity. For over a century we cut a swath through continents. A hundred years, she never stopped surprising me. Never stopped taking me to new depths. I was a lucky bloke just to touch such a black beauty.'

Notes: 'Even if I did have a crush, he wouldn't notice in a million years. Spike's totally into you.' A compelling look at unrequited love and obsession which begins by showing Spike as sympathetic and ends with him as simply pathetic. One of the best scripts of the season, with a ton of clever set pieces and brilliant wordplay. A gem.

Willow is still experiencing headaches and nosebleeds after her teleportation spell in **91**, 'Blood Ties'. Dawn says she was not originally human. 'I was,' notes Spike. 'I got over it' (see **85**, 'Fool for Love'). Spike asks Drusilla: 'Darla got mojo'd back from the beyond. You vamped her and now she and you are working on turning Angel into his own bad-self again?' Dru replies: 'Didn't care for Angelus setting us on fire,' a summation of the *Angel* episodes 'To Shanshu in L.A', 'Dear Boy', 'The Trial', 'Reunion' and 'Redefinition'. Dru still carries the burn scars from the latter. Drusilla wants Spike to return with her to Los Angeles so that they can be a family again. Spike says he has 'done the L.A. scene' and it didn't agree with him. He mentions Dru leaving him for a chaos demon (see **42**, 'Lover's Walk'; **85**, 'Fool for Love'). The *Sunnydale Press* headline is: METROTRAIN MURDER. SIX FOUND MURDERED ON TRAIN AT SUNNYDALE STATION. The newspaper costs 35¢ daily. The article was written by Jeannie Lozammo.

Soundtrack: 'Key' by Devics, and two songs by Summercamp: 'Play It By Ear' and 'Happy'.

Critique: 'A deliciously twisted, funny valentine, just missing the jugular by a crucial inch,' wrote Mark Wyman in *TV Zone*. 'The Bronze nightclub's reopening mirrors the series' revivification. Harmony role-plays as Buffy to arouse Spike, while a railway massacre points to a rarity: a dangerous vampire at large in Sunnydale . . . James Marsters' brilliantly shaded performance [makes] Buffy (whose response to him is morally accurate) seem the cruel-hearted one.'

Did You Know?: Sarah Michelle Gellar used an interview with *Cosmopolitan* to pay tribute to her mother: 'Everything I am is because of my mom,' Gellar says of the woman who guided her between auditions and school. She is less effusive about her father, who divorced her mother when Gellar was seven, describing him as non-existent in her life. Pressed to elaborate, she borrowed Keanu Reeves' famous line from *Parenthood*: 'You need a licence to go fishing, you need a licence to drive, but any butt-reaming asshole can be a father.'

93

I Was Made to Love You

US Transmission Date: 20 Feb. 2001
UK Transmission Date: 13 Apr. 2001 (Sky)

Writer: Jane Espenson
Director: James A Contner
Cast: Gil Christner (Resident), Paul Darrigo (Driver),
Amelinda Embry (Katrina), Shonda Farr (April),
Kelly Felix (Teenager), Paul Walia (Friend)

A pretty girl, April, arrives in Sunnydale looking for her boy-friend, Warren. After proving herself to be extraordinarily strong, the gang deduce she is a robot, built by a lonely teen-ager who couldn't get dates. Buffy tracks down Warren and his creation and stays with the android until her power runs out. Arriving home, Buffy finds Joyce motionless on the couch.

Dudes and Babes: April arrives at the Spring Break party and makes many heads turn. Anya graciously allows Xander a moment's distraction, although Tara is surprisingly jealous by Willow's sudden loss of concentration. When Spike tries to chat April up, she throws him through a window. 'She's a sexbot,' notes Xander, and asks what guy doesn't dream about such a concept. Looking up, he finds Anya, Willow, Tara and Buffy scowling at him. 'Too many girls,' he laments. 'I miss Oz. He'd get it. He wouldn't say anything, but he'd get it.'

At the party, Buffy and Ben cautiously arrange to go for a coffee, with the hope that it won't lead to anything further (like Ben having to leave town, for instance). Joyce has a date with Brian, a 'nice normal guy' who works for a publishing house and sends her flowers thanking her for a lovely evening. Joyce teases Buffy that she may have left her bra in Brian's car.

Instant Karma: Anya is familiar with the Hindu philosophy of karma (the law of cause and effect, rebirth and spiritual release) and expects an instantaneous reward for allowing Xander to dance with a depressed Buffy.

Babysitting: Giles's evening with Dawn consisted of listening to 'aggressively cheerful music sung by people chosen for their ability to dance', then eating cookie dough and talking about boys. How awful.

Denial, Thy Name is Buffy: Despite Giles and Xander's assurances that Buffy can't be held responsible for what Spike feels, Buffy stills considers that 'something about me had to make him feel . . . "that's the one for me!"' Coming so soon after Riley's defection, Spike's attraction to her seems to have shaken Buffy more than she is willing to admit.

Denial, Thy Name is Spike: Spike goes to the Magic Box and talks to the Scoobies about misrepresentations, misunderstand-ings, slurs and allegations, claiming that he and Buffy were working together to get rid of Dru (see **92**, 'Crush'). 'We are not your friends,' Giles tells him. 'This thing. Get over it. Move-the-hell-on.' Unfortunately, Spike's idea of moving on is to commission Warren to create a Buffy robot for him (see **96**, 'Intervention').

Denial, Thy Name is Warren: 'So you have girl troubles?' Buffy asks. Warren confirms this – he couldn't get a date, so he created April to love him: 'I didn't make a toy. I made a girlfriend.' But Warren found April too predictable and she became boring. 'She was exactly what I wanted and I didn't want her.' Then he met Katrina in his engineering seminar. She was funny and cool and built model monorails that run with magnets. Warren fell in love with *her*. Left with the complex issue of what to do with April, Warren simply abandoned her in his dorm room believing that whilst he was away her batteries would run out.

The Conspiracy Starts at Home Time: Buffy tells Warren, 'My name's Buffy Summers. We were at Sunnydale High together. *Do you know who I am?*' Warren replies 'Yes, I know.' It's clear that they're talking about the knowledge among Buffy's contemporaries about her status as Class Protector and that she is the girl who fights the monsters that terrorised their childhood (see **54**, 'The Prom').

Technophobia!: Anya says computers were once confusing to her. 'I'm eleven hundred years old. I had trouble adjusting to the idea of Lutherans.' She has, however, become addicted to online trading. The secret, she says, is to avoid tech companies, and go with smaller firms that supply basic components. Her initial investment tripled and she is now thinking of buying something expensive. Maybe an antelope. She designed a website for the Magic Box with a huge photo of herself on it. Anya is also the first to spot something odd about April, noting that the girl speaks with a strange evenness and selects her words too precisely. Tara admits that she goes online occasionally but 'everyone's spelling is really bad'.

Among the programs Warren installed in April are kissing_01.gfd, kissing_02.gfd, lstn sympthtc.gfd, gv_hm_prsnts.gfd, *four* sex files, praise.gfd, neckrubs.gfd, three fetish files and at least *six* positions files. Underneath 'Warren' and 'Boyfriend' appear other identifiers: really smart, handsome, best lover, snappy dresser and good dancer. She is also programmed to fight, with disciplines including kung fu, judo and karate.

Work is a Four-Letter Word: When Tara notes that April at least didn't do much damage, Xander looks at the broken window and replies: 'Double-glazed windows ain't cheap. The jamb needs to be completely repaired. Dear God, I'm the grown-up who sees the world through my job. I'm like my uncle Dave, the plumber.' When fixing the damage later, Buffy asks if he really understands the terminology he's using. Xander confirms that he does: 'Scary, isn't it? I've turned into someone you want around after a crazed robot attack.' 'If you ever start your own business,' Buffy replies, 'you have your slogan right there.'

It's a Designer Label!: Buffy thinks Joyce's dress is not mom-ish at all. 'It's sexy. It screams, "Randy-sex-kitten, buy me one drink and I'll . . ."' Buffy's purple hooded top appears again. April's pink flowery dress and Buffy's sparkly gold top.

References: The title is from Lorraine Cato's 1996 hit. There's a possible oblique reference to the Who's 'The Kids Are Alright' and a direct one to the Beach Boys' 'Do You Wanna Dance?' Also, actor Warren Beatty, President Warren Harding (1865–1923), Prince Charming from *Cinderella*. The plot may have been influenced by *Weird Science*, *Westworld*, *Wonder Woman* and *Mannequin*.

Bitch!: Buffy, after April has thrown her across the room: 'I've had it with super-strong little women who aren't me.'

Tara: 'Do you have any books on robots?' Giles: 'Dozens. There's an enormous amount of research we should do . . . No, I'm lying. I haven't got squat, I just like to see Xander squirm.'

Awesome!: Buffy taking out her revulsion at Spike's attraction on a hugely padded 'Puffy Xander' ('I'm alive,' he tells her when the assault is over, 'I can tell 'cos of the pain'). Also, Ben standing in the middle of the apartment wearing Glory's red dress after getting off the phone and Buffy's fight with a growling April. There's also the first presentation of a harder Giles (see **100**, 'The Gift') in his confrontation with Spike. And, of course, the final scene (see **94**, 'The Body').

'You May Remember Me From Such Films and TV Series As . . .': Adam Busch was Kyle in *Magic Rock* and Manolo in

Léon. Shonda Farr appeared in *What Friends Are For*, *Idiot Savants* and *Jack Frost 2: The Revenge of the Mutant Killer Snowman*. Kelly Felix was in *Sally and Johnny* and *A.I. Artificial Intelligence*. Gil Christner was Ed the Hippy in *More American Graffiti* and can also be seen in *Mystery Men* and *Masque of the Red Death*. Amelinda Embry was in *Romy and Michele's High School Reunion*.

Don't Give Up The Day Job: Paul Darrigo was a casting apprentice on *Piranha*.

Valley-Speak: Buffy: 'You're one creepy little *dweeb*.'

Logic, Let Me Introduce You to This Window: Who invited Ben to the Spring Break party at Sunnydale U? Come to that, who invited Warren and Katrina, both of whom attend another college? When April throws Spike through the window, it's obviously a dummy. When Katrina walks out on Warren, she leaves wearing a green T-shirt and with no bags (that, in itself, is hard to believe, though she's clearly acting on impulse). Next time we see her, she's acquired a thick ginger cardigan.

Cruelty to Vampires: 'That's my secret to attracting men,' Buffy tells Xander. 'You slap 'em around a bit, torture 'em, make their lives a living hell ... Sure, the nice guys, they'll run away, but every now and then you meet a real prince-of-a-guy like Spike who gets off on it.'

Quote/Unquote: Buffy: 'I'm very sorry, but if it makes you feel any better, my "funtime-Buffy-party night" involved watching a robot throw Spike through a window, so if you wanna trade ... No, wait, I wouldn't give *that* memory up for anything.'

Notes: 'This is something that you can't possibly know. She's a robot.' Another episode that got a generally less-than-favourable review from the *cognoscenti* but, again, it's hard to see why. A serious study about male obsession (almost all of the male characters have something to be ashamed of) and its mirror image, female denial – but with enough laughs to cheer up even a professional misanthrope if you don't step on the cracks. I love it. Magic Jane *again*, doing the seemingly impossible and gently debunking a standard media cliché, in this case the image men have in their search for the perfect woman. A nice juxtaposition with the *Angel* episode 'Happy Anniversary' shown two weeks before and dealing with broadly similar subjects but in a very different way.

Warren went to Sunnydale High with Buffy for a semester, then graduated to technical college in Dutton. Dawn refers to the events of **23**, 'Ted' – a further example of the way in which *Buffy*'s past now, seemingly, includes Dawn as part of it (see **91**, 'Blood Ties').

Soundtrack: Mellonova's 'Hideeho', 'Kawanga!' by Los Straitjackets and Caviar's 'OK Nightmare'.

Did You Know (Maybe)?: A popular fan rumour is that the robot-girl, April, was written specifically with Sarah Michelle Gellar's friend, teen-pop sensation Britney Spears, in mind. No one from the production has yet confirmed this although before the season began Marti Noxon told *Entertainment Weekly* that a Britney appearance was 'very likely'.

Jane Espenson's Comments: 'I love Giles making a joke,' Jane told *Xposé*. 'Because you expect him to be a stuffy fellow. It's nice to let him have some fun.' Jane's first comic, *Jonathan*, was based in the alternative universe she created in **73**, 'Superstar', and she was also writer of the one-shot *The Lone Gunmen* comic for Dark Horse, based on the popular characters of Byers, Langly and Frohike created by Chris Carter in *The X-Files*. This summer she's contributing to an eagerly awaited comic anthology called *Tales of the Slayer*. '[There'll be] much growth and change,' she notes, 'but with the same delicious *Buffy* flavour.'

94

The Body

US Transmission Date: 27 Feb. 2001
UK Transmission Date: 20 Apr. 2001 (Sky)

Writer: Joss Whedon
Director: Joss Whedon
Cast: Tia Matza (Teacher), J Evan Bonifant (Kevin),
Rae'ven Larrymore Kelly (Lisa), Kelli Garner (Kristie),
Kevin Cristalon (First Paramedic), Stefan Umstead (Second Paramedic),
Loanne Bishop (911 Operator), John Michael Herndon (Vampire)

Joyce is dead, despite Buffy's frantic efforts to save her. Buffy,

Dawn and their friends must each deal with the loss as best they can. But, on the Hellmouth, life goes on.

Dreaming (As Blondie Once Said) is Free: The Christmas flashback that opens the episode. Plus the extraordinary use of imaginary sequences of Joyce recovering, slipping in and out the narrative.

Dudes and Babes: Tara says that Willow likes it when she rubs Willow's tummy.

A Little Learning is a Dangerous Thing: Concerning Santa, Anya says it's a myth that *he's* a myth. He's been around since the 1500s. He wasn't always called Santa, but Christmas night, flying reindeer, coming down chimneys is all true. Of course, he doesn't traditionally bring presents so much as disembowel children.

Work is a Four-Letter Word: When Xander punches a hole in Willow's wall, he notes: 'In my defence, some crappy wallmanship.'

It's a Designer Label!: 'The first person I ever lost, I had to find a black tie, because I thought you *had* to wear one to a funeral,' Joss told an online interview. 'Of course, it was California, so people showed up in Hawaiian shirts, but I didn't know that. I couldn't find one anywhere in L.A. I was sweating, like, "If I don't find this, it'll be *sacrilege*." That's where the Willow-thing came from.'

References: Allusions to *Xena: Warrior Princess* ('Strong like an Amazon') and Marvel's *The Avengers* ('Gotta get with the assembling', see **57**, 'The Freshman'). There's a SMOKING SUCKS poster on the school corridor wall. Willow and Tara's room has a poster for String Cheese Incident. 'The Body' is the title of a Stephen King novella (filmed as *Stand By Me*) which is thematically very similar to this – young people's reactions to death as a rite of passage.

Awesome!: The Christmas memories. That awful moment where Buffy, administering CPR, snaps one of Joyce's ribs. Buffy straightening Joyce's skirt as the paramedics arrive. The first imaginary sequence ('It's a beautiful miracle') and the relief the audience feels, which is suddenly crushed when you realise that this is all going on in Buffy's head. The strange camera angles reflecting Buffy's dislocation and inability to look the paramedic in the face as he tells her that her mother is dead. The incredibly voyeuristic moments of Buffy alone, wandering around the house in a state of shock, sinking to her knees and vomiting. Dawn's school life: how clever and yet obvious that she should have her own versions of Willow, Xander and Cordelia. Dawn's drawing. Willow's frustration at her inability to find appropriate clothes. *The kiss.* Xander's impotent anger at the unfairness of it all. Anya's confusion on how she should act – leading to one of the finest moments in the series as she tearfully remembers the things that Joyce liked to do. Tara's numb empathy with the pain of others. Dr Kriegel lying to Buffy in voice-over – 'to make you feel better'. Tara telling Buffy about her own mother's death ('I know it's different for you . . . It's *always* different'). The vampire waking up in the morgue as Dawn looks at Joyce's body. The final extraordinary lines.

'You May Remember Me From Such Films and TV Series As . . .': J Evan Bonifant was Buster in *Blues Brothers 2000*, Steven in *Dottie Gets Spanked* and Tum Tum in *3 Ninjas Kick Back*. Kelli Garner was in *Bully* and *Hometown Legends*. Tia Matza played Vicky in *Jackpot*. Loanne Bishop appeared in *Kiss the Girls*, *Kalifornia* and *Hill Street Blues*. Stefan Umstead was in *The Ice Cream Man*. Rae'ven Larrymore Kelly was Wanda in *Maximum Bob*, provided voices on *The Dead Presidents* and appeared in *The Ditchdigger's Daughters*, *A Time to Kill* and *Flossin*.

Valley-Speak: Lisa: 'That was when you were wiggin' out about your family.'

Kevin: 'Kirstie, man. It's like she thinks, "I'm so hot, everybody should just bow down before me." And I'm, like, *whatever*.'

Cigarettes and Alcohol: Dawn says her nog tastes funny; she thinks she got one with rum in it. Giles is seen opening a bottle of red wine.

Logic, Let Me Introduce You to This Window: As several fans with medical backgrounds pointed out (loudly) on the Net, some of the paramedics' actions are inaccurate. They shouldn't have called time of death (in most states, including California, only a doctor can do that). Joyce should have been taken to hospital where she would have been declared DOA. Once CPR has been started by paramedics, it cannot be stopped until the patient is transferred to someone with a higher degree of medical training, and certainly not for the reason that the paramedics have another call to go to. It's also unlikely (although not inconceivable) that Buffy would have been left alone with the body. Chest compressions should be done with straight arms, at a 90 degree angle to the ground, slower than depicted by either Buffy or the medic and much deeper. For Buffy this is to be expected but, for trained medical staff, it's inexcusable (although, to be fair, doing compressions 'properly' on an actor is probably not good for their health). The police should also have been called to conduct a preliminary interview and determine cause of death (although there's nothing to indicate that this wasn't done off-screen). Why is Dr Kriegel, Joyce's surgeon, doing her autopsy? Shouldn't a pathologist do that? It seems churlish to mention this but Kristine Sutherland does, briefly, appear to breathe during Buffy's frantic attempts to revive her.

Motors: Xander now owns a car.

Quote/Unquote: Willow: 'Why can't I be a grown-up?'

Anya: 'I don't understand how this all happens. How we go through this. I knew her, and then she's just a body, and I don't understand why she just can't get back in it and not be dead anymore. It's mortal and stupid. And Xander's crying and not talking, and I was having fruit punch, and I thought, well, Joyce will never have any more fruit punch ever. And she'll never have eggs, or yawn or brush her hair, not ever, and no one will explain to me why.'

Dawn, poised to touch Joyce's body: 'Is she cold?' Buffy: 'It's not her . . . She's gone.'

Notes: 'We're not supposed to move the body.' A bittersweet symphony. A thing of grace, power and immense beauty, 'The Body' is like an act of flagellation; painful, but necessary. It asks some hard questions about *Buffy*'s traditionally blasé attitude to mortality by making the death of a much-loved character, itself, almost a throwaway prelude to the *real* horror that follows – the horror of coping with death. The characters move around the subject, circling it, avoiding dealing with it.

Death depersonalises Joyce, stripping her of an identity until she is merely 'the body'. But the vampire in the morgue is the body too. Everything is reduced to incidentals – particularly the vampire attack on Dawn. This takes on an operatic quality of side-theatre dismissed by an outraged Buffy with a smile on her face as she decapitates the series' most extreme presentation of a vampire-as-non-human (deathly pale, naked, autopsy scar still visible) whilst her sister shows no interest in the event. There is so much to appreciate in this extraordinary piece of work. The story develops in an impressively non-linear fashion without traditional signposts that tell the viewer what a dream sequence is trying to say. There's also Tara and Willow's kiss – not erotic or out-of-place but genuine and loving in a moment of abject defeat. The performances are wonderful: Amber Benson's anguished silence; Alyson Hannigan's portrayal of Willow facing her up to the realisation that the world will not allow you to remain a child forever; Emma Caulfield's finest hour. Sarah Michelle gives a stunning turn, full of tiny details. And then there is Michelle Trachtenberg. Her performance is worthy of a very experienced and mature actress. Which, of course, she is. She's also *fifteen*. And the fact that this lyrical piece didn't even earn a *nomination* for an Emmy is one of the most shameful disgraces in the history of those most arbitrary of awards.

Buffy asks Joyce and Giles to stay away from the band candy (see **40**, 'Band Candy'). 1630 Rivelo Drive is near Hadley. Dawn's best friend is called Lisa. Last week Kevin Berman said she was 'freaky', though he turns out to be sympathetic and likes Dawn a lot. Her nemesis is a bitchy girl called Kirstie. Tara's mother died when she was seventeen.
Soundtrack: The only music heard is a brief snatch of the Christmas Carol 'The First Noël'.
Critique: 'Emmy voters take note,' wrote *TV Guide*'s Michael Ausiello, 'last week's haunting episode of *Buffy* in which the Scooby Gang mourned the death of Buffy's mother instantly earned a place as one of the finest hours of television ever produced.' 'There was a lot of integrity in this,' added Matt Roush, 'not just in how it played, but in how it wasn't oversold.' The *Guardian*'s Gareth McLean was moved to write:

'Again the allegation that *Buffy* is just another schmaltzy American teenshow (*Dawson's Creek* with fangs) is refuted. This episode was a brave, honest and wrenching portrayal of death and loss. This is a world in which death is commonplace, but *this* death moved away from cartoonish vanquishing of vampires and was all the more devastating for it. Joyce died on her couch looking as surprised as the rest of us at her passing. She died as *people* do.' Mark Wyman in *TV Zone* described the episode as 'A painful, grief-stricken drama played out in four acts, largely in real-time – with no music, precious little fantasy, and a numbing sadness throughout. Quite rightly, it's been hailed as one of *Buffy*'s finest hours.' In *SFX*, Paul Cornell added that the episode is concerned with reality: 'Whedon directs our attention to the oddness of real life ... The acting honours go to Kristine Sutherland. Here's a woman who's willing to abandon dignity altogether for her craft, and play a corpse in an unflattering, knocked-about, utterly real way.' An editorial on the website *teevee.org* considered 'the fact that this episode was not nominated for any Emmy awards is all the proof you need that the Academy is comprised of a half-dozen drooling, comatose octogenarians. In what may be the best single hour of network drama in the past five years, Gellar's performance was positively searing, especially the opening ten minutes when the Slayer finds her mom splayed out on the couch. Buffy aged twenty years before the hour was over and Gellar pulled off a minor miracle in turning her snappy-but-weary-twentysomething into a crushed soul.' 'One of the toughest hours of television I've ever weathered,' noted Susan Kuhn at *scifi_ign.com*. Praising the episode's occasionally claustrophobic camerawork, lack of soundtrack and almost no supernatural influences she drew particular attention to Emma Caulfield's performance. 'Anya has her purest expression of emotion. When she starts to cry and express those feelings of a being who has never dealt with death or loss before, it's a beautiful thing, a manifestation of the deepest of human aches.'

Did You Know?: At the *Angel* seminar at the Museum of Television and Radio's 18th annual William S Paley Television Festival in Los Angeles, Charisma Carpenter asked a question that many fans wanted the answer to: 'Why didn't you close [Joyce's] eyes?' Joss replied: 'To make it worse.' He also confirmed a long-held fan suspicion, that the production team purposely tries to pair a really dark *Buffy* episode with a lighter *Angel*, and vice versa.

Nick Brendon's Comments: 'I thought it was going to be much more sombre,' Nick told *E! Online*. 'It did really affect people. It was a lot warmer on the set than I'd anticipated. People were kind of reminiscing and going through that. It was a blessing.'

Kristine Sutherland's Comments: 'Joss wanted to make it clear that this was *real* death. This wasn't about vampires. Our society doesn't grapple with death at all,' Kristine told *SFX*'s Paul Simpson and Ruth Thomas in a revealing interview. 'I thought that in closing a person's eyes, it's a way of telling ourselves that they're asleep, and not really dead. We make up dead bodies so they look like they're still alive, and shove them off to funeral homes and pretend they don't exist. Europeans don't have that same "let's clean death up" attitude. Their reaction to death is not quite as antiseptic as ours. At an Irish wake you lay the body out on the kitchen table and everybody comes to look at it and have a big party. So, not closing Joyce's eyes was definitely scripted that way. The make-up was scripted as well. Todd [McIntosh, head of the make up department] structured it so that it was a gradual progression until, in the morgue, I was literally grey-blue.' Asked when she knew that Joyce was going to suffer an illness and die, Kristine's answer will amaze many: 'Before I went to Italy [at the beginning of Season Four]. I probably wouldn't have known that early but, when I told Joss that I was planning on going away for a year, he said "But you have to come back. I need to kill you! And it's really important!"'

'Strangely enough, my mother had an aneurysm,' Kristine continued, before explaining that, at one stage in the planning of the arc, Joss's idea was that Joyce had 'adopted a young girl, maybe five or six years old, so it was interesting how the adoption became [Dawn]. I knew that Joyce was going to get ill, then get better, then suddenly be gone. After I had the surgery, people had the idea that I would have my head shaved and wear a wig. I said "You can't do that", because I knew from my mother that would not happen.' She also revealed that in most of the episode, she is playing Joyce's body. 'There might have been some times during the fight in the morgue where it was so in the background that they put in a mannequin, but I did an awful lot of laying around dead.' Another revelation was that the Christmas scenes were filmed first. 'All the stuff where [Joyce was alive] was shot the first day. We did the Christmas scene and then did the waking up in the ambulance stuff, and by the time that we started to do that, the mood on the set really changed. It was a very sombre set.'

The death of a much-loved character can be hard on the viewers, but Joyce's many fans can take comfort from the fact that there are plans for the character to return in the future and Kristine says she's looking forward to this. But only in flashbacks and dream sequences. 'There will be no real return for sure, because I *am* dead.' As for regrets: 'I always wished to do more of Joyce at work. Have a chance to explore her as a working woman. She had a job and provided the money for herself and the house and her daughter. Her capabilities as a single mother – they often explored her at home. I would've liked to have ventured into that area a bit more.'

Joss Whedon's Comments: Explaining the purpose of the Christmas flashback to *TV Guide*, Joss noted: 'I wanted to get the credits over with. I knew that I had to have opening credits and I knew that there was no way that I was going to put them over the 911 sequence.' Hence, the Christmas gathering: 'It gave me a great transition from happy-to-dead,' he continued, adding that: 'Music would have been too easy. It would [tell you] to feel sad. I wanted to not have that safety net.' On Willow and Tara's overdue kiss: 'They are living together so they're probably already kissing. To make a big deal of it would've been wrong.' He waited for the right moment to script the scene. 'It belongs somewhere you least expect it.' WB execs, however, asked Whedon to cut the kiss, a request he flatly refused. 'I said "the kiss is in, or I'm walking." This belongs in the show . . . There was one discussion and only one.' A WB representative responded: 'We had questions, but after reviewing the final cut, we chose to air it.' The brutal realism of the episode was interrupted by the vampire in the final act. 'I stayed away from unnatural things as much as possible,' Joss admits. 'I didn't have Glory or even Spike in the episode because I wanted everything to be very real. But because the show is *Buffy*, vampires are part of that world. So I wanted to have the vampire fight, but put it in the context of this occasion, because life is still going on . . . This tragedy has occurred and the world is supposed to stop. Some people thought that at the beginning of the next episode, Dawn was going to touch Joyce and heal her. I'm like, "Missing the point!"' Joss adds that the idea to leave Buffy and Dawn orphans was conceived some time ago, and that 'If you brought [Joyce] back, it would have to be extremely earned, and there would have to be a good reason for it.'

'This is a rite of passage that people go through. That I went through myself,' Joss told *scifi_ign.com*. 'I lost my mother several years ago. I wanted to capture something much more abstract. A morbidly physical reality of death and grief, of that first few hours. Just the incomprehensibleness of it, and the different ways everybody deals with it. My whole cast was extraordinary. But I really thought people were going to hate it, because the whole point was, there's no catharsis. It was just, "My mother is a dead body. And that's all." But people actually *did* get a catharsis from it. A lot of people who have experienced loss said it helped them to deal with it or that it moved them. I was surprised by that.'

95

Forever

US Transmission Date: 17 Apr. 2001
UK Transmission Date: 27 Apr. 2001 (Sky)

Writer: Marti Noxon
Director: Marti Noxon
Cast: Andrea Gall (Customer), Alan Henry Brown (Funeral Director),
Darius Dudley (Minister), Annie Talbot (Lady with Baby),
Noor Shic (Lady with Rosary)

Joyce's funeral is held, and Angel returns to comfort Buffy. Dawn, with Spike's help, visits Doc, an expert in resurrection, in an attempt to bring Joyce back. Despite being warned of potentially dire consequences, she casts the spell, only to change her mind at the last moment.

Dudes and Babes and Those of Indeterminate Origin: When Jinx tells Ben, 'every moment you fight Glory, you're only fighting yourself,' he's talking literally. Ben attempts to kill Jinx to protect Dawn's secret, but the minion survives, and Glory now knows that The Key has human form. Whatever Doc is, he isn't human. He has a tail and his eyes turn black when he tells Dawn to keep in touch (see **99**, 'The Weight of the World').

A Little Learning is a Dangerous Thing: Giles keeps most of his potent texts and potions away from the public on the first floor of the Magic Box.

What is Willow playing at? Here we see the basic difference between being a witch and being Wiccan. Tara understands her relationship to the universe and has no intention of messing with it. For Willow, magic is still a game. She can see, intellectually, why some things shouldn't be attempted, but underscored by her grief and her desire to make Dawn less miserable once her platitudes have failed, this leads her to do an *extraordinarily* stupid thing, giving Dawn access (indirectly) to the resurrection spell.

Denial, Thy Name is Summers: Buffy's reaction to Joyce's death is a terrible guilt for not having arrived home ten minutes earlier. She becomes morose and obsessive before the funeral, through which she is able to avoid reality for a few more days, before (as she tells Angel) she is required to face a future that she isn't prepared for. Dawn, due to immaturity possibly, can't see that her sister is clinging to mundane details by her fingertips to avoid dealing with larger issues (several of which involve her). Dawn is in pain and (not entirely unreasonably) wants everyone else to share it. It's unfortunate that, given where she lives, dark forces are such a temptation. It's to her credit that Dawn realises her mistake.

It's a Designer Label!: Dawn's 'panther' T-shirt. Tara's red leather funeral coat. Glory's figure-hugging dress.

References: The episode is a variant of the traditional short story *The Monkey's Paw*. And of Stephen King's *Pet Sematary* (though the former was an influence on the latter so we're into wheels-within-wheels territory). Doc hums Prokofiev's *Peter and the Wolf*. Anya asks Dawn: 'Don't you watch television? I thought all children despise effort and enjoy cartoons.' Also, the Prodigy's 'Breathe' and *Star Trek: The Next Generation* ('Proceed'). Dawn's spell is to the Egyptian death god, Osiris.

Awesome!: Giles playing 'Tales of Brave Ulysses' in tribute to an almost perfect day he once spent with Joyce (see **40**, 'Band Candy'). Spike arriving with flowers. Xander and Willow assume they're for Buffy but find, after he's left, that there's no greetings card. Angel and Buffy reunited, briefly, in tragedy. Anya and Xander's existential post-coital ruminations on the purpose of sex. The introduction of the dryly sinister Doc (Joel Grey is *fabulous*). The tearful climax. Not a lot of laughs, but many memorable moments.

'You May Remember Me From Such Films and TV Series As . . .': A cinema legend for his Oscar-winning performance as the emcee in *Cabaret*, Joel Grey's career stretches back to 1952's *About Face*. He can also be seen in *Venus Rising*, *The Player* and *Man on a Swing*. He played the Devil in the final episode of *Dallas* and appeared in *Maverick* (as Billy the Kid) and *77 Sunset Strip*. Todd Duffey was in *Don't Try This At Home* and *Office Space*. Annie Talbot appeared in *Down Periscope*. Andrea Gall played Tracey Ullman in the spoof *Allyn McBeal*.

Valley-Speak: Xander, to Spike: 'We're all hip to your doomed obsession.'

Glory: 'Jinx, you robed-stud, you're my man! I'm even gonna let you slide on the lame toadying on account of your dying and stuff.'

Willow, on Tara's breakfast: 'Two eggs sunny-side-up. I remember 'cos they were wiggling at me like little boobs.'

Logic, Let Me Introduce You to This Window: At some point Wiccans took an oath never to perform resurrections. What, *all* of them?

Cruelty to Stuffed Animals: Trying to cheer Dawn up, Willow says she could do a spell to make a stuffed animal dance.

Quote/Unquote: Spike: 'Joyce was the only one of the lot of you that I could stand.' Xander: 'And she's the only one with a daughter you wanted to shag. I'm touched.' Spike: 'I liked the lady. Understand, monkey boy? She was decent. She didn't put on airs. She always had a nice cuppa for me. And she never treated me like a freak.'

Angel: 'I can stay in town as long as you want me.' Buffy: 'How's forever? Does forever work for you?'

Notes: 'I wanna bring Mom back.' Hard work, though Marti writes Dawn better than any of the other staffers. But there's a sense of everything standing still for a week – the ongoing plot doesn't advance an inch (except for the introduction of Doc, and even that is handled in an oddly dispassionate way). Ultimately 'Forever' is flawed by its own inertia, despite many moments of gut-wrenching beauty.

Buffy has been unable to contact her father in Spain to inform him of Joyce's death. Willow says she intends to visit her mother before going home (see **45**, 'Gingerbread') and that she has been doing this a lot since Joyce's death. Xander notes that *he* called to see Willow's mom (with whom he has always got on well) too, though he certainly isn't going to his own parents – 'Those people are scary.' The book Willow makes sure that Dawn has access to is *History of Witchcraft* (she considers it merely a history book, though Tara feels it is much more than that). Among its chapters are 'Age of Levitation', 'War of the Warlocks' and 'Resurrection: A Controversy Born'. Willow has started to keep a journal. The Ghora demon that Spike has to steal an egg from to aid Dawn's spell has its nest in the sewer near Tracey Street.

Soundtrack: In addition to the Cream song, 'Tomorrow We'll Awake' by Splendid.

Critique: The *National Review* called *Buffy* 'One of television's most morally serious shows. One of the show's most powerful themes is that the vampires often seem to have the better deal. An eternity of leather, sex, and will-to-power can seem very attractive to your average school kid. Vampires are not hobbled by conscience and seem to be masters of adult indulgences. One minute, a high-school guy is nervously babbling as he tries to ask Cordelia out; the next he's confident, sexy, mysterious. You just don't see him much during the day. But again and again, *Buffy* shows that this rock-star life is empty and brutal compared to the more difficult and more rewarding business of becoming a responsible adult, soul intact.'

Did You Know?: In Britain during early 2001, the Broadcasting Standards Commission criticised an early evening broadcast of *Buffy* as being too sexually explicit for its pre-watershed time slot. Viewers (no numbers were given) objected to sex and violence in **59**, 'The Harsh Light Of Day', shown on BBC2 at 6.45 p.m. in October 2000. The BSC ruled: 'In relation to the sex scene, it considered that it had exceeded acceptable boundaries for broadcast at a time when young children could be watching.' The BBC said the show's time slot was specifically to appeal to a teenage audience. In a statement to the commission, it added: 'There was a sexual aspect to scenes in this episode but, in all these sequences, sexual activity was implied rather than depicted and more comic than erotic.' Complaints over offensive language were not upheld. The incident provoked utter hilarity in the US media and a dignified 'No comment' from Mutant Enemy and Fox.

96

Intervention

US Transmission Date: 24 Apr. 2001
UK Transmission Date: 4 May 2001 (Sky)

Writer: Jane Espenson
Director: Michael Gersham

Spike's Buffy-robot is completed just as the real Buffy goes out of town on an enlightenment quest. Spike is captured by Glory's minions and tortured to reveal the identity of The Key but, in a noble gesture, he refuses to betray Dawn.

Dudes and Babes: Willow loans a fellow student a book containing last week's notes and says that she wants it back by Thursday. And not to write in it. Or put a coffee mug down on it. Or fold the page corners.

Authority Sucks!: Buffy tells Dawn that if there are plates in her room, they should be cleaned 'before they get furry and we have to name them'. 'I was, like, five then,' replies her sister.

Denial, Thy Name is Spike: 'I feel kinda bad for the guy,' notes Xander. 'Gets all whupped and his best toy taken away.' Spike's refusal to betray Dawn despite being horribly tortured by Glory does bring the reward of a kiss from the real Slayer.

The Conspiracy Starts at Home Time: Glory says that Ben is getting stronger and she is losing control of him. When it's pointed out that she is a god, she says: 'A god in *exile*. Sharing my body with an enemy.' She deduces that The Key is someone known to the Slayer and orders her minions to find out who is new in the Slayer's circle. Buffy previously described Glory's minions as 'hobbits with leprosy'. Glory cannot brain-suck vampires (possibly because they are impure).

Technophobia!: Warren says the Buffy-robot has everything Spike requested including real-world knowledge, family and friends' profiles, scenario responses and 'special skills'. The robot tells Spike that she wants to hurt him but can't resist 'the sinister attraction of your cold and muscular body'. Amongst her program folders are *Slaying*, *Locate Spike* and *Make Spike Happy*. The program files include two kissing and at least five positions options (see **93**, 'I Was Made to Love You'). Xander's listed attributes include: friend, carpenter, dates Anya. Anya's state: dates Xander, likes money, ex-demon. Willow's list is: best friend, gay (1999–present), witch, good with computers. The robot cannot pronounce Giles's name properly. Although broken in the fight with Glory's minions, Willow believes she can fix it (see **100**, 'The Gift').

It's a Designer Label!: The robot's girly-pink skirt and sweater. Buffy's suede jacket. Glory's green negligée.

References: Spike quotes U2's 'Even Better Than the Real Thing'. Willow wants to see a History Channel documentary on the Salem witch trials (this proves upsetting and she and Tara watch koala bears on Discovery instead). Also, Plasticine™, the Four Tops' 'I Can't Help Myself', Xander quotes from 'For He's a Jolly Good Fellow' and Spike tells Glory that The Key is *The Price Is Right* host Bob Barker. Visual references to the *Star Trek* episode 'What Are Little Girls Made Of?'

Bitch!: Glory, on Spike: 'What the hell is *that*, and why is his hair that colour?'

Xander: 'No one is judging you. It's understandable. Spike is strong and mysterious and sort of compact but well-muscled.' Buffy: 'I am *not* having sex with Spike. But I'm starting to think *you* might be.'

Spike, to Glory: 'The god of what, bad home perms?' And: 'The Slayer is going to kick your skanky, lopsided ass back to whatever place would take a cheap, whorish, fashion victim ex-god like you.'

Awesome!: Everything the robot says is hilarious (it's a *wonderful* performance by Sarah) from her cheery discussion with Willow about making love to Spike in lots of different ways ('I could make sketches') to her Spike-influenced description of Angel as: 'Lame. His hair grows straight-up and he's *bloody stupid*'). The finale, Buffy impersonating the robot to give Spike a reward, is incredibly touching.

Valley-Speak: Glory: 'That's *fantabulous*!'

Buffy: 'The who whating how with huh?'

Logic, Let Me Introduce You to This Window: After Spike agrees to tell Glory who The Key is, we next see him drinking water. His face is much more lacerated than it was a moment earlier. It's possible that Glory tortured him a bit more in the interim just because she felt like it. Some of Spike's wounds disappear when he's in the elevator, only to reappear later. During the subsequent fight, Xander's hairstyle changes (probably these are the scenes that saw Kelly doubling for Nick). What's the significance of Dawn pocketing those earrings? Are they Anya's and she's stealing them? The shot seems to get far more prominence than it needs. Willow began her relationship with Tara in 2000 rather than 1999.

Quote/Unquote: Buffy, on the ritual: 'How's it start?' Giles: 'I jump out of the circle and then jump back in it. Then I shake my gourd.' Buffy: 'I know this. The ancient shamans were next called upon to do the hokey-pokey and turn themselves around!'

Tara: 'People do strange things when someone they love dies. When I lost my mother, I did some pretty dumb stuff, like lying to my family and staying out all night.' Anya: 'Buffy's *boinking* Spike.' Willow: 'Tara's right. Grief can be powerful. We shouldn't judge . . .' Tara: 'Are you, kidding? She's nuts.'

Buffy, to Spike: 'The robot was gross and obscene . . . It wasn't even real. What you did, for me and Dawn, *that* was real. I won't forget it.'

Notes: 'You look just like me. We're very pretty.' After two episodes with barely a laugh in sight, we all probably needed this more than we realised and Magic Jane comes up with the goods. A delightful slab of slapstick amid a story about trust and destiny. Another superb episode from a gifted writer.

Some Slayers before Buffy found it helpful to regain their focus and learn more about their role by visiting a sacred place and undergoing a quest. The (mental) location is a secret and Giles is unable to take Buffy there, so he has to perform a transference of his guardianship to a guide. A mountain lion leads Buffy into the dreamscape of **78**, 'Restless', and to a meeting with the guide, in the form of the First Slayer. Buffy believes she is losing her ability to love, and her humanity. The Slayer forges strength from pain, she is told. 'Love will bring you to your gift.' Which is death (see **100**, 'The Gift'). Anya was at Salem during the witch trials.

Did You Know?: In January 2001, *Associated Press* announced *Buffy* had been nominated at the 12th annual Gay and Lesbian Media Awards, which honour 'Accurate and inclusive representations of the lesbian, gay, bisexual and transgender community.' Other nominees included *Queer as Folk*, *Dawson's Creek*, *Popular* and *The West Wing*. Although generally praised for its sensitive handling of the issue, *Buffy* has come in for some mild criticism from the gay community over the way Willow's sexuality is referenced in both **89**, 'Triangle', and **93**, 'I Was Made to Love You'. Willow seems to be bisexual given that she had such an intimate and loving relationship with Oz. It's therefore difficult to believe that she's completely unattracted to men. One theory put forward is that Americans associate bisexual women with porn videos and *Jerry Springer*, so they're not comfortable with using the term.

Jane Espenson's Comments: Asked on the *Posting Board* about the kiss Buffy gave Spike, Jane noted that 'It was [in] gratitude and forgiveness.' Answering another question about how she began writing, Jane replied: 'I watched a lot of TV and wrote sample scripts that I sent to *Star Trek: The Next Generation*. So all you kids out there. Watch TV! It's good for you.'

97
Tough Love

US Transmission Date: 1 May 2001
UK Transmission Date: 11 May 2001 (Sky)

Writer: Rebecca Rand Kirshner
Director: David Grossman
Cast: Anne Betancourt (Principal Stevens),
Leland Crooke (Professor Lillian), Alan Ketz (Slook)

Threatened with having Dawn taken into care, Buffy tries to become a parent. Glory comes to the conclusion that Tara is The Key. Realising her error, she brain-sucks Tara. Willow stages a revenge attack and, with Buffy's help, survives. But Tara, in her deluded state, reveals Dawn's identity to Glory.

Dudes and Babes: Ben hasn't been to work at the hospital for two weeks (which seems to surprise him – presumably neither he nor Glory are aware of the passage of time when they are not occupying the body) and is thus fired. Tara tells Willow that it frightens her how powerful a witch Willow is becoming. The discussion moves onto other matters. 'I'm really sorry I didn't establish my lesbo street-cred before I got into this relationship,' Willow says angrily. Willow adds Tara has been 'out' longer than her, indicating that Tara was already describing herself as lesbian when they met in **66**, 'Hush'.

Authority Sucks!: Dawn has missed lots of school without telling Buffy. When Giles refuses Buffy's request to be the authority figure, Buffy realises that she will have to do the 'strong guiding hand' stuff herself. She then finds Dawn apparently messing about with Xander, Willow and Anya. In vain Willow protests that they were acting out a geometry problem. Buffy looks unamused, despite some nice obtuse and acute puns. After a huge argument about homework and chores, Buffy tells her sister that, if Dawn continues to miss school, Buffy will be declared unfit to be her legal guardian.

A Little Learning is a Dangerous Thing: Buffy has decided to drop out of college for the semester (though she says she may return). She tells Lillian that she really enjoyed his poetry class but doesn't have time for poetry now. Not even short ones like Haiku ('those Japanese ones that sound like a sneeze?') Willow says 'I took Psych 101 ... from an evil government scientist who was skewered by her *Frankenstein*-like creation before the final' (see **69**, 'The I in Team'). The book that Willow uses is called *Darkest Magick*.

The Conspiracy Starts at Home Time: Glory says that her brain-suck feels like the victim is 'in a noisy little dark room, naked and ashamed. And there are things in the dark that need to hurt you because you're bad. Pinching things that go in your ears and crawl on the inside of your skull. And you know that if the noise and the crawling stop that you could remember how to get out. But you never, ever will.'

Capitalism is a Ten-Letter Word: Anya has been reading about the USA and embracing the 'extraordinarily precious ideology that's helped to shape and define it'. She proudly explains that the free market depends on the profitable exchange of goods-for-currency. 'It's a system of symbiotic beauty.'

It's a Designer Label!: Buffy's leather skirt. Anya's green dress. The reappearance of Glory's red dress and the debut of Tara's silly stars-and-moons pants.

References: Xander alludes to Wolfgang Amadeus Mozart's opera *Don Giovanni* (1797). Giles misquotes George Harrison's 'All Things Must Pass'. There's a John Lennon poster on Lillian's wall. Xander seems to be reading a copy of *The Incredible Hulk*. Also, Freudianism (see **23**, 'Ted'), Frances Hodgson Burnett's *A Little Princess* ('Miss Minchin's Select Seminary For Girls').

Awesome!: The blindfolded minions. Glory's hand-crushing and brain-sucking attack on Tara. Giles getting Slook to talk by doing something whilst Willow and Anya's backs are turned. A black-eyed, floating Willow's revenge-attack on Glory – the first indication that Tara is right, and that she's becoming frighteningly powerful. Buffy's confrontation with Glory: 'They used to bow-down to gods. Things change.'

'You May Remember Me From Such Films and TV Series As . . .': Anne Betancourt was in *Code Blue*, *Sliver*, *Life Stinks* and *Passions*. Leland Crooke appeared in *Dirt*, *Scorchers*, *Dead Man Walking* and *The Lone Gunmen*.

Don't Give Up The Day Job: *Buffy*'s three casting directors, Anya Collof, Jennifer Fishman and Amy McIntyre Britt worked together on *Bones*, *The Hollywood Sign*, *Rats in the Can* and *Class Warfare*.

The Drugs Don't Work: Willow is given medicine to keep Tara calm.

Valley-Speak: Willow: 'I was snippy-gal.'

Glory: 'I think I'm a little buzzed from eating that witch.' And: '*Nummy* treat.'

Cigarettes and Alcohol: Glory drinks a mimosa in her bubble bath.

Logic, Let Me Introduce You to This Window: Willow's definition of a Freudian slip isn't, strictly speaking, accurate (it's usually regarded as a subconscious substitution of one word with another which reveals a repressed emotion rather than, as with Tara here, merely a slip of the tongue revealing a repressed fear) though Freudian scholars themselves don't seem able to make up their minds what the term refers to. Glory says witches used to be crucified. Although there were a few isolated incidents of this in the Middle Ages, the practice certainly wasn't widespread. What sort of slides are being used in a poetry lesson? Willow and Tara's dorm-room is on the second floor (see **94**, 'The Body'). But when Glory bursts through the wall, it's clearly on the ground floor. Why doesn't Tara react like all the other brain-sucked people who encounter Dawn until the moment that Glory appears.

Quote/Unquote: Anya tries to comfort Willow by saying she can sleep with her tonight: 'That came out a lot more lesbian than it sounded in my head.'

Spike: 'So you're saying that a powerful and mightily pissed-off witch was planning on going and spilling herself a few pints of god-blood until you, what, "explained"?'

Notes: 'It's not like I don't have a life. I have Dawn's life.' A powerful episode, dealing with raw, bloodied emotions. Little fun for the viewer, but lots of intense frustration and anger which (after a while) becomes strangely compelling.

Tara mentions having to deal with her brother's problems after their mother's death (possibly Donny from **84**, 'Family'). Willow likes chicken salad sandwiches. Buffy prefers eggplant and Dawn goes for salami and peanut butter.

Critique: In an amateur publication *TV24* (associated with the website *www.offthetelly.co.uk*), someone called Robin Carmody notes that: '*Buffy* – well, it's trash . . . Parts of it are absolutely hilarious and, if they had a sense of irony, they'd be wonderfully camp. But I got the disturbing feeling that they mean it . . . You want to kick their straight faces in.' Wonder if anybody's alerted Joss or his lawyers to this?

Did You Know?: Ian Stratton, a 24-year-old Bath student, plans to spend the next six years watching *Buffy* videos, all in the name of research. Ian's PhD thesis, as widely reported in the UK press, is on the psychology behind monsters and why 'civilised 21st-century society' still has a need to be scared. Nice work if you can get it.

David Fury's Comments: 'To the few of you who don't [think] this season's been as strong as any year of *Buffy*: "The Body", "Fool for Love", "Blood Ties", "Family", etc., all I can say is go watch some reality-programming. This stuff's wasted on you,' David memorably told the *Posting Board* on 18 April. 'And anyone who doesn't know that Marti Noxon is one of the prime reasons for the greatness of this show is a complete and utter moron.'

98
Spiral

US Transmission Date: 8 May 2001
UK Transmission Date: 18 May 2001 (Sky)

Writer: Steven S DeKnight
Director: James A Contner
Cast: Wade Andrew Williams (General Gregor), Karim Prince (Dante),
Jack Donner (Cleric #1), Mary Sheldon (Nurse)

Fleeing from Glory, the Scoobies find themselves also pursued by the Knights of Byzantium who are determined to destroy The Key to prevent Glory from using it. Hiding at a disused gas station, Buffy telephones Ben to come and give medical attention to the injured Giles. Little does she know that she is bringing Glory closer to Dawn.

Dudes and Babes: Glory, not unexpectedly, can run at super-human speed. Gronx tells Ben that he exists only because of Glory, and asks if, after 'her magnificent incandescence was returned to this manly and painfully handsome assemblage', he might have noticed The Key.

A Little Learning is a Dangerous Thing: Dawn is pleased to be skipping town – she won't have to study for a geometry test.

Denial, Thy Name is Buffy: Stubborn, to a point beyond sense, Buffy abandons strategy in favour of retreat, and compromise for dictatorship. The Scoobies follow her without question, saying much for their trust in Buffy. She's never let them down before. But there's always a first time (see **99**, 'The Weight of the World').

The Conspiracy Starts at Home Time: Gregor says that Glory is from a demon dimension of unspeakable torment. She ruled as part of a triumvirate, but her power grew beyond that of her fellow gods and 'they looked upon what she had become and trembled.' They feared Glory would attempt to seize their dimension and struck first. A great battle erupted and Glory was cast out, banished to a 'lower plane of existence', and forced to live and eventually die trapped within the body of a new-born male, created as her prison. That's her only weakness – kill the human and she dies too (but, see **100**, 'The Gift'). 'You have seen a glimpse of the true Beast,' Gregor tells Buffy. Her power was too great to be completely contained. She found a way to escape her mortal prison for brief periods, until her energies are exhausted and she's forced back into her 'living cell of meat and bone.' The Key, Gregor continues, is almost as old as Glory herself (see **91**, 'Blood Ties'). Where it came from and how it was created are mysteries. Countless generations of the Knights have sacrificed their lives in search of it, to destroy it before its wrath could be unleashed. But the monks found it first. Buffy asks why *they* didn't destroy it, if it's as dangerous as Gregor suggests. 'Because they were fools,' he replies. 'They thought they could harness its power for the forces of light.' Dawn asks why she was created. Gregor says her purpose is to open the gates that separate dimensions. Glory will use Dawn's power to return home and seize control of the Hell she was banished from. But, once The Key is activated, it will not merely open the gates to Glory's dimension. The walls separating realities will crumble, dimensions will bleed into each other, order will be overthrown and the universe will tumble into chaos. Gregor tells Ben that if The Key is not destroyed 'unimaginable legions will perish, including everyone here. You can stop this. You can save all their lives by ending one. The little girl. Destroy it, and the will of the Beast will be broken.'

It's a Designer Label!: The Knights' baseball caps! Willow's orange pants.

References: *Indiana Jones and the Last Crusade* (visually and the Knights' *raison d'être*). Inspired by probably every road-trip movie ever made. Allusion to *Bring It On* and *Dead Man Walking*. Bugs Bunny – Anya suggests dropping a piano on Glory because 'It always works for that creepy cartoon rabbit when he's running from that nice man with the speech impediment.' Also, *Monty Python's Holy Grail* ('Run away!') and *Flying Circus* (Anya's tin of spam), *Batman* (Xander refers to his car as the 'Xandermobile'), *Sergeant Rock*, obliquely to Italian poet Dante Alighieri (1265–1321), author of *Inferno* and *La Vita Nuova*. Another epic, 'Ozymandias' by Percy Bysshe Shelley (1792–1822), *The Simpsons* ('Shouldn't someone be saying "Are we there yet?"'), Crimean war heroine Florence Nightingale (1820–1910), *Scarface*, *Julius Caesar* ('Honourable men'), *The Outer Limits* and the Animals' 'It's My Life'. Spike calls the Knights 'role-playing rejects'. Xander has a poster in his apartment of the cover of a pulp novel seemingly called *Tough Love*.

Bitch!: Gronx: 'No one can stand against her blindingly scrumptious luminescence.'

Awesome!: The truck hitting Glory. The chase, and Buffy fighting the Knights on top of the Winnebago. Willow's energy barrier spell and the Knights flying backwards as it takes effect. The injured Giles's admission that he is proud of Buffy. Gregor explaining, sanely, to Buffy and Dawn what will happen if Glory gets The Key.

'You May Remember Me From Such Films and TV Series As . . .': Mary Sheldon was in *The Young and the Restless*. Karim Prince played Cestro in *Mighty Morphin Power Rangers* and Stanley in *Malcolm in the Middle*. Jack Donner was in *Stigmata*, *Soulkeepers*, *Star Trek* and *The Monkees*. He played Commander Kinwon in *Power Rangers in Space*. Wade Andrew Williams was Ted Daniels in *Erin Brockovich* and can also be seen in *Terror Tract*, *Route 9* and *Star Trek: Voyager*. Lily Knight appeared in *Little Girls in Pretty Boxes* and *Static*.

The Knights Who Say 'Key': 'The Knights' sole purpose has always been to destroy The Key, *not* the Beast,' Steven DeKnight told the *Posting Board* on 11 May. 'Gregor says that if The Key is destroyed, the will of the Beast will be broken and she will fade. He also says that The Key is almost as old as the Beast (Glory says the same in **91**, 'Blood Ties'). So, the Knights are an ancient order bent on destroying The Key before someone (NOT just Glory) screws the universe.' He added: 'As for Buffy killing the Knights . . . Buffy would never kill a *defenceless* person, even if they had the potential to do great harm (i.e. Spike). But guys trying to kill her and everyone she loves with pointy weapons? Sometimes you just don't have a choice. Also, you might have noticed that Buffy wasn't exactly her normal self, as witnessed by the catatonia at the end of **98**, "Spiral". I'm sure this explanation won't please everyone, but we're really pressing for the *Buffyverse* to become less black-and-white. Like it does when you grow up (hence next season's theme).'

The Drugs Don't Work: Ben says that one of the reasons he wanted to be a doctor was the drugs and the possibility of finding the right combination to keep Glory buried inside him.

Valley-Speak: Spike: 'Buckle up, kids. Daddy's puttin' the hammer down.'

Xander: 'How're your feelers?' Spike: 'Nothing compared to the little bits we're gonna get chopped into when the Renaissance Faire kicks the door in.'

Cigarettes and Alcohol: Xander helps Spike to light a cigarette after the vampire injures his hands.

Logic, Let Me Introduce You to This Window: Gregor specifically says that 'the identity of the human vessel has never been discovered'. Yet a scene later, he seems to recognise Ben. Presumably they have met (which would also explain how Glory knows Gregor's name). All the Knights of Byzantium appear to be American. When Glory runs at speed after Buffy and Dawn, one of the people she rushes close to looks in completely the wrong direction after she passes him. During Buffy's battle on the Winnebago, the face of Sarah's stunt double can be seen at least twice. The number of Knights involved in the chase fluctuates wildly from shot to shot.

Motors: Spike steals a decrepit Winnebago as the Scoobies' getaway vehicle. Giles says he's driven tricycles with more power. Spike wanted to obtain a Porsche.

Cruelty to Animals: When the Knights attack the Winnebago and Giles shouts 'Weapons?' Spike suggests that he's driving one. 'Don't hit the horsies,' pleads Willow rather pathetically. '*Aim* for the horsies,' Buffy orders.

Quote/Unquote: Ben: 'I didn't ask for any of this. I just want to be normal . . . Nothing's mine, is it? This life, this body, it's all infected. The only thing I ever cared about she's taken away from me.'

Xander, when the Knights discover the Scoobies' location: 'We got company. And they brought a crusade.'

Buffy, to Gregor: 'She doesn't remember anything about being this Key you're all looking for. The only thing that she remembers is growing up with a mother and a sister that love her. What kind of God would demand her life for something she has no control over?'

Notes: 'At least things can't get any crazier.' Who'd have thought that such a talky episode, with the information-overload that this one has, would have been so entertaining? Base under siege-type drama needs a lot of suspense and good acting to keep it from collapsing under its own weight and 'Spiral' succeeds on both counts.

Xander mentions using a rocket-launcher to kill The Judge in **26**, 'Innocence'. Buffy tells Giles: 'We're not gonna win this with stakes or spells or pulling out some uranium power core' (references to **12**, 'Prophecy Girl'; **34**, 'Becoming' Part 2; and **77**, 'Primeval'). Xander gets travel-sick. Glory's brain-sucked victims appear to share a mental link.

Critique: In another glowing piece in *TV Guide*, Matt Roush noted that: '*Buffy* layers its violent allegories with emotional empathy, nimble wit and barbed humour,' and described the likely pairing of *Buffy* with *Roswell* on UPN as: 'displaying a Picasso alongside an *Archie* comic'.

Joss Whedon's Comments: Quizzed by *Horror Online*, Joss revealed some of his plans for *Buffy*'s future: 'I don't have an end of the show in my head,' he noted, 'because at the end we'll start making expensive movies every four years, not unlike *Star Trek*, only with somewhat younger and more compelling people in them. *Buffy* is not a show I feel I can wrap up neatly with a ribbon.'

99

The Weight of the World

US Transmission Date: 15 May 2001
UK Transmission Date: 25 May 2001 (Sky)

Writer: Douglas Petrie
Director: David Solomon
Cast: Alexandra Lee (Young Buffy),
Matthew Lang (High Priest Minion)

Buffy's friends search for Glory without Buffy's help, as the shocked Slayer has lapsed into a catatonic state. Willow goes into Buffy's mind to get her back. But on their return to reality, Giles has some unpleasant news.

Catatonia is Free: Entering Buffy's mind, Willow finds a six year old Buffy on the day that Joyce and Hank brought Dawn home. Buffy is frightened that her parents will pay more attention to the baby. Joyce tells Buffy that she can be the one to take care of Dawn. Next, Willow encounters Buffy filing a book in the Magic Box. Then Buffy's meeting with the First Slayer from **96**, 'Intervention', and finally another Buffy who stands by Joyce's grave and tells Willow that she understands the First Slayer's prophecy 'Death is your gift'. 'It's what I do,' she notes, picking up a pillow and smothering Dawn. Willow is particularly interested to know why Buffy keeps on returning to the tiny fragment in the Magic Box. 'This was when I quit,' Buffy tells her. 'Just for a second . . . I put a book back for Giles, nothing special about it. Then it hit me. I can't beat Glory. And in that second of knowing it, I wanted it to happen.' If Glory wins then Dawn dies, Buffy continues. She would grieve, people would feel sorry for her and she imagined the relief it would be. Her belief that she condemned Dawn to death is what has sent Buffy into the trance. '[When] Glory took Dawn, I know I could have done something. But I was off by some fraction of a second.' Willow realises that Buffy is simply suffering from guilt. 'You've carried the weight of the world on your shoulders since high school. I know you didn't ask for this, but you do it every day.'

Dudes and Babes: Spike confirms that Doc is 'not so much a bloke, more a demon. All tuned into the nastier corners of this our magic world.' When he and Xander visit Doc they discover that he is also in league with Glory. 'You think only underworld bottom-feeders worship the Beast?' he asks. Doc's blood is blue, he has a lizard-like tongue and is not killed when stabbed by Xander's sword in the chest.

The Conspiracy Starts at Home Time: Dawn's blood is 'the key to The Key'. Glory must bleed Dawn for the portal to open. Spike is the only one able to remember that Ben and Glory share the same body (see **98**, 'Spiral'). Glory has worked some magic where anyone who sees the change instantly forgets (see **91**, 'Blood Ties'). Spike, being non-human, is immune. Later, Glory complains that the cloak between her and Ben is fading: she can remember what happened when Ben was in control of the body. When Dawn confirms that she too has these memories, Glory says: 'She's not supposed to remember that. Nobody should.' Significantly, when Xander is in Doc's presence, the fog clears and he also remembers.

When Buffy returns to the Magic Box she asks Giles if he has checked the ritual texts and found a way to stop Glory. He confirms that he has. Once Dawn's blood is shed, the fabric which separates realities will rip apart. 'How do we stop it?' asks Buffy. The portal will close once the blood stops, Giles tells her. The only way is to kill Dawn.

It's a Designer Label!: Glory's ceremonial gown. Buffy's tight black jeans and matching top.

References: Spike compares Ben and Glory sharing a body to apartment-sharing sitcoms. Also Kewpie dolls, Armageddon (the final battle between good and evil as predicted in Revelation), *The Prisoner* ('We need information'), a THERE'S MONEY IN ARC WELDING! poster, Glory alludes to a famous quotation by English writer and humanist HG Wells (1866–1946): 'In the Country of the Blind the One-Eyed Man is King'. Spike uses the finger-on-the-nose 'correct answer' sign from charades.

Bitch!: Willow, to Spike and Xander: 'Glory has Dawn. Sometime real soon, she's gonna use Dawn to tear down the barrier between every dimension there is. So if you two wanna fight, do it after the world ends.'

Awesome!: Spike discovering Ben's rather pathetic little room in Glory's palace, and smacking Xander on the head to get him to remember the Ben/Glory link. Glory's rant to Dawn on the madness of humanity (which actually makes a lot of sense). Spike and Xander's confrontation with Doc.

'You May Remember Me From Such Films As ...': Alexandra Lee was in *Alone With a Stranger*.

The Drugs Don't Work: When Spike tries to convince the Scoobies that Glory and Ben share the same body, they look blank. In exasperation he asks: 'Is everyone here very stoned?'

Valley-Speak: Glory: 'Why am I not popping your head like a zit right now?'

Xander: 'I'm so *large* with not knowing.'

Willow: 'I think we already *deja*'d this *vu*.'

Logic, Let Me Introduce You to This Window: 'The Knights weren't formed to fight Glory. They were formed to find and destroy The Key, which has existed in our dimension for just this side of forever. Glory was cast out from her dimension and into baby Ben 25 years ago. She only recently gained the strength to emerge from her "prison",' Steven DeKnight told the *Posting Board*. 'Hope that clears it up.'

Yeh, it pretty much does, actually. On the other hand why, if the alignment takes place now and it's only at this time that Glory can use The Key, has she been so desperate to get her hands on it for four months? Murk says the big event will be tonight, but Glory tells Dawn she will be bled tomorrow. If what Willow sees are really Buffy's memories, and not her imagination, then it seems that Hank left a six-year-old girl on her own whilst he went to pick up Joyce and Dawn at the hospital. Of course, this could be Buffy's subconscious view of her father abandoning her. Giles was severely injured in **98**, 'Spiral', yet after minor hospital attention he's able to discharge himself. Willow changes clothes between bringing Buffy out of her catatonia (which took place at Xander's apartment) and the final scene in the Magic Box. Ben says Glory can't die, that she's immortal, completely contradicting what was said in **98**, 'Spiral' (see **100**, 'The Gift'). The young Buffy is a lot blonder than the young Buffy seen in **30**, 'Killed By Death'.

I Just *Love* Your Accent: Spike's attempt to get through to Buffy: 'Oi, rise and shine, love!'

Motors: Spike hotwires Ben's car, noting that a better part of a century spent in delinquency just paid off.

Quote/Unquote: Glory, on humanity: 'How do they function like this in the world with all this bile running through them? You have no control. They're not even animals, they're just these meatbaggy slaves to hormones and pheromones and their *feelings. Hate 'em* . . . Is this what the poets go on about? Call me crazy, but as hard-core drugs go, human emotion is just useless. People are puppets.'

Notes: 'I look around at this world you're so eager to be a part of and all I see is six billion lunatics looking for the fastest ride out. Everyone's drinking, smoking, shooting-up, shooting each other, or just plain screwing their brains out 'cos they don't want 'em anymore. *I'm* crazy? Honey, I'm the original one-eyed chicklet in the Kingdom of the Blind.' A fragmented story, trying to tie-up many strands for the big finale. It just about works although the viewer really has to concentrate to catch the explanations. Don't blink, or you might miss two or three. Clare Kramer is fabulous, as she has been all season.

Joyce's gravestone reads 'Joyce Summers 1958–2001'.

Buffy once told Willow in chemistry class that she talks funny.
Did You Know?: Early 2002 will see the release of Amber
Benson's independently produced movie *Chance*. Directed,
written by and starring the actress, and featuring her *Buffy* col-
leagues Emma Caulfield and James Marsters along with
Angel's Andy Hallett and Nick Brendon's fiancée, Tressa
DiFiglia, the film is described as 'a black comedy about how
hard it is to find "the one".'

100

The Gift

US Transmission Date: 22 May 2001
UK Transmission Date: 1 Jun. 2001 (Sky)

Writer: Joss Whedon
Director: Joss Whedon
Cast: Craig Zimmerman (Minion #1),
Josh Jacobson (Teen), Tom Kiesche (Vampire)

Buffy and her friends prepare for the final battle with Glory.
Giles's common sense approach suggests killing Dawn, but
Buffy will not consider it. Meanwhile, Xander proposes to
Anya, Spike's rehabilitation into humanity continues and
Willow attempts to reverse Glory's brain-suck on Tara. Glory
is defeated when Giles kills Ben, but not before Doc cuts
Dawn to open the portal. This leaves Buffy to make the ulti-
mate sacrifice.

Dudes and Babes: Glory tells Dawn that Ben is probably the
reason Buffy and her friends are still alive. 'That little nagging
pinch of humanity that makes me go for the hurt instead of the
kill. Lowering myself to trade blows with the Slayer when I
should have just put my fist through her heart.' Willow's
powers seem to be growing daily. She produces spells that pull
Tara back from Glory's influence and parts the crowd of
Glory's minions to allow Spike to climb the tower. She also
displays telepathic ability.

Work is a Four-Letter Word: Spike describes Xander as 'a
glorified bricklayer'.

References: The tower construction is reminiscent of one in the *Doctor Who* story 'Genesis of the Daleks'. *X-Men* (not only does the climax resemble the movie – bound girl on a tower – but Willow has *become* Marvel Girl – telekinesis and now telepathy), *The Omen*, *Monty Python* ('a pointy stick?'), *Scanners* ('it might make all our heads explode') and Badfinger's 'Come and Get It'.

Murder: It's Xander who first suggests the alternative to killing Dawn might be to kill Ben, though he's clearly disgusted with himself for even voicing the idea. Giles, however, coldly and clinically does the deed to end the insanity of Glory's plans. This is a very different Giles from the one we're used to. He does what has to be done, knowing it's a dirty job but that, ultimately, *someone* has to do it.

Awesome!: Buffy's surprise at finding a vampire who doesn't know her reputation. Giles's anger at Buffy's refusal to consider the possibility of killing Dawn to prevent the ritual. Dawn telling Ben to become Glory – they're both monsters, but at least Glory is open about it. Xander and Anya in the basement, from the ridiculous (the discovery of the toy bunny) to the sublime (Xander's proposal). Anya's decision to accept, but wait for the world not to end, indicates her faith in his belief of their mutual survival. She'd been sure they would die, reinforced by the bunny-omen, but now she says their love will see them through the apocalypse. Spike telling Buffy that he will protect Dawn 'until the end of the world'. Tara calling Giles a killer and Giles fulfilling this prophecy by calmly smothering Ben. Buffy disinterestedly pushing Doc out of the way as she reaches the top of the tower. Buffy diving from the platform. Spike weeping as Buffy lies dead before him.

'You May Remember Me From Such Films and TV Series As . . .': Tom Kiesche was in *The Animal* and *3rd Rock from the Sun*. Craig Zimmerman appeared in *Sabrina the Teenage Witch* and *In the Light of the Moon*. Josh Jacobson was in *Not Another Teen Movie*.

Anya's Ideas Work: Despite Giles's withering sarcasm, Anya comes up with several ways of stopping Glory, including the Dagon-sphere (see **83**, 'No Place Like Home') and Olaf the Troll's enchanted hammer (see **89**, 'Triangle'). Whilst the others seem immobilised by fear, Anya's self-preservation instincts re-emerge. But, unlike **55**, 'Graduation Day' Part 1, her love for Xander means that she is leading the battle rather than fleeing. It was possibly also Anya's idea to use the Buffy-robot (you can certainly hear Buffy thanking Xander and Anya for *something* when they emerge from the basement).

Valley-Speak: Xander: 'Smart chicks are *SO* hot!' And: 'Shpadoinkle.'

Murk: 'Take mine, oh *groovetastic* one.'

Logic, Let Me Introduce You to This Window: 'We set up in "Blood Ties" that Buffy and Dawn were true blood relations, that their blood was the same, so the portal would be sated when EITHER stopped flowing,' Joss told the *Posting Board*. 'Nobody ever took orders from the Buffybot. Buffy gave the gang the speech in the magic shop then went down to change clothes with the bot. At the tower you hear Buffy give Willow an order and then see the bot,' he continued, explaining the rationale behind two often-quoted 'errors'. Joss also revealed, to *TV Guide*, the meaning of the mysterious '730' references that first surfaced in Buffy's dream-encounter with Faith in **56**, 'Graduation Day' Part 2. As many fans had suspected, it's a reference to the number of days in two years. Of course, the year 2000 was a leap year . . . Doc's shallow cuts to Dawn don't seem to pierce her flesh. In the next shot, the blood is pouring out. Given the location of the cuts, the blood should drip down the front of the dress, rather than running down Dawn's legs. As with Dracula's castle in **79**, 'Buffy vs Dracula', didn't anybody notice the construction of a massive tower of scaffolding in the middle of Sunnydale? Maybe we can let them off with that one – this *is* Sunnydale after all, and denial is rife.

I Just *Love* Your Accent: Giles and Spike hilariously misquote the St Crispin's Day speech from *Henry V* (Giles: 'We few. We happy few.' Spike: 'We band of buggered').

Quote/Unquote: Teen: 'How'd you do that?' Buffy: 'It's what I do.' Teen: 'But you're just a girl.' Buffy: 'That's what *I* keep saying.'

Anya: 'Usually when there's an apocalypse, I skedaddle. But now I love you so much instead I have inappropriatelytimed sex and try to think of ways to fight a god . . . I honestly don't think that I could be more nervous than I am right now.' Xander, holding out a diamond engagement ring: 'Care to wager on that?'

Spike, to Buffy: 'I know you'll never love me. I know that I'm a monster. But you treat me like a man.'

Ben: 'She could've killed me.' Giles: 'No, she couldn't. And sooner or later Glory will re-emerge and make Buffy pay for that mercy. And the world with her. Buffy even knows that and still she couldn't take a human life. She's a hero, you see. She's not like us.'

Notes: 'Dawn, listen to me. I will *always* love you. But this is the work that I have to do. Tell Giles I figured it out. And I'm OK. Give my love to my friends. You have to take care of them now . . . You have to be strong. The hardest thing in this world is to live in it. Be brave. Live for me.' An episode about sacrifice. Xander refers to Ben as an innocent but not innocent the way Dawn is. He's closer to the truth than he knows. Dawn is ready to sacrifice herself for others to save the world. Anya and Xander have sex while looking for the sphere, a very human moment in a time of inhumanity. 'The Gift' is about choices, about priorities in a world where the only escape from the delicious ironies of life is through love. Willow has been busy working to help Tara and believes that she's let Buffy down but is told that Tara should come first. Spike again shows himself ready to die because of 'a promise to a lady'. This is a story about life's little victories. About how we are born to die but are redeemed through our fear of that death (the new dawn that rises as Buffy throws herself from the tower is a literal and a metaphorical acknowledgement of this). It's a life-affirming message that, even in death, the memories we leave behind guarantee us a kind of immortality.

The Apocalypse Will Not Be Televised: 'This is how many apocalypses for us?' Buffy asks. 'Six at least,' replies Giles referring to **12**, 'Prophecy Girl'; **26**, 'Innocence'; **34**, 'Becoming' Part 2; **47**, 'The Zeppo'; **56**, 'Graduation Day' Part 2; and **77**, 'Primeval'. 'Feels like a hundred,' he continues. Buffy mentions sacrificing Angel to save the world (see **34**, 'Becoming' Part 2).

Spoiled Rotten: In America, despite the presence of accurate rumours on the Internet, the secret surrounding the season's shocking climax was pretty well kept from those who didn't go looking for it. In Britain, however, because 'The Gift' was shown ten days later, it was virtually impossible to avoid knowing. The *Evening Standard*, for instance, ran a 'Buffy Dies' exclusive a few days before the final episode. Prize for the most banal action, however, went to the normally reliable Sky who, after their broadcast of **99**, 'The Weight of the World', showed a trailer for 'The Gift' which included the final lingering shot of Buffy's gravestone. They then repeated this, *ad nauseum*, throughout the week leading up to 1 June.

Did You Know?: 'The WB either misplaced the media roll, or someone has taken it,' Emma Caulfield told Australian magazine *Big Heat*. 'Media rolls are shown to selected media groups to help them promote *Buffy*. They get a two or three month ahead sneak-peek. We wrapped up filming of the season finale then Sarah flew out to the Gold Coast for *Scooby-Doo*. She was flown back on Sunday night to re-shoot the stolen scenes. It's been panic here because we had to change the whole last fifteen minutes because of the stolen footage. Joss is far from impressed.' This revelation has given rise to a popular fan-rumour that the ending of the episode as originally filmed was to have featured Dawn sacrificing herself instead of Buffy.

Did You Spot?: The 'Previously on *Buffy the Vampire Slayer*' reprise includes clips (often as short as a single frame) from all 99 previous episodes. See how many you can identify.

Joss Whedon's Comments: 'I did warn UPN,' Joss told *DreamWatch*. ' "Guys, you might see something in the final episode that disturbs you slightly!" ' After the episode's broadcast, Joss told panicking fans on the *Posting Board* that the series *will* return. '*Buffy* will be back next season, starring Sarah Michelle Gellar, on UPN, Tuesdays at 8 p.m. How will we bring her back?' he rhetorically asked. 'With great difficulty, of course. And pain and confusion. Will it be cheesy? I don't think so. The fact is, we had most of next season planned before we shot this episode. Same writers you know, same actors you love, same crappy little warehouse in Santa Monica we've been shooting in for five years. Different network. But we've never been controlled by the network. An ensemble this brilliant could easily carry the show even without the Slayer. But even though she reached some closure, Buffy's story isn't over. When it is, I'll know. And we'll stop.'

> BUFFY ANNE SUMMERS
> *1981–2001*
> *BELOVED SISTER*
> *DEVOTED FRIEND*
> *SHE SAVED THE WORLD*
> *A LOT*

The Buffy Novels

Published in the US by Pocket Books, the novels arrived in Britain before the series did, via import book stores like Forbidden Planet. Although they often contradict established continuity, most are well written (notably Christopher Golden and Nancy Holder's impressive characterisation). It's tempting to wonder whether some of the ideas from the books influence the series itself (there are certainly some coincidences).

Halloween Rain

Writers: Christopher Golden and Nancy Holder
Published: November 1997
Tagline: He walks . . . He talks . . . He kills . . .
Setting: 30–31 October 1996

It's Halloween; Giles expects trouble. Sure enough, vampires are out in force, but the biggest danger comes from Samhain, who raises the Sunnydale dead as zombies, fulfilling a local legend concerning walking scarecrows. Buffy almost loses her nerve, while Willow, Giles and Xander face a zombie attack . . .
Authority Sucks!: 'Xander, do not argue with me. I'm your school librarian.'
Mom's Apple Pie: Buffy and Joyce indulge in a horror-movie fest on Showtime.
Denial, Thy Name is Sunnydale: 'The rest of the town is psycho,' says Willow. 'They all want to pretend Sunnydale is as sunny as Sunnybrook Farm . . . The stories are all there . . . but nobody connects the dots.' 'Because nobody wants to,' Buffy says.
References: 'Sometimes it concerned [Buffy] that her head was filled with so many pop-culture references.' *The Twilight*

Zone, Heathers, Indiana Jones ('If adventure has a name, my dear, it's Xander Harris'), Jackie Chan, *The X-Files*, *Mission: Impossible*, *Pinky and the Brain*, *The Pirates of Penzance*, *The Addams Family*, *The Wizard of Oz*, *Star Trek: The Next Generation*, James Bond, *Star Wars*, *Superman*, *The Jetsons*, *Grease*, *Back to the Future III*, *Dawn of the Dead*, *Nightmare Before Christmas*, *The Terminator*, Roy Rogers and Dale Evans ('popular American cowpeople'), *Zorro*, *Macbeth*.

Logic, Let Me Introduce You to This Window: Giles expects Halloween to be a big time for vampires, though **18**, 'Halloween', tells us exactly the opposite. Buffy is sixteen, although her seventeenth birthday in **25**, 'Surprise', comes after Halloween 1997. As this is set during the first season, Buffy must have been fifteen when she arrived in Sunnydale. Buffy has a phobia about clowns – it's actually Xander who has this. (See **10**, 'Nightmares'.)

Notes: The first original novel could be a television script, if it didn't contradict so many later-established concepts. Xander and Willow discuss whether vampires can enter public places long before **30**, 'Killed By Death'; Mr Flutie is one of the raised zombies. Samhain claims to be the instigator of all the nightmares Buffy suffered as a child. Buffy originally runs away from Samhain, before realising that her destiny is to be the Slayer. She promises Giles she'll never shirk her duty again.

Coyote Moon

Writer: John Vornholt
Published: January 1998
Tagline: Humans by day . . . Evil by night . . .
Setting: Late August 1997

A carnival comes to town, at the same time as a coyote pack. When Willow and Xander fall under the spell of the carneys, Buffy and Giles must prevent the resurrection of Spurs Hardaway, a 'werecoyote' buried in Sunnydale, and save their friends from sacrifice.

References: Bela Lugosi's *Dracula*, Stephen King's *Cujo*.

Logic, Let Me Introduce You to This Window: Buffy is in

Sunnydale during the summer. Not according to **13**, 'When She Was Bad', she wasn't (and babysitting at that). Willow is allergic to dogs (does Oz know?). Giles doesn't recognise candy floss.

I Just *Love* Your Accent: Giles raised hounds for a local fox hunt.

Notes: A werewolf story, competently told, but done much better in **27**, 'Phases'. There are some nice continuity touches – Angel is mentioned but not present, Xander doesn't like clowns. One line stands out: 'We need to start using trickery, though, or the next mayor of Sunnydale is going to be a werebear!'

Night of the Living Rerun . . .

Writer: Arthur Byron Cover
Published: March 1998
Tagline: The stage is set for a killer performance . . .
Setting: Late 1996

Buffy has weird dreams, linking her to Samantha Kane, one of the Salem witch-hunt victims. Xander and Giles suffer similar nightmares and four ghost hunters arrive in Sunnydale hot on the scent. Buffy has to discover why history is repeating itself and what it has to do with a statue in her mom's gallery.

A Little Learning is a Dangerous Thing: We learn far more than we ever want to about the Salem trials, mixing rather too much fiction with the facts.

Denial, Thy Name is Sunnydale: It's stated – as a fact – that there is a 'forgetfulness spell' over Sunnydale. Joyce worries that Buffy won't keep her skin's 'youthful quality' if she keeps getting bruised.

References: *Kolchak: The Night Stalker* (one of the ghost hunters is a reporter called Darryl MacGovern), Taster's Choice coffee commercials, *Romeo and Juliet*, game show *Jeopardy*.

Logic, Let Me Introduce You to This Window: When told to prepare for death, Buffy says, 'Been there, bought the T-shirt.' Her 'death' doesn't occur until a later date in 1997.

Notes: The Master was responsible for the events of the Salem witch trials, apparently. Lora Church (one of the hunters) was at Oxford with Giles and remembers his interest in the paranormal, though they lost touch after graduation. The theme of possession is handled far better in **31**, 'I Only Have Eyes for You', while a possessed artefact would later feature in **36**, 'Dead Man's Party'. Buffy disguises herself in a burger joint uniform – as she would do in **35**, 'Anne'. (See *Prime Evil*).

Blooded

Writers: Christopher Golden and Nancy Holder
Published: August 1998
Tagline: Buffy's new enemy is close to her heart . . .
Setting: Impossibly, after **34**, 'Becoming' Part 2, but before **35**, 'Anne'

On a school trip to the museum, Willow cuts herself on a Japanese artefact and she is possessed by an ancient vampire, Chirayoju. When Xander is possessed by Chirayoju's ancient enemy, Sanno, a fight to the death ensues . . .

References: *Pulp Fiction, William Shakespeare's Romeo and Juliet, Hamlet, Casper, Rocky, Poltergeist, ER, Deep Space Nine* ('Principal Snyder looked only slightly more human than one of the Ferengi on *Star Trek*'), *The Absent-Minded Professor, Batman, Star Wars, Mission: Impossible.*

Bitch!: 'You could use some time on self-improvement, Cordelia. Maybe then people would stop mistaking you for Barbie's friend Skipper turned crack-ho.' This, from Willow!

Logic, Let Me Introduce You to This Window: Angel has stopped being Angelus and everyone is friendly with him – even Giles! Cordelia says Xander 'doesn't usually snore', suggesting they have slept together (Xander is still a virgin until **47**, 'The Zeppo').

I Just *Love* Your Accent: 'It was times like this that Giles wished he was back in the land of tea, crumpets and baked beans for breakfast.' As Giles would say, 'Americans!'

Notes: The first book to try to deal with the aftermath of season two is hampered by clearly not knowing what happened in **33/34**, 'Becoming'. Additionally, it's set within 1998 –

SATs are next year – but Angel is, critically, one of the gang after 'the Angelus crisis'. We meet Willow's mom for the first time in another tale of possession (this time much closer to **31**, 'I Only Have Eyes for You', in form). Oz is experimenting with heavy chains as a werewolf-containment system. Buffy's driving is as excruciating as her attempts in **40**, 'Band Candy'.

Child of the Hunt

Writers: Christopher Golden and Nancy Holder
Published: October 1998
Tagline: Only his soul was human . . .
Setting: Autumn 1998

As Joyce becomes involved with parents searching for their missing children, a Renaissance Faire comes to Sunnydale – bringing with it the Elf Hunt and its leader Herne the Hunter. When Giles, Willow, Xander and Buffy are captured, it's up to Cordelia to save the day.

Mom's Apple Pie: Joyce insists on some quality time with Buffy, Slayer or not.

Denial, Thy Name is Sunnydale: 'Typical Sunnydale denial,' Willow says when Cordelia wonders why no one noticed 'spooky horse guys snatching people and . . . killing babies'.

Denial, Thy Name is Joyce: Joyce still can't understand why Buffy has been chosen and ends up clutching a stake as a comforter and moaning, 'It wasn't meant to be like this.'

References: *Camelot, Who Framed Roger Rabbit?, Jeopardy, Star Trek, Rain Man, The Addams Family, Hamlet, Batman, Mary Poppins, Something Wicked This Way Comes, Hansel and Gretel, The Hobbit, Bewitched, The Wizard of Oz, The Silence of the Lambs.*

Cigarettes and Alcohol: Giles remembers escaping into the bottle in **20**, 'The Dark Age': 'The one and only time he had gotten drunk in Sunnydale he had so badly frightened Buffy that he had vowed never to be so self-indulgent again.'

Logic, Let Me Introduce You to This Window: Although Buffy's disappearance to LA is mentioned, Angel is still part of the team and even agrees to share a beer with Giles.

Notes: Another story that could work on screen (it's similar in places to **45**, 'Gingerbread'), bringing fantasy into the Buffy universe. Willow's parents (and their disapproval of Oz), Xander's parents (who ignore him) and Cordelia's parents (who disapprove of Xander) all appear. Giles uses a phone card to avoid questions about all the long-distance calls from the library. Cordelia has visited England and seen a fox hunt.

Return to Chaos

Writer: Craig Shaw Gardner
Published: December 1998
Tagline: Under the cover of Darkness . . .
Setting: Spring 1999

All the signs point to a major event at the Hellmouth. Plans for the Spring Formal Dance are put aside when a group of Druids invade Sunnydale and Cordelia is bitten by a former rival, who is now a vampire, under the thrall of a demon called Eric . . .

A Little Learning is a Dangerous Thing: The origins of the Druids are explained.

References: *Batman*, *Sesame Street*, *Masterpiece Theater*, *Lost in Space*, *Mad* Magazine, *Mission: Impossible*, *The Man From UNCLE*, *Rebel Without A Cause*, *Jeopardy*, *Superman*.

Logic, Let Me Introduce You to This Window: The relationship between Buffy and Angel is not as on screen by this time – and Xander and Cordelia are still an item.

Notes: A much simpler novel than the two predecessors, although for once the British contingent are portrayed accurately. Cordelia beat Naomi to become chief cheerleader. Research shows that Drusilla was a regular user of a spell that would explain how she killed Kendra so easily. The high mortality rate of principals is referred to: 'Cordy hadn't gotten in real trouble at Sunnydale High for at least the last three principals. That was probably close to two years around here.' The most prophetic line is, 'An alliance between us [a vampire and a druid] will allow you to control the Hellmouth for a hundred years.' Ascension, anyone?

The Gatekeeper Trilogy Book One: Out of the Madhouse

Writers: Christopher Golden and Nancy Holder
Published: January 1999
Tagline: Evil is eternal . . .
Setting: Spring 1999

Weird things start happening in Sunnydale, with the arrival of Springheel Jack, the Kraken, storms of toads *and* a mysterious brotherhood stalking Buffy. Giles believes the Gatehouse – a mystical gateway between dimensions – is under attack and he, Buffy, Cordelia and Xander head to Boston, where they discover that the Gatekeeper is dying. The Brotherhood of the Sons of Entropy (who are killing Watchers around the world) nearly destroy the Gatehouse and the only hope is the Gatekeeper's son – who is in the hands of Spike and Drusilla!

Denial, Thy Name is Sunnydale: Xander: 'Maybe [my parents] live on the Hellmouth, but like everyone else in Sunnydale, they somehow manage to get by without acknowledging how crazy that is.'

Denial, Thy Name is Joyce: 'Mom had been in denial ever since Buffy told her the truth.'

References: The Energizer Bunny, *Rocky the Flying Squirrel*, *The Beverly Hillbillies*, Elmer Fudd, *My Own Private Idaho*, *Dawson's Creek*, *Reservoir Dogs*, *Jeopardy*, *Thelma & Louise*, *Supergirl*, *Sabrina The Teenage Witch*, *The Wizard of Oz*, *Alice's Adventures in Wonderland*, *Peanuts* and Charlie Brown, *Batman*, *Ricochet Rabbit*, *Star Wars*. Oz's infrequent gigging with Dingoes Ate My Baby is causing rifts (the band refer to Willow as 'Yoko'). There's an oblique reference to Golden's excellent vampire trilogy, *The Shadow Saga*.

Logic, Let Me Introduce You to This Window: Giles seems to think that all nurses are called 'Sister' in Britain. They aren't. This is set in the same alternate universe as *Child of the Hunt*, with Giles accepting Angel, and Cordy and Xander still dating in Spring 1999.

Notes: Lots of running around and action sequences that would make this a terrific movie, but they just don't work on paper. Half the fights are unnecessary and the chapters within the Gatehouse go on far too long. However, it's a continuity-fest both to the series and to the books, with Roland from *Child of the Hunt*, and Kobe Sensei from *Blooded* both appearing. Travelling the ghost roads between dimensions, Oz meets Kendra, while Angel sees Jenny.

The Gatekeeper Trilogy Book Two: Ghost Roads

Writers: Christopher Golden and Nancy Holder
Published: March 1999
Tagline: Last exit before fear . . .
Setting: 30–31 October 1998 (impossibly out of sequence with the others in the trilogy)

Buffy, Angel and Oz travel the ghost roads around Europe, visiting London and Paris, before a dream guides them to the Sons of Entropy in Florence, where they are saved by Il Maestro's daughter, Micaela, and rescue the Gatekeeper's son from Spike and Dru. Meanwhile Giles visits the *Flying Dutchman* and Joyce is captured by the Sons of Entropy in a bid to get Buffy to surrender. Xander is shot during a rescue attempt . . .
References: *Casper*, *E.T.*, *Little Shop Of Horrors*, *The Addams Family*, *Batman*, *Someone's Killing The Great Chefs of Europe*, *Casablanca*, Daffy Duck, *Superman*, Xander misquotes John Masefield, *Star Trek*, *Star Wars*, *West Side Story*, TS Eliot's *The Wasteland, Man of La Mancha, Invasion of the Body Snatchers*, *The X-Files*, *Armageddon*, the game Cluedo.
Logic, Let Me Introduce You to This Map: There's some weird geography going down. The Cotswolds are apparently to the East and slightly south of London. Travelling from there, they arrive on Hampstead Heath!
Logic, Let Me Introduce You to This Window: Joyce moves in with Giles for safety, with no reference to **40**, 'Band Candy'.
Cigarettes and Alcohol: In an effort to fit in, Angel smokes a cigarette at a Paris café, while Giles gets drunk on board the *Flying Dutchman*.
Notes: Middle books of trilogies tend to drag, and this is no exception. The *Flying Dutchman* incident is pure padding and

Spike and Dru are underused. Like episode three of your average *Doctor Who* story – loads of running around, and the plot barely progresses. One neat reference is Amy Madison helping out in Sunnydale, since there's no Slayer around.

The Gatekeeper Trilogy Book Three: Sons of Entropy

Writers: Christopher Golden and Nancy Holder
Published: May 1999
Tagline: The final battle has begun . . .
Setting: Spring 1999

Willow and Cordelia take Xander to the Gatehouse where he is saved. When the Gatekeeper is killed, Xander becomes acting Keeper. With Ethan Rayne's help, Buffy rescues Joyce and Angel and Oz escort Jacques, the new Keeper, to Boston. Il Maestro is in alliance with the demon Belphegor, but realises that he's on the wrong side as Buffy defeats Belphegor.

References: *Batman*, *The Wizard of Oz*, Ethan refers to Buffy as 'Slayer Spice', *Spider-Man*, *Star Trek* (Xander realises he is now 'Picard, Kirk, Sisko and – God help him – Janeway, all rolled into one'!), *Alice in Wonderland*, *Apollo 13*, *I Was A Teenage Werewolf*, *Sliders*, *Silent Night*, *The Addams Family*, *The X-Files*, *The Shining* novel, *Pleasantville*.

Logic, Let Me Introduce You to This Window: Despite no mention being made of Joyce and Giles's exploits in **40**, 'Band Candy', Buffy refers to this episode when talking to Ethan.

I Just *Love* Your Accent: Ethan: 'Good Lord. Who died and made you Xena?' Buffy: 'Same people who made you Dr Smith.' 'Sorry, I don't follow,' Ethan told her. '*Lost in Space*?' Buffy prompted. 'The cowardly bad guy?' 'We're from Britain, Buffy,' Giles informed her. 'We had *Dr Who*.'

Notes: More running about, and the cue for some great special effects, but they don't work on paper. There are a couple of neat ideas (Xander as the Gatekeeper), but none of it lives up to the promise of the first book.

Visitors

Writers: Laura Anne Gilman and Josepha Sherman
Published: April 1999
Tagline: The Slayer is being stalked . . .
Setting: Spring 1999

Buffy has problems when a group of student teachers get the hots for Giles and infest the library; Ethan Rayne returns to Sunnydale; the Watchers' Council sends a Watcher to watch Giles, and the korred – a creature that makes people dance themselves to death – arrives.

Mom's Apple Pie: Buffy and Joyce have a weekly quality time set aside, which seems to be painful for both sides.

References: *Batman*, Leonardo DiCaprio, *Wheel of Fortune*, *Macbeth*, *Gunfight at the OK Corral*, *West Side Story*, *All's Well That Ends Well*.

Logic, Let Me Introduce You to This Window: Ethan's return here takes place not long after **40**, 'Band Candy' – just as in *The Gatekeeper Trilogy*. A wonderful mistake that went unspotted: Willow refers to 'The Dingoes' *Ate My Babies*'. Cordy and Xander are *still* together.

Notes: Back to the younger readers range, with a weak plot. The Council sending someone to check out Giles had been seen on the series (although not before this was delivered) and Willow possibly becoming a Watcher is one fans had debated.

Unnatural Selection

Writer: Mel Odom
Published: June 1999
Tagline: An environmental evil haunts Willow . . .
Setting: Spring 1999

Gallivan Industries' plans for a local park disturb the inhabitants – a bunch of Soviet faeries, who need a witch's blood for one of their rites. The faeries start stealing babies, Buffy and Angel have to pose as a married couple, Xander discovers that a new friend is not all he appears to be and Willow must be rescued from the middle of a faerie civil war.

Denial, Thy Name is the Summers Family: 'Both [Buffy and Joyce] knew that each time [Buffy] stepped out the door to go Slaying could be the last time they saw each other, but they couldn't act that way.'

References: The works of James Fenimore Cooper, *Dragnet*, *NYPD Blue*, Jerry Springer, *Good Housekeeping*, Bugs Bunny, *Scream* (Willow is babysitting for the Campbells when their baby is taken), *The Godfather*, *Dirty Harry*, *The Smurfs*, *Scooby Doo*, *Duck Tales*, *Yogi Bear*, *The X-Files*, *Dick Tracy*, *Small Soldiers*, *Butch Cassidy and the Sundance Kid*, *Pinky and the Brain*, Superman's foe Brainiac, *The Twilight Zone*, *Lassie*, 'Santa Claus Is Coming To Town', *Star Trek: The Next Generation*.

Logic, Let Me Introduce You to This Window: Cordy and Xander are *still* dating! Do the editors of the two ranges talk to each other? Buffy encountered the faerie folk in *Child of the Hunt*, and briefly in *Out of the Madhouse*, yet here she's never heard of them.

Notes: A convoluted plot that just about manages to keep going for 210 pages – but there's precious little of the Slayer, compared with normal. Notable for being the first original novel *not* to feature Sarah Michelle Gellar on the cover.

Obsidian Fate

Writer: Diana G Gallagher
Published: September 1999
Tagline: A dark force shows the Slayer her destiny . . .
Setting: Mid season 3, directly between *47*, 'The Zeppo', and *48*, 'Bad Girls'
(the bomb has been found in the school basement, but Mr Trick is still alive)

A buried Spanish expedition on the outskirts of Sunnydale is discovered along with an obsidian mirror containing the soul of Aztec evil darkness god Tezcatlipoca. As it possesses the archaeological team, it plans to bring eternal night to Sunnydale, something with which Mr Trick is eager to assist.

Authority Sucks!: Snyder's mission statement: 'I've got teachers to harass and students to intimidate.'

Denial, Thy Name is Joyce: 'Apparently, her mother didn't want to spend the morning discussing her dangerous duties as the Chosen One either.'

Denial, Thy Name is Sunnydale: Joyce: 'Look at all the strange things that happen in this town that nobody ever talks about.'

References: *The Lone Ranger*, *America's Most Wanted*, *Silas Marner*, James Bond, *Star Trek*, Han Solo, Joshua 6 (the fall of Jericho).

Bitch!: 'Have fun playing together in your super sandbox.' Cordelia's on form.

The Drugs Don't Work: Willow gets stoned on Aztec hash.

Logic, Let Me Introduce You to This Window: Reference to the line of Slayer succession, which ignores Faith, yet a few pages later Faith is referred to in the past tense. Angelus is constantly called 'Angeles'. Despite being set mid season three, 13 August 1999 is in the past. Mayor Wilkins is spelled 'Wilkens' throughout.

Notes: Mayor Wilkens [sic] is financing the dig. Giles has visited archaeological digs in Egypt and the Congo. Each of the Slayerettes faces their worst nightmares in the mirror: Xander returning to his hyena state, Willow failing as a witch and a student, Giles having Jenny erased from his life, Buffy facing an eternity of demons and claws, Oz gaining the knowledge of what he's like as a werewolf and Cordy . . . 'Life was so much easier when I only cared about me!' A lot of resonances of season four and *Angel* season one.

Immortal

Writers: Christopher Golden and Nancy Holder
Published: October 1999 (hardback); May 2000 (paperback)
Tagline: As long as there have been vampires, there has been the Slayer. One girl in all the world, to find them where they gather and to stop the spread of their evil and the swell of their numbers. She is the Slayer.
Setting: February 1999 (during season three)

Veronique is an Immortal – a vampire who can switch bodies when they're destroyed. She's preparing the way for the Three Who Rule, the Triumvirate of demons who'll bring the

Apocalypse. But Buffy is distracted from the fight – Joyce may be suffering from cancer.

Denial, Thy Name is the Summers Family: The main theme is learning to deal with things you can't do anything about.

References: *Peter Pan*, *Felicity* (Buffy doesn't want to miss it), *Frankenstein*, Nancy Drew, The Hardy Boys, *Night of the Living Dead*, *All My Children*, *The Mod Squad*, *Mystery Men*, *The Avengers* Marvel comic, *Psycho*, Jennifer Love Hewitt, gymnast Kerri Strug, the *Chicken Soup* self-help books, *Walker: Texas Ranger*, the song 'Strange Things Happen', *Batman* ('Come on, Boy Wonder,' says Angel), Indiana Jones, *The Terminator*, *Mary Poppins*, *Psalm 23*, *Taxi Driver*, New Match Game, *Jack and the Beanstalk*, *Star Trek*, *The Lone Ranger*, Archie Comics, *Aliens* ('Get away from her, you bitch').

Cigarettes and Alcohol: Angel has a beer at Willy's bar.

Notes: The first Buffy hardback deals with adult themes, with the vampires-as-cancer subtext brought to the fore. In common with the rest of Golden and Holder's work, there are plenty of flashbacks, following Veronique's history – including her responsibility for the deaths of the Knights Templar in the fourteenth century – as well as Angel's appearance in Manhattan in 1944. There's continuity to *The Gatekeeper Trilogy*, with the reappearance of former Slayer Lucy Hanover (see **1**, 'Welcome to the Hellmouth').

Power of Persuasion

Writer: Elizabeth Massie
Published: October 1999
Tagline: Sunnydale's hit with a girl-power trip . . .
Setting: Late in season three, impossibly both before and after **54**, 'The Prom'

An innocent wish brings three Greek muses to Sunnydale. They soon have all of the women under their control. When they turn their attention on the men, Xander and Giles fall prey. But to defeat this menace, Buffy needs to ally herself with her normal enemies – the vampires.

References: *Dark Shadows*, the Three Stooges, *The Twilight Zone*, *Jeopardy*, Bruce Willis, *Titanic*, *Night of the Living Dead*, *The World According to Garp*.

Logic, Let Me Introduce You to This Window: This is very late in season three, around the time of the Sunnydale High Pageant and after Buffy learns of Cordelia's family problems – but no one mentions Ascension. Or Faith. Or the Mayor.

Notes: Xander had a two-month-long crush on a Greek exchange student during the second season. Viva and her nest of vampires are somewhat reminiscent of Sunday and her group in **57**, 'The Freshman'.

Sins of the Father

Writer: Christopher Golden
Published: November 1999
Tagline: The past revisits both the Slayer and the Watcher . . .
Setting: Spring 1999

Buffy's former friend Pike turns up in Sunnydale, with a stone demon, Grayhewn, on his tail. Giles is distracted by Karen Blaisdell – a *glamour* working for a demon who appears to be Giles's father.

Mom's Apple Pie: . . . Is shared with a new man, Alan Wicksham.

References: *The Godfather III*, *Batman* and Two-Face, *Superman* and Mysterio, *White Fang*, Hugh Grant, Nigel Bruce as Doctor Watson, *MTV Unplugged*, James Bond, *Nightmare on Elm Street*, John Wayne, *Dr Laura*, *NYPD Blue*, Wagner's Ring Cycle, *The Mighty Thor*, *Robin Hood*, James Dean, *Rain Man*, *Pulp Fiction*, *I Love Lucy*.

I Just *Love* Your Accent: Giles's manic 'colloquial' English-speak is gently brought to a halt by Buffy.

Notes: Xander notices that Joyce is a babe (**78**, 'Restless'). Pike's relationship with Buffy is based on Golden's version of the movie from *The Origin*. Pike has encountered Lyle Gorch. Buffy hurt Pike in Las Vegas, which was partly why they separated. There's an unfortunate coincidence as Giles, Xander, Cordy and Snyder come under the influence of another female member of staff (see *Power of Persuasion*). At the end, Giles heads back to Britain.

Resurrecting Ravana

Writer: Ray Garton
Published: January 2000
Tagline: A dark evil is rising . . .
Setting: Impossibly, post **38**, 'Beauty and the Beasts', and before **42**,
'Lover's Walk', but Spring 1999 and after
the SAT results

Guidance counsellor Promila Daruwalla's interest in Hinduism comes at the wrong time, when a set of hellhounds from that religion's beliefs attack Sunnydale, forcing friends to be at each other's throats. When Giles spots Ethan Rayne, he's sure there is something else going on.

Mom's Apple Pie: Some standard Joyce nagging and she and Buffy face the Rakshassa.

References: Jerry Springer (being a werewolf is said to be like watching him), 'The Member of the Wedding' by Carson McCullers, *Beowulf*, *Tarantula! Wheel of Fortune*, *Jeopardy*, *Must See TV*, the Sci-Fi Channel, Conan O'Brien, *La Femme Nikita*, Ward Cleaver from *Leave it to Beaver*, Stephen King, Dean Koontz, Sherlock Holmes, Alanis Morissette, Jewel, the Waco massacre, *Carrie*, Daffy Duck, *Jurassic Park*, BBC America, Beanie Babies, *Scanners*, *Poltergeist*, *Weekly World News*, *Politically Correct* (and its host Bill Maher), Marilyn Manson, *South Park*, *The Shadow*, *The Twilight Zone*, Aleister Crowley, *Mission: Impossible*, *Gremlins*, *Batman*, *Star Wars*, *Star Trek*, *Star Search*, Betty Crocker.

Bitch!: Brilliantly, Cordelia's website is *www.shrew.com*

Logic, Let Me Introduce You to This Window: The timeframe for the story doesn't work – Xander and Cordelia are still an item, but we're definitely in Spring 1999.

I Just *Love* Your Accent: 'Forget you're British and step on it!' Buffy tells Giles. 'Such an economy with words, the English,' Xander comments and Giles finds himself thinking in a cod German accent.

Notes: Ethan's appearance is wasted – makes you wonder

whether it was someone else originally, and Ethan was suggested in his place.

Deep Water

Writers: Laura Anne Gilman and Josepha Sherman
Published: February 2000
Tagline: Can Willow's new friend be trusted?
Setting: Spring 1999, as Cordelia starts being friendly to the
Scooby Gang again

Willow finds a *selkie* – a seal-woman – on the shore after an oil spill and she and the others have to protect her from merrows (sea monsters), as well as humanity.
Denial, Thy Name is Sunnydale: Giles muses that Xander refers to the collective forgetfulness as 'Total Cluelessitis'.
References: *The Little Mermaid*, Fred Astaire, *Jaws*, *Animal Planet*.
Logic, Let Me Introduce You to This Window: It's another full moon and Oz has to be guarded but, during the fight on the beach between merrows and vampires, Oz wishes it was a full moon.
Notes: The most simplistic plot yet. To be read when you've got a spare, oh, twenty minutes should do it.

Prime Evil

Writer: Diana G Gallagher
Published: March 2000
Tagline: Infinity awaits an ancient evil
Setting: Late in season three, before *52*, 'Earshot'

New teacher, Crystal Gordon, takes a dislike to Buffy – and starts to form a witches' coven in Sunnydale – affecting Willow, Anya, Cordelia and Buffy in various ways. They realise that she is a lot older than she looks.
Mom's Apple Pie: Joyce joins the Slayerettes. She hates snakes.
References: *Mr Roger's Neighbourhood*, *Godzilla*.
Logic, Let Me Introduce You to This Window: Angel's age

is given as 250, contradicting numerous *Buffy* and *Angel* episodes.

Notes: Written with the benefit of having seen all of season three, this tries valiantly to fit into continuity – with Joyce and Giles uncomfortable in each other's company for reasons Buffy can't yet fathom and Cordelia anxious about her father's tax position (but not telling the others) – while following the novels *Obsidian Fate, the Gatekeeper Trilogy* and *Immortal*. Shame that the Buffy–Willow relationship takes yet another battering. Cordy helps Giles with compiling a Slayers' database – foreshadowing some of her work on *Angel*. The ending is neat – but Crystal Gordon's fate is unfortunately reminiscent of that of the Mummy in the 1999 movie. This eliminates *Night of the Living Rerun* as a possible past for the Slayerettes, as Crystal, rather than the Master, was responsible for the Salem Witch Trials.

Here Be Monsters

Writer: Cameron Dokey
Published: June 2000
Tagline: Family ties that bind
Setting: Late season three

When Buffy dusts vampire twins, she has to deal with their mother – who calls on the Balancer, Nemesis, to assist. Mama's first move . . .? Snatch Joyce.

Mom's Apple Pie: 'Things at home were, well, sort of peaceful,' Buffy muses. Doesn't last.

References: *Gone with the Wind*, Hannibal Lecter, Disneyland, *Pleasantville, Happy Days, Spider-Man*, Lewis Carroll, *Big Trouble in Little China*, Pillsbury Doughboy adverts, *The Blob, Superman, Star Wars, Leave it to Beaver, Star Trek*: 'Arena', *This is Your Life, Psychology Today* magazine, *Charlotte's Web*, Little Miss Muffet.

Bitch!: 'Cordelia, why don't you let me get you something?' Xander asks. 'What a truly fabulous idea,' Cordy replies. 'How about a tetanus shot?'

Notes: A simple novel that could easily be a stand-alone episode. We see a Summers family photo album, which could be interesting bearing in mind Dawn's arrival. Buffy is helped by her younger self.

The Evil That Men Do

Writer: Nancy Holder
Published: July 2000
Tagline: An ancient betrayal threatens the Slayer
Setting: Season three between **40**, 'Band Candy',
and **52**, 'Earshot'

The vicious Helen wants to bring Meter, a dark god from Caligula's Rome, to the present world – and sends Sunnydale mad in the process.

Dudes and Babes: Buffy in a leather gladiatorial bikini. Why don't these books come with illustrations?

Denial, Thy Name is Sunnydale: Xander asks Giles what the official explanation for a town gone mad will be: 'Let me guess. PCP?'

References: Hellboy (Chris Golden's comic strip character), *Shakespeare in Love*, *ER*, *Star Trek: The Next Generation*, Sam Peckinpah, poet John Ireland, Eric Clapton, *Beverly Hills 90210*, *Titanic*, *Star Trek*: 'The Omega Glory', *Teen Wolf*, Jack the Ripper, Hannibal Lecter, Brendan Fraser, Madonna, *Batman*, the Spice Girls, Drew Carey, David Letterman, *Rambo*, *The Wizard of Oz*, *The X-Files*, *Hamlet*, Sylvester the Putty Tat, *Oedipus Rex*, James Dean, *House of Style*, *W* magazine, Brad Pitt, *The Addams Family*, *The Justice League of America*, *The Mousetrap*, *The Rocky Horror Picture Show*, *Fiddler on the Roof*, *Julius Caesar* (from where the title quotation comes).

The Drugs Don't Work: Everyone has a bad trip.

Logic, Let Me Introduce You to This Window: Helen is meant to have killed hundreds of Slayers, with Angelus watching, during the nineteenth century . . . Hundreds during a century? That's at a rate of several a year . . .

I Just *Love* Your Accent: Giles suggests cucumber sandwiches for tea. Angel was in Yorkshire in 1897 (an allusion to Bram Stoker writing *Dracula* that year in Whitby).

Notes: Originally intended for publication in July 1999, but postponed after the Columbine High School massacre – a more understandable reaction than the delay surrounding **56**, 'Graduation Day' Part 2, since the novel begins with a high school massacre. How odd that there was a novel about a massacre at Sunnydale High being written at the same time as **52**, 'Earshot'. There's a gladiatorial contest between Angel and Buffy that has elements of *Angel*: 'The Ring'. One of the pursuers of Marc Dellesandro wears a 'Wilkins for Re-Election' cap.

How I Survived My Summer Vacation Volume 1

Writers: 'Dust' by Michelle West, 'Absalom Rising' by Nancy Holder,
'Looks Can Kill' by Cameron Dokey,
'No Place Like' by Cameron Dokey,
'Uncle Dead and the Fourth of July' by Yvonne Navarro,
'The Show Must Go On' by Paul Ruditis
Published: August 2000
Tagline: What really happened the summer after sophomore year?
Setting: Between seasons 1 and 2

Buffy learns to accept her own mortality. A new vampire, Absalom, comes to town and seeks The Master's remains. A shapeshifter tries to get Angel and Giles at each other's throats. Buffy helps a ghost family reunite. Giles, Jenny and Angel battle a resurrected war hero and his zombie army. Willow and Xander become caught in a vampire-run theatre production.

Dad's Apple Pie: Buffy spends her time with Hank Summers in LA.

References: 'Absalom Rising': Sherlock Holmes, *Jack and the Beanstalk*, Houdini, Byron's 'She Walks in Beauty', *The Ghost and Mrs Muir*, *The Alamo*, Batman, *Dust in the Wind*, 'Looks Can Kill': *Funniest Home Videos*, *Jeopardy*, 'No Place Like': *Cathy*, *Ghostbusters*, *Mighty Morphin Power Rangers*, *The Wizard of Oz*, *It's a Wonderful Life*, 'Uncle Dead and the Fourth of July': The American War of Independence. 'The Show Must Go On': *Macbeth*, *Hamlet*, Thornton Wilder's

'Our Town', Euripides' 'Medea', *Romeo and Juliet*, *Superman*, *Jesus Christ Superstar*.

I Just *Love* Your Accent: 'Uncle Dead' is based around different views of the war of Independence.

Notes: These short stories neatly tie **12**, 'Prophecy Girl', with **13**, 'When She Was Bad' – the stories are interconnected, as Absalom comes to town, Cordelia is spectacular by her absence, Mayor Richard Wilkins and Allan Finch make cameo appearances and there are numerous pieces of foreshadowing (Willow asks if there are such things as werewolves). We also see more of the affair between Giles and Jenny Calendar, and the growing trust between Angel and Giles.

Paleo

Writer: Yvonne Navarro
Published: September 2000
Tagline: Evil is never extinct . . .
Setting: Season three, post-Cordy/Xander break-up

Buffy meets *Jurassic Park* when an old incantation has the power to infuse dinosaur eggs with life. And someone's trying to con the Dingoes into signing themselves onto a contract . . .

A Little Learning is a Dangerous Thing: Lots of palaeontology.

Denial . . . Generally: 'There was something . . . off about Sunnydale,' a newcomer to the area realises. 'People aren't always what they seem,' he's warned by a teacher.

References: *Leave It To Beaver*, *Jurassic Park*, *Dinotropia*, *The Wizard of Oz*, *Godzilla*, *Peter Pan*, Pierce Brosnan, the Cookie Monster, *Star Trek*, and the novel *Child of the Hunt*.

Notes: Fun, but never quite sells the dinosaurs well enough to be credible even in the Buffy-verse.

Ghoul Trouble

Writer: John Passarella
Published: October 2000
Tagline: Evil walks by day . . .
Setting: Season three, post-Xander/Cordelia break-up

The Scooby Gang encounter Solitaire, seemingly a vampire who can walk in the daylight, and a bunch of ghoul-girls who want to attract more groupie-food for their rock band . . .

Authority Sucks!: Buffy falls foul of an over-efficient school counsellor.

Mom's Apple Pie: Joyce is kidnapped.

References: The Grateful Dead, Baby Huey, KFC, *Geraldo*, *Night of the Living Dead*, Celine Dion, Hieronymus Bosch, *Oprah*, the Spice Girls, *The Brady Bunch*.

Bitch: 'Hussy, thy name is Cordelia,' Willow says innocently.

Logic, Let Me Introduce You to This Window: Thinking they're about to be killed, Xander and Willow admit – for the first time – that they're fond of each other. What caused the break-up with Cordelia then?

Notes: Buffy does *Blade*. Solitaire isn't a vampire.

Spike & Dru: Pretty Maids All in a Row

Writer: Christopher Golden
Published: October 2000
Tagline: One Slayer dies, another is called –
unless Spike and Drusilla have their way . . .
Setting: Various locations (mainly in Europe),
9 March 1940–14 September 1940

At the start of the World War II, Spike does a deal with the demon Skrymir to obtain Freyja's Strand as a birthday gift for Dru. His fee: to kill all the Slayers-in-Waiting and end the line of succession.

References: World War II generally, *The Three Musketeers*, *Paradise Lost*.

Logic, Let Me Introduce You to This Window: American proofreaders don't seem to realise Silk Cut is a brand of cigarettes.

Notes: A nicely written period piece. Unfortunately much of the story was rendered uncanonical by **85**, 'Fool for Love'. The human William is described as a 'wild young man'. The Slayer in 1940 was Dane Sophie Carstensen, accompanied by her Watcher, Yarna Narvik. She was killed by Spike and replaced (after another girl, Isobel's, brief reign) by Eleanor

Boudreau. Amongst the Slayers-in-Waiting (there are said to be several at any time – which ties in with **22**, 'What's My Line?' Part 2) are Ariana de la Croix and Rita Gnecco, an Italian–American from Boston, Massachusetts. The Council of Watchers is based in Great Russell Street, London; their members included Harold Travers (father of John and, presumably, grandfather of Quentin – see **46**, 'Helpless'), Mrs Giles (possibly Rupert's grandmother, mentioned in **5**, 'Never Kill a Boy on the First Date'), Marie-Christine Fontaine, Sir Nigel Rathbone and Trevor Kensington. Faith's nemesis Kakistos was in Louisiana at this time.

Doomsday Deck

Writer: Diana G Gallagher
Published: December 2000
Tagline: Who's dealing out trouble?
Setting: Season three, six months after **34**, 'Becoming' Part 2. Anya is pursuing Xander, but pre-Cordelia working in the shop in **53**, 'Choices'

Joyce asks the Scooby Gang to help protect the Sunnydale Sidewalk Art Festival, but the Festival attracts a Tarot-reading artist who is in league with Kali to conquer the universe.
Mom's Fettucine: Buffy and Joyce bond over an Italian meal.
References: *Peter Pan*, Charles Dickens and *A Christmas Carol*, singer Mel Tormé, Spider-Man, Gandhi.
Notes: 'We've upgraded from saving the world.' A well-paced novel, with excellent characterisation explaining the increased maturity in the characters towards the end of season three. A shame, though, that two books in a row feature members of the gang enthralled by a female villain.

Revenant

Writer: Mel Odom
Published: January 2001
Tagline: A foreign evil has a new address . . .
Setting: Begins 5 April 1999

Hong Kong businessman Chengxian Zhiyung wants to take

over Sunnydale's underworld and brings the demons Black Wind to help.

Mom's Apple Pie: Joyce plays dodgem cars with a group of vampires.

Cigarettes and Alcohol: Willy's bar is trashed.

Bitch!: 'There's an unexpected compliment . . . Of course, considering the source, I'm not going to swoon in delirium,' Xander is told by Cordelia.

References: *Better Homes and Gardens*, Barry Manilow, *Cosmopolitan*, *Star Trek*, Batman, Captain America, the X-Men, Spider-Man, *Lost in Space*, the novel *Where the Wild Things Are*, *Baywatch* icon Pamela Anderson Lee, Discovery Channel, Mr Potato Head, Kryptonite, fashion labels Versace and Gucci, *TV Guide*, *Kung Fu*, Metallica, the Grateful Dead, Risk™, Monopoly™, Gene Simmons of Kiss, *The Hobbit*, *Alice's Adventures in Wonderland*, Harry Houdini, *Butch Cassidy and The Sundance Kid*, Jean-Luc Picard, *Night of the Living Dead*, *World's Most Incredible Police Chases*, Rock 'em Sock 'em Robots™, *Xena: Warrior Princess*, *The Stepford Wives* and *The Wacky Races*. Angel paraphrases *Dirty Harry*'s 'do you feel lucky, punk?'

Logic, Let Me Introduce You to This Window: Given the setting, no Wesley and no Faith?

Notes: Odd coy references to superheroes, rather than naming them, but otherwise this is *Buffy: The Movie*. Good characterisation, action and a new foe – all the classic ingredients.

The Book of Fours

Writer: Nancy Holder
Published: April 2001
Setting: During season three, post-Xander/Cordy break-up.
The book claims that *The Gatekeeper Trilogy* was the previous summer (which doesn't fit with chronology)

The Gatherer is ready to walk the Earth again, bringing his four Wanderers – Earth, Air, Fire and Water – together. Only four Slayers can stand against him, but, while Faith and Buffy are alive, India Cohen and Kendra are dead . . .

Authority Sucks!: Snyder commandeers the library for a nursing station when disasters hit Sunnydale.

Cigarettes and Alcohol: Watchers who lose their Slayers hit the bottle – and Giles seems to be starting early.

References: Martha Stewart, Pepe LePew, astronaut Neil Armstrong, *Star Trek: Voyager*, *The Godfather*, James Bond, Johnny Bravo, Lord Byron, *The Twilight Zone*, Tori Amos, *A High Wind in Jamaica*, Matthew Broderick, Genesis 37 (the story of Joseph), *The X-Files*, *Titanic*, *ER*, *Vogue*, Marvel's *Avengers*, serial killer Ed Gein, *GQ*, *The Rainmaker*, Clint Eastwood, *Bride of Frankenstein*, *The Simpsons*, Mr Spock, *Bambi*, Boris Karloff, *The Mummy*, *Jeopardy*, Batman, Irish dramatist and short-story writer Lord Dunsany.

Logic, Let Me Introduce You to This Window: Faith, but no Wesley?

Notes: Much of this can be regarded as canonical. Buffy's predecessor was India Cohen, called 1993, died in San Diego 1996; Xander has a cousin in San Francisco who needs bone marrow from him. Spike and Dru were in Spain in 1995 (see **25**, 'Surprise'). Buffy perversely suggests that Willow should dream about Seth Green. There are a lot of characters from, and reference to, other books' mythology, particularly *The Gatekeeper Trilogy*, *Immortal*, and *Pretty Maids All in a Row*.

The Outsiders

'The brilliant thing about Joss is he's got all these people sucked in watching this fantasy, but in the meantime he's making them think about the kid that they've ostracised and the kid who's in trouble . . . He explores a lot of things that are going on with kids today.'

– Kristine Sutherland

'I don't want him to be lonely. I don't want anyone to.'

– 'Passion'

For some people memories of school are as Muriel Spark describes them in *The Prime of Miss Jean Brodie*: 'the happiest days of their lives'. For most of us, however, it was a time of intense pressure and loneliness when, cruelly, we were nowhere near mature enough to deal with these emotions. That's the central paradox of the teenage years that *Buffy the Vampire Slayer* articulates. Many TV series have talked about how hard growing up can be (from *Happy Days* and *The Wonder Years* to *Press Gang*). Few, however, have been as honest or as painfully accurate as *Buffy*. When Buffy is overwhelmed by the thoughts of her fellow students in **52**, 'Earshot', from the cacophony certain phrases stand out: 'It's got to get better. *Please* tell me it gets better'; 'I *hate* my body'; 'What if I *never* get breasts?'; 'I *hate* her'; 'No one's *ever* gonna love me.'

'I was a pathetic loser in school,' confesses Joss Whedon but, despite his stated intention to make Buffy's conflict with the monsters she fights 'a metaphor about just how frightening and horrible high school is', there are few metaphors in *Buffy*'s treatment of the teenage years themselves. Here, an outsider *is* an outsider. The aspirations of parents and teachers place a burden on young shoulders that needs no subtext to amplify it. Self doubt, especially in those with identity or image problems, is never far from the surface. (Xander acknowledges his shortcomings in **3**, 'The Witch', saying, 'For I am Xander, King of Cretins. May all lesser cretins bow before me.') The fear of failure and peer rejection is a topic of many conversations. As Willow tells Xander in **6**, 'The Pack', 'You fail math, you flunk out of school. You end up being the guy at the pizza place that sweeps the floor and says, "Hey kids, where's the cool parties this weekend?"' The obsessions of sex and peer acceptance are crucial to the way that characters regard themselves. Cordelia's dream in **3**, 'The Witch', is: 'Me on the cheerleading squad, adored by every varsity male as far as the eye can see. We have to achieve our dreams, or else we wither and die.' In **11**, 'Out of Sight, Out of Mind', Cordelia seems sympathetic towards Marcie, the Invisible Girl saying, 'It's awful to feel that lonely.' When Buffy asks how *she* would know, Cordy replies, 'You think I'm never lonesome 'cause I'm so cute and popular? I can be surrounded by people and be completely alone. It's not like any of them really know me. I don't even know if they like me half the time. People just want to be in the popular zone.' When Buffy asks why, if Cordelia feels like this, she works so hard at being popular, Cordelia says simply that it 'beats being alone all by yourself'.

'The anger of the outcast', central to **11**, 'Out of Sight, Out of Mind', is a touchstone for the entire series. 'On the exterior it's about demons and vampires and the mythology of the Slayer, but underneath it is strictly about growing up and all of that stuff just becomes a metaphor,' said Kristine Sutherland in a recent interview with Paul Simpson. Most *Buffy* episodes concern one form of outsider or another. Buffy herself, from the first episode, is a textbook example. A girl in a new town and school, struggling to keep her head above waves that could drown someone with less mental toughness (as it does Marcie). Battling the preconceptions of others, whether those of hated authority figures like Snyder, or of her friends. In **23**, 'Ted', after she has apparently killed her stepfather-in-waiting, Cordelia asks Willow, 'Shouldn't there be different rules for her?' 'In a fascist society,' notes Willow. 'Why can't we have one of those?' asks Cordy. Others deal with the pressure in different ways. Willow keeps her head down and hopes to avoid Cordelia's sarcasm. Xander becomes the class clown, with a witty comeback for every 'loser' put-down. When Willow asks Giles why Marcie is doing the terrible things she does, he replies, 'The loneliness, the constant exile. She's gone mad.' It's a simplistic answer but, in essence, it describes a heightened version of a form of trauma that many teenagers experience.

In **3**, 'The Witch', Amy is seen as a victim of the aspirations of her 'Nazi-like' mother. The issue of parental pressure here (the implication of Amy as a little fat girl beaten into agreeing to Catherine's mad schemes), along with **23**, 'Ted' (a potential stepfather who likes to slap young girls about), and **24**, 'Bad Eggs' (Joyce at the nadir of her *Mommie Dearest* period), reaches a violent climax in **45**, 'Gingerbread'. Here, it's no longer a case of 'I want my kids to be just like me' but rather 'what are my children up to behind my back, and how can I put a stop to it?' The episode's witch-hunt plot concerns attacking the right to freedom of speech, but the belief systems into which Buffy and Willow find their mothers trying to push them are much more frightening. As Buffy tells Joyce when the demon manifests itself, 'Mom, dead people are talking to you. Do the math.' See, also, **84**, 'Family'. The aftermath of Joyce's death in **94**, 'The Body', sees Buffy attempting to take on a parental role that she is manifestly ill-equipped for (**95**, 'Forever'; **97**, 'Tough Love'). Dawn's introduction and meta-morphosis from a bratty annoyance to Buffy into the key (in several senses) to her sister's future helps change the focus of both the series and the characters. 'She still thinks I'm just her dumb little sister,' Dawn notes in **80**, 'Real Me'. 'Is she in for a surprise.'

Bullying is also a central prop. 'Every school has them,' notes Xander in **6**, 'The Pack'. 'You start a new school, you get your desks, your blackboards and some mean kids.' Whether it's Jack O'Toole pulling a knife on Xander in **47**, 'The Zeppo', or Larry's outrageous sexual innuendo in **27**, 'Phases', the threat of humiliation and pain is never far from the minds of the audience. 'Testosterone is a great equaliser,' notes Giles in **6**, 'The Pack'. 'It turns all men into morons.' In **27**, 'Phases', Buffy tells Willow, 'Welcome to the mystery that is men . . . It goes something like, "They grow body hair, they lose all ability to tell you what they really want."' 'That doesn't seem like a fair trade,' notes Willow. Ultimately, the theme is examined to breaking point in **38**, 'Beauty and the Beasts', which fudges the tricky subject of male domestic violence, but accurately captures the confusion on both sides when trying to maintain relationships. By the time they reach college, bullying has become intellectual rather than physical, something Xander (as an outsider within his own peer group) feels particularly strongly (see **60**, 'Fear Itself'; **61**, 'Beer Bad'; **77**, 'Primeval').

The second year of *Buffy* was the point at which a promising idea suddenly (and, given the formulaic nature of American TV, quite unexpectedly) grew up and got serious. If the initial episodes had been a dip of the toe into a pool of delicious irony, in which teenagers fought vampires between homework and dates, then the second season was a fully clothed dive into the murky waters of the adult world. We had no reason to expect anything so daring, so *challenging* as this. Previously, *Buffy* had been about teenage dreams and desires: Xander's helpless love life, Willow's quest to make Xander notice her. The great taboo 's' word ('sex') was finally spoken (by of all people Joyce) in **29**, 'Passion', after the heroine's virginity was lost in **25**, 'Surprise'. Even Giles was not immune from the great hormonal upheaval going on around him, first winning Jenny Calendar, then mourning her.

Giles is another outsider. The Englishman abroad, lost in a school situation he doesn't understand, working with a girl who speaks a language he doesn't, having to put aside all his preconceptions about what a Watcher is, to deal with the realities of life in Sunnydale. 'But Giles is not a fool,' says Tony Head. 'He's deeply learned. One of the choices I made at the beginning was that [Giles has] prepared for this for some time. There's a lot of theory gone into it, but that [he's] had absolutely no practical experience. So when we first get into the affray, it's a bit of a shock.' In **42**, 'Lover's Walk', when Buffy tells him that when her mother saw her SAT scores 'her head spun around and exploded', Giles asks, 'I've been on the Hellmouth too long. That was metaphorical, yes?' **41**, 'Revelations', sees Buffy keeping Angel's return from Giles and, upon discovering this, Giles is furious at her betrayal: 'I won't remind you that the fate of the world often lies with the Slayer. What would be the point? Nor shall I remind you that you've jeopardised the lives of all that you hold dear by harbouring a known murderer. But, sadly, I must remind you that Angel tortured me. For hours. For pleasure. You should have told me he was alive. You didn't. You have no respect for me or the job I perform.' But he *knows* Buffy and is able to spot Faith's lies about her in **49**, 'Consequences'. Of course Giles was an outsider even as a teenager and in **40**, 'Band Candy', we see evidence of his way of dealing with responsibility: 'Let's find the demon and kick the crap out of it!' 'Did anyone ever tell you you're kind of a fuddy-duddy?' Jenny asks him in **20**, 'The Dark Age'. 'Nobody ever seems to tell me anything else,' he replies. In season four, as David Fury notes, Giles becomes the equivalent of a father who has seen his children leave home. He feels abandoned by them and struggles to create a new identity for himself (see **57**, 'The Freshman'; **74**, 'Where the Wild Things Are'), a metaphor that **68**, 'A New Man', takes literally. It's almost a relief for him in **66**, 'Hush', when everyone loses their voice and, at last, he has something that connects him with his young friends again.

In Xander we have a paradox. Someone who is (according to **47**, 'The Zeppo') 'not challenged', but who finds school such hard going that he has surrendered his intellect to the clouds and spends his days dreaming about sex (hinted in **10**, 'Nightmares'; **26**, 'Innocence'; and **47**, 'The Zeppo'; and confirmed in **52**, 'Earshot'). But Xander is, as Oz notes in **52**, 'Earshot', 'a very complex man'. 'You are strange,' Ampata notes in **16**, 'Inca Mummy Girl'. 'Girls always tell me that,' confesses Xander, 'right before they run away.' The only time we see Xander enraged about the abject unfairness of a system to which he is a crushed victim is in **32**, 'Go Fish', when Willow is told by Snyder to up the failing grades of one of the swim team. Xander knows, however, that life is seldom fair (it's a system that, he acknowledges, 'discriminates against the uninformed'). In **17**, 'Reptile Boy', having suffered from a ritual frat-party humiliation, his way of dealing with his feelings is mind-numbing violence. Hints of domestic horror (see **78**, 'Restless') give this recurring theme a contextualisation.

Willow's story is different. In **1**, 'Welcome to the Hellmouth', she is simply looking for a friend to call her own. ('Aren't you hanging out with Cordelia?' Buffy asks, 'I can't do both?' 'Not legally,' Willow replies.) Willow never surrenders to the cruelties of life (not even Xander's failure to notice her increasingly desperate advances), but sometimes longs for change. By **50**, 'Doppelgängland' she is bemoaning the one quality she can be proud of: 'Yeah, that's me. Reliable Dog Geyser Person.'

There's also Faith, whose way of dealing with the 'outsiderness' of being a Slayer is radically different from Buffy – as shown in **48**, 'Bad Girls', and her random sexual exploits. 'How many people do you think we've saved by now. Thousands? And didn't you stop the world from ending? Because, in my book, that puts you and me in the plus column,' she says in **49**, 'Consequences', as the cracks begin to open. Faith turns to the dark side because she's an outsider within the Scooby Gang – none of them really want her around. Whereas, with the Mayor, she's cherished in a home rather than alone in a motel room ('This place is the kick,' she says when entering her new apartment). In **51**, 'Enemies', her sleeping with the enemy is revealed as she tells Buffy, 'I'll be sitting at his right hand. Assuming he has hands after the transformation. I'm not too clear on that part. And all your little lame-ass friends are gonna be Kibbles and Bits.' Ultimately it could have been so different if only she'd had any love in her life. But at every step, from her mother's rejection onwards, it was not to be. In **38**, 'Beauty and the Beasts', Buffy calls her 'all men are beasts' view cynical. 'It's not . . . It's realistic. Every guy, from *Manimal* to Mr "I Love *The English Patient*" has *beast* in him. I don't care how sensitive they act. They're all still just in for the chase.' Redemption is key to Faith, an anguished and world-weary figure; a girl sick of all the horror in her life and of the taint of evil within her. In **71**, 'This Year's Girl', and **72**, 'Who Are You?' (and her subsequent two-part appearance in

Angel), we see Faith reaching, literally, the end of the line. Sadistically torturing her former Watcher, Wesley, for the simple reason that it will make Angel interested enough to kill her. That she chooses the path of redemption in *Angel*: 'Sanctuary' is almost entirely down to Angel's refusal to play the vengeance game, however much Buffy may want him to.

Angel doesn't fit in either. He's shaken to his core by Buffy's arrival. (In **19**, 'Lie to Me', he tells Willow, 'A hundred years just hanging out feeling guilty, I really honed my brooding skills. Then *she* comes along.') His curse puts him on the outside of his own kind *and* humanity. 'The last time I looked in on you two,' says Spike in **42**, 'Lover's Walk', 'you were fighting to the death. Now you're back to making googly-eyes at each other again like nothing happened. Makes me want to heave.' When Angel loses his soul in **26**, 'Innocence', note how happy Angelus is to be back with Spike and Drusilla.

For Buffy, the constant struggle is to balance the different elements of her life. In **40**, 'Band Candy', she challenges Joyce and Giles saying, 'You're both scheduling me twenty-four hours a day. Between the two of you, that's forty-eight hours.' But her rebellion against her destiny is only a tiny part of the complicated double life she is forced to lead. On occasions (**3**, 'The Witch'; **17**, 'Reptile Boy'; **37**, 'Faith, Hope and Trick') she longs for a life free of the burden of her Slayer duties. In **39**, 'Homecoming', she even tries to put it into practice ('This is just like any other popularity contest. I've done this before. The only difference being this time I'm not actually popular'). And with her off-on-off-on-again relationship with an older man (old enough, in fact, to be her ancestor) Buffy's confusion reaches critical meltdown. Even when she *tries* to find a normal boy (Owen or Scott), Slaying gets in the way. 'Obviously my sex appeal is on the fritz today,' she notes in **32**, 'Go Fish', when Gage calls her a 'psycho bitch'. It's the five episodes that detail the climax and breakdown of the Buffy–Angel relationship (**25**, 'Surprise'; **26**, 'Innocence'; **29**, 'Passion'; and **33/34**, 'Becoming') that identify the biggest change to *Buffy*. These are episodes in which we see a young girl being given some heartbreaking lessons in the horrors of the adult world. In the teen-suicide drama **31**, 'I Only Have Eyes for You', Buffy spends the episode believing that the haunting of the school by the restless soul of James is just retribution for what he did to Grace, until Giles tells her, 'To forgive is an action of compassion. It's not done because people deserve it. It's done because they *need* it.' It's only when she realises, in **54**, 'The Prom', that what she is doing has not gone unnoticed that Buffy's defences crumble. 'It was a hell of a battle,' she says at the end of **56**, 'Graduation Day' Part 2. She could be talking about her own struggle to find a purpose in the madness around her.

Denial, thy name truly *is* Sunnydale: how do the average people of Sunnydale look at Buffy and her friends? What do the good townsfolk make of Giles, for instance? While he was the school librarian, he at least had an excuse to be hanging around with teenage girls and boys. But he never seemed to have a steady girlfriend, apart from his brief interlude with Jenny Calendar. His home is filled with books on black magic, weapons, shackles and handcuffs. Then, after losing his job, young men and women are regularly seen coming and going from his house at all hours of the night. It's obvious that he must be selling drugs. And surely the delivery boy has noticed that Giles keeps a blond man tied up in a chair in his living room.

Look at Buffy herself. How many times is she seen in public with ugly bruises on her face and arms, or cuts on her lip. To anyone who knows her, it must seem that she is being regularly abused. And since Buffy never complains to anyone, the natural assumption must be that she tolerates it. The neighbours *must* assume that Joyce, and possibly Giles, are beating Buffy in sick and twisted sadomasochistic games. It's a wonder the child welfare department haven't been around long before now. In previous seasons we knew that Buffy was leaving her house every night to hang around the park. Clearly she was a teenage prostitute, often seen in the company of a much older man who, we can only guess, is her pimp. As for Xander, he was recently observed taking a man home to his basement apartment and the man was wearing handcuffs and tied with ropes. What are the Harris's neighbours supposed to believe about him? In fact, what does his family believe? When you look at the Scooby Gang from this perspective, they seem a bunch of perverted dysfunctional weirdos.

In **52**, 'Earshot', Buffy finds Jonathan alone on the top of the school clock tower with a gun in his hand. We've seen him in several episodes before, always the butt of cruel jokes by the likes of Harmony, or intimidated and bullied by others. Buffy tells Jonathan that she's never thought much about him: 'Nobody here really does. Bugs you, doesn't it? You have all this pain, all these feelings, and nobody's really paying attention . . .' Jonathan says, 'You think I just want attention?' 'No,' replies Buffy sarcastically, 'I think you're up in the clock tower with a high-powered rifle because you want to blend in! Believe it or not, I understand about the pain.' Jonathan is incredulous: 'Oh, right! Because of the burden of being beautiful and athletic, that's a crippler!' he says echoing Buffy's own disbelief at Cordelia in **11**, 'Out of Sight, Out of Mind'. 'I was wrong,' says Buffy. 'You *are* an idiot. My life happens, on occasion, to suck beyond the telling of it. Sometimes more than I can handle. Not just mine. Every single person down there is ignoring *your* pain because they're dealing with their *own*. The beautiful ones, the popular ones, the guys that pick on you, everyone. If you could hear what they're feeling, the loneliness, the confusion. It looks quiet down there. It's not. It's deafening.'

Analysing the success of *Buffy the Vampire Slayer* requires us to look hard at our own experiences in our teens. Joss Whedon and the other writers, in using the clichés of horror movies – vampires, demons, possession, robots and so on – to represent the terrors of being a teenager, have managed to tap into something buried deep within all of us. It's the subtext stuff – parental pressure, bullying, fear of sex, social exclusion. The characters in *Buffy* are characters that we empathise with, because we were all once like them. Outsiders.

> Cordelia: *'Are we killing something tonight?'*
> Buffy: *'Only my carefree spirit.'*
>
> – 'Band Candy'

Demonising America

'This is not gonna be pretty. We're talking violence, strong language, adult content.'

– 'Welcome to the Hellmouth'

Shortly after *Buffy*'s BBC debut, the media critic AA Gill wrote a hysterically overblown review of the series in the *Sunday Times*:

> This is a High School where even the plain girls are models . . . And they're all remorselessly Anglo-white. If I were writing a communication studies thesis on *Buffy* . . . I might go so far as to say the allegory of vampirism has been subtly shifted from sex to outsiders. The monsters have the look of the underclass, the leather-jacketed, dangerous drifting denizens of street corners and recreation areas, the gangs of lost youth that prey on middle-class America.

Opinionated stuff but not without an element of truth. In Sunnydale there are not only no drug dealers but also no homeless people (Spike mentions one in **42**, 'Lover's Walk', but we never see him) and frequently no ethnic diversity – something Mr Trick spotted in **37**, 'Faith, Hope and Trick'. Not a haven for the bruthas, indeed. Instead, these pariahs of society have been replaced by 'the forces of darkness'. A new underclass of demonised nightmares. When we *do* see the underbelly of Sunnydale (the prostitute in **26**, 'Innocence', for example) it's the cosiest underbelly imaginable. This is a small town with no sleaze, no junkies and no dog shit. In any sort of real-world-type scenario, Cordelia should be doing five lines of cocaine a day, Xander would be asking serious questions about his sexuality and Buffy would be living on the street selling her body to finance her smack addiction. 'Buffy's school,' added Gill, 'is an embattled fortress of learning and the old Eisenhower American way of life, full of beautiful, rich middle-American kids. It doesn't take a huge stretch of the imagination to see that this is how a lot of Americans view their current predicament, and there's no doubt where the real power lies.'

In other words, American small-town *gothica* in the dying days of the millennium, and America is *scared*. If you tolerate this, your children will be next. 'Pre-wedlock humping isn't the fate worse than death that keeps American mothers awake worrying about their daughters,' Gill continued, and concluded:

> It's crack and gun control and the waves of ethnic visigoths that are sucking the blood right out of the nation. And it's no great stretch of the imagination to set *Buffy* in the long line of separatist white xenophobia that is a continuing riff in American films and television. In fact, she has a lot more in common with John Wayne than she does with Peter Cushing.

In many ways this view of contemporary America is *de rigueur*. One doesn't have to be a genius to spot the link between series that use science fiction and horror as an audience grabber while simultaneously pointing the finger at politicians and the media and the paranoia of many of the people who are vocal in their admiration of such series. Some people may watch *The X-Files* for revelation. More watch it as, they believe, an act of rebellion. In the words of one of the true philosophers of the age, Bruce Willis, 'You're either part of the solution or you're part of the problem.' *Buffy* is part of the solution, even if this is sometimes *in spite* of itself. Its agenda is specific, measurable, achievable, realistic and timebound,

'It's a very ambitious show,' says Charisma Carpenter, and she's right. Put simply, *Buffy the Vampire Slayer* might (just) have been a series about post-millennium neuroses but, unlike *First Wave*, *Dark Skies*, *Millennium*, *Brimstone* and (during its po-faced early days) *The X-Files*, it *knows* that. In this regard, *Buffy* is closer to the spirit of Homer Simpson, *Friends* and *Ally McBeal* than it is to Mulder and Scully or the kids of its WB network neighbours *Dawson's Creek*, *Felicity* and *Popular*.

Self-awareness is not, in itself, something to shout about too loudly. Being self-aware simply means that when you're bad, you *know* you're bad. (The volume of television-industry one-liners that Xander is given suggests that self-awareness *is* a deliberate part of the mix.) Where *Buffy* scores again, and more tellingly, is that, in addition to the knowing glances it gives to viewers and critics alike (let's remember, at one time the series' critical standing was far higher than its audience appreciation), it seems to have an uncanny knack of hitting weak spots at the heart of the intellectual demonisation process of American youth culture, the era's great trio of evil – television, rock music and the Internet. All of the elements, in other words, that *Buffy* itself satirised as 'evil' in **37**, 'Faith, Hope and Trick' (the 'hankering for the blood of a fifteen-year-old Filipina' sequence) and **45**, 'Gingerbread'. But sometimes we must pay the price for being ahead of the game.

In April 1999, two students from Littleton High School in Denver took guns into their school cafeteria and opened fire. It wasn't the first such incident to shock America in recent years and it won't be the last (indeed, within weeks, a similar if less fatal event had taken place in Georgia). That evening on *Newsnight*, the BBC's America correspondent Gavin Esler gave a critical summation of the mood of the country when he reported that, as with previous incidents of this kind, America was in a collective state of shock but with an equally collective determination that such a thing should never, ever be allowed to happen again. However, when it came to the actual apportioning of *blame*, this consensus had quickly evaporated. Each time something like this happens, noted Esler, within hours the TV screens are filled with people with easy answers and easy solutions. Blame the violence on TV or in the cinema. Blame the power and lack of control of the Internet. Blame satanic messages in rock music. (In the particular case of Littleton, all three were combined by a media desperate to make some *sense* out of the tragedy, though it's noticeable that the Marilyn Manson angle was quickly pushed to one side when the controversial rock star actually stood up and defended his right to freedom of speech under the First Amendment of the Constitution.) Sadly, noted the reporter, this deflects the argument away from the *real* cause of such cases and, after much wringing of hands, everybody quietly forgets about such events until the next one happens. As Elizabeth Wurzel wrote in *Bitch*, discussing the case of Amy Fisher, a sixteen-year-old high school girl who in 1992 shot her lover's wife, 'Bad people and bad parenting are what made Amy bad, not rock music or the Internet.'

None of this stopped the *Buffy the Vampire Slayer* episode 52, 'Earshot', from being postponed a few days after the Littleton incident. By a horrible irony, the episode concerned just such a scenario. The decision to pull the episode by WB executives *was* understandable – indeed, given the circumstances, it was probably the only thing to do. Sometimes we do the right things for the wrong reasons. Sometimes, we can't even manage that. WB's subsequent decision to also postpone the *Buffy* season finale, 56, 'Graduation Day' Part 2, four weeks later was a knee-jerk reaction which probably did more harm than good. By initiating headline-making cancellations, one tends to draw media attention *to* such episodes that may otherwise have passed by unnoticed. When Associated Press's Ted Anthony called *Buffy* 'a vivid piece of hip TV splatterpunk, a hybrid of *Fast Times at Ridgemont High*, gothic romance and one of the video games you might think was favoured by Columbine's "Trench Coat Mafia" ', at least he tempered this with an interesting observation: 'While peppered with cartoonish violence – choreographed kung-fu, blood rites and the occasional stabbing or vampire-related blood feast – *Buffy* is actually pacifist in many ways.'

That *Buffy the Vampire Slayer* touched a raw nerve in the American psyche with these episodes and others is evidenced by the very nature of the episode cancellations themselves. They were pulled because they had *predicted* events rather than reacted to them. One should, perhaps, be grateful that 52, 'Earshot', wasn't shown a week earlier as there would be those who would have used such a coincidence to suggest that *Buffy* had actually *caused* Littleton. Appearing on CNN, Sarah Michelle Gellar was asked whether she thought the violence in *Buffy* and programmes like it was in any way responsible for such acts. She responded, 'Our show is broadcast in England, throughout Europe and throughout the world. And apparently only in America do we have this problem. Why?' Why indeed?

Seth Green also expressed anger at the suggestion that controversy should be avoided just for the sake of it: 'The simple fact is, this is a topical issue,' Green told *Entertainment Weekly*. 'It's a growing problem and Colorado isn't the only place it's happened. We just don't want to think these things happen, but they happen all the time.' The actor was bothered that the shootings had *again* provided a target for criticism on violence in entertainment. 'Instead of focusing on the real issues and the fact that guns are so easily and readily available to kids and that people aren't watching their kids carefully enough or monitoring the emotions of their students, they'd rather say, "Oh, that guy's got a Mohawk", or "That guy's got a leather jacket on, and *Natural Born Killers* is a film I don't like, and Marilyn Manson scares me, so all that shit should be put on a funeral pyre." I think that's the wrong way to go.'

Ultimately, we need television series and films that tackle issues that concern society. Sometimes the medium genuinely *is* the message and, if only briefly, a well-written teenage horror-comedy-soap-drama can have its finger so on the pulse of a nation that it hurts. In the spring of 1999 *Buffy the Vampire Slayer* for one brief moment got to the absolute heart of what currently makes America tick. What it found was *fear*.

In the preface I said that *Buffy the Vampire Slayer* shares more in common with *Hamlet* than a blond hero and death on a large scale. Shakespeare too was writing his stories at a time of great change and his audience were presented with plays that dealt with things that they could recognise in their own lives. In *Hamlet* (Act III, Scene II), the Prince tells the First Player that the purpose of drama is 'to hold, as t'were, the mirror up to nature'.

Sometimes we need that mirror very badly.

Buffy and the Internet

Jenny: 'In the last two years, more e-mail was sent than regular mail. More digitised information went across phone lines than conversations.'
Giles: 'That is a fact that I regard with genuine horror.'

– 'I Robot . . . You Jane'

Buffy the Vampire Slayer is TV's first *true* child of the Internet age. Even more than *The X-Files*, *Buffy* not only saw its fans embrace new technology to (articulately) spread the gospel, but the Net itself became part of the series iconography. Within weeks of *Buffy* beginning, flourishing fan communities had spawned newsgroups and websites. As with most fandoms there is a lot of good stuff to have emerged, and a little that's downright scary. This is a rough guide to the bewildering world of *Buffy* on the Net.

Newsgroups: The usenet group, alt.tv.buffy-v-slayer, discusses the merits of new and old episodes, rumours and likely developments. In the past it's been a stimulating forum with debate encouraged; however, it has recently begun to attract a distinctly aggressive, overly vocal contingent who are unhappy with the current direction of the show and want the world to know it. Hell hath no fury, it seems, like overgrown school-children with access to a computer. The group also features that curse of usenet, 'trolling' (people who deliberately send abusive and offensive messages to see what reaction they get). alt.fan.buffy-v-slayer.creative is a fan-fiction forum and carries a wide range of 'missing adventures', character vignettes, 'shipper' (relationship-based erotica) and 'slash' (same-sex erotica), some of it of a very high standard. uk.media.tv.buffy-v-slayer features gossip from the States, but also *stars* a number of obnoxious individuals, so is probably worth avoiding if you want a quiet life. There are also lively newsgroups in Europe (alt.buffy.europe) and Australia (aus.tv.buffy) where *Buffy* has big followings and groups devoted to both Sarah Michelle Gellar and Alyson Hannigan (although neither alt.fan.sarah-m-gellar or alt.fan.hannigan at present generate large numbers of posts).

Mailing Lists: These give fans a chance to talk in a more relaxed forum than usenet. At http://groups.yahoo.com/ you'll find numerous *Buffy* groups listed. Many are members only, such as the impressive *JossBtVS* discussion list that also features daily newsflashes on the activities of the cast and crew. Amongst the public ones are *BuffyScripts* (which provides a 'unique look at *Angel* and *Buffy,* including rarities such as early episode drafts, stage direction notes and special "written-but-not-seen" tidbits'), *skyonebuffythevampireslayer* (for viewers in the UK) and *BuffyWatchers* (basically a group of friends, including this author, who allow visitors to join us for after-dinner chats. A *Buffy* version of The Algonquin club, if you will). Also members only is *Buffy-Christian,* a group that prides itself on being 'Christians who love *Buffy.* No small-minded bigots. Positive talk and fun only.'

Posting Boards: www.buffy.com/bronze_home.jsp is where you can find the official *BtVS Posting Board*, which includes regular contributions from Joss Whedon and other members of the production team and cast (writers Jane Espenson, David Fury and Steven DeKnight show up regularly). This is an excellent forum (particularly as it features a direct line to the production office). The only problem is the sheer size. When asked about his Internet usage, Joss Whedon told *DreamWatch*: 'I came to it late. I'm still: "What's download?"'

Websites: There are literally thousands of sites relating to *Buffy the Vampire Slayer.* What follows is a (by no means definitive) list of some of the author's favourites. Many of these are also part of webrings with links to related sites. An hour's surfing can get you to some interesting places.

Disclaimer: websites are transitory things at the best of times and this information, though accurate when it was written, may be woefully out of date by publication.

UK Sites: www.watchers.web.com/ (*The Watcher's Web*). An award-winning and invaluable source of information and analysis from a largely British perspective. Includes exclusive interviews, probably the most up-to-date news service on the Net, ratings figures and fan fiction. You can, literally, get lost in it for days.

The BBC's *Buffy Online* (www.bbb.co.uk/cult/buffy/index.shtml) has become a terrific news resource and features numerous exclusive interviews. Also has a good message board.

Other UK sites include *Dusk til Dawn* (www.dusk-dawn.co.uk/) and *Bonkers About Buffy* (www.geocities.com/bonkersabout buffy/index2.html).

US Sites: http://slayground.net (*Little Willow's Slayground*) is a delightful melange of photos, articles and reviews, plus all the latest news. Includes the VIP archive of the *Posting Board*, fun sections like 'The Xander Dance Club', filmographies and official pages for Danny Strong (Jonathan) and Amber Benson (Tara). Also as a useful link to the *Keeper Sites* (www. geocities.com/stakeaclaim), a webring with numerous pages. Again it's possible to find something new on each visit.

http://buffyguide.com (*The Complete Buffy the Vampire Slayer Episode Guide*) is one of the best general review sites, with excellently written, intelligent summaries. The legendary www.angelicslayer.com/tbcs/main.html (*Buffy Cross and Stake*) includes a huge range of material such as character biogs, a weekly media update, an extensive episode guide, impressive links and a famous 'spoilers' section. Whilst not always 100 per cent accurate, they often get the exclusives on hot *Buffy*-news.

www.buffymusic.net/ (*Buffy the Vampire Slayer: The Music*), Leslie Remencus's beautiful and frequently updated site, is devoted to the music on *Buffy*, including interviews, tour details, musical allusions, etc. An absolute gem.

www.geocities.com/Hollywood/Boulevard/4065/ (*For Every Generation There Is Only One Slayer!*) features a plethora of information, including quotes, photo galleries and biographies. http://www.enteract.com/~perridox/SunS/ (*Suns – The Sunnydale Slayers*) was, according to the authors, set up by 'a gang of people . . . who wanted to talk about, lust after and discuss in depth *Buffy*.' It's great fun and includes fiction and well-written reviews. Love the *FAQ* where they answer the question, 'So, this isn't just a women's drool fest over David

Boreanaz, Anthony Stewart Head, Seth Green and Nicholas Brendon?' with 'Nope, we have male members too!' www.hannigan.com/altar/ (*The Alyson Hannigan Altar*), a lovely site dedicated to all things Alyson that includes news, quotes and photos. Well worth dropping in. *The Sarah Michelle Gellar Fan Page* (www.smgfan.com) is the largest of the hundreds of SMG sites, and is a good place to start if you're looking for Sarah-related stuff. http://members. Tripod. com/anyanka/ (*All For Anya*) is a smashing unofficial Emma Caulfield site, whilst www.geocities.com/Hollywood/Land/ 1702/ (*The Seth Green Megasite*) is a must for the actor's many fans. www.geocities.com/gylzgirl/ (*The Anthony Stewart Head Shrine*) is the best of several unofficial Tony sites. Eliza Dushku's legion of fans should definitely check out www.efanguide.com/~eliza/updates.html/ (*Everlasting Eliza*). http://www.angelfire.com/wa/SpikesPrincess/ (*He's To Die For: James Marsters Fan Page*) has amusing subsections like 'All I Needed to Know in Life I Learned from Spike' ('If you're going to hit a girl, make sure her mother isn't standing behind you with an axe') and the bitchy 'Why Spike is Better than Angel'. www.jamesmarsters.com/ (*JamesMarsters.com*) is also recommended for Spike fans. 'I'd like to know what he was before being a vampire,' James says about his alter ego. 'I have a feeling he was pretty much an asshole. I don't think being a vampire is what made him evil. Perhaps Mommy didn't love him enough!' http://slayerfanfic.com/ (*The Slayer Fanfic Archive*) is, as the name suggests, dedicated to *Buffy* fan fiction with links to related pages. www.geocities.com/Kleysa/buf1.html (*Bad Girls*) is a *must* for those adults yet to discover the joys of *shipper* and *slash* fanfic. www.dreamwater.com/peopeomoxmox/ (*Queen of the Damned*) and www.tdsos.com/ (*The Darker Side of Sunnydale*) and http://anya4xander.homestead.com/ (*The Fruit Rollups of Love*), a Xander-and-Anya-shippers delight, are also excellent. 'I love fanfic,' Jane Espenson told the *Posting Board*. 'I'm not really allowed to read *Buffy* [stories] but I do read other fandoms. There's some great stuff out there. Also some crappy stuff, but people should feel free to read/write that as well.' On the same forum, Joss Whedon commented: 'On the subject of fanfic I *am* aware that a good deal of it is naughty. My reaction to that is mixed; on the one hand, these are characters played by friends of mine, and the idea that someone is describing them in *full naughtitude* is a little creepy. On the other hand, eroticising the lives of fictional characters you care about is something we all do, if only in our heads, and it certainly shows that people care. So I'm not really against erotic fic and I certainly don't mind the other kind. I wish I'd had this kind of forum when I was a kid.' Marti Noxon, meanwhile, is full of praise for the genre. 'We're in a weird position,' she told the *Washington Post*. 'It's flattering because a universe you're part-of has inspired people to continue imagining.' The writers, however, have to be careful as a TV story with similarities to previously published fanfic could result in accusations of plagiarism. 'Because of legalities, we have to be judicious how much we read.'

http://www.chosentwo.com/buffy/main.html (*Much Ado About Buffy the Vampire Slayer*) is another terrific site featuring a fine episode guide, spoilers, extensive coverage of the comics and sections like 'Be A Watcher'. Fan-written transcripts for all *Buffy* and *Angel* episodes can be found at www.psyche. kn-bremen.de/

Miscellaneous: Space prevents a detailed study of the vast array of *Buffy* websites around the world, but a few deserve to be highlighted: *Buffy*'s popularity in Australia is shown by the number of impressive Aussie sites, including: http://members. tripod.com/~sbia_becki/ (*Save Buffy in Australia*), which gives an excellent insight into the bewildering way in which *Buffy* is shown state-to-state. www.buffydownunder.com/ (*Buffy Down-Under*) is a classy site described as 'the ultimate Australian resource for *Buffy* and *Angel*'. Danny Sag's www.geocities.com/ glpoj/buffy (*Episode Title Explanations*) is worth a visit; also www.jenniferdudley.com/buffy/ (*Slayer Sheila*), which promises '*Buffy* from an Australian perspective'.

For European readers, http://bite.to/Buffy (*Buffy in Ireland*), France's http://destinbuffy.ifrance.com/destinbuffy/Sommaire. htm (*La Destinée de Buffy*), the Netherlands' http://members. tripod.lycos.nl/dutchbtvs/ (*Dutch Buffy*), Germany's www. buffynews.k-babes.de/ (*BuffyMedia*), the Italian site www.

just-dreaming.com/buffy/ (*Just Dreaming*), Iceland's http://oto. is/buffy/inngangur.htm (*Blódsugubaninn Buffy*), Portugal's www.geocities.com/edilal/novaserie.htm (*Buffy, a Caça Vampiros Page*) and www.geocities.com/TelevisionCity/Station/9409/ (*Buffy in Israel*) offer impressive local coverage of the *Buffy* phenomena.

www.synapse.net/~dsample/BBC/ (*The Buffy Body Count*) contains 'an ongoing count of the number of dead bodies which have shown up on school property'. www.geocities. com/TelevisionCity/Loy/7330/index2.html (*Beneath the Bronze*) has an impressive sound archive. http://gurl/pages.com/ jennifer-jcbuffyfan/IQuitMain.html (*I Quit*) is devoted to characters who have left the series. http://home.4w.com/ pages/btvs/index.html (*All Things Philosophical on BtVS*) debates serious ethical and metaphysical questions and the moral ambiguities of *Buffy*. www.geocities.com/angeliklee/ BandCandy.html (*Band Candy*) takes pride in being a site for *older* fans. www.gethomebeforedark.com/ (*Get Home Before Dark*) features sections like 'What's the Sitch?' http://members. aol.cm/lostgiant/buffy/buffy.htm (*BtVS Series Timeline*) is an impressive attempt to pull the entire backstory of *Buffy* into a single chronology.

www.dymphna.net/loaded/ (*Loaded*) is the place for all Giles and Oz fans, whether your interest is their Zen-like connection, the shared passion for rock'n'roll or just some quality slash-fic, there'll be something here for you. http://pages. zoom.co.uk/kfantastico/frames/index.htm (*The Miss Kitty Fantastico Appreciation Society*) merits recognition for being so delightfully daft. Although it mainly concentrates on *Angel*, http://ljconstantine.com/doyle/ (*Doyle – Glenn Quinn*) is a beautiful celebration of both the series and the actor, with lots of *Buffy* crossovers. www.concreteelephant.com/Telly/ buffy_guide/buffy_index.htm (*Concrete Elephant*) has in-depth *Buffy* episode commentaries (along with lots of swearing and bad jokes) whilst www.geocities.com/shvcat/cityhall.htm/ (*Sunnydale Town Hall*) is the site of the 'somewhat official' Harry Groener homepage. The regularly updated www. fortunecity.com/lavender/rampling/271/ (*You Thought YOU Were Obsessed with BtVS*) assures readers that, no matter how much you think you love *Buffy*, somebody out there is more sad than you are. If you want some cool *Buffy* quotes to slip into the conversation, www.mindspring.com/~suzecamp/buffy.html/ (*Camp Suze*) has several pages full of them.

Finally, www.buffysearch.com/ ('your portal to the *Buffy* and *Angel* community') is an invaluable search engine that includes links to most of the above sites and hundreds more.

Select Bibliography

The following books, articles, interviews and reviews were consulted in the preparation of this text:

'Angel Restores Faith', *DreamWatch*, issue 68, April 2000.

'. . . and finally', *Metro*, 12 July 2001.

Anthony, Ted, '12 Weeks After Columbine, Delayed "Buffy" airs', *Associated Press*, 12 July 1999.

Appelo, Tim and Williams, Stephanie, 'Get Buffed Up – A Definitive Episode Guide', *TV Guide*, July 1999.

Atherton, Tony, 'Fantasy TV: The New Reality', *Ottawa Citizen*, 27 January 2000.

Atkins, Ian, 'Homecoming' to 'The Zeppo', *Shivers*, issues 70, 71, October, November 1999.

Atkins, Ian, 'Superstar' to 'New Moon Rising', *Shivers*, issue 81, September 2000.

Baldwin, Kristen, 'Green's Day', *Entertainment Weekly*, May 1999.

Baldwin, Kristen, Fretts, Bruce, Schilling, Mary Kaye, and Tucker, Ken, 'Slay Ride', *Entertainment Weekly*, issue 505, 1 October 1999.

Behr, Jason, 'Behr Essentials', interview by Paul Simpson and Ruth Thomas, *DreamWatch*, issue 68, April 2000.

Benson, Amber, 'Every Little Thing She Does . . .', interview by Matt Springer, *Buffy the Vampire Slayer*, issue 8, Summer 2000.

Benz, Julie, 'Little Miss Understood', interview by Ed Gross, *SFX Unofficial Buffy Collection*, 2000.

Bergstrom, Cynthia, 'Slaying With Style', interview by Matt Springer, *Buffy the Vampire Slayer*, issue 3, Spring 1999.

Betts, Hannah, 'And now, ladies, just for yourselves . . . When Harry met Garry', *The Times*, 7 July 2001.

Bianco, Robert, 'Holiday Ghosts haunt the Vampire Slayers: A "Buffy" with a "Christmas Carol" bite' ('Amends' review), *USA Today*, 15 December 1999.

Bianculli, David, '"Buffy" Characters Follows Her Bliss', *New York Daily News*, 2 May 2000.

Billings, Laura, '"Like, Duh," says Gen Y', *St Paul Pioneer Press*, 10 October 2000.

Binns, John, 'No Place Like Home' to 'Shadow', *Xposé*, issue 52, January 2001.

Binns, John, 'Listening to Fear' to 'Into the Woods', *Xposé*, issue 53, February 2001.

Blucas, Marc, 'Slayer Layer', interview by Paul Simpson, *SFX*, issue 75, March 2001.

Boreanaz, David, Landau, Juliet, and Marsters, James, 'Interview with the Vampires', by Tim Appelo, *TV Guide*, September 1998.

Boreanaz, David, 'Leaders of the Pack', interview (with Kerri Russell) by Janet Weeks, *TV Guide*, November 1998.

Brendon, Nicholas, 'Evolving Hero', interview by Paul Simpson, *DreamWatch*, issue 53, January 1999.

Britt, Donna, 'The Truth About Teen TV', *TV Guide*, 28 October 2000.

'Buffy move will alter little, creator says', *Indianapolis Star*, 18 July 2001.

'Buffy: The Animated Series', *Starlog*, issue 14, June 2001.

Bunson, Matthew, *Vampire: The Encyclopaedia*, Thames and Hudson, 1993.

Campagna, Suze, 'Bite Me: The History of Vampires on Television', *Intergalactic Enquirer*, October 2000.

Campagna, Suze, 'The World of Joss Whedon', *Intergalactic Enquirer*, February 2001.

Campagna, Suze, 'True Romance', *Intergalactic Enquirer*, February 2001.

Campagna, Suze, 'TV Tid Bits', *Intergalactic Enquirer*, June 2001.

Carpenter, Charisma, 'Charismatic', interview by Jim Boultier, *SFX*. issue 40, July 1998.

Carpenter, Charisma, 'Femme Fatale', interview by Mike Peake, *FHM* issue 117, October 1999.

Carpenter, Charisma, 'Charisma Personified', interview by Jennifer Graham, *TV Guide*, 1 January 2000.

Carpenter, Charisma, 'In Step With . . .' interview by James Brady, *Parade*, 5 March 2000.

Carrillo, Jenny, 'Buffy Round Table', *DreamWatch*, issue 80, May 2001.

Carter, Bill, 'Dawson's Clones: Tapping into the youth market for all it is, or isn't, worth', *New York Times*, 19 September 1999.

Caulfield, Emma, 'Insider: She Hath No Fury', interview by Michael Logan, *TV Guide*, 25 December 1999.

Caulfield, Emma, 'Anya Horribilis', interview by John Mosby, *DreamWatch* issue 70, June 2000.

Caulfield, Emma, interview, *Big Hit*, June 2001.

'Celebrity Shame', *Dolly*, October 2000.

Chavez, Paul, 'Suspect's family "heartbroken" over son's role in UCSB deaths', *Los Angeles Daily News*, 28 February 2001.

'Cheers and Jeers' ('Hush' review), *TV Guide*, 1 January 2000.

'Cheers and Jeers' ('The Body' review), *TV Guide*, 17 March 2001.

Clapham, Mark and Smith, Jim, *Soul Searching: The Unofficial Guide to the Life & Trials of Ally McBeal*, Virgin Publishing, 2000.

Collins, Scott, '*Buffy* star goes to the woodshed over remark about sticking with the WB', *Los Angeles Times*, 30 January 2001.

Cornell, Paul, Day, Martin, and Topping, Keith, *Guinness Book of Classic British TV*, 2nd edition, Guinness Publishing, 1996.

Cornell, Paul, Day, Martin, and Topping, Keith, *X-Treme Possibilities: A Comprehensively Expanded Rummage Through the X-Files*, Virgin Publishing, 1998.

Cornell, Paul, 'Ally the Vampire Slayer', *SFX*, issue 60, January 2000.

Cornell, Paul, '20th Century Fox-Hunting', *SFX*, issue 63, April 2000.

Cornell, Paul, '*Buffy*: The Body', *SFX*, issue 80, July 2001.

Darley, Andy, 'Waiting for Willow', *Science Fiction World*, issue 3, August 2000.

DeCandido, Keith RA, *The Xander Years, Vol. 1*, Archway Paperback Publishing, 1999.

Denisof, Alexis, 'A Revival of Spirit', interview by Simon Bacal, *Xposé*, issue 43, February 2000.

Denisof, Alexis, 'Vogue Demon Hunter', interview by Matt Springer, *Buffy the Vampire Slayer*, issue 7, Spring 2000.

Dougherty, Diana, 'Oh, Jonathan', *Intergalactic Enquirer*, April 2000.

Duffy, Mike, 'All seems to be rotating perfectly on Planet *Buffy*', *TV Weekly*, October 1999.

Dushku, Eliza, 'A Little Faith Goes a Long Way!', interview by James G Boultier, *Science Fiction World*, issue 3, August 2000.

Dushku, Eliza, 'Keeping Faith', interview by Ed Gross, *SFX Unofficial Buffy Collection*, 2000.

Espenson, Jane, 'Superstar Scribe', interview by Joe Nazzaro, *DreamWatch*, issue 74, November 2000.

Espenson, Jane, 'I Journalist, You Jane', interview by Lisa Kincaid, *Xposé*, issue 58, August 2001.

Fairly, Peter, 'Last Night's View' ('The Puppet Show' review), *Journal*, 4 March 1999.

Ferguson, Everett, *Backgrounds of Early Christianity* (second edition), William B Eerdmans Publishing, 1993.

Francis, Rob, '*Buffy the Vampire Slayer* Season 4', *DreamWatch*, issue 71, August 2000.

Gabriel, Jan, *Meet the Stars of Buffy the Vampire Slayer: An Unauthorized Biography*, Scholastic Inc., 1998.

Gellar, Sarah Michelle, interview by Sue Schneider, *DreamWatch*, issue 42, February 1998.

Gellar, Sarah Michelle, 'Star Struck Slayer', interview by Jenny Cooney Carrillo, *DreamWatch*, issue 55, March 1999.

Gellar, Sarah Michelle, interview by Jamie Diamond, *Mademoiselle*, March 1999.

Gellar, Sarah Michelle, 'Staking the Future', interview by John Mosby, *DreamWatch* issue 61, September 1999.

Gill, AA, 'A Teeny Pain in the Neck', *Sunday Times*, 24 January 1999.

Giglione, Joan, 'Some Shows Aren't Big on TV', *Los Angeles Times*, 25 November 2000.

Golden, Christopher, and Holder, Nancy (with DeCandido, Keith RA), *Buffy the Vampire Slayer: The Watcher's Guide*, Pocket Books, 1998.

Golden, Christopher, Bissette, Stephen R, and Sniegoski, Thomas E, *Buffy the Vampire Slayer: The Monster Book*, Pocket Books, 2000.

Gray, Ellen, 'The gay joke is becoming a staple of network TV', *Philadelphia Daily News*, 1 September 1999.

Green, Seth, 'In Step With . . .', interview by James Brady, *Parade*, 17 December 2000.

Green, Michelle Erica, 'Darla and Topolsky Are More Than Bad Girls', *Fandom Inc*, September 2000.

Gross, Ed, 'Triangle' review, *SFX*, issue 75, March 2001.

Hallett, Andy, 'Smells Like Green Spirit', interview by Tom Mayo, *SFX*, issue 81, August 2001.

Hannigan, Alyson, 'Slay Belle', interview by Sue Schneider, *DreamWatch*, issue 43, March 1998.

Hannigan, Alyson, 'Net Prophet', interview by Paul Simpson, *DreamWatch*, issue 55, March 1999.

Hannigan, Alyson, 'Willow Blossom', interview by John Mosby, *DreamWatch*, issue 73, October 2000.

Head, Anthony Stewart, 'Bewitched, Bothered & Bewildered', interview by Paul Simpson, *DreamWatch*, issue 54, February 1999.

Head, Anthony Stewart, 'Speaking Volumes', interview by David Richardson, *Xposé*, issue 39, October 1999.

Head, Anthony Stewart, 'Heads Or Tails', interview by Paul Simpson and Ruth Thomas, *DreamWatch*, issue 69, May 2000.

Head, Anthony Stewart, 'My Kind of Day', *Radio Times*, 30 September 2000.

Head, Anthony Stewart, 'Ripping Yarns', interview by Paul Simpson and Ruth Thomas, *SFX*, issue 80, July 2001.

'Hell is for Heroes', *Entertainment Weekly*, issue 505, 1 October 1999.

Hensley, Dennis, 'Sarah Michelle Gellar Vamps it Up', *Cosmopolitan*, June 1999.

Highley, John, 'Beer Bad' to 'Pangs', *Xposé*, issue 42, January 2000.

Holder, Nancy (with Mariotte, Jeff and Hart, Maryelizabeth), *Buffy the Vampire Slayer: The Watcher's Guide Volume 2*, Pocket Books, 2000.

Huff, Richard. 'WB Net Returns to Gender-Build on Initial Appeal Among Young Women', *New York Daily News*, 14 September 1999.

Hughes, David, 'Slay Ride', *DreamWatch*, issue 42, February 1998.

Johnson, Kevin V, 'Fans Sink Teeth into Bootlegged "Buffy"', *USA Today*, May 1999.

Johnson, RW, 'The Myth of the 20th Century', *New Society*, 9 December 1982.

Keveney, Bill, 'When it's quality vs ratings, casualties abound', *Charlotte Observer*, 31 August 2000.

King, Stephen, *Danse Macabre*, Futura Books, 1981.

Kurtz, Frank, 'Whedon Talks *Buffy* Resurrection', *New York Daily News*, 17 July 2001.

Lambert, Brian, 'The WB network contemplates life after *Buffy*', *St Paul Pioneer Press*, 17 July 2001.

Lane, Andy, *The Babylon File*, Virgin Publishing, 1997.

Littleton, Cynthia, 'UPN sked has WB feel; Fox goes Conservative', *Hollywood Reporter*, 17 May 2001.

Lowry, Brian, 'Actresses Turning Down Roles of Teens' Mothers', *Los Angeles Times*, 29 April 1999.

Lowry, Brian, 'WB Covers A Trend Too Well', *Los Angeles Times*, 29 June 2000.

MacDonald, Ian, *Revolution in the Head* (second edition), Fourth Estate Ltd, 1997.

Madden, Michelle, 'Total Faith', *Mean*, July 2001.

Marsters, James, 'Sharp Spike', interview by Cynthia Boris, *Cult Times* Special 9, Spring 1999.

Marsters, James, and Caulfield, Emma, 'Vamping It Up', *Alloy*, Summer 2000.

Marsters, James, 'It's Only Rock & Roll, But I Spike It!', interview (with Four Star Mary) by Tom Mayo, *SFX*, issue 81, August 2001.

Mauger, Anne-Marie, 'Staking their Claims', *Sky Customer Magazine*, January 2001.

Mayo, Tom, *SFX Presents Buffy the Vampire Slayer The Unofficial Episode Guide to the First Four Seasons*, Future Publishing, 2000.

McDaniel, Mike, '*Buffy* Lauded for Gay Character', *Houston Chronicle*, 18 May 2000.

McIntee, David, *Delta Quadrant: The Unofficial Guide to Voyager*, Virgin Publishing, 2000.

McIntyre, Gina, 'Slay Anything', *Hollywood Reporter*, 21 May 2001.

McLean, Gareth, 'Last Night's TV: A real death in Buffyland', *Guardian*, 21 April 2001.

Metcalf, Mark, 'Buffy's Master', interview by Mark Wyman, *Starburst*, issue 245, January 1999.

Miller, Craig, 'Xander the Survivor', *Spectrum*, issue 17, March 1999.

Miller, Craig, '*Buffy the Vampire Slayer* Fourth Season Episode Guide', *Spectrum*, issue 25, January 2001.

Moore, Ronald D, 'Moore the Merrier', interview by Jim Swallow, *SFX*, issue 74, February 2001.

Mosby, John, 'UK-TV', *DreamWatch*, issue 71, August 2000.

Newman, Kim, *Nightmare Movies: A Critical History of the Horror Movie From 1968*, Bloomsbury Publishing, 1988.

Noxon, Marti, 'Soul Survivor', *DreamWatch*, issue 63, November 1999.

O'Hare, Kate, 'Silent Buffy', *Ultimate TV*, 13 December 1999.

O'Hare, Kate, 'WB's Core Series *Buffy* and *Angel* Cross Time and Space', *TV Weekly*, 12 November 2000.

O'Hare, Kate, 'While *Buffy* Rages, *Angel* Still Flies', *St Paul Pioneer Press*, 15 April 2001.

O'Hare, Kate, '*Buffy* reaches end of run on the WB', *St Paul Pioneer Press*, 20 May 2001.

Owen, Rob, '*Pow! Bash! Bam!* WB, UPN trade barbs over *Buffy*', *Post-Gazette*, 17 July 2001.

Peary, Danny, *Guide For the Film Fanatic*, Simon & Schuster, 1986.

Pirie, David, *The Vampire Cinema*, Galley Press, 1977.

Plath, Sylvia, *Collected Poems*, Faber & Faber Ltd, 1981.

'Potty About Paganism', *Alternative Metro*, 24 August 2000.

Pruitt, Jeff and Crawford, Sophia: 'The Hitman and Her', *Science Fiction World*, issue 3, August 2000.

'Queen of the Damned', *FHM*, issue 114, July 1999.

Richardson, David, 'Snyder Remarks', *Xposé*, issue 37, August 1999.

Robins, J Max, '*Buffy* Goes Too Far for the British', *TV Guide*, 17 March 2001.

Robson, Ian, 'Action Replay: Buffy's Show'll Slay You' ('The Freshman' review), *Sunday Sun*, 9 January 2000.

Roeper, Richard, 'Buffy Crackdown Won't Strike Heart of Problem', *Chicago Sun Times*, 27 May 1999.

'Role Offers New Blend', *Evening Chronicle*, 12 February 2001.

Rose, Lloyd, 'Outcast Buffy Embodies Teen Angst', *Washington Post*, October 1998.

Roush, Matt, 'The Roush Review', *TV Guide*, 3 April 1999.

Roush, Matt, 'The Roush Review – Buffy Rocks: Better Late Than Never', *TV Guide*, 10 July 1999.

Roush, Matt, 'Shows of the Year '99', *TV Guide*, 25 December 1999.

Roush, Matt, 'The Roush Review', *TV Guide*, 1 April 2000.

Roush, Matt, 'The Roush Review: End Games', *TV Guide*, 16 June 2001.

Roush, Matt, 'Spaced Out – *Roswell* Beams to UPN with *Buffy*', *TV Guide*, 7 July 2001.

Rubinstein, Julian, 'Politically Correct', *US Magazine*, October 1999.

Sachs, Robin, 'The Eyes Have It', interview by Paul Simpson and Ruth Thomas, *DreamWatch*, issue 68, April 2000.

Sansing, Dina, 'Secrets of Sarah', *Seventeen*, August 2001.

Sangster, Jim and Bailey, David, *Friends Like Us: The Unofficial Guide to Friends* (revised edition), Virgin Publishing, 2000.

'Sarah gets a spanking: *Buffy* star forced to eat humble-pie after "Quit" gaff', *Daily News*, 30 January 2001.

'Sarah Michelle Gellar: American Beauty', *FHM*, issue 128, September 2000.

Schneider, Michael, '*Roswell* Joins *Buffy* for UPN Fall Lineup', *Variety*, 16 May 2001.

Sepinwall, Alan, 'Delaying episode could make *Buffy* target of witchhunt', *Network Star-Ledger*, May 1999.

Sepinwall, Alan, '*Buffy* network switch could slay TV industry practices', *St Paul Pioneer Press*, 29 April 2001.

Simpson, Paul, 'Red Shirt Robia', *DreamWatch*, issue 59, Summer 1999.

Simpson, Paul and Thomas, Ruth, 'Interview With The Vampire', *DreamWatch*, issue 62, October 1999.

Simpson, Richard, '*Buffy* bites the dust', *Evening Standard*, 25 May 2001.

'Single Women: If The She Fits, Air It', *St Paul Pioneer Press*, 6 January 2000.

Silverman, Steven S, ' "Buffy" on Big Move: Nervous', *People*, 17 July 2001.

Spines, Christine, 'Getting Buffed!', *Glamour*, October 2000.

Spragg, Paul, 'Welcome to the Hellmouth', *Cult Times* Special 9, Spring 1999.

Springer, Matt, 'Crusin' Sunnydale', *Buffy the Vampire Slayer*, issue 3, Spring 1999.

Stanley, John, *Revenge of the Creature Feature Movie Guide*, Creatures Press, 1988.

Stanley, TL, 'Is it the end of the road for *Buffy–Angel* connection?, *Los Angeles Times*, 21 May 2001.

Steel, Bill, 'Beautiful Buffy's Back, Big Boy' ('Anne' review), *Journal*, 31 March 2000.

Streisand, Betsy, 'Young, hip and no-longer-watching-Fox', *US News & World Report*, 15 Nov 1999.

Strong, Danny, 'Big Man on Campus', interview by Matt Springer, *Buffy the Vampire Slayer*, Fall Special 1999.

Summers, Montague, *The Vampire, His Kith and Kin*, Kegan Paul, Trench, Truber & Co., 1928.

Sutherland, Kristine, 'Source of Denial', interview by Paul Simpson, *DreamWatch*, issue 58, July 1999.

'The Boo Crew', *Entertainment Weekly*, issue 505, 1 October 1999.

'Today's Trout' ('Earshot'/'Bad Girls' preview), *St Paul Pioneer Press*, 27 April 1999.

'The Top Fifty SF TV Shows of All Time!', *SFX*, issue 50, April 1999.

Topping, Keith, '*Buffy the Vampire Slayer* Season One', *DreamWatch*, issue 55, March 1999.

Topping, Keith, '*Buffy the Vampire Slayer* Season Two', *DreamWatch*, issues 57, 58, May, July 1999.

Topping, Keith, '*Buffy the Vampire Slayer* Season Three', *DreamWatch*, issues 60, 61, August, September 1999.

Topping, Keith, 'The Way We Were', *DreamWatch*, issue 58, July 1999.

Topping, Keith, *Hollywood Vampire: A Revised and Updated Unofficial and Unauthorised Guide to Angel*, Virgin Publishing, 2001.

Topping, Keith, *High Times: An Unofficial and Unauthorised Guide to Roswell High*, Virgin Publishing, 2001.

Topping, Keith, 'Body Rock', *Intergalactic Enquirer*, March 2001.

Topping, Keith, 'Teenage Kicks', *Intergalactic Enquirer*, April 2001.

Topping, Keith, '*Sed Quis Custodiet Ipsos Custodes*?', *Intergalactic Enquirer*, May 2001.

Topping, Keith, 'It's Called *What*?!', *Intergalactic Enquirer*, July 2001.

Topping, Keith, 'Changing Channels', *Intergalactic Enquirer*, August 2001.

Trachtenberg, Michelle, 'Summer's Dawn', interview by Ian Spelling, *Starburst*, issue 272, April 2001.

Tucker, Ken, 'High Stakes Poker', *Entertainment Weekly*, issue 505, 1 October 1999.

Udovitch, Mim, 'What Makes *Buffy* Slay?', *Rolling Stone* issue 840, 11 May 2000.

van Beek, Anton, 'Bite Me!', *Total DVD*, issue 21, January 2001.

Wagner, Chuck, 'Punk Shocks', *SFX*, issue 49, March 1999.

Whedon, Joss, 'How I Got To Do What I Do', interview by Wolf Schneider, *teen movieline*, issue 1, March 2000.

Whedon, Joss, 'Whedon, Writing and Arithmetic', interview by Joe Mauceri, *Shivers*, issue 77, May 2000.

Whedon, Joss, 'Blood Lust', interview by Rob Francis, *DreamWatch*, issues 71–72, August/September 2000.

Whedon, Joss, 'Prophecy Boy', interview by Matt Springer with Mike Stokes, *Buffy the Vampire Slayer*, issue 20, May 2001.

Whedon, Joss, interview by Gina McIntyre, *Hollywood Reporter*, 21 May 2001.

Whedon, Joss, 'Buffy R.I.P.?', interview by John Mosby, *DreamWatch*, issue 84, September 2001.

Wilson, Steve, 'Web Sucks TV's Blood – *Buffy* Fans Bite Back', *Village Voice*, May 1999.

Wright, Matthew, 'Endings and New Beginnings', *Science Fiction World*, issue 2, July 2000.

Wurtzel, Elizabeth, *Bitch*, Quartet Books, 1998.

Wyman, Mark, 'The *Buffy* Guide Season Two', *Xposé*, issue 29, December 1999.

Wyman, Mark, 'Anno I', *Cult Times* Special 9, Spring 1999.

Wyman, Mark, '*Buffy* Joins The Banned – A Fable For The Internet Age', *Shivers*, issue 68, August 1999.

Wyman, Mark, 'Crush' to 'The Body', *TV Zone*, issue 140, July 2001.

Grrr! Arrrgh!

It was the TV story of the decade, though it had little to do with what was taking place in Sunnydale. Tension erupted early in 2001 when *Buffy*'s production company, Fox, asked the WB to pay $2 million per episode, effectively doubling the cost of carrying the series. WB executives replied that they would up their ante to $1.6 million, but no higher. Although only the WB's third-highest-rated series (behind *7th Heaven* and *Charmed*), *Buffy* was easily its biggest revenue generator, with 30-second advertising spots believed to be worth $100,000 each. The resulting impasse sent shockwaves through the TV industry with other networks keen to jump in at any sign of a terminal break between the parties. 'If we end up somewhere other than the WB, we'll be exactly the same show. Fox have supported us on everything,' Joss told the press. 'I think the fans will find it.' Still, Whedon was hopeful that *Buffy* would remain on familiar ground. 'I keep thinking it will be best for everyone if the show stays where it is.' He wasn't the only one. 'I will stay on *Buffy* if, and only if, *Buffy* stays on the WB,' Sarah Michelle Gellar told *E! Online* in an unguarded moment of clarity at the Golden Globes. The remarks enraged Fox executives, considering that Gellar is under contract until 2003 regardless of where *Buffy* runs. If the star was announcing serious intentions to quit, the studio's bargaining position would be seriously undermined. What happened next shows how frantic Hollywood players become when a major deal is on the line. Firstly, according to the *Los Angeles Times*, Joss expressed his severe displeasure to Gellar. Then Fox executive Sandy Grushow, who is not one to pull his punches, rang up Gellar's representative Debbie Klein – whom he has known since they were classmates in fifth grade – and reminded her of her client's binding contract. If Gellar left the show, a studio insider noted, she would be sued for breach of contract: 'Every penny she's made would come back to us.' Subsequently, a wholesale retraction from the contrite star appeared: 'I'm not going anywhere,' Sarah said, adding that, 'Fox has been very good to me. I intend to stay with *Buffy* no matter what.' Soon, she wasn't alone in feeling the heat.

Various comments attributed to WB's chief executive, Jamie Kellner, made Joss Whedon's blood boil. Kellner had argued vigorously against paying more for *Buffy*, telling *Entertainment Weekly* that it wasn't the network's top-rated series and insulting the series' many adult viewers by asserting that it appeals mainly to teens. 'It's not a show like *ER* that stands above the pack,' he added. 'It makes me angry to see the show belittled,' Joss told the *Daily News*. 'For Jamie Kellner to call *Buffy* a teen-show and dismiss his own product angers me. It doesn't breed love.' WB spokesman Brad Turrell manfully tried to defuse the row: 'We have tremendous respect for Joss, Sarah and everyone associated with *Buffy*. They have delivered a consistently excellent program for five seasons.'

A late-February deadline passed and negotiations ground to a halt. Fox were now free to consider bids from such parties as ABC and UPN. The latter was an interesting, if unexpected, player. Home to the *Star Trek* franchise, WWF Wrestling and not a lot else, UPN made a bid in March. Nick Brendon broke the news of the approach in an interview with *Zap2it.com*. Asked if such a move would affect *Buffy*, Brendon replied: 'We would still be shooting in the same place, but we'd have more money to work with.' Finally, in April, Fox announced that *Buffy* would be relocating from season six; UPN agreed to a two-year, 44-episode deal, reportedly paying $2.3 million per episode (and, it later emerged, broadcasting at a loss). UPN President and CEO Dean Valentine said, 'We are incredibly pleased to have *Buffy*, not just because it is one of the best shows on air and represents a new era in UPN's direction, but because Joss is one of the finest writers and producers in television.' Advertising revenue also played a huge part in the decision – Adam Ware, UPN's chief operating officer, credited *Buffy* and *Roswell* (which UPN bought after it was dropped by the WB) with attracting advertisers such as The Gap and Maybelline. Although the media had considered UPN a longshot, the network was said to be passionate about the series and 'invested in its long-term success'. Needless to say, the WB were *not* impressed – in a terse statement they suggested Fox had made 'an inauspicious decision for the television industry by taking one of their programs off a non-affiliated network and placing it on a network in which they have a vested interest' (Fox and UPN are allegedly discussing a merger). 'We wish Sarah, Joss and David Greenwalt well,' it concluded flatly. The price UPN eventually paid for *Buffy* made no sense to the WB, largely because (according to Brian Lambert in *St Paul Pioneer Press*) it only made sense *at all* as part of a broader deal that guaranteed UPN continued affiliation in New York, L.A. and other large markets. The acquisition of *Buffy* may have, effectively, guaranteed UPN's continued existence.

Joss, interviewed by *E! Online*, was asked if he actually watched UPN. 'No,' replied the producer, 'but I don't watch the WB either, apart from my own shows. You'll find that people who make TV seldom have time to watch it. The exception is *The West Wing* [NBC's acclaimed political drama and Joss's favourite show]. I'm never home.' He also noted: 'My entire meeting with the executives at UPN was about the ways in which *Buffy* will not change. They've got a sort-of testosteroney rep and the first thing I described to them was the musical episode I'm planning. I said "Your blood's running cold now." They [replied] "Bring it on!"' Writer Steve DeKnight, in one of his regular Internet postings, added: 'Let me assure you this is very good for the show. UPN is crazy-happy to have *Buffy* and will really push support through the stratosphere. And, hey, this might even mean free *WrestleMania* tickets. Woo-hoo! Beer hat!'

Meanwhile, plans were already in place for not-one-but-two further *Buffy* spin-off series. In February, it was announced that Fox were to produce *Buffy: The Animated Series*. A potential cartoon seemed to dismay some of the less broad-minded parts of *Buffy* fandom, but for fans like this author who grew up on *Scooby Doo* and DC comics, it seemed such an obvious idea they wondered why nobody had thought of it sooner. Joss told the *New York Daily News* that producing an animated show would provide 'an opportunity to take our characters back to the beginning of their adulthood and tell the stories we

never got to tell. It's a chance to recapture those years of heart-
ache and confusion.' Maureen Smith of Fox Kids added:
'We're excited to bring the talent and creativity of Joss to Fox
Kids and we look forward to building on this franchise's loyal
following.' Though it's unlikely that any *Buffy* stars will
provide the voices, most of the writers will be from the Mutant
Enemy stable. David Fury excitedly commented: 'The premise
is, it's all the episodes you didn't see that took place when Oz,
Angel and Cordelia [were] there.' Another name associated
with the show, as executive-producer, is the great Jeph Loeb,
writer of legendary superhero comics such as *Batman*, *Superman* and *Daredevil*. 'I got a call asking whether I was a *Buffy*
fan,' Jeph told Susan Kuhn. 'I think both Joss and I [wanted] to
meet each other as fanboys. I wanted to meet the *Buffy* guy, he
wanted to meet the *Batman* guy. For somebody that's had his
kind of success to be so open to someone else's talent is – at
least in Hollywood – extraordinary.' Their visions meshed
immediately. 'It all built to a single moment where I was asked
"How do I see the show?" I thought, Is this a trick question?
Because I'm not sure what to say other than "Like *the
show* ...?" They all started smiling. I [said] "you guys have
100 episodes of some of the best television on the air. Why
wouldn't the cartoon reflect that?"' Whedon and Loeb are currently aiming for an autumn 2002 debut. Though it's too soon
to say how the animation will look (Loeb hints it may be
heading in a *Batman Beyond*-ish direction), it's been determined that the series will return the Slayer to her roots,
Sunnydale High. 'Joss came up with a unique way of doing
things,' says Loeb. 'It's what people refer to as Year One. The
first year of Buffy's life, she's a sophomore in high school.
Stories that would work in terms of Buffy aged 15 or 16, you
couldn't do [once] she became 17 and graduated high school.
So Willow's first babysitting job, Buffy going for her driver's
licence – those are the kinds of teen-angst moments that they
never got around to doing. An expression used a lot is, "We
were always going to . . ."' The chance to work with the man
who wrote **94**, 'The Body', was, for Loeb, too good to miss.
'When Buffy's mom died in the "The Body", I sat and wept,'
he says. 'I was watching with my son, who's 13, and there was

just silence. He turned to me and went, "*Whoa!*" I'm hoping that at least some of the animated series will have *that* texture.' Loeb was also keen to assure fans that the animated series will follow established continuity. 'The great majority of the episodes are going to be written by the guys and gals who write *Buffy*,' he noted. 'Joss and I are working on the pilot, but everybody on the staff has expressed an interest. I'm hoping that Marti Noxon does one. I know that David Fury and Doug Petrie will. Jane Espenson would write the entire series if I had my way – I call her Magical Jane. Steve DeKnight has done two that are amazing.'

Excitement about the *Buffy* animated project was nothing compared to that for a proposed Giles spin-off series. In April *Ain't It Cool* reported that Tony Head had confirmed such a project was being explored. Joss told the *Los Angeles Times* that the show would be 'a grown-up, quiet show about a cool, grown-up non-teenage man quietly solving ghost stories'. Compared to *Buffy*, the intention was to make something 'slower. More like the series already on TV there,' he added. Joss noted that, again, he and the regular *Buffy* writing team would script this series. A pilot episode would be shot in America before production moved to Britain, allowing Tony to spend more time in the UK with his family. Giles would also remain an, occasional, part of the main *Buffy* series and other cast members had expressed interest in making guest-appearances. 'I've asked Joss to talk to the BBC about setting it in the West Country, where I live,' Tony told *SFX*'s Paul Simpson and Ruth Thomas. 'It's got an incredible amount to draw on: Wells, Glastonbury Tor, Bath has a huge wealth of history, stuff relating to the English Civil War.' Joss was clearly excited by the project, telling the *Posting Board*, 'One of my writers was like, "He could just walk into a room, make a drink, sit down and think. That can be a scene!" I said, "Exactly! That's *just* the kind of show I want to do." The BBC [said], "Not *too* British. *Something's* going to happen, isn't it?" I said, "Yeah, there'll be monsters."' Although, at the time of writing, there's still no confirmation of *The Watcher* being commissioned, it seems likely that such a potentially fascinating cross-pollination of genres could happen as early as 2002.

Joss told the audience at the N3K convention in London that
things were progressing; he claimed to be shocked that Jane
Root, controller of BBC2, had said they were thinking of doing
six to ten episodes. 'My plan is to direct the first episode as a
template and just for the experience to direct something in the
UK,' he confirmed. 'One of the chief greatnesses of *Buffy*,'
Tony acknowledges, 'is that it can make you laugh – with
witty, sardonic humour – and the next moment, scare the living
Jesus out of you.' Describing *The Watcher* as '*Cracker* with
ghosts' to *DreamWatch*, Tony added that Joss has mapped out
a format and even gave *SFX* a list of British actors he'd like
to work with including Michael Bryant, Phil Daniels, Ray
Winstone and Michael Kitchen. *Buffy*'s many British fans
eagerly await the outcome.

Speaking of Brits, there's one in particular that Marti Noxon
would love to see on *Buffy*, as she told *zap2it.com*. 'Eddie
Izzard. He's dangerous. I have tremendous respect for him. If
he ever would deign to visit our universe, we'd be glad. We
have lists of people we'd like to have on. The problem is you
think, I work on a hit show. I'll go up and tell them that I work
on a hit show and maybe they'll be a fan or something. Nine
times out of ten, they're like, "Is that animated?" They're
lovely, but they have no idea what we're talking about.'
Apparently first contact has been made with the great British
comedian. 'I think he knows about us,' says Noxon. 'He once
sat next to Anthony Stewart Head on a plane. Tony's a personable guy and did say "You should come and be on the show."
We all wish that would happen.'

As for *Buffy* itself, *SciFi Wire* announced that the series
would make its UPN debut in a two-hour special on 2 October
2001. 'When you bring somebody back to life,' noted Joss at
the UPN's fall preview in Pasadena, 'you have a lot of disbelief. You have to always make the characters feel the way
the audience does. You have to earn it. Make it very visceral.
It's not going to be simple or a cheat. We did this knowing that
we were going to have to bring her back, and we're going to
have to do it legitimately and with integrity.' Joss added that
the show won't rely on a gimmick for Buffy's return. '*Dallas*
was lame,' he continued, killing suggestions that the season

would begin with Xander stepping out of the shower. The cast also acknowledge that resurrecting the show won't be easy. Asked, by the Television Critics Association, what changes she'd like to see in her character, Sarah Michelle Gellar replied, simply, 'Alive!' Joss added that *Buffy* will probably not feature any direct crossovers with *Angel*, which remains on the WB. 'We had a couple of notions that were embryonic, but it was never crucial,' Whedon said. 'I want the shows to stand on their own.' Amongst other changes in the upcoming season: Willow will assume more of a leadership role in the Scooby Gang, Willow and Tara's relationship may undergo changes, Anya will take over the Magic Box in the wake of Giles's return to England and there will be no new Slayer called as a result of Buffy's death as the line now goes through Faith. And Amy, the rat girl, will *finally* return to human form. 'As God is my witness, I will de-rat that woman this year for sure,' Joss promised. He added that he was aware of the WB's decision to shut the official *Buffy.com* website and its message board, *The Bronze*. Concerning a replacement, 'I said to [UPN] "Get that thing ready." I'm hoping it will be soon.' Adam Ware told *SciFi Wire* that UPN will work with Fox to revive the site. In response to a question about rumours on *Ain't It Cool*, Joss said that some were accurate but wouldn't elaborate (in a subsequent interview, Marti Noxon confirmed that the production team sometimes plant bogus spoilers to confuse the situation. 'That's the fun part,' she says. 'We're trying to track down genuine leaks, so there's stuff out there that's pure hokum'). At the Comic-Con convention, in San Diego in July 2001, Joss said that the writing staff is currently kicking around a few ideas involving Buffy's chirpy doppelgänger, the robot.

Further rumours appeared in late July. In the first episode, it's alleged, the robot fills in as Slayer and accompanies Dawn to parent–teacher meetings, totally humiliating her; Willow uses a spell to bring back the real Buffy from the dead which coincides with the arrival of Razor, a Freddie Kruger-like demon biker; Willow increasingly dabbles with dark power and is tempted to misuse it – much to Tara's consternation; Jonathan makes a reappearance as part of a *troika* who conjure demons and Buffy finds herself once again struggling with the dramas that Joyce used to handle. There are also that Buffy and Spike become more than friends. At least some of these are probably wholly inaccurate but, as with every year, sorting out the wheat from the chaff is a necessary part of fan-life during the summer. 'What's the goal for season six? To not suck,' says Marti Noxon. 'We don't want to jump the shark. If we can avoid that for another couple of years, I'd be a happy girl. I'm really excited about this coming season. It's good, old-style *Buffy*.' Noxon reveals that there's plenty planned for Willow and that the passing of Joyce has set up all the characters (including the resurrected Buffy) for more adult responsibilities. Well, maybe not all of them. 'Except Spike. He's not about responsibility.' The musical episode is planned for November. Joss told *TV Guide* 'I think of it as kind of a sequel to 66, 'Hush', in the sense that [it's] about when you stop talking, you start communicating.' He also told *scifi_ign. com* of his love of the genre. 'I'm a Sondheim fanatic and I studied musical-film in college. Musically, what I'm going for is somewhat more pop-y than the movies I watch. People like Elvis Costello and Aimee Mann have very structured lyrics, are storytellers, but still write extraordinarily catchy pop tunes. That's the sort of sensibility I'm trying for. *Rent* kind-of did it. I can only play five chords, so we'll see. But hopefully I know the characters well enough that I can write songs that reflect emotionally what they're going through. Also, I know the ranges of all my actors.'

But, despite having planned season five as early as two years ago, Joss has no thoughts on how *Buffy* will end. He told *Horror Online*, 'I don't have an ending because I think of Buffy as life and I don't like to think about the end of that. We know after the final frame of whatever episode ends the show that these lives will go on. Nothing is frozen in time. That's the whole point of the show, that we're always changing and growing.'

A natural evolution in the lives of these characters that we have grown so attached to, then. One thing is certain, however *Buffy* itself will remain what, arguably, it has been for the last five years – the most unique TV series in the world.